SKIN DEEP

Liz Conor is an ARC Future Fellow at La Trobe University. She is the author of *The Spectacular Modern Woman: Feminine Visibility in the 1920s* [Indiana University Press, 2004] and editor of the journal *Aboriginal History*.

SKIN DEEP

First published in 2016 and reprinted in 2016 by
UWA Publishing
Crawley, Western Australia 6009
www.uwap.uwa.edu.au

THE UNIVERSITY OF
WESTERN AUSTRALIA

UWAP is an imprint of UWA Publishing
a division of The University of Western Australia

This book is copyright. Apart from any fair dealing for the purpose of private study, research, criticism or review, as permitted under the *Copyright Act 1968*, no part may be reproduced by any process without written permission. Enquiries should be made to the publisher.

The moral right of the author has been asserted.

Copyright © Liz Conor 2016

National Library of Australia Cataloguing-in-Publication entry

Creator: Conor, Liz, author.
Title: Skin deep : settler impressions of Aboriginal women / Liz Conor.
ISBN: 9781742588070 (paperback)
Notes: Includes bibliographical references and index.

Subjects: Pioneers—Australia—Attitudes.
Women, Aboriginal Australian—First contact with Europeans.
Women, Aboriginal Australian—Public opinion.
Aboriginal Australians and mass media.
Mass media and public opinion—Europe—History.

Dewey Number: 305.89915

Typeset by J & M Typesetting
Cover design by Kathryn Bird
Printed by McPherson's Printing Group

uwapublishing

Author's note

This book reproduces certain historic terms now considered derogatory and offensive in order to trace the cultural recurrence of racism and misogyny. In their first appearance I signify their origin through the use of quotation marks but thereafter assume the analysis and historical arguments they appear within indicate my rejection of them. I wish to advise Aboriginal and Torres Strait Islander readers that this work includes images of people now deceased but whose families could not be traced.
Warning: This book contains the names and images of Aboriginal people now deceased.

*For my parents John and Betty O'Connor
and the flying fox that gave me wing.*

CONTENTS

Acknowledgements	ix
Introduction: 'Her mind was vacant'	1
1 'A full account of the inhabitants': name-dropping in early encounters	44
2 'A species of rough gallantry': impressions of gender status	90
3 'If they be facts': infanticide and maternity	152
4 Footfall over thresholds: in and out of the settler-colonial domicile	239
5 'Black velvet' and 'purple indignation': sexuality and 'poaching'	284
6 'Absolute frights': appearance and elders	326
Conclusion: The anatomy of racism and misogyny	365
Appendix: Journal publications dedicated to Australian Aboriginal women until 1959	371
Notes	375
Bibliography	458
Index	505

Acknowledgements

This book was long in the making, over a decade. By its nature any tracery of racism and misogyny can only be written through with regret. What it documents necessitated the utmost deliberation. The help and encouragement it received was thus keenly appreciated.

Initially supported by an Australian Research Council postdoctoral fellowship in the Department of Culture and Communication at the University of Melbourne, it was lent further support through an Interrupted Career grant there. I thank colleagues at Melbourne and at Monash in the National Centre for Australian Studies for their encouragement. Particular thanks go to Jane Lydon (also for her friendship and gentle acumen), Lynette Russell, Maryrose Casey, Rachel Standford, Jan Richardson, along with Odette Kelada and Sally Rose for advising on the ethical considerations the research entailed. I am grateful to the Indigenous women who generously gave me their time at Hopevale, Yarrabah, the Flinders and Grampian Ranges, in Melbourne and on the Coorong.

Earlier versions of some chapters appeared in the journals *Settler Colonial Studies*, *Aboriginal History*, and the *Journal of Australian Studies*. The research was assisted by Michelle Smith and Eve Vincent. Colin Chestnut generously opened his private collection to me. John O'Connor translated exploratory French. Denis and Gerald O'Connor and Trisha and Brian Wadley shared their research into the historical accidents of our forebears' arrival in Australia. My girls, Faith and Harriet O'Connor, tolerated a much distracted mother but their own curiosity and merriment gave me respite and kept me on track as did their brother Jake Ludowyke – master of absurdity. Nevertheless, I sought silent sabbaticals at Wye River (sadly no more since the Christmas day 2015 fires), Cape Liptrap, Maleny and Harrietville, for which I have to thank Betty and John O'Connor, Kate and Madhu Kazony, Julian Burnside and Kate Duhram, and Meryl and Butch Thomas.

I am grateful to figure in the publication catalogue of UWA Publishing. Terri-ann White and Kate Pickard entrusted the book with their patience. Thanks also to Kelly Somers for her fastidious editing. Kathryn Bird's arresting jacket design covered and exceeded my hopes. Publication subsidies were gratefully received from the Australian Academy of the Humanities and La Trobe University, along with a research fellowship in the Department of Archaeology and History. Permission to reproduce images is noted with the captions but I thank particularly the families for their kindness again here.

Such a protracted preoccupation could not have come to completion without personal buttress and buoy. My irrepressible little girls grew into maidens throughout its many interruptions and their patient father, Jeremy Ludowyke, bore me with unstinting and impeccable grace through its meditations and excavations. My sisters, Jenny, Katy, Angie and the niece I've always counted as one, Cait, sustained me. Thanks also to cherished friends Madeline Toner, Jordie Albiston, Clare Sawyer, Kathryn Bird, Ross Gibson, Guy Rundle, Deborah Kelly, Jasmine Salomon, Eric Raymond, Deborah Hart, Zelda Grimshaw, Shelley Marshall, and so many more. The loss of the brilliant and ebullient Patrick

Acknowledgements

Wolfe enlarges the inspiration of a confrere and comrade. And my cosmic Dad Jock, and my Mum Biddy, who took on so much childcare and yappercare, I wonder which of us felt each trial and feat more acutely.

For the mothers and daughters of the country I tentatively call home, with deepest respect I thank you for your custodianship, and regret the invective you have withstood with such mettle and valour, and acknowledge that your sovereignty was never ceded.

Introduction

'HER MIND WAS VACANT'

Someone called her gin, someone else lubra, but I never heard anyone call her girl or woman.[1]

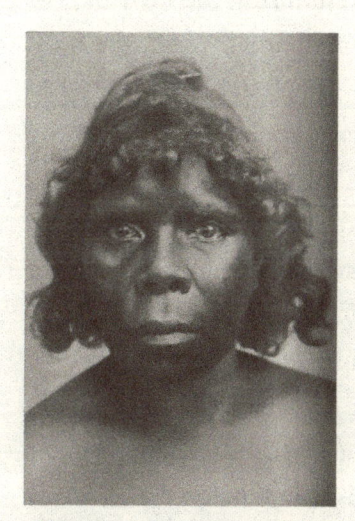

Figure 1 A. M. Duncan-Kemp, Where Strange Paths Go Down, Brisbane, W. R. Smith and Paterson, 1964, p. 297.

There were many names by which the Aboriginal woman portrayed in this photograph might have been known to settler-heritage Australians, but few of them were likely to have been her own, or of her choosing. Depending on the time or place this woman might have been typecast as a 'lubra', 'native belle', 'sable siren', 'spinifex fairy', 'stud' or 'gin'. In most forms of colonial knowledge production and in most of the mediums of its dissemination, her names, her work, where she belonged and who and what belonged to her were deemed largely immaterial to the meanings she ought to impart about herself or her people. What names she might have called newcomers was also of little interest to the historical record. For nearly all settlers, seeing that she was Aboriginal and typecasting her as such through various colloquial subject-effects, or name-calling, sufficed to evoke an understanding about her, one as surface-based, half-knowing and compelling as this image: a way of knowing that was skin deep.

The encounter encapsulated by this photograph was experienced within the pages of a hardcover, now collectible, 1960s edition of an outback woman's 'life among the blacks'[2] – a book in the tradition of better-known authors such as Mrs Aeneas Gunn, Daisy Bates and Mary Durack.[3] In this instance Alice Duncan-Kemp gives an account of life on a cattle station in the Channel Country of Southwest Queensland. The caption merely states, 'This photograph was taken during the early days of white settlement.' It has the shimmer of albumen silver, the most commonly used processing technique for photography between 1857 and 1895. For over a decade I have attempted to trace the woman in this photograph as part of this study of settler print impressions of Aboriginal women, to repatriate her image to her descendants and seek their permission and cultural clearance. Visual anthropologists and curators of Aboriginal family history in museums and state libraries and public record offices – people who spend months, sometimes years, sorting family biscuit-tin collections into records that Indigenous descendants might identify themselves by – have never seen this image before. The family of Duncan-Kemp believes the publishers of the second edition of *Where Strange Paths Go Down*, W.R. Smith & Paterson, held a number of such photographs of Aboriginal people unrelated to the Duncan-Kemp station and scattered them throughout her book, perhaps against her wishes.[4] Duncan-Kemp wrote about the Karuwali, Marrula and Mitaka peoples. Like Bates herself and the photographs she sometimes even misattributed to people she claimed to know,[5] Paterson may have used a postcard, or a plate cut from a book, or bought it from a studio as a print, though the quality suggests he had a good print and perhaps the original.

In settler-colonial Australia this woman had long been typecast under already established, even entrenched, conventions for knowing Aboriginal women. From the 1790s around Sydney, she was known as a 'gin', and from the 1830s around Tasmania and then into Victoria, a 'lubra'. The failure to credit her own name was an erasure of her identity – at least from the settler perspective. Other categories were called upon to construe her meaning, in a process of what we might call 'cultural captioning'. Her photographed image evoked recurrent meanings of Aboriginal femininity for white consumers through the machinery of print, namely through its repetition. As an Aboriginal woman she was positioned at the 'intersection of "race" and gender (as markers of difference)', as Marcia Langton has put it.[6] As I have explained elsewhere, 'lubra' was quite possibly a misinterpretation by the 'conciliator' George Augustus Robinson at Oyster Cove, Tasmania, in 1826 whereby he may have mistaken the local word for penis as referring to wife.[7] Lubra became a settler construct that spread through the settler imagination with alacrity, sweeping aside local language use, totemic distinctions, restricted nomenclature, mortuary protocol and permissible forms of address. All Aboriginal women become lubras, whether they were married or not. Very often this classified them with the social phenomenon of 'black velvet', that is, as a class of Australian women to whom sexual access was assured for settler men, particularly on the remote pastoral, mining and pearling frontiers – the 'stud' was said to be 'easy for the taking.'[8] From this survey of white imaginings of Aboriginal women, the lubra type became a masthead of sexual and racial difference localised to Australia. And like *terra nullius*, despite being incorrect, it attained the status of a sustaining national fiction that absented the identities of Aboriginal women, or imagined them within a particular frame, or a sort of cultural skin.

Since the photograph gives nothing away about the woman it takes as its subject, a kind of over-determined anonymity was imposed over her surface – skin, hair, expression – which then carried the burden of her meaning. As Homi Bhabha writes, 'skin, as a signifier of discrimination, must be produced or processed as visible.'[9] In the annals of costume history, it is usually the task of 'native' women to display the meanings of traditional dress. When the native woman was naked, interest was focused on her exposed skin and sometimes its markings. It may be ironic, or telling, that the English word 'skin' was adapted by Aborigines to explain cosmologies of kinship and marriage laws, such as 'skin' relative, or to describe the contravention of those laws by the expression 'wrong skin'. But the concentration of melanin in our epidermis determined what Frantz Fanon dubbed a 'racial epidermal schema',[10] namely the investments, operations and entanglements of settler-colonial institutions that sheathed Aboriginal men, women and children as Other. There were other perceived determinates – hair structure, occipital ridge, evenness of teeth, ratio of arm length to trunk, prehensility of toes, acuteness of vision, lack of reflection, depth of female genitalia – most of which were clearly confected, but that nevertheless defined the physiognomy of Aboriginality. But skin was undoubtedly foremost in assigning group membership to the 'native'. Said to be uniquely 'velvety', colonised women's skin also intimated touch, or unmediated contact, a very different contact to that with Aboriginal men.

In the colonial visual archives the pathos and beauty of this woman's photograph make it a singular portrait. By my reading – and I take ownership of this as a subjective reading – it seems an expression rent, dissembled, and yet defiant. A scholarly response should couch it in the repertoire of meanings construed about Aboriginal women for white consumption since settlement, and that is certainly what this book will attempt. Popular understandings of human variation were informed by racialist thought, which despite a postwar coyness about the very concept of race, nevertheless continued to be shaped by comparative anatomy, physiology and zoology. These disciplines were originally forged from 'data' extracted during exploratory voyages from the 1760s and they played critical roles in the development of the discipline of anthropology. Along with this epistemological circumstance the image also draws on the conventions of nineteenth-century photographic portraiture, a format that from around 1900 colonised people showed 'mounting enthusiasm' for, commissioning studio portraits, Anne Maxwell argues, as a 'mechanism to recover pride

Figure 2 Hugh Maclean, 'Dry Gin', Bulletin, 1929

and dignity.'[11] As with any image, multiple meanings threaten to capsize the determinates of skin colour, nakedness, hair grooming and expression.

Under the cultural rubric of settler-colonialism, representations of Aboriginal women became part of an invented system of type-portraits whereby the nation of Australia was imagined as a shared experience and, as Anne McClintock has argued, 'all nations depend on powerful constructions of gender', some of them outright 'dangerous'.[12] There is no question that much of the imagery and textual description of Aboriginal women in the colonial archive undermined their wellbeing and safety. Denigrating cartoons in print culture, such as this one from 1929 (Figure 2), had been standard fare over which Australians buttered their toast without batting an eye.[13] The simian features, ragged Mother Hubbard dress, oversized feet and spindly limbs formed a visual blazon reserved for Aboriginal women, along with the inference that their access to modernity was always compromised by a tattered hem, a misappropriated utensil, a missed button.

When I first came across such cartoons in Australian 1920s print (I was researching a PhD on modern girl types, such as the flapper, and their relation to industrialised image production),[14] I reacted at first with repugnance and cuffed over the pages, thinking some things are best consigned to history. At this moment, 1998, then Prime Minister John Howard was decrying a 'black armband' view of history and arguing we needed to focus on our national achievements. He'd lifted the term from historian Geoffrey Blainey,[15] reacting to the confronting revelations arising from new research in the areas of Indigenous studies and imperial history. While people were then exposed to more historical detail of conflict and discrimination, there was less work on the everyday perceptions so well captured in the (increasingly digitised) print archive. I was torn between believing that non-Indigenous, particularly settler-heritage Australians should know more of the racism of our everyday ephemera and doubting that Aboriginal women needed any reminders of these malicious descriptors. Perhaps they have preferred not to pass on their memories of this racism to spare their children and grandchildren the pain of their humiliation. As such there lies a conflicting warp in the very spine of this book. Its intention is to counter the amnesia besetting those who fanned the history wars, to bring about a reckoning in settler-heritage Australians about the entrenched cruelty with which racism and misogyny hinged in our nation's public. But with that comes the potential risk of reinscribing trauma for Aboriginal readers. The material comprising this archive is deeply offensive, it is often shocking and sometimes nauseating. It should disturb all Australians, but I hope its potential to incite a reckoning offers some safeguard for Aboriginal readers, especially women.

There was also remarkable variety in the 'image-objects' through which Aboriginal women were imagined and desired, disregarded and absented. The engraving that graces the cover is taken from a photograph of two young women in the Herbert River area of Queensland, so the women may have been of the Nawagi, Bandjin or Warakamai peoples.[16] The engraving was captioned 'Civilised girls from the vicinity of Townsville' and signed CPAULLK.A.[17] It was published in the travelogue of a Norwegian zoologist, Carl Lumholtz, in his 1889 *Among Cannibals,* which was translated into four languages.[18] Despite its jarring and sensational title, Lumholtz's account is relatively considered and sympathetic for its time. This striking image illustrates the ambivalence with which 'civilised' Aboriginal women were met. The dilly bag slung over the headscarf and the missed buttons intimate their

Figure 3 'Dark Ladies', Walkabout, May 1964.

assimilation can never be complete – and indeed that it may even be resisted – while the panniers indicate their usefulness for domestic service. For Lumholtz, 'civilised' women made useful servants, but despite their original 'modesty' their first contact usually with 'rough settlers' invariably led to prostitution, at first by force and then as a means of survival.[19]

Nearly a century later this affirming image of a mother laughing and going about her day, indifferent to the camera, appeared in a feature on Aboriginal women in the popular tourist magazine *Walkabout*, entitled 'Dark ladies' (Figure 3).[20] There are many such admiring, even fond, images of Aboriginal women, yet others in the colonial archive are breathtakingly offensive.

'Her mind was vacant'

Figure 4 'Goodbye Mother', Thomas Cleary (1854–1899) 1896. Photograph: albumen silver; 22 x 26 cm. Acc. no: H96.160/468, State Library of Victoria

'Goodbye mother' (Figure 4), taken by New Zealand commercial photographer Thomas Cleary, probably in either Benalla in 1896 or Wahgunyah in 1897, is one of a series of photographs of Victorian Aborigines discovered in 1988 in the shed of a photography student's uncle.[21] The woman has been identified as Kate Friday and was possibly Kwat kwat or Pangerang. Aboriginal artist Tommy McRae sued Cleary for failing to pay Friday and other Aboriginal people the £10 he had promised.[22] The photograph was said to be a 'parody on the "irrational costume" affected by lady cyclists.'[23] It was not the first use of the 'primitive' to parody white women's modernity and it would not be the last, for it was woman, as Deborah Poole writes, 'who embodied the purest means of perceiving [racial] difference.'[24]

Of critical importance to these ways of apprehending and appraising Indigenous women was the historical coincidence of print and colonialism, and the dissemination and synchronisation such knowledge was afforded through the industrialisation of print. It is also true that Indigenous Australians engaged with this technology, printing their own newspapers such as *The Abo Call* in 1938, writing protest letters, and accessing print imagery and text. Jack Patten was this shortlived newspaper's editor and he was acutely aware of the consequence of this medium. He made 'propaganda for the emancipation and betterment of the Aborigines' the first objective of the new organisation, the Aborigines Progressive Association. He determined to 'print, publish and circulate books, papers, pamphlets and leaflets to promote the objects of the association.'[25] Through this 'alter/native'[26] use of print, Patten sought to counter the 'libel'[27] that had been reiterated since the time of Dampier and the 'cruel joke' of the 'jacky-jacky' type by 'comic cartoonists'.[28]

Aboriginal readers also took a keen interest in print. Visitors at nineteenth-century reserves noted hut interiors were decorated with cuttings from the illustrated press,[29] and the consumption of newspapers at Coranderrk was reported in 1879.[30] Anecdotally, Aboriginal people in the Northern Territory were avid readers of Eric Jolliffe's 1950s cartoon booklets *Witchetty's Tribe*. Our focus will stay with print because it was the dominant media form of the colonial era, and sifting through its remarkable offerings allows us to consider, as Michael Taussig urges, the 'capacity of the imagination to be lifted through representational media, such as marks on a page, into other worlds.'[31] Print not only reported events, but circulated meanings of Aboriginality from archives and events that historians often treat as distinct from print, such as public lectures, excerpts from new publications, and the documents of governance such as the findings of select committees and royal commissions. This study follows the methodological devices Edward Said set out in his foundational work, *Orientalism*. He asks us to look for the 'strategic formation' of texts, that is, 'the relationship between texts and the way in which groups of texts, even textual genres, acquire mass, density, and referential power among themselves and thereafter in the culture at large.'[32] It is an approach wholly suited to the principal function of print: to copy and to imprint by reproducing en masse.

Let's consider the scaling of grey in this print copy of the unnamed woman reproduced in *Where Strange Paths Go Down*. It calls to mind a line from Taussig: it is poised between 'fidelity and fantasy, between iconicity and arbitrariness, wholeness and fragmentation.'[33] For all we know about the formal properties of photography and print, this image still affects me through a set of emotional responses influenced through childhood exposure to the growing disquiet about colonial legacies, spurred by Aboriginal activism of the time. I have been asked why I undertook the research and writing of this book. Without wanting to cross the very fine line between self-indulgence and accounting for my standpoint, it is a question a white scholar in Indigenous studies should be able to honour.

The disclosure in the documentary *The Last Tasmanian*[34] that settlers buried Aboriginal babies up to the neck and, forcing their mothers to watch, kicked off their heads, was among many I found sickening and shameful. This documentary by Tom Haydon, released in 1978, created controversy as descendants challenged its premise that Aboriginal Tasmanians had been eradicated. At twelve years of age, I wasn't aware of the contestation surrounding the screening of this widely viewed documentary. Michael Mansell refuted that the atrocities committed in Tasmania in the nineteenth century were part of 'the swiftest and most complete genocide on record.'[35] Tom O'Regan, too, argued, 'the Tasmanian Aborigines have no existence in the present' in the film.[36] Nor did I then know that reactions to the film marked a turning point in white representations of Aboriginal and settler history, and influenced the politicisation of anthropological and archeological methodology.[37] At that age it seemed unfathomable that generations of an entirely unfamiliar people had lived out their lives over millennia in a place where I felt at home and at peace but from which they were now entirely erased – if we generalised, as I did, from the contention of *The Last Tasmanian*. If I really was 'fifth generation', I wondered, had my forebears been involved in their eradication?[38] During this period of widespread changes to the Australian historical consciousness,[39] and intensified Aboriginal activism,[40] like many settler-heritage Australians my sense of national identity became deeply unsettled.

But, as Sara Ahmed has warned, 'declarations of shame can work to bring "the nation" into existence as a felt community.'[41] Without providing any relief to Aboriginal suffering, such sentiments might be mawkish to Indigenous Australians. These feelings can appropriate their suffering as 'our shame', which is then expunged through public declarations.[42] Insofar as adopting a political stance requires public display, anti-racism is performative, which is not to suggest it isn't genuinely and profoundly felt. At times among settler-heritage Australians I've wondered if there isn't a degree of competitiveness in fawning displays of anti-racism, which I've sensed on a few occasions makes for tiresome company for Aboriginal and Islander peoples. In his study of whiteness Richard White has remarked that even lacerating ourselves with admissions of guilt, 'bears witness to the fineness of a moral spirit that can feel such guilt.'[43] Reconciling the past means not only knowing it, but knowing how it has been constructed to nationalise historical imagination. Reconciliation means uncovering our individual and shared historical inheritance and understanding the processes by which it became shared. Racial difference imposes profoundly determining identifications, and neither whiteness

'Her mind was vacant'

nor womanhood can be shed like a skin. As a white woman I'm positioned on either side of the dominant/subordinate power dyad. In other words, I know one type of subjugation and I know *of* and have benefited from another.

Wanting to know more, in my early twenties I thought I knew who to best ask about the first people of the poplar-scented Ovens Valley, where an intergenerational aura enfolded me in a sense of place. Edith Hoy (1905–1996) was a woman who in hindsight was steeped in history. As a child she knocked about with Ned Kelly's nephews and nieces in the bush hamlet of Greta West in north-eastern Victoria. Writing under a male pseudonym – notably her boss's – she was a reporter for Wangaratta's *Chronicle Despatch*. She 'pioneered' a number of business ventures into the Ovens Valley, including Hoy's Buses and the Bon Accorde Hospice. She was president of the Harrietville Historical Society and energetically planted plaques among the heath over the Victorian Highplains to commemorate the cattlemen and drovers. After she retired she wrote a history of gold mining in the Ovens Valley, particularly on the Buckland Valley riots and the Chinese expulsion,[44] along with a pamphlet on Guide Alice (Manfield) of Mount Buffalo,[45] another early tourist operator with whom she may have identified. Every January 26, Mrs Hoy was Harrietville's Australia Day impresario, inviting dignitaries to hoist the flag in the Historical Park and breaking the celebratory crust of almond icing. Finally, she installed a waterwheel in the Historical Park to commemorate her late husband. She was also my maternal grandmother.

Before all these flags and fruitcakes, plaques and historical parks became apparent to me as artefacts of a very orthodox form of colonial history – one in which Aborigines were notably absented – I thought Haha, as we called her, was the obvious person to ask about the region's colonial past. On a drive out to the Greta

Cemetery I asked, 'What happened to all the Aboriginal people here?' She raised the imposing span of her palm to me and said, 'They ran away into the hills', then turned and resolutely scanned the horizon, not to be drawn. Granted, Haha might simply have grown tired of my blathering, or was deep in remembrance for the people reposing beneath the Greta sky, but it nevertheless struck me as a telling omission from a local historian.

Given that seven or eight shepherds were speared and one Aborigine shot in the 'Faithfull massacre' on the Broken River near Benalla in 1838, the 'frontier skirmishes' first described in the works of Richard Broome and Henry Reynolds is a more accurate description of interracial relations in the area.[46] The Faithfull brothers' men were killed by a sanctioned avenging party of 150 Pangerang men in retribution for the shooting and injuring of a number of Aboriginal men following an attack on the Faithfulls' overlanding party on the Ovens River a week before.[47] The suspicion of an impending attack was aroused among the Faithfull party through the absence of women at the Aboriginal meeting place they were befouling with their camp and stock. As was the case in many violent reprisals in the incendiary violence on the colonial frontier, the misuse of women, or failure to properly recompense for the exchange of women, was one of the motivations for the assault. The ratio of European men to women on the rapidly advancing Victorian pastoral frontier was twenty to one and sexual outlet was assumed to be a universal constant in white men.[48] As Patrick Wolfe has argued, territoriality is not encountered without gender, itself foundational to the world-historical project of settler-colonialism.[49]

But violence in the northeast predated even the Faithfull reprisals. Around 1838, William Thomas, the Protector of the Port Phillip, Westernport and Gippsland districts, described the individual men who comprised the native police in Victoria under Captain Dana. 'Yupton – (Yeap-tune)' was highly regarded for his restraint in action, particularly given 'his father, mother, and elder brother were shot by the settlers in a sheep robbery between the Goulburn River and the Ovens.'[50] The deaths of the Faithfulls' shepherds occurred during a series of raids against stations being established along the Port Phillip route from Sydney to Melbourne, soon after the government in 1836 issued annual licences for the depasturing of stock 'beyond the limits of location' to shore up the wool export market, by then the colonies' largest.[51] Dispatches from Governor Gipps show him to resist pressure from squatters overlanding stock to form 'militias' though this meant their punitive raids on Aboriginal camps could appear 'administratively clean'.[52] Overlanders from Sydney pushed south. They set up their stations during a drought, prompting the local people's requests for food – though they may also have been seeking recompense for the use of their lands, waterholes and access to women. Following a raid on his Ovens station, Faithfull led a counter-attack during which sixty rounds were fired on a camp of men, women and children. He reported, 'I trust and believe that many of the bravest savage warriors bit the dust.'[53] In Grenfell Price's brief 1949 history he noted that George Faithfull knew his name to be 'a terror' among Aborigines in the vicinity of Wangaratta. In one disturbing incident Faithfull recovered a boy sheltering under a log, 'took him home and tamed him, and he became very useful to me.'[54] A raid on George Mackay's Whorouly station on the Ovens and King rivers in 1840 was attributed by the Chief Protector of Aborigines, George Robinson, to the many 'collisions' which he feared to have been of a 'fatal character' perpetrated by one of Mackay's shepherds.[55] One of Mackay's men, perhaps the same, had recommended to the local protector that since 'Blacks' were cannibals they 'ought to have bullets put through their heads.' (Haha's home, where my mother was raised and we kids had holiday visits, was in Mackay Street, Wangarrata.) In 1839, in response to eighty-one petitioners, a letter from a Port Phillip administrator informed the Colonial Office that a party had been dispatched, 'consisting of an officer and twelve men of the mounted police, to the River Ovens, as soon as he heard of the late massacre of Mr. Faithfull's men, and that this party has since been increased to twenty-one.' The group soon swelled to forty-four with 'a discretionary power' given to the police magistrate in Melbourne 'to cause parties of infantry to advance, if necessary, into the interior.'[56] In all but name these Border Police, stationed along the river crossings on the Port Phillip Overland Route, were the militia pastoralists had earlier demanded. The number of deaths they caused is unknown.

No doubt running for their lives into the hills was one response to the violent incursion of Europeans into the Aboriginal homelands of Victoria's North East, which took in the people of Bidawal, Monero-Ngarigo, Gunai-Kurnai, Jaithmathang, Taungurung, Mitambuta, Ngarigu-Currawong, Dhudhuroa, Waywurru and Wurundjeri. In fact, Aborigines waged hit-and-run strikes on stations throughout the region, though only fifty-nine Europeans were killed by Aborigines on the Victorian frontier while 800–1,000 Aboriginal lives are estimated to have been lost in conflict. Attacks in the North East, such as that on Mackay, in which his house and stores were fired, a shepherd killed and thousands of pounds of stock stolen,[57] were met with paramilitary-style raids on camps.[58] Reprisal attacks were led by Fitzherbert Mundy and parties of Europeans assembled from the neighbouring stations of William Bowman, Henry Yaldwin and John Hutchinson. They were among the eighty-one settlers who had threatened to take matters into their own hands if the

'Her mind was vacant'

government did not retaliate by raising a militia.[59] Fighting was reported in the area again in 1841, when Aborigines were said to be using firearms.[60] The Aboriginal population of Victoria was halved and halved again through two onslaughts of smallpox in the 1790s and again in the 1830s.[61] James Boyce writes in his history, *1835*, that thirty years after the founding of Melbourne, population decline across Victoria was at least 80 per cent.[62]

The discovery of gold in 1852 occasioned a massive influx of men into the valley of the Minjambutu/Mogullumbigj.[63] Very often Aborigines acted as guides to the goldfields including men documented at Omeo and on the Ovens.[64] But through violence and disease, by 1901 the area was thought to have become entirely 'devoid' of Aboriginal people.[65] The dramatic depopulation was descriptive of the Australian frontier wherever it pressed forward into Aboriginal homelands. In 1934 Polish anthropologist Ludwik Krzywicki assembled a tribe-by-tribe breakdown of Aboriginal depopulation and found most groups had halved within twenty years of contact with Europeans. The Kundangora (one division) of the Ya-itma-thang people (Omeo, high plains) were counted at 500–600 in 1835. Krzywicki claimed that by 1862 only four or five of its people remained.[66] In an 1877 census only thirty-four people were listed as living off-reserve in the North East.[67] In 1942 Charles Barrett, naturalist and prolific publisher, wrote in his booklet *Blackfellows* that the 'Oven River blacks' had 'long been extinct.'[68]

This may have been wishful thinking. Survivors did not simply run into the hills as Haha told me. Mary Jane Milawa ('mil' = eyes, 'wa' = water in Pangerang)[69] belonged to 'the Wangaratta tribe' and lived in her 'miam' on the banks of the King River (see Figure 5). Sally Corbett 'belonged to the Maragan (Broken River) tribe' (see Figure 6). Both women were

17

Figure 5 Sally Corbett. Science of Man, *vol. 3, no. 3, 23 April 1900.*
Courtesy of the National Library of Australia JAF 572.06 SCI

Figure 6 Mary Jane Milawa, Science of Man, *vol. 3, no. 3, 23 April 1900.*
Courtesy of the National Library of Australia JAF 572.06 SCI

'Her mind was vacant'

profiled together in *Science of Man* in 1900. Sally (who married twice) and Mary Jane visited each other, and Mary 'lived the old camp life on the site of a very old camping ground' about 2.5 miles from Wangaratta. Corbett was described as 'the last female representative' of the Wangaratta tribe and 'an intelligent black' with 'a kind disposition', showing 'a strong attachment to those who had treated the blacks with kindness.' Yet Pangerang elder Freddie Dowling advises me that Corbett died a few weeks before Milawa. *Science of Man* records that Corbett 'liked to talk of old camp life' but 'her mind was vacant' of any religious belief and 'had the usual dread of evil spirits.' Though married twice and known to have had children, it was doubted if any of them were living.[70] As it transpires, Mary Jane Milawa was the sister of Luana, Freddie Dowling's great grandmother.[71] By his account Luana and Mary Jane were taken by Wiradjuri people to safety at Wahgunyah near Lake Moodemere, but Mary Jane pined for her country and, still a girl, walked back to the river flats east of Wangaratta below the township of Milawa where she camped until she died in 1888.[72]

Mary Jane Milawa and Sally Corbett lived before Haha's time. Whether my grandmother was aware of the people of the North East who remained, and whatever she knew of the destructive events that went unmentioned in her carefully stage-managed Australia Day revelries, her explanation to me was nevertheless pervaded by a sense of unmentionable history. It's unlikely that in her time even such an inquiring amateur historian would have known that the local Aborigines called the Ovens River the 'Torryong', the King River the 'Poodumbia' and their junction 'Burawang'. There is nothing in her five scrapbooks, including hundreds of pages of closely typed transcripts from the *Ovens and Murray Advertiser,* pertaining to Aboriginal history (although

19

she was unusual to have taken such an interest in the Chinese). Sally Morgan's grandmother has called this distinct unknowing of white Australians 'living a half-life.'[73] I first felt its peculiar pall between Haha and I there on the Kingswood's baking nylon seat on the way out to the Greta Cemetery. Bhabha takes the question into new territory when he asks how this might be experienced by the colonised: 'If, as they say, the past is a foreign country, then what does it mean to encounter a past that is your own country reterritorialized, even terrorized by another?'[74]

As it transpires Haha did take an active interest in local Aboriginal history, but as distinct from the terrorising by settlers. She knew of rock art in caves at Mudgegonga near Myrtleford, and didn't tell anyone for fear of them being vandalised, but later gave their whereabouts to the anthropologist John Mulvaney, whom she took to the site in December 1965, and who gave assurances the site would be protected.[75] She sought references from the Australian Institute of Aboriginal Studies.[76] She also talked of her great grandfather who had dark colouring on his back, perhaps from labouring with coal, and who worried about taking off his shirt when working or boxing for fear that his dark skin might imply Aboriginal heritage.[77]

The concealments of colonial history require the intimate and informal discretions of rolled-down shirtsleeves and clandestine caves. But they also rely on sanctioned, ritualised, spectacular displays — of flags, plaques and waterwheels. Haha was a custodian of a form of history that I came to understand as particular to settler-colonialism as both arbitrary and archived. As Chris Healy has argued, the 'intercultural space of Aboriginality' is 'constituted by strange and transient patterns of remembering and forgetting.'[78] The things Haha vouchsafed to display or keep secret marked the distance Ann Stoller has charted 'between recognized and disqualified knowledge, between intelligible accounts and those deemed appropriate for exchange.'[79] She gave careful consideration to where and how imperial signs should be made known and remembered as part of our national and local heritage. Her stalled remembrance of North East Victorian Aborigines stands in direct contrast to her energetic and insistent memorialising of white 'pioneers'.[80] Healy is prescient when he asks if it is enough to 'simply incite more memories' or whether it's more critical 'to remember white forgetting.'[81] His argument is linked to Bhabha's that,

> It is not adequate simply to become aware of the semiotic systems that produce the signs of culture and their dissemination. Much more significantly we are faced with the challenge of reading, into the present of a specific cultural performance, the traces of all those disciplinary discourses and institutions of knowledge that constitute the conditions and contexts of culture.[82]

With this in mind, Healy's contention that settlers were 'desperate to fill, to replace bodily absences with body traces that could be studied',[83] helps to explain Haha's interest in the cave outside Myrtleford. Such a site of remembrance, once revealed to authorised custodians, might create an alternative to her cattlemen plaques, yet also address the 'permanent emergency of authenticity'[84] that Healy sees as luring tourists to such sites, arguably questing for a national origin other than land theft and violent incursion.

It was through this sense of mired history that I viewed this photograph of the woman 'taken during the early days of white settlement.' The fact that the woman herself went unnamed and could not be traced places her within 'spaces blanked out by that ruthless whiteness'[85] that Robert Young has described. Blanking out is not merely passively absenting an omission, or forgetting. It is an active part of the production of historical understanding. It constructs the Other as for consumption within the dominant Western culture, projecting and disavowing her difference. On the one hand this unnamed woman's story – arguably best told by her descendants – fills in a blank. It assigns a position from which her content can be shared. But since the content of that story has been blanked out, the other task this image assigns is to understand the processes by which her individual, rather than typecast, identity was effaced, paradoxically by that most individuating of artefacts, the photographic portrait. She appears within the frame of the coloniser. Yet, a number of portraits of Aboriginal women taken at this time suggest through their address to the camera that many women had become 'practised' sitters.[86] It is similar in composure and technique to a portrait of Ngilgi, a Bibbulmun woman Daisy Bates counted as a friend, which appeared in her *Passing of the Aborigines,* but I have not been able to trace the photographer to locate it within any body of work.[87] The unnamed woman's address to the camera is arresting and unassimilable to the categories available at this time within which to apprehend her. Her resolute individuality punctures any imposition of type. It is not merely that some residue of the self is extant in every photographic portrait. Her expression belies any attempt at silent extirpation, any foreclosure of her life experience. As far as I can tell (and again I make no claim over any correct reading, but take ownership of this reading as subjective) it seems to animate her face with anger, grief and possibly trauma. Caught between this ineradicable expression of self and the photograph's cultural framing of the Other woman is a certain indeterminacy. She remains unknowable to authorised colonial knowledge. Yet, because her image has been consumed by white Australians it has become part of a shared story of intercultural encounter.

Understanding the processes of these attempts to know, remember, forget and blank out within the figurative space of the Aboriginal Woman might tell us something about colonial forms of knowledge production. As Bhabha reminds us, 'the image is only ever an *appurtenance* to authority and identity; it must never be read mimetically as the appearance of reality.'[88] Nevertheless, it is hard to turn away from her expression even in an effort to avoid an overdetermined typecast. Gayatri Spivak has warned against 'the slippage to rendering visible the mechanism [of occlusion of the subaltern subject] to rendering vocal the individual.'[89] There is indeed no way to fill this cultural frame with her identity by making visible the ways this woman was effaced. What it meant for this woman to directly look down the lens, and whether this contravened protocols for perceptual relations, such as eye contact between men and women, we cannot know. Whether the photographer had offended her or her husband through inadequate recompense, or in requiring her to bare herself, as far as we can see, to at least her shoulders, or come indoors, stand or sit against a sheet, where perhaps a brother-in-law had just been seated, to put to one side her child, head covering, pipe, her digging stick…for all this exposure, she remains 'doubly in shadow.'[90] We cannot access the emotional triggers for her arresting address to this camera. Nor can we assume she had any sense that we might, decades later, engage with her address. Did she associate the click of the shutter with the mechanics of incursion, or was this woman, cast as primitive, familiar with or even inured to this quintessentially modern machinery? We could resign ourselves to never knowing, or attend to the task that remains of 'measuring silences...into the object of investigation.'[91]

Since 1970, the colonial archive, occluded and partial though it is, has become an important source for Indigenous activists, including native title claimants, and stolen generations connecting back to family and country, and artists wanting to dispel settler-colonial icons and stereotypes.[92] The gleanings from this same archive have been contested by historians accusing each other of selective, tendentious readings and partial interpretations. All are invested in shaping national memory either as reckoning or redemption.[93] It has long been apparent that any historical work is necessarily selective, mediated by text – document, image and artefact – themselves created and preserved by partisan institutions and traditions, their significance often fermented in the distillery of nationalism.

The authors were, of course, largely settler men wanting to account for racial difference, within a context of colonial dispossession, and usually not wanting to leave much trace of individuals who might make unsettling claims as landowners, heirs and custodians. It is also important to remember, as Robert Kenny writes, that there is 'as wide a gulf between the mind-set of the world we inhabit and the mind-set of the colonists...as there was between those colonists and the Aboriginal peoples they confronted.'[94] The more information we have about historical texts, the greater empirical basis we have to assign fresh meanings and significance to them, and from this reinvent national remembering. However, more and more historians are drawing upon remnants and filling in the gaps with broader context and imaginings, acknowledging that even the most comprehensive sources are partial and require additional referencing through subjective analysis and creative connections to a variety of contexts. The colonial archive is now intercepted with 'the triple imperative to throw past light on ambiguous present usages, to dereify the concept of race, and to keep encounters and local agency at the forefront of analysis.'[95]

Despite the intentions of the publishers to convey something typical about her race, this photo is ineluctably a portrait. It is a mutable amalgam of bared yet imperceptible emotions. Again, by my reading, the halves of her face seem split unevenly by the spread of light, and each seems to be held in tension between a distinct and irreconcilable disturbance. The left, in darkness, seems wrathful, yet this anger appears to be contained within an intelligent management of that emotion's causes and sensations. The right, pressed with a handprint of exposure, seems bright with the trauma of newly slapped shock. The brow seems drawn into a scarcely traceable expression of anxiety. There appears an edge of scorn arcing over the plains of her face. That and an excruciating vulnerability, caught off guard yet composed in the face of history, unifies this face, for me, into the most compelling and compromising human visage. She looks to me devastated yet non-compliant.

No name, no date, no place – hardly a working basis from which to understand colonial relations as imprinted through its print archive. Ordinarily the difficulties such an image presents would render it historically impermissible. Yet, these are in themselves descriptive difficulties. This woman's imposed anonymity interpellates her into the prevailing type of lubra or gin. In my book, it is descriptive of racial encounters to which we still need to reconcile ourselves.

In her esteemed history of images of Andean Indians, Deborah Poole found such colonial images provide an impetus to 'examine the role of visual images in the structuring and reproduction of the scientific projects, cultural sentiments, and aesthetic dispositions that characterize modernity in general and modern racial discourse in particular.'[96] A similar archive of images and descriptions of Australian Aboriginal women can be found in the holdings of museums, public record offices and state libraries around the world. They reference much earlier conventions of iconography of indigenous women who, as Phillipa Levine observes, 'bore an enormous symbolic burden as writers from Walter Raleigh to Edward Long employed them to mark metaphorically the symbiotic boundaries of European national identities and white supremacy.'[97] As Levine notes, subsequent writers borrowed freely from one another, superimposing imagery from enslaved and colonised women from diverse scenarios of racial difference. These earlier archival holdings also provide the basis for mapping out shifting discourses of racial difference within the amalgam of gender. But in terms of trying to account for white imaginings, this particular study focuses on how these images, textual descriptions and material products were circulated and reiterated for white consumption in travelogues, settler autobiographies, illustrated encyclopedias, pictorial atlases, newspapers and magazines – that is, in print media. It is striking that before 1967, Aboriginal women were largely depicted unnamed, or given white names, often Mary or Topsy, or typed as lubras and gins throughout popular print.

Yet, by the time Duncan-Kemp's book was published, Indigenous women had been appearing as public figures, such as the community advocate Faith Bandler[98] and Pearl Gibbs.[99] In addition, white women involved in Aboriginal reserves had become public advocates, including Mary Montgomery Bennett[100] and Caroline Kelly.[101] The publication of anthropologist Phyllis Kaberry's *Aboriginal Woman: Sacred and Profane* in 1939 redressed the gender partiality of male anthropologists and their failure to credit women their distinct role in ritual, the 'matriarchal transmission of rights'[102] to perform ceremonies, along with their interests in land tenure law.[103] Aboriginal women gained increasing recognition after the 1967 referendum, through the unrelenting activism of Marcia Langton, Bobbi Sykes, Oodgeroo Noonuccal (Kath Walker) and many others, through the international champions Evonne Goolagong and Cathy Freeman, and through biographers Margaret Tucker, Ruby Langford Ginibi and Sally Morgan. Also noteworthy were a series of biographical essays on Koorie women by anthropologist Dianne Barwick,[104] a collection edited by Fay Gale,[105] the award-winning television series *Women of the Sun* in 1981,[106] anthropologist Dianne Bell's 1983 *Daughters of the Dreaming* and an exhibition of the same name at Museum Victoria in 1990.[107]

Before these post-referendum additions to understandings of Aboriginal women, newcomers craved to know the specifics of Aboriginal women's lives, such as how they grieved, birthed and were married, but then usually erased their individual identities. In the most obvious sense, one explanation has to be the dispossession of identity and the role it played in what Patrick Wolfe influentially identified as the settler-colonial 'logic of elimination.'[108] It created a space divested of individual women in the white imagination, which was then supplanted by types, tropes, obfuscations and sometimes outright lies. It is these supplanted imaginings that form the basis for this book. It is a print history of settler impressions of Aboriginal women situated at that most potent juncture of racism and misogyny. This is a book of lies.

The colonial archive largely consists of accounts by white men. It is not only delimited to their worldview, but it is also marked by a particular disregard for the identities of individual

Aboriginal women, more overt than the disregard for Aboriginal men. It is also replete with fantasies, projections and caprices. To give another example, in 1946 Norman Laird wrote a vignette about an unnamed 'Aborigine girl' standing by a railway siding on the Nullarbor while his train was being rewatered. The quotation that kicks off this introduction comes from Laird. He saw her 'cracked and bleeding feet', her 'matted and untidy hair' and wrote that her 'European rags hung upon her like a blanket of darkness choking the life-green from a struggling plant.' Even though the girl seemed to 'shrink into space', Laird wanted to see into the 'sheltered caverns of her eyes.' He imagined he saw 'a fellow creature who, having lost so much on the margins of existence, seemed now to watch wistfully for a new signal from life.' Laird is contemptuous of white superiority and 'civilised stupidity', displaying his fine moral spirit. Nevertheless, he attributed her impoverishment to an inherent Aboriginal incapacity to take on the mantle of civilisation. The girl may be of a 'vanishing race' but Laird passionately hopes for a better future, and by 1946 he is also aware of the importance of perceptual relations. He wishes her people are never permitted to be 'publicly humiliated with remarks, jokes or ridicule that directly reflect upon their mental status.'[109]

The author is caught up in the prevailing ideas of his time and his cackhanded sympathy ought to be a warning for how fine feeling is not enough. From today's vantage he was wrong on a number of counts; most obviously and against all odds, the young woman's people did not 'vanish'. He was wrong to conflate the undoubted loss of knowledge, language and ceremony with dying race theory. And he writes, 'If it is pointed out that the aborigines are unable to learn calculus, let us also remember that we cannot learn black-tracking.' Racial difference is granted latitude

'Her mind was vacant'

through a peculiar mix of patronising self-apology. Laird's piece is embroidered with the fortifying regret of tenderfoot occupants. Still, in the end all that we know about the young woman he describes comes from his side of the tracks. He never crosses over, asks her name or attempts to find out anything about her. This appraisal from a distance characterises the gendered and racialised perceptual relations of the settler.

It is clear newcomers have always been deeply ambivalent about the processes of colonisation they were complicit in and accrued dividends from. Perhaps it was this that prompted them to concoct entire narratives of Aboriginality working off glimpses.

Figure 7 'Aborigine Nellie', in Walkabout, *1952, Courtesy National Library of Australia. Rex Nan Kivell Collection NQ 919.4WAL*

In 1952 a TAA passenger, Eric White, penned a vignette of 'Aborigine Nellie', a young woman travelling on her own with a hessian bag to Katherine (see Figure 7). He claimed she 'rolled big, frightened eyes' at the plane because she was 'a mute and lonely symbol of her race, a stone-age victim of the machine age.'

Even so, he notes 'her deportment would have excited the envy of many a model or ballerina of the south.' Clearly intrigued, White continues, 'Every movement had a natural grace; each gesture was smooth and dainty. The print frock emphasized the slimness of her waist.' Then he snuck a snapshot of her and, again, to my reading, she seemed to huddle dejected on the lowest step leading up to the Cloncurry passenger lounge. It is remarkable from today's vantage that White did not make any attempt to speak to her. Instead he lifted her name from the passenger list. And the name she gave may have been how she preferred to be known by whitefellas. The name or names she knew herself by were either immaterial to whites or perhaps something of herself she preferred to keep to herself. If she was coming from home she may have been a Kalkadoon, Pitta Pitta or Mitakoodi woman. White watched her every move, even though he knew she 'crouched' in her seat, 'intent on keeping out of sight' and was 'trying to be as inconspicuous as possible.'[110] That sense of entitlement to visual access pervades perceptual relations from settlers to Aboriginal women. Is it any wonder she crouched in her seat? Laird left her historically stranded; today an anthropologist at the Northern Land Council is unable to identify 'Aborigine Nellie.'[111] The question for us is do we leave this woman consigned to history or, having attempted to identify her and contact her descendants, do we ask why Aboriginal women were granted this oneiric presence in the national optic?

Under this unrelenting gaze, of following and noting their every move, yet not wanting to include their voices or lived experiences, it isn't hard to imagine Aboriginal women keeping things back, such as their names, their destination, their business. Their sacred knowledge has been denigrated as 'superstition', even suspect, such as during the Hindmarsh Island affair, in which a proposed bridge in South Australia was disputed by Ngarrindjeri women as infringing on sacred 'secret women's business' they could not reveal.[112] Indigenous intellectual property has understandably become a site of heightened protection. When contacting Aboriginal women's organisations to repatriate images such as that of 'Nellie', this has been raised as a concern.[113] As such, this isn't a book about Aboriginal women's stories, but rather about the stalled encounter within which whites wanted to know Aboriginal women – without actually speaking to them. It is an attempt to reconcile this failure of recognition with regard.

The article on 'Nellie', like that on Sally Corbett and Mary Jane Milawa, is centred on a named woman. In the vast print literature on Aboriginal women up to 1967 I've been able to locate twelve such articles in journals and magazines (including some newspapers). Nine are obituaries in the 'last of her tribe' genre, including three on Trugernanner and another on Fanny Balbuk-Yooreel of Swan River, which shows a photograph of her corpse.[114] One article features a tree climber.[115] Another queries whether Fanny Cochrane Smith was in fact the last Tasmanian.[116] The last is a story on 'Black Aggie' in a journal entitled *Wild Life*.[117] Three of these stories are written by the amateur anthropologist and well-known journalist Daisy Bates, who camped at Ooldea for sixteen years and devoted her life to collecting information and artefacts while tending to the sick. Along with her widely read 1938 book, *The Passing of the Aborigines*, Bates published 270 newspaper articles on her 'natives and I'. These articles on women she knew consolidated her claim to having intimate knowledge of the 'dying tribes', as she called them.

It seems Aboriginal women were mostly named in print after they died in what we might call obituary hubris. In the John Greenway bibliography of some 20,000 references (which we will come to in the next chapter), largely listing journal and magazine articles on Australian Aborigines until 1959, there is one lonely publication authored by an Aboriginal woman. It was written by Ngoondaw Gladys, a fourteen-year-old girl at the Mount Margaret Mission in Western Australia in 1937, rather forlornly about Saint George, and was published by the mission to showcase her progress after two years of schooling.[118] Yet, literate and educated Aboriginal women, such as Bessy Cameron (nee Flowers), teacher at Ramahyuck, wrote letters to the press but weren't listed in the Greenway bibliography.[119]

Does recirculating these unnamed images simply reinstate settler presumptiveness about visual access? Does it merely consolidate a vantage over Indigenous women where, to paraphrase Bhabha, they are not?[120] Or is it justified by what they can tell us about settler imaginings of Aboriginal women and the part they continue to play in shaping non-Indigenous responses to Aboriginal women? Certainly the textual imaginings of Aboriginal women that comprise this study confirm Langton's crucial argument that, 'The densest relationship is not between actual people, but between white Australians and the symbols created by their predecessors.'[121] More circumspect settler observers, such as Victorian squatter Edward Curr,[122] whom we will meet again in this work, knew that the knowledge most Australians had of Aborigines was derived purely from read sources which were themselves 'little better than a tissue of errors', intimating also the flimsiness of evidence for white perceptions.[123] Women were particularly obscured to predominantly male observers by their reserve, as they protected restricted knowledge, and by their being subsumed under the category 'native' and collectivised into types such as lubra and gin. When in 1934 Krzywicki singled Aboriginal women out for particular attention (attempting to verify whether women ever induced abortion), he complained, 'The life of Australian women is to this day a closed book in many respects: we know little about it.'[124] European-heritage authors compensated the gap with much speculation and little regard.

Under these conditions it is remarkable that Aboriginal women themselves have still felt generous enough to share some of their knowledge with non-Indigenous Australians, no doubt to counteract the 'tissue of errors' but perhaps also in reaction to having been 'wilfully concealed or carefully forgotten.'[125] It has meant we can now look back on this colonial record circumspectly and rethink the meanings circulated in this little-known compendium of banal description of Aboriginal women. By not intervening in that tissue of errors, non-Indigenous disregard for their concerns, their demands and their defiant custodianship of land, livelihood, law, language and lineage will continue, as will a concentrated scrutiny of Aboriginal women, over which they have little say and which paradoxically fails to represent them. Aileen Moreton-Robertson gives a sense of being caught within this tissue of errors and how it creates 'the complexities Indigenous women face in a world under conditions not of their choosing, where they must translate and interpret whiteness, while being "Other".'[126] Indeed, in a bracing critique which the underlying predicament of this book resonates with, Moreton-Robinson has also argued, 'White feminist academics engage with women who are "other" predominantly through representations in texts and imaginings. The "Other" offers no resistance and can be made to disappear at will.'[127] Undertaking a cultural history *of* that process risks amounting to nothing more than another distancing device. It is all the more reason to engage as much as possible with Indigenous women.

The Australian Institute for Aboriginal and Torres Strait Islander Studies' 'Guidelines for Ethical Research in Australian Indigenous Studies' explains that it is important to 'recognise that Indigenous individuals or communities may have more pressing priorities, that may impinge on the research time frames.'[128] Whenever photographs gave any sort of hint to the whereabouts of descendants – and the absenting of identities meant few details of such coordinates were forthcoming – I have attempted to repatriate them to communities, but I've rarely heard back. Engaging with the project may not have been a priority and it was impossible for me to build personal relationships through such a geographical spread of sources. This means the principle of 'appropriate negotiation and consultation about the aims and objectives, and… meaningful negotiation of processes, outcomes and involvement' hasn't been realised as fully as I'd hoped. This book does not deal with cultural heritage, nor is it localised to one community where I could over years build collaborative relationships. It surveys print representation intended for white consumption – textual, visual and material – since Dampier and beyond our shores. Nevertheless, images of Aboriginal women, perhaps since deceased, are included and engaging with their descendants was therefore critical. As Eric Michaels has explained, photography, as a mass medium, poses special problems because the unauthorised display of people may violate mortuary restrictions or invade privacy, and of course people have become sensitised to 'paternalistic imagery which makes Aborigines appear exotic.'[129] Michaels' influential essay puts complex cultural differences around photography in simple terms. He writes,

> One could pursue at length the ethnographic significance of people's fear of cameras and accusations of spirit

theft. Or one might simply admit that there is a certain sense to the proposition that using someone else's image, property or life as a subject to be recorded, reproduced and distributed is a kind of appropriation.[130]

Focusing at times on unnamed women, that is, women already subjected to this very appropriation, creates a dilemma: should such images be left outside the historical account, when they have played a significant role in shaping ongoing imaginings of Aboriginal women?

I was fortunate to be given time in the communities at Hopevale and Yarrabah and by women in the Flinders Ranges, the Grampians and by the Wurundjeri Council Elders, to whom I showed most of the images comprising this study and asked if they could identify the woman I had made a particular focus. None could. But many made suggestions which I hope I have given due credit. I thank Aunty Di Kerr and Fjorn Butler of the Wurundjeri Council Elders, Shirley Costello of the Hopevale Indigenous Knowledge and Technology Centre, Shirley Hartman and family at the Indigenous Ngarrindjeri Centre, Lillian Holt, women of the Yarrabah Women's Resource Centre, and Brambuk – the Gariwerd National Park & Cultural Centre. Thanks also to Freddie Dowling, elder of the Pangerang people of North East Victoria, for his comments on this introduction. I am of course solely responsible for any shortcomings in this work.

The cultural inclination to consume images of mostly anonymous Aboriginal women is what this book tries to understand, a facing that attempts to eclipse difference and reduce it to appearance, 'an entity without materiality.'[131] That very inclination may have contributed to Aboriginal women's distrust of any form of white 'interest'. Approaches to Aboriginal women's organisations prompted questions about how their input into my project might address any of their immediate concerns – housing, safety, education, discrimination – which of course it does not. However, women I spoke to did feel it addresses their shared disquiet that many non-Indigenous Australians don't understand the pervasive and particular racism that has dogged Aboriginal women. In one instance, after warning that many of the images I would show were offensively racist and potentially hurtful, a woman shrugged and replied, 'We've seen and heard it all before.' Despite these constraints on 'consulting', all the women I met with encouraged me to continue with the research and publish it, even when I expressed my trepidation that I could be recirculating damaging, hurtful material. The aim to challenge amnesia about our history of everyday cultural racism was nevertheless encouraged. Settler accounts of Aboriginal women's violent subjugation and the 'savage' nature of pre-contact sexual politics is unavoidable for any researcher in the colonial archive. Since the damaging Northern Territory 'Emergency Response' intervention in 2007, researchers have engaged with this material in the context of gut-wrenching disclosures of Aboriginal family violence that have then been misappropriated as the rationale for discriminatory welfare and lease occupation policies. However, it is not within the scope of this book to assay the disjoint between the need to address contemporary disclosure and the representational contrivances of ethno-history.

This book historicises a way of relating in which dialogue is eschewed and talking *about* is the sole point of reference. By bringing this largely unfounded gossip before contemporary readers I hope non-Indigenous Australians can reflect on how it continues to haunt white perceptions of Aboriginal women, shaping policy directions, government interventions and daily interactions. One of the most helpful examples of overcoming these tensions can be found in Shino Konishi's refutation of the historical misuse of Aboriginal men's violence.[132] She charts the shift from ethnography – of speaking of and about Indigenous peoples – to representation – of reading European sources critically, holistically and sceptically for what they reveal about imperial investments, mirrored in the move from 'archive-as-source to archive-as-subject.'[133] The 'linguistic turn' in historiography draws on poststructural methodologies of semiotics and iconography to take sources as mediated, implicated in the parameters of identity and needing to be read 'against the grain'. Thus 'the complexities and contradictions' of early culture-contact sources can be drawn out with an astute eye, as can their unwitting disclosure of European interests, not to mention their 'ethnocentrism, imperial agenda, and narcissistic self-regard.'[134] Checks and balances need to be applied, such as querying the reliability of sources which claim to quote Aboriginal individuals who weren't proficient in English, or comparing 'generalized and speculative' third-person accounts involving unnamed people with detailed eye-witness descriptions. I want to contribute to this the technique of surveying across a critical mass of sources with an eye out for the reiteration of those unverified tropes, most of which, unsurprisingly, rationalise the colonial project. The careful sifting, contextualising, verifying or refuting of sources shows a strategic deployment of reading critically. I want to propose a practice of reading across (as well as against and along[135]) the recursive grain and, since this archive is constituted through print, of reading *across the typeset*, of looking for reiteration and immersion within discursive fields, of keeping an eye out for the moment that representation becomes instated as the unmediated presentation of fact. I want to add to the repertoire of refutation by postcolonial scholars and to their identification of the colonial archive as comprising politically invested representations, by conducting a tracery of amassed reiterations of these tropes of savage sociality and typecastings. Part of what this book attempts is to document, historicise and understand the peculiar disregard that comes with knowing from one side of the tracks, while acknowledging my standpoint as a white feminist hoping to politically intervene in these enduring distortions.

Skin Deep looks at the distinct but related preoccupations of European-Australians in their encounters with Aboriginal women and the tropes, types and perceptions that seeped into everyday thinking. The organising fields in European imaginings of femininity frame the following chapters: first (early) impressions, then gender status, maternity, domesticity, sexuality and appearance. Aboriginal women were, unsurprisingly, thought of within the same domains by which European women were appraised, all overlapping, interacting and enmeshing in this singular yet subsumed entity, the Australian Aboriginal woman.

Chapter 1 explores first-contact descriptions of Aboriginal women, looking at the coincidence of colonial expansion with developments in print media; for instance, total newspaper sales in Britain reached 16 million by 1790.[136] It lays the basis for the central argument of the book: that colonial racism and gender relations hinge in particular ways and depended on the facility of print to reiterate and thereby entrench meaning as truth. It looks at the circulation of early images, particularly an engraving of the woman Arra-Maïda, through European print media. It contextualises this within the textual description of exploratory voyages and knowledge regimes that shaped perceptions of 'native' women and how they were entwined by the observational ethos of ethnography and exoticism. Chapter 2 is concerned with settler perceptions of Aboriginal women's gender status. It traces the 'bride capture' trope and shows how preoccupations with the tribal status of women allowed white men to disavow their own atrocities (also detailed). Additionally renounced were the impacts of colonialism on Aboriginal gender relations, so newcomer men could conceive of their 'civilising' as part of a grand design of colonial chivalry. Chapter 3, on maternity, traces the confronting trope of the Aboriginal mother as infanticidal cannibal. Reading through select reports from an almost definitive study of every press mention of Aboriginal mothers as infanticidal cannibals, it finds no credible evidence. Instead, it finds an upsurge in print reports of court proceedings against white women 'of the serving-girl variety' charged with infanticide. It relates this trope to dying race theory and also to shifts in European ideas of maternity and the primordial, 'primitive' mother. Chapter 4, on domesticity, examines white imaginings of the Aboriginal domicile through cartoons of women's exaggeratedly outsize feet. The oxymoron at the heart of *migrating settlers* was dodged by focusing on the footfall of Aboriginal women over domestic thresholds in print descriptions of nomadic comportment. Europeans' imposition of their limited ideas of the home utterly disrupted the domicile of Aboriginal women that had been ordered around an economy dependent on their harvesting, communal eating and shared childcare. This undomesticated and abject Aboriginal mother justified the 'race rescue' of her 'piccaninnies' by the paternal state – conveniently also removing the evidence of white men's sexual use of Aboriginal women. The place for Aboriginal women in the nation's home became the domesticated 'house gin' often figured in bric-a-brac ceramics and tourist memorabilia tea towels. Chapter 5, on sexuality, focuses on the 'black velvet' trope that emerged under pastoral and mining expansion into remote areas. Sexual access to Aboriginal women was dismissed as a necessary evil in terrain unpopulated by white women. Yet longstanding indifference, or ineffective moral outrage, turned overnight into moral panic when prostitution with Japanese pearlers was revealed just before World War II. The absence of the term 'black velvet' in the print panic that ensued points to the use of colloquial language to shore up national borders against the intimate exchanges endemic to trade and frontier. In Chapter 6, on appearance, the 'look' of Aboriginal women is shown to be at times fascinating and abhorrent to Europeans. They either demanded a guise of primitive authenticity or assimilated modernity from Aboriginal women, all the while assessing their racial character. Europeans vacillated between the romance of the primitive and unaffected native belle type to revulsion at elder Aboriginal women and their apparent embodiment of the 'Hobbesian nightmare'. The reaction of European and newcomer men to the appearance of Aboriginal elder women exposed their delimited vision of permissible expressions of feminine visual identity in a constantly changing colonial public sphere. From the early descriptions of the native belle to the dystopian visions of the elder woman succumbing to the logic of dying race, the book cycles through the disrupted life cycle of Aboriginal women in the white imaginary, as brides, mothers, homemakers and matriarchs. These idealised social positions for women were intercepted by counter-narratives of prostitution, infanticide, fringe-dwelling and the malevolent presence of unsightly elder women.

This book conducts a very broad survey, ranging through a number of shifts in racial thought, from the physiological taxonomies of the eighteenth century, the legal distinctions enforcing racial difference in the nineteenth century, the focus on family and the domestic and moral coordinates of the early to mid-twentieth century, and the cultural racism of the postwar era's representations. What is evident in the latter, through the tracery we will follow over print representations of Aboriginal women, is the reinscription and recovery of older racial discourses and the 'layering of sedimented hierarchal forms.'[137] Starting with early impressions, the book charts their ongoing hold and reiteration, and their disruption and demise through shifts in public discourse. As the categories of gender status, maternity, domesticity, sexuality and appearance were applied to Aboriginal women, they were both shored up and contested. These understandings were distorted by hidden elements, such as settler men disavowing their promiscuity. What becomes clear is that the enmeshment of racism with misogyny is not merely an addendum to an already fully operational set of understandings, but indispensable to settler-colonialism's operations of power, its technologies and mechanics of rule.

Ordinarily, historians attentive to an image's production – and many aren't – would foreground the photographer, their body of work, the subjects' names and dates, and less often how and where the image was published and exhibited; in other words, its attribution. The unnamed woman photographed (Figure 1) and her community may have been involved in intense negotiations in the taking of her photograph. As just one example, one photographer in 1944 first had to explain to women on Groote Eylandt that he was married and then parley that he was classified as the brother of one of his guides, which meant some of the women could not exchange looks with him, before they would consent to be photographed.[138] The omission of this woman's name from the caption may have been in response to her having a number of skin names. For example, the Walpiri of Central Australia have more than one skin name depending on their relationship to who addresses them, where and when. And as Dianne Bell observed from her fieldwork in 1970 with the Walpiri, 'what is stressed when identifying a person, alive or dead, is their relationship to others, their dreaming affiliations and their ritual associations.'[139] These are entirely abstract determinates of identification from those that inform photographic portraiture. And yet Susan Sontag's analysis resonates with this portrait: 'the camera cannot help but reveal faces as social masks.'[140] Her picture still 'calls for a *lexis*', one inscribed through the enterprise of settler-colonialism and through differentiating into racialised collectivities or designated types.[141] Her portrait 'imposes meaning at one stroke', as Barthes wrote,[142] allowing for the intensified focus applied to Aboriginal women.

The very absence of the names this woman knew herself by and the country that defined her place in the world is descriptive of what colonial occupation took from Aboriginal women. The compulsion to displace their voices with images and description was inscribed in the everyday rounds of banal ephemera in newspapers, postcards, ceramic bric-a-brac, cartoons, fabric design, lithographs, magazines, children's storybooks, tourism pamphlets, gallery catalogues, breakfast cereal tie-ins and published settlers' accounts of their lives 'among the blacks'. For a nation that sustained the fiction of *terra nullius* by taking lives, 'dispersing' people from their homelands and removing children, the cultural presence granted to a people who were not even counted in the census until 1967 is remarkable. It showcases the settler-colonial impulse to 'get hold of something by means of its likeness.'[143] In the instance of Aboriginal women, that something was contact beyond copy, displaced by commodity fetishism in the 'mighty mimetic machineries'[144] of camera and print. Race relations are displaced onto relations among things, often bric-a-brac 'used like gum trees to mark Australian distinctiveness.'[145] Some have commented that a kind of proximity, a quest to belong as kindred, shaped the need to prop images and ceramics of Aboriginal women around our homes as if to keep a trace of them among us. They comprised a kind of colonial publicity, that is, publication mediated by colonial organisations, 'with publicity merely staged for manipulative ends',[146] or what we've also called propaganda. Within a public sphere 'transmogrified into a sphere of cultural consumption',[147] colonial publicity about Aboriginal women helped settler-heritage Australians ignore how the women depicted had been displaced from their homes. Nicholas Thomas's analysis of appropriation lends itself to the ornamentalising of Aboriginal women. He writes,

> the business of simultaneously exhibiting and exterminating the native is consistent with the enduring, invasive logic of a settler-colonial nation. On the one hand, a self-conscious national culture that seems permanently in the making required Aboriginality for its localizing effect; on the other, Aboriginal sovereignty and autonomy diminished the authority and coherence of the settler nation, and were persistently repressed.[148]

It excused a long tradition of publicity that was constituted through a colonial economy of image and text and which, in the main(stream) 'cant of conquest',[149] rendered Aboriginal women as unnamed, as anonymous, as a particular formation of *nullius*.

1

'A FULL ACCOUNT OF THE INHABITANTS': NAME-DROPPING IN EARLY ENCOUNTERS

> It is only through the knowing of blackness in Australia that whiteness has been felt to be real.[1]

A cursory glance though the *Bibliography of the Australian Aborigines and the Native Peoples of Torres Strait to 1959*[2] reveals three points of interest in the 'native' for the medium of print. They are strictly for 'things' left behind: implements, place names and skulls. Knowing what has been lost (as distinct from taken) is an enduring quandary for the settler-colonial imaginary. Through the artefacts of antiquity, settlers and visitors hoped to glimpse something of their origin in the 'fossil men' of the Antipodes.[3] Through their isolation Aborigines had preserved intact, or so it was thought, our prototypical, earliest and least complicated forms of human economy, kinship structures, language forms, religious and aesthetic traditions and even physiology. At least the men had: the women just bookended the gender divide common to all humankind, attracting some interest in their youth and thereafter merely trudging after their 'lords'...or so it was thought.

This remarkable bibliography is a compendium of all the journal and magazine print articles on Australian Aborigines until 1959. It surveys the inventory of thinking about Aborigines by settlers, Europeans, Americans, anthropologists, missionaries, administrators and an array of informal observers into the mid-twentieth century. Cranial articulations and dimensions, artefacts, weapons, rock paintings and carvings, district dialects and word lists, marriage laws and sexual taboos, burial rites, ceremonies, habits, customs, manners and 'superstitions'—all incised a discursive frieze of the primeval across the nation's pages. Pre-settlement ways of being were imagined as having not been impacted by settler-heritage observers peering in from cities appliquéd on the continent's hem. It is as though the only real Aborigine were a pre-contact one,[4] and male.

The bibliography was compiled by John Greenway, a folklorist, who went on to pen some of the foremost studies of protest song. Greenway came to Australia as a Rhodes scholar to record Aboriginal songs. His bibliography of some 20,000 citations includes the entries, 'On a numerical determination of the relative positions of certain biological types in the evolutionary scale, and of the relative values of various cranial measurements and indices as criteria';[5] *Fossil Men and Their Modern Representatives*;[6] 'The teeth of some Australian Aboriginal natives, and comparisons with the teeth of prehistoric man';[7] and even *Australian Aboriginal Signs and Symbols for the Use of Boy Scouts*.[8] Also to be found in Greenway's unstinting bibliography, after careful excavation, are works that single out Aboriginal women. In most of the more general works women are appended to men, under a subheading or particularised under their separate chapters or paragraphs. For instance, in the 1880 *Natural History of Man*, the first chapter has as its subheading: 'The native Australians – The general conformation of the head and features – Their average stature and form – The women and their appearance – Character of the natives – Their thievish propensities – Their cunning, and power of disimulation'[9] – I need hardly go on. Similarly, William Ramsay Smith, in his entry on Aborigines in a 1927 encyclopedia, gives a very detailed description of initiation and then writes, 'For women, too, there are special initiatory ceremonies, in many ways analogous to those of the men. Fuller accounts of all these ceremonies will be found'...in other books cited in the references, he says.[10] Soon after, a photographed man is said to best represent the race as 'a fine physical example of the aboriginal.'[11] The psychologist Porteous in 1929 published his study of Aboriginal intelligence. The claim he made in his *Psychology of a Primitive People*[12] – that the average brain capacity for Aborigines was between twelve and thirteen years – was based on a study of 257 Central Australians.[13] It included eleven women.[14] Arguably it reflected rather worse on men's cranial capacities that it did on Aborigines'. In another example of the elision of women, the same year C. S. Browne speculated on the rapid decline of the Aboriginal population, completely disregarding women's primacy in reproduction. He wrote, 'the aboriginal has succumbed with terrible rapidity to Western pestilences – tuberculosis from the wearing of clothes, syphilis, from the intercourse of white and yellow men with his womenfolk, the ravages of alcohol.'[15] Here the universal category 'man' has segued into actual men. That women suffered and transmitted syphilis was immaterial. In these iterations, women are both within the category of Other and without.

Dedicated titles on women in the Greenway bibliography are in the very slimmest minority, forty-four in all. They are trifling enough to compile a sequential list provided in this book's Appendix. A glance through gives a lightening tour of the shifts in settler thinking about Aboriginal women. (The Greenway bibliography referenced few newspapers, so his survey can't be said to be definitive of print culture.) It shows that childbirth, fertility, mourning rites, implements, singing and marriage laws remained constants, while an interest in pubescence, domesticity, labour, status and property came to the fore in the early twentieth century. The language in the few newspaper articles listed is notably more sensational, and while these articles tended to be reprinted a number of times, there is little crossover from scientific journals to newsprint. In the last entry of 1958, women's distinct relation to sacred rites finally appears. Among settler-observers a greater emphasis was placed on Aboriginal men as bearers of the past through the type of the 'myall', the 'wild' tribesman, and due to the precedence anthropologists placed on men's ceremony, business and traditions. Women were less subject to either the romanticism or the scholastic hustle for tribal custom. Instead, their traditions were largely subsumed under those of men or failed to register with most observers until the emergence of women anthropologists Phyllis Kabbery, Olive Pink and Ursula McConnel from the 1930s.[16] The emphasis on childbirth in our forty-four citations is telling. As mothers, Aboriginal women carried the future of the race; yet newcomer interest in Aboriginal maternity focused on parturition while care, nurturing and provision for their children hardly bears mention.

As we observed in the introduction, the historical coincidence of industrialised print with colonialism invites us to reflect on print as a media form in which thoughts were pressed into permanent patterns on collated sheets that, through their dissemination, were capable of conquering space. Print and colonialism were interdependent, enmeshed, expansionist economies. Tony Ballantyne has written of the central place of print in the age of empire-building. The printing press was a 'crucial instrument' for colonial administrators, missionaries, social reformers, pioneering nationalists, Indigenous leaders and for members of international scientific, humanitarian and political communities.[17] These settler imaginings accrete into a cultural inheritance. The reiteration of these tropes of aboriginality aggregate patterns of meaning within a pastiche of cultural productions. Through repetition, and through the immersion that it creates, racial differences become entrenched.

The new intelligence about humankind shipped in from the New World needed to be not only documented but maintained over time through the multiple dissemination of copies, syndications and reprints. Conceptions of racial difference did not take hold when first set down, but rather amassed over decades into the guise of commonsense understandings through the repetition that is intrinsic to print. They piled up through popular imperial culture to consolidate what J. A. Hobson, in 1901, called a 'psychology of jingoism'. Analysing imperial culture around the Boer War, Hobson argued this jingoistic patriotism circulated through music halls and popular culture, transforming 'the love of one's own nation…into the hatred of another.'[18] Ideas of nation closely align with the ideal of racial homogeneity. Hobson paid close attention to the role of the press in producing jingoism. It worked, he thought, to consolidate a 'concurrence of opinion' due to its standing as 'by far the most potent instrument in the modern manufacture of public opinion.' He detailed the networks of journalism, noting that most newspapers syndicated and referenced uncritically from two major London dailies, *The Times* and *The Daily News.* They themselves sourced from certain press offices in Capetown, which Hobson dismissed as a 'bought and kept press' owned by an elite group of men who happened to also own or control diamond mines at Kimberley and goldfields on the Rand. These men had, as company directors, 'assessed the business value of a war at several million extra profits per annum.' Hobson also noted the colonies were every bit as jingoistic in their sympathy for the Boer War, because the Australian press took all its cablegrams from the same London correspondents as a means to pool their expenses. Ultimately, they distorted public opinion.[19]

Hobson didn't much credit readers with any capacity for critical or even circumspect reading, though few readers would have been aware of the financial interests linked to the major dailies and the effects of sourcing from limited correspondents and cablegrams. Nothing much has changed. What he schematises, however, in this notion of jingoism is a certain relation between imperialism and repetition that we can call 'imperial copy'. As the province of print, copy is both literal and peculiar to its professional and corporate networks. Copy stems from a limited pool of correspondents, the vested interests of editors, the uncritical syndication of the same reports or simply the circulation of a broadsheet. Copy constitutes code. It establishes discursive coherence through certain 'features as criterial'[20] to national inclusion.

This kind of 'looping' has more recently been theorised by Deb Verhoeven in her history of sheep in Australian cinema, wherein 'a set of stock visual and thematic motifs' was employed.[21] In the context of my study a sameness of identity is reiterated through stock imagery and description – the figure of the Aboriginal woman – that does not add up to comprehension but rather to the directionless circuitry of 'originary thinking'.[22] Reiteration doesn't foreclose meaning, but by its nature suspends it in a loop without culmination in a relay of differentiation without end. Racism and misogyny are the twin sides of a möbius strip. In this chapter we trace a few of the early settler impressions of Aboriginal women – in Dampier's earliest descriptions, an engraving by John Webber illustrating Cook's published journals, an illustration and description in John White's journals, and the travels of a French engraving of the Tasmanian woman Arra Maïda – to chart their circulation through print and gain a sense of its constitutive role in the colonial project.

Let's take a buccaneer as our first exemplar of the loopiness of racial thought as facilitated by print. William Dampier was the first Englishman to collide with the continent and scribed some of the originary denigration of Australian Aborigines from his two visits to the North West in 1688 and 1699.[23] An ambivalent figure, Dampier morphed from sea bandit to man of science, largely through the publication of his journal, *New Voyage Around the World* (1697), which ran to five editions before 1706 and gained him the notice of the recently established Royal Society.[24] Having attained the standing of a natural philosopher and author,[25] his observations did not set him apart from Europeans traversing the globe at this time. Spanish, Portuguese, French and Dutch privateer mariners formed a 'literate and literary buccaneering fraternity',[26] whose exploratory publications frequently engaged in ethnological observations, or 'buccaneering ethnography' as Anna Neill has dubbed it.[27] Their ships at times acted as 'floating laboratories'. Exotic Others were perceived collectively, that is, grouped within a unitary category, variously expressed through the types barbarian, heathen, infidel, Indian or savage. Langton describes this tendency as, 'an ancient and universal feature of racism: the assumption of the undifferentiated "Other".'[28] It is also a function of typecasting to set up significatory frameworks through which meaning can be slotted in. These racialised types were generally judged deficient in terms of morality, law, religion, governance, trade, attire, agriculture, dwellings and the status of women. In that regard they preceded and offset the cult of the noble savage – the rational man living in a state of paradisiacal nature, a type that emerged in response to eighteenth-century

A full account of the inhabitants

exploratory voyages and the discovery of Tahiti.[29] Earlier, in 1688, when Dampier came ashore at King Sound, northwestern Australia, he was famously underwhelmed:

> The inhabitants of this country are the miserablest people in the world...and setting aside their shape they differ little from the brutes. They are tall, straight-bodied and thin, with small long limbs. They have great heads, round foreheads, and great brows...They have great bottle-noses, pretty full lips, and wide mouths...They are long visaged, and are of a very unpleasing aspect, having not one graceful feature in their faces.[30]

Significantly, Dampier barely commented on the women, nor distinguished them from the men.

The entire passage was reprinted in the rather premature 1787 *History of New Holland*.[31] It reappeared in an 1854 dictionary, under 'Races of men in Australia.'[32] Then in 1857 the Sydney magazine *Empire* extracted it from a public lecture in which it was likened to a sketch in *Punch* as 'by no means a fair portraiture.'[33] The speaker, J. H. Palmer, was the first and only author to challenge Dampier before 1952! The passage found its way into Albert Calvert's 1893 *Discovery of Australia*.[34] In fact, it was reprinted fifteen times in Australian newspapers between 1890 and 1948 as well as in *Walkabout*, the widely read travel magazine, in 1947.[35]

Another passage completes a similarly circuitous print circuit. Dampier unsuccessfully attempts to involve Aborigines in the colonial exchange of labour for cast-offs. He wrote, 'we clothed some of them, designating to have some service of them for it.' They gave them an old pair of breeches, a 'ragged shirt', and a jacket 'scarce worth owning.' 'We put them on them, thinking that this finery would have brought them to work heartily for us', but when his men placed the six-gallon barrels across their shoulders, 'they stood like statues, without motion, but grinned like so many monkeys, staring upon one another; for these poor creatures seem not accustomed to carry burthens.'[36] A poor existence indeed. Dampier and his crew were 'forced' to carry their own water. So it was Dampier's observations that initiated, and through reiteration entrenched, the idea that Aborigines are lazy.[37] The *History of New Holland* used these comments to support the contention that New Hollanders were 'totally unused to laborious work, and particularly not having the least idea of carrying burdens.'[38] The passage is given another airing in 1865 in Samuel Bennett's *History of Australian Discovery*. To clarify that he is not citing Dampier almost two centuries later in order to historically distance his viewpoint, Bennett adds, 'What Dampier wrote of the aborigines of that part of Australia, nearly two hundred years since, is as true now as it was then.'[39] Thirty years later, Calvert reprinted the same passage and commented,

> This refusal to work is highly characteristic of the Australian native of to-day, for they have a strong objection to anything in the nature of work as the European understands it; though, of course, their whole life is one of constant arduous toil to keep body and soul together.[40]

Subsistence survival should not be confused with productive labour. A decade on, Anthony Trollope, novelist and indefatigable traveller – often in his capacity as a representative of the British Postal Service[41] – published his travelogue of Australia and New Zealand[42] citing Dampier's comments in order to refute the belief that Aborigines have 'a certain dignity of deportment which is natural to them.' He sneers, 'To my eyes the deportment of the dignified aboriginal is that of a sapient monkey imitating the gait of a do-nothing white dandy.'[43] Trollope's perspective may have been influenced by his son working as a sheep-herder in New South Wales, yet he was also cognisant of the 'injury' being done to the 'blacks' and their 'not unnatural hostility' in the face of the loss of their land and livelihood.[44] While at times sympathetic, particularly to Aborigines being subjected to 'incompatible' laws,[45] he nevertheless quotes approvingly from Dampier's passage describing Aborigines as 'having the most unpleasant looks and worst features of any people I ever saw.'[46] Significantly, both Dampier and Trollope felt their keenest disappointment over any hindrance to Aboriginal labour. The same excoriating remarks found their way into five Australian newspapers between 1904 and 1925.

In 1906 Dampier's journals were republished and his comments given another outing:

> Their Eye-lids are always half closed, to keep the Flies out of their Eyes; they being so troublesome here, that… they will creep into ones Nostrils, and Mouth too, if the Lips are not shut very close: so that from their Infancy being thus annoyed with these Insects, they do never open their Eyes as other People: And therefore they cannot see far, unless they hold up their Heads, as if they were looking somewhat over them.[47]

This passage appeared in two Perth newspapers, in 1898 and again in 1935. In 1929, Sir Hal Colebatch, writing a history of Western Australia, cites Dampier's observation of the half-closed eyes. But

Colebatch intervened in Dampier's images of 'The poor winking people of New Holland' (which also appeared in Calvert and in two Perth newspapers, in 1898 and in 1906). He suggested Dampier should've explained the 'full glare of a burning northern sun' and 'the irritation caused by the troublesome fly.'[48] Likewise, Calvert comments wryly that Dampier 'evidently was much impressed with their optical eccentricities',[49] and he construes Dampier's finding that New Hollanders were afforded no food by the earth as an 'erroneous first impression.'[50] Only from 1930 does Dampier's account begin to be read a little more circumspectly until finally, in 1952, a NSW school magazine narrates Dampier's contact with a little more caution.[51]

When it comes to exploratory writing, what goes around certainly comes around. Dampier was not only circulated within histories and dictionaries, he was also instated into the literary canon. Jonathan Swift's 1726 description of the Yahoos in *Gulliver's Travels* is said to be based upon Dampier's observations of Aborigines.[52] Swift borrowed Dampier's map for his 'country of the Houyhnhnms.'[53] Calvert claimed that Defoe based the rescuer of Robinson Crusoe, the character Selkirk, on Dampier.[54] (In fact, Defoe based Crusoe on the castaway Alexander Selkirk whom Dampier put ashore on an island off Chile and rescued four years later.) Snippets of Dampier's phrases slid off pen nibs and were stamped by typewriters, unacknowledged, like a cultural contagion.

Miserable, winking, brutish, unpleasant and optically eccentric: and that is just for starters. Having had a taste of print tracery, let's turn again to the subject matter of this book, newcomer impressions of Aboriginal women. Dampier made quite detailed observations of women at other landfalls, particularly the women of the Isle of Mindanao, yet of the women of the Kimberley coast he notes only that, along with the men, they practised tooth avulsion and may have cohabited 'promiscuously'. On coming ashore an island in King Sound, the 'lustiest of the women, snatching up their children, ran away howling.' Those that couldn't stir lay still by the fire, but when it became clear the Englishmen didn't intend them any harm they sat quietly and the others returned.[55] This earliest recorded encounter between European men and Aboriginal women (and it would be almost solely European men until the First Fleet arrived with its cargo of 180 convict women in 1788) was written up in the context of Dampier wishing to portray his activities as legitimate and state-sanctioned privateering as distinct from piracy, and this influenced his description of the Aboriginal woman. Piracy was increasingly criminalised and officially condemned due to changing notions of sovereignty as well as Spain and England's tenuous trade relations.[56] As Neill has found, during the 1690s buccaneers were likened to stateless and uncivilised barbarians, even cannibals. They were also racialised through comparisons to mulattos. Dampier's description of native women thus needed to convey a clear distinction between civilised and uncivilised femininity; it also needed to communicate his courtliness through the respectful behaviour of the crew over which he had command.

A tradition of feminising and sexualising new lands was already prevalent in the protocolonialist discourse of discovery in Western Europe.[57] Whether Dampier's account bore much relation to actual events will never be known. His desultory descriptions are in part due to his judgement that New Holland and its people offered little prospect for the expansion of merchant capital. Since it was the lot of the native to be drawn into the various economies of colonialism, and since Dampier wasn't settling, but instead canvassing prospects for exploitation, Indigenous women might be appraised as augmenting commerce between native producers and British traders. Nevertheless, as far as Dampier could see there appeared to be no discernible economy of exchange the British could exploit. The natives' enslavement was implausible given New Holland's prohibitive distance from British colonies. Women might be appraised as principally, but not exclusively, a sexual expropriation, which tended to figure more as extracted resource than labour. Their custodianship over land and children needed to be entirely discounted to obviate any inheritance under the 'logic of elimination'[58] by which settler-colonials assumed proprietorship. Discerning no prospect for either mercantile or settler expansion, Dampier was indifferent to Aboriginal women; they barely rated a mention. His observations, however, could serve state objectives for the production of ethnological knowledge, within the purview of Enlightenment scientific exploration. As Neill argues, knowledge of the manners and dispositions of 'savage' peoples confirmed the legitimacy of colonial and commercial expansion into the far-flung reaches of the globe, along with the authority of the sovereign.[59] Dampier needed only to set Aborigines apart to vouch for his own civility and to convince the elite men of letters who would read his published account that he no longer conducted his foreign encounters beyond the strictures and protocols of state-sanctioned exploration. Native women were savage by dint of their nakedness and they overreacted to the benign presence of Englishmen.

Captain James Cook invoked Dampier's failure to sight any women during his second visit in 1699 to argue that New Hollander women 'shewed' particular reserve. The women Cook saw on the Endeavour River when his ship foundered during his first voyage of 1768–71 never approached the ship and kept to the other side of the harbour. In Van Diemen's Land, they were sent away by the men 'upon the slightest approaches made by the officers to any familiarity with them'. Cook was credited with these words in the aforementioned 1787 *History of New Holland*.[60] Early contact accounts, such as in the publications of Cook's voyages, intone a certain disappointment that the women showed quite so much reserve.[61] As Deidre Coleman has documented, an elaborate game of coaxing and withholding was pursued by explorers and early settlers in their attempts to draw women out.[62] In 1770, Cook's men tried to follow people with beads, 'hoping that they would conduct us to some place where we should find more of them and have an opportunity of seeing their women; but they made us understand by signs that they did not desire our company.'[63] They were struck, at Endeavour River, that the women 'were stark naked', and seemed to think this was why they 'did not approach nearer.'[64]

Nakedness paradoxically clothed the native in a kind of legibility, at least for the nascent science of physiognomy. Johann Caspar Lavater's *Essays on Physiognomy*, published in 1775–78[65] and widely read throughout Europe, sparked the quest for the hidden principles of character that might be discerned through physical traits. It linked colonialism and science in the charting and measuring of racial difference by nineteenth-century anthropometry.[66] The uncovered body was invested with conflicting meanings that were racially graded.[67] Yet, feminine nakedness paradoxically was an unnatural state for Cook's contemporaries. He recorded in his journal, 'We could very clearly see with our Glasses that the Woman was as naked as ever she was born; even those parts which I always before now thought Nature would have taught a woman to Conceal were uncovered.'[68] Nakedness in 'Indian' women described not untainted innocence but a deficit of naturally inhering feminine shame. The fact that people were 'clad in nature's dress' was listed in the London press as being among a number of traits by which voyagers could identify New Holland as 'the outcast of God's works', along with living in 'miserable' huts and subsisting 'chiefly on fish and nuts.'[69] Curiously, part of the New Hollanders' degraded state was attributed to their not suffering 'their women to be seen if they can avoid it. This miserable state of the natives appears to me to be a sure sign of the poverty of the country.'[70] Ironically, unfettered visual access to women seemed an important testament to Englishmen of a reputable, advanced society. And doubtless it assisted them in the objectives of these scientific voyages, to observe and document the native woman, who was all the more comprehensible when uncovered.

The economic, strategic and scientific prospects of New Holland were of a different order in the time of Cook's voyages than they had been for Dampier. Knowledge of the inhabitants was critical to determining the viability of expansion, particularly in terms of their capacity for opposition and resistance to invasion. The British interest in Indigenous women was mostly couched in scientific terms. Unstated is their undoubted erotic enthralment, notwithstanding standards for proper deportment for state-appointed mariners. If it goes without saying (in both senses) in the colonial record, it is nevertheless evident that heterosexual desire was a clear and present danger to the locals, who set strict parameters around visual and other access to women. This would soon be construed as men protecting their property. The British themselves conferred only the most limited property rights on women until the Married Women's Property Act of 1882,[71] and they understood women's relation to production and labour in terms increasingly differentiated to men.[72] The sexual

A full account of the inhabitants

appropriation, even assault, of women and girls was thus rarely thought of in terms of the harm it did to women themselves, but rather as an infringement of men's property.

Cook and the official artist, John Webber, on the HMS *Resolution* during his third voyage of discovery around the Pacific (1776–80) were literally on a mission and a description of the women of New Holland was always requisite, if usually appended, to a full account of the inhabitants. Webber has been described by esteemed art historians Bernard Smith and Rudiger Joppien as a 'Captain's artist' due to his visual collaboration and close witnessing of Cook's vision.[73] As such, many of the scenes, artefacts or people Webber depicted were also described in Cook's journals, as was this 'Woman of Van Diemen's Land'. Figure 1.1 is a drawing derived from an encounter at Adventure Bay in late January 1777,

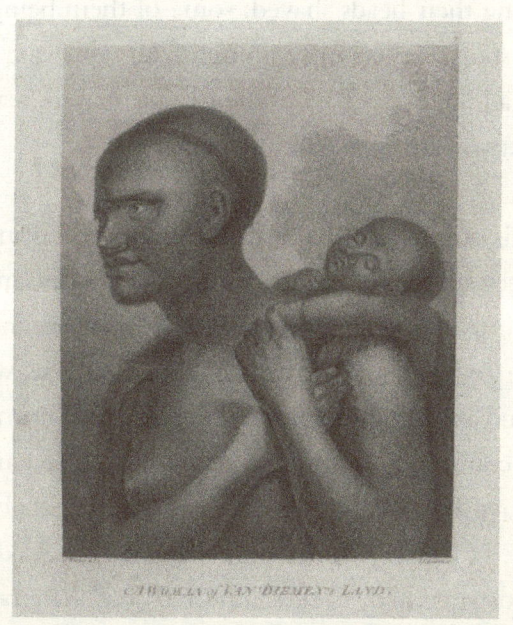

Figure 1.1 'Woman of Van Diemen's Land', engraved by John Caldwell after design by John Webber, in Captain James Cook, A Voyage towards the South Pole, and Round the World, *London, 1777. Courtesy National Library of Australia. Rex Nan Kivell Collection NK1426.*

which was also narrated in a number of works that drew from Cook's journals. The confident manner of the people was noted, and their weapons, nudity, lack of ornaments, cicatrised markings, stature, skin colour, hair texture and features were judged to be 'far from being disagreeable.' On this occasion a group of women joined the men,

> some with children on their backs, and some without children. The former wore a kangaroo skin fastened over their shoulders, the only use of which seemed to be, to support their children on their backs, for it left those parts uncovered which modesty directs us to conceal. Their bodies were black, and marked with scars like those of the men; from whom, however they differed, in having their heads shaved; some of them being completely shorn, others only on one side, while the rest of them had the upper part of their heads shaved, leaving a very narrow circle of hair all round.[74]

Through this ethnographic textual description the image undergoes a process of cultural captioning that guides an otherwise roaming eye over the surface of Webber's image and attributes significance to particular features, notably those which mark off racial and sexual difference. These include immodesty, the manner of conveying children and the circlet of hair. This last can only have been strikingly distinct from European women, who displayed their wealth through elaborately dressed, perfumed, powdered, ornamented, even sculpted 'big' hair raised with a pouf, while men's gentility was flaunted by wigs.[75]

European and Indigenous peoples' face-off in these early colonial encounters impelled new and enduring literary, scientific and artistic conventions, themselves enmeshed in prevailing textual and image production. As Philipe Despoix argues, these published accounts of British circumnavigations in the 1770s and 1780s 'effected the passage from complex knowledge inscribed in logbooks, astronomical and longitude calculations, charts and natural history drawings to a new type of illustrated travelogue that associated the art of writing with techniques of visualising the unknown'.[76] The Webber image is contemporaneous with the type of the noble savage mentioned earlier – the ideal of primitive man existing in a state of original grace and simplicity – which had been foremost at the time of Bougainville's first incursion into Tahiti in 1768.[77] Diderot's version of Tahitian ease and hospitality within a landscape of tropical plenitude was published after Rousseau's eulogy to the innate transparency of primitive social organisation, grounded in natural laws that were universal and harmonious.[78] The noble savage, with its roots in classical antiquity, conferred certain virtues on Enlightenment man, since the ideal of reason was thought to develop from a natural state.[79] Its gendered bookend was the native belle (which I've written about elsewhere[80]). At this time her sexual accessibility was considered an expression of unconstrained nature and was thereby innocent.

This cult held sway for the chroniclers of the exploratory voyages of the Pacific, including Parkinson in 1773,[81] Banks in 1771,[82] Cook in 1777,[83] and Anderson in 1784[84] as well as Diderot writing on Bougainville's trip in his supplement to Hawkesworth in 1773.[85] But it increasingly washed against a growing tide of evangelical opinion, which was scandalised by descriptions of native morality and advocated Christian obligation to the pagan savage. The noble savage type was revised after the killings of prominent explorers: Cook at Hawaii, Marion du Fresne at New

Zealand and the crews of Furneaux and La Pérouse. The assigning of immodesty rather than innocence to New Holland women's nakedness by Cook was a major shift that would thereafter sexualise them.

Webber's image appeared in a number of illustrated publications that collected accounts of these voyages, such as Anderson's *A New, Authentic, and Complete Collection of Voyages Round the World*. This sumptuous publication featured twelve similar folio copperplate engravings of male and female bust portraits, each facing away from its partner, and representing the people of New Zealand, Bolabola, Easter Island, Mallicolo, Tanna Island, New Caledonia, Christmas Sound, St Christina, Sandwich Island, Prince William Sound, Oonalashka and Kantschatta, as well as Van Diemen's Land. Seen in its printed context Webber's image appeared within a cosmopolitan tour of men and women each of whose features, hair and ornaments were carefully detailed as a means to catalogue racial difference. The face became a site of variable criteria, by which geographic type could be identified through a morphology of features. This gallery afforded the viewer a comparison, albeit scattered throughout an 800-page text. In the purview of such publications, the 'natives of New Holland and Van Diemen's Land' figured within a visual and textual repertoire that was comparative due to its global reach. These constituted important shifts in the production of knowledge about racial identity within the context of large-scale formations of empire and colony.

The 'Woman of Van Diemen's Land' is not seated, giving the sense of her being drawn 'from nature' as she goes about her life. She is also the only 'native' woman in the series carrying her child. In Webber's image it is the primordial mother who bookends the warrior. As I will discuss in Chapter 3, primeval maternity was embodied by the 'native' mother. Universal and idealised principles of the feminine became exotic when realised under the rubric of racial difference. The primordial mother conveyed the sense that maternity is an impervious, natural category of human existence, aesthetically and spiritually uplifting. For Europeans at this time, maternity evinced the natural state for womankind, as variously 'sacred, dangerous or even polluting', and this most feminine principle increasingly required regulation and rationalisation by men of science.[86] The native mother consolidated reproduction within the universal kinship of shared human experience. She confirmed that reproduction was the universal function and role of sexual difference.[87]

As Londa Schiebinger has carefully detailed, the inclusion of humans into the tripartite division of animal (alongside mineral and vegetable) in naturalists' taxonomies was highly contentious in this period of exploration: in the Middle Ages humans had been excised from nature and linked to angels.[88] The rise of comparative anatomy to tabulate the masses of unidentified species extracted by the exploratory voyages put the classificatory systems deriving from the Aristotelian *Scala natura* all at sea. In 1758 Linneaus had changed the category *Anthropomorpha* to rank humans with primates, outraging naturalists at the imputation that humans weren't made in God's image but were animals.[89] As Schiebinger explains, he also made the capacity for women to breastfeed the icon of a new defining category he coined *Mammalia*,[90] his only zoological division based on a capacity of the female body, which was widely accepted. The troubling question of why men's teats did not issue milk Linneaus compensated for by devising the category for mankind, *Homo sapiens*, by which man's capacity for reason distinguished him from all other categories of life. The identification of the feminine with nature in Western knowledge and aesthetic traditions[91] informed Linneaus's category of *Mammalia*. It also informed his sentiment about mothering, for Linneaus joined the eighteenth-century campaign against wet-nursing and advocated for its abolition.[92] The primitive mother was evoked in this discourse of natural mothering as exemplary of nurturance, yet Indigenous wet nurses were decried as corrupting.[93]

The prematernal shape of Webber's breast conveys his sympathy for this mother for it was more common to ascribe pendulous, 'udder' shaped breasts to Indian, Hottentot and native women, not to mention the practice of suckling animals. A deeply ambivalent sensibility about the nature of the maternal itself can be gleaned from the observations of Indigenous maternity by Europeans. Yet, the beauty of Webber's woman's face is also overtly inscribed, albeit Europeanised, and there is a sense that maternity and exotic desirability could coexist in the figure of the native mother.

Webber came to be appointed topographical artist to the expedition after three of his works, exhibited at the Royal Academy, were noted by Daniel Solander, a friend and colleague of Cook's botanist Joseph Banks (and incidentally a favourite student of Linneaus). This woman, whose name was dropped since it was also deemed immaterial to knowing who she was, was thus perceived within particular colonial networks of knowledge exchange.

Bernard Smith concludes his classic survey *European Vision in the South Pacific* noting that, 'it was the initial impressions of the early navigators in the Pacific which made the most fundamental and lasting impression upon the European imagination.'[94] The images taken during these exploratory voyages were critically important to the consolidation of scientific authority in this era of far-flung encounter with human difference. Webber submitted some 200 works to the admiralty. He reworked many drawings and oversaw their engraving and printing over four years from

1780. They were prepared for publication under the direction of Lord Sandwich. This image was thus prized among high-ranking colonial administrators; the Gallery of New South Wales holds a copy that was once in the collection of Lord Hobart (Secretary of State for War and the Colonies from 1801 to 1804). But it also played an important role in the growing appetite for print culture, with its diverse offerings ranging from staid private collectors' albums of zoological etchings to popular magazines circulating 'curiosities and wonders'. The relation of image to text is also of interest in colonial-era print culture, in the reiteration of cultural captions of Aboriginality.[95]

For all the blindsiding, evasion and outright gaping of these pre-settlement forays, the arrival of the First Fleet in 1788 saw the appraisal of Aboriginal women entangled within intercultural exchanges that were now invested with visions of settlement, as distinct from scientific exploration, though of course these objectives were strategically linked. But as Nicolas Thomas argues, 'the point to grasp about intercultural entanglement is that histories may be linked but not shared.'[96] As with his analysis of European descriptions of indigenous cultures in the Pacific, though many accounts derive from encounters where an exchange of some sort occurred, rather than a one-sided observation, Thomas reminds us they did so 'from cultural ground that is fundamentally distant.'[97] It was a distance members of the First Fleet, such as John White, sought to bridge with physical contact by enjoining Aboriginal women in an exchange that was inflected with soliciting.

John White was chief surgeon on the First Fleet. He was an amateur naturalist and accompanied Governor Phillip on two voyages of exploration from Sydney Cove, from which he collected many specimens. Over sixty plates, some of which he may have drawn, appeared in his *Journal of a Voyage to New South Wales*, published in London in 1790.[98] It gained wide circulation and was translated into German, Swedish and French. White's New Holland encounter was first narrated in text as an 'Anecdote' and then drawn, engraved and printed in England by artists familiar with his journal, but not with the settlement at Sydney Cove, we can assume, by the length of the adorned woman's untied hair in this image (Figure 1.2).[99] It was drawn by Charles Ansell (b. 1752), better known for drawing horses (which may explain the odd join of the woman's abdomen to her legs) and who, in his short life, never visited Australia. It was then engraved by Birrell for the periodical *Historical Magazine, or, Classical Library of Public Events*.

Figure 1.2 'Mr White Decorating a Female of New South Wales'. Charles Ansell, 1790, Courtesy National Library of Australia, Rex Nan Kivell Collection, Acc. No. NK5687

A full account of the inhabitants

Copperplate engraving had gained precedence over the woodcut in image production but there had been a revival of wood engraving, going across the grain and achieving a much finer line than the plank edge could. New etching and engraving techniques, such as stipple (punched patterns of dots) wax and acid etching, and drypoint on steel and copper surfaces, enabled a refining of the graphic dimensions of print, particularly in the relatively fledgling medium of the magazine.[100] This particular publication was destined to fail within its first year, as would over half the new magazines of the time. London print culture was nevertheless the epicentre for the circulation of aboriginality until the mid-nineteenth century, before an Australian press began to secure its hitherto hesitant footing.

Colonial printed records, such as charts, maps, government gazettes, edicts from the colonial office, published journals, botanical prints and missionary pamphlets, have, of course, always been primary sources for historians of empire. In her foundational history of print, Elizabeth Eisenstein presciently noted that 'constant access to printed materials is a prerequisite for the practice of the historian's own craft'. But in terms of the hitherto absence of historicising print itself, she adds, it can be 'difficult to observe processes that enter so intimately into our own observations.'[101] Scholars attracted to the 'elusive quarry'[102] of print culture, because of its intimate relation with everyday cultural meaning and its wide circulation, have to contend with a number of methodological problems, as have I. These include giving coherence to a source that is by its nature strewn across time and space, of providing context for often unattributed, syndicated material and, not the least, of accounting for its reception and readership. There is also the problem of undue focus on the written record, thereby privileging elite 'men of letters' in accounts of the past and marginalising oral-based cultures, and to some extent women, whose literacy rates in the West still trailed those of men. Reading itself, an activity increasingly centred on 'the public sphere's preeminent institution, the press',[103] mirrored the social hierarchies of race and gender. Wherever typographic men went with their press machines, print media was introduced into 'a bewildering array of social structures and linguistic contexts.'[104] Because of print's industrialisation and the altered relation of readers to texts through the rise of literacy and a mass reading public,[105] print has been designated by Eisenstein as an 'agent of change.'[106] In the instance of colonial print, it may also have been an agent for consolidating power through the coincidence of the printing revolution in early modern Europe with European exploration and colonisation.[107]

This dispersal of meaning and diffusion of ideas enabled by print has been described as 'transtextuality' since meanings were scattered across borders and seas.[108] Through images such as Webber's and White's, the native belle became portable and was able to transgress visual thresholds, playing a key role in creating a cosmopolitan readership for a vernacular ethnography. In Ansell's image the entry into this visual vignette through the textual portico – much in vogue in print culture from the seventeenth century – creates a sense of access to the far distant portal of New Holland. The spatial distinction marks off an otherworldly moral vestibule, wherein genteel Englishmen face off with entirely naked women, even outdoors. White joins a number of French and Englishmen whose impulse was to proffer clothes, even pantaloons in one instance, as a response to first-contact encounters. The year before, in dispatches to the admiralty, Commodore Phillips had explained, 'It was a practice with the seamen in these intercourses to dress up the inhabitants with shreds of cloth, and tags of coloured paper; and when they surveyed each other, they would burst into loud laughter, and run howling to the woods.'[109]

The ocularcentric impulse of colonial modernity, that is, the quest to visually account for the racial Other, compelled the transference of this 'Anecdote – Mr White decorating a female from New South Wales' from text to image. This engraving also illustrates the increasing enmeshment of image and text in the production of knowledge through print culture. Such ephemera shaped the stories of empire, themselves determined by gender relations across the cleave of race. White tells of his encounters with native women with saucy verve.

In late August 1788, White was with a party exploring Broken Bay. They returned to Manly Cove (so named by Phillip because of the 'manly conduct' of the men he met there on his first visit) and found a group of people fishing. The Englishmen each singled out a woman and made presents of trinkets to her and her family. White notes that the little finger of the left hand on all the women and girls had been removed at the second joint. He admired the surgical appearance of the well-covered stumps.[110] White then combines courting ritual with ethnological observation. He asks the woman to whom he has paid attention for some of the fish she is broiling and she rather indifferently obliges. He then relates,

> Many of the women were strait, well formed, and lively. My companion continued to exhibit a number of coquettish airs while I was decorating her head, neck, and arms with my pocket and neck handkerchiefs, which I tore into ribbons, as if desirous of multiplying two presents into several. Having nothing left, except the buttons of my coat, on her admiring them, I cut them away, and with a piece of string tied them round

her waist. Thus ornamented, and thus delighted with her new acquirements, she turned from me with a look of inexpressible archness.[111]

In another popular magazine White's account continues. He suffers a disenchantment with the native belle when, soon after, an older woman, 'perfectly grey with age, solicited us very much for some present; and, in order to make us comply, threw herself, before all her companions, into the most indecent attitudes.'[112] Aged Aboriginal women came in for the most virulent racism, as we shall see in Chapter 6. Their racial difference was not mollified by their exotic appeal and European men were completely unaccustomed to the public nakedness of aged women, certainly men of White's age, though they likely had some exposure to classical and romantic nudes and presumably the indoor intimacies of bordellos. In a discussion of interracial sex in the voyages to the South Seas, Laura Rosenthal writes that, 'transracial sex in travel journals and satires functioned as a trope for contact in general, potentially suggesting a range of relationships: cooperation, pleasure, escape, conquest, scandal, danger, disease, pollution, and exploitation.'[113] Naked elderly women, however, proffered none of the pleasures of such encounters, and when observers referred to them at all it was with revulsion or sympathy. They overlooked the women's authority and their particular role in mediating intertribal and, later, transracial interactions.

Earlier in his journal White evinces the travelling Englishman's general interest in women of different climes. His preoccupation with new specimens paralleled that with women of different lands, in the sense that they typified discernible groups. Not dissimilarly to his interest in fish, birds and reptiles, White took every opportunity for 'inspecting more minutely into the manners and disposition of the women' at each landfall en route to Botany Bay. A description of the women – who are generally distinguished from 'the inhabitants', whose gender is unmarked – is requisite to any account within this genre of the travel journal. At this time a separate paragraph or even a chapter devoted to the women formed a necessary addendum to any traveller's or scientist's account of any nation or people distinct from his own. Sexual commerce was a preoccupation, along with what could be gleaned through gender relations about the polity of these nations.

Perhaps anticipating the sexual adventure still reverberating from accounts of the French and English visits to Tahiti, the predominant themes were visual appearance and moral disposition of foreign women, the first often taken to indicate the second. In yet another reprinting of White's journal in a popular magazine, White is attentive to the morals of women at Santa Cruz, Tenerife, who were said to be of an 'amorous constitution, and addicted to intrigue.'[114] His lengthy description of Rio de Janeiro assays its women much as it describes its churches, streets, harbour and commerce. In the spirit of empiricism he tested the honour of the women by considering 'every woman as a proper object of gallantry.'[115] He concludes that the women of the higher classes are undeserving of any imputation as to their 'turn for intrigue.'[116] We might take that to mean he had no luck. Indeed, he and a number of other 'gentlemen belonging to the fleet' took to courting novices, since they might choose a husband over the veil. In yet another masthead, a passage reads much the same as hundreds of passages describing Aboriginal women. White reports to his readers,

> The women, when young, are remarkably thin, pale, and delicately shaped; but after marriage they generally

incline to be lusty, without losing that constitutional pale, or rather sallow, appearance. They have regular and better teeth than are usually observable in warm climates, where sweet productions are plentiful. They have likewise the most lovely, piercing, dark eyes, in the captivating use of which they are by no means unskilled. Upon the whole, the women of this country are very engaging; and rendered more so by their free, easy, and unrestrained manner.[117]

This blazon of visage, shape, colouring and racialised features, such as teeth, lips or hair, was informed by Blumenbach's and other naturalists' comparative anatomy.[118] But it included a nod to beauty as a racially distinguishing mark. The frisson created by the allegedly unregulated sexuality of non-European women underpins so many such descriptions of racially differentiated women, they start to read like some kind of self-pleasuring pulp-ethnography.

White's motivations become more overt in the comparisons between nations afforded to the travelling gentleman. He was able to contrast the women of Cape Hope with the ladies of Rio de Janeiro.

Among the latter a great deal of reserve and modesty is apparent between the sexes in public. Those who are disposed to say tender and civil things to a lady must do it by stealth, or breathe their soft sighs through the lattice-work of a window, or the grates of a convent. But at the Cape, if you wish to be a favourite with the fair, as the custom is, you must in your own defence (if I may use the expression) *grapple* the lady, and paw her in a manner that does not partake in the least of gentleness.

Such a rough and uncouth conduct, together with a kiss ravished now and then in the most public manner and situations, is not only pleasing to the fair one, but even to her parents, if present; and is considered by all parties as an act of the greatest gallantry and gaiety.[119]

The observational ethos of ethnography and exoticism are already entwined. As such White's encounter with the young woman pictured is shaped by an observational technique of 'external mastery'.[120] Jonathon Crary has postulated this technique is specific to the modern subject through the rise of the empirical sciences from the 1830s and due to the new vantages afforded by visual technologies with their 'promiscuous range of effects.'[121] I would add the settler-observer, due to the new vantages afforded by mobility and the distance this created from accustomed morality, instated a particular visual field that was shaped by new observational techniques. Gender was critical to this practice. Perceived through the prism of gender, for instance, White brings to bear his own presuppositions regarding the native belle type. It seems comportment is highly adaptable in the face of new opportunities for sexual expansion by the gallant but open-eyed colonial traveller.

At Sydney Cove and on the journey thence, gender relations were always defined by the behaviour of the women. White writes of the women convicts at Port Praya that, despite the oppressive heat, nothing could dampen 'the warmth of their constitutions, or the depravity of their hearts' in the 'promiscuous intercourse' taking place between them and the seamen. White makes many references to the abandon of convict women,[122] among the first European women to enter this exclusively masculine terrain of voyaging to colonial outposts. He reported that their desire was 'so uncontrollable', that nothing could deter them from 'making their way through the bulkheads to the apartments assigned the seamen'. It is as though on disembarking England, sex seeped through class and racial boundaries, through bulkheads, convent grates and torn handkerchiefs. White himself was not immune to such temptations. His fourth child, Andrew Douglas, was born to White by a convict, Rachel Turner, in Sydney and was brought up in England as a member of the White family.[123]

If White obeyed Phillip's instructions not to 'molest' or 'interfere with' the natives, this did not prevent him from courting favours from the women, making detailed observations of their forms, features and airs, stringing their waists with his buttons and draping them with his handkerchiefs. We can surmise White's observations were of a very different order of things to those charged with purely ethnological data collection. The French, whose visits to Australia during these early years are often sidelined in historical accounts, were intent on the observation of *natifs* of the New World and their methodology emphasised contact and interpersonal relations. But making contact with women in Van Diemen's Land evidently entailed very different understandings of gender relations, contributing to a series of misunderstandings and upsets that played a role in deposing the noble savage, itself a type construed by the French.

If the young medical student François Péron (1775–1810) had not argued a special case for the new importance of anthropological observation, he might never have found a post aboard the Nicolas Baudin expedition, departing 1800. During a visit of some weeks in Van Diemen's Land, Peron encountered an Aboriginal woman at South Cape who would be painted in watercolour and ink by Nicolas-Martin Petit, in 1802, as *Femme de la terre de Diemen* (Figure 1.3). Her name was Arra-Maïda but, in the reproduction of her image through engraving and its circulation in European print over subsequent decades, her name was dropped and her identity reassigned from a nominated individual to a racialised type, a primitive woman, or *Femme de la Tasmanie*.

Figure 1.3 'Femme de la Terre de Diemen', Nicolas-Martin Petit, 1802, Water colour and ink portrait, painted at South Cape, Museum d'Histoire Naturelle, Le Havre.

The encounter created for readers by Arra-Maïda's documentation in print culture, and the circulation of her image for consumers, reveals the transnational circuits of information exchange Aboriginal women were situated within. Through engraving and textual description, Indigenous women were positioned in particular ways in a public sphere that was itself being redefined by a confluence of changes: in print and publishing, colonial expansion and gender regimes. Arra-Maïda was made legible to a readership through the stamping of her image in the inherently visual, graphic medium of print. It was an altered public, a dispersed community of anonymous and simultaneous readers, consuming shared yet scattered meanings. As her image was 'poached' by mastheads around Europe, Arra-Maïda went unnamed.[124] She was rent from the narrative Péron provided, as shaky as his grasp was on what transpired between them.

Dispatched under Napoleon's orders and sponsored by the Institut National with the express aim of collecting and documenting zoological specimens, the Baudin expedition was, like Cook's, principally scientific in nature.[125] Péron's initial application was declined but he managed to gain an interview with a member of the committee who had appointed the expedition's naturalists. He was invited to submit a memoir in which he argued the necessity of a medical naturalist to the expedition. Napoleon's interest in science was, of course, part of his expansionist enterprise. According to John West-Sooby, Napoleon, then First Consul,

> saw the prestige of science as being vitally important to the French nation and its image and to the enlightenment project which was the Revolution, spreading science and the light of knowledge throughout the world, and he saw that France needed to play a major role, if not the major role in that.[126]

Napoleon remarked in 1797, 'The true power of the French Republic must henceforth consist in not allowing there to be new ideas which do not belong to it',[127] underscoring the critical role of knowledge production, and presumably its dissemination in print, to imperial nations. The Baudin expedition aspired to position the French at the frontier of knowledge and at the forefront of scientific inquiry. But almost from the moment it embarked the expedition haemorrhaged zoologists, either through death or desertion. Péron and the illustrator Charles-Alexandre Lesueur worked closely together and assumed the task of publishing the findings of the voyage on their return.[128] It was a mammoth undertaking: Lesueur made some 1,500 drawings of more than 100,000 zoological specimens, an unprecedented number, higher than all the previous exploratory voyages combined. Such a mass of data necessitated more refined classification in the organisation of material through indexing, cross-referencing and cataloguing, principles derived from print culture.

These new ideas which the French aspired to own, including anthropology, were published just before the industrialisation of print.[129] Though the all-metal Stanhope press, with a 'platen large enough to print a complete folio at one pull',[130] was invented circa 1800, the steam-driven press would not appear until 1807, just two years after Péron published the first edition in French of his *Voyage of Discovery to the Southern Hemisphere* (as it was translated in English).[131] This work coincided with the rise of mass literacy.[132] The French publications market had been deregulated with the dismantling of monarchal controls, becoming more fiercely competitive and open. The revolution created the appetite for political news, making Paris the 'centre of the information industry in Europe' through an explosion in newspaper circulation.[133] Napoleon's new ideas were thus fomented within a public sphere whose 'preeminent institution' was indeed the press, as Habermas noted.[134] Péron's publication was no doubt self-consciously intended for the 'Republic of letters', composed of secular readers, limited to men, yet nevertheless imagined as egalitarian. Images were obviously more accessible to the non-literate, and also accessible across vernacular boundaries, very often corresponding to the national boundaries that print played a role in consolidating in this period. Engravings and lithographs were made after drawings, watercolours and pastels, and were published in sumptuously illustrated travel volumes, such as Péron's *Voyage of Discovery*. They provided for the growing interest in new worlds, furnished also by English publishing houses such as Havell & Son in Oxford Street and Ackermann in the Strand.[135] The reprinting of such imagery over the ensuing decades, in different countries, showed a particularly transnational reception of meanings for Australian indigeneity.[136] Pictorial statements such as Arra-Maïda's likeness were inherently cosmopolitan: it came to appear in French, German, Italian and English publications. Such volumes have been recognised by Benedict Anderson as 'the first modern-style mass-produced industrial commodity', exemplifying the emergence at this time of 'print capitalism'.[137] The role of indigenous content within the pages of this print commodity warrants closer attention.

Illustration in these publications presented the anthropological encounter as a scenario in which the reader could also participate. Scientific observation and its ensuing records became commodities in these early years of exploration publishing, particularly through the growing interdependence of text and image to convey knowledge.[138] In its fulsome commendation from Lesueur, the Baudin expedition committee noted the importance of graphic illustration in lending accuracy to text:

> A description, nevertheless, how complete soever it may be, can never give a sufficiently just idea of those singular forms, which have no precise point of comparison in objects previously known. Correct figures alone can supply the imperfection of language.[139]

The committee hastens to add that Lesueur's ethnographic drawings were no less important than the zoological reproductions:

> All the details of the existence of the natives have been designed by him with the most scrupulous accuracy. All their musical instruments, those of war, of hunting, of fishing, their domestic utensils; all their peculiarities of clothing, of their ornaments, of their habitations, of their tombs; in a word all that their rude ingenuity has been able to accomplish, is found united in the productions of this skilful and indefatigable artist.[140]

As the expedition was in part designed and propelled by the newly formed Societe Observateurs d'Homme (Society of the Observers of Man), the observation and documenting of the *natifs* formed a significant portion of the project's achievements.[141] Along with the hundreds of thousands of specimens they returned with – from which 2,500 new species were identified – they had also been asked to bring back 'Savages of both sexes' and, if possible, a 'whole family'.[142]

Firsthand observation and immersion in the host society were central tenets of this newly self-conscious anthropological enterprise, as advised by Joseph-Marie Degérando (1772–1842). His *Observation of Savage Peoples* (1800) was specifically addressed to the Baudin expedition, requiring them to carefully observe the 'physical nature and circumstances' of native peoples.[143] After extolling the virtues of comparative analysis, Degérando advised that no subjects were more fascinating and fruitful than savage peoples belonging to the simplest societies since they could provide the 'material needed to construct an exact scale of the various degrees of civilization.' Since the development of native 'intellectual faculties is much more limited', their nature could be more easily 'penetrated' to determine their 'fundamental laws'.[144] By using scientific methods, explorers would become 'philosophical travellers' in the 'systematic study of simple societies for the edification of humankind.'[145] Degérando pitched this notion of embedded observation against the explorers who had 'given us bizarre descriptions which tickle the idle curiosity of the many, but which offer no useful instruction to the philosophically minded.'[146] He was marking a distinction between erudite and sensational accounts of indigenous peoples. But this most curious of guides gave no instructions about women whatsoever. The men of Baudin's party, however, would fail to follow his instructions on a number of counts, not the least failing to learn to fully converse in the host language, but also in the attentions they paid to the women of Van Diemen's Land.

Figure 1.4 'Terre de Diémen, Arra-Maïda', Charles-Alexandre Lesueur and Nicolas-Martin Petit, in François Péron, Voyage of Discoveries in Terra Australis, *1807, Courtesy of Allport Library and Museum of Fine Arts, Tasmanian Archive and Heritage Office.*

As mentioned above it was the portraitist Nicolas-Martin Petit (1777–1804) who took the likeness of the woman the French knew as Arra-Maïda that would become the 1807 French engraving *Terre de Diemen,* of the woman *Arra-Maïda* by Barthelemy Roger (1761–1841) (Figure 1.4). Petit was, as Bernard Smith describes him, 'no unthinking exponent of that noble savage primitivism'; indeed, he 'did his best, within the conventions of neoclassicism, to draw what he saw to be characteristic and typical.'[147] Arra-Maïda then was a woman whose features characterised the female *natif* of 'Van Diemen' and, as with most typifications of the native from these early encounters, the name of the subject is still attributed, fulfilling Degérando's instructions for firsthand observation.

Arra-Maïda's likeness was taken a few days after an encounter between Péron and a group of women. As this series of events has already been skilfully detailed by Shino Konishi,[148] I will only sketch them here. Konishi argues Péron's encounter with the woman Arra-Maïda was a turning point in his perceptions of the noble savage and, I would add, its female counterpart, the native belle. Péron encountered this particular woman just as the Tasmanians were, over a number of weeks, demonstrating the kind of resistance to French presence that challenged the concept of the noble savage. On a number of occasions these two peoples, worlds apart, understandably misunderstood each other and, although we have only the French account to draw upon, it seems that both sides took offence at the other's inscrutable demands and reactions. The Baudin expedition was one of ten French expeditions to the Antipodes during the 'Age of Discovery'. It was in this period that the noble savage underwent a cultural demise due to the killings of the explorers Marion du Fresne in New Zealand in 1772 and Cook in Hawaii in 1779.

Arra-Maïda was not shaped in the same mould as either the primordial mother or native belle. Péron had met two other women who had fulfilled his expectations for these two types. The first he described as carrying a

> little girl, who she still suckled…[her] eyes had expression, and something of the spiritual which surprised us… She appeared to cherish her child very much; and her care for her that affectionate and gentle character which is exhibited among all races as the particular attribute of maternal tenderness.[149]

But Péron was also taken aback by the fire in her eyes when she unabashedly met his stare. This woman later screamed out when one of the Frenchmen removed his glove. They thought that she thought he had removed his hand. The native belle was embodied by the lovely young Tasmanian woman, Ouré Ouré, through her naked and 'delicate' form, hospitable gestures and 'tender expressions'.[150]

Arra-Maïda's indomitable behaviour was thus an affront to Péron's impetus to classify, that is, to assign her group membership within the native belle type. With the women in her company she demanded the Frenchmen, who had approached them on a beach, sit. As Konishi describes the encounter, Péron felt the women criticised the Frenchmen's appearance and laughed 'heartily at their expense.' When the surgeon Bellefin tried to win their esteem by singing to them, Arra-Maïda mimicked his movements and tone, and began to dance in a manner that Péron found 'very indecent'. She then approached Péron, crushed charcoal between her palms and proceeded to apply it to his face, much pleased at the result.[151] The women accompanied the Frenchmen to their boat, but seemed to become alarmed at the number of men there. When the Aboriginal men arrived on the scene they looked 'fierce and menacing', some gathering up their spears. One attempted to remove one of the Frenchmen's swords.

This likeness of Arra-Maïda was taken a few days after this cack-handed encounter, when the French were once again rebuffed by the Tasmanians without quite understanding why. Péron felt they had displayed nothing but conciliation towards the natives and was disappointed enough by their reactions to frankly declare, 'that whole tenor of their conduct shewed a treacherous disposition, and a degree of ferocity that disgusted both me and my companions.'[152] The noble savage was deposed, but it is significant that this masculine type was in part destabilised by a woman, the indomitable Arra-Maïda, whose forthright behaviour shocked Péron, but also uncovered the extent to which the primordial mother and native belle types were contrived around ideals of European feminine gentility, modesty and welcoming supplication, positioning women as guardians of propriety.[153]

While Petit's portraits, as Smith notes, contain a touch of the 'elongated Mannerist affection present in much of the French neo-classical draughtsmanship of the time', he was attentive to the 'characteristic and typical' features of his subjects, sufficiently for his Tasmanian and mainland subjects to appear quite distinct.[154] At this stage Péron was one of the first observers of people from other cultures who was not a well-placed yet informal bystander, such as a ship captain, but instead a self-consciously scientific observer of racialised Others. Arra-Maïda was a woman Péron wished to show he had personally interacted with, their contact evincing important data about her race, such as language and kinship. Arra-Maïda commences her print tour of Europe as an individual whose stated name credits Péron's anthropological practice. Though initially named, Arra-Maïda's identity would soon be lost through print's necessitating of a new ordering of data, most obviously through its recourse to alphabetic sequence in indexing and cataloguing but also through a 'new alertness to the individual and the typical' deriving from fifteenth-century

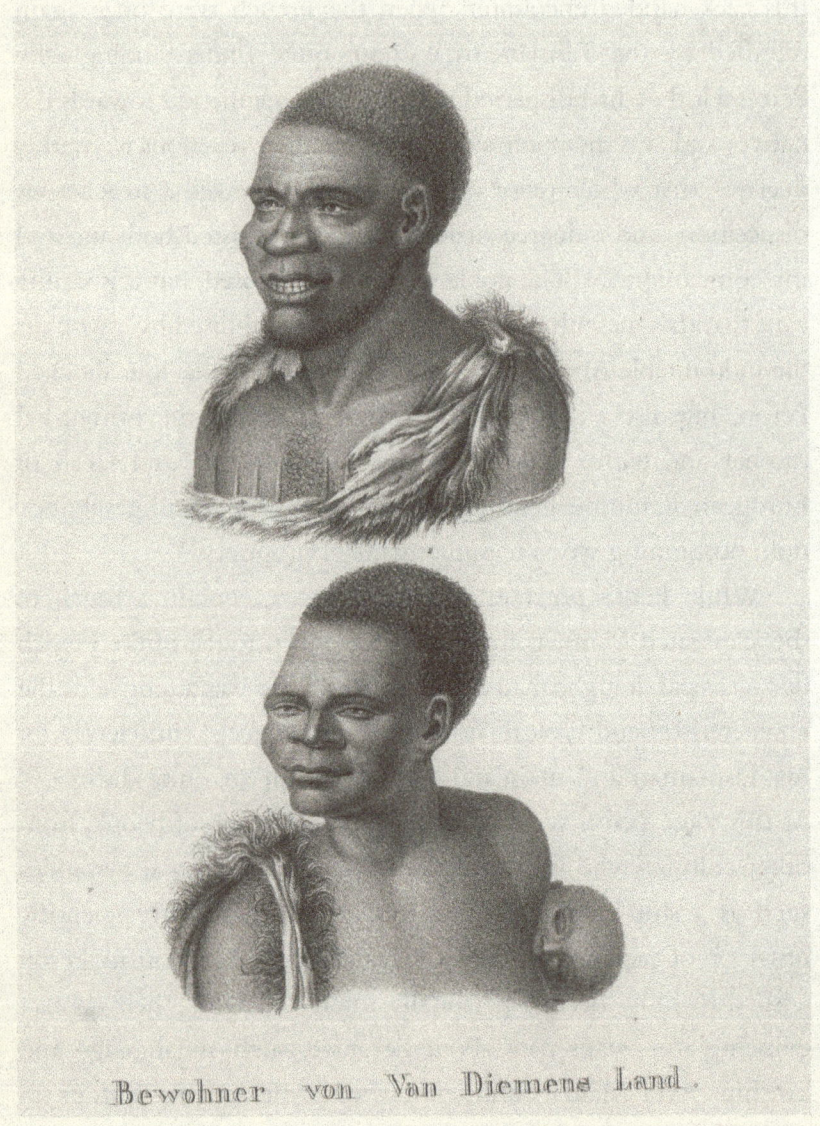

Figure 1.5 'Bewohner von Van Diemens Land'. Courtesy of State Library of Tasmania.

A full account of the inhabitants

regional guides, costume manuals, illustrated guidebooks and genres of literature.[155] Over the coming decades she would be typecast as a native woman, whose physical characteristics, as visually apprehended from her image, were sufficient to typify her racial difference.

As mentioned, Arra-Maïda's likeness first appears in Péron's atlas of historical views, *Voyage of Discovery to the Southern Hemisphere*, which included the first printed map of the entire continent, and predated Matthew Flinders's map by several years. It also included the first European notation of Aboriginal music. While the fate of Arra-Maïda herself is unknown, and may well have been unpromising, her image took on a life of its own. She reappears in a lithograph by a German publisher, captioned 'Bewohner von Van Diemens Land', circa 1815 (Figure 1.5). Also

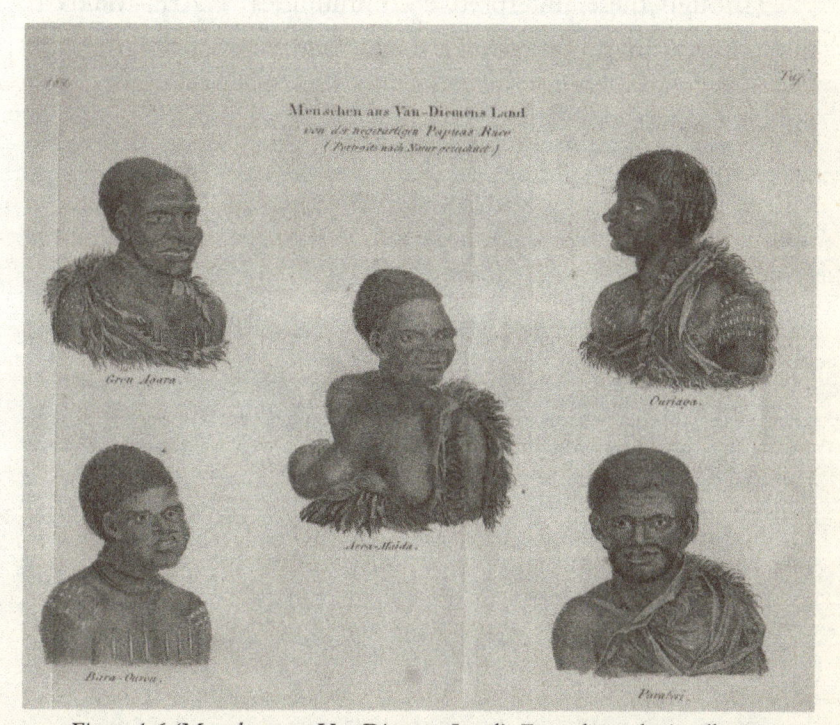

Figure 1.6 'Menschen aus Van Diemens Land'. From the author's collection

in this year, her image is printed on a folded sheet which was slipped into a German edition of Baudin's journal (Figure 1.6) (an untinted print appeared the following year in an edition published in Prague). Her likeness is then printed as Plate 59 (Figure 1.7) with two bust portraits of Tasmanian men, now also unnamed, from an aquatint engraving by Castelli in *Le Costume Ancien et Moderne*, published in Milan by Ferrario and reprinted from 1816 to 1827. (Plate reproductions from this lavishly illustrated volume, which freely borrowed from the exploration publications of the previous decades, are currently being sold by dozens of online art print vendors.) Soon after, Arra-Maïda appears again alongside another bust portrait, this time under the image of a burial ceremony, in a steel plate engraving from the *Voyage pittoresque autour du monde* published in Paris between 1822 and 1843 (Figure 1.8).[156]

Through these 'interpretive communities',[157] Arra-Maïda is situated within the particular social field reproduced through

Figure 1.7 'Three inhabitants of New Holland', aquatint engraving by Castelli from Le Costume Ancien et Moderne, 1816-1827. From the author's collection

A full account of the inhabitants

Figure 1.8 'Enterrement des Naturels de l'Australie / Naturel de'l Australie/ Femme de la Tasmanie', Jules Boilly after Louis Auguste de Sainson, for Rear Admiral Dumont d'Urville, Steel plate engraving from the Voyage pittoresque autour du monde: avec des portraits de sauvages d'Amérique, d'Asie, d'Afrique, et des îles du Grand ocean; des paysages, des vues maritimes, et plusieurs objets d'histoire naturelle, *Paris, Louis Choris, De l'Imprimerie de Firmin Didot, 1822. From the author's collection*

print culture. The men who consumed and circulated her likeness created a certain *habitus* for themselves within colonial social space, one exacted through observation of the racially differentiated Other. Her image was a symbolic good in Bourdieu's sense. Its consumption and reception designated not only class, but also more overtly racial distinctions. Print played a decisive role in the encoding and entrenching of national vernaculars that distinguished themselves sharply from oral-based cultures. The recording of indigenous knowledge traditions within those vernaculars profoundly altered them, as Ballantyne argues, disembodying and 'wrenching them free of the traditional social contexts of knowledge transmission to revalue them as an aid to the operation of imperial authority'. But while he argues the '"textualisation" of indigenous cultures was a crucial foundation of colonial rule',[158] it also created a blind spot through limited awareness of indigenous knowledge, this being orally comprised with access to it restricted, and as it suffered rapid destruction.

Arra-Maïda's preservation and reappearance in print illustrates Bourdieu's definition of social capital as the 'sum of the resources, actual or virtual, that accrue to an individual or a group by virtue of possessing a durable network of more or less institutionalized relationships of mutual acquaintance and recognition.'[159] These relationships point to the enmeshment of illustrators, printers and publishers with colonial explorers. As Martyn Lyons notes, 'it was from European bases that printing colonized the world.'[160] The recurrence of Arra-Maïda's likeness supports Eisenstein's argument that the central feature of print is not merely permanency, but repetition. This repetition suggests that the new intelligence about humankind provided by indigenous peoples needed to be not only ordered but maintained through reiteration over time. Arguably, the new ideas Napoleon wished the French to lay claim to did not so much take hold on first telling, but rather created significatory frameworks reinforced over decades through the slotting in of new information via repetition.

Arra-Maïda was typed in both senses of the word. The dispensing of her identity, by replacing her name with a type, was effected through captioning. The relation of image to text, particularly where they intersect in the caption, is a productive site for investigating the role of Aboriginal content in print culture, and querying how the more mutable and undefined meanings of images are pinned down, often through typecasting, itself a confluence of typography and typology.[161] Typecasting went hand in glove with typesetting not only in the sense that both terms derive from print culture, but also in the sense that unfamiliar people such as Arra-Maïda were 'smelted' into 'common groupings',[162] or racial types, in the marketplace of colonial print media.

The colonial networks of information exchange provided a new context for Arra-Maïda. The confluence of print and type, or typography and typology, nested Indigenous women within the Enlightenment 'catalogue of creation', as Edward Duyker has dubbed it.[163] Through the coincidence of the printing revolution in early modern Europe with European exploration and colonisation, depictions of racial difference literally expanded the horizons of European readers – who were at this time mostly elite, propertied men. In print accounts of the native, European readers traversed the border between tribal and scribal. The accounts of Dampier, Cook, White and Péron were recirculated again and again, like a discursive tic, in the industrialised and commodified print culture of the coming centuries, particularly in the ephemeral form of the newspaper. The Aboriginal woman was cast in these print impressions within the same organising domains as European women – status, maternity, domesticity, sexuality and appearance. What remains to be seen was the impression their racial difference left.

2

'A SPECIES OF ROUGH GALLANTRY': IMPRESSIONS OF GENDER STATUS

> It is as if the weakness and powerlessness of the women rendered Aboriginal society familiar and decipherable.[1]

In an 1869 illustrated collection of frontier travel adventures, Queensland police magistrate Charles Henry Eden recounted the search for a missing schooner, the *Eva*, in the Palm Islands off the coast of northern Queensland.[2] The search was spurred by reported sightings of four white men on Hinchinbrook Island allegedly being kept prisoner by 'the blacks',[3] and no doubt given heightened urgency by retellings of the Eliza Fraser story, the tale of a white women captured by Aborigines in 1836.[4] Eden's party had planned to (likewise) 'capture a *gin* (native woman) and gain all the intelligence we could from her.'[5]

Targeting women as forced informants was common practice on the frontier. In one instance in the same decade, a woman was reportedly partly hung by the neck by police near Booligar, New South Wales, until she revealed the whereabouts of her husband, who had allegedly killed a Glaswegian at a river crossing.[6] According to settlers themselves, women on the frontier were singled out after massacres and threatened with murder if they did not heed the warning.[7] They were 'run down' and forced to direct explorers to water.[8] In Eden's unconfirmed report he claimed to intercept and trap a large group, during which the men 'broke in every direction.'[9] As Eden relates his story, he then had on his hands a group of unprotected, terrified women and children, who clearly had met the likes of him before, for

> the gins and piccaninnies threw themselves into a heap, one on the top of the other, until they formed a mass of naked arms, legs, and heads. If they are surprised, and there happens to be water near, they always tumble into it, piccaninnies and all, for they swim like fishes, only showing their heads above; but in the absence of water, they generally fling themselves into a heap and talk. The confusion of tongues at Babel must have been dulcet melody to the sounds emitted by a mound of gins and youngsters.[10]

After gathering up the weapons of the men who had fled, Eden and his party surrounded the women and children, sat themselves down and took in a meal. In his narrative Eden next ruminates at his leisure on the status of Aboriginal women.

> Certainly the Australian gin is no beauty, or if she has ever possessed any it is soon knocked out of her by the life of privation and misery which she leads, and the brutal conduct of her husband. As with most savages, the black looks upon a woman merely as child-bearer and slave, and the more physical strength a warrior has, the more wives has he at his beck and nod, for he appropriates freely the domestic treasures of his weaker brother, knocking him on the head if he demurs. To the women fall all the drudgery of moving the goods and chattels, during the constant changes of locale, lugging along

the babies, carrying firesticks, digging yams, cooking the food, weaving the beautiful baskets in which they carry their little knickknacks, or, to sum it up in a few words, they do everything, except make the weapons and hunt. Of food their share is the scantiest, consisting only of the fragments their devoted consorts pitch over their shoulders when they have finished gnawing them themselves, and even these they have to divide with the half-starved dingo curs that form a necessary portion of the black's camp. For the slightest neglect, or if the noble savage happens to have 'turned out on the wrong side of his bark blanket,' they are cruelly beaten, often killed, and the sight of a gin without ghastly scars, telling tales of this gentle mode of marital connection, is rare.[11]

Eden is content, through the expertise gained from his experience – for you can tell a lot about a people by piling them into 'mounds' – to circulate unsubstantiated indictments, some of which had already been challenged in the public domain by 1869. Clearly he is engaged with the myth of manliness[12] forged on the frontier, in which his restrained gentility is contrasted with the brutality of native 'subordinate' masculinity.[13]

But it is not constructions and performances of frontier masculinity this chapter is concerned with; rather, I will rent apart Eden's 'tissue of errors' by selecting the predominant trope from his very representative textual description – of bride capture – and situating each within its field of reiteration as it was constituted by nineteenth-century print culture. We can then compare these printed accounts against reports of white men's gendered and racial violence, wherein it becomes all too clear that Aboriginal women were the playthings of settler sadism. Aside from the documentation of these attacks by sympathetic, even appalled settlers, these women found no redress nor protection from colonial administrators or the judiciary. Indeed, the particular distortions that Eden directs at Aboriginal women found purchase because they reiterated well-worn meanings about Aboriginal gender relations in print. A particularly specious species of racialised gallantry was in play that had discernible political effects: the ranking of Aborigines as primitive through their treatment of women and the assigning of a race destiny that was ultimately oblivion. Needless to say, this had a significant role to play in the settler-colonial 'logic of elimination', as Wolfe has defined it.[14] Racial and sexual conquest were welded together within a discourse of settler-colonial gallantry. Given sexual relations with Aboriginal women dared not be spoken of, interracial sex was simultaneously disavowed and then transferred onto fetish tropes such as bride capture. They were also infused with aggression, as we shall later, belatedly, bear witness.

The trope of bride capture was principally and pervasively entrenched through the reiterative cycles of print culture. When historian Inga Clendinnen claimed in *Dancing with Strangers* that Aboriginal men were customarily violent to their women, she supported her argument with a critical mass of references: 'too many' accounts, she claimed, 'reported violent rape as commonplace'. While the first half of this chapter traces bride capture reports beyond Clendinnen's focus on the First Fleet of 1788, up until they were finally refuted by Malinowski in 1913, this tracery across the typeset demonstrates that these 'too many' reports were simply recirculations derived from a mere handful of speculative and unsubstantiated textual contrivances.[15] Towards the end of the chapter we'll see that these reports were quite differently recorded compared to reports of white men's violence. A sample of the few that came to public attention were detailed with names, localities, circumstance and corroboration, as distinct from recycled generalised anecdote. And the same disparity, between speculation and substantiated instance, occurred with infanticide, as we'll see in the next chapter.

Scholars have visited the trope of bride capture and dubbed it 'courtship with a club' (by Nicholas Ruddick) or the 'marriage-rites genre' (by Lisa O'Connell).[16] Most recently Shino Konishi has examined wife capture, focusing on early exploratory and settlement accounts by Europeans in Australia.[17] I would like to add another aspect to this work by bringing in new sources from print culture, for the enmeshment of this commercial venture with imperial expansion during the nineteenth century created a particular place for exotic sexualities. As Konishi also notes, perceptions of Australian Aborigines were a significant part of this discourse. For English newcomers, marriage had been redefined by the Marriage Act of 1753. This reform eradicated clandestine marriage forms, and it formalised marriage as 'a practical reiteration of governmental regulations that bound citizens to the nation-state.'[18] It was well entrenched by the time of Eden's ruminations. In O'Connell's study of the emerging interest in global nuptial practices, European indissoluble consensual monogamy was pitted against polygamy and 'primitive' rites as the apex of 'enlightened national and imperial culture.'[19] Not to be missed in Eden's print offering is the disturbing disavowal by white men of their own violence (not that it ever came to prominence beyond court reports). Consider the scene again: Eden is reflecting on Aboriginal women's degraded status while he and his men surround a group of women who have so little recourse to defending themselves that they throw themselves over their children's and

A species of rough gallantry

each other's bodies. I believe Eden is then able to hear their distressed cries as 'infernal jabbering' because he and his critical mass of settlers thought that merely with their presence Aboriginal women had recourse to protection, in what we may identify as a discourse of settler-colonial gallantry.[20]

Eden's cant should be contextualised within well-established European tropes of traditionally living Aboriginal women as battered, downtrodden, half-starved camp drudges who were routinely passed between men against their will. In hundreds of printed accounts that reflected on gender relations in Aboriginal society, settlers routinely believed women were utterly subjugated by their 'tyrannical' men, whom they pilloried as 'lords and masters'. This is not to suggest that every report is hearsay and fabrication, only that most are. It is to argue that attributing the undoubted upsurge in violence towards Aboriginal women, particularly in the two decades following first contact, exclusively to Aboriginal men and, worse, as descriptive of their pre-contact sociality, was an expedient contrivance.

During this period, as we saw earlier, print underwent dramatic and sweeping changes due to industrialised production and dissemination and new demographics entering its readership, including women.[21] A similar leap in production occurred due to the mechanisation of paper manufacture, the invention of the Linotype in 1886, the invention of the telegraph in 1844 and the laying of transatlantic cables in the 1850s and 1860s,[22] which established print as a truly global enterprise.[23] It is the interplay between the promulgation of the ostensibly exotic and violent sexuality of Aborigines, settler-colonial discourse and print culture, with its particular facility to recirculate and thereby entrench racialised thinking, that brings together the focus of this chapter.

But as the last section on print reports of violence by white men demonstrates, print also harboured the potential for intervention in established patterns of perception.

The violent subjugation of Aboriginal women was secured in place as a discursive fixture recurring over an extensive timeframe and across a number of representational genres. Arising from this exhaustive survey of print culture, the tropes of Aboriginal women's subjugation figured, in order of predominance, as captured brides, then as victims of brutal violence, as the carriers of burdens, as camp drudges, followed by the trope of the child bride, with settlers fixating on women's unequal access to resources (particularly food), the polygamy of their men, exclusion from practising law and ceremony, neglect as elderly women, forced prostitution and, lastly, lack of formal marriage or burial ceremonies. Before they landed on the shores of New Holland, Europeans already held the belief that savage nations were characterised by the subjugation of their women. But the 'chattel and slave' trope was provided with new imagery from New Holland, particularly of women as 'sumpter-animals',[24] which perhaps offended most because it gave Aboriginal women propriety over belongings that were essential to the workings of economy, while women as load bearers contravened the rarely lived ideal of the passive ornamental wife.[25] The image of women sitting impassively behind men having their fill, waiting to be tossed food scraps over his shoulder, also stuck in the settler craw. These purported characteristics of Aboriginal gendered sociality were advanced as fully intact ways of traditional living, entirely unaffected by colonisation. This was a falsehood of epic proportion and impact. As we will see by the end of the chapter, it enabled settlers to get away with murder.

the more physical strength a warrior has, the more wives has he at his beck and nod, for he appropriates freely the domestic treasures of his weaker brother, knocking him on the head if he demurs

There are several persistent tropes at work in these lines of Eden's: bride capture, polygamy and a third that often accompanies them of child bestowal.[26] Also in play is the gendered, misaligned notion that women are the cause of conflict between men. Eden is not unusual in mentioning the competition between men for wives and assigning women as the principal cause of all violence, both intertribal and interracial. Making rare appearance into settler discourse is the notion of women as agitators.

These women, usually older, were described by respected anthropologists such as Brough Smyth as 'termagants' and the 'instigators of many of the quarrels inflaming disturbances in the camp.'[27] Elder women were said to scold, ignore and 'loudly remind' men of their 'holiest office of revenge',[28] and to have 'great influence' in irritating their peaceful husbands into 'killing parties'.[29] Aboriginal women could use these powers against settlers as did Walloa, whom James Bonwick in 1884 described as rising against the Van Diemen's Land 'conciliator' G. A. Robinson, 'like a Joan of Arc, amidst a nation of warriors, to deliver her people.' She led the Port Sorell tribe in pursuit of Robinson for five days. Bonwick admiringly relates, 'She gathered a party together by her eloquence, urging a band to violence and war by her appeals, and by her courageous conduct in the field.'[30] Bonwick was unusual in his approbation.

One image that certainly offers a 'contrapuntal intrusion'[31] into the stock of colonial images of Aboriginal women's subjection is a little-known French engraving titled *Vieille femme haranguant des natifs* (Figure 2.1) that appeared in Henri Perron d'Arc's 1869 *Aventures d'un voyageur en Australie*.[32] The image illustrates d'Arc's textual description of *natifs*, the scope of which reaches beyond the 'set-piece'[33] on Aborigines as they were appearing in a number of French travel accounts on Port Phillip. D'Arc writes of a nine-month stay with the 'Nagarnook' people, a group of Aborigines in the Murray–Darling region, during which this elder woman

Vieille femme haranguant des natifs.

Figure 2.1 'Vieille femme haranguant des natifs', in Aventures D'un Voyageur En Australie: Neuf Mois De Sejour Chez Les Nagarnooks, *2nd edn, Hachette, Paris, 1870. Courtesy National Library of Australia N 919.4 PER*

incites the men to avenge the death of her grandson, Warburg.[34] The inference that women played a determining role in intertribal conflict perhaps resonated with the potent feminine symbol of the French revolution, the figure 'Marianne', who rouses men to action in Eugene Delacroix' 1830 painting *Liberty leading the people*, which commemorated the July Revolution of that year.[35] Putting to one side the pernicious confusion of battle adrenalin with sexual arousal, this feminine allegory of Liberty expressed Enlightenment ideals of reason and the republican ideal of equality (even though the actual political agency of women was actively suppressed following the French uprisings).[36] Alternatively, the *femme natif* rouses men not to national destiny, or progressive ideals, but to a rabble of purposeless violence in avenging deaths, the cause of which were childishly misconstrued as sorcery.

In the chapter d'Arc devotes to translating the songs of women, the woman depicted – 'the finest example of sorcery which one would ever see' – delivers a 'wild' song to the young men. In riveting prose d'Arc describes his chanteuse as 'swaying from right to left, like a polar bear fascinating its prey; with disheveled hair, glaring dark eyes, her front tattoed white, and her body – haunches on her knees – enveloped in a red loincloth.'[37] The stanzas are no less compelling:

> O Warburg, my dear young son!
> Golam-biddies, you who have been always brave,
> Your short javelins – are they well sharpened?
> The quartz (edges) of your hatchets – are they
>   sufficiently cutting?
> So that their wounds shall fall as the rain, as the
>   thunder,
> Upon the boyl-yas.

The 'shrew' does not cease her invective until she runs out of breath, whereupon her 'rant' is taken up by another 'ancient fury'. She also has a 'prodigious' effect on the 'finest' of the men, spurring them into battle 'with the same ardour which impels the French soldier into the drum-charge of his regiment.' Hardly the battles that forged nations, these were instead thought to be 'quarrels', half of which were behind the murders and reprisals occurring within families or between tribes, which had 'mostly no reason to take place other than these fierce rants, always demanding death or blood.'[38] Luckily d'Arc has recourse to illustration, since 'no pen, no phrase, will ever be able to convey perfectly their fearfulness of appearance, their turbulence of gesture, their metallic voice-claps.' In the engraving assorted unattended babies throw the 'shrew's' disengagement with maternity into relief. Tellingly the men are passively attentive, mumbling 'Goran-win, goran-win (well said, well said)'.[39] Her features, long hair and breasts, were by 1869 atypical of the flattened nose, cropped hair and pendulous post-maternal breasts routinely ascribed to older Aboriginal women.

As the origin, or cause, of most of the violence between men, women agitators inverted the gender order, emasculating men and their standing as warriors. 'Savage' conflicts were too often incited by the irrational, and decidedly unfeminine, impulses of Aboriginal women whose outbursts men could not control. The trope, though infrequent, persisted, so that in 1913, Thomas Welsby's memoirs of exploratory surveys of Moreton Bay stated, 'an elderly and spiteful female, who possesses musical and poetic gifts, can set a score of warriors thirsting for each other's blood.'[40] The archival residue of these accounts, when read both against the grain or across the typeset, is the intimation that song was a cultural site within which women held significant authority and influence. Indeed, the second of the forty-four citations in the

Greenway bibliography that explicitly reference women is of the Menero tribe women's song.[41] There is an inkling of recognition betrayed here which may derive from the awe the most skilled and talented divas in Europe commanded, such as Pauline Viardot.[42]

From this mesh of gendered causalities accounting for Aboriginal conflict, the most conspicuous trope to emerge is undoubtedly that of bride capture. It drew on established conventions across a variety of print forms, from ethnography, satire, travel writing, pornography and journalism, to explore the particular offerings the Antipodes might make to the exotic and erotic in print culture. O'Connell notes the shift from religious categories of marriage rites in the earliest text of the marriage-rites genre (de Gaya's 1680 *Ceremonies nuptials de toute les nations*)[43] to geopolitical categories in subsequent publications. She argues that this shift sets out 'the terms within which the genre goes on to reproduce an imperialist ethnography of marriage for which English masculinity and femininity and English statist, consensual, monogamous marriage are a hypercivilised global example.'[44] The marriage rites of Aborigines, by their purported cruelty, reflected rather well on this exemplary frontier manliness.

As mentioned, Eden's story was presaged three decades earlier by the Eliza Fraser shipwreck off the southeast coast of Queensland. As Kay Shaffer demonstrates, this captivity narrative also persisted through 160 years of retellings in a number of 'fields of meaning'.[45] Schaffer finds these adaptations of the event were variously framed within imperialism, evangelical Christianity, scientific racism and 'gender divisions within Victorian sexual politics'.[46] Like bride capture, captivity narratives were advanced as a 'foundational fiction'[47] of colonial culture, inviting both mass prurience and the attention of natural science. Both reflect on a racialised masculinity at a time when violence by British men was being 'quarantined' to the armed forces and police, out of the purview of the respectable, hard-working settler, whose interactions on the frontier, as Angela Woollacott contends, defined a manliness 'built into colonial culture and politics'.[48]

As such, by the time Eden's story was published the Australian native offered some variation within a commercially proven, entrenched imperial publishing system. Aboriginal women starred as the spoils of intertribal conflict, or as objects abducted by gangs of men or beaten into submission. None of the print accounts particular to Australian Aboriginal marriage rites were captioned with the terms then used to depict sexual assault and partner violence in European societies: 'outrage of a woman', 'ravishment', 'wife beating' or 'rough usage' and 'marital cruelty'.[49] They were instead captioned 'courtship', inhering a cosmopolitan universality of humankind, while also demarking racial difference through geographically determined variety. The Australian contribution to the marriage-rites genre that O'Connell has identified does not take into account impacts of disease and settler violence against Indigenous people, nor of groups pushed into hostile territory, nor of the untimely death of sanctioned marriage partners. It is feasible that Europeans witnessed an upsurge in the abduction of young women in early contact scenarios. Assailants may have been enforcing retribution for the loss of a wife, sister or daughter. It is simply impossible to know from these accounts; indeed, the earliest bride capture account was plagiarised, as we shall see, within an elaborate publishing scam.

The original and first of three generations of the bride capture trope in Australia is found in judge advocate and secretary of the colony David Collins's *Account of the English Colony in New South Wales: with*

Remarks on the Dispositions, Customs, Manners, etc. of the Native Inhabitants of that Country, which appeared in 1798.[50] Native women are the victims of 'lust and cruelty (I can call them by no better name)' by 'the males (for they ought not to be dignified with the title of men)'. Women from enemy tribes were 'stupefied with blows' until streaming with blood the victim was,

> dragged through the woods by one arm, with a perseverance and violence that one might suppose would displace it from its socket; the lover, or rather the ravisher, is regardless of the stones or broken pieces of trees which may lie in his route, being anxious only to convey his prize in safety to his own party, where a scene ensues too shocking to relate.[51]

These words were lifted and recycled like newspaper fish wrapping, again and again. As Konishi observes, it is notable that Collins was not a firsthand witness of the incident, but rather gave a general account. His account was intended to apply not to 'ravishment', but to all Aboriginal marriage rites. Tellingly, the trope of bride capture was soon transferred from this reputable and credible colonial administrators' travelogue to a publishing con.

The next instalment is also significant because it includes the first bride capture image (Figure 2.2), created by London engraver and printer Vincent Woodthorpe and published in 1802 in *The History of New South Wales*, a volume falsely credited to legendary Irish thief George Barrington (Waldron).[52] Barrington was appointed superintendent of convicts and constable of Parramatta though he had been originally transported as a pickpocket. His career in crime, and his own eloquence and talent for class passing, lent him such notoriety that this 'Prince of Pickpockets'[53] was closely

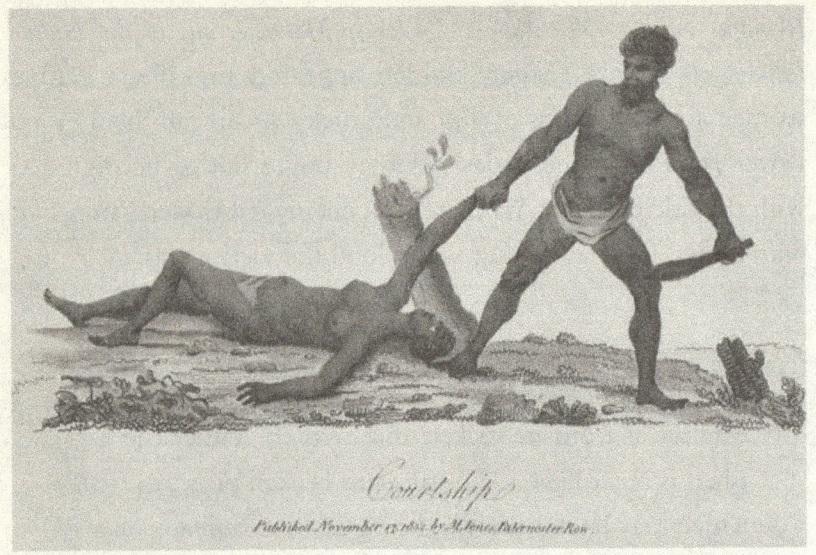

Figure 2.2 'Courtship', George Barrington, The History of New South Wales: including Botany Bay, *London, M. Jones, 1810. Courtesy National Library of Australia FRM F485A.*

followed by the press. He was credited by scurrilous journalists with a number of publications, none of which he authored.[54] The vivid description of bride capture attributed to him was liberally plagiarised from Collins by London hacks within the 'shadowy world of popular publishing',[55] in which Barrington's notoriety was a selling point.

'Barrington' paraphrases that the 'disgusting' conduct of the male natives of New South Wales 'renders them considerably inferior to the brute creation', who seek only 'the gratification of their brute desires.'[56] He then details the stupefying blows a suitor rains down all over his intended's body, which 'streaming with blood' is then dragged through the woods to his own tribe whereupon, 'Barrington' coyly writes, 'a scene takes place with the relation of which I shall neither stain my pages nor offend my reader.' We are then given to understand the 'greatest subjection' in which native women are kept, their frequently fractured skulls, their ravished contentment and their occasional retaliation, such that the 'analogy' between 'savages and the lower classes' becomes 'too obvious to escape attention.'[57] This confirms Robert Hogg's analysis of the middle-class notion of 'character' as distinct from worker masculinities, which were associated with the primitive.[58] London publishers would continue to exploit this potent trope intended for salacious consumption by flirting with the genre of pornography.[59]

'Barrington' then relates at length the romantic tale of a young native who attempts to avenge his beloved sister's abduction by seizing a young woman from a neighbouring tribe. Yet the brother becomes so enamoured by the girl's beauty and gracious form that he instead lowers his club, gathers her to his breast and henceforth the amorous couple live with the young man's sister near Barrington, who teaches them to read. His refining influence, it is to be surmised, sets the lovers and the sister on the course to civilisation, despite their being, in fact, entirely fanciful characters. The 'money shot' in the narrative of bride capture is gang rape, and having freely indulged these imaginings – facilitated by the already naked forms of the protagonists and including a reference to stained pages – readers could then regain their moral footing through the narrative resolution of civilised natives succumbing to the refined feelings of romantic love as distinct from the savage passions of brute desire. Reinstated are the ideals of courtly love with sexual self-mastery and rebuffed is the unrestrained passion of the New Holland native with his lack of control over primitive urges.[60] It is little wonder bride capture was fully exploited by spurious London publishers. Under their imprint it was heady reading. Indeed, if the same scenario and images were attributed to Europeans it would within a few decades come to be classified as pornography, as moral reform movements such as the Society

Figure 2.3 'Ceremonies preliminaires d'un mariage Australien', in Dumont D'Urville, Voyages pittoresque autour de monde, c1835. Steele plate intaglio print with watermark,1835, Jules Boilly after Louis Auguste de Sainson. Courtesy of the private collection of Brook Andrew

for the Suppression of Vice[61] would eventually influence the passage of the Obscene Publications Act in 1857.[62]

Konishi has drawn attention to contradictory sources on bride capture which could already be found, such as Watkin Tench's firsthand description of young men displaying their prowess to young women aspiring to be chosen.[63] In particular, Konishi has contextualised French discourses on Aboriginal sexuality within the 'contemporary scientific, cultural and political milieu' and strategically counterposed these sources against violent accounts.[64] She analyses a Sebastian Leroy engraving of bride capture (Figure 2.3) made after a lost sketch by Petit, the artist travelling with the

A species of rough gallantry

Baudin expedition of 1800.⁶⁵ Konishi situates the production of this image within the increasing state policing of sexuality aimed at monitoring population growth, along with the

> context of certain pressing concerns within the metropolitan and peripheral realms of the late eighteenth century (health and procreation, gallantry, modesty and marriage, women's emancipation) and, of course, redeployments of long-standing European myths of savage sexuality.⁶⁶

Also of interest here is the extent to which it reappeared due to print's readiness to exploit such material. As Konishi has explained, the original Petit drawing was not related to any textual description of an eye-witnessed assault by any of the crew of the Baudin voyage, as such its 'veracity as an ethnographic study' is in doubt.⁶⁷

This engraving (Figure 2.4) derived from Leroy appeared in 1836 in another French publication, this time by the travel writer

Figure 2.4 'Australie', Domeny de Rienzi, Océanie; ou, cinquième partie du Monde. *Courtesy of the National Library of Australia FRM F2173A*

107

Figure 2.5 Hochzeits-ceremonie der Neuhollander, Ceremonie d'un mariage. *Unknown artist, c.1840. Lithograph. Courtesy Art Gallery of Ballarat*

and illustrator Domeny de Rienzi in his *Océanie; ou, cinquième partie du monde*.[68] This 'highly derivative' but widely read book was created by an independent traveller who, after five voyages, documented in detail the peoples of 'Oceania'.[69] Yet, de Rienzi was credited by the Bibliothèque Nationale de France as an 'illusionist, creator of a fantasmagoric autobiography'.[70] We can see de Rienzi altered the left half of Leroy's engraving so that the woman is viewed kneeling from the front, perhaps to display her breasts. Her hair is not pulled by the man with the raised waddy and one of the Leroy assailants, tugging on her left arm, has been excised along with a figure in the background. De Rienzi rendered all of his many figures of Oceania peoples as classical forms and in this image softened the assault not only through the omitting of assailants, but through Europeanised features. In 1840 the image was printed as a lithograph in a German publication (Figure 2.5). The woman's anguish is emphasised as is the brutality of her assailants, her breasts are made more pendulous and all their limbs are attenuated.[71] The stereotyped physiognomy of Australian Aborigines is literally drawn on stone in transnational circuits of print imagery.

Following Petit (notwithstanding its reiterations into 1840) and Barrington, the next print instalment of the bride capture trope in 1829 skitters back to the publishing genre of the imperial travelogue. It also omits time, place or named individuals, and relies on the ready credence of unsubstantiated reports. Robert Mudie's travelogue cites Collins's description, extrapolating that 'every marriage…in the neighbourhood of Port Jackson…is attended with more violence than the rape of the Sabine women by the ancient Romans.'[72] To underscore that these courtship and marriage rites reflect 'savage character', Mudie adds that 'native Australians' are 'wholly wanting' in the 'foundation of the kindly affections',[73] a telling remark in this period of the 'remarkable growth of the ideology of companionate marriage.'[74] In O'Connell's study, the Roman practice of divorce (along with Eastern polygamy) was also deployed to 'generate an imperialist typology of sex',[75] but here other rites are associated with primitive sexuality through violence.

The Collins citation jumps genres again to reappear in 1854 in a geographical dictionary authored by the economist and newspaper founder John Ramsey McCulloch. Under 'Races of men in Australia', the entry reads: 'The treatment of females in Australia is in the last degree brutal. Wives are not courted or purchased, but are seized upon, stupefied by blows, and then carried off to be the slaves of their unfeeling masters'.[76] Paradoxically, just as ethnography was gaining the legitimacy of science and being calibrated in the dictionary format (three years before the Oxford English Dictionary began to be compiled), Collins was cited once more in 1873 in a four-volume vernacular ethnology called *The*

Races of Mankind by the botanist Robert Brown (who travelled mostly in British Columbia). Brown cites the entire passage, complete with stupefying blows, streams of blood, the dragging by one arm, 'with a perseverance and violence that might be supposed would displace it from its socket' over 'stones or broken pieces of trees' until we find ourselves once again at a scene 'too shocking to relate.'[77] Bride capture has by this time acquired a permanent cultural imprimatur, across a number of genres within print culture's self-referencing imperial circuits of information exchange. Under this licence, the identity of Aboriginal women was principally 'stupefied', a far cry from the 'outraged' white women of captivity narratives.

To recap, thus far the recurring image and trope of bride capture has been detached from firsthand observation (in Petit), engraved decades later based on this original drawing (in Leroy), reworked by a reputed 'illusionist' (in de Rienzi), plagiarised from another generalised account (from Collins), and falsely attributed to a notorious pickpocket in a dubious publishing venture (Barrington). Yet the plot of bride capture continued to thicken. It was recirculated for another half-century to come. A sample includes Lieutenant R. N. Breton, who stated in his travelogue of 1834, 'All the tribes procure their wives by treachery, and always from some other tribe: on these occasions the unhappy woman is often most dreadfully beaten.'[78] Likewise the former Reverend William Yate (expelled from New Zealand for scandalous practices with young Maori men and who may have felt an uncomfortable resonance with coercive sexual behaviours)[79] was asked in evidence before the 1837 Select Committee on Aborigines in the House of Commons whether rites of marriage were practised among Aborigines. He replied, 'Nothing more I

A species of rough gallantry

Figure 2.6 'Courtship in Australia. Contracting an alliance with a neighbouring family'. P.H.F. Phelps, Native Scenes [snakes, birds & marine life], *c. 1840–1849, unpublished album. Courtesy Dixon State Library of New South Wales.– DL PX 58/1*

believe than merely seizing by force the person they intended to marry; the strongest gains the day.'[80]

Increasingly inhering in settler masculine identity was the position of observer, which, as noted earlier, positioned humans in the modern perceptual field to allow for 'optimum conditions of circulation and exchangeability, whether it be of commodities, energy, capital, images, or information.'[81] Within colonial modernity, visual access to the native by the settler-observer was confirmed by a certain logic of exposure that informed print culture. Observations of the racial Other were yet to be circumscribed by the rigours of systematised data collection under the strictures of anthropology. It would come.

A decade on, in 1849, NSW settler P. H. F. Phelps installed the next image of bride capture (Figure 2.6).[82] This is an interesting

111

case, for Phelps's caricature was never published. However, the captions to his scenes of Aboriginal life suggest he may have intended to sell his images as a book of cartoons, perhaps encouraged by the success of illustrated humour in magazines such as *Punch,* which had recently inaugurated the use of the 'cartoon' for this genre.[83] Many of the drawings were framed and titled, and the pages of the albums were inserted with a sheet of explanatory text. Although the drawing, captioned 'Courtship in Australia: contracting an alliance with a neighbouring family', was never published, its creation was informed by publishing conventions Phelps perhaps aspired to emulate. The inserted sheet gave another third-person account of bride capture commencing with, 'The aborigines of Australia have the most singular and barbarous mode of obtaining their wives known to exist amongst savage nations.' The image shows a raid that, in the text, includes men seizing young women by the hair, dragging them while stunning them with 'terrific blows upon the head' said to leave scars for life. Phelps claims women showed them with pride and as proof of the strength of their husband's attachment, 'as if the greatest beating showed the most ardent love.' Significantly, then Phelps let on that the 'sable ladies' sometimes hinted that the captures were made through a 'previous arrangement between the parties' although such an admission impugned the 'warlike prowess of their lords.' The seizure is then followed by a public duel, 'according to established forms and rules between the bridegrooms and selected champions from the opposite party', then celebrated with a corroboree and 'festive meeting' of both parties.[84] Phelps's caption intimates bride capture may have been a highly mannered and formalised rite, but it was impossible for Europeans to distinguish between performance and their overriding sense of the impulsive satisfaction of 'primitive' urges.[85]

The question of scarification requires a momentary deviation from the trajectory of bride capture. Far from women being scarred by men's violence, in fact, over twenty years earlier women in Van Diemen's Land had been said to be the operators in the scarification of men's thighs, shoulders and breasts.[86] Scarification was among a number of 'mutilatory rites', such as the boring of the septum of nasal cartilage (less common in women than men); tooth avulsion, which was widespread; circumcision and introcision – in women the cutting on the perineum to ease birth; and cicatrisation, which was sometimes ornamental – one 'Arunta' woman was observed to have forty raised scars. In the Northern Territory it was most often used on the death of a relative.[87] Highly regarded social anthropologist Malinowski, who we will see finally laid to rest the bride capture trope, in 1913 surveyed all the literature that attested to women as chattels and refuted that their scars and wounds were evidence of male violence. The claim was 'obviously unreliable, at the same time being typical of a whole class of statements based upon insufficient and superficial observations.'[88] He also notes they are more often than not anecdotes conveyed by 'civilised blacks', which 'suggests to us that much of the ill-treatment was due perhaps to the "civilization" of the blacks.'[89] He concludes his exhaustive survey with what amounts to an intervention.

> Here we have a great diversity of statements and much contradiction. We read of barbarous ill-treatment and of deep affection; of drudgery and slavery imposed on wives, and of henpecked husbands; of fugitive men having recourse to magic, and of women mercilessly chastised, prostituted…our authors were lost in the diversity of facts and could not give an adequate generalization.[90]

Figure 2.7 Newsletter of Australia: A Narrative to Send to Friends, no. 58, June 1861, 'Aboriginal Courtship', University of Melbourne Archives, John J English, 1963.0008.0001

Nevertheless, claims of scarification had commenced half a century earlier with Sir George Grey writing,

> The early life of a young woman at all celebrated for beauty is generally one of continued series of captivity to different masters, of ghastly wounds, of wanderings in strange families, or rapid flights, of bad treatment from other females, amongst whom she is brought a stranger be her captor; and rarely do you see a form of unusual grace and elegance, but is marked and scarred by the furrows of old wounds…[91]

This is quoted by John McLennan in 1865 in his major anthropological work, *Primitive Marriage: An Inquiry into the Origin of the Form of Capture in Marriage Ceremonies*, to which we will return. It reappears as late as Alan Moorehead's 1966 *Fatal Impact*.[92]

Earlier, in 1861, another salacious engraving of bride capture, captioned 'Aboriginal courtship: carrying off a lubra' (see Figure 2.7), appeared in a print 'Newsletter of Australia: A narrative to send to friends.'[93] It was reprinted the following year in the *Illustrated Melbourne Post*.[94] This violent scene of abduction is surrounded by vignettes of industry, mining, horseracing and droving, while uncommonly handsome settlers – a punter, a cricketer, a soldier and highlander (!) – lounge amid bales of wheat and wool. Contained by it all is the flailing woman, her distress and helplessness, and firm breasts no less, presenting an occasion for readers to deride frontier masculinities.

Let us complete our tour of this first generation of bride capture circulation, originating as it did principally in Collins. In 1846 a newspaper review of Charles Baker's advice book, *Sydney and Melbourne*, informed prospective emigrants that the young initiated 'Cœleb' made his 'introductory salutation' to his chosen bride with a 'stunning blow from his club – under the lulling effect of which she of course falls "head over ears in love".' She was then carried off to become the 'lawful "lubra", *alias* wife, of an arbitrary lord.' Baker argued that such a system, if adopted in England, would save much anxious and frequently unsuccessful manoeuvring on the part of the fair sex, not to mention spinsters who 'would not mind the blow, if it were certain to be followed by the honours of the married state.'[95] These little asides become more frequent from this point and betray a shift from salacious interest and fetishising to identification or a need to theorise racial decline.

Thus, in 1854, Finney Eldershaw, a squatter in New England, published his rather assuredly titled, *Australia as it really is,* which details his seeking of runs in Queensland in 1842 when he *really was* still in England.[96] Nevertheless, he managed to claim he was an 'eye-witness to the facts recorded'. These included the lack of marriage ceremony and the fact that 'proprietorship of wives, or "gins", was generally maintained by force of arms.'[97] He added that polygamy and infanticide were the principal cause for the decline in numbers of Aborigines and rather candidly admitted his motive for understanding this decline was that it 'relieves us from the onus of being the immediate instrument of their apparently inevitable destruction.'[98] To these causes of population decline he added the 'fearfully degraded position of their women, (who are literally the beasts of burden to the community)'. With remarkable detachment, Eldershaw also claimed to have taken part in a massacre of some 200 'insatiable wretches' to avenge the deaths of three shepherds at one of his outposts. Since it's hard to pin the man down, of more interest here is that Eldershaw was careful to tie his theories of demise to race destiny. He stated,

> if it be true that the status of the women of a country is a fair criterion of the civilization to which its people have attained, verily no stronger proof of humanity's deepest degradation need be cited against the Australian Aborigines.[99]

It was this degradation that positioned Aborigines on the decaying bottom rung of the ladder of race destiny, their treatment of women another unsustainable load that would see them fall into oblivion.

Eldershaw's entry is noteworthy for it shows the significance of bride capture in legitimating the moral basis for the discourse of settler-colonialism with its recurring references to Indigenous eradication. Eldershaw probably concocted this account far removed from the Australian frontier. His familiarity with settler-colonial formations of mobility and morality had to be enacted through circuits of print dissemination and, through reiterative tropes such as bride capture, identification with frontier manliness was as ready to hand as the morning paper. For Victorian anthropologists, as we'll see, bride capture would become a descriptor of human antiquity and European origin, along the trajectory of racial succession.

In 1864 a second generation of bride capture citations would emerge from the pen of an anonymous writer in the widely read London (originally Edinburgh) magazine *Chambers's Journal of Popular Literature, Science, and Arts*. The article commences with the 'beasts of burden' trope then moves on to courtship. The suitor seizes a 'leubra' from a rival camp and, 'With a blow of his nulla-nulla (war-club)' by which he 'stuns the object of his "affections", and drags her insensible body away to some retired spot, whence, as soon as she recovers her senses, he brings her home to his gunyah in triumph.' A raid on a sleeping camp is then described in which 'quite naked' men creep into the camp of sleeping 'leubras':

> then one of the intruders stretches out his spear; and inserts its barbed point amongst her thick flowing locks; turning the spear slowly round some of her hair speedily becomes entangled with it; then, with a sudden jerk,

she is aroused from her slumber, and as her eyes open, she feels the sharp point of another weapon pressed against her throat. She neither faints nor screams; she knows well that the slightest attempt at escape or alarm will cause her instant death, so, like a sensible woman, she makes a virtue of necessity, and rising silently, she follows her captors.[100]

When they reach his camp, 'they are received with universal applause, and highly honoured for this *gallant* exploit.' This very same article appeared the following year in a magazine called *The Golden Era*.[101]

Remarkably, the entire unauthored and uncredited piece was reprinted the same year as a key source in McLennan's *Primitive Marriage*.[102] This beggars belief given that natural science was now going to great pains to demarcate itself from pseudo-science in periodical literature.[103] The transfer from ethnographic publications to newspapers is an established pathway, most obviously in the form of book reviews and extracts.[104] The passage of ethnological data from popular magazine to scientific text, however, is less documented. This instance appears to have slipped through before the discipline of anthropology moved to question the scientific credibility of casual observers and, from around 1870, formalised its data sources into systematised knowledge production through statistics and metrical comparison, professional accreditation and peer-reviewed disciplinary journals.[105]

McLennan, who is credited with coining the terms 'totemism', 'endogamy' and 'exogamy', was an influential cultural evolutionist who, in keeping with Victorian anthropology, took particular interest in Australian Aborigines because they were thought to embody the testimony of fossilised early man. As an evolutionist he was influenced by Charles Lyell's *Geological Evidences of the Antiquity of Man* (1863), and the doctrine of uniformitarianism, in which forces shaping the earth in the present have antecedents reaching back into deep time. The gradualism of Darwinian natural selection confirmed McLennan's thinking about the 'primitive' kinship and marriage forms of Australian Aborigines by which he could formulate Victorian marriage customs as transcending the primal horde. Bride capture evidenced the evolution of monogamous matrimony from the most elemental form of social relation, promiscuity. In 'horde' social forms, the scarcity of women, said to be effected by female infanticide, 'and the instinctive recoil from incest, prompted 'exogamy' under which wives were obtained from outside groups. Since hordes existed in a state of competitive hostility with these outside groups, bride capture was the only means to avoid incest. According to John Lubbock, who challenged McLennan's thesis in 1870,[106] 'modern savages' were only able to practise exclusive love relationships (and advance from primal promiscuity towards modern monogamous marriage) by capturing from other tribes who would otherwise demand communal access to a chosen wife.[107]

As Patrick Wolfe has extensively detailed, McLennan's 'wild scenario of marriage by capture' was in fact a 'rhetorical device' which, with others, became 'debating-effects, theoretical reaction-formations whose elaboration was to give evolutionary anthropology its propositional shape.'[108] McLennan substantiated and defended propertied patriarchy by separating kinship from residence through the ruse of matrilineal nescience – ignorance of maternal origin due to the unstable circumstance of bride capture. Feminist anthropologist Micaela di Leonardo has noted the 'anthropological tradition of dichotomising "male" public kinship and "female" domestic kinship – and, of course, of providing "thin descriptions" of the latter', when in fact women's kinship struggles 'are concerned, after all, with the distribution of whatever domestic power is available to women and often also entail female influences on male political actions.'[109] In McLennan's schema, consanguinity comes into being first through territory, not kinship, which he set at a later stage. Wolfe explains the twists and turns by which McLennan ultimately legitimated property-owning patriarchy as a higher evolutionary stage:

> the famously shocking saga of violent wife-capture [was] a means of interrupting the continuity of a naturally given maternity. By filiating children to the horde on the ground that their mothers could vanish at any moment, McLennan made nescience of maternity underwrite the exclusively territorial basis of the wife-capturing primal horde. Having in turn suppressed both naturally given maternity and naturally given territoriality, he was able to reintroduce them on his terms, terms which sanctified patriarchal property and subordinated the female principle in order to furnish the twin foundations of human society.[110]

The descent of the Australian Aborigine within this schema was to an elemental stage of origin for Victorian anthropologists, who imagined they were observing across vast expanses of time when, in fact, the distance was purely spatial, as indeed were their sources – not to mention inflected with imaginary tendencies. These exchanges may well constitute one instance when print culture did not conquer space, but attenuated it. Notable is the attempt to apply the abstract paternal principle, which introduced territorial consanguinity and inheritance, by entirely devoiding mothers,

A species of rough gallantry

women and daughters from property rights. Bride capture was a means to imagine that so-called primitive peoples could not observe matrilineal kinship or the maternal principle. Bride capture then became a means by which Victorian evolutionary anthropology could enact, as Wolfe puts it, 'a gendered variant of *terra nullius*.'[111]

McLennan's second source on these 'modern savages' came from an early travelogue: John Turnbull's *Voyage Around the World* (1805).[112] Yet, as Konishi shows, Turnbull had stated New Hollanders only 'sometimes marry into other families', and he also claimed colonists were informed by young women that they were not 'forced away against their inclinations', but rather 'this mode of gallantry was the custom, and perfectly to their taste.'[113] McLennan thought Turnbull's qualification 'suspicious', no doubt because that much agreement might suggest prior knowledge, even arrangement of the exchange of daughters and sisters. This would compromise his theory that primitive people were unable to observe who their mothers were; rather, it suggests they formally arranged matrilineal kinship. But from Turnbull also came the notion that bride capture was 'rather relished by the ladies as a species of rough gallantry.'[114] McLennan himself offered another important qualification: bride capture was no longer the 'sole or regular mode of getting a wife among the Australian tribes'; however, he still claimed it was common enough to be considered a 'system'. Relying on an anonymous contributor to a popular magazine, along with an 1805 travelogue, McLennan felt equipped to argue that the 'system of betrothals points unmistakably to a previous stage when wives were captured', which graduated to exogamy.[115] McLennan's third and last source was Sir George Grey, 'a good authority', who had written of the 'many plots' to carry young women off, who are speared should they refuse.[116]

Remember McLennan is ultimately seeking to defend and legitimate Victorian patrilineal propertied inheritance through his theories of pre-social origins. A certain identification was enabled by the much attenuated link to these supposed early sexual forms for McLennan and his readers: the fantasy of promiscuity, which in Victorian England was proving irrepressibly present and, indeed, capable of assuming new social forms through prostitution intersecting with urbanisation and capitalism.[117] In our time the theory of bride capture has been discredited as 'largely a fantasy of the Victorian male anthropological imagination',[118] though we can see these men of science were themselves beholden to the fantasies of purportedly less discriminating observers. Nevertheless, at the time, McLennan's text gave the imprimatur of science to earlier iterations of bride capture, legitimating its circulation as empirically substantiated. Thus, in the same year botanist and zoologist Augustus Oldfield published his study of the people near Port Gregory in which he referenced back to earlier by now stock descriptions of men who 'discover an unprotected female' whose,

> proceedings are not of the most gentle nature. Stunning her by a blow from the dowak…they drag her by the hair to the nearest thicket to await her recovery. When she comes to her senses they force her to accompany them, and as at worst it is but the exchange of one brutal lord for another, she generally enters into the spirit of the affair.[119]

Oldfield is then quoted in Brown's *Races of Mankind* in 1873. Brown seamlessly reiterated the passage:

> [when Aboriginal men] discover an unprotected female, their proceedings are not of the most gentle nature. Stunning her with a blow from the waddy (to make her love him perhaps), they drag her by the hair to the nearest thicket to await her recovery. When she comes to her senses they force her to accompany them; and, as at the worst, it is but the exchange of one brutal lord for another, she generally enters into the spirit of the affair, and takes as much pains to escape as though it were a matter of her own free will.[120]

Brown added, 'Between the wives and the husbands little real affection can be expected.'[121] Brown, whose work was replete with 'finely gradated'[122] tables, was ordinarily a careful empiricist.

This brings us to the third generation in the rickety discursive scaffolding of bride capture, following Collins and McLennan. This was unwittingly provided by the unusually sympathetic and experienced Victorian Assistant Protector William Thomas, whose jurisdiction was the Port Phillip, Westernport and Gippsland districts. He wrote around 1838 that men have the right of giving the women away, and 'sulky' brides who crept back to their mothers in the night were knocked about by their enraged fathers 'with his bludgeon or tomahawk', and dragged by the 'head to her koolin', where she got 'another drubbing'. After two or three days of this treatment 'the poor creature is regularly broken down. She resigns to her fate, and generally proves a constant and affectionate wife.' Thomas added a qualifying footnote, 'Of course these scenes are not practised now in my encampment, I merely state their customs as I found them.'[123] So incompatible are these customs with European civility and gentility as ensconced in the identity of frontier manliness, it is inferred that merely by dint of settler presence, or perhaps example, they cease to be practised.

Thomas was generally a sympathetic observer and advocate for Aborigines. Acting as district protector under George Augustus Robinson, he concentrated less on Aboriginal salvation than their practical needs under the impact of incursions onto their land.[124] Significantly, his ethnographic notes and collections became a critical source for Robert Brough Smyth's influential *Aborigines of Victoria*. In this 1878 work, Brough Smyth included a lengthy description of bride capture.

> Seizing her by her long hair, the stern father drags her to the home prepared for her by her new owner…If she attempts to abscond the bridegroom does not hesitate to strike her savagely on the head with his waddy; and the bridal screams and yells make the night hideous.[125]

Brough Smyth introduces the new element of rivals attacking the new husband's dwelling and while he is fending them off, 'the bride rushes to her mother, and with streaming eyes and heaving breast begs vainly for protection and help, which her mother dare not give her.' She is then dragged back, and sometimes speared. 'Beaten, frightened, and at last completely conquered, she resigns herself to her hard fate.'[126] As a respected meteorologist, Brough Smyth was known to be cautious about premature and speculative data.[127] Yet, *Aborigines of Victoria* was highly derivative,[128] particularly depending on the unpublished notes of Thomas. Curiously, the 'streaming eyes and heaving breast' phrase can be traced to a 1774 pamphlet, 'Thoughts on slavery', by emancipist and founder of the Methodist Church, John Wesley.[129] His phrase was soon disassociated from racial subjection and had done the rounds of poetry,[130] essay[131] and memoir[132] before Thomas resurrected it in the Australian context. According with Konishi's finding that contradictory sources were paid little heed,[133] it is telling that Brough Smyth didn't also publish Thomas's relating of the enactment of a creation story of 'Murrina kooding, or strength lost', at a large gathering of Goulburn, Mount Macedon, Barrabool, Yarra and Western Port peoples on the Yarra. Thomas's account rather confounds Brough Smyth's reiteration of bride capture. He wrote,

> The Goulburn lubras, quite naked, stole upon seven young men. No sooner had the women their hands on the heads of the young men than the latter appeared helpless; they cut from each young man a lock of his hair. As soon as the hair was cut the young men fainted; the women took the ornaments from the men's heads and decamped.[134]

The men reportedly then underwent a ceremony over three hours to save their lives. Nevertheless, bride capture was given a new lease of life in settler-colonial discourse largely through Brough Smyth's text – and such elisions.

In 1881, the prolific ethnologist and journalist Augustus Keane drew heavily on Brough Smyth's account of a forced marriage in *St James's Magazine*. Here we see that part of the crossover between print genres rests on the authors themselves writing across professions.

> When we read the accounts of the barbarous treatment to which they are habitually subjected, all our preconceived notions of the 'noble savage' are quickly

dispelled, and we begin to wonder how the human race could have ever succeeded in struggling upwards to a higher state.[135]

The article includes the passage we already know verbatim, including

> seizing the bride by her long hair, [he] drags her to the home prepared for her by her new owner. Further resistance often subjects her to brutal treatment. If she attempts to abscond, the bridegroom does not hesitate to strike her savagely on the head with his waddy, and the bridal screams make the night hideous…During the fight the bride rushes to her mother, and with streaming eyes and heaving breast begs vainly for protection and help, which the mother dare not give her…Beaten, frightened, and at last completely conquered, she resigns herself to her hard fate, and becomes the willing obedient drudge to her new master.[136]

Keane concludes, 'Such the fitting preclude to a monotonous life of incredible hardships and prolonged misery.'[137] In the 1890s Keane, a professor of Hindustani at University College, London, based his work on linguistic classification rather than the dominant physical anthropology. He disputed the theory of common origin in part due to his 'extremely antagonistic attitude towards the blacks.'[138] Despite the new strictures imposed by the discipline of anthropology, he drew on travel literature to advance his theories of the natural inequality of racially categorised human beings. Scientific racism had taken hold and bride capture, by now a transplatform media trope, was cast in a particular role. It meant that the egalitarian and cultural relativist intervention of early sociologist Edward Westermarck would be largely ignored. In his 1891 *Origin of Human Marriage,* Westermarck refuted primitive promiscuity, arguing instead that monogamy prevailed in primordial sexual relations rather than polygamy and that chastity was more closely observed among savages than civilised. He attributed the 'wantonness of savages' to 'the dregs' within the 'higher culture', yet his argument was rejected by Freud and others who maintained the theory of primitive promiscuity progressing to civilised monogamy.[139]

As such, in the account Keane cites, Brough Smyth referenced evangelical missionary John Bulmer, of Lake Tyer mission, who claimed he had seen with his own eyes a woman dragged by the hair.[140] In all the bride capture references I surveyed, Bulmer is the only observer who claims to see a woman dragged by her hair firsthand, and he does not specify that she was a bride. The next closest eye-witness account comes from the popularist Edward Curr, in his *Recollections of Squatting in Victoria*, detailing the decade from 1841. Yet even his story was provided by a 'blackfellow who was present.'[141] Curr installed himself in his informant's standpoint as witness and, with a talent for amplification, embellished the story. He describes the entrance of a new young wife, Kilbangaroo, to the camp of her betrothed, Wawgroot, and his first wife, Polly, a 'lubra', and herself 'decidedly a belle amongst the blacks; a sprightly, arch-spoken, laughing young lady.'[142] Kilbangaroo ignores lengthy pleas from her father, who finally loses patience and raises his waddy, but is stopped by her mother who gets the girl on her feet and marches her off to her new home. Curr believed Kilbangaroo did not want to give up ideas of a bachelor from another camp, or that she considered it the 'proper thing to give as much trouble as possible on these occasions.'[143]

The next day when Wawgroot was hunting, 'the first wife, after abusing the younger one in the choicest Billingsgate, took the opportunity of beating her soundly with her yamstick'. Wawgroot then saw fit to 'admonish the lady of his early affections with his nulla-nulla, in a style which would probably have killed most white women, reducing her temporarily to complete obedience.' He then retrieved the absconding Kilbangaroo with her father but 'it was not until a year or so had elapsed, and the young wife had received two or three severe beatings that obedience became habitual.' After which Curr reports Kilbangaroo later carried 'a little black thing', 'peeping over her shoulder' that even Polly seemed 'fond of'. He remarks,

> As a proof of the general prevalence of such wooden admonitions, it may be noticed that most women bore about their persons proofs of savage treatment at the hands of their husbands; but, putting aside occasional ill-usage, it always seemed to me that the women were happy enough, and got on very comfortably with their lords.[144]

To give a sense of the ongoing popular purchase of bride capture, Curr's entire, lengthy passage was extracted and printed in *The Sydney Mail*.[145]

While Curr appeared to convey an unmediated report of the violence inflicted on this young woman by her father, husband and his first wife, there is something in the perceived submission of this arch belle of a young woman that Curr quietly approves of. When he next reflected on the subject, Curr showed deference to the increasingly complicated understandings of bride capture by then in circulation and to which we will come. In his 1886 four-volume *Australian Race,* he cited a report on the 'Bahkunjy' from the Darling River. A newly wed girl had to report to her parents after a few days and, 'if the inquiry put to the girl by her mother as to whether she is happy could be answered satisfactorily, the pair continued to live together; otherwise they separated – that is, the girl went home again.'[146] The contradictions within Curr's accounts are descriptive of the beginnings of a wider questioning of these accepted print sources, most of them, as we've seen, being anthropological texts sourcing from popular magazines or travelogues. Alongside this new stipulation for credible sources comes the authority to extrapolate the meaning of bride capture to racial inferiority and its correlate, racial demise. Credible sources, however, could prove inconvenient.

In 1879 anthropologist and prolific author James Anson Farrer in his *Primitive Manners and Customs* discussed marriage outside the same 'stock', no doubt influenced by McLennan, as a

> mark of higher conception of social organization, when people have learned to classify themselves with respect to their neighbours, when tribal and personal property is well established, and when, consequently, marriages between the groups can be effected by purchase better than by violence.[147]

From these Victorian standards Farrer defended Aborigines against the record. He wrote, 'That force was ever the normal method by which marriages were effected in Australia, there is no proof; that, on the contrary, mutual likings often set the law.' He cited the case of a 'native captive girl' who, 'after living among the colonists for some time, expressed a desire to away and be married to a young native of her acquaintance.'[148] After three days she returned, 'sadly beaten and jealous of the other wife.' While this hardly disproved violence and polygamy, Farrer uses this 'case' of yet another unnamed woman to dispel the theory that bride capture was prevalent.

The first major rupture to bride capture discourse came from anthropologists Lorimer Fison and Alfred William Howitt in their foundational and highly regarded anthropological work, *Kamilaroi and Kurnai*.[149] As we've seen, kinship, marriage and courtship had been a central preoccupation for Victorian anthropologists and periodical print. It was now demarked as a site of complex, localised and erudite knowledge production. Fison and Howitt explain, 'A girl, if she fancied a young man, might send him a secret message, asking "Will you find me some food?" And this was understood to be a proposal.'[150] 'The young Kurnai', the authors go on, 'can, as a rule, acquire a wife in one way only. He must run away with her.' This important shift from abduction to elopement was possibly merely a refinement of understanding of what previous settlers had observed. Fison and Howitt argued that the eloping couple might face severe punishment until the family tired of objecting. When he was challenged on his thesis of elopement by Bulmer of Lake Tyers, Howitt did something not tried since Turnbull made reference to women's accounts in 1805. He went to Ramayuck mission and spoke to four women, one of whom, 'Nanny', 'stated positively that the rule was that young women ran off with their husbands.'[151] Aboriginal women's voices finally rent the tissue of errors. Their words would reverberate, crossing into the factual calibration of the *Encyclopedia Britannica* in an 1890 entry by popular science author George Bettany, who did not quote Fison and Howitt but repeated their passage on girls initiating proposals by asking men to provide food.[152] The discourse of bride capture was now vacillating between older assumptions which tended to persist in newspapers and more qualified, localised assertions in publications increasingly formalised by their scientific discipline.

The Reverend George Taplin, missionary at Point McLeay in South Australia (now renamed Raukkan and administered by the Ngarrindjeri people) explained in 1897 that the 'Narrinyeri' do not abduct their wives and that consent 'is always regarded as desirable'. He added,

> It is regarded by the females as very disgraceful not to be given away in exchange for another. A young woman who goes away with a man and lives with him as his wife without the consent of her relatives is regarded as little better than a prostitute. She is always open to the taunt that she had nothing given for her…A woman is supposed to signify her consent to the marriage by carrying fire to her husband's wurley, and making his fire for him. An unwilling wife will say, when she wishes to signify that she was forced into marriage with her husband, 'I never made any fire in his wurley for him.'[153]

Taplin nevertheless saw 'bartered' wives as the 'absolute property of their husbands', and he contradicted himself in claiming there were no marriage ceremonies and women were 'simply ordered to take her bag and join the camp of the man on whom she was bestowed.'[154] Soon after, in 1882, Howitt and Fison (whom W. E. H. Stanner believed instituted new standards for data collection and analysis of social organisation in the field of anthropology[155]) agreed that Narrinyeri women were 'bartered' by their male relatives but they qualified that a perpetual reproach lay against a woman if she went to her husband for nothing.[156]

Spencer and Gillen's 1899 foundational study *The Native Tribes of Central Australia* asserted, 'the method of capture which has so frequently been described as characteristic of Australian tribes, is the very rarest way in which a Central Australian secures a wife.'[157] This could be interpreted as either an affirmation of the new thinking in anthropology or a backhand endorsement of bride capture as practised everywhere but in Central Australia. Regardless, more popular publications reverted to the more salacious line, which suggests that although they clearly depended on new scientific findings, their commercial interest compelled them to hold the line. The *Illustrated Handbook of Western Australia* in 1900 shored up 'the native type' by dint of a series of tropes: nomadism, intertribal warfare and interchanging of 'women folk by the rough and ready method of capture.'[158] This was contradicted in 1905 by a newspaper review of Howitt and Fison, Spencer and Gillen, proclaiming new information that proved that 'so-called "wife-captures" are very often only prearranged elopements.'[159] As mentioned, newspaper reviews were the principal means by which scientific racial thought gained mass exposure. Yet, the trope persisted, even in the vernacular works of credited anthropologists. Thus, with condescending candour, anthropologists N. W. Thomas and Athol Joyce in their *Women of All Nations* (1908) revealed, 'In some tribes it was a point of honour for the bride to appear unwilling to join her husband, and even carry her resistance so far as to use her yam stick upon him, if she wished to be ultra fashionable.'[160] The slavish following of social trends, along with feigned resistance and veiled ardour, were particularly feminine and universal traits, ones that any man could feel familiar with if snubbed by a woman. Threaded through all these accounts, I think, is a discernible identification with the savage warrior, whose sexual conquests were no doubt enviable.

Certain journalists remained committed to keeping bride capture discourse in circulation, failing to notice that ethnology now demanded a more rigorous system of referencing instead of falling back on habituated allusions. In 1908 G. Fox dredged up the 1864 anonymous *Chambers's* piece that McLennan had used as his primary source for Australian bride capture. In a *Science of Man* article on marriage, Fox paraphrased the article with 'he stuns the object of his affections with a blow of his nulla nulla or club, and while she is recovering her senses takes her home to his hut...to commence a life of toil from which she finds no release until death.' This enabled Fox to define the 'Position of Women' as 'a very subordinate one' since women were regarded 'only as articles of personal property, to be bartered or sold at their owner's pleasure.'[161] Fox does make an attempt to assimilate the latest findings but becomes bamboozled by the intricate rules of marriage, finding it 'almost incredible that a race with absolutely no literature and with a brain only capable of understanding the most primitive sensations and emotions, should be able to evoke rules and regulations regarding marriage and relationship so extremely complicated.'[162] The *Chambers's*/McLennan nulla-nulla was even used in the Education Society's 1910 *Series of Lessons on Aboriginal Life*. It read, 'If bride unwilling, clubbed with nullah by husband – still unwilling, clubbed till exhausted. Then so proud of husband's strength she is willing to marry.'[163]

As noted earlier, it was finally social anthropologist Bronislaw Malinowski who, in his 1913 *The Family Among the Australian Aborigines*, examined exhaustively the available literature on 'Modes of Obtaining Wives'. As with scarification, he roundly rejected the repeated statement that Aborigines had no marriage ceremony, stressing such fallacies were due to 'the slight and superficial acquaintance these observers had with the aborigines.'[164] He, too, noted the central role of repetition in recirculating the same publicly held fallacy writing:

> It is characteristic that all statements reporting the prevalence of marriage by capture refer to New South Wales, and more especially to the neighbourhood of Sydney. But I think that it would be inadvisable to attribute this to a local peculiarity of those tribes. It appears more probable that as all these reports date back from the early days of the settlement, and were written nearly at the same time, their opinions cannot be considered as independent, and they are probably repetitions of the same erroneous view which may be assumed to have been held by the general public in the settlement.[165]

He asserted, 'in utter contradiction with those few statements, made by some early observers in New South Wales, capture is usually reported to be merely an exceptional form of contracting marriage.'[166] In addition, the girls had to be unappropriated and of the right class. Malinowski also exposed the gender blindspot in theories of betrothal, pointing out a number of times that neither young women nor men had any choice.[167] He stuck with earlier theories of marriage wherein elopement was the exception, but argued that only elopement provided real choice for women or men. However, in the 'normal cases neither of them had any voice in the matter at the time of actual marriage.'[168] As for the bestowal of young girls to old men (which curiously does not figure in the bride capture trope), Malinowski believed a certain equity presided since young girls were allotted to older men and boys were assigned to older women. He finds the difference of age to be around thirty years and this 'disparity of age in marriage seems to be quite a universal feature in Australia.'[169] It begs the question how much of the authority assumed to pertain to older men was about age and how much about gender. It also, to my mind, suggests that the care of elders may have been tied into the objectives of betrothal and marriage, something that settlers may have been incapable of understanding.

Malinowski also included the finding from the Narrinyeri that it was a 'social disgrace' for a girl not to be given away. A girl who went to live with a man of her own volition was regarded as 'little better than a prostitute.'[170] He attributed this finding to Meyer, however, rather than Taplin. By 1930 the distinction between abduction and ceremonial 'capture', though present from Turnbull in 1805, was lent scientific credence through tabular form in which bride capture was quantified at about half the rate, at least among 'lower hunters' who were confined to Australians.[171] As anthropologists tabulated the 'consideration' shown to prospective brides' families through payments and percentages, and the 'required consent' of brides in hunter, agricultural and pastoral gradations of social formations, a certain episteme of gallantry was enshrined in social evolutionist anthropology. From the beginning of the twentieth century it was scientists who knew about primitive and modern social forms, and principally by how they were assigned within sexual, marriage and kinship relations. As the variables of cranial articulation and hair structure, et cetera, overwhelmed the clear distinctions of race taxonomy through sheer weight of varied data (for example, 'Australoid' skulls were turning up in South America and northern Europe), men of science continued to look to sexual and gender relations to demarcate themselves once and for all from primitive masculinity. They also sought to demarcate their published findings from that of popular print, but ultimately could not control the dependence of commercial print on their work, nor its contradiction as periodical print continued to profit from circulating the by now roundly refuted trope of bride capture. Bride capture was but one ready-to-hand trope by which Europeans assigned themselves the standing of refined gentility in their relations with women. The inventory of tropes snaking through Eden's disavowing diatribe proffered many such focal points by which to reconfigure the compounding harms done to women as benevolent gallantry.

It must have been cold comfort to European women, struggling for the vote and other basic rights,[172] to see the fascination European men paid to the subjugated native woman. The violent oppression of Aboriginal women by their own men, yet no others, was undoubtedly a critical discourse in realising the settler-colonial project. The manifold tropes of feminine subjection acted as a kind of discursive fretwork, interlacing some of the organising fields of sovereignty: gender asymmetry, frontier manliness, primitive social relations, race destiny and indigenous eradication, or in the very least, the necessary eradication of purported traditional living, including the brutalisation of women, to assimilate to settler standards of decorum in marriage rites. The rationale of assimilation within the discourse of settler gallantry prosecuted the converse race destiny of white and black men and the discourse of supersessionism. Men that brutalised their women must relinquish such impotent expressions of masculine power and adopt the demeanour of civilised manliness. They must attract their spouses through an unspoken contract of physical protection in exchange for consensual monogamy which, formalised as marriage, bound subjects to the imperial nation – or they must vanish into the oblivion of the primeval horde.

A species of rough gallantry

The demarcation of primitive and civilised manliness was stated ad nauseum. As such George Bennett, a naturalist, wrote in his 1834 travelogue that it is 'but too well known in what degradation the female sex are held among savage nations, so different from the deference and respect so justly given to that amiable and gentle portion of the creation in civilized life.'[173] On his travels Bennett, a fellow of the Linnean Society and first secretary of the Australian Museum, had himself gallantly rescued a young girl from the New Hebrides, named Elau, whom he said was about to be sacrificed – only for her to die in Plymouth.[174] Race rescue was part of the benevolent imperial project, according to James Dredge, who would become Assistant Protector of Aborigines. After all, Aboriginal women were 'subjects of the most illustrious among women – our most gracious Queen'. Their 'miserable and truly pitiable' state was due to the 'cruel and tyrannical despotism' of their husbands and presented 'loud and just claims upon the royal attention.'[175] The characterisation of violent subjugation as the arbitrary force of unmanly races was reiterated by British poet and traveller Kinahan Cornwallis in 1859, who wrote in one of his many travelogues of the New World that Aboriginal men were 'lords' to their women who, 'alike with their sisters of all such nations, were used and looked upon as drudges and vassals, rather than companions.'[176] The *Argus* newspaper went in for the kill when it opined in 1860 on the 'ultimate extinction' of the Aboriginal people of Victoria, whose demise 'will not be regretted when they are gathered to the blankets of their forefathers, and can beat their lubras no more.' Having explicitly linked their demise to gendered violence, the paper continued,

> Barbarians must give place to civilized men. Wherever the whites choose to settle upon the domains of coloured

tribes, the latter must resign their ancestral possessions, and, if they cannot lose themselves amongst the invaders, must retire or perish beneath their onward march. This has for centuries been the invariable law, to which the boldest and most intelligent, as well as the most brutish savages have alike succumbed. But if the whites become the instruments of fate, they are bound to perform their mission with tenderness, and to postpone as long as they can the inevitable conclusion.[177]

The tenderest expressions of these self-identifying settler-gentlemen were reserved for the women, in the bona fide expression of settler-colonial gallantry. But this affectation was undone by the violent actions of so many newcomer men, and needless to say these were rarely accounted for in print culture, let alone reiterated from implausible sources for decades across the typeset. The ethnologist we met above, A. H. Keane, known for his extreme racial bigotry, again made the link between race destiny and the savage treatment of women explicit in a magazine in 1881, averring that the 'lot of the female sex is seldom an enviable one in savage life, but that that of the Australian lubra is exceptionally hard.'[178] But more, the status of women, like their linguistic and kinship structures, figured in the Australians' 'low state of culture' in Keane's *Man, Past and Present*. It contributed to the 'retarding effect' of their isolation and why they were 'doomed gradually to disappear.'[179]

Merely by their watchful presence, settlers imagined they ameliorated the plight of Aboriginal women. But if Aboriginal men restrained their inherent violence, it was not from finer feeling but because they valued their wives as property. Thus, Wood in his *Natural History of Man* describes women as 'much his chattel as his spear or hut, and he would no more think himself cruel in beating his wife to death than in breaking the one or burning the other.'[180] However, Aboriginal men soon learned that 'breaking a wife's limb with a club, piercing her with a spear, or any other mode of expressing dissatisfaction, shocked the prejudices of the white men', so they 'ceased to mention such practices, though they did not discontinue them.'[181] On the one hand, Wood abhors 'the utter contempt which is felt by the native Australians for their women' and yet, like many settlers, he paradoxically harbours respect for feminine docility, as they saw it, such that, 'in spite of this brutal treatment, the women often show a depth of affectionate feeling which raises them far above the brutal savages that enslave them.'[182]

Also reliant on Aboriginal women's subjugation to justify, in a real sense, their very existence, were Christian missionaries. In 1944 Reverend J. H. Sexton of the Aborigines' Friends' Association described 'the wild state' as including 'cruel rites, causing needless suffering and shameful mutilation, which shock all ideas of decency and propriety.' He claimed women of the Musgrove regions were 'crudely deflowered, beaten, and terrorized, lent to strangers', and 'enslaved in scores of unseemly ways.'[183] It is only through the redemption of missionary work that the 'lubra' can find new hope and the 'black' can be retrieved from the 'backwash',[184] by coming to a 'new conception of the relationship of wife and husband.' But more than redemption was on offer. Sexton proselytised, 'The Australian aboriginal is in the same category as other primitive races where women's place is low down in the scale. It is only where Christianity comes that she gets her chance at emancipation.'[185]

By the mid-twentieth century the language was changing; though this idea of colonial emancipation persisted. Aboriginal women, as anthropologist Diane Barwick would later argue of the women on stations, were to find 'new emancipation',[186] paradoxically through their assimilation to settler domesticity. Barwick proposed that the movement of women onto European mission, pastoral and government stations permitted new roles for women, encouraging them to participate in religion, politics and economy. As proof she described women at Framlingham signing petitions and in 1880 conducting a dormitory strike. They also used a sewing machine in 1873, and dressed with 'quite remarkable elegance.'[187] Barwick's revision of Aboriginal women's status, however, was specific to women who, through mission life, were in many, but not all, senses removed from traditional life. Women anthropologists such as Catherine Berndt disputed the 'chattel and slave' construct as the projection of male observers of their own striated gender relations. Berndt saw Aboriginal women's position as 'enviable' since they fended for themselves and, while their main area of authority was the domestic field, they were not confined to the kitchen.[188] She saw their place as not restricted to the camp fire, but within the wider economic world in which they were self-sufficient,[189] even the 'bread-winner' and 'backbone'.[190] Moreover, as life givers women were the 'first sex' at a 'symbolic and latent level.'[191]

The rich, flourishing, separate, secret life of Aboriginal women was never revealed to settler men and was restricted to women anthropologists who had not accrued authority as mothers.[192] In the 1930s anthropologist Phyllis Kaberry explicitly and carefully argued against the position routinely adopted by male ethnologists, even Malinowski who, despite his intervention, still believed 'the relation of a husband to wife is in its economic aspect, that of a master to its slave.'[193] Kaberry countered:

> If it was compulsory to search for food, at least they did not travel like beasts of burden, with timorous docility and bovine resignation. They were not driven forth by the men; they departed just as leisurely, chose their own routes, and in this department of economic activities were left in undisputed sway. If it was left to them to provide certain goods, at least it was a province in which they were their own mistresses, acquired their own skill from the older women, and served no weary apprenticeship to an exacting husband or father.[194]

Kaberry also notes that women's work day compared favourably to the eight-hour day. It was Kaberry who instated Aboriginal women in the white imagination as 'wielders of the digging-stick' and brought to the fore that their labour meant they were highly valued as wives and elders for their distinct skills and specialised economic contribution. These challenges to the confirmed view of Aboriginal women's subjection did not puncture public perception, until Aboriginal women activists argued for autonomy from the 1930s and the figure of the Aunty, particularly 'Aunty Marg' (Margaret Tucker), came to the fore in the 1970s.[195] How then did newcomer violence figure in this litany of colonial calumny?

As we have observed, accounts of Aboriginal men's ill-treatment of Aboriginal women are overwhelmingly generalised, speculative, decontextualised and unnamed. A representative sample of accounts of Aboriginal men's violence finds the same pattern of speculative print reiteration as for the bride capture trope. Women were 'brutally beaten and ill-used on the most trivial provocation.'[196] They were speared 'for the most trifling offence.'[197] They were 'cruelly beaten or ill-treated'[198] and silenced 'with a club.'[199] In the Kimberley, they were said to be 'clubbed to death, amid much pomp and ceremony, by the old men of the tribe' on the death of their husbands.[200] Should a wife 'make a slip, forget something, or spill the water and her lord and master may beat her to the ground with a club.'[201] As late as 1964 it was claimed girls as young as three years had their craniums tapped 'as a precautionary measure' to thicken the skull in preparation for marriage.[202] It is easy to see why historians might conclude from the overwhelming number of citations that Aboriginal men were traditionally 'very' violent to their women – until you consider them in the context of other tropes of maltreatment that entrenched such understandings by the same means, of print reiteration.

Needless to say, print accounts of violence against Aboriginal women by white men took a discernibly different form. Some were generalised, noting, for instance, that stock-keepers 'take their women and do them various injuries besides'[203] or that sealers were in the habit of tying them up to trees for twenty-four hours or longer, and 'if they proved stubborn, killed them outright.'[204] Yet, the distinguishing feature of settler accounts of white men's violence is that names, localities, circumstances and often assailants are given, and not always because they were detailed from court proceedings. Having charted a comprehensive survey of bride capture, the remainder of this chapter will sample representative printed reports of newcomers' violence against Aboriginal women. That white men did not subject women, black or white, to an imperious gender regime is the premise of the 'chattel and slave' race claim. The irony of Europeans – and not only humanitarians – using metaphors of enslavement, in many cases before abolition, is searing. Although largely restricted to reports of court proceedings, a sampling of white men's violence did appear in print. These cases were often pursued due to the indignation of sympathetic men who sought redress or even public notice of the atrocities being perpetrated around them.

There are approximately thirty-five reports of Aboriginal women murdered by white men between 1833 to 1949, and since none of these occurred in the course of punitive raids, or 'dispersal' exercises, the figure is demonstrably an understatement. Recent histories of frontier violence by Timothy Bottoms and Dirk Moses have built on the earlier work of C. D. Rowley, Lyndall Ryan, Raymond Evans and Henry Reynolds.[205] The deaths of women in frontier violence, like those of children, tend to indicate the indiscriminate and callous nature of massacres, which is superfluous when we consider that Aboriginal weapons were hardly a defence against European firepower, and very often men were avenging assaults on women and girls.

Nevertheless, due to the threat Aboriginal men had posed on the frontier, they came under intense and exaggerated policing. In the states surveyed (excluding Tasmania and New South Wales) these reports of violence against Aboriginal women from the mid-nineteenth century peak in the two decades following the establishment of the frontier. The incidence of women murdered by Aboriginal men, numbering close to eighty deaths, thus came under closer scrutiny and police action. Fifteen women were reported as assaulted by white men and approximately forty were reported as assaulted by black men from 1857 to 1953, overwhelmingly in what we would today call alcohol-fuelled domestic violence. Around sixty women were reported to have caused violent incidents predominantly between black men. Nearly forty women were reported as abducted, again overwhelmingly by black men. The nine reports of sexual assault were couched in language such as 'used her very roughly', 'took indecent liberties', 'interfered' and even that the 'details were unfit for publication.'[206]

These figures in no way represent the actual rate of violence. They tell us only what newcomers were willing to report, act upon and print. Massacre scenarios tended to surface in this deeply skewed record from humanitarians, missionaries and sympathetic settlers. Given white men's violence was overwhelmingly disavowed, on the rare occasions it came to print it was under very restricted circumstances: as court reports, as exposing the excesses of the native police,[207] as derring-do pioneer memoir,[208] or from humanitarian settlers who cast other white men, paradoxically, as 'barbarous' and 'savage'.

Nevertheless, what is clear is that the frontier and its aftermath was an extremely perilous place for Aboriginal women. The sheer sadism is appalling. Boys 'pelting' an aged woman with flour, urged on by a crowd. This case came to light because a witness who chased the boys away was then assaulted by one of the group of crowing bystanders.[209] A 'black gin' known as Topsy was inveigled by two men to search for their tobacco. While she was squatting with her face to the ground they ignited gunpowder they'd spread over the spot.[210] The right hand of a 'young lubra' was blown off after she rejected the advances of a 'murderous Chinaman' who threw a dynamite cartridge at her, also injuring her face and arms along with a nearby woman.[211] Aboriginal women were singled out in massacres such as at Cape Otway,[212] or caught in the crossfire, such as at Bearpurt (later Melbourne)[213] and on the Upper Barwin.[214] Women were summarily punished for minor offences. After stealing grapes from a store and throwing stones at its window, a 'black gin' was dragged by the hair, doused repeatedly in a ditch, and kicked over and over. The incident came to light because the woman was defended by a doctor – who was then charged with assault. No charges were brought against the assailant.[215] Women and girls were abducted, imprisoned and raped. A woman was manacled near Lake Kinross by dog-chain.[216] Girls were dressed as boys by cattle drovers to travel as their servants, after 'brushes' with their male relatives who were 'shot down'.[217] The particular vulnerability of Aboriginal women and girls is little considered as part of our history, of shaping who we are.

As Reynolds has found, urging redress for violence could be dangerous for humanitarians.[218] In Ipswich in 1861 Doctor Challinor came under attack for pushing for an investigation into a massacre at Mr Hardie's station at Fassifern, which prompted a select committee on the native police.[219] Challinor was requested by the coroner to attend an inquest held upon a 'black gin', who was disinterred from a paddock adjoining Hardie's house. While Challinor was stooping over the body, taking notes of the number and type of wounds, he was shoved onto the corpse, grazing his skull on the dead woman's fractured skull. Richard Spencer, Hardie's superintendent, had fallen on him and was thought to have fainted. But when Challinor accepted Spencer's apology, the superintendent then saw fit to add that 'he only wished the body had been as putrid as it could be, and that instead of falling on her as he did – the remainder of the speech being much too filthy and disgusting to appear in print.'[220] In print reports such as this, it was sympathetic settlers' sense of public duty that compelled them to bring such incidents to light. Challinor became a target because he'd been effective in calling for a major inquiry. More often, such disclosures not only went unheeded but the violence of their countrymen was dismissed as accidental.

Time and again, settlers who violently attacked or even killed Aboriginal women were acquitted. On a number of separate occasions Aboriginal women were shot dead by settlers who pointed loaded guns at them and fired, yet they were found to have been accidents because they claimed they didn't know the gun was loaded and they'd pointed and fired in jest. In 1867, *The Brisbane Courier* reported the shooting of a woman by five 'lads' at a camp near Maryborough. They had demanded the people corroboree and when refused threatened to shoot them, but were sent packing by other whites visiting the camp. A short distance away the boys encountered a smaller camp and 'commenced teasing one of the gins who was lying by the camp fire'. One of the boys, only twelve years old, 'presented a double-barrelled gun at her'. The clearly alarmed woman took refuge behind a burning stump. He put a percussion cap on the nipple of the gun, and 'putting the muzzle close to the gin, fired, shooting her through the apex of the heart and the lungs'. The report queried whether the boy knew the gun was in fact loaded with a charge of heavy shot and slugs, claiming this information had 'not yet come out.'[221]

Similarly, a series of reports were printed in the *Argus* in 1881 that Mr R. A. Boyd, the manager of Caiwarro station on the Paroo River in Queensland, was arrested on a charge of 'shooting a black gin.'[222] Within a few days it was followed up with a report that 'the occurrence was purely accidental.'[223] The woman had been shot through the brain after Boyd had presented a breech-loading revolver at a 'favourite black gin' and, 'believing that all the cartridges were discharged, in fun' pulled the trigger. It reads, 'to his horror she fell dead' and concludes it was just one of 'those ghastly accidents.'[224] Another one. A *Townsville Herald* report of yet another accidental shooting of a woman was reprinted in *The Northern Territory Times and Gazette* in 1882. A mailman, Thomas, called at Byerwen station every week while riding the mail from Birralee to Nebo. He shared the lumber with a saddler who left his gun loaded in the room. The report reads,

> A black gin named Emily, who was employed on the station, came into the room and sat down watching Thomas handle the gun. It was at half-cock, and went off when he lowered the hammer. Its contents were lodged in the gin's head, and she fell back dead.[225]

Thomas was found looking 'stunned' and an inquiry determined that it 'seems certain, from the evidence, that the affair occurred in the manner stated, and was a pure accident.' And again, in 1885 the Thornborough correspondent of *The Herberton Miner* gave an account which was also reprinted in *The Northern Territory Times and Gazette*. Mrs Leon Cravino shot dead a 'black gin and a blackboy', her young son, aged eleven. The gin was shot through the left breast and the boy in the head. Five shots were heard by neighbours. Cravino stated that she 'only fired off the revolver for the purpose of unloading it, and that one shot caused both deaths, the whole affair being an accident.' She was committed for trial on the charge of murder and was tried at Cooktown.[226]

When Aboriginal women met untimely and violent deaths, their lost lives incited little more than a judicial shrug. In 1863 a report from *The Clarence and Richmond Examiner* was reprinted in *The Courier*, on the dismissal of sub-inspector Galbraith, stationed at Grafton, after 'the death of a lubra (black gin)' by the 'accidental discharge of firearms carried by Mr. Galbraith, when routing the blacks, who were very troublesome to the inhabitants.' The local people had been 'committing depredations', namely drinking alcohol that had been washed down in a flood.[227] Similarly, as late as 1910 at Lawlers near Perth, a jury found police to have exercised 'reasonable precautions' when they shot a woman named Annie through the head while they were 'rounding up and arresting natives for theft.'[228] In 1933 *The Canberra Times* reported a case in which Constable Stott was acquitted of killing 'a lubra named Dolly.'[229] Stott was 'bringing in' fifteen 'blacks' on a charge of cattle spearing and handcuffed Dolly to a chain. She slept in Stott's tent along with the 'police boy'. When Dolly tried to run away Stott beat her and tied her to a tree all night in the rain. A witness alleged that Stott hit Dolly 'until she could not talk.' She died that night.[230] Although the coroner found that Dolly had been assaulted by Stott and a tracker, Donegan, 'he was unable to say whether the assault had contributed to her death.'[231] Minister for the Interior J. A. Perkins decided to take proceedings against Constable Stott,[232] yet Judge Wells acquitted him with his 'sympathy' and adjourned the case to decide whether he could force the Crown to pay Stott's costs. Stott was reinstated with six months' pay.[233]

White police had another alibi when they were accused of killing women in conflict – the unmanly, unrestrainable savagery of their native police. In 1875 *The Brisbane Courier* reported the case of William Indane, charged with the murder of Nelly, a 'black gin', at Kilkivan. Indane and most of the witnesses were employed at the Mount Coora mine. Late on Saturday night Indane had been seen 'dashing her down on the muddy ground' and accusing the woman of stealing money. She cried for help and was dumped again and again for an hour and a half. Indane was later seen hanging 'the unhappy creature' over a fence by her knees, her head almost to the ground, while Indane held her in place by her knee-caps. After she was released on the entreaty of onlookers, she tried repeatedly to run but fell. She was taken by the onlookers to the 'blacks' camp, and left with her 'own blackfellow, who appears to have been very drunk.' Her body was found behind a witness's house on a bark sheet the next morning. Indane was acquitted, the author remarking, 'You will not get a jury, at least in Maryborough, to bring in a verdict of murder for the killing of a black.'[234] Indeed.

Interracial violence was not divided neatly between incursive and Indigenous. In 1895 *The West Australian* reported on a prisoner at Coolgardie who, while out bringing in water, had assaulted a 'black gin' by shattering a beer bottle over her head. The woman dropped to the ground and was taken to hospital, having received a 'frightful gash'. This time onlookers followed the prisoner, 'with the object of dealing out justice, but he found refuge in gaol'.[235] Clearly, there was strong feeling across a variegated scene of players. While these cases were often only brought before the courts due to the insistence of humanitarian whites, the disregard for Aboriginal women permeated the prosecution. A Protector of Aborigines' annual report detailed the chaining of an Aboriginal woman to a verandah post for three days by a settler named Gurriere at the Vasse, 'proposing thereby to induce her husband to bring in a stray cow.' She died almost immediately after her release, yet her death was attributed to 'a severe attack of influenza, doubtless aggravated by her illegal detention, and the fact of her being near the time of her accouchement.' Gurriere was committed for trial on a charge of manslaughter, but was fined £5 for aggravated assault 'and severely reprimanded'. His 'high character' was cited along with his 'total absence of malicious intent.'[236] Similarly, *The Brisbane Courier* reported in 1881 on the failure of the New South Wales police to prosecute a case against a 'naturalised Dane' who 'committed an unmanly and dastardly assault on a black gin on the Queensland side.' The witnesses were 'a blackboy and two gins.' The woman had refused to leave her camp at night with the man so he thrust a spear two inches into her left breast below the heart. She was attended by a chemist, but was 'spitting blood and unable to move'.[237] Three years on *The Argus* reported on the rape and murder of Matilda Walker at Strathmerton, who was robbed alongside her husband by three men, McKinnon, Mansell and Jeffries. The men assaulted Edward and 'outraged his wife', also burning her body, which then 'presented a shocking appearance, the lower extremities and breast being disfigured by wounds which appeared to have bled profusely.'[238] A magisterial inquiry concluded, however, that Matilda died from natural causes, 'though, according to medical evidence, death might have been accelerated by violence.'[239] It was her husband Edward who was instead accused of ill-treating Matilda. McKinnon, one of the original defendants, gave evidence for the prosecution and the bench dismissed the case.[240]

This disregard and indifference to the harm perpetrated against Aboriginal women was encapsulated in a blithe description of Sal's Gully on Kangaroo Island, which appeared in *The Advertiser* in 1901: 'quite a romantic spot, so called from an aboriginal woman having been killed somewhere near.'[241] Yet, the sympathy of settler men forged a communication conduit exposing and impressing on record a modicum of their countrymen's violence. Letters appear replete with recrimination at the pleasant talk of 'black crow shooting', the boasting of rows of shot 'stuff uns'. These were bitterly decried as 'English justice'. Such circuits intimate that print on the one hand impressed warps upon the national imaginary, such as with bride capture, yet it also could intervene in these racialised imprints. It has often been noted that Indigenous women and men were colonised differently and it is clear from these print accounts the distinction hinges on forms of violence. Rare mentions in print were also made of the transmission of venereal disease and the abduction of children. In incremental clustered patterns, the machinery of letterpress cast Aboriginal women as subjugated, yet print also proffered a serrated surface of infinite meaning with which to both reprise and recast the restless grammar of tiny stamps. The intricate trails of ink, when traced, scanned and sampled across the typeset, confirm that sexual difference is complicated by race and confers intelligibility to it. Aboriginal women were cast in a starring and often salacious role as brutalised and docile. However, we also catch glimpses of a backdrop of gendered colonial violence, even sadism. Aboriginal women's battered bodies were used to cast them as 'less a woman than a display of impressive but verbally inexpressive femininity.'[242] Their cries went largely unheard in the graphic yet silent dramaturgy of colonial print.

3

'IF THEY BE FACTS': INFANTICIDE AND MATERNITY

'It was not a happy lot' for the children of the 'Queensland blacks', declared the popular American travel and fiction author Louise Jordan Miln in her 1899 compendium of cosmopolitan childhood, *Little Folks of Many Lands*.[1] In a disturbing entry that references the beasts-of-burden and discarded-scrap tropes mentioned in Chapter 2, Miln's description of Aboriginal maternity is stock standard for the savagery it attributes to infanticidal mothers. It also anticipates a certain relish in her readers for another form of consumption – of print:

> Score upon score of babies were slaughtered by their own mothers every year – indeed, I may almost say every month. If a baby was in the way they dashed its brains out and left the bruised and broken little corpse to the indescribably horrid obsequies performed by the beasts and the bird-beasts of the bush. And babies often were in the way – very often! When the tribe was on the march the women carried everything. They were the tribe's only beasts of burden. Many a wretched jin flung her child in desperation from her overburdened back. Had she dared to cast away her load of kangaroo flesh, or her heavy dilly-bag, it would have cost her a terrible thrashing, or, like as not, her life. Baby the

'If they be facts': infanticide and maternity

father was not apt to miss, especially if Baby were a girl! And the children who were let live, lived lives as unpampered as we can well imagine. Did the tribe have a feast, a grand feast of half-raw, half-charred kangaroo meat, or opossum flesh, or roasted snake, the children sat with the jins, behind the man, and ate such refuse portions as the man threw to them, or fasted if those men were very hungry. Small wonder that they were meager of limb, 'pot-bellied,' and hopeless of face, those poor little black children.[2]

Having recovered from Miln's white-supremacy splatter, a starting point might be the throw-away droplet 'I may almost say'. Miln trips over the void in her sources but quickly recovers her stride to malign the Aboriginal mothers of Queensland. She was able to regain her momentum, I will argue, because of the paper tide of reticulated reports of Aboriginal infanticide awash in newspapers and magazines, popular travelogues and vernacular ethnology, each entry accruing to the weight of public opinion, each recycled fibre of invective meshing into the 'tissue of errors'. In this sense print culture reproduced the figure of the 'native' or 'primitive' Aboriginal mother. For Said this naming of the Other describes the 'life-giving' power of the 'creator': that is, the discourse of the Other is itself a 'means of *creation*'.[3] It conferred the limits of Aboriginal mothers' intelligibility through a series of denigrating and enduring tropes, reissuing her reproductive powers as 'copy' for colonial print culture.

The insistent appeal to settlers about the adversity and privation of Aboriginal children had to be navigated across the asperities of typeset carefully, particularly before the policy of assimilation was federalised at the conference of state officials in 1937, mandating paler-skinned children's removal from families and communities. The idea of racial decay, central to the settler-colonial enterprise, depended on exposing the alarming extent of child mortality and duress. Notions of child rescue did, too, as the suffering of children compelled settlers to initially 'civilise' and later assimilate them through their removal. Print culture could graphically elaborate on that suffering only if it had recourse to an alibi, lest doubts be cast over the providence of colonialism. In the face of manifest child mortality and disease on the frontier, newcomer observers resorted to the ready defence of the incompetent and unnatural 'native' mother (an allegation that has been revived through the NT Intervention).[4] Child mortality thereby fitted neatly within, and even magnified, dying race theory for over a century from the 1830s. For sympathetic newcomers, infanticide provided an explanation for the tragic decline in fertility and the visible absence of children in the camps. For the righteously imperial, it provided more than a cause for that decline, but an injunction to take up emptying lands. The assumed ineptness of Aboriginal mothers, gathering their children into the cul-de-sac of racial decline, was conveniently accomplished through the damning indictment of infanticide with the additional provocation of child cannibalism. Added to these spooling tropes were the 'barbaric' funeral rites of carrying the body parts of deceased children, prolonged breastfeeding and hasty postpartum recuperation, the charge of suckling whelps,[5] along with overindulgent parenting and cloying attachment.

This chapter presents characteristic selections from print of the predominant trope of infanticide and its shifts and interactions with Aboriginality over the period it prevailed from around 1830 to 1940. A chronology of the origins and print reiterations of this trope of 'primitive' maternity divulges a great deal of rumour, hearsay, exaggeration and regurgitation. Significantly, and unlike the salaciously graphic trope of bride capture, print readers were rarely given lurid detail on infanticide, at least not until the early twentieth century. A lack of accurate and credible observation was compensated by misinterpretation and distortion. Just as imaginings of bride capture may have had some tenuous point of reference in the ritualised performance of abduction (in fact, prearranged elopement), on exceptional occasions infant anthropophagy was attributed as the motivation for infanticide, but it referenced highly constrained mortuary rites that were very rarely observed firsthand by settlers, and for that reason could be easily misinterpreted. Infanticide was never witnessed, yet it provided an alibi for staggering and manifest infant mortality, along with declining fertility, in the contact zones. Congenital syphilis was the most likely cause for this infant mortality, it being noted by a number of observers, including Port Phillip Assistant Protector William Thomas and medical dispenser Henry Jones.[6]

A greater emphasis on the reported testimony of explorers, missionaries, government officials and settler-observers thematises infanticide. It parallels the credibility increasingly attributed to personal testimony over that of circumstantial evidence in legal processes, along with the shift from informal observation and vernacular ethnology to expert evidence in select committees – all, however, conflicting with Aboriginal testimony, which was deemed inadmissible. Where such testimony contradicted these allegations – for example that of Mahroot, who was directly questioned on the subject at the 1845 Select Committee and strenuously denied its existence – this refutation barely appeared in newspapers. Nevertheless, the practice was declared to prevail and to 'materially aid the other causes of decrease' of population.[7] As noted, unlike the trope of bride capture, infanticide was not graphically described as a means of bolstering the sale of newspapers – these were hardly edifying details for print consumption. That is until Daisy Bates found a way to embellish its reiteration with sensationalist language in the lead-up to tabloid journalism in the mid-twentieth century.

Infanticide and cannibalism were, even before European settlement in Australia, already entrenched tropes in imperial culture. Along with polygamy they comprised the trilogy of savagery, discursively deployed by colonial powers around the globe to denigrate and dehumanise first nation peoples as savage and primitive. Yet, throughout the centuries of exploration and colonisation, infanticide had been practised extensively in the West and rather than being exceptional, scholarship has found 'it has been the rule.'[8] In Europe the myth of the 'changeling' as the issue of witches consorting with devils, and the notion of Christian baptism as tantamount to exorcism were superstitions informing infanticide well into the nineteenth century. It was practised among all people lacking fertility control as a response to privation, illness, deformity, illegitimacy or population pressures, but was increasingly criminalised in Europe from the late medieval period.[9] Anthropologist Gillian Cowlishaw argues, however, that the notion that Aboriginal mothers obediently took the lives of their newborns, countervailing all the 'phylogenetic heritage' of hormonal changes associated with birth and lactation, in the interests of her group's undefined target for sustainable numbers, is implausible.[10] Prior to reliable contraception, infanticide gave women in straitened circumstances the only means to hide illegitimacy and, as we shall see, it was widely practised by vulnerable colonial women of the 'serving-girl variety'. Unmarried domestic servants likewise dominate recent historiography of infanticide in Britain. They contributed to a sense of deviancy or moral responsibility around women and crime, which humanitarians related to their subordinancy and dependence on men. This in turn led to greater leniency in sentencing due to interventions in statutory legislation from 1770 bringing about the lesser charge of concealment.[11] Nevertheless, the documented use of foundling homes to dispense with unwanted babies considered alongside the ratio of girls to boys in European cities demonstrates the practice was widespread and, as Judith Allen's study of infanticide in colonial New South Wales shows, largely concealed.[12]

Aboriginal restrictions on the practice of newborn infanticide may have been unravelling under frontier conditions of disease, starvation, illegitimacy, violence and, as this chapter uncovers, the threat of child removal. These conditions, however, were largely attributed to tribal contingencies, in what Marguerita Stephens calls an 'inversion of colonial cause and effect',[13] which effectively made Aboriginal people culpable for the impacts of colonisation. The high rate of child mortality and infecundity in Australian contact zones is given slanting reference in the records, though it can be inferred as elevated from colonial reports of dramatic population decline and of camps virtually bereft of 'pickaninnies' – regularly attributed to infanticide.[14] Moreover, at the time of early settlement European meanings of childhood were changing and an outcry against the practice of infanticide arose in the medical community.[15] A number of high-profile cases in nineteenth-century Australia[16] revealed the true purpose of baby farms,[17] as did public concern following notorious cases in England in 1870.[18] It annealed the view of infanticide as monstrous and unnatural. From the 1850s the number of white women in Australia charged with infanticide far outweighed speculative claims made about Aboriginal mothers – none of which, I venture, would have stood up in a court of law. Yet, despite a print panic in mid-Victorian

Britain and Australia over an apparent rise in convictions, it was never said that infanticide comprised white custom when white women murdered their children or that this was a practice that characterised white maternity in general. Accusations of infanticide, which had been concentrated on Aborigines from the 1830s, shifted to other ethnicities following the Indian mutiny in 1857,[19] along with the influx of Chinese onto the Australian goldfields. As a trope, infanticide was readily transmuted across the colonies to serve the interests of expansion: in terms of settlement, in terms of defending against insurrection and in terms of competition with new arrivals. It had come to the attention of the British through the Bengal code of 1795 and then again in 1824 when the House of Commons released East India Company reports. It travelled around with surveyors, settlers and missionaries, fast becoming a staple in colonial print.

Aboriginal infanticide became a key trope in the humanitarian and religious networks within a combative ecclesiastical public sphere. Disputes and legal stoushes over the efficacy of missions in evangelising Aborigines were waged in the colonial press between protagonists often competing for land originally set aside for missions. Quelling the practice of infanticide became an important defence of missionary work and in vying for land and government grants. From the 1860s ethnological fieldwork mostly recycled earlier speculation as new findings, simply because it had never been questioned. (This study does not survey the anthropological record and engages with it only insofar as it appeared in newsprint.) By the 1930s, as women writers assumed more presence in print, Daisy Bates attempted to clinch a causal relation between infanticide, population decline and racial decay, but she added her own lurid signature by claiming Aboriginal mothers ate their babies because of their taste for 'tender' baby meat. Bates 'jumped the shark' on infanticide, to the extent that her calculated embellishments served to caricature this longstanding trope. Attacks on her credibility by men of science meant the trope of infanticide waned from this point.

Confirmation for the practice seemed to come early from an elder of the Yarra tribes, Billibellary, who told Assistant Protector Thomas in 1843 that women used strangulation and suffocation to make away with their newborns. Stephens shows how Billibellary did not specify the circumstances of any such practice and she argues it isn't clear whether he is talking about women of his own tribe or disparaging feared 'others' from the 'Murry'. She argues that fears of the 'other' by settlers mirrored Aborigines' fear of people beyond their own country and that the two men were 'jointly speculating on the uncouth habits of outsiders.'[20] In Stephens's most recent examination of the dissonance between Thomas's personal and public records, she finds that the word Billibellary used, 'weikite', does not mean 'to kill', but 'are dead'.[21] She uncovers the explanation of women likely to have been involved in any such killings and finds the woman Wurrun adapts Christian numinous causality to explain the deaths of newborns showing all the signs of syphilis.[22]

Credible reportage of infanticide was nevertheless published. In a 1978 survey of late nineteenth and early twentieth-century settler-observers of different standing, Cowlishaw rightly explains that there are 'no a priori grounds on which authors can be judged for reliability', and thus we can only trust that people were not lying. But wilful distortion or fabrication are quite distinct from an unconscious desire or even tendentious will to deploy a commonly circulated trope that, through its reticulation, entrenched shared and uninterrogated meanings of savagery. Cowlishaw examines those writers who seemed most intent on reporting objectively, including Taplin, Meyer, Curr, Howitt, Dawson, Roth, Spencer and Gillen. Arguably the authors that are regionally specific are most credible, yet the possibility that they were all citing from each other is not considered. In citing Taplin, who we will come to, Cowlishaw doesn't allow for him drawing from Meyer, or indeed for Gason then recycling Taplin's figure of thirty per cent of newborns being killed. Cowlishaw challenges some of the shared claims of these authors by exploring psycho-social dynamics with male kin as a factor. She argues infanticide is an expression of women's autonomy, even resentment, in otherwise constrained circumstances. She describes the conditions and processes that might spur the 'frequent rejection of motherhood',[23] yet these remain ahistorical contingencies and the pressures of contact, with its incumbent poverty and disease, are not considered.

They are, however, given careful consideration in Lynette Russell's analysis of Aboriginal women sealers of the Bass Strait and the autonomy they exercised by practising infanticide. She looks at the reports of the Tasmanian 'conciliator' George Augustus Robinson, in which women recount instances by named women and backs up Cowlishaw's contention that infanticide afforded women 'levels of resistance and autonomy.'[24] Any such agency contradicted settler imaginings of Aboriginal women. If children embodied the future, by their hand Aboriginal mothers decreed the incumbency of their people's future and thereby the racial make-up of a nation that aspired to racial homogeneity.

In popular print the Australian Aboriginal mother was cast in a principal yet mute role in the unfolding drama of her people's race destiny, purportedly eating her babies and suckling puppies instead. Moreover, by producing 'half-caste' children, the Aboriginal mother was merely the conduit for the issue of white men, children who were thereby the prerogative of the paternal state. Aboriginal maternity was repudiated in the colonial imagination, most tragically in terms of the claims of their own children. By the twentieth century it was reassigned towards the fantasy of white Australia. The depth of national investment in this fantasy can be gauged by its counterintuitive premise that Aboriginal mothers could be recruited as bearers of the white race, extinguishing their own via the reassigned conveyance of their wombs. The figure of the Aboriginal mother – whether 'detribalised' or 'civilised' and mother of either 'full-bloods' or 'half-castes' – has thus been critical to the development, enactment and enforcement of all state policies directed at Aboriginal Australians, including the administrative regimes of protection, assimilation and less formally of national gestures towards segregation, preservation, appropriation and intervention. As Stephens and others have argued, infanticide has stood as a leitmotif for savagery, inviting 'the surveillance and the interrogative operations of the colonial state [and] bolstering colonial projects ranging from extermination to missionary salvation to humanitarian civilising.'[25] It was centrally and crucially the interruption of the mother–child relation, principally through widescale child removal, that animated the twentieth-century aspiration to divest Australia of its original custodians.

Under the policy of assimilation (the formal federal adoption of which was delayed by World War II), Aboriginal mothers were the cargo-carriers of white Australia, effecting through their perversely non-generative wombs the extinction of their own race. The disturbing history and legacy of state intervention into Indigenous families has been extensively documented in recent years, through the Human Rights and Equal Opportunity Commission's 1997 *Bringing Them Home: Report of the National Inquiry into the Separation of Aboriginal and Torres Strait Islander Children from their Families*[26] and most comprehensively (and movingly) in the work of Anna Haebich.[27] Rather than reprise these findings here, this chapter will focus on print imaginings of Aboriginal maternity as infanticidal, which came to inform the paradoxical public demand on the procreative capacities of Aboriginal mothers to expire their own race while reproducing another. Of course, the maligning of Aboriginal maternity in colonial print served the settler-colonial project of eradication of native custodianship over their lands and particularly the disinheritance of their rightful successors. But also of interest is the way Aboriginal reproduction was rendered unproductive 'copy' for white consumption through the recursive workings of print. In this form it provided the rationale to remove Aboriginal children, effecting, among other things, their disinheritance.[28] Aboriginal maternity thus became unproductive, even monstrous. The wresting of labour from native women was prioritised and their bodies sexualised through a process equivalent to land extraction. Assaying a select tracery of the trope of infanticide, we will see how it provided an alibi for the devastating impacts of dispossession, violence, disease and malnourishment. It disavowed grieving and distorted birthing and funeral rites. So shocking were these recursive claims, they found ready reception when reproduced within colonial newsprint and were reissued until infanticide become a banality of savagery.

As observed, accusations of native infanticide in Australia were not unprecedented. A regulation of the Bengal code of 1795, which decreed that infanticide be punished as murder, had been preceded by journals of exploratory voyages to the Pacific, such as Hawkesworth's visit to Otaheite as excerpted in the *London Magazine* in 1773. Otaheite was said to be a society 'in which every woman is common to every man' and paradoxically that the women conceived 'less commonly than when they cohabit with one man.'[29] Oh, and they smothered their offspring. This causality between native women's promiscuity, infertility and unnatural mothering persisted, at least in popular print, until around 1860. Effectively it indicted them for 'self-extinguishing' their race (as Patrick Brantlinger aptly puts it)[30] by, of all things, having indiscriminate sex. A century on, an infamous yet uncharacteristic assertion by the geologist Paul de Strzelecki persisted for many years in popular circuits despite being disputed by Darwin in 1879.[31] He claimed there existed a 'remarkable physical law in connection with the rapid decrease of the aboriginal races of these colonies' because Aboriginal women, 'after connection with a European loses the power of conception on a renewal of intercourse with the male of her own race, retaining that only of procreating with the white man.'[32] Aside from a facility for racially selective procreation, Aboriginal women were also made infertile simply through contact with civilisation through a metaphorics of race suicide. The native woman's fertility euphemistically 'disappeared like melted snow before the sun',[33] or 'withered away before the touch of civilization.'[34] When reproduction with Aboriginal women was described it was also euphemised as 'absorption', 'admixture' and 'amalgamation'. When these ethnocidal affronts are compared with the 'language of increase' – meaning the capacity of slave women to bear children, who then by law became the property of her master – as deployed in the slave colonies of the Barbados, the permeation of the settler-colonial logic of eradication is thrown sharply into relief.[35]

Native maternity was also associated with animalistic meanings through prolonged breastfeeding and ease of birth. The alacrity by which native women purportedly gave birth and recovered inferred they were not subject to God's curse upon Eve – the pain of childbirth that Christian women bore. Before the privations of dispossession became visibly manifest on the bodies of Aboriginal mothers and children, native maternity encapsulated the indelibly generative cycle of life, which in harsh, 'primitive' conditions was perhaps cause for wonder. On these distant shores, men far from home may have recognised their common human origin in the native mother, all the while confirming their civilised status by recalling and comparing the motifs of their mothers' domestication, such as clothing, medical attention and wet-nursing and, perhaps, if they were lucky, protracted 'lying in'.

But the native mother was set apart from the British matron, just as constructions of maternity were shifting in the mid-eighteenth century through the invention of bourgeois, asexual, sanctified motherhood in the conduct and medical literature of Britain. Ruth Perry ties this maternity to the 'heady new belief in the manipulation of natural forces for greater productivity' from the economising of agriculture to textile manufacture and, we might add, in the reproduction of print.[36] A growing emphasis was placed on demographics and population 'increase' to meet the demands of the military and the labour needs of industrialisation. New meanings of childhood as dependency associated maternity with natural resource. Felicity Nussbaum also perceives a shift in constructions of the maternal in which 'Englishmen largely defined themselves, sexually and materially, as fully outside the scope of the maternal yet eager to intervene within it.'[37] These meanings were transferred, via transnational mobility and print, from the metropole to the periphery where native maternity was set in contradistinction, as promiscuous, unproductive and unnatural. But as Perry argues, British motherhood was itself a 'colonial form – the domestic, familial counterpart to land enclosure at home and imperialism abroad.'[38] Constructions of native

'If they be facts': infanticide and maternity

maternity provided that othering against which motherhood of empire could be articulated.

In New Holland infanticide came to the fore in travelogues from the 1820s when the frontier, though still contested, was more assured ground. The following survey depends on the exemplary scholarship of Stephens, who has traced the reification of infanticide in the nascent colony of Port Phillip from settler hearsay to ethnological exchange, administrative policy and government legislation. Stephens convincingly concludes there was no basis for the oft-repeated charge that Aborigines routinely killed and sometimes ate their children, especially if they were 'half-caste' or girls. She sifts through foundational Port Phillip sources and traces their reiteration, in her study, through nineteenth and twentieth-century anthropological texts, notebooks, testimony and correspondence.[39] Here I focus on the implications for meanings of Aboriginal maternity created through the transference of these fragments into print culture, and the subsequent circulation of this 'convenient colonial invention' into the wider colonial public.

From the first, observers attributed infanticide to a mix of barbarity and desperation ensuing from frontier conditions, betraying the ambivalence that structured colonial perception. As with any recurring trope, these early accounts laid down the template for forthcoming imaginings of Aboriginal maternity. As with bride capture, it started with Collins in 1798 with an account of the burial of Col-bé's live child with its deceased mother.[40] The claim was reprinted in 1854 by the economist and newspaper founder John Ramsey McCulloch in a geographical dictionary under the entry, 'Races of men in Australia'.[41] Given McCulloch's profession, we should be alert to the untested nature of such claims. Collins had contextualised the child's live burial within the devastation of the smallpox epidemic in 1789 in which Col-bé was forced to take the life of his baby because of its infection and due to the death of its mother and the loss of substitute breastfeeding. As Stephens argues, this account was probably extrapolated by political economist Thomas Malthus in his influential essay in 1798 on population. But Malthus then merged constructs of the native woman as chattel to substantiate infanticide as one response to her 'unremitting drudgery'.[42] The Col-bé story also reappeared in an 1853 feature in a magazine called *Empire* in which a 'party of officers' was said to witness the 'internment of a female whose surviving infant was thus interned by the Father.' This version ascribed the infanticide to other women being 'averse' to taking care of the child and even though the officers purportedly witnessed the live burial, they did not 'have time to interpose their influence to save the little victim.'[43] Contradictions such as this pervade accounts of infanticide.

Despite the imprimatur of Malthus, infanticide did not come to the fore in print until the 1830s when, as Stephens shows, a number of elements converged. Sturt's narrative of expeditions in New South Wales was published in which he 'loosely' records a report by a European stockkeeper, though admits he was unable to corroborate it. The Poor Act of 1834 prompted an increase in prosecutions for infanticide in Britain. The Commons Select Committee on the Aborigines in 1835–37 circulated testimony of infanticide in New South Wales (despite the only murder of a newborn being perpetrated by its convict father, who hid the body, afraid the evidence would reincarcerate him).[44] And with the frontier expanding exponentially in the southeast after Batman's arrival in Port Phillip, colonials sought explanation for dramatic population decline.[45] Satanda Sen has found female

'If they be facts': infanticide and maternity

infanticide also came to the fore in India in the 1830s,[46] brought to public attention through calls by Thomas Buxton in 1823 for dispatches on infanticide from 1789 to be tabled in the British parliament.[47] The ensuing surveillance of female infanticide influenced Australian observers for whom, as Cowlishaw found in her survey of settler-observers, the targeting of Aboriginal girls became orthodoxy in late nineteenth and early twentieth-century descriptions of infanticide. Even so, Cowlishaw finds more denials than confirmations in the early literature.[48]

Infanticide began to surface from this point in generalised travelogues, such as an unattributed 'Journal of an excursion to Brisbane Water' in *The Australian* in which it is itemised in an inventory of custom, appearing between lack of marriage ceremony (the bride's company being simply requested) and the 'magic' throwing of the 'Bomarang or crooked stick'. *The Australian* was edited by liberal pro-emancipist barristers and it challenged government censorship. It had attracted a wide readership since its establishment in 1824. It stated, 'Infanticide is too common among the black women, they will not be troubled with the rearing of children, and mostly take them up by the heels and knock their brains out against a stone.'[49] A much longer version of this passage then appeared in another unattributed 'Rambles in New South Wales', in *The New Monthly Magazine and Literary Journal* in 1828. To give a sense of the attitude adopted towards the 'black gin', the author laments the policy of separating female convicts from newcomers, for a fisherman at Broken Bay had just 'lost' his Aboriginal 'housekeeper'. The author wrote,

> I blushed to think that any man, bearing the name of Englishman, should form a cool, deliberate connexion with a female savage, who must have been unlike her

race if she ever washed herself, if she was not eaten up with vermin, legs ulcerated, blotches on her head, and in manners and habits everything that is not base and disgraceful.

Should the fisherman have been assigned a female convict instead, the author continued,

this old man would have been most likely a happy, cleanly and creditable husband, with everything around him comfortable and tidy, and half a dozen chubby children to make this stage in the journey pleasant and interesting. As it was, no doubt the black woman was getting more civilized; but the white man was approaching the savage state of indolence and filth.[50]

The contributor, clearly also an emancipist, scripted the role white women ex-convicts were assigned in reproducing settlement, producing 'cleanly' and 'interesting' home fronts, and the disturbance to that domestic economy – at this stage of settlement – should they be contaminated by Aboriginal women whose services exceeded the bounds of domestic labour. As Lorenzo Veracini argues in his study of the settler-colonial formation, 'the establishment of normative familial relations is a crucial marker of a successful settler project.'[51] This norm had to be forged at first from transported convicted criminals who, it was hoped, by their respectable yeomanry would establish a domestic-based sovereignty by expropriating the labour of the native before they obligingly disappeared.

The year before, naval surgeon Peter Cunningham (who received three land grants on the upper Hunter River)[52] had published his widely read *Two Years in New South Wales*. In it he claimed that newborns were killed 'when means of support are denied' and that grief 'though brief, is acute', but that children reared were 'tended with great affection.'[53] His account foreshadowed the principal contradiction in settler accounts of infanticide, between attentive and murderous parents, and between indulged and deprived children. In another popular travelogue of 1834, Lieutenant W. H. Breton observed that infanticide, though greatly exaggerated, was a consequence of famine, but he qualified that New Hollanders were not alone in this 'act of necessity'.[54] It was with very mixed feelings that newcomers attempted to know Aboriginal maternity, a half-lament that disavowed the impact of their own incursion. Breton had also encouraged making a 'strong impression' during reprisals on natives since, 'if only one or two be killed, the sole effect is to instigate them to revenge their companions.'[55] Breton's reflection on infanticide, placed against his calls for indiscriminate slaying (that don't explicitly rule out women and children), lend his observations a degree of deflection. The prolific naturalist Robert Mudie also published in his travelogue that Aboriginal 'female honour' had been compromised by the settlement of the colony and that when 'children of a mixed blood make their appearance among the natives the husbands of their mothers are very apt to destroy them.'[56] It wasn't known at this time that darker-skinned babies gained pigment some hours to days after birth, and given newborns were said to be targeted, settlers may have confused newborn mortality with 'half-caste' infanticide. Mudie also repeated Collins's claim that children at the breast were 'cast alive into the graves of their mothers'.[57]

Two further themes emerge here. The first, that the native father rather conveniently dispensed with the evidence of white men's sexual demands on Aboriginal women, was probably more wishful thinking than substantiated fact. The children resulting from these unions were perhaps so beyond the ken of some newcomers it was easier to imagine them dead, and the fantasy was conveniently expedited through the figure of the infanticidal Aboriginal mother. In bearing 'half-castes', indigenous maternity forced an exposure of sorts: it betrayed colonialism's bastard secret, before the scientific racism of biological absorption resolved the difficulty through child removal. In fact, as Annette Hamilton's research of nineteenth- and twentieth-century mission records found, the number of half-caste children rose throughout the period it was claimed they were targeted for infanticide.[58] A second theme is that of burying live children with their deceased mothers and here we can perceive a colonial blindspot that structured accounts of infanticide. Should this claim be credited as corroborated, it begs the question: of what precisely were young mothers dying at such rates, and why did their deaths entail a complete loss of alternative means of sustenance within extended kinship networks? To give another instance of the way newspapers scrapped and snipped complex phenomena, eliding explanatory context, in 1835 a lone sentence appeared among items in a miscellaneous column. It simply read, unattributed, without any context or qualification, 'The Aborigines about Port Phillip, it appears, are cannibals and practice infanticide.'[59] *The Hobart Courier* was conveying short items, such as shipping news, from the nascent settlement, and as the colonial public sphere was transitioning from penal to settlement interests, pastoral expansion began to assume more influence in the institutions shaping print. As Anna Johnston writes, 'It was not only the land that needed to be cleared for settler expansion, but the conceptual space in which white colonial subjects could flourish'.[60] The stance in relation to native infanticide was a key defence of

'If they be facts': infanticide and maternity

the newcomers' moral surety and entitlement to compete for and claim that land.

The coupling of infanticide and cannibalism was particular to Australian truth claims. Cannibalism, in Theodore de Bry's 1590 engravings based on the voyages to America,[61] was presented (for reader consumption) as the nadir of not only civilisation but of human identity. As noted earlier, cannibalism was a key trope of savagery.[62] In Australia, cannibalism was also repeated in print culture, across the spectrum of travelogues, settler reminiscences, missionary pamphlets, ethnology and newsprint; however, in Australian colonies it took a particularly nasty turn. It was run together with infanticide and directed at Aboriginal mothers either as active participants or as resigned to the devouring of their children by brutal fathers and tribal men. Although Captain Cook had not seen any evidence of it,[63] it sufficed that the practice had already been popularly attributed to all 'savages' for the surgeon Peter Cunningham to assert in his travelogue that cannibalism was practised in New South Wales simply because it was a 'very general custom among all nations in the early stages of civilisation.'[64] This is a descriptive entry in this inventory of Aboriginal maternity: Cunningham mistook reiteration for substantiation. Before long Aboriginal mothers would be implicated in infant cannibalism. While there was mounting public concern about infanticide in Europe, as a motivation for cannibalism in New Holland it provided the means to single out a particularly savage maternity.

Print accounts associating infanticide with cannibalism began to proliferate from the mid-1830s[65] and they derive principally from a report by John Helder Wedge, the Port Phillip Association's surveyor, concerning an exploratory journey taken with the newly repatriated and yet to be pardoned William Buckley, an escaped convict who had lived with the Wautha wurrung for thirty-two years.[66] Wedge wrote that Buckley confirmed the 'natives' practised infanticide and cannibalism – without specifying which group Buckley referred to. The failure to make this distinction between informants and whom they informed on beset many infanticide accounts. Under the umbrella of pan-Aboriginality, the Wautha wurrung's disparagement of their adversaries was counted as self-description.[67] A tendency to disparage rival clans or peoples beyond territorial boundaries was documented by more sympathetic newcomers. Robert Dawson, the NSW Chief Agent of the Australian Agricultural Company, in 1830 roundly rejected accusations of cannibalism, reporting that he had 'investigated officially' a charge in Sydney and found 'it was a tale fabricated solely to excite a prejudice against the natives.' He argued, too, that rival groups made the charge against their adversaries, 'knowing that they cannot, in any way, so much degrade their enemies in the eyes of white people as by calling them cannibals.'[68] Wedge claimed to have had pointed out to him a woman who had 'destroyed' ten of her eleven children because of a preference for 'nursing' until three or four years of age. Wedge's narrative, however, did not find any traction in the colonial press, which at this stage tended to rely on anonymous 'reports' relating to prospects for settlement at Port Phillip.[69] Wedge was making a report to the surveyor-general on the prospects for settling Port Phillip. He created the impression that the 'natives', though practising 'horrid' customs, nevertheless, if 'worked' on and with 'great forbearance', might come to see the advantages of 'intercourse with us' along with 'habits of industry'.[70] As we shall see, government and missionary claims of tempering the practice of infanticide – along with cannibalism and polygamy – were portents of colonial beneficence.

'If they be facts': infanticide and maternity

As Stephens shows, Wedge got his information by probing Buckley, leading with questions on infanticide, seeking confirmation from a man returning to his mother tongue only weeks after some thirty-two years' absence. In his *Journey to Examine the Country West of Indented Head*, he attributes the infanticidal tendencies of the mother said to have killed ten of her babies to 'mere wantonness' and to a 'total absence of maternal feeling.'[71] As Stephens reasons, the period spanned ten to twelve years, yet was recalled by Buckley while probably struggling to express himself in his native tongue. More importantly, as Stephens shows, Wedge would have been influenced by his role as surveyor of the Port Phillip Association, the corporate body proposing to settle the Port Phillip district. Although its 'treaty' with the Wurundjeri was invalidated by the colonial office in London in 1836, the association's 'application' for land acquisition was encouraged. In this context the testimony Wedge took from Buckley was circulated in London as part of the lobbying by the association. Buckley's revelation of infanticide was 'perfectly tempered to commend the Aborigines of Port Phillip to the British philanthropic movement as people in need of Christian salvation.' Stephens points out that Buckley was soon after pardoned and appointed superintendent and interpreter over the Port Phillip tribes.[72]

Within this tangle of motives, what Buckley relayed to Wedge was contradicted by his account to George Langhorn, in which he modified cannibalism as ritual mortuary practice on children who had died of natural causes and said he had lived with large and attached families.[73] Wedge's report, originally printed in the *Van Diemen's Land Monthly Magazine,* was circulated as far as Perth but there it was gainsaid in print by the observations of an interpreter, Francis Armstrong, who argued infanticide was not practised in southern Western Australia.[74] Interestingly, Armstrong also noted there was no 'barrenness', nor discarding of children if one was already 'suckling'; indeed, women were known to have up to seven or eight children.[75] A year later, however, Armstrong attributed infanticide to mothers 'labouring under some superstition.'[76] His about-face brought him into the fold of by now accepted wisdom on infanticide, wherein such fealty to the trope required no further elaboration in the form of substantiated, detailed evidence.

The Port Phillip Assistant Protector William Thomas believed 'the fruit of the womb', girl newborns, were strangled or smothered until a male was born and that this happened on their ninth or twenty-first day.[77] He famously reported in 1845 that a chief had conveyed the belief to him that as they had 'no country; no good have pickanineys.'[78] This oft-used quote came from the Woiwurrung tribesman Billibellary, whose words, as we earlier observed, may have been misinterpreted.[79] Billibellary sought rationale for the massive infant mortality. To give another indication of the local devastation, Stephens finds in his notes that Thomas tallied seventy-six deaths (all ages) and only twelve births across six years.[80] He recorded only twenty births in Port Phillip before 1849 within seven language groups around Melbourne. These humanitarian and government appointees were often champions of the Aboriginal people they nevertheless sought to 'civilise'. Infanticide thus assisted in painting a picture drastically needing Christian intervention and guidance. Yet, between the lines, contradictory inferences were made that infanticide was both traditional and circumstantial, a response to 'famine' and denied 'means', which hardly gave the whole frontier picture.

Stephens sets out the theories abounding in Port Phillip that Aboriginal mothers were devoid of feeling. These paralleled mounting calls by colonial administrators to remove Aboriginal children as they struggled to contain clans to designated stations

'If they be facts': infanticide and maternity

and keep them out of towns, away from 'lower orders' of white 'vice'. They also sought to stop parents forcibly retrieving children, causing clashes, as had taken place at the Merri Creek Baptist Mission School. In early reports and dispatches to the colonial office, administrators called increasingly for the incarceration of children and used infanticide as their rationale.[81] This is about the time that reports began to circulate in the press on Indian and Chinese infanticide.[82] And significantly, throughout the decade newspapers reported on the court proceedings of a series of infanticide cases perpetrated by lower-class settler women, often servants attempting to conceal illegitimacy.[83] Yet, as noted above, no one deduced from these instances of convicted white assailants that infanticide was an observance of white custom, or that these mothers identified their race by their actions. These cases show that the designated circumstances for legitimate maternity were tragically constrained for colonial women. And clearly infanticide was a preoccupation, for a 'domestic drama' of that name played at the Sydney Royal Victoria Theatre in 1840. Concealed illegitimacy was given salacious overtones in the tag line, 'Infanticide: or the Bohemian Mother.'[84]

By now Aboriginal infanticide was simply 'fact, which is too well substantiated', according to Reverend Joseph Orton, a missionary travelling from Hobart Town to Port Phillip with a view to establishing a mission. Orton, like many to come, was influenced by Malthus when he asserted that mothers killed and ate their children because their 'wandering habits render it inconvenient to carry about their young infants.'[85] It seems the quandary newcomers experienced countenancing women carrying 'burdens' extended to even Aboriginal children. As if, in a robust and intricate network of care and family, there were no available arms but those of mothers. By 1840, however, accusations

175

of cannibalism specified children in a pamphlet advising prospective immigrants to 'Australia Felix'. It averred that 'the natives of Australia can only be placed in the great animal family as one degree above the brute creation' since 'there is no doubt that the lives of infants are often taken, and the bodies converted into food.'[86] In the instance of the trope of cannibalism we can rely on an exhaustive survey of the colonial literature undertaken by Michael Pickering. He found that, of the minority of settler observations that can be credited, elements of mortuary anthropophagy were overwhelmingly misconstrued as evidence of cannibalism.[87] Pickering critically reviewed 440 accounts of cannibalism in 298 published and unpublished sources. He found seventy-two per cent derived from unsourced and second-hand observations. Only eight per cent of observers claimed to have witnessed cannibalism and these were likely to have been misinterpretations of mortuary rites including the smoking of corpses and bone cleansing in preparation for burial.[88] We can here add to his findings that the warming of newborns in earthern hollows was also misconstrued as roasting.

Cannibalism of children reversed the natural order of birthing. The macabre spectre of Aboriginal mothers reabsorbing their children evoked fear of the oceanic primordial mother. As Anne McClintock has argued, 'the fear of engulfment expresses itself most acutely in the cannibal trope',[89] and infanticide undoubtedly made the link more direct. So predisposed were settlers to believing native mothers ate their own babies, so invested were they in subscribing to the tropes of savagery, they overcame their own doubts with aphorism and anecdote. For example a 'Lady's' notes about taking up a run near Geelong had ready recourse to these truth procedures. She explained, 'When a black woman has a second child before the first can run about and take care of itself, it is said they eat the second one. I have been told this several times, but am not certain if it is really the case, it is so very unnatural; but it is well known they are cannibals.'[90] These notes appeared in the same weekly magazine, *Chambers's Edinburgh Journal,* from which McLennan appendiced that anonymous screed on bride capture to his authoritative text *Primitive Marriage.* Only a decade old, *Chambers's* already had a wide circulation and a secure place in the very competitive newsprint market due to the broad appeal of its articles. Whether Australian Aboriginal women ate their babies or were dragged off by their hair to their married lives was immaterial to the market objectives of *Chambers's* in the prevailing print culture. Infanticide was not supplied with quite the same lurid detail, however, until Daisy Bates's print forays – although the author of our opening quote clearly anticipated her.

Early missionary observers were often in close contact with Aborigines and, although sympathetic, failed to relate the 'custom' to contact conditions. German Lutheran missionary C. G. Teichelmann wrote in 1841 that infanticide was practised 'chiefly on female children' and was a means to 'keep down their number', and it was 'very likely that those children who are the offspring of indiscriminate intercourse, become the victims of this practice; as this is carried on between whole tribes.'[91] Teichelmann was collecting the language of the Kaurna and advocating for the amelioration of their plight. His writing can be situated in the 'emergent genre of missionary ethnography, a form of writing about the heathen other that enacts the new "scientific" mode of early nineteenth-century evangelising.'[92] It meant his reports were not generalised constructs but localised and peopled instances. He wrote that the fourth wife of a man named King John said her child was stillborn, 'but we knew this was not the case.' King John came to his wife's defence, arguing that 'the child has been very small, had been possessed of a bad soul, and such children their forefathers had taught them to kill.' When the missionary remonstrated with the father he angrily replied, 'Am I the wife? Have I born the child? Why do you scold me?'[93], suggesting any such decision rested with the mother, confirming the argument shared by Cowlishaw and Russell.

King John was in fact a 'Burka' man, that is, a mature man, whose authority was in part accrued by the number of wives and children he could support. He was a Parruwonggaburka man, meaning he had responsibility for the dreaming lore of the 'pankarra', a stretch of land from Mypolonga to Echunga of the Mount Lowry area. His extended forebears had numbered 400 people before the first outbreak of smallpox in the area in 1789. Another epidemic in 1829, along with other introduced diseases, reduced his family group to sixty people and when he died of tuberculosis in 1845 only thirty remained. Over his life ninety per cent of his family group died. Another mother believed to have killed two of her newborns, and it seems a Malthusian, reasoned with Teichelmann, 'how could I accompany my husband, and how could I supply food enough were I to bring up so many children?' But this woman also said of another mother, 'she has been too lazy to nurse the child.'[94] Placed in the context of this devastation, it becomes clear that missionary accounts of infanticide, even those that contextualised and claimed to directly quote the people involved, did not allow for the determinants of almost incomprehensible loss of life, in this case, largely through disease, and how grieving, traumatised people made sense of it within their cosmology of life and death. If this account can be credited it needs to be asked, did the Peramangk people of the woman quoted have reason to believe these newborns were afflicted, or were more likely to become so? Were they sparing these newborns the dreadful fate of older siblings, by disease, privation or dislocation, or of being orphaned?[95] Did 'laziness' here refer to resignation to being unable to support children under contact conditions? There is also in Teichelmann a sense of powerlessness in the face of purported tribal custom. This helplessness may have derived from Europeans' own struggle with child mortality.

During the nascent years of colonial New South Wales the rate of infant mortality was an astonishing 41.3 per cent.[96] The decline of child mortality (which had peaked in Britain at 73.4 per cent in 1730–49) coincided with the increasing depiction of mothers as primarily concerned with 'the fate of the family, [for] the stability of the class, and [for] the vitality of the race.'[97] The fragility of child life no doubt impacted on colonial imaginings of maternity. Rather than life-giving, maternity may have been increasingly associated with frailty and loss. Within this milieu of unstable, unpredictable maternity, the growing population promulgated a sense of national vigour. Teichelmann himself fathered fourteen children, four of whom predeceased him.

As Johnston writes, evangelical missionaries 'sought, by their zeal, to remake colonial projects in the image of religious conversion'.[98] In their attempt to forge civilised identities through conversion, missionaries sought to claim an end to the practice of infanticide as insignia for their victory. 'With regard to infanticide', the *South Australian* wrote in a report on a lecture on the Milmenrura 'natives' (as though it could reasonably assume the question arose whenever the 'natives' were mentioned), 'there was great reason to hope this darkest spot on the native character might be removed.' Indeed, as the surgeon Penny argued, dissuading mothers from infanticide 'afforded an evidence that their prejudices were not unassailable and opened a breach through which the whole of their superstitions could be assailed.'[99] Curbing the practice was as irreducible to the civilising mission as settling the native down to industry. It remained to be seen through what breach the prejudice of settlers might be assailed.

The discourse of savage infanticide consolidated over the 1840s as observers attempted to substantiate allegations with more formalised firsthand observation. A number of questionnaires were circulated to settlers, some of which appeared in print. As Stephens details, the British Association for the Advancement of Science sent out a questionnaire in which colonists were effectively asked to keep a look out for the practice – as if that were not a leading question.[100] It was reissued by the Select Committee of 1858–59 with a question tellingly added about Aborigines' likely objection to their children being removed.[101] The NSW Select Committee of 1845 had also sent out a questionnaire which included a prompt on infanticide,[102] as did former assistant protector James Dredge, who also asked for reports of cannibalism.[103] From only eight respondents associating the reduced numbers of children with infanticide, it was Henry Bingham's reply that appeared in the press. Bingham was a commissioner for crown lands and replied to a question concerning the disposition, usefulness and possibility of attaching 'natives' to establishments for labouring. He answered that 'gins' destroyed the 'half-caste' babies in the 'wild bush' because the men could not bear to see them. Bingham was commenting on ill-feeling from the 'natives' towards assigned white servants of settlers on their land. Their 'promiscuous intercourse' with the women caused dislike from the native men, dissuading any attachment to settler 'establishments' and thereby depriving them of a source of labour.[104] If this 'intercourse' was in fact rape, the likelihood that assaults on kinswomen might occasion more than dislike was not considered. Dredge, too, had

'If they be facts': infanticide and maternity

taken his conjecture to the press, publishing florid descriptions of this 'long established and heartless usage' in a series of articles in *The Geelong Advertiser*.[105] In this decade reports of infanticide from credible journals were reprinted in newspapers, such as that of R. H. Davies, who argued there was no evidence infanticide existed in Aborigines' 'wild state', but that they were driven to it by the 'continued harassing of the whites.'[106] Also advanced was the view that Aborigines were 'diminishing their own numbers by deliberate infanticide.'[107] The disjoint between low fertility, child mortality and infanticide that Thomas wrestled with was not pursued as a contradiction, but instead was resolved simply with the expedient yet lamented observation that there would soon be 'no more infants to sacrifice.'[108]

Cannibalism would soon become especially topical for the British readership as they grappled with the implications of the Irish famine of 1845–50. Its newsprint included many references to Irish cannibalism as an alibi for the starvation of one-eighth of the Irish population.[109] It was in this context, in which doubts were raised about the sclerotic British colonial administration, that firsthand accounts of child cannibalism emerged in Australian print. A key and widely reprinted testimony appeared as a letter in *The South Australian Register,* South Australia's first newspaper (soon to become a daily after changing hands). The author of the letter, Kenneth Campbell, a stock importer and inspector, claimed he had himself witnessed a 'most revolting instance of cannibalism.'[110] His eye-witness story was submitted expressly to convince 'those ultra-philanthropists of their error, who either deny the fact, or argue the impossibility of the "harmless, and innocent aborigines" being guilty of such atrocities.' In fact it was Campbell's shepherd who claimed he'd been asked by a newly delivered mother and another woman to dash the baby against a tree. When he refused, and told them it was wrong to kill the baby, they apparently said it was 'very good to eat.' The next morning Campbell asked to see the child and when told it was dead he accused them of killing it, which they 'persisted in denying'. Campbell assumed the child was being 'roasted' when he insisted on seeing the remains and 'at length they pointed out a native oven in the miami.' When shown the remains, Campbell wrote, '----------. The very remembrance of what I saw fills me with horror and I fervently pray that I may never behold the like again.' He later saw a number of the 'natives' at the sheep-yard, 'several of them having portions of the infant with them, which they were eating.' This he took as 'further convincing proof' and 'drove them away'. Campbell said another woman, when asked of the fate of her 'white child', had said, 'it plenty cry; we plenty waddy it', and that another native told him this child was 'likewise eaten'. Campbell forestalls reader accusations that he did not intervene in the babies' fate with the telling defence, 'Place yourselves in the bush, like myself, with a couple of white men, in the midst of perhaps thirty or forty savages, and you will see the danger of attempting to interfere with the customs of a barbarous and revengeful people.' Editors at the *Register* then 'candidly admit' they had been previously 'sceptical in reference to the existence of habitual cannibalism in Australia.' They had believed the 'extreme pressure of hunger' may have 'produced occasional instances'.[111] But Campbell's statement is 'authenticated' and, placed together with 'testimony we can rely' on (but don't reference), they conclude cannibalism 'is generally prevalent in the Tatiara country.' 'Parties' had assured them they had seen the 'gnawed limbs of immolated infants' carried about in the baskets of the 'lubras as provision for the next repast.' They extrapolated that women themselves 'attracted the horrid gastronomic propensities of the blacks' and at Mr Power's station, near Mount Muirhead, 'two lean lubras' were offered in exchange for a 'well favoured lubra' who 'was wanted to be made a feast of.'[112]

Despite a show of protestation to the contrary, newspaper editors were disposed to circulate as credible these extrapolations from a second-hand account of infanticide and, most likely, eye-witness misinterpretation of mortuary rites. It suggests that print editors now sought to substantiate mere speculation, and wished to convey a more critical, circumspect and rigorous relation to reportage through firsthand testimony. Campbell himself had an established relation with print to advance his business aims. He advertised stock or mutton weekly and contributed to the *South Australian Magazine*. Notices were regularly posted about his inspection of sheep scab as inspector under the Sheep Act. A 'sensation' had been occasioned by his discharge in 1841 and the *Register* printed an unattributed letter calling for a protest meeting of flockmasters and his reinstatement.[113] A pamphlet he penned on sheep shearing in South Australia was advertised weekly. More to the point, he is listed as applying for an occupation licence in the same county a month after his letter was published.[114] Campbell actively sought new pastures and when he died of a lung infection on the Victorian goldfields he was obituarised as 'a successful explorer of the interior, so far as relates to penetrating beyond other adventurous spirits in search of new country for grazing purposes.' Significantly the *Register* editors do not make enquiries as to how Campbell 'drove away' the people that so outnumbered him. His letter was reprinted in five colonial newspapers, so as to dispel any doubts about the practice of Aboriginal infanticide and child cannibalism.[115] It appeared in the *London Journal* in April the following year, suggesting that its topical value, within a mediascape now contoured by pastoral expansion, was enduring.[116]

The notable natural history artist and traveller George French Angas wrote in an illustrated folio volume the same year that the people of the Murray 'kill boys for the sake of their fat, with which to bait their fish-hooks!'[117] Angas toured South Australia with Governor George Grey and his lithographs were displayed in the SA Legislative Council Chamber.[118] His words would have carried repute. In 1847 Angas repeated the supposition originally taken by Collins, writing of New South Wales, 'Should a woman die having an infant at the breast, the living child is buried with her.' He elsewhere adds, 'the natives argue that as no one could be found to nurse the child, it is better for it to lie with its mother, than to be left to pine to death.' Like the *Register* editors, Angas qualified his information with the impression that children were devoured only 'in times of scarcity'. But he, too, weighted his account by claiming a man was pointed out to him who had 'destroyed two children for that purpose.' Moreover, he claims 'none of them', unnamed as they were, denied having recourse to 'so dreadful an alternative when pressed with hunger.'[119] Angas, however, intimates that consuming the flesh of dead children was 'a token of grief and affection for the deceased', citing a Moravian missionary on the east coast of New South Wales as an eye-witness.[120] He also reported in 1847 that he had never witnessed 'more attenuated or wretched looking beings' than the Port Fairy Tribe at Portland Bay:

> It appeared unaccountable, that a race of people living a primitive life, amidst the aromatic fragrance of these woods, with their dwellings upon the green and flower-spangled turf – breathing the pure transparent air of this part of Australia, and enjoying one of the finest possible climates – should be so low in the scale of humanity as

'If they be facts': infanticide and maternity

are these degraded creatures, when all around is fair and beautiful.[121]

The promise of a new land was compromised by the spectacle of Indigenous degradation and destruction. Angas described a scene that he also sketched (see Figure 3.1):

> But the most extraordinary and revolting spectacle...was an old woman, reduced to a mere skeleton, with an idiotic child – apparently four or five years old, but unable to stand erect – to which she was attempting to supply nourishment from her shrivelled and flaccid breast. Both were utterly destitute of clothing; and the spectre-like form of the aged hag, as she sat in the ashes before the hut, was loathsome: one of my companions actually turned sick and vomited at the sight.[122]

Figure 3.1 S.C. Jackson, engraver, 'An Old Woman', in George French Angas, Savage Life and Scenes in Australia and New Zealand, Smith, Elder, *London 1847. Courtesy National Library of Australia, FRM F4456*

This was not a spectacle descriptive of the tragic impacts of starvation, disease or dispossession. It was the spectacle of Aboriginal maternity as abhorrent and unable to reproduce, and thus as an anomaly in an arcadian paradise better suited to a virile race.

By this time John Morgan's ghostwritten narrative of Buckley was being anticipated in the press through advertisements for preview readings. The notoriously reticent Buckley purportedly described a deformed baby's brains as 'dashed out at a blow' and of its brother being 'made to eat the mangled remains' to prevent 'evil' befalling him. Morgan also quotes Buckley as saying firstborns were killed if the mother had earlier been promised to another man.[123] As Cowlishaw argues, the killing of firstborns was commonly asserted, despite contradicting the belief that women could not carry or breastfeed two or more children.[124] Readers would nevertheless reasonably assume that Buckley's account was verifiable. Four years later Buckley's story was contextualised by other accounts of infanticide and cannibalism in James Bonwick's *William Buckley, the Wild White Man, and his Port Phillip Black Friends*.[125] Bonwick repudiated Morgan's narrative since all accounts of Buckley were of his extreme reserve – and given what Wedge had done with his words, this was perhaps understandable. Indeed, Stephens notes, 'there is a clear reining in of his account between 1835 and 1837.'[126] Under the subheading 'Infanticide and cannibalism',[127] Bonwick referenced widely, starting with Wedge purportedly quoting Buckley, whom Bonwick had earlier established was monosyllabic, also by referencing widely. He quoted a Dr Ross, who in turn quoted Wedge, pointing out the woman who destroyed her ten babies. He drew on Assistant Protector Thomas, who had, as Stephens found, given second-hand evidence to McCombie's Select Committee, trying with caution to account for the dearth of children by the deaths of babies born so diseased, most likely with congenital syphilis, they were 'literally rotten'.[128] Stephens sifts through Thomas's claims, comparing his language with that of other administrators, missionaries and pastoralists alleging infanticide and using his case to illustrate how infanticide was fabled. We can add that infanticide was then circulated in print culture, directly shaping public opinion specifically about Aboriginal maternity and thereby the viability of Aborigines as a race.

A report by William Westgarth, later a respected parliamentarian, drew from testimony before the 1845 NSW Select Committee, including that of Thomas. Printed in *The Moreton Bay Courier*, it more explicitly linked infanticide to depopulation. Infant mortality was said to arise from infanticide, and 'aboriginal mothers' were named as destroyers of 'their half-caste children'.[129] The *Courier* additionally has Westgarth concur with Strzelecki – that Aboriginal women became infertile to their own men having had intercourse with white men – when, as Stephens shows, Westgarth in fact disputed the theory.[130] He does, however, not only claim infanticide to be 'well-authenticated' but the means to dispose of the 'additional number of helpless offspring'. Infanticide thus directly accounted for infant mortality and population decline. Reprinted not two months later in Hobart's *Courier*, the report asserts 'the general prevalence of infanticide is established beyond any reasonable doubt', yet it also includes the testimony of settler-observers who said it was 'unknown' on their stations. The accusation also had to be reconciled with mothers' obvious 'great affection' for their children as commonly observed by witnesses. Such 'strong maternal feeling' led some witnesses to believe infanticide 'if it exists at all' to be 'very rare, and occasioned by the deepest misery and want.' The report was forced to declaim, 'The unnatural coldness on the part of a mother, that might be expected to accompany such a practice, does not appear to exist as a necessary associate; at least, there is on occasions no want of maternal feeling, notwithstanding the apparent inconsistency of such a circumstance.'[131] Nevertheless, it was 'the interference of the whites' which saved particularly 'half-caste infants' from the practice, and in districts 'where the Protectorate influence is felt' it was said to have nearly ceased.

The one and only eyewitness to infanticide appeared before the select committee in the person of Captain Fyans, who claimed to have seen a child 'dashed' against a tree by a man. Stephens shows, however, that Fyans was recalling an incident from 1838 that he originally said he had seen, only to later speak of not seeing the actual event, but rather the remains on a trunk.[132] There is no way to verify whether Fyans saw the hair and brain matter of a child or a possum. These purportedly firsthand and authenticated accounts, which were never actually witnessed, were then reprinted in *Simmon's Colonial Magazine* and *The Moreton Bay Courier* under the title 'The Aborigines of Australia', as though infanticide furnished all there was to know about them.[133] An unbroken thread within infanticide discourse began to stand out in bold relief, namely its use as an alibi for the dramatic depopulation newcomers observed. It advanced a curious paradox: that settlers believed their own incursions brought about such desperate want that Aboriginal mothers took the lives of their newborns, particularly those fathered by their kind. Infanticide thus became a leading cause of Aboriginal depopulation, elided with race destiny and settlers' natural succession to the land.

Also in 1847 a contributor to *The Geelong Advertiser* using the pseudonym 'A Bushman' disputed the charge of infanticide and cannibalism by another contributor who had written under the pseudonym, 'Friend of the Aborigines'. 'Bushman' claimed he knew the identity of this 'Friend' and that his intention was only to 'gratify the ill-feeling of the Colac gentry', since his real objection was that land had been set aside for the Buntingdale mission on which he himself had hoped to depasture stock. 'Bushman' shows the intense competition for land directly playing into unsubstantiated claims of infanticide. He relates a story of grief displayed for a lost child by the Colac tribe, disputing the charge of infanticide and directly challenging 'Friend' to 'prove the contrary'.[134] While humanitarians and missionaries sometimes attributed the charge of infanticide to rumour or ill-feeling, this was the second instance, following Campbell's, of the allegation being associated with applications for occupation of land. The letter from 'Bushman' was resoundingly endorsed by the Buntingdale missionary, Francis Tuckfield (who had surveyed for a mission site in the area around Geelong with Buckley). Interestingly, despite depending on Buckley's knowledge of Aboriginal ways, Tuckfield did not come away from Buckley's company with a confirmed belief in Aboriginal infanticide. Instead, he challenged 'Friend' to 'tell us of a single case' of infanticide and exposed the scheme to get the reserved land for the mission 'into the possession of five settlers.'[135] Undeterred, 'Friend' made his opposition to the mission clear, insisting, 'the establishment at Buntingdale is an improper and unjustifiable appropriation of the lands of the colony.' Questioning how much material aid and moral instruction the establishment was in fact providing to the Colac tribe, 'Friend' furnished three examples of infanticide, two related by the 'natives themselves': one of a woman whose husband had beaten her for killing their child, another of 'Beoc' who was said to have pulled a child from a woman's back and knocked it on the head with a 'liangle', and the third of a 'gentleman' who related seeing a woman hanging her child who then told him it was 'merrijig (that is very good) to strangle it.' Using infanticide as an alibi for infecundity and child mortality, 'Friend' then asks Tuckfield how he accounts for there being no children under five years in the area.[136] These mordant stories came second-hand, from a witness with vested interests in misappropriating mission land. Since the Colac tribe was said to be fated to soon disappear, infanticide became central to this expedient depopulation. It seems this pressure from 'Friend' was felt by the government for the mission closed the following year, after the government announced it intended to cancel its grazing licence in 1850.[137] Infanticide was still given as a chief reason for the decline in the Colac tribe in local print histories in 1889 and lack of children on the mission was deemed proof of its failure.[138]

Yet, Tuckfield's denial of infanticide also stood as proof of the mission's success. In their forays into print, the Wesleyans listed the cessation of infanticide as a key rationale for their civilising efforts. A meeting of the Wesleyan Missionary Society detailed in the *Bathurst Free Press* declared, 'The enormities of murder, infanticide, cannibalism, and suicide were of common occurrence in heathen nations, and were only to be checked by the civilizing influences of the Christian religion.'[139] A letter from the Lord Bishop of Adelaide reporting on progress at the mission at Port Lincoln lists infanticide alongside 'tyrannical polygamy' and 'promiscuous intercourse' to illustrate the 'degraded state' of these 'bond-slaves of Satan'.[140] The Benedictines also had recourse to infanticide in claiming success in not just evangelising but also civilising. Benedictine missionary Rosendo Salvado included infanticide of the third girl child in his vivid account of entering the Victorian Plain of Western Australia to establish his New Norcia mission. He gives no incident of maternal infanticide yet says, 'Such was the degraded state of these unhappy people on our arrival in the lonely bush where we founded our mission.' Within two years

'If they be facts': infanticide and maternity

of evangelising, Salvado claimed these people had 'become more or less civilised human beings.'[141] His memoir was published in Naples, Rome, Barcelona and Paris and raised funds through the ecclesiastic networks of Europe. In such stories infanticide became a custom stemmed only by missionary intervention. As Johnston has detailed in her study of epistolary networks and print in the colonial 'field of textuality', competing land claims between, in this instance, missionaries and pastoralists, were waged within partisan newspapers. The 'prolific missionary media machine' created a textual landscape in which the rousing deeds of 'missionary heroes' were eagerly reported.[142] Evangelical humanitarians, such as Tuckfield, claimed to be tempering infanticide to assert the moral civility they saw as central to forging a settler polity, within textual circuits in which settler masculinities competed for standing. Infanticide was a recurring motif in colonial knowledge production. Such ethnological sleights of hand accrued credibility merely by the reiteration of Indigenous birthing and funeral practices that were in fact inaccessible and incomprehensible to settler men, due to the separate sphere of women and their custodianship of this knowledge.

This did not prevent more heavyweight colonial men weighing in. Westgarth's widely reviewed *Victoria: Late Australia Felix*,[143] published in 1853, linked population decline to infanticide, thus providing the rationale of race extinction. Westgarth was an examplar of mid-Victorian gentlemen imperialists. A colonial official, merchant, member of the NSW Legislative Council, historian and prolific author, he formed the Melbourne Chamber of Commerce and a number of colonial institutions. As an associate of *The Argus*, Westgarth was a respected commentator, informed by Alexis de Toqueville's theory of democracy, which he aspired to apply to Victoria's protean social and political institutions.[144]

Westgarth was a public figure with a vision of equality, male suffrage and emigration, and was credited with taking his 'full part in the 1852 campaign for unlocking of the lands', or surveying for lease or auction.[145] As he travelled back and forth between metropole and colonial periphery, he relayed his vision of the British Empire, networking extensively through his business and institutional affiliations. As an author, Westgarth fully participated in the burgeoning of colonial print titles. The following extract imbricates general history with print review. Having declared that cannibalism was a 'constant habit' of this 'degraded race', the review of Westgarth continues,

> Nor can the Infant claim any security from the mother who bore it, against some ruthless law, or practice, or superstition, that on frequent occasions consigns the female proportion, and sometimes both sexes, to destruction. On authentic testimony, bodies have been greedily devoured even in a state of obvious and loathsome disease; and a mother has been observed deliberately destroying her youngest child, serving it up as food, and gathering around her the remainder of the family to enjoy the unnatural banquet. Facts like these, if they be facts, would certainly soothe the regrets so deeply felt by high-minded observers, that in the march of those providential events which serve to plant the whiteman, with all his resources of power and knowledge, on the shores of the great continents and islands, the coloured skin is fated to disappear. Attempts at conversion and assimilation have both signally failed in Australia – nor has it yet been found that any other race than the Negro can take root and flourish in the same soil with the European.[146]

'If they be facts': infanticide and maternity

'If they be facts.' The same little trip we saw in the opening quote from Miln reappears here and it is clear that settlers must constantly attend to the implausibility of the charge of infanticide, dispelling, proving beyond doubt and cautioning even as they go ahead and insist on the practice. We have established that Westgarth's accounts hinged racism and misogyny on the particular odium settlers reserved for Aboriginal mothers. We know there was insufficient 'authentic testimony' to make the claims he did. We see the extrapolation from what has come before, the indulgence of the prose and the way the edge of Westgarth's text stands thickly with the reviewer's consignment of the native to oblivion. First nation peoples are cast as 'disappearing' while the enslaved 'Negro', reserved for labour, is opportunely increasing. Perhaps we can grant some latitude to colonists like Westgarth who had no means to interpret the dramatic infant mortality and the mortuary rites rumoured. Westgarth provided a finger for this reviewer, and no doubt for countless readers of the *Launceston Examiner*, to point down the tunnel of race extinction, via the extinguishing effects of Aboriginal maternity. The trope of infanticidal native mothers racially distinguished 'natives' from the 'whiteman' of empire – a type comprising men like Westgarth questing to create a self-governing federation – through the organising principle of imperialism: that of civilising. It consigned Aborigines to the 'worldwide category of the doomed',[147] their imminent loss obviating any need to expend funds on them. As a well-connected radical liberal trader, Westgarth looked forward to unoccupied lands unimpeded by the claims of inheritance that surviving native children might one day have asserted. Thanks to the self-extinguishing proclivities of native mothers, Westgarth was able to continue tirelessly advancing investment in the newly minted colony of Victoria as a soon-to-be vacated property prospect. Yet, the leitmotif of native infanticide was about to metastasise into the white community, rescinding its use as a descriptor of Aboriginal barbarity.

The decade of 1850 was marked by a notable upsurge in charges and convictions of infanticide by colonial women (and, very seldom, fathers). Newspaper reports specialising in these uncorroborated speculative statements about 'native' infanticide were themselves eclipsed by reports of court proceedings against named white women committed to trial for the crime. A case in point is the trial of Ann Malcolmb, sentenced to two years' imprisonment for concealing the birth of a child, a lesser charge than murder, after knocking her baby on the head and throwing it down her employer's well. Malcolmb had travelled to Australia pregnant, hoping no doubt to find refuge from shame. She delivered her baby alone in a water closet, found smeared with blood.[148] *The Geelong Advertiser and Intelligencer* was correct in observing that 'scarcely a week went by' without such a new case reported in the press and a number of editors began to express alarm at what appeared to be a dramatic increase in court proceedings for white infanticide.[149] Perhaps chastened, there followed a trailing off of extracted travelogues and reports generalising that 'native' infanticide was a more common occurrence. Another marked shift in the discourse in this decade was an almost corresponding increase in generalised reports of Chinese and Indian infanticide, just as the presence of the Chinese grew on the goldfields and in the months following the Indian Insurrection in May 1857.[150] It seems even when located firmly in the metropole and in the colonial periphery, infanticide was a transferable, ready-to-hand, racialised denigrator.

The policing of permissible forms of maternity across race and class was cruelly exacted; despite anxiety about the upsurge in

'If they be facts': infanticide and maternity

white infanticide cases, they were policed as an aberration. Those still attributed to Aborigines, notably without sufficient evidence to advance them to trial (until 1890),[151] gained legitimacy through their reiteration in government reports as an Aboriginal custom. For instance, a public lecture by J. H. Palmer was transcribed in the Sydney magazine *Empire* in 1857. Palmer was recommended to readers as a 'short-hand writer to both Houses of the Legislature' who drew from his official position, which 'laid open to him the evidence given before the committees of the Legislature in reference to the aboriginal inhabitants', including the testimony of 'Captain Grey, E. J. Eyre, Count Strzelecki, Sir Thomas Mitchell, Westgarth, Hodgkinson, and others.' He thus mediated the transference of early ethnology into print. But Palmer was a bit of a wag. He delivered an ironic reading of Aboriginal customs, commencing with Dampier's overworn 'miserablest people in the world' passage, which he dismissed as unfair caricature. Yet, he continues mocking Aboriginal mothers as just as likely to gaze 'fondly upon the well flattened nose and incipient wool just springing from the round bullet head of that black bundle of mortality, as did the lovely Ino upon her infant Bacchus'. Proffering an example of cannibalism Palmer writes, 'I have myself met with a woman at Carrington, who having killed her child ate it, and afterwards carried the bones about in her net'. And he backs up this misreading of mortuary rites with 'personal inquiries, as well as from the replies sent to the queries forwarded by the committee on the aborigines to the benches of magistrates throughout the country', citing

> in confirmation of my statement, the names of F. Fyans, Esq., late Commissioner of Crown Lands at Port Phillip, Mr. Protector Sievewright, and Serjeant Windredge,

who was sent out with a party of men to Gipps Land, in 1846, in the hope of recovering a white woman, who was then said to be in captivity among the blacks.[152]

We already know of Fyans's trustworthiness as a witness. Sievewright in fact argued that the Barabool people concocted tales of cannibalism to play on the gullibility of settlers and a medical officer at his protectorate station stated, 'I have never known an instance of it.'[153] As for Windredge, he was willing to lead an expedition in search of a white woman rumoured to be held captive by Gippsland tribes, also entirely unsubstantiated and never since proved.[154] On this authority Palmer attributed the apparent 'disproportion' between the sexes — which no one else noted — to infanticide. Palmer was then in a position to describe the birth of an Australian baby as 'not to its parents a matter calling forth the most lively emotions of gratitude and delight.' No Aboriginal father could thereby enter into the 'feelings of intense joy with which an Englishman would address his child' and no 'grand preparations' were made to welcome it.

Palmer is quite specific about what that welcome should occasion, including 'swathing it in long bandages', 'a beautiful net cap, surrounded by some score yards of lovely thread lace' and 'long garments ornamented with profusion of needlework'. We can conjecture these items were not part of the clothing rations being provided for displaced Aborigines at this time. The newborn was instead 'wrapped in a greasy opossum cloak, or a still more filthy blanket' and 'suspended from the back of its mother, its head scorched by the rays of the summer's sun, or exposed to the "pelting of the pitiless storm".' Moreover, insufficient 'restraint' was imposed by Aboriginal parents, yet there were 'exceptional cases' — which Palmer evenhandedly shares among 'our own

'If they be facts': infanticide and maternity

colour' – in which Aboriginal mothers 'behave with great barbarity' towards their children. What counts for this 'knowing' can be ascertained to some extent by Palmer's use of a bride capture passage. He writes of the unwilling bride being waddied senseless, after which her beau 'drags her to his hovol [sic], regardless of her striking against shrubs or stones.'[155] The rest we could, like Palmer, almost recite verbatim.

The following year in 1858, Sydney's elite welcomed the Austrian frigate the *Novara* into the harbour (engaged in a circumnavigation of the globe between April 1857 and August 1859). Some of them assisted with this scientific expedition by furnishing specimens. Naturalist and trustee of the Australian Museum Edward Smith Hill guided the party through the Illawarra and with a whistle summoned a group of Aborigines living with the elder Tullimbar. Hill was a regular contributor to *The Herald* and *The Sydney Mail*, served as a New South Wales commissioner for exhibitions in Philadelphia, Paris and Sydney, and through the museum board was connected to George French Angas. In his obituary it was said that when Aborigines visited Sydney they made his grounds their headquarters and saw him as a friend and 'chief'.[156] The historiographer of the expedition, ethnologist Karl Scherzer, wrote of the 'natives' of the Murray, Clarence and Brisbane rivers that, 'Infanticide, especially of female children, is of very frequent occurrence. Abortion is also so frequently practised that they have a word (*Mibra*) to express it!' Scherzer was shown a tour of the museum by Angas and exchanged items, and Hill took him to Kogerah Bay to collect Aboriginal skeletal remains. During his five-week stay he made a number of cranial and other measurements of Aborigines.[157] Scherzer was, unsurprisingly, particularly interested in the mortuary rites of a boy who had died in the vicinity of Moreton Bay, whose head and skin, according to the savage habits of the natives, were separated from the rest of the body and dried over a fire. The father and mother were both present and uttered loud cries. The heart, liver, and entrails were divided among the warriors, who carried away with them pieces stuck on their pointed spears; while the upper part of the thigh (apparently the tit-bit) was roasted and eaten by the parents themselves! The skin, the skull, and the bones were, on the other hand, carefully packed up and taken away with them in their grass sacks.[158]

Scherzer surmised that it was 'not usual for a mother to devour her own child, that she may thereby regain the strength which the fruit of her womb had abstracted from her!' Given that the *Novara* did not land at Moreton Bay and his contact with Aboriginal people, and any specimens expropriated from them, was through his contacts with ethnologists at Sydney, we can infer Scherzer rehearses information mediated through Angas, George Bennett and the well connected of Sydney. Scherzer's account thus reflects on the knowledge institutions and their circulation through transnational networks of correspondence, visits, specimens and print at this time. The pomp and ceremony occasioned by this visit, from formal dinners, tours, meetings and concerts to a 21-gun salute and a lord mayoral fancy dress ball, suggests the knowledge production of international scientific expeditions depended on access to the highest levels of government administrators and their links to local scientists and patrons among the wealthy and connected. Hill was, for instance, brother of Richard Hill, a justice of the peace and member for Canterbury, and George Hill, Mayor of Sydney and a member of the Legislative Assembly and the Legislative Council. Infanticide was here a knowledge

'If they be facts': infanticide and maternity

artefact exchanged unquestioned between elite colonials through international scientific networks.

By 1859, features on infanticide in Australian print looked outward to reports of Chinese and Indian infanticide, but overwhelmingly the local focus of news reports remained on white women committed to trial. Headlines now had to specify which infanticide they referred to, such as an article subtitled 'Infanticide of black children.'[159] No doubt influenced by the rise in criminal proceedings against white women, this article was the first to call for charges against 'black' mothers who continued the 'time immemorial...custom' against 'half-casts' for whom mothers 'have even less care' than they did for their 'genuine black progeny' (Aboriginal wombs also had the remarkable facility, it seems, to issue fake children). The legalities of charging 'ignorant black gins' presented problems, however, since 'considerable difficulty would be found in procuring evidence of such misdeeds, as in the majority of instances blacks would be the only witnesses.' Yet, the contributor then relies on Aborigines – 'if the blacks are to be believed' – to report on a newborn purportedly thrown on a fire, allegedly crying until burned to death.[160] 'Newborn roasting' tended to be reserved for such calls to police Aboriginal mothers, though they fell on deaf ears. Another pastoralist called for Aborigines, as the Queen's subjects, to be subject to her laws, invoking the 'lubra...roasting her child as an easy way of getting rid of it' to bolster his argument that the death of one of his black 'workmen' during a tribal affray should be dealt with as a criminal matter. He accuses the protector (whom he mistakenly infers was the local missionary Taplin, to whom we shall soon turn) of writing glowing annual reports while 'keeping behind the scenes the writhing body of some insignificant black piccaninny that the mother thinks too much trouble to rear, and so roasts.'

The complainant, Tilney Cotton, was much inconvenienced and possibly even bereft at the loss of an Aboriginal labourer, Jack Hamilton, but it is infanticide, which he verifies on the authority of 'E.C. Hughes Esq., J.P.', that he details so luridly, to bolster his demand that charges be laid. When Taplin was defended a few years later as not in fact the protector but rather the agent of an evangelical society, working without government authority, it was still argued that if British law is used in India to 'put down' infanticide, it should equally be applied here to Aboriginal customs.[161] As attention swung from Aboriginal to Indian to Chinese infanticide, comparisons were made between colonies and local meanings were revised. But a legal approach as called for may have individualised Aboriginal infanticide rather than attributed the cause to race, and indeed exposed this axiomatic trope as lacking evidence. Moreover, Aboriginal testimony was inadmissible until 1876 (in New South Wales) and prospects for recognising customary law had been increasingly curtailed from 1835 in the colonial justice system.[162] Instead, from this point, calls for the removal of children grew, regardless of their relation to mothers and clans.

The findings of the 1860 South Australian Select Committee were published in *The South Australian Advertiser* and infanticide figured as the first cause of depopulation.[163] One of the principal concerns of the Select Committee was population decline and whether it could be attributed to colonisation. Prostitution, promiscuity, intoxication, the wearing of wet European clothes in place of hygienic skins, people's vulnerability to pulmonary disease and syphilis were all considered. But 'infanticide, to a limited extent' was – despite these obvious injuries sustained from European occupation and contact – given as the first cause of decrease.[164] The committee was largely initiated by a settler contesting the land claims of the missionary we met earlier, Taplin, and disputing his success in evangelising Aborigines. By this decade newcomers were evincing a strange mix of misericordia and inverted causality around the manifest loss of Aboriginal tribes. Dying race theory provided some surety around the thorny moral question of colonisation which, as the southeast frontier was secured, could now be unambiguously referred to in terms of 'title', 'lands virtually dispossessed' and of people 'deprived through our occupation of their inheritance'. The prospect of 'awarding compensation' was even raised, but only because any special fund or additional reserves of land recommended were unlikely to tax the colony for long due to 'the melancholy fact' of the race being doomed to extinction, meaning it was 'only a question of time when these reserves would again revert to the crown.'[165] Overall the cause of decline was attributed to 'contact with Europeans', but the *Advertiser*'s editors were able to dispute this since the first named cause, infanticide, was not learned 'from Europeans'.[166] The fifth cause, infertility, was said to result from promiscuity. But this was not related to venereal disease since the third item stated that syphilis had existed prior to 'occupation' – it was merely a more 'aggravated form' that Europeans had introduced. Along with recommending the appointment of a chief protector, the committee examined the outcomes of the reserves and the stations at Poonindie, Point McLeay and Wellington. It submitted, with 'strong conviction', that hopes to Christianise and instil 'steady industrial habits' in the tribes could 'only be expected by separation of children from parents and the evil influences of the tribe to which they belong'. While this practice might 'grate' on 'pseudo-philanthropists', only 'complete isolation' could provide the 'work of mercy to the rising generation of aborigines.'[167]

Infanticide underpinned this inchoate complex of casuistry and cant on depopulation. The language of a 'remnant' and 'pitiable' race was now in mainstream circulation, as observers sought a consensus, one writing of 'the gradual extinction of the native races being considered the natural but inevitable sequence of colonization. On this point alone all are agreed.' For this sympathetic resident of 'Robetown', infanticide, though discouraged by 'occupation', continued to 'secretly' lurk as a cause for 'excessive' mortality, mostly attributed to the 'vicious propensities' contracted from 'intercourse with the white population.' Even though Aborigines' sustaining 'mode of living' was 'completely subverted', this contributor still claimed it was simply a 'stern unflinching decree' of nature that 'barbarism' succumbs to 'civilization'.[168] It was baffling sophistry, that a black population was destined to die out because children born to white fathers were subject to infanticide. Perhaps it presaged the logic of biological absorption which would follow in the early twentieth century; white-fathered children, by one means or another, spelled the demise of the black population.

In order for colonials to shrug off responsibility, the logic of dying race discourse contorted. The Reverend Dr McCombie, editor of the *Port Phillip Gazette*, claimed in 1861, 'They have recently destroyed a large number of their children, fearing that they would become the victims of the superior race.'[169] Bonwick had made the same claim in his narrative of William Buckley.[170] But rather than illustrating the crisis conditions Aborigines were managing, by the 1860s the context of dying race theory instead lent McCombie's claim the spectre of race suicide. This variety of victimhood was less direct than settler destruction at least and it sustained a sense of inevitability for 'melting' and other disappearing acts. A shift occurs after the middle of the nineteenth century, in which mothers become culpable, rather than having their hands forced by overbearing husbands, tribal custom, promiscuity, defect, gender or, less openly stated, frontier conditions. Thus *The Courier* reported in 1862 that a 'black gin' gave birth to a child in a paddock near Fortitude Valley and 'was seen immediately afterwards to dash the infant's brains out.' The expression comes from Shakespeare's *Macbeth* but a reference to so destroying babies can also be found in Psalm 137.9. From the mid-nineteenth century it recurred in print to describe the atrocities of savage custom. She allegedly 'went into the bush' and was not heard of again.[171] The report is left stranded, as though an explanatory context had not yet been imagined. It would come.

From the 1860s infanticide was taken up to rubricate the ambitions of prominent settlers and adjudicate their disputes. For instance, another wild white man narrative emerged in a book by the prominent Presbyterian clergyman, reformer, journalist and newspaper proprietor John Dunmore Lang. This story concerned the escaped convict, James Davis, who lived among Queensland Aborigines for fourteen years until 1842. Like Buckley, he was reputed to be extremely reserved and reticent. Nevertheless, Lang somehow managed to winkle his story out, an extract of which circulated in *Empire, The Courier* and the shortlived *Ipswich Herald & General Advertiser*.[172] Davis 'acquits' the people of Moreton Bay and surrounds of infanticide, which Lang localised as different from other regions. Lang followed up by alleging infanticide and cannibalism in a pamphlet promoting Protestant immigration to Queensland.[173] An anonymous newspaper review of Lang introduces the grisly tidbit that parents feasted 'very comfortably on the bodies of their children, and are even in some places accused of practicing infanticide for the purpose of gratifying their tastes.'[174] The accusation that Aborigines ate babies for the taste of their meat takes off from this point to climax with the apocryphal account of Daisy Bates, as we shall see.

In Johnston's close study of Lang's very public stoush with the missionary Threlkeld, she found he made use of his own mastheads, the weekly *Colonist* (1835–40), *The Colonial Observer* (1841–44) and *The Press* (1851), to stage attacks on dissenters and defend his rather provocative actions by printing polemics that targeted adversaries and promoted his projects (assisted migration, education, the separation of New South Wales from Port Phillip and republicanism). He was sued for libel, accused of slander and directed his abhorrence of convict morality at the convict and emancipist press. Though accused of self-aggrandising, Lang's titles were widely read and he contributed daily letters or articles to a range of newspapers. He was, Johnston surmises, 'a master manipulator of public opinion.'[175] He used his newspapers extensively to attack Threlkeld's mission at Lake Macquarie, accusing him of extravagance and disputing the viability of the mission.[176] It is probably quixotic to ponder whether the loss of five of Lang's children in infancy[177] contributed to his sense of the fragility of life and informed his take on dying race theory. His reports of infanticide should be seen in the context of fierce contest between humanitarians and clergymen over their reputations. Within settler bloviation in print, the meaning of infanticide shifted from unnatural mothers to race suicide, to disappearing acts, to concealing or avenging illegitimacy, this last just as a rash of infanticide cases by white women spread over the colonial pages.

At the end of 1861 the most plausible, graphic and confronting report of infanticide appeared in *The South Australian Register,* signed only G.T. but undoubtedly penned by the missionary George Taplin. It's an exemplary instalment of colonial rivalries working this trope to their advantage within the recursive tendencies of print. From 1859 to 1879 Taplin ran the mission at Point McLeay (or Raukkan), administering to the people of the lower Murray. His approach was unusually enlightened for the time and his commitment to the welfare of the Ngarrindjeri continues to stand. He learned their language and preserved Aboriginal nomenclature in surnames, sought freehold title for cottage builders, argued against the removal of children, respected many traditional customs and practices and left a detailed anthropological record still of significance to descendants.[178] Taplin claimed his information came from the 'Narrinyeri' themselves and, indeed, he had worked closely with the Ngarrindjeri for two years by the time this account appeared in print. Like the missionaries discussed earlier, Taplin's work with communities and his close association did not dissuade him from pursuing a program of Christianising by which Ngarrindjeri civilisation should ultimately be abandoned.[179] Taplin 'assisted in undermining their government and social structure, further weakened traditional discipline and morale within the confederacy and provoked strong opposition from conservative tribal members.'[180] His purported success at stemming the alleged practice of infanticide was key to demonstrating his mission's progress. His publications were publicity for the Congregational church, which was yet to ordain him, and for the Aborigines' Friends' Association (AFA), which employed him to establish the mission at Point McLeay.

Like Tuckfield at Buntingdale and Threlkeld at Lake Macquarie before him, Taplin faced opposition, in this instance from a local pastoralist, a formidable parliamentarian with extensive pastoral interests, John Baker. Baker initiated and sat on the board of the South Australian 1860 Select Committee into the conditions of the Aborigines.[181] He used the proceedings to attack both Taplin, for failing to provide adequately for the 'natives' in his charge, and the AFA that employed him. Taplin had wholehearted support from AFA witnesses and was able to disprove Baker's accusations of laziness, of profiteering from the Ngarrindjeri fish trade and of being motivated by self-interest. At a later annual general meeting of the AFA it was reported that infanticide was diminishing, 'in consequence of the assistance rendered to the mothers by the Government'. Taplin's work at Point McLeay was the centrepiece in the meeting's claims to be ameliorating the plight of Aborigines, and his success in instructing children was keenly reported. Taplin was at this time tendering to extend the schoolhouse where thirty-three boys and girls already resided. He was no doubt especially pleased to report that young men shearing on Baker's station walked the five miles to attend Sunday worship. In a letter defending the mission in 1876, Taplin claimed to have stopped the practice of infanticide 'altogether'.[182] And when his book was reviewed in 1874, it was noted that infanticide 'disappeared' following the provision of government rations to nursing mothers.[183] If this was more than a defence of his missionary work and ancillary support, we should query how rations were given to newborns. If speculation about mothers with older siblings killing newborns can be credited, it suggests prolonged breastfeeding could in some areas have been lengthened as a response to child malnutrition rather than Aboriginal convention. Newborn infanticide could then have been understood as in direct proportion to older child preservation. Such reasoning was rarely applied to living children, and mothers, following dispossession. The politics of the leitmotif of infanticide for rivalrous white settler men was suppressed, and the discourse went unchallenged. Nevertheless, over twenty years the mission advanced apace; the Ngarrindjeri population stabilised at 600 in the 1870s – from

'If they be facts': infanticide and maternity

3,000 in the 1840s – comparing favourably with groups that had no such support.[184]

Taplin's contribution to the infanticide trope was significant, despite its being enmeshed in conflicting land objectives. It was also ghastly, for he claimed the usual method for killing newborns was by inserting a red hot ember into either ear 'as far as it could be thrust' and covering the orifice with sand.[185] As we've seen, such graphic detail was unusual in the circulation of the infanticide trope. As a missionary wanting to furnish, specifically publish, proof of his Christianising influence, Taplin claimed that infanticide was so prevalent 'before the commencement of this colony' that more than half of all newborns were destroyed. This figure is a far cry from the single child murder he documented during his time at the mission.[186] He touted that one 'intelligent woman said she thought that if the Europeans had waited a few more years they would have found the country without inhabitants', a startling preemption of dying race theory and one many settlers would no doubt be relieved to hear. Taplin wrote that this woman had herself destroyed one infant and that he personally knew 'several women' who had each put two or three of their newborns to death. He was at pains to reveal that since his mission had commenced, infanticide had decreased to a third of newborns, a figure that demonstrated his efficacy in evangelising while evidencing urgent need for ancillary support. Taplin also said that the 'terrible crime of infanticide is covered up and concealed from the observation of the whites with extreme care.' Somehow Taplin managed to attest to these numbers with grisly description despite avowing that he was himself 'for some time in ignorance that it existed to such an extent as it does. Only very intimate acquaintance with the natives led me to discover its prevalence.'[187]

Taplin had testified to the 1860 Select Committee that infanticide existed 'to some extent', although more so on the Coorong, yet he also testified that no case had come to his knowledge. He reported an innkeeper's wife at Guichen Bay had related a story of people eating twins. The panel noted this did not appear to be a 'well-authenticated case' and Taplin himself admitted it was 'third-hand'.[188] Taplin was more credible than most newcomers but his testimony to the select committee was contradicted by his print account the following year. After one year of careful concealment it seems he knew personally of a number of cases. Yet thirteen years later, when he recycles his 1861 copy with few alterations in his 1874 book he is unable to furnish any more instances. In addition, advanced pregnancy hardly requires intimate observance. Surely a heavily pregnant woman delivers a baby and returns to camp with or without a baby. The many possible explanations for loss of a newborn under contact conditions are myriad and it was highly unlikely Ngarrindjeri women would have shared information about birthing with an unauthorised male.[189] As was the case with Buckley, Taplin's informants may have been conveying their attitudes to foreigners – Aborigines beyond or even remote from their territorial boundaries – which Taplin then assumed to have pan-Aboriginal applicability. As Stephens argues in relation to the transmission of Aboriginal confirmation of infanticide in Port Phillip, the women may have betrayed their imaginings of rival clans or their fear of alien tribes beyond their country, a projection that coincided with newcomer imaginings.[190] The women may have been talking up to power or fulfilling a perceived expectation in Taplin's line of questioning. His confidence about his mastery of their language may have been misplaced. Or his informants may have been describing the distressing and extreme circumstances afflicting Ngarrindjeri child mortality.

'If they be facts': infanticide and maternity

Well before the time of Taplin's published infanticide claims, the Ngarrindjeri confederacy, comprising eighteen tribes, had been critically depleted by a smallpox pandemic around 1830. The Foundation Act of 1834 had alienated the Indigenous people of South Australia from their land with a 'stroke' of King William's pen from twenty thousand kilometres away.[191] Invasion of their lands began in 1837 and was formalised by the Waste Lands Act of 1842, but they had long endured raids on their camps for women by escaped convicts from Van Diemen's Land, as well as whalers and sealers on Kangaroo Island prior to 1820, who introduced venereal disease which profoundly impacted on fertility and the birthrate. As Russell argues, despite the violence, women exerted agency within their relations with the sealers, passing language and ceremony on to their children and possibly resorting to infanticide as an expression of autonomy. Russell, however, does not claim this infanticide was the principal explanation for low birthrates.[192] When the surgeon Dr Richard Penny established himself at Encounter Bay in 1840, venereal disease was 'rife'. The Milmenrura had also suffered a punitive expedition. Although Penny had successfully treated twenty-four cases of the afflicted he was retrenched by Governor Grey in 1841. Their next champion was Dr David Wark, who noted the infertility and 'abortive' impacts of venereal disease.[193] In 1856 the protectorate was abolished, leaving the Ngarrindjeri with little material and medical aid. Their loss can be compared with the depopulation experienced by other tribes and compiled by a Polish anthropologist in the 1930s. Krzywicki assembled a tribe-by-tribe breakdown of depopulation. If he can be credited, most populations continued to dramatically decline within twenty years of contact with Europeans: by 1880 the Booandik at Mount Gambier were 'reduced' to seventeen from an estimated 900; 700 Toolooa (Dandan) on the Boyne

River in 1854 were 'reduced' to forty-three by 1882; the Kurnai of Gippsland were numbered at 1,000–1,500 in 1839 on first contact – 140 remained by 1877. Of the 3,000 Bakunji of the Lower Darling in 1845, not more than eighty survived in 1880.[194]

The Dresden missionary H. A. E. Meyer, working in the same area at Encounter Bay, had written a pamphlet in 1846 which stated that children were 'frequently put to death.'[195] Taplin seems to have drawn upon Meyer, insofar as some of his phrasing is similar: fathers nursing children 'for several hours together' is read in Taplin as 'for hours at a time.'[196] Taplin may have relied upon Meyer to state that deformed, illegitimate children or children born to a mother already raising two children were killed. He extrapolates, naming parents and describing his intervention to save the life of their child, who later dies 'suspiciously'. As noted, when he recycles his 1861 copy with few alterations in his 1874 book, he is unable to furnish any more instances.[197] He argues in his book that infanticide is not prevalent and restates that the figure of one-third of newborns applied thirteen years ago. But given that he claims to have only become aware of it through 'intimate acquaintance' it is indeed suspicious that another thirteen years of close observation did not yield any further examples.[198] Taplin also downgrades his 'proof' between 1861 and 1874 of the *kaininggi* apron which he said girls wore until they became mothers. He first noted in 1861 that many girls discarded the kaininggi without 'living offspring', assuming most of the children had been killed. Taplin seems more open to the incidence of infertility by 1874, noting instead that the husbands of girls who did not bear children took their kaininggi and burned them.[199]

As a missionary Taplin was typically focused on the 'rising generation' of children, persuading their parents to send them to school and hoping to dissuade them from their parents' way of life. As hopes grew for the conversion of children due to their now tested 'aptitude for learning', greater interest was taken in their welfare and emphasis placed on overcoming the 'tenacity with which the natives clung to their old customs, and the anxiety they evinced to initiate their children into their superstitions.'[200] Aboriginal children were thus a focus of the select committee in more ways than one. Noting they had been successfully educated at two schools, it recommended founding an institution in an 'insulated position'. This meant the children's 'perfect isolation was considered as necessary to relieve the rising generation from the evil influences and example of their parents.'[201] Taplin was more prescient than most colonial administrators, however, and knew removing children from parents against their will was inhuman. He did institute a dormitory system at Raukkan so his portrayal of children as vulnerable may have worked in favour of this approach. Yet, he was acutely aware of the rate of infant mortality, which he estimated at seventy-five per cent, linking it to traditional shelters, immoderate tobacco use and mothers' lax morality.[202] In his 1874 book he was also very aware of the losses suffered by the Ngarrindjeri, noting their game had been largely exterminated, the reeds they built their houses from were now 'useless', and their overall condition was 'broken and scattered.'[203]

Finally, in disproving this most graphic of infanticide reports we need to assess the likelihood of the method described. Given Taplin was so aware of the devotion and dedication of Ngarrindjeri parents and vividly describes the inconsolable grief they suffered on the loss of a child, he appears to have discounted the likely distress caused by the alleged method of killing. The efficacy of this method in bringing about a quick death to newborns should be considered, though there would have been far less prolonged and painful ways of killing an infant.[204] We should note that Taplin also claimed that mothers who smoked produced 'excessively fat' babies.[205] Moreover, how exactly could hot coals be handled, let alone inserted into the tiny orifice of a newborn's ear, and why would sand be used to close over the hole? Taplin was the first to report this practice and perhaps it struck a wrong note, even in colonial print of the time, for it was not repeated again until 1890, where it was embellished with 'sharp cries of agony' and 'spasmodic jerking of the little limbs', probably by the editor Charles White, in the rather obscure *Bathurst Free Press and Mining Journal*.[206] This quote then appeared in the *Shoalhaven Telegraph* in 1905.[207] Much later, in 1936, the author of *Back in the Stone Age*, a popular book on Central Australia, claimed to have been made aware of two instances of infanticide and included live coals in the mouth among the methods. As with Taplin, this is then contradicted by the fond indulgence attributed to Aboriginal mothers, who always 'give them the last bite of food.'[208] The long gaps in recycling the hot coal method suggest two things: that white readers did not want the details of infanticide and that it was simply the phantasm of infanticide which sufficed as a signifier of savagery. In a widely circulated lecture to the Australian Natives Association in 1889, three nights before his death in a fire, Taplin noted merely that infanticide was practised, without elaborating further.[209]

Such graphic detail had a long cultural memory, however. Fieldwork by Ronald and Catherine Berndt in the region in the 1940s (but not published until 1993) did not challenge Taplin's reportage, though it noted the opinion that 'more than half' of newborns were killed was a distortion of traditional life that was 'most unreliable, grossly exaggerated'.[210] In addition, the Berndts document a number of contraceptive measures, such as a thistle herb called a 'talgi', along with purgatives, such as the 'pangki' root, to induce menstruation, information which would have been kept from unauthorised men like Taplin, no matter how 'intimate' his 'acquaintance'. The Berndts found that illegitimate children would have been incorporated into the father's clan and any 'shame forgotten', and that it would have been 'virtually unheard of' for a legal father not to be found for an unmarried woman's child. When mothers were unable to look after their children they were adopted by the father's sister.[211] The Berndts believed infanticide was resorted to in cases of deformity, but that it was always as a 'last resort'. They were, however, appraising claims made a century earlier by Taplin, who wrote within a public sphere that we've seen was fraught by public relations between newcomer men of different castes, here missionary and pastoralist, and their competing land claims.

Speculative reports in the press continued to be outweighed by criminal proceedings against named white women by roughly eight to one.[212] A Society for the Prevention of Infanticide was proposed in London as cries against this English 'fashion' became increasingly shrill.[213] It was renamed the Society for the Preservation of Infant Life and it argued that bastardry laws 'pressed too severely on the mothers of illegitimate children', yet it called for harsher laws against infanticidal mothers. It advocated for foundling homes to accommodate mothers with their children and it recommended an increase in the payment of medical expenses by fathers and a weekly payment to mothers. This shift in sentiment towards Aboriginal mothers can also be discerned in Australia in an 1865 article calling for a protector to be stationed in Adelaide following reports of ill treatment and drought in the north. The author argued, 'It is firmly believed that so great have been the sufferings of some of the tribes that infanticide and cannibalism have prevailed amongst them to a considerable extent.

We should not be surprised, then, that poor wretches who under the pressure of starvation will kill and eat their own children should not respect the cattle of a stranger.'[214] Public exposure of infanticide in England along with print reports of local white cases brought to court undoubtedly altered the readiness with which colonists were prepared to accuse Aboriginal mothers. Indeed, by 1865 so alarmed was the English-speaking public by such repeated convictions that one report read, 'No longer can we reproach the natives of India, China, or the South Seas with their special addiction to this practice. Few nations would appear to be more guilty in this respect than Christian England.'[215]

Aside from a new interest in idolatory practices in Fiji, including infanticide, the focus of print now was on the almost weekly cases of 'child-dropping', 'seduction' and 'concealment of birth' by mostly servant girls, and in 'baby-farming'. Aboriginal infanticide was next mentioned in a series of asides as having ceased at a number of missions. Yet in 1873 it was reported as 'common' at a mission at Noosa in Queensland, under Methodist missionary Reverend Edward Fuller. Infanticide was here for the first time explicitly an outcome of white men 'living with' black women, linking it with the seduction and abandonment of white serving girls. Together the mission and the 'decently disposed' white population in the area were overwhelmed by these 'numerically strong' and 'bad' elements. The mission closed four years later and the Aboriginal Reserve was cancelled with the announcement that 1,700 acres would be opened for selection from January 1879 at the price of seven shillings and sixpence per acre, and 8,250 acres would be surveyed for auction.[216] In the same year, 1873, Aboriginal infanticide was circulated through three newspapers in a review of Samuel Gason's manuscript on the tribes around Lake Hope. Significantly the review follows a disapproving report on delays in the surveying of land in what would become the Northern Territory.[217] Gason was stationed there as the police-trooper and the review notes that infanticide is 'singular' given the 'tenderness' with which the people 'cherish' their offspring.[218] As the cases of white infanticide streamed in, the question of legal responses to Aboriginal 'custom' arose, and the 'strong hand of the law' was counselled as appropriate for infanticide along with the custom of 'carrying about their dead'. Arguably unsubstantiated generalised references to Aboriginal infanticide were difficult to sustain against the 'epidemic' of white charges, for child murder was presented in far more graphic detail in court reportage. As soon as the question was begged – why weren't Aboriginal women charged? – it could only be answered that, unlike white cases, no incidents evidenced by infant corpses were coming to light.[219] Speculation about Aboriginal infanticidal mothers literally dropped off the page.

As with bride capture, in the 1870s men of science carried the requisite authority to confer intelligibility on the trope of Aboriginal infanticide. Their work gained presence in print through reviews which sometimes departed from their texts. It was incumbent on scientists to demonstrate their findings had some basis in fact and to distinguish their work from the conjecture of settler observers, which had assumed the weight of fact merely through unquestioned repetition. Yet, in many cases scientists continued to rely on this very conjecture. Reviews of Edward M. Curr's four-volume *Australian Race* said it was 'aided by the experience and inquiries of observant men scattered through the island-continent', and while some caution was expressed over 'assigning to human testimony its true value', any doubts were assuaged by Curr's own 'years of close and personal intercourse with the blacks.'[220] The botanist

Robert Brown (whom we recall lifted his passage on bride capture almost verbatim from Collins for use in his four-volume *Races of Mankind* of 1873) corroborated his allegation of Australian infanticide with that of cannibalism in Papua writing, 'As cannibalism is so marked a feature of the Papuan race, it would be remarkable if the Australian, so low in type, was altogether free from suspicion in this respect.' That Aboriginal 'participation in this loathsome practice is not, however, perfectly made out' did not restrain him from having 'little doubt but that in times of scarcity they will eat their relatives' and that certain unnamed tribes mixed the flesh of children with dogs. He generously qualifies this florid assertion with the pressing fact that 'even civilised races have been driven to the same extremity' of cannibalism.[221] The swathe of press reports over the previous two decades on white infanticide forced this qualification again in a newspaper review of the influential 1878 book *The Aborigines of Victoria* by anthropologist Robert Brough Smyth. The reviewer drew on Malthus to link Aboriginal infanticide to the status of the 'wretched black mother' in marriage who killed her first child because it was 'too heavy a burden to carry about in the discharge of her other domestic duties.' The reviewer was careful to note that the practice of infanticide is 'certainly far more merciful than to place an infant in a baby farm, with a *faiseuse d'angers*, to be starved to death by inches.'[222] Similarly, in 1880 a newspaper article argued that infanticide 'does not appear to have been more frequent amongst Australian aborigines than among the most highly civilised people of Europe.' Indeed, 'black husbands' were 'like white husbands in the exaction of [these] domestic attentions.'[223] Recalling from Chapter 2 that Brough Smyth was highly derivative,[224] depending particularly on the unpublished notes of Thomas, we can place this with Stephens's discussion of Thomas described earlier, which found he gave second-hand evidence to McCombie's Select Committee, in an attempt to account for the dearth of children in the camps. Accusations of infanticide appearing in print were clearly changing in tone, cowed by the ongoing charges being brought against white mothers. *The Australasian Sketcher* republished a long essay from *The Argus* in which it argued that the 'low barbarism' that infanticide evidenced was never compared with the rate among the 'most highly civilised people of Europe.' Moreover, among Aborigines it was never 'resorted to as a means of destroying the proof of social indiscretions', but in cases of deformed offspring or to give adequate care to an older sibling.[225] Henceforth, in print Aboriginal infanticide appears as a custom staunched by the presence of missionaries,[226] or in a growing number of general histories of early settlement, still as an ethnological characteristic generalised to contemporary Aborigines from pre-settlement practices. As Aboriginal women were increasingly being sought for indentured service to settlers, this then had to be qualified by how 'fond of their charges' they nevertheless were when 'utilised as nurses' in this domesticated, displaced expression of maternity.[227]

In 1881 a review appeared in *The Argus* that gave an unprecedented imagining of mortuary rites. It moved away from the notion that cannibalism was motivated by hunger to it showing esteem for the departed. The book's author was well placed to introduce more considered and detailed analysis into the discussion, for James Dawson was a protector who vigorously championed the Djargurd wurrung people from the Camperdown area, erecting a granite obelisk to the memory of his friend Wombeetch Puyuun. His *Australian Aborigines: The Language and Customs of Several Tribes of Aborigines in the Western District of Victoria* was written with the help of his daughter, Isabella Park Taylor. Though accused by Curr of being unreliable in parts, it occasioned an extraordinary comparison of Aboriginal mortuary rites and meat eating. *The Argus* ironically conjured this corporeal crypt:

> To provide the dead with a living tomb, such as we ourselves offer to oxen, sheep, pigs, poultry, fish, and molluscs was certainly an ingenious idea and a most delicate mark of attention, and to feel that the fragments of a departed friend, transformed by the chemistry of the stomach into warm blood, were coursing through his veins in red corpuscles and were passing through his heart itself, must have been a thrilling sensation to the eater.[228]

That *The Argus* should review Dawson's book so unsparingly is all the more curious, given that he had reputedly taken to the editor, Frederick Haddon, with his umbrella when he refused to run Dawson's expose of maltreatment of Aboriginal people in Camperdown after locals declined to contribute to his memorial to the Djargurd wurrung.[229] Dawson was not singled out in being queried by Curr, who also criticised Brough Smyth, Howitt and Fison, but his work at least provoked a rethink on meanings of anthropophagy before Curr's loose and derivative claim that, 'Abortion is practised occasionally throughout the continent, and infanticide generally.'[230]

Print reviews of the well-regarded ethnology *Kamileroi and Kurnai* by Fison and Howitt reconsidered infanticide as not merely stemming from 'idle caprice'. One qualified that even 'the fearful practice of infanticide' had been traced to a 'sort of system of social economy', in which many of the customs which were 'so revolting to civilized men and so brutal in their nature' were simply the 'outcome of native necessity.'[231] Such allowances were made for the hardship of traditional living rather than for any imposed by

'If they be facts': infanticide and maternity

contact. As Stephens observes, Howitt had in fact been informed by the Kurnai that instances of infanticide were unknown, though children were on occasion left behind. Stephens argues that Howitt concluded they were being exposed, rather than left behind for other kin to take up.[232] She also notes that an informant of Howitt, Bairuk, was unable to remember any instance of child desertion or infanticide save by that of Bunjil, a mythical figure.[233] The review also fails to resolve the paradox between the evident and extreme fondness for children against the 'expediency' of infanticide due to their 'encumbrance' for nomadic tribes.[234] Given the effect of prolonged breastfeeding on the suppression of ovulation, it is ironic in the extreme that colonialists attributed 'suckling' as a rationale for infanticide, rather than a cause of low birthrate, the very phenomenon they were trying to explain. Curr, for instance, gave 'half-castes' and prolonged breastfeeding as causes for depopulation among the Wongatpan, noting food was 'hard', but not allowing for mothers who could feed more than one child at a time.[235] While Curr could not have known that breastfeeding inhibits ovulation, he may well have been aware of the newfound healthful effects of colostrum and indeed the longstanding use of breastmilk in a range of medicinal salves and treatments.[236] An assumption of high fecundity in Aboriginal maternity is dispelled by Cowlishaw who argued in 1981 that low birthrate could be attributed to the structural tensions in male–female relations and the suppression of ovulation due to nutrition, lactation, introcision and the low ratio of subcutaneous fat.[237]

Print reviews of credited ethnologists continued to compete with vernacular ethnology as observation became a gentlemen's pursuit in the newer reaches of settlement. The contributions of those who fashioned themselves as dauntless frontiersmen pacifying the blacks and protecting settlers from their 'depredations' proffer new data on people they saw as not impacted by their sometimes violent incursions. A review of his 'Aborigines of Central Australia' credits mounted constable W. H. Willshire as 'cultivating close relations with the natives', though he has since become better known for, and at the time was charged with, shooting them. Willshire reports on bride capture and on infanticide as a common crime. He details a 'sable matron' carrying portions of a 'cooked child' and reportedly remarking, 'Only eat him piccanniny when big fellow hungry.'[238] Willshire was notable for being the first policeman to be charged with murder after a series of 'dispersals' with his Native Police Corps on the Daly, Finke and Victoria rivers, including one attack on a sleeping camp and another in which chained, escaping men were shot in the back. Flourishing his pen, Willshire wrote in response to a call from the Royal Australian Geographic Society and produced a number of pamphlets since 'distinguished more for their sexual overtones, boastful sadism and racial triumphalism.'[239] His intimacy with Aboriginal mothers, such that he could quote them on infanticide, may have been more the result of his view that 'perhaps the Almighty meant them for use as He has placed them wherever the pioneers go.'[240]

Willshire's prompt from the Geographic Society was mirrored by the recently formed Royal Society of Queensland which put out a call in 1889, under ten headings, seeking to 'throw light upon the complicated ethnological problems set for solution by our indigenous decaying nomads.' Complicated they were, for *The Brisbane Courier* took pains to add its own notes under the headings, each informed by the recent ethnological publications and evincing a more detailed, nuanced and informed approach to data collection, with questions aimed at Aboriginal territorial limits, assemblies and councils, property held in common and

'If they be facts': infanticide and maternity

individually, and the division of labour. Infanticide was not a heading but it was discussed within *The Courier*'s additional observations, many of them referenced, under a heading on the rights and titles of each sex before and after maturity. The paper repeated long-held beliefs, by now only substantiated by reiteration, that 'half-caste', deformed, illegitimate babies, and those born with an older sibling still in arms were 'put to death', more often when a girl. Infanticide was a 'corollary of polygamy in a life of constant migratory hardship.'[241] This survey enjoined autodidacts in remote regions to report back on a sophisticated line of questioning, so much so that participation may have afforded far more nuanced observation and dispelled supposition. One such contributor in 1899, in a long and detailed essay, written after a lifetime of close association with the people around Sydney, said of infanticide, he 'never saw nor heard of it during the many years I was among them.'[242]

The collocation of infanticide and declining population earned it a place in the Darwinian doctrine of survival of the fittest as it continued to bolster dying race theory in print. Infanticide was thought to be a 'natural check' on overpopulation universally which also had the benefit of eliminating the feeble and deformed who, under civilised nations, were preserved by medicine and then passed on their defects to their young. Under this rubric, infanticide was not particularised to Aborigines, but rather was invoked to illustrate the implications of eugenics as formulated by the eugenicist Francis Galton with his crusade against miscegenation and degeneration of the 'Caucasian races'.[243] These impulses towards population control raised uncomfortable corollaries between savage custom and any civilised program of merciless elimination, one essayist argued in *The Queenslander*, of 'every living element likely to vitiate the corporate organism.'[244]

As we've seen, infanticide itself had by now been subjected to new forms of sustained and detailed fieldwork, and qualified by decades of public concern about the concealment of white illegitimacy and recourse to baby farms. That infanticide might become state sanctioned under the doctrine of survival of the fittest prophesied for this contributor the extreme manifestation of an uncharitable yet civilised doctrine. Already inured to the unsubstantiated claim that half-caste babies were targeted, a growing abhorrence of the half-caste took hold under the rising influence of eugenics. A glance through *Pastoral Pioneers of South Australia,* which uses 'stud' and 'buck' to describe fertile Aboriginal women and men on outback stations, suggests the focus on stock breeding by pastoralists may have played a role in their receptivity to the language of social Darwinism and eugenics.[245]

Social Darwinism increasingly buttressed dying race theory as infanticide continued to explicate observations of dramatic depopulation in print from the 1890s. Drawing now on the writings of Matthew Moorhouse, Edward John Eyre and Francis James Gillen, one report generalised about infanticide not only prevailing, but 'accelerating the work of decadence and death.'[246] Infanticide remained 'the clearest token of the savagery of the native race.'[247] Particularly in the rural press, infanticide was revived as the principal cause of 'dying out' by a range of commentators.[248] Reviews of Spencer and Gillen's seminal *The Native Tribes of Central Australia*, based on fieldwork, noted it was practised only on newborns when the mother was still 'suckling' an older infant, and they added the finding that the spirit was believed to return to the 'particular spot whence it came' to be 'born again at some subsequent time.'[249] By the turn of the twentieth century newsprint had reformatted the trope of infanticide a number of times. It followed the arc of frontier expansion and was

'If they be facts': infanticide and maternity

interestingly most animated in South Australian newspapers. The accusation slewed from Aboriginal to Chinese, Indian and even Polynesian 'custom' as competition for land and various challenges to imperial rule arose.[250] It was revived as Aboriginal 'practice' – against the rising panic around white women concealing illegitimacy – as ethnology absorbed the contributions of amateurs and began to formalise its data collection from the late 1860s, notably in the work of Howitt and Fison, Spencer and Gillen, and Brough Smyth.

One such man of science, an author whose ethnographic publications were respected, was Queensland northern protector Walter Edmund Roth. This awarded and well-reputed administrator remains a credible source and was willing to challenge prevailing views.[251] He published notes from the explorer, surveyor and commissioner of crown lands Robert Austin and reported that 'infanticide was not practised', on twins nor on any other children, and mothers were often seen 'suckling' two or more infants simultaneously while raising three or four children.[252] Though it is hard to gauge his impact, from this intervention onwards Aboriginal infanticide tended to be constrained to generalised histories, where it remained a 'foul blot' which to the 'European eye appears the clearest token of the savagery of the native race.'[253]

Men of science, such as Roth and Howitt,[254] did not agree on the question of infanticide and in print they and their male colleagues competed with an emerging genre of women writing about their reminiscences of growing up with or 'living among the blacks'. Their work had quite distinct inflections of racialised domesticity and maternity. Whereas lay gentlemen observers tended more to catalogue ethnological description, women middlebrow writers such as Mrs Aeneus Gunn, Daisy Bates, Ernestine Hill and Alice Duncan-Kemp, who came to the fore from this point, penned amusing or poignant vignettes in 'sketches of bush life'.[255] Apparently they were less deterred by the panic over white women wrapping their newborns in bloodied rags and dispatching them in drains, logs and under floorboards. Indeed, they seemed more intent on reviving the earlier frontier focus on savage infanticide as part of their nostalgia for the lost tribal camp. A review of Rosa Campbell Praed's *My Australian Girlhood* in 1902 gives a shrill description of parents feasting 'very comfortably on the bodies of their children…for the purpose of gratifying their tastes.'[256] For Praed, as for Hill later, the remoter reach of the Australian outback was a lonely, desolate 'eucalyptic cloister' where hardy stockmen got 'bushed' and died of thirst, and where 'children falling by the wayside are devoured by soldier ants.' Infanticide was another descriptor of the Australian bush gothic. The gruesome primeval bleakness of Aboriginal infanticide was thus pitted against the innocent calamity of the lost white child separated from her isolated mother.

The beginning of the twentieth century saw a revival of this trope as the findings of a royal commission into the declining birthrate in Australia in 1904–05 linked infanticide to women's emancipation, garnering widespread anxiety.[257] While the loss of black children assured the natural order of race destiny, fewer white children was said to 'strike at the welfare of the white race in Australia.'[258] The language altered at this time. If, aside from Taplin, there had been reluctance to detail methods of this key insignia of savagery (in contrast to the recycled language of bride capture), from this point authors were more willing to sensationalise the trope. In 1908 G. Fox wrote in *Science of Man* that it was the 'decree' of husbands if a newborn was to die and the 'poor mother' with 'babe in arms' and 'all her tender feelings wrung', must strike her child's head or strangle it in a secret spot. He also claimed, without any corroboration, that women's breasts were mutilated to hinder them from nursing.[259] This unsubstantiated claim was derived from Curr, who had said that women's nipples were sometimes cut off as a measure for reducing children.[260] Polish anthropologist Krzywicki makes the claim again in 1934,[261] citing Lumholtz who published an account of his fourteen-month stay with people near Herbertvale under the capricious title *Among Cannibals*.[262] Again, the irony of white men failing to understand the suppression of fertility by breastfeeding is striking. By now the more rigorous work of Malinowski had appeared. He does not deny the practice but finds no evidence for the central conjecture, that a distinction was made between male and female children, either in affection or in selection for infanticide.[263] His assertions did not dissuade popular authors, such as W. J. Sollas (*Ancient Hunters and their Modern Representatives*) and N. W. Thomas and T. A. Joyce (*Women of All Nations*), in drawing on Taplin's one-third figure or, in 1904, Howitt's reference to babies being fed to older siblings respectively.[264] Even Strzelecki continued to be cited by a contributor to *Science of Man* in 1908: 'Truer words were never written', he added to the sophistry that after intercourse with white men, Aboriginal women lost the power to procreate with their countrymen.[265] A feedback loop continued between men of science and casual observers who drew upon each others' testimony, sourcing, citing and recycling without the kind of scrupulous rigour that a charge of infanticide should surely demand. It was a loop that fed the self-gratifying impulse to malign the racial Other, and women, together. Thus, the ordinarily assiduous natural scientist William Ramsay Smith lazily referenced infanticide in the Australian encyclopedia entry he co-authored with the esteemed Baldwin Spencer.[266] And even Spencer and Gillen's *The Arunta* mentions infanticide as a means to restrict family size and an explanation for rapid depopulation without going into any detail, referencing or attempt to substantiate the claim.[267] Their authority then fuelled contestation between contributors who cited these unreferenced infanticide findings.[268]

In the middlebrow genre it was Irish-born self-appointed journalist and imperialist Daisy Bates who best exploited the fissure between fieldwork and print, filling it with cannibalism and infanticide as central tropes in her macabre pulp polemics of the camps she lived in at Eucla, Yalata and Ooldea. Bates's crude exposés did more to revive and entrench white belief in customary infanticide motivated by cannibalism than that of any other author, amateur ethnologist or casual observer. Her livelihood, and often the provisions for the people she privately tended, yet publicly vilified, was supplemented and sometimes dependent on the 270 articles she published, including a series encouraged and assisted by journalist Ernestine Hill, 'My natives and I', commissioned and syndicated by *The Advertiser,* which she reworked into her 1938 international bestseller, *The Passing of the Aborigines.* Bates's rich store of cultural recordings, comprising nearly 100 boxes donated to the National Library, is compromised by 'her well-known profligacy with autobiographical truth on the one hand and her claims for producing objective knowledge about Aboriginal people on the other.'[269] For Bates was a bigamist whose origins in Anglo-Irish gentility were self-invention.[270] In a letter published in 1928 in defence of her 'personal integrity' after her claims were questioned, Bates ascribed cannibalism to Aboriginal mothers who professed to her an appetite for baby meat. She claimed her findings were grounded from 'steady, quiet, concentrated, investigations extending over 27 years among the circumcised groups'. Like so many missionaries,

'If they be facts': infanticide and maternity

Bates also claimed that 'cannibalism automatically ceases on their entry into civilized areas',[271] including within the purview of her desert encampments.

Her 1930 article, 'Our cannibals', in *The Sydney Morning Herald* was typical of the 'palimpsest-like quality' of her print contributions.[272] She asserted the central desert Aborigines were 'the most lawless mob of human beings on this earth' who went in for an 'orgy of human meat.' Of a group coming to Peak Hill from Central Australia in 1908, Bates claimed 'every woman in the group had given birth to a baby and eaten it' and so captioned a photograph of herself standing with the group – which does not bear republishing here. Suffice to say Bates appears under a fly veil, buttoned up tightly in the middle of a line-up of Aboriginal women. In another group travelling from beyond the Musgrove and Everard Ranges to Bates's Aoloca camp in 1920,

> there were two pregnant women. One killed and ate her baby a mile west of my camp, sharing the food with the baby's sister – a child of two or three years. I had followed Nyan'-ngua-era's tracks for about 12 miles, but she doubled back on her tracks and before I could find her again the baby had been cooked and eaten. The charred remains of the little skull are now in the Adelaide Museum.[273]

Bates sent bone remains from such cannibalistic 'orgies' to the Adelaide University for investigation. They were found to be 'undoubtedly those of a domestic cat.'[274] Bates wrote 'the outstanding reason put forward by the women themselves, for the prevalence of infanticide, is their liking for the tender meat, and the fact that it is the only full meat meal they can eat without interference from their mankind.'[275] In 1934, Bates gave yet more 'grim revelations' of 'present-day cannibalism' from her camp in Ooldea. She claimed the 'natives' coming along the east–west line from the Central and Western 'reserve' 'stalk each other and kill and eat, annexing the women and children' and said she'd had 'three cases of infant cannibalism.' While claiming her provisions eased the practice, there was 'no hope for those promiscuous hordes' still 'wandering the Plain's edge.'[276]

What is striking about this copy was the explanation given for infanticide, said to have come from the women themselves.[277] When Bates began her forays into print in 1906, her account of infanticide was clearly derivative, sourced probably from Howitt and even Collins.[278] And like Taplin, decades of 'life among the blacks' at her desert camps did not furnish further testimony, for she made the same presentation in 1930 in Melbourne as she had in 1914.[279] The accuracy of her account was challenged by the Sydney Anglican Rector, Phillip Micklem, who queried her motive for her fatalistic and damning portrayal of traditional life as wanting to prove 'a case against communism as a social or political system.'[280] Bates's journalistic works indulged in self-mythologising as a leader and welfare worker among remnant tribes, whose knowledge and artefacts she exploited to provide the revenue she could not always secure from government. Her profound hatred of half-castes, who interrupted her deeply held conviction in dying race theory, and inherently vicious vilifying of Aboriginal mothers as infanticidal cannibals found a ready market in print towards the emergence of tabloid in the interwar period. Editors were keen to have her graphic, lurid copy and went to lengths to credit her as being respected. Indeed, in the 1930 *Advertiser* newspaper, in which Bates recycled the Peak Hill claim that every mother arriving had killed, cooked and eaten her

'If they be facts': infanticide and maternity

baby — her explanation for why there were no children among them — Bates was exalted as the 'best informed authority' on Aborigines following the death of Baldwin Spencer.[281]

Bates was a highly controversial figure among anthropologists, most of whom dismissed her as an amateur and excluded her from the scientific fraternity. She accused Radcliffe-Brown of plagiarising her but corresponded with Howitt and Spencer and Gillen. A number of anthropologists, including Basedow and T. H. Strehlow, cast doubt on her assertions of maternal infanticide and cannibalism.[282] Through her meticulous cultural recording she created an enduring and extensive archive on kinship and linguistics, the value of which, as Ann Standish argues, is largely due to the otherwise dearth of such records.[283] Bates can be positioned within the beginnings of a global indigenous or first nation identity, which revived the classification of aboriginal peoples by their shared 'barbaric practices' including infanticide, exchange of wives and the 'circumcision' of females.[284] Her diehard insistence on 'dying race' was disproven by the increase in Aboriginal population from the 1920s, although she would not have included 'half-castes' in her cohort. She was decried by feminist and Aboriginal rights activist Mary Bennett as 'one of the worst enemies that our poor natives had.'[285]

Bates was, however, championed by the widely read journalist Ernestine Hill, who encouraged her to write and claimed to have ghostwritten *Passing of the Aborigines*. Hill wrote about visiting her friend Bates (whom she declared 'Queen of the Blacks') and together they 'track up on a woman' due to give birth that Bates had suspected of intending to eat her baby. Instead they find a 'proud mother, beyond reproach', whose 'grisly hunger for human meat — "meeri-coonga" — had been staved off for the time.' If this phrase is in fact Pitjantjatjara, it could possibly translate as

229

either 'miri-kungka' (dead-body woman) or 'mi<u>r</u>i-kungka' (skin woman).[286] Hill cackhandedly remarks, 'Even so, I could not help thinking, purely as a journalist, that God and Daisy Bates had robbed me of a thundering front-page story.'[287] Hill is similarly nonchalant when a white father of four Aboriginal children asks for her help with his 'poignant little problem'. The Northern Territory Chief Protector of Aborigines from 1927 to 1938, Dr Cecil E. Cook, was sending a policeman with a pack-horse to remove his children to 'an institution for vocational training in Alice Springs.' The bereft father pleads that the children are happy and well, and that if they are taken, 'the old woman will break her heart.' But the mothers' feelings are immaterial to Hill in this 'vitally interesting ethnological experiment' of submerging the progeny of the black race into the white, effecting their 'complete disappearance' by 'breeding him – or rather her…with the whites to every possible extent.' Indeed, for Cook 'the quickest way… to write the end of the story' is to 'breed him white.' Thus, Hill assures her readers of the 'eradication' and 'elimination' of the half-castes whom, like Bates, she vilifies as 'pitiable', 'menacing', 'human misfits', 'cursed with a dark skin in a white man's country.'[288] Other authors also drew a chilling causal link between infanticide and conditions imposed by contact and, disturbingly, white administration: they claimed mothers preferred to kill their half-caste baby girls rather than 'get sore hearts at losing them later' on their removal.[289]

Between them, Hill and Bates consolidated these recrudescent meanings of Aboriginal maternity: it was blighted by infanticide which was motivated by cannibalism. The emphasis both authors place on documenting as a means to preserve the mythologies of black primitivism and white pioneering is key to their freelance entrepreneurship since, as Meaghan Morris argues, 'writing is

'If they be facts': infanticide and maternity

really the border that separates white from black, life from death, and history from oblivion.'[290] Their work was influential as they both wrote for all the Australian mastheads in the lead-up to the introduction of the new tabloid format in 1942, the year Hill's *Great Australian Loneliness* was published. Hill also had enduring relationships with the tourist magazine *Walkabout* and the Australian Broadcasting Commission.[291] Hill and Bates mark a shift in the moveable feast that was the amateur ethnologist: from explorer and travellers' journals such as Collins, to government administrators and protectors such as Thomas, to missionary cultural recorders such as Taplin, to settler-observers such as Curr, to policemen such as Willshire, to fieldwork anthropologists such as Spencer, to journalists such as Hill. Bates cut a perturbing figure, as she sought scientific authority but had to draw her income from newspaper contributions. She did not report from field trips like her male contemporaries, but was the first to set up camp.[292] Clearly, it was no guarantee of accuracy.

In the interwar period, anthropologists knew their work could play a role in renting the 'tissue of errors' by now piled up underfoot in the print archive, but their own unexamined sources could see them adding to the pile. Krzywicki, in his *Primitive Society and its Vital Statistics*, is exemplary in his dependence at this time on a confusion of interstitial sourcing. He cites Curr to claim that infanticide was 'a very ancient custom' that took place in all parts of the Australian continent. He also cites Brough Smyth, Peggs and Lumholtz to argue that in rare instances, 'child-murder was committed not only from necessity but also for reasons of mere gluttony.' This notion that Aboriginal mothers ate their babies purely out of an appetite for their flesh was recent and appears to have been presaged by Praed before it was really given wing by Bates. He continues, 'The existence of this eating of children is testified to by all too numerous facts.' By now this sort of assertion ought to alert us to hypertrophied leitmotifs in which 'facts' swim to the surface from a moire pattern of sourcing. For instance, Krzywicki cites the itinerant swagman Phil Mowbray, who related that he personally found in the basin of the river Mitchell Aborigines 'roasting and eating their own children.'[293] Mowbray was an outback raconteur and eccentric who contributed stories and snippets to the *Bulletin*'s 'Aboriginalities' page.[294] Krzywicki's was an exhaustive literature survey depending mostly on the questionnaires returned to Curr which, as we've seen, were largely anecdotal observations from stockholders for whom ethnologising could help to shore up their status as gentlemen. But he also drew on Spencer and Gillen, Eyre, Brough Smyth, Basedow, Taplin and Gribble, among others, to detail instances of infanticide. For all that, he wasn't aware, for instance, of explanatory practices such as the cremating of babies, the stabilising of newborns' temperature in stone-warmed earthern hollows nor of mortuary rites involving consumption of specified parts of corpses.

Even so, Krzywicki was circumspect and believed the 'Australian mother' was 'often accused of hardness towards her progeny.' He found these accusations were 'extremely unjust' and arose 'merely from ignorance of Australian custom.' It was also due to 'lack of comprehension' that under the conditions 'natives' lived, 'infanticide was often the only thing possible for the mother if she did not want to sacrifice an older child' and he attributed any infanticide to conditions of extreme privation arising from 'white invasion'. In trying to quantify the average number of children a woman bore Krzywicki wrote, 'we may get a very inexact idea from loose and scanty statements left by first-hand observers.' Nevertheless, he estimated 4.6–5 babies of which 1.8–2.3 might be reared in pre-contact scenarios by women who, on average, became mothers 'at about the age of fourteen.' He calculated forty per cent of children died within their first few months, but then noted that around the same number died before the age of fifteen in some European countries. He then calculated child mortality rates and argued that infanticide removed a certain number of children who would have died a natural death shortly after birth. Krzywicki makes the clear correlation between low birthrate and colonialism, writing that 'Contact with civilization had an unfavourable effect on fertility', yet he stops short of relating this to venereal disease. Indeed, in an echo of Strzelecki, he writes that Aboriginal women's fertility 'when mated to a native would be sometimes exceedingly small and in any case smaller than when in marital relations with a white.'[295] Within this mesh of citation and calculation, perhaps the most glaring methodological flaw is the distinction made between child mortality and infanticide. How could it be made when no one at all actually witnessed a newborn being put to death? In the meantime, high rates of child mortality were beginning to attract attention, notably from women humanitarians.

A new comparison between modern mothers and 'native' mothers emerged in this period of increasing government intervention into birthing and postnatal practice, along with the advocacy of maternal feminists such as Mary Bennett, who denounced the cruelty of child removal, as did Constance Ternent Cooke.[296] In testimony before the Moseley Commission they defended the right to family life, mobilising the support of women's organisations, the Anti-Slavery Society and the Aborigines' Protection League.[297] Bennett drew attention to Aboriginal child mortality in a paper delivered before the British Commonwealth League in London which brought a response from the Western Australian government.[298] She certainly made sensational claims about

Aboriginal maternity but in direct contravention of Bates. She accused police officers of fathering children and then removing them, of wholesale prostitution of Aboriginal women and girls to white men, and of their appalling living conditions due to dislocation and inadequate rations. No rations were provided for children in Western Australia under three years of age. Bennett reported on shocking instances: of a baby dying on a veranda due to insufficient food and of pregnant women unable to access natal care.[299] In view of this, perhaps the most startling aspect of Bates's allegations of infanticide was that she herself tended women and children suffering severe deprivation, but unlike Bennett attributed the lack of children in camps not to child mortality, venereal disease and food shortage, nor to lack of natal care and rations, but to mothers' craving for baby meat.

Whereas the modern mother had recourse to 'birth control literature' or asking the 'milkman to leave an extra supply on the doorstep',[300] it was now asserted that native mothers 'suckled' their children for several years because they had no other means to feed them. Reaction to the expediency of contraception drew equivalences between savage infanticide and modern fertility control, allowing men to express horror at white women's new-found reproductive autonomy. The link is unsurprising given the racial dimensions to the birth control movement that Jane Carey has uncovered through its intertwining with eugenics and origins in Malthusian population theories.[301] In a letter that appeared while Bates's 1930 'Lawless cannibals' article was being reprinted – tellingly, at least seven times – the contributor compares infanticide to birth control, which he decries as so immoral that it cancelled out any basis for the 'civilised' to condemn savage infanticide.[302] Arguably, the trope of Aboriginal mothers' infanticide has always acted as a catalyst for the anxiety provoked by white women's increasing and inherent reproductive autonomy. It was embellished with cannibalism to racialise infanticide as savagely distinct from the desperate recourse of ill-used European women.

For over a century – coinciding with the expansion and reformatting of print media – the trope of infanticide was reissued as a point of reference for settler imaginings of Aboriginal mothers. There was a handful of credible reports, it should be stressed, against fistfuls of actual convictions of white mothers. In an effort to explain away the lack of children in camps it was easier to claim that Aboriginal mothers killed and ate their own babies than admit that white men infected them with syphilis. The contradictions were manifest: that half-caste children were targeted when their numbers were in fact growing on the missions; that firstborns were targeted because subsequent babies were too much a burden to carry, though they were also targeted; that Aborigines were inordinately fond and indulgent of their children – whom they sometimes ate; that mothers docilely did away with the babies they had carried and birthed to meet somehow approved population levels, which were calculated by whom, and how? If we understand infanticide as mothers' universal response to the cruel constraints placed on their maternity and a tragic expression of sovereignty over their bodies, we can sense the anxiety it created in the race/gender complex of settler-colonialism. On the one hand, its invocations furnished a convenient alibi for infertility and child mortality in the contact zones. Infanticide became the orthodox way to usher extinction into public opinion. On the other hand, it left the race destiny of the nation effectively in the hands of Aboriginal mothers, women credited with no active roles in any field, who then had complete and discretionary power over the racial mix that would people the colonies, and later the newly federated nation. As eugenics and the policies of White Australia and assimilation came to dominate racial thought, a deep ambivalence emerged around Aboriginal infanticide. It begat a natural process of racial decay, yet it was conducted by women attributed with an abject deficit of any form of agency – except, that is, as infanticidal mothers. Much as newcomers abhorred the chattel status of Aboriginal women, the idea that they might act autonomously in denying both black and white menfolk their children was a far worse prospect.

European patriarchal familial relations were firmly entrenched in the operations of the political state. Nevertheless, it was Thomas Hobbes who declared the right of dominion over the child inhered in the mother, since men could not claim their progeny with the certainty of women. This natural dominion of maternity was counterintuitive to the imposed laws of nationhood which secured the patrilineal inheritance of property. By the mid-eighteenth century, middle-class women's reproductive capacity overshadowed that of their intellectual or economic production. Civilised English mothers were pitted against savage mothers in an 'interlocking network of hierarchies'.[303] The regulation of women's fertility should have assured rightful lineage in the inheritance of natural wealth. It was for white men, through the rhetorical device of nescience, to assign property and identity, as can be seen in Wolfe's analysis of McLennan's *Primitive Marriage*.[304] Somehow reproduction had to be harnessed to the settler-colonial project without crediting mothers. For instance, in 1867 David Page penned a natural history that delved into the antiquity of 'man'. Having discussed the geological and climatic influences on the degrees of man's civilisation, Page reasons,

'If they be facts': infanticide and maternity

> The relative superiority and inferiority of the varieties of mankind is so obvious, that it need not be further dwelt upon, unless to show that as the White man advances and spreads over the continents of the world one of two things must follow – viz. either the coloured and inferior races will be absorbed into his race and partake of his improvement, or in time be utterly extinguished.[305]

Since this process was an 'invariable method of nature', meaning it was devoid of violence, it positioned Aboriginal maternity as inherently unproductive and Aboriginal mothers as surrogates of race suicide. Page appears to be talking about the large-scale issues of nation-building and race destiny. Actually he is talking about mothering, about a sphere of human activity in which women can reasonably claim primacy. The spectre of the savage mother departed from European conventions in the organisation of care for children and in the duty of raising citizens that would contribute to the national project. Doubtless this is the 'end' Reverend Dove referred to when in 1840, as chaplain of the reserve settlement at Wybalenna on Flinders Island, he claimed that Aboriginal parents' feelings for their children were 'more of the nature of an instinct than a principle' and thereby 'directed to no high or worthy end.'[306]

The leitmotif of infanticide was a means to discursively dispense with Aboriginal maternity in the machinery of race perpetuation. It retrofitted theories of dying race to staggering rates of child mortality. In this print recursion of Aboriginal infanticide, the slew across sources finds its most recent revival, rather predictably, with Pauline Hanson. In 1997 she cited Daisy Bates in federal Parliament, drawing on her 1908 Peak Hill claim that every woman of that group arriving in camp had killed, cooked and eaten her baby.[307] Hanson wanted to 'refute the romantic view of the Aborigines held by the new class' and to assuage prevailing 'guilt' about settlement.[308] She added insult to the injury of former federal Minister for Aboriginal Affairs Peter Howson (1971–72), who had defended decades of child removal as in fact the rescuing of thousands of babies from infanticide. These modern-day echoes should give us pause when relegating this trope to the unrigorous standards of past knowledge production. They remind us that a plethora of sources in furious agreement should engender suspicion more than credit confidence and that entrenched meanings linger unless recursively challenged.

4

FOOTFALL OVER THRESHOLDS: IN AND OUT OF THE SETTLER-COLONIAL DOMICILE

In 1949 *The Herald and Weekly Times* released a pictorial atlas, *Wonderful Australia in Pictures,* that ranged its lens across picturesque landscape, picaresque industry and 'Vanishing Aboriginals'. Under this heading the chapter commences,

> At a lonely, wayside halt on the great Nullabor Plain of Southern Australia it is today possible for the traveller to make, in a stride, the longest journey possible to man. For here, at the ancient 'soak' of Ooldea, on the edge of the desert, modern man may meet his primitive ancestor – across a gap of only a yard or two of space but of thousands of years of anthropological time. Here he may meet face to face the original Australian aboriginal.[1]

It is by now a commonplace in colonial cultural histories that Australia's Aborigines were construed in the settler imagination as 'stone age', 'living fossils' and 'curiosities' displaced by the 'atomic age' (this last epithet came after World War II).[2] Our atlas, one of many picture books fostering tourism, goes on to explain that a 'long trek' after a 'sea passage' had brought Aborigines to this 'Island Continent' and, after being cut off here for millennia, they now afforded the anthropologist a study in 'undiluted antiquity'. Evolutionary succession was a coefficient of the passage of deep time and, as we saw in the last chapter, for some decades the ascendance of social Darwinism provided new ways to racialise the principle of gradation. But racial difference was by then defined not only in terms of taxonomic branches and nested categories, but also through Einstein's space–time continuum,[3] from which Emile Durkheim could then advance the social relativity of time, relating time-keeping and the occupation of space to social organisation.[4] Nevertheless, for all this new-found temporal and spatial heterogeneity, ideas of racial decay, progress and social advancement continued unabated. Indeed, settlers seemed to map them as organising principles over their dwellings and occupancies, demarking their surrounds with every possible sign of their onward and upward putting down of roots.

Actual dispossession was supplanted by the 'mystery' of Aboriginal origin and identity, which, I want to argue, was bound up in racialised traits of comportment. The sense of rightful dominion over this continent was in part decided by a metaphorics of movement. Race traits were differentiated by boundary markers, such as fences and walls, which contained difference within permissible confines. An inordinate interest was thus displaced onto colonial thresholds – doorways, stoops, verandas, gates – those 'contact zones' where exclusions and inclusions were enacted and enforced.[5] The manner in which those thresholds were traversed marked bodies as racially different. Specifically, it was footfall and even footwear – or lack thereof – that drew the gaze of settlers and provided another leitmotif on which to hinge race and gender, particularly as Aboriginal women's labour became indispensable to the remote settler domicile. Images of Aboriginal women's feet assumed a recurring role in what I've elsewhere called the discourse of settler homelands.[6] They became splayed, engorged, disproportionate and 'unshodable', and this nasty, shoddy jibe was reified in print through reiteration.

This chapter, on settler print imaginings of Aboriginal women's domesticity, does not single out a predominant trope and trace its insignia reticulations across the typeset as in chapters 2 and 3. Instead it takes an idiosyncratic, little noticed but recurring visual motif, one that lampooned the comportment of Aboriginal women as they crossed over the thresholds of the settler domicile in inter- and postwar cartoons – the period in which Aboriginal women were being formally and intensively indentured to white homemaking through state protection and welfare boards. It sets the scene for colonial domesticity in the industrial revolution ideology of separate spheres presaged by the agrarian household. It then contextualises this leitmotif of unshodable feet within competing and often conflicting understandings of mobility circulating in print at this time as newcomer women's relation to public thoroughfares, homemaking and remote spatiality itself shifted around within modernity. The chapter detours into the middlebrow genre to gain a sense of how comportment was racialised by tourists and travellers in the outback in the first half of the twentieth century. I'm interested here to trace the progress of racialised, gendered modes of comportment as they came to influence the visual motif of Aboriginal women's feet through mid-twentieth-century Australian print culture. In this chapter 'print culture' will take in cartoons and the middlebrow travel genre in which we can situate the work of Daisy Bates, Ernestine Hill, Alice Duncan-Kemp and a number of the authors with whom we are acquainted, for this threshold imagery predominantly concerned cross-cultural domesticity between Aboriginal and newcomer women.

The settler domicile, particularly the outback homestead, was a site inflected by gender, as interiors and exteriors mapped out the inclusions and exclusions by which white women negotiated their dependency on black women. And as Haskins points out, due to domestic service, Aboriginal women underwent 'new patterns of mobility' from the outback to the coastal suburbs of Australia's urban centres. Their sexual vulnerability and removal from communities for placement in distant white homes rendered them 'human flotsam', in the words of white women activists at the time. On occasion it took them to places they wanted to stay, where they demanded 'liberty' from the service contracts that constrained their movement. The thresholds of the colonial domicile also varied across contact zones.[7] Russell's study of the sealing frontier of the Bass Strait, for instance, uncovered examples of domesticity which 'evidenced accommodation, creolization, and the women's independence.' Careful not to downplay the abduction and sexual abuse endured by many, Russell found that some women 'moved across and between the worlds of the newcomers and their traditional culture. They developed domestic spaces that can be seen as both a place of and a constraint to colonialism.'[8] How the distinct 'races' negotiated the boundaries and thresholds established by settlement became an abiding fascination to settlers. I suggest it was due to the disavowal of domestic intimacies and dependencies that so much interest turned around the figure of the Aboriginal woman on the threshold. The Missus, often standing guard, maintained the corporeal boundaries that sanctified her whiteness by assigning the most menial tasks to her Aboriginal charge. In many of the cartoons we'll see later in the chapter, the white mistress stands as a sentinel figure on the threshold of settler occupancy, guarding against or strictly regulating the terms of Aboriginal women's entrance.

Soon after our atlas was published, the filmmaker couple Elsa and Charles Chauvel were putting the finishing touches on their film *Jedda* (1955) and were approached by the BBC to film a travel series throughout Australia. The Chauvels rolled their swags and went into the outback as tourists – which is to say, they had a home to return to. 'Home' figures prominently in the book account of their outback adventures. Elsa is particularly attentive to the homemaking of Australian white women in these remotest reaches of the continent. At Coober Pedy she marvels at the dugout homes and how each is kept 'spick and span' with the 'fanaticism of a high priestess':

> I found this leaning towards extreme domestic fastidiousness rather typical of outback women, one of whom confided to me that it was her defense against the toughness of her surroundings, and the outcome of her fear that she and her husband (particularly her husband) might be ensnared in, and finally submerged by the rougher elements of their living. 'Men like to "live it easy"', she continued. 'They slip a bit here and there, then finally start walking into supper in their bare feet and forgetting to shave. Then they get to feel like a black fellah, and before you can count to ten, they're going downhill, going native. So a woman must keep herself and her home attractive and never give in to the climate or the environment, for degradation can creep up like a thief in the night. And so the civilized woman's crusade goes on – to keep her man from her greatest rival, the primitive – which fundamentally is his prototype.[9]

This guarding against an encroaching, felt-footed primitivism draws on explicitly gendered tropes of an evolutionary regressive masculinity, while feminising the primitive as a sexual rival who creeps into dugouts and entices hapless, unshod men into the night. The significance of bare feet, as an emblem of the primitive, perfectly describes the anxieties attendant on the footfall of Aboriginal women over thresholds. The white woman must act as shod sentry, vigilantly guarding against myriad transgressions.[10] In Figure 4.1 Elsa and her high priestess are pictured smiling up from the dugout doorway, impressing their wifely attractions and domestic proficiency into the stony entrance with heeled sandals. Put together with the text this is one of those images that conjures the predestine gender strictures and racial exclusions of quotidian imperial domesticity. In what historical frame can we situate this image? What are the socio-economic coordinates that precipitated these two women displaying their station in this manner?

Figure 4.1 'Elsa with her landlady on the Cooper Pedy opal-field', in Charles and Elsa Chauvel, Walkabout, W. H. Allen, London, 1959. Courtesy of the Charles Chauvel Film Trust

Historians have noted the irony of a nation initially based on convict *transportation*, and settled through assisted *passage* (funded, for instance, through the Australian Waste Lands Act of 1842) and *migration*, admonishing the natives for their 'roving propensities'.[11] Victoria Haskins has drawn attention to the centrality of mobility to colonialism, defining it 'as a specific mode of imperialism [that] entailed the movement of people over the course of the nineteenth and twentieth centuries in particular directions and with particular consequences.'[12] Marilyn Lake and Henry Reynolds have shown how 'the perfect liberty of locomotion' was enshrined in international treaties of the nineteenth century as a doctrine of freedom of movement. It was, however, the preserve of Anglo-Saxon working men who tied it to the assertion of their democratic rights, albeit trespassed upon by the mass movement of millions of Chinese and Indians from the 1850s.[13] Opportunities were also afforded to women travellers by rail and steamship.[14] And Indigenous whalers and sealers had long been 'roving mariners', complicating meanings of mobility by race.[15] It was thus within the context of international arguments over free migration and trade that Australian newcomers looked upon the cyclic movement of tribes through horde countries as 'the natural restlessness' of a 'shiftless, aimless life',[16] that was simply 'the disposition of the savage mind'.[17] 'Locomotion', it was observed in 1842, 'seems essential to their very existence'.[18] Just as white men were asserting that rights to untrammelled movement were theirs exclusively, they tracked up on the idea of nomadism almost with the sense that it tread on their immigrant toes. And women nomads were thought to be mere followers of their men, laden with their trappings and trudging behind in obedience.

The nomadism of Australian Aborigines was said to have marooned them in a temporal dead end, their wanderings – unlike the newcomers' – failing to effect any progress through time and paradoxically fixing them in a lost primeval past. They had ceased passage and were now, with the ethnocidal imprimatur we can recall from Daisy Bates's book title, 'passing' – a very different thing it seems to coming or going.[19] Accordingly, our roving pictorial atlas asks how did this most ancient race remain 'in such a primitive state'?

> The answer is probably to be found in the fact that he is, above all, nomadic. Of all the great steps which mankind has taken in his climb to higher standards of life and greater mastery of natural forces, the act of settling down in one place and tilling the soil has not been the least.[20]

And therein lies the foundational paradox with which colonial scholars are by now familiar, the unresolved contradiction that continued to unsettle colonial discourse: the great 'step' of settlement defines historical progress, while nomadism defines not just the stand-still but the backward march of a people. That is, migrants travelling often thousands of kilometres between metropole and periphery accused Aborigines, harvesting, trading, initiating, marrying and burying within defined parameters, of wandering aimlessly.

Transporting tropes was certainly easier than spanning the 'vast distances' of the continent's immensity. Its 'long miles' needed to be overcome and, indeed, a later chapter of the atlas is titled, 'Conquest of vast distances'. It was the far-flung conveyance of scattered raw materials from distant markets that created an impediment to Australia's industries and 'national prosperity'. Further rail track and road were laid, but really it was aviation that provided new prospects for travellers, who had to then disprove that the epithets laid at the feet of the 'wandering savage' did not apply to them. For postwar Australians began to tour extensively on the 'open road'. They were even said to be 'fond of travelling'. One way to sort these categories of mobility into a non-contradictory national pastime was appropriation:

> the traditional 'walkabout' urge of the Aboriginal has to some extent communicated itself to a restless people; and though they are not all cosmopolitans, the variety and vastness of their own land is a lure to their curiosity.[21]

The critical import of the settler appropriation of 'walkabout' becomes clear.[22] Let's allow the atlas to spell it out for us again:

> the true native Australian black simply cannot settle down for long in any one place. He is a wanderer. And though his wanderings, complete with family and tribe, follow a general route or are confined to the same general areas, he is a true nomad none the less. This native desire to 'go walkabout,' as the black describes it, has deprived the aboriginal of the opportunity of gaining a knowledge of house-building, agriculture or other of the fine arts.[23]

Authenticity of the 'native' is here tested against modes of comportment. From this point, the text launches into a description of Aboriginal deficits and 'evidences of arrested development', from superstitions to primitive weaponry – the leitmotifs of the primitive we've seen rehearsed. But as soon as we turn to Aboriginal advancement towards the European criteria for becoming civilised,

Skin Deep

for those who survived the initial 'shock of white contact', we read that, 'The art of horse riding and car driving have been easily mastered.'[24] Yet, there was an impasse for those Aborigines who had 'come into contact' and were adapting white modes of transportation: they were also decried as compromised, sometimes corrupted and 'very poor specimens'. And so, despite the overall push for assimilation, a place of exceptionalism was reserved in the national character for the roaming, vanishing, naked hunter, full-blood, myall type. We remember him still in the iconic personage of One Pound Jimmy (see Figure 4.2).

Figure 4.2 Gwoja Tjungurrayi, 'One Pound Jimmy', Wonderful Australia in Pictures, *Colorgravure, Melbourne, 1949.*

Jimmy, or Gwoja Tjungarrayi, was in fact a survivor of the 1928 Coniston massacre. For all his 'contact', for which he no doubt suffered considerable 'shock', many have noticed he managed to stand up rather well. Ironically, Tjungarrayi's impressive physique could be as much attributed to hunting as to labouring on the Napperby and neighbouring stations, which included sinking boreholes, mining and stock mustering.[25] This iconic photograph of Tjungarrayi was staged in the early 1930s by the tourism executive Charles Holmes and photographed by Roy Dunstan. A crop of Tjungarrayi's face was distributed to 99 million people in the form of a 1950 Commonwealth postage stamp. Holmes was instrumental in opening new tourist routes into Australia's 'Dead Heart' as the manager of the Australian National Travel Association, which published *Walkabout*, and through his other publications.[26] As Jill Barnes argues, representations of the indigenous have 'long been used to promote tourism to remote regions by colonising powers.'[27] Aboriginal women assumed quite distinct and contradictory mantles of comportment within this increasingly criss-crossed terrain – as burdened and downtrodden, yet also as the bearers of regal grace. The 'dignified carriage' so striking in Aboriginal men (recalling Manly was so named after the 'confident' men at Sydney Cove) inspired newcomers to call them 'Lords of the Soil' in countless print invocations. Aboriginal men were said to be 'tall, graceful, and muscular...lithe and active even in old age' and white men, perhaps not always quite so active and 'deep-chested', were 'forced to admire the graceful walk and dignified carriage of the aboriginal'.[28] The noble savage type persisted into post-settlement notions of Aboriginal authenticity and aims of preservation, but in the twentieth century it was moved into the interior and north as the tribal myall type. As the opening quote suggests, the Australian tourist was keen to encounter this apparition by the roadside and perhaps imagine that they, too, expanded into the surrounding vastness with a newfound noble bearing. The splitting of colonial logic, its underpinning contradiction between mobile settlers and stagnant nomads, invested notions of comportment and modes of propelling the racialised body through space into an organising principle of colonial discourse. This 1921 advertisement from *The Bulletin* of non-skid Boomerang tyres (Figure 4.3) stages the appropriation of Aboriginal dominion and mobility through white technological

Figure 4.3 Barnet Glass advertisement, The Bulletin, *15 September 1921. Courtesy State Library of Victoria. Newspaper collection, NMR_ – Sydney – 0 1883–1984*

mastery of space. Significantly, it is the woman on the ground attempting to gather up the clay tread, this remnant imprint of an insignia of modern propulsion through space purportedly shared between white and black men.

It has often been noted that the reign of empire was critically enforced through the organisation of domesticity to secure the overthrow of traditional economies by land-owning capitalism, creating a 'home rule' dimension to settler-colonialism.[29] As McClintock has argued, 'colonialism took shape around the Victorian invention of domesticity and the idea of the home.'[30] A paradigm of separate spheres was by now ingrained through industrialisation, urbanisation and the introduction of large-scale wage labour, which historically coincided with colonial settlement.[31] The socio-economic upheavals of British colonialism also warped contradictions within its lived spaces as well as ambivalence about settlers' sense of place. Ann Laura Stoler has written on Dutch-Indonesian colonialism and intimacy, and has explored this highly productive tension, 'between a culture of whiteness that cordoned itself off from the native world and a set of domestic arrangements and class distinctions among Europeans that produced cultural proximities, intimacies, and sympathies that transgressed them.'[32] Arguably, because of its dependence on Indigenous women's domestic labour, the contact zones of colonial occupation everywhere comprised a home front within the walls of permanent residence.

Since Britons at the time of first settlement were flush with the success of the agrarian revolution (or at least those beneficiaries of the Enclosure Acts were), the perceived scavenging for food and subsisting by the New Holland native discounted a number of key ideas emanating from Enlightenment Europe. The utilitarians, for example, believed in the deferment of gratification, thereby casting nomadism as a moral failing that obstructed the evolutionary fiscal progression from 'hunter to shepherd to farmer to merchant'.[33] Thus, in 1843 a newspaper editorial could opine, 'The grand and radical evil in the present conditions of the Aborigines…is their roving vagabondage.'[34] Another chided in 1853, 'They live in detached groups, subsisting by the chase, having no practice in building, or domesticating animals, or cultivating the ground.'[35] This visible neglect of domicile was to be clearly distinguished from the aspirational departures of immigrating white men. European domestic space, at the time of incursion into Australia, was also being increasingly cleaved by gender, through the beginnings of industrialism and the shift of the workplace away from the household economy.[36] The eighteenth-century cult of motherhood encouraged middle-class Englishwomen, 'formerly producers of things as well as of life…to limit themselves in the newly emergent money economy to producing life.'[37] While increasingly working outside the home, men yet maintained ownership of the domestic layout: the armchair, table, hearth and bed being the hub of domestic space, around which the tending and servility of women revolved. Land and occupancy were thus deeply gendered placements: contact with new worlds exacerbated the association of women with nature by identifying native women with the raw materials of colonies in which they supposedly voluntarily exchanged their labour to receive the benefits of white civilisation.[38]

The socio-economic transformation of wasteland into productive estate was deemed to be for the greater good and it required that land be marked as property through stocking and fencing. The material culture of Aborigines struck Europeans as a primitive form of communalism, devoid of property, unmarked by

'Goodbye Mother', Thomas Cleary (1854–1899) 1896. Photograph: albumen silver; 22 x 26 cm. Acc. no: H96.160/468, State Library of Victoria

Fem'me de la Terre de Diemen', Nicolas-Martin Petit, 1802,
Water colour and ink portrait, painted at South Cape,
Museum d'Histoire Naturelle, Le Havre.

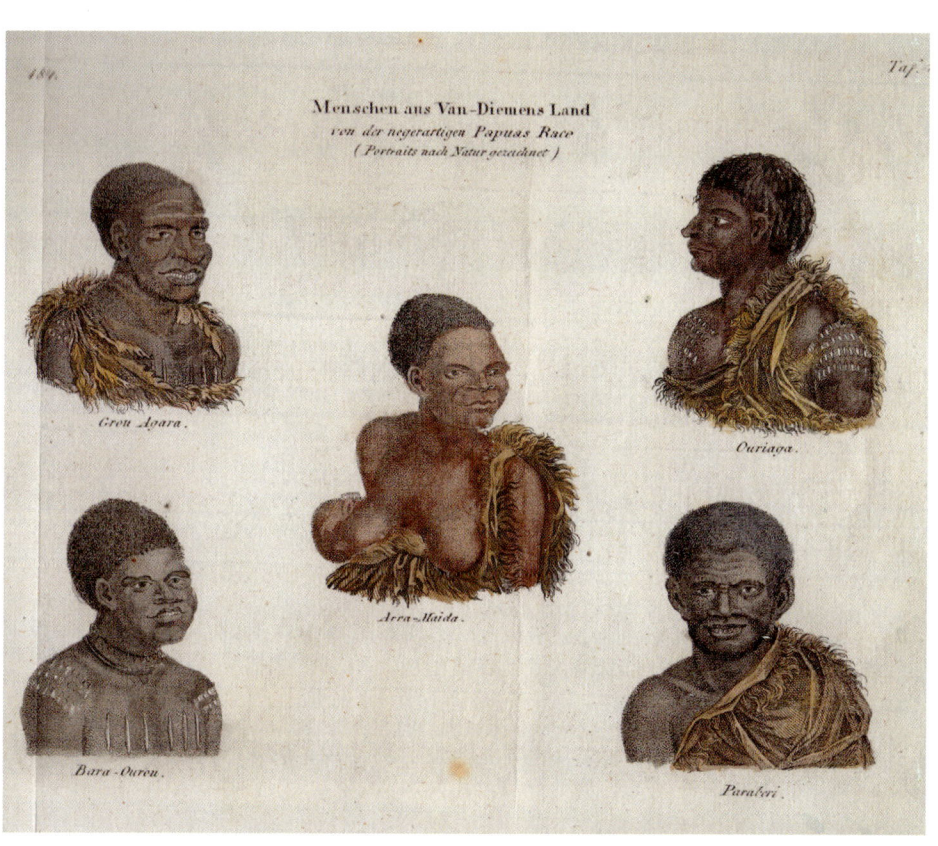

Menschen aus Van Diemens Land'.
Original stipple engraving (with later hand-colour)

'Courtship', George Barrington, *The History of New South Wales: including Botany Bay*, London, M. Jones, 1810.
Courtesy National Library of Australia FRM F485A.

Automobile Richard Brasier 1904 Paris Poster.

Hand painted wall plaque, made in Western Australia.
Courtesy of the Queensland Museum, Glenn Cooke Collection E20733.

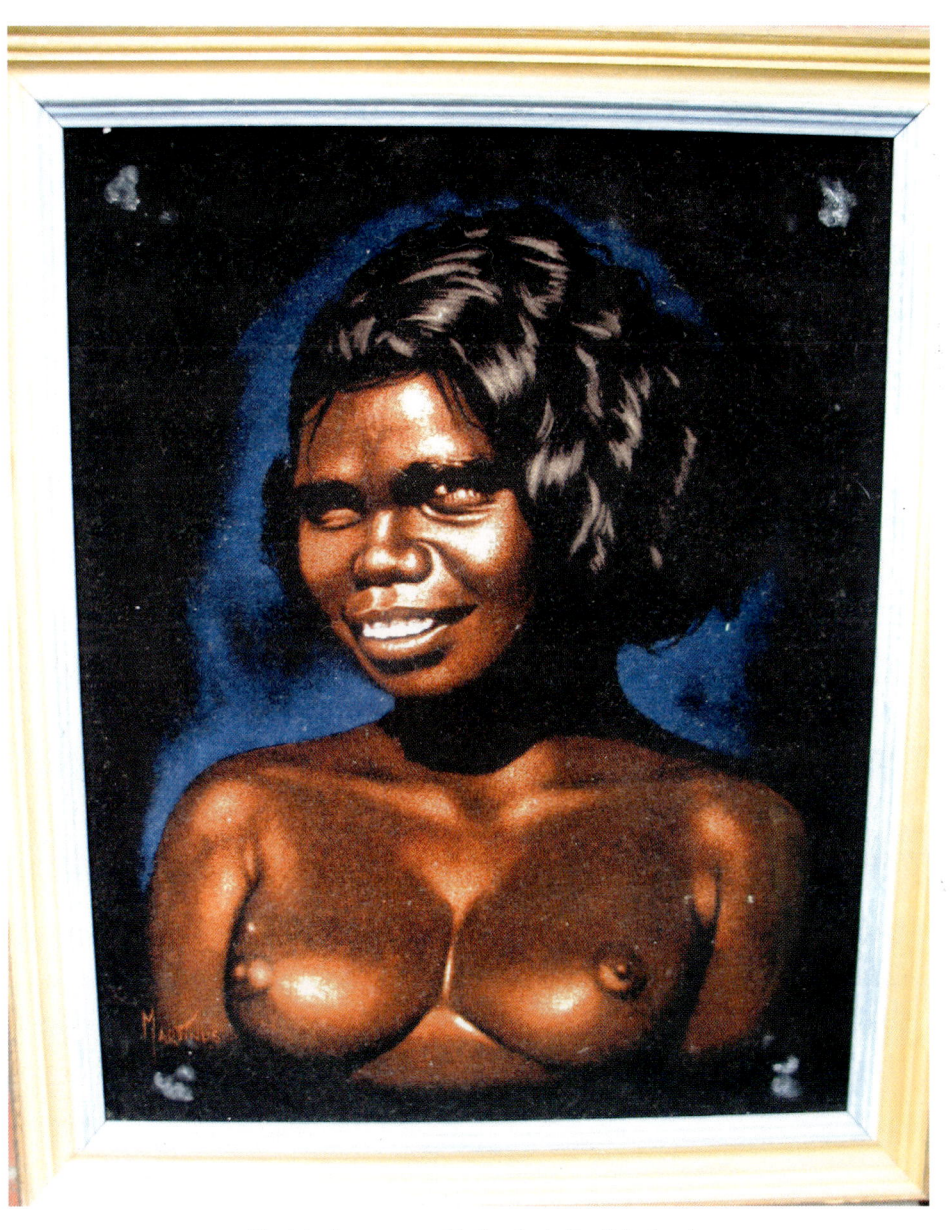

*Aboriginal woman on black velvet. By 'Martinos'.
Hanging in the Union Hotel, Gore St Fitzroy.*

Ceramic ashtray. Private collection of Colin Chestnut

enclosure. In 1858, the South Australian government had erected a row of pisé huts on North Park Lands for the Kaurna, who nevertheless remained in their 'spontaneous pervious mansions of gum-branches and sheoak.' The Kaurna used the building instead as a windbreak for 'their customary umbrageous dormitories.'[39] Colonials approved the Lockean supposition that agriculture supported larger populations: it was a more efficient use of land. Aborigines were thought to make a disproportionate and excessive spatial claim and this casuistry was still in play in 1924, when British geologist and anthropologist W. J. Sollas admonished the 'extravagant demands made by a hunting life on the land', claiming that in fertile districts more than 100 square miles was required 'to support 300 people.'[40] By 1930 this purportedly inefficient use of resources by the original inhabitants had nevertheless produced ideal conditions for occupation. The encyclopedia *People of All Nations* claimed,

> Nature [thus] seemed to be working, as though consciously, for the making of a place uniquely fitted for peopling by a white race, while at the same time ensuring that its aboriginal inhabitants should not be able to profit by its resources, and thus raise themselves to a degree of social organization which would allow them to resist invasion.[41]

Given that the intensive domiciliation of this land was in fact largely by cattle and sheep, it remains an open question how long it might have been before these bovine and bovid tenants raised themselves to a degree of social organisation sufficient to pose a threat to the white occupants. And given that the often poorly watered land of Australia required large tracts of pasture to sustain this stock, settlers' descriptions of Aborigines grazing across expanses of country[42] ought to have resonated with pastoralists. There was little 'ecological humility',[43] as John Gascoigne puts it, to be found in settler-colonialism even though in many instances of early settlement, colonists and their families survived only because of Aboriginal knowledge of resources, particularly the location of waterholes.[44]

Despite this dependence, under settler-colonialism's imperative to eradicate Indigenous proprietorial presence, 'natives' were 'in the way' simply by staying at home.[45] They were accordingly shunted out of the way onto missions and settlements under protection-era segregation. This shifted under the national policy formalised as 'assimilation' in 1937. The demand that Aboriginal women display European standards of domestic competency – stage-managed through state removal concentrated on 'half-caste' girls for their training in institutions and white homes – intensified through to the era of 'self-determination' which commenced in 1972.[46] These dramatic policy swings meant that Aboriginal women's homemaking was impacted by myriad contingencies. It was realised and resisted within the local variants of pastoral, mining, sealing and pearling industries, as well as within the very different approaches of missionary and government settlements, and not least the changing ideals of the home in Australia and the British metropole. Traditional Aboriginal homemaking was imperceptible to the majority of newcomers; when assimilated, it was overseen as an indice of civilisation by state administrators.

The rich, flourishing, separate life of Aboriginal women was never revealed to settler men, nor to women anthropologists who had not accrued authority as mothers.[47] A blind spot in colonial perceptions of Indigenous gender relations was critically influenced by the inability of European observers to discern the separate but interdependent economies of Aboriginal men and women. The scheduled harvesting and generation of foodstuffs were particularly invisible to colonial men, largely because it was labour performed by women. Where women's labour was noted, it was used to explain the low status accorded to agriculture by Aborigines. Thus Archbishop Polding was able to advise the Select Committee on the Condition of the Aborigines in New South Wales in 1845, 'They have very low ideas of obtaining food from the earth, inasmuch as they only employ their women for that purpose.'[48] Aboriginal women living traditionally were literally hard to place within the colonial schema of homemaking;[49] their labours were hardly sedentary as they moved beyond the home into diverse, seemingly unscheduled activities, and yet also into a realm separate from men's hunting. Ominously, their work of childrearing, health care, religious responsibilities, harvesting and regeneration were quite obstructively within the workspaces of white male pastoralists, shepherds, farmers and miners, who looked upon Aboriginal women's work and agricultural capacities with incomprehension. This separate economy appeared to them as a form of exclusion assigned to women due to the low status accorded to them by men.[50] In 1915 the Reverend John Flynn accounted for Aboriginal women's place in and out of camp as gender segregation, but notice how he stumbles through his schema of home: 'A black woman never shares her husband's table, she merely takes the crumbs that fall – no, our figure breaks down for crumbs never fall from the blackfellow's table, they can't – she gets what he can't eat single-mouthed.'[51] Without a table at which a man sits and on which a woman waits, the newcomer becomes disoriented, and little sense can be made of the camp scene except as a site of women's supplication. This unsettling black camp encapsulates Bhabha's argument of 'the estranging sense of the relocation of the home and the world – the unhomeliness – that is the condition of extra-territorial and cross-cultural initiations'.[52] Part of the disorientation pivoted around this blind spot over women's contribution.

It was not until women anthropologists undertook fieldwork in communities that any recognition came of Aboriginal women's status as landowners and breadwinners or of the gendered organisation of the Indigenous economy.[53] We saw in Chapter 2 how anthropologist Phyllis Kaberry rejected the view expounded by male anthropologists such as Malinowski that 'the relation of a husband to wife is in its economic aspect, that of a master to its slave.'[54] She noted women's workday compared favourably to the eight-hour day. It was Kaberry who dubbed Aboriginal women 'wielders of the digging-stick' and who recognised that because of their labour, their distinct skills and specialised economic contribution they were highly valued as wives and elders. Newcomers were unable to perceive, due to their own myopia and sometimes because it was actively kept from them, the autonomy and authority women enjoyed within homosocial patterns of relating. Significantly, it was their perfect liberty of locomotion that enabled Kaberry's refutation of Aboriginal women as downtrodden.

Ironically, the autonomy Aboriginal women had always experienced within their expansive spatial homemaking was lost even on some feminist anthropologists and much debated. As we saw in Chapter 2, like Diane Barwick, anthropologist Catherine Berndt argued that the movement of women into European missions, pastoral and government stations at this time, 'allowed and encouraged new economic and religious roles for women, and invited their political participation.' But, unlike Barwick, Berndt did not construe this as a 'new emancipation'[55] because she refuted that traditional family and economic structure was patriarchal, specifically because women did not economically depend on men. Berndt attributed the 'chattel and slave' view of Aboriginal women's status to a projection of male observers, reflecting more on their own gender relations. Berndt saw their position as 'enviable', since

> they were normally in a position to fend for themselves and for their young children. Although their main area of authority was the domestic field, they were not confined to the kitchen. Their place was not only by the camp fire, but in the wider economic world in which they moved more or less independently – independently of their menfolk.[56]

Berndt notes that at the time of her writing, white Australian women were seeking equal pay for equal work and greater presence in public life to counter discrimination. And yet she pointedly notes an incommensurability in ideas of equality, one that sharply rebuked the very premise of not only liberal feminism, but also assimilation – 'how to measure equality, except on the basis of similarity? – a question which, insofar as Aborigines asked it, they answered differently.'[57] She compared the vulnerability of white deserted wives and widows with Aboriginal women, whose labour was valued and made them economically self-sufficient. But although independence was entirely lost on some observers, they saw it as embodied in other aspects of Aboriginal womanhood. For some women the comportment of Aboriginal women assumed a certain descriptive value for the freedom of movement they coveted.

Visual access to Aboriginal women's unclothed bodies and their unrestrained movement in early print invocations had forged a discernible trope in colonial discourse of the lithe, supple gait of Aboriginal women, which we can trace through to the first half of the twentieth century. Aboriginal women were inexplicitly exotic when still at home outdoors. William Henry Suttor, a member of parliament, recalls in 1877 meeting Maria, alias 'The Soldier' or 'Jacky's mother', when she rescued a young man from his upset canoe:

> She had her masculine nickname from her majestic walk, and tall upright figure. A Roman empress, full of pride of royal beauty and of imperial power, could not have moved with a more graceful and dignified freedom. She dropped her opossum's fur cloak – her garment – from her shoulders, and posing on the bank for a moment, a splendid, nude, and breathing bronze.[58]

Maria retrieves the boy and replaces her cloak, laughing and gasping as she wrings her hair. It is through Suttor's account that Maria's unwitting beauty is salvaged from the ruin of the tribal,[59] for he later saw her diseased and dying, breastfeeding an ailing sister. Suttor initially admires the stock qualities of the feminine counterpart to the noble savage type, the native belle – her untutored dignity, grace and beauty – and he distances his desire with artistic objectivity by bronzing her nudity, cloaking it in classical conventions. No doubt Suttor was unaccustomed to seeing naked women outdoors and with such active engagement in, even life-saving command of, their surrounds. Though, like the admiration for Aboriginal men's agile physiques and manly bearing, it was split with ambivalence, for this comportment would later come to characterise women's perceived degree of assimilation to domestic labour within white homemaking.

Often the Aboriginal woman's comportment appeared within an ethnological inventory of physical traits, confused with a blazon of features that ranged over the 'coarse' hair, 'prognathous' head, 'deep set' eyes, 'dilated' nostrils and 'thick' lips, as in this 1894 description by a surgeon on a survey ship in northwest Australia.[60] He was, like many others, struck by the seeming contradiction that their legs had 'practically no calf muscles', yet they walked 'great distances; their carriage, especially among the young women, or "lubras," being graceful and pleasing, as springy and upright as possible.' The ease of comportment of the native belle was no doubt especially fascinating as white women, particularly of the middle class, were at this time challenging the constraints on their movement, striking out over the private threshold into public space. Within two decades a critical mass of shopping, working and leisure-seeking white women, such as the business girl and outdoor girl, would take to the streets, yet their movements were characterised quite differently to Aboriginal women's comportment. In 1924, for instance, Mr C. Price Conigrave noted in a public lecture that 'some of the ladies of Perth, elevated on stilt-like heels, did not compare favourably, so far as grace and deportment was concerned with the lubras of the North, who walked gracefully and correctly, as the creator intended them to walk.'[61] The modern girl was tied to her mobility as a corollary of her whiteness. How they traversed urban space was of considerable interest to commentators, columnists, moral hygienists, legislators, doctors, cartoonists, filmmakers, advertisers and cultural producers of all persuasions of the interwar period. I briefly track this detour to set the wider scene for perceptions of Aboriginal women's footfall.

Figure 4.4 Automobiles Richard-Brasier 1904 Paris Poster. Author's collection

Speed itself had been signified by the feminine, as were many of the innovations of modernity, such as electricity. Borrowing from earlier uses of the feminine to signify such intangible imperial ideals as victory and nation, the feminine body figured the illusion of speed in advertising of the interwar period (see Figure 4.4). As I've argued elsewhere, the productiveness of the city depended on the orderly movement of crowds through its thoroughfares and the increasing presence of women in city traffic caused the disruptions of proximity, sexual attraction and consumer distraction.[62] Women 'held up the traffic', obstructing the footpath by being unable to look away from the diversions of shop window displays, advertising and commodity products. City types rerouted the seat of masculine urban productivity, providing much material for cartoonists who portrayed men as bewildered and disoriented. In this fast-moving realm of motorised mobility, trams, ferries, cars and even aeroplanes facilitated an exchange of looks that was bereft of the traditional virtues of contemplation and therefore thought to be promiscuous. City variations of the modern girl, including the flapper as well as the business girl and outdoor girl, cast the 'glad eye' from these proliferating vantages, exchanging anonymous, soliciting glances. They 'caught' the eye of passing men and 'picked' them up, installing themselves in their motorcars for joy rides. The spatial transgressions of modern girl types were overlayed onto sexual transgression as the enthusiasm with which they stepped over the domestic threshold into public urban space caused considerable consternation among print commentators.

Ambivalence over the modern girl's newfound freedom of movement carried over to Aboriginal women's comportment in their assigned roles as sashaying native belle and as feltfooted house lubra. Newcomer observers situated their freedom of movement in romanticised visions. Prolific nature writer Charles Barrett wrote in his circa 1936 illustrated booklet *Blackfellows of Australia*, 'The walk of the women in particular, and of all aborigines, is stately and graceful.'[63] An observer in 1934 wrote 'the most graceful walkers I have ever seen were native women (gins, or lubras, as they are customarily named), in Central Australia, where still some untamed tribes may be met with.'[64] When they were successfully assimilated to servicing white domesticity, women could bring this comportment to new roles in service. A 1934 essay on the beauty of the McDonnell Ranges described two Aboriginal women shepherding goats as 'walking with the ease and grace of carriage for which these people are famous.'[65] In 1953 a travelogue by hitchhiker Coralie Rees called *Spinifex Walkabout* describes a visit to Hermannsburg: 'As the donkey-wagon moved off into Missionary Plain the black milkmaids came in from milking the small dairy herd. They walked in procession barefoot across the sand, carrying billies. They made a pattern of simple dignity, like a frieze on a vase.'[66] So romanticised was this native comportment and the sense of dominion it carried, it appeared on biscuit tins,

Figure 4.5 Hand-painted wall plaque, made in Western Australia. Courtesy of the Queensland Museum, Glenn Cooke Collection E20733

in garden ornaments and on many vases and wall plaques such as the one in Figure 4.5.[67] Similarly, Alan Marshall's 1948 travelogue to the Torres Strait describes his visit to the Aurukun mission. 'Slender girls, beautifully erect walked by' carrying pineapples, water, bananas or kindling balanced unsupported on their heads: 'Their carriage, the dignity and grace of their slow stride, excited me, as if I were witnessing some rare work of art.' He notes, as had many newcomer observers before him, the 'thin legs of the natives', often described as a 'deficiency of limb'. But to Marshall they came to assume a 'beauty of their own', in harmony with the slender trees, moving here 'tirelessly and gracefully'.[68]

Many observers, such as Barrett, were doubtful about the imposition of European clothing, robbing Aborigines of their unrestrained grace and, unstated, observers' visual access. He notes elsewhere, 'Aborigines, the women especially, walk in a stately manner; they possess a natural dignity, camouflaged when they wear European clothes.'[69] It was a common lament that Aboriginal women, contrary to European women, lost dignity once clothed. Recalling A. M. Duncan-Kemp and her appositely named *Where Strange Paths Go Down,* she describes the way a 'gin crept up' with a parcel of fish, handed it over and 'glided off, firestick aloft towards the camp, her naked body seamed with tribal cicatrices gleaming mahogany brown where the torch light shone upon it.' Kemp then refers to the clothing 'ensemble' of a shepherd gin, which included glistening mourning kopi, faded green overalls missing their buttons, and a 'pair of outsize elastic-sided boots, above which her thin legs looked more than ever like a couple of broomsticks.'[70] Across these textual snippets a sense of grace and poise is attributed to traditional young women's movements, while older women, especially if they were station-based, appeared in the much derided outsize elastic-sided boots, clumsily shod.

When women in service transitioned from 'wretched humpies' into clean smocks to pass over the threshold of white homemaking, white women found refuge from the potential boundary confusion by turning Aboriginal domestics into entertaining spectacle. Kemp typecast them as 'house gins' who 'went about their work bright-eyed and chattering like a lot of playful monkeys'.[71] Perhaps the most iconic 'good fella missus' in Australian national folklore was Mrs Aeneas (Jeannie) Gunn, who became mistress at the remote Elsey cattle station in 'never-never' Northern Territory in 1902. As Margaret Macquire has written, the legend of the good fella missus (in fact a type) took her cue from the imperial mother, Queen Victoria, conferring maternal authority within her domesticated domain and implementing the spatial distinctions by which white feminine identity could remain unsullied and sanctified.[72] Gunn reported, 'The lubra's methods of housekeeping were novel in the extreme'; they were 'apt, and merry and openhearted, and wayward beyond comprehension.'[73] Gunn divulges her role as overseer, supervisor, soap dispenser and idler in the shade,

> When washing is done by black lubras, the fun is always fast and furious...Directly after breakfast, which was usually after sunrise, there was a wild scramble among the bundles of soiled clothes, followed by a go-as-you-please race to the billabong, or water hole. Each lubra, as she ran, looked like a big snowball with twinkling black legs; while, perched on top of two or three of the snowballs, sat little shiny-black piccaninnies.[74]

This lively vignette of docile, childlike washer-women is intended to amuse, but it also marks out the precincts of race around the homestead through their distinct footfall. Gunn issues orders seated in the shade. Aboriginal women scampered and scrambled under their load through the bush and splashed about in the waterhole, none of which seems much like work. In a *Walkabout* feature on the vast NT station Victoria River Downs, having provided an inventory of outstations, outcamps and paddocks, the author describes the homestead as ensconced in a tropical island of shaded garden, tended tennis courts and vegetable fields through the mistress's command of 'toiling black labour', and her 'personal fight to subdue the wilderness to civilized man.' This 'native labour had to be broken in – everyone individually' by Mrs Martin, who had acquired the necessary 'severity', 'authoritative speech' and 'commanding manner' by homeschooling her six children. Here the 'walkabout' was the 'age-old custom' of the

"Life in and around the homestead is ruled by Mrs. Martin, the First Lady of Victoria River Downs."

Figure 4.6 'Cattle Kingdom', Walkabout, March 1942. Courtesy National Library of Australia, Rex Nan Kivell Collection; NQ 919.4 WAL

'blackfellow' and the 'nightmare of every station manager'. As such, this image (Figure 4.6) of women in their Mother Hubbard print frocks and one man thronging the back steps of the homestead imparts the domestic order imposed on tribal 'unruliness'.[75] In her collaborative oral history of the area Deborah Bird Rose describes the Victoria River frontier as a 'death-scape', particularly during the posting of the murderous Willshire, whom we met in Chapter 3. Bird Rose writes that death 'still bore heavily'[76] on the Aborigines in the 1940s, and the extreme brutality that had marred frontier relations in the region was likely carried in the memory of the people standing unpaid on this threshold, no doubt informing their comportment.

So essential were Aboriginal women's domestic services that Chief Protector of Queensland J. W. Bleakley justified locking women servicing Darwin's homes in the compound at night as 'made necessary by the fact that, owing to climatic and other conditions, life in Darwin for many of the white families would be almost impossible without some cheap domestic labour, and the aboriginal is the only suitable labour of the kind procurable.'[77] Darwin Aborigines lived under a curfew, ostensibly for their 'protection' from men from the meatworks and 'aliens' (Southeast Asian workers, to whom we will turn in Chapter 5). Women who were scrubbing floors and waiting on tables, and upholding all the mores of white bourgeois femininity, then returned to their camps where accommodation, water supplies and sanitation were rarely supplied. Neither was adequate medical attention, contributing

Figure 4.7 'Coloured Characters' in Walkabout, *vol. 11, no. 8, 1 June 1945. Courtesy National Library of Australia. NQ 919.4WAL*

to high rates of disease and infant mortality.[78] Housing provision was inscribed with evolutionary gradation, so that the Minister for Territories, Paul Hasluck, writing in 1957 of the 'houseless nomad', advised that the 'first step' to house Aborigines must be gradual. By resorting to the doors, or boundary markers so elemental to settler sociality, for firewood, and 'quite casually, tear[ing] off doors', Aborigines showed that they needed to be 'assisted to follow a slow evolutionary path' in making the 'leap from his primitive wurlie into a modern house.'[79] Despite the oxymoron of slow leaping, this language of comportment over thresholds was extensively deployed under the policy of assimilation. Indeed, Aboriginal women were often portrayed as maintaining those thresholds – under their missus's supervision. In Figure 4.7, the young woman sweeping is used to illustrate a series of homestead vignettes by novelist Henrietta Drake-Brockman which included an occasion when she reprimanded a 'house native' after he called upon his wife to pick up paper on a shell path rather than obey the 'Missi' himself. Drake-Brockman put on her 'best army manner' from the veranda, roused by her 'Rights-of-Women prejudices' at this 'lazy fellow's' misuse of his wife's labour.[80]

In the 'pioneering' experience of the far-flung homestead, white women were a long way from their own homes, very often arriving as new brides to established pastoral stations which were demonstrably the home of the Aboriginal women. This peculiar 1885 engraving (Figure 4.8) intended to convey the 'surprise and possible disgust of the new chum lady at the unceremonious entrance of the daughter perhaps of a king amongst his own people.'[81] The 'ladies' were just 'settling down' on the station and putting the house in order when they were paid a visit by an 'ebony princess'. The explanatory text describes the newcomer as a 'city exquisite' who will, in time, like her bemused but

Figure 4.8 'Christmas Day in the Far North – A Royal Visitor', Supplement to the Illustrated Australian News, *19 December 1885. Courtesy National Library of Australia, Rex Nan Kivell Collection; NK3822*

more accustomed companions, learn to greet native nobility at her door with 'kindlier feeling'. This curious image shows that men – artists and editors – were interested in the phenomenon of women meeting over ambiguous thresholds. It was a rare nod to the dominion over country represented by Aboriginal women on stations and the confused status of the newly arrived station mistress, trying to set up home in territory over which they had no claim to.

The more likely scenario was that the station mistress was entirely dependent on the labour of such women, creating an awkwardness around who was more at home in which spaces. Duncan-Kemp later describes the 'blacks' as the 'saviours of the lonely bush where lie the scattered homes of white women with young children'.[82] White women would have 'found this life well-nigh unbearable had it not been for the gins who did the roughest of the housework'.[83] The pastoral industry and 'outback economy' were said to be 'absolutely dependent' on the domestic and field labour of 'the blacks'. In a rare acknowledgement, Bleakley looked back from the vantage of 1928 and said that without 'the lubra' it would have been impossible for the white man to have carried on, especially where 'conditions were practically impossible for a white woman, and even where, as in the towns or in places in touch with civilization, the white woman has braved the climate and other discomforts, the lubra has been indispensable to make life possible for her.'[84] Bleakley's acknowledgement came at the price of preserving white woman's delicacy, while the 'camp lubra' could be extolled as the 'mainstay' of the NT frontier because of her rough hands and endurance. Ann McGrath has detailed the activities incumbent on being a mainstay in the NT and they went far beyond our present-day imaginings of roughest housework. They included mustering cattle, accompanying camel teams, working as shepherds, road and fence building, and ochre mining. In addition, this work was performed 'usually in conjunction with sexual services.'[85]

White women were seen to be out of place in the outback. Angela Woollacott finds a pervasive assumption 'that for women the city was a more congenial place than rural or frontier society.'[86] And, indeed, Hill wrote of white women living on the rim of the 'sinister country' of Arnhem Land, and that 'it is scarcely within the bounds of credibility that white women could exist for one year, much less ten, under even the friendliest conditions, in such an environment.'[87] White women's absence was noted and seen as symptomatic of a nation somehow out of keeping with itself. Elsa Chauvel remarked of Abmimga station, near Finke in the Northern Territory, 'there seems to be something biologically wrong about a place like this fettlers' camp – set in a wilderness, with not a single woman in one hundred miles, unless she is black.'[88] Hill decries the dearth of white women in the north, citing statistics of less than 1,500 white women in the territory, 'one to every 360 square miles.' The white woman, as McGrath wryly notes, was a 'rarer commodity'.[89]

Once installed, white women were thought to have a startling effect on the outback; they domesticated the frontier and made a home by putting things in place, creating a boundary between the frontier and the settled, the blacks' camp and the white homestead. Hill proselytises:

> Wherever there is a white woman on a station – and sadly few there are – that station is a pleasant and prosperous one, and her influence is deep and illimitable. The blacks are clean, the homestead is clean and pretty, the stockmen are cheery – they have a home to come to, someone to listen to their troubles, and see that they change their shirts, and write to their mothers, and jest with them, and keep them human.[90]

In this 1940s image (Figure 4.9) from another pictorial atlas,[91] the presence of black women is acknowledged as an afterthought, a footnote. Lack of footwear grounds them to the earthen floor their mistress's feet are elevated above. The distinctions of womanliness are made through which parts of which bodies are in contact with what surfaces or have jurisdiction over traversing which thresholds. As McClintock says, 'Housework is a semiotics of boundary maintenance.'[92] At Kenmore Park Homestead, Musgrove Range,

> Lois paid her girls a small wage and kept them in dresses. Each morning they came to the house, washed and put on clean house smocks. She never allowed them

Figure 4.9 From The Australian Countryside in Pictures, *Herald Gravure, Melbourne, 1953.*

to handle the food – very few white women do – but they washed up, made the beds, swept the floors and did the washing and scrubbing, all with lots of gossip and shrieks of laughter. Then they went off back to their humpies along the creek.[93]

These homebody white missuses articulated racial distinctions through the demands of propriety and the delegation of tasks, yet they also depended on Aboriginal women's traditional skills. These skills were hybridised in the colonial economy, which had unsettling implications for the belief that industrialism was the pinnacle of labour efficiency. Hill is struck by the paradox of 'ancient' people performing modern labour. Yandying grass-seeds or ant's eggs is adapted to condiments, and Hill describes the process almost as a fairground act: 'I have seen a lubra, with just this quick flutter of dish and hands, manipulate a quantity of tea, sugar and sand that a station-owner had deliberately mixed together. She handed it back miraculously divided into three distinct heaps in less than five minutes.'[94] The mechanical yandy installed at great cost was abandoned to 'wilt in the sun. The hands of the lubras were infinitely more efficient than the machine'. Appropriated as labour, 'primitive' skills were more efficient than machinery, that is, until they were paid for.[95] There is a sense in the writings of white women in the twentieth century, from Gunn, Chauvel, Duncan-Kemp, Hill and Bates, all of them far from home, that the work of Aboriginal women is uncanny. Their exposés speak of their own displacement, but more so of the seepages of place between the homestead and the camp in home country. They confirm Bhabha's idea that displacements force upon us 'a vision that is as divided as it is disorienting...the "unhomely" is the paradigmatic colonial and post-colonial condition.'[96] How very comforting Aboriginal women's skills must have then seemed in maintaining the distinctions of tea, sugar and sand; how reassuring the cartoons preoccupied with footfall over thresholds in newspapers on white breakfast tables, waited on by black women.

Crossing the threshold into white domesticity, Aboriginal women often had to dress and wash and give every appearance of not living in shelters made from scraps of hessian, bags and iron tins hammered flat.[97] That is, it was incumbent on them to

Footfall over thresholds

disguise their exploitation. This contradiction between the living standards in white homes extracted from exploited Aboriginal women and their own appalling living conditions in station camps and town compounds fed the impetus for threshold and interior imagery which placed great emphasis on the feet of Aboriginal women. However dependent industries may have been on the domestic labour of Aboriginal women (leaving the light work to the 'real' women), they were represented again and again in the mainstream press as figures on the threshold of white domestic space, comically confusing the boundaries of inside and outside, the purpose of domestic tasks, or calculatedly extracting benefits for themselves from the miscomprehension. The artists from these cartoons (Figures 4.10–4.15), B. E. Minns (*The Bulletin*), Hugh Maclean, Stan Cross (*Smith's Weekly* and *The Herald*) and Mick Paul

MISTRESS: "Mary, it's no use putting fly-paper outside the house—put it inside."
MARY: "Well, Missus, you can catch a lot more out here."

Stan Cross SMITH'S WEEKLY 1921

Figure 4.10 Stan Cross, Smith's Weekly, *1921 from Vane Lindesay*, The Inked-in Image, *Hutchinson, Richmond, 1979.*

Skin Deep

NO TIME LIKE NOW.

THE MISTRESS: *"What a big baby for six months old! Tell me when he has a birthday, Mary, and I'll give him a present."*

MARY: *"My word, Miss. Mine tinkit this pfella have birthday longa sarf'ernoon."*

Figure 4.11 'No Time Like the Now', Mick Paul.

"There's a bottle of cooking wine missing, Mary; I hope your Jackie hasn't taken it!"
"My word missus, I tink so; that pfella that drunk las' night I see him double."

Mick Paul AUSSIE 1926

171

Figure 4.12 Mick Paul in Aussie, *1926 from Lindesay,* Inked-in Image, *p. 171.*

Footfall over thresholds

"Was Jacky pleased when the twins were born, Mary?"
"No fear, missus; he gibbit plurry black look."

Figure 4.13 Hugh Maclean, in The Bulletin, *1922.*

"My word, Mary, there's not much left of that skirt I gave you!"
"No, Missie; on its last plurry legs, minethinkit!"

Figure 4.14 Hugh Maclean in Aussie, *1928.*

THE UNION LEVY.
MISTRESS: "Here, Mary Ann, I want you to do a day's scrubbing."
MARY ANN: "How much you gib it?"
MISTRESS: "I'll give you three shillings."
BILLY (chipping in): "By cripes, I go halves."

Figure 4.15 'The Union Levy', B.E. Minns, The Bulletin, 1919.

were popular single-panel and strip cartoonists as well as members, some foundational, of the Society of Australian Black and White Artists.[98] The motif of enlarged feet was shared between them and by other artists such as Phil May, and it came to the fore in the 1920s just as urban white women were crossing over the domestic threshold in a critical mass. The bareness and 'unshodability' of Aboriginal women's feet situated them as remote from the fast pace of modernity. They were said to lumber around the outback homestead, in direct contact with the earth, yet strangely disconnected from it as displaced; inept yet calculating with splayed feet, which seemed to comment on their nomadic origin, now in service to the daintily shod mistress. It was, of course, part of the ugliness ascribed to Aboriginal women, as a way to deflect that the threshold was a sentry post for white mistresses to ward off the potential intimacies incumbent and unspoken around Aboriginal women's servitude.

Boundary hygiene had been a preoccupation for middle-class Victorians. The colonies, far-flung from these strictures of social order, were seen as realms of contamination where lines demarking sexual, class and gender distinctions were regularly perforated. Kate Bagnall has found the same recurrence of threshold imagery in cartoons of Chinese hawkers in their interactions with white women.[99] Moreover, as Mary Douglas influentially wrote, 'dirt is essentially disorder',[100] and in the settler domicile, service was not merely about 'help' but about delegating away tasks that might defile white women, from discarding night soil to meeting the sexual needs of white men – outside the prescribed sexual role of the sanctified wife, perhaps in terms of acceptable frequency or even certain acts.

As white women began to move into the north, their demands on Aboriginal women's labour were exacting. Diane Bell found that,

> women emphasize that it was the arrival of the 'white missus' which created the role of domestic labourer for Aboriginal women; the missionary presence which created shame; the institutionalization of settlement life which created households wherein women were dependants.[101]

Their sexual labour was forced underground and the paternity of their children was less likely to be acknowledged. Larissa Behrendt's work on sexual consent found that Aboriginal women were 'able to exert their own power and control through their relations with white men and, once there was reliance on black labour, were able to exert more control over the situation.'[102] But the arrival of white women on the frontier compounded Aboriginal women's loss of economic status. Along with assimilating Aboriginal women into the European domicile, the white missus was also there to insulate white men from their sexual dependency on 'black velvet' and 'spinifex fairies'.

In service Aboriginal women should enshroud and stifle their presence as much as humanely possible. Frank Clune's 1947 travelogue *Roaming Around Australia* thus described the 'Mission-trained' girls at Ivanhoe on the Ord River as 'clean at housework', but was struck by one thing: 'How heavy-footed is the Abo lubra! In Java and India the house-boys slink like wraiths, very soft-footed, but, in North Australia, when the native girls promenade around, doing their work, it sounds as if Jessie the elephant had arrived to pay a sociable visit'.[103] Clearly, 'help' should be neither seen nor heard. Clune then segues into a justification of White Australia, saying white women wouldn't have to depend on any coloured labour if every house north of the Tropic of Capricorn was air-conditioned. He, too, noted the 'splayed feet' of a 'Bush Black' woman coming to the station store with her seven children. Conversely, the girls who waitressed at the manager's table were 'nattily dressed' in cream printed frocks. They brought the meal 'like the Charge of the Light Brigade': 'Advancing in formation, like a musical comedy ballet, they deploy around the table, put down their dishes, and retire in good order and "at the double".' Clune was 'delighted' by this swooping, rushing 'tropical troupe'. The manifest inconsistencies disclose how ambivalent settlers were about the tread of Aboriginal women, how heavy or light, its shape and step, its nature and adaption. It seems the Aboriginal women and girls who discreetly and docilely stepped over the threshold of white domesticity were also valued for adapting their light step to the interior. Ernestine Hill applauded the 'soft' gliding feet of the house girls in her *Great Australian Loneliness*.[104] When properly assimilated to domestic service, and properly discreet, the 'age-old' traits of the nimble-footed nomad could find new quarters within the bounds of settler occupancy.

This emphasis on footfall was, of course, a distraction from the reality of working in white homes, which so often led to economic exile rather than the integration that was attempted through the policy of assimilation. Sub-protector and retired constable George Aiston, writing in 1935, bemoaned the farce of removing young girls from camps – where they would have learned from their mothers how to provide for themselves and their children – to be placed in white homes and then banished to the town fringe camp when 'the inevitable baby arrives.' He fulminated,

> They are absolutely helpless, and have to get a living the best way they can. It always seems pitiful to me to see girls that I have known as clean house-servants living in dirty camps ignorant of how to keep themselves clean and half starved because they never learnt how to find food for themselves.[105]

In these lifelong sagas of separation, absorption, exploitation and abandonment – forced movement in fact – the policy of assimilation was rarely held to account. Aiston was not a lone voice as the 'Women Protector campaign' gained momentum from the late 1920s, in which white women activists 'sought an important role in "civilizing" colonialism and imperialism' by pressing for women protectors to prevent the sexual abuse of domestics, particularly 'half-caste' girls.[106] The labour of the 'house-gin' within the pastoral, mining or pearling economies was essential. But her impoverished living conditions were often romanticised as part of primitive itinerancy. In Western Australia, Commissioner H. D. Moseley found in 1935 that workers 'want for nothing; they are well fed and clothed and the huts in which they live, made of bush material, bags or sometimes flattened petrol tins, are suitable to their needs; anything more would not be appreciated by them – indeed, they would not be used.'[107] He added that in the Kimberley the native was not paid: 'it appears to be of no great disadvantage to the native; he has not acquired, and I doubt if (generally speaking) he will ever, acquire, any real sense of property: he will give away anything he has.' Early recruitment by pastoralists could be with 'gun in hand' while native administrators could recruit by removal and coercion, with threats to stop rations, remove children or banish people from reserves – again through forced movement.[108] Until 1892 Aborigines and Europeans were subject to the Masters and Servant legislation, which enabled pastoralists to require police to recapture any women, men or children who had left their employ by running away. Under this legislation they could be imprisoned for three months and disobedience was punishable by flogging.[109] For all their lightheartedness, the print invocations of Aboriginal women's comportment concealed a deeply constricting administration of their actual movement, threatened by a mobility which might propel their autonomy.

While living in a 'blacks camp' Dairy Bates scrupulously maintained her own boundary rituals to manage close contact. Bates described trudging miles through marsh, bog and sand in her own 'high-heeled footwear', but it was her gloves that seemed to demark boundaries for her, and this is no doubt because Bates insisted she was no mistress of her 'friends', and 'never made servants or attendants of them'. Rather she saw herself as in service to Aboriginal people. She famously wore gloves in her 'handling of the blacks' and when caring for the sick. She explains,

> Many people, both in private and in the Press, have expressed amazement in that, in the heart of the Australian desert, I have always adhered rigidly to the incongruity of gloves. The explanation is simple. From the time of my first ministrations to the diseased – often repulsively diseased – natives of the north-west and the south-west of Australia, gloves have been my safety from contagion. I have kept dozens and dozens of the cheapest always ready, and immediately on my return from the anointment of sores, the bathing of eyes, and septic wounds, and other dangers of infection, both gloves and hands have been steeped in boiling water. It was a drastic safeguard but a very necessary one.[110]

Bates's gloves, like the Coober Pedy landlady's scrupulous housekeeping, guarded against the various contagions of the primitive. She participates in 'the protection of social "orifices"'[111] since she 'never in the slightest degree "went native"'[112] and this she achieved through careful and diligent maintenance of the trappings of Edwardian dress, described as withstanding heat, infection and flies. In case it wasn't abundantly clear that Bates never compromised her whiteness, she was extolled for maintaining her 'soft pink Irish complexion to the end of her days.'[113] Bates also made a point about her never offending strictly observed Aboriginal propriety, for people in her camp were scandalised by her granting the state governor entrance into her tent. If the threshold of her domicile went uncrossed it was in deference to camp standards and not at her insistence.

Bates was unusual in that she maintained distinctions by imposing her own as well as adhering to those that she understood to be important to the people around her. And no doubt women negotiated many of the incommensurabilities incumbent on lived, shared space divided by service, gender and racial difference. It was an uncanny doubling by which white women in settler occupancies cleaved – in both senses, to and from – Aboriginal women. Their dependency and proximity was disavowed by recurring motifs of comportment and footfall, which became points of reference in the early to mid-twentieth-century middlebrow and newspaper cartoons as a means to enforce and distinguish white and black women's respective place in and around settler occupancy. The tread of the tribal myall and station buck assigned authenticity, dominion and adaptability to white labour. The footfall of the house or camp lubra and gin – just as urban modern girl types were entering metropolitan space and as Aboriginal women's misappropriated labour became government policy – stood them apart from settler-colonial modernity, even while serving its domestic regime.

Quintessentially a contest over space, settler-colonialism produced a 'halfway house of racial and cultural origins',[114] which required the reiteration of racial difference through a constant maintenance of boundaries. This spatial delineation would ideally manage the intimacies and interdependencies that crept in with the indenture of native labour. Antoinette Burton's influential idea of the 'porousness of colonialism'[115] has become a home truth in histories of settler-colonial domesticity. The terrain of cultural and political displacements endemic to various home fronts was unsettled by the presence of the dispossessed. They were perhaps more of a corrosive than a porous presence. The contradictions and elisions endemic to settler and indigenous mobility, migration and movement show that modalities of movement were thought to be 'nation-making'. Their pathways, laid down by trade and print syndication, were racialised. Under the rubric of colonial mobility, incursion, arrival and the stepping onto purportedly untrammelled soil characterised the colonial comportment of newcomer types such as the navigator, explorer, surveyor, overlander, drover, boundary rider, even the bushranger. Their passage was opposed to the 'passing' of Aboriginal types such as the myall, tracker, lubra and gin. Sense of place and use of space were critical to newcomer imaginings of the 'camp lubra' and her purported evolutionary progression to the 'house gin'; in print culture these became mnemonically bound up in her footfall over the domestic threshold.

5

'BLACK VELVET' AND 'PURPLE INDIGNATION': SEXUALITY AND 'POACHING'

In 1936 a flurry of print reports alleged widespread prostitution of Aboriginal women and girls to Japanese pearlers. The revelations had a dramatic impact. Within weeks of them being aired a report was placed before the Department of the Interior. A vessel was commissioned to patrol the Arnhem Land coast. The allegations were raised at the first meeting of state aboriginal protection authorities. Cabinet closed Australian waters to foreign pearling craft and a control base was established in the Tiwi Islands. Japanese luggers were fired upon with machine guns and a crew detained in Darwin. These escalating events occurred within five years of a series of attacks on Japanese by Aborigines[1] and only five years before Australian and Japanese forces waged war. Much ink was spilt over the course of this print scandal, and while reports made use of established language such as 'vice' and 'outrage', a telling omission was the well-known expression 'black velvet'. Tracing its use through print reveals that the phrase exclusively pertained to white men's sexualisation of Aboriginal women. Aboriginal women were never referred to as 'black velvet' as a colloquial jeer of their relations with Japanese men, for whom they were quite literally out of bounds. This indicates this phrase played a role in establishing white men's sense of proprietorial ownership of Aboriginal women's bodies.

'Black velvet' and 'purple indignation'

The pearling scandal played out principally in print and this chapter follows the use of the term 'black velvet' through the ensuing media panic. Taking a new tack to previous chapters, we'll attend to the absences more so than reiterations. As I've elsewhere published a more detailed history of the pearling/prostitution scandal, we'll sample print reports of this episode as it unfolded along Australia's northern shore to show how frontier sexuality was mapped onto national borders and racial and gender identifications.[2] As Stoler argues in her work on carnality and imperial power,

> the management of the sexual practices of colonizer and colonized was fundamental to the colonial order of things and...discourses of sexuality at once classified colonial subjects into distinct human kinds while policing the domestic recesses of imperial rule.[3]

This chapter draws attention to the impressions made in print by these categories, by looking at print's expressions as well as its countervailing suppressions. It divulges the role of colloquial language or slang in the ordering of social kinds (grouping people by shared traits that are socially determined). It shows that the epidermal enmeshments of interracial sexuality constantly undermined the categories that were reiterated and racialised through colloquial language. Terms historicised in this chapter remain offensive and have continuing power to offend. This chapter attempts to dispel and challenge the meanings conveyed by the term 'black velvet' by tracing its use in print media and exposing the attitudes it disseminated.

'Black velvet' made explicit reference to tactile sensations from illicit white contact with racialised genitals. The oblique use of the term in print worked to shore up racial designations in which Aboriginal women were construed as susceptible to white men's purportedly unrestrainable soliciting, as distinct from their depiction as vulnerable to 'Asiatic' supposed degeneracy and aggression. Meanwhile Aboriginal men, said to be the real instigators of the traffic in Aboriginal women, were accused of prostituting their women and thereby of being profligate with their own property rights, not to mention of instigating unsanctioned trade across borders and shores. The presence as much as the absence of 'black velvet' in print shows that colloquial language was a means for white colonisers to boast ownership over Aboriginal women's bodies. The scandal erupted around the trade in pearl shell – a sensory opposite to 'black velvet' – yet the two were construed as commodities and overlayed with a sense of settler entitlement to the bounty of the land that expressly denied 'Asiatics' right of entry.

Print coverage of the Japanese pearler scandal mediated a tension between foreign trade and the territorial claims of settler-colonialism through the vector of sexual access to Indigenous women. It showed that these incursions of capital introduced competing claims from other nation-states, in Japan's case one with rising imperial ambitions. The relations then forged between competing masculinities on the northern frontier pushed to the fore the intimacies that trade invariably relied upon and the challenges they posed to established and tolerated patterns of interracial sexuality, as blithely and even boastfully encapsulated in the colloquialism 'black velvet'. As Ruth Balint has argued,

> At the farthest edge of the continent from the centers of European power, pearling and the seascape it inhabited came to embody the possibility of the erosion

of officially sanctioned notions of home and nation, a threat personified by the presence of Asian men and their unions with Aboriginal women.[4]

If we look at newspaper reports of these interracial sexual unions we can see the discrimination against, and regulation of, relations between peoples without citizenship, Asian and Aboriginal, under the White Australia policy[5] along with 'the ambivalence of "nation" as a narrative strategy.'[6] The history of Australia's northern shore, as a number of scholars have argued, reveals the complex interplay of migration, diaspora and identity, and realigns the axis of colonial history from Indigenous/settler relations to a conflation of identity categories forged through multiculturalism and migration.[7] Peta Stephenson has detailed Asian–Aboriginal relations in the north and argued their sexual liaisons played a role in Aboriginal communities maintaining a degree of autonomy from white administrators.[8] They also undermined white men's exclusive sexual access to Aboriginal women. The 'interior frontier'[9] accustomed by settler/Indigenous exchange was impinged by the exterior frontier presented by the pearlers, yet internalised by the intimacies and heterogeneity initiated along its contact lines. Within print reports non-white interracial sex could only be imagined as prostitution or sexual aggression, which implicated the hostile infringement of national borders.

The scandal is an instance of the 'concrete linkages between forms of love and forms of governance'[10] that Elizabeth Povinelli has explored. The sexual labour of Aboriginal women, inferred as an aberrant trade when between Aboriginal and Japanese men, was newly imagined on the nation's daily pages within a metaphorics of 'poaching', and metastasized into diplomatic tensions. In stark contrast, sexual unions between white men and Aboriginal women were either silenced, decried by humanitarians on rare occasions, or euphemised by 'black velvet'.

Indigenous women's sexuality had long been deemed a frontier resource, a 'necessary evil' required for irrepressible colonial manliness in regions unpopulated by white women. 'If you were to put rams in with ewes what would you expect?', one sheep farmer explained to the South Australia 1899 Select Committee, adding that 'men are placed in positions where for ten or fifteen years they never see a white woman. In the interior, there are a lot of these flash young lubras about, and you can hardly expect men not to touch them.'[11] The right of extraction – a tenet of settler-colonialism – found ready application over the bodies of Indigenous women. Nevertheless, 'interfering', particularly by 'lower-caste' white men, was far from encouraged. Aside from the indignation of a handful of sympathetic humanitarians or piously appalled missionaries and clergy, encounters with white men were secreted from the wider public or given glancing acknowledgement in descriptions of remote regions as suffering a 'frightful want of females.' Under protection-era state administrative regimes a number of legislative measures were designed to guard women and girls from any sexual activity with white men, be it abusive, contractual or consensual (usually involving their removal to training homes and reserves).[12] In 1934 Minister for the Interior J. A. Perkins issued an exhaustive statement on the Commonwealth's policy for dealing with the Aboriginal population of the Northern Territory, under which the protection of Aboriginal women 'from moral abuse on the part of Europeans and other races' numbered as the fourth objective.[13]

'Asiatic' men's sexual involvement evidently presented a far worse evil. This episode of 'lubras on luggers'[14] revealed these women were decisively debarred to 'Asiatic' men. A new element had been introduced to the degenerate frontier – non-white interracial sex. It exposed an unstated, even deeply repressed, logic of the protection and assimilation regimes: the regulation and containment of Aboriginal women's sexuality within nationally inscribed limits of access. The press treatment of the pearling incident underscored the active repression of interracial sex in public discourse – except when it involved 'coloured aliens'. The racially delimited slang 'black velvet' was indicative of this cordoned access. The expression was racialized not only in terms of the women involved, but insofar as it specified their procurers or partners or perpetrators as white men. The pearling scandal and the 'lubra trade' proffered an opportunity to reconfigure and reinforce a discourse of colonial chivalry: 'White men are saving brown women from brown men', as Spivak has described it.[15] Yet, here the 'brown men' were not just the Aboriginal men accused of prostituting their women. 'Brown men' also referred to the Japanese men who were both trade competitors and non-assimilative to national masculinity. The scandal provided another opportunity to shift culpability from white men to other groups. The pearlers were perhaps the very thing white men could least face about themselves, being invaders.

The pearling print scandal rent apart the veil conventionally drawn across interracial sexual activity. The concealment had been enabled by what Ganter identifies as 'the indistinctness between corroboration and reiteration' through the characterising of all interracial gendered contact as prostitution. Much as we saw in print accounts of bride capture, Ganter finds in missionary and ethnographic accounts a 'mirroring of accounts which then became cemented as the master narrative of race relations of the pearling and *bêche-de-mer* industry of North Queensland.'[16]

Frontier sexual activity has been documented mostly within pastoral,[17] mining and sealing scenarios,[18] but also within the domestic labour of Aboriginal women in settler homes.[19] Recent scholarship has explored the 'spectrum' of sexual relationships in frontier and post-frontier settings, which ranged from abduction and aggravated rape to consensual, companionate marriage between settler men and Aboriginal women. Arguably, lack of consent disaggregates any such spectrum since aside from penetration, pregnancy and venereal disease, no other commonality exists between sexual assault and sexual relations. However, in the print coverage examined, Aboriginal women's consent is almost impossible to gauge for a number of reasons. Firstly, interracial sex comprised such a violation of social norms it was confused with violation itself. Secondly, Aboriginal women were characterised as so devoid of chastity or modesty as to be unable to be 'outraged'. Thirdly, as we saw in the second chapter, they were routinely typed as 'chattels', so subjected to their men's tyranny that any agency was subsumed beneath Aboriginal men's trafficking of their bodies.

The prohibition on cohabiting and marriage between Japanese men and Aboriginal women in the 1905 Aborigines Act created longstanding regulation and discrimination against couples,[20] along with the concentrated removal of their children to missions and reserves.[21] It presumed that women who engaged in consensual relations were prostitutes. In all of the diverse scenarios characterised as miscegenation, sexual exchange across racial boundaries was profoundly destabilising in terms of the devastating spread of venereal disease. Miscegenation became a heightened preoccupation for administrators just as the assimilation regime adopted by some states sought to resolve the half-caste 'menace' through a policy based on the spurious scientific premise of biological absorption. In addition, settlers on the frontier found it difficult to perceive within rites of sexual exchange a range of traditional women's practices which might include barter, the establishment of diplomatic relations, negotiating riparian rights and those of ingress, and sourcing food including from settlers. For Europeans, sexual activity outside marriage could rarely be perceived outside the terms of one-off prostitution, longer-term concubinage or abduction and rape. They were largely clueless about their obligations should their sexual involvement draw them into kinship and totemic relationships based on reciprocity and ongoing outlay. Their subsequent sexual activity with impermissible women, or failure to meet their obligations, could be met by violent reprisals from Aboriginal men. These, on many tragic occasions, became the grounds for indiscriminate, wholesale massacre which itself might include sexual violence and the abduction of women and girls. The Coniston massacre of 1928, for instance, was a 'punitive expedition' precipitated by retribution from Walbri for the reneged payments by a dingo trapper, Fred Brooks, and another white man.[22]

The dispute over Aboriginal cohabitation with Japanese pearlers contrasts sharply with years of ineffective intervention by state protection administrations, ostensibly to protect Aboriginal women and girls from white sexual aggression. Yet, while these reports occasionally surfaced in print, we'll never know to what extent the abduction, rape and prostitution of Aboriginal women and girls by settlers went unmentioned, elided and silenced. Moreover, as noted, settlers considered consensual interracial sexual unions as much an offence against social standards as sexual violence, due to their contravention of racial boundaries. Many accounts of sexual violence are confused by the equation of 'seduction' by white men with 'violation'. Despite decades of reports of violence towards Aboriginal women by white pearling masters,[23] it was finally Aboriginal women's use by 'alien' men, particularly 'Asiatics', which prompted dramatically contrasting government interventions, media scandal and exposure, not to mention heightened white feeling. The Pearl Shell Fisheries acts in Western Australia in 1871, 1873 and 1875 came about after the colonial secretary became aware that women and children were being abducted in raids and forced onto boats where conditions were so deplorable that forty women were known to have died of scurvy in the industry in the 1860s on the Western Australian coast.[24] Aboriginal women were prohibited from employment on pearling operations and vessels.[25] Nevertheless, violence against them had been largely met with pervasive apathy, evasion, resignation, winking and looking the other way. Instead, anxiety was focused on Asian–Aboriginal cohabitation, which was itself precipitated by state ambivalence towards Aboriginal employment in the pearl-shell industry. Also shaping reactions was the competition for depleting shell beds outside the three-mile territorial limit with the more organised, efficient and entrepreneurial Japanese divers, though the crews were exempted from the provisions of the Immigration Restriction Act of 1901.[26] The prostitution scandal broke as fears of espionage and alien intrusion, debates over territorial boundaries and poaching, and Japanese technological, numerical and market dominance reached a climax. But these resource, property and trade relations were applicable also to women's bodies, and their distribution and allotment also came under state jurisdiction.

This little-known episode mapped interracial sexuality onto national borders and racial identifications. Clearly, 'black velvet' already specified interracial sexual relations since Aboriginal women were never said to be such to their own men. Rather,

'Black velvet' and 'purple indignation'

Aboriginal men were said to consign their women to 'black velvet' by trafficking them. The expression made slanting reference to the genital interior of Aboriginal women as inducing a particular sensation in white men. When the faltering usage of the term is contextualised in the print scandal around Japanese pearlers, it reveals that this contact was colloquially restricted to white men. The reiteration and avoidance in print of 'black velvet' secured the discursive borders of Aboriginal women's sexual 'susceptibility' to white men's incorrigible seduction and soliciting, as distinct from their vulnerability to 'Asiatic' degeneracy and violence.

The trope of 'black velvet' is specific to Australia yet it derives from long-established notions of black women's inherent lasciviousness. In European colonies, 'natives' were figured 'as gender deviants, the embodiments of prehistoric promiscuity and excess.' So entrenched was the association of race with sexual transgression that during the Middle Ages sexuality itself was referred to as 'the African sin'[27] and black skin was said to be caused by syphilitic sores.[28] Interest in the sexual availability of indigenous women had been heightened by European exploratory accounts of the Pacific in the writings of Bougainville, Hawkesworth, Banks and Diderot. Climate was thought to favour a promiscuous disposition and the bountiful ease of living in the tropics was said to encourage moral degeneration and vice.[29] Hawkesworth wrote of 'rites of Venus' performed before a crowd 'without the least sense of its being considered indecent or improper' and of a dance called 'Timorodee', performed by girls, 'consisting of motions and gestures beyond imagination wanton.' He notes Europeans should have no expectation of natives that 'chastity should be held in high estimation.'[30] Part of what made the native woman such a highly libidinised entity was her sexual knowledge, even or perhaps particularly when still a virgin, in marked contrast to the repression of sexual and reproductive knowledge European girls endured.[31] Yet, it was hardly a free for all, and in an anonymous letter from the *Endeavour* voyage to Otaheite of 1768, a crew member admitted to purchasing a 'virgin', of nine or ten years, with three nails and a knife. 'I own I was the buyer of such commodities', he admits and laments having to leave behind one such 'nut-brown sultana' whom he had married.[32] As Michael Taussig has argued, 'Racism is the parade-ground where the civilised rehearse this love-hate relation with their repressed sensuosity', projecting an animality onto the racial Other through their sadistic degradation.[33]

Cook, like many who followed him, noted the extraordinary decorum and strict regulation of interaction between the sexes among the New Hollanders. Much to their frustration women kept themselves out of sight in many first-contact encounters. In one interaction he records that the crew of the *Discovery* 'paid their addresses, and made liberal offers of presents'. Yet they were spurned for reasons Cook would not 'pretend to determine'.[34] This acknowledgement of the European limits of understanding about native protocols for sexual transactions, or rites of cohabitation, would soon give way to the assertion of certainties about Aboriginal women's lack of modesty, virtue and inherent shame, for a preoccupation of European exploration was sexual rites in other lands.[35] Joseph Banks lamented that their connection with women had been limited to one landing. 'Yet we saw them with our eyes or glasses many times', and he added with some satisfaction, 'our glasses might deceive us in many things, but their colour and want of clothes we certainly did see.'[36]

Also in play was a clear sense of resistance by Aboriginal women that both intrigued and frustrated European explorers.

As Konishi documents, Cook attributed the reticence of native women to the jealousy and control of their men, itself a marker of 'uncivilised peoples'.[37] French explorers of the Baudin expedition claimed that since they did not batter women over the head with sticks, they could have no intercourse with the women of Van Diemen's Land. As such their civility 'barred them from emulating Aboriginal men's barbaric technique.'[38] Given both the proprietorial basis of European marriage along with routine frontier abduction and rape by settlers, this denigration of 'barbaric' native rites, such as bride capture and polygamy, provided a means to allot chivalry to newcomer men. It depended on a blind spot in the operation of power and asymmetry in their own sexual rites and relations. In McGrath's analysis of the variegated formations of marriage across the Australian frontier, she shows the dependence of eighteenth-century notions of civilized marriage on rebuffing those of the primitive, and discusses the significance of property to the ordering of monogamy. The union of marriage required the right of exclusive property in individuals and its regulation became an object of state policy: 'Thus property, and the institution of marriage, mutually confirm each other.'[39] Property under settler-colonialism was land entitlement but its settlement entailed family relations and inheritance. Sexual violence against women and girls divested Aboriginal men and women of property relations as determined by marriage and inheritance. Following incursion onto homelands Aboriginal women became a resource whose extraction was either veiled beneath courtly conventions or scapegoated onto lower orders of non-Indigenous men. This purported tyrannical sexual custody so marked in the second chapter continued as a key trope of primitivism into Japanese pearler prostitution. Aboriginal men were less often attributed with the 'feeble', despondent virility of the American 'savage' before them,[40] but rather with a brutish, calculating bent to prostitute their wives and daughters, which only confirmed they were essentially squanderers of property.

By the time of settlement of New Holland, the sexuality of the indigenous was less often described in terms of a simplicity of response to natural urges under the guise of the noble savage and its female counterpart, the rather obliging native belle; rather it began to the bear the marks of European corruption, provoking missionary zeal. Moral degeneracy played its part also in the emergence of dying race theory. As we saw in Chapter 3, venereal disease and infertility were seen as causing a 'certain deperishment of the aboriginal race.'[41] George Barrington, our ghostwritten pickpocket from Chapter 2, perhaps predictably reported in 1810, 'chastity is not one of the virtues they boast.'[42] As early as 1791, Clendinnen finds evidence of some Aboriginal women bartering their favours to convicts, 'presumably with the permission of their men.'[43] Although Konishi shows Clendinnen to have 'misplaced confidence'[44] in British ethnography, I think it is reasonable to assume that the direct contract by which settlers sought to engage the services of Aboriginal women left Aboriginal men, traditionally the brokers of this exchange, 'abruptly outside the loop.'[45] There is much testimony by Europeans that the contravention of Aboriginal men's rights incited retribution against both white men and Aboriginal women. But when violence flared, Europeans seldom recognised that Aboriginal men might simply love their wives, daughters and mothers and despair at their vulnerability to white men's violence. One such rare acknowledgement came in 1851 from NSW Presbyterian minister John Gibson, who declared,

> The amount of misery inflicted on the Blacks by the Whites is ample excuse for their depredations: their

wives enticed or forced from them; their female children violated in the most brutal manner; their encampments and implements burnt and destroyed; is it to be expected that they will bear this quietly – that they will not retaliate?[46]

It was more usual for Europeans to entirely fail to distinguish between consensual sex and rape since the real transgression, interracial sex, was common to both. Gibson's observations intimate – far from a purported lack of shame in native women[47] – the corroding influence of European sexual commodification under capitalist models of exchange, along with sexual violence, and the disastrous upheaval these caused within complex Indigenous kinship relations and totemic systems of obligation as they continued to play out around the question of the prostitution of Aboriginal women and girls. Arguably, after exploratory parties' initial reliance on local people as guides for water and to negotiate rights of ingress, once their land was taken and with it their livelihoods, Aboriginal men and women on the frontier and town fringes remained in possession of one sure commodity: sexual access to women. White men sought to negotiate that access directly with the women, forever altering its meaning and central role within interracial and possibly intertribal and interfamilial relations.

This first 'contact' could also mean the earliest 'civilising influences' were intimated to women, who might be the first to acquire the language and customs of the intruders and pass them on to their camp.[48] Newcomers also excused their abuse as a better fate than women's sexual relations with their own men. In 1915, a letter to the *Northern Territory Times and Gazette* responded to allegations by a Mr Beckett of mistreatment 'meted out to half-castes' by white men. The author wrote 'on behalf of the white men in the N.T. who, owing to the exigencies of climate etc., have been forced to keep half-caste or black women in the N.T.' He demanded the claims of cruelty be proved and asserted the idea that 'these women are practically slaves' was 'utterly ridiculous', after all 'their lot is far better than those of their unfortunate sisters who have submitted themselves to the tender mercies of nigger husbands, and the filth and bestiality of a black's camp.'[49] This newcomer rival would hardly countenance competition from outsiders. The very visible outcome of interracial sex in diseased women and 'half-caste' offspring could not be reconciled with settler self-perception as bestowing a civilising presence. Responsibility was transferred to convicts, low-class white men and, later and most visibly, 'Asiatics'.

If the circulation of tropes and types, such as the lubra, piccaninny, jacky-jacky and King Billy, among many others, was a mainstay of the very enterprise of colonial print culture, 'black velvet' stood apart. Unlike stud or gin stud,[50] it did not denote a type but rather, like bride capture, a social phenomenon, specifically a sexual relation. 'Black velvet' was barely present in print. While the requisite search through digitised newspaper archives uncovers an abundance of ribbons, trimming, bodices and bonnets, it is noteworthy how little this typology of interracial sexual transaction is made mention of. Given its common usage the omission, I will argue, is telling of more than simply editorial tact. What is evident in this print archive is the striking contrast between white women clothed and trimmed in black velvet, and Aboriginal women construed as naked by this expression, their skin rendered a more tactile surface by its colour. 'Black velvet' evoked a racialised register of touch, not only of Aboriginal surface, but also of white touch. A number of authors commented on the skin of Aboriginal women, such as

'Black velvet' and 'purple indignation'

Victorian squatter Edward Curr, as 'particularly velvet-like to the touch'.[51] In the 1912–13 *Cyclopedia of Western Australia*, the skin of Aborigines is described as 'of a dark copper colour…particularly soft and velvety to the touch.'[52] In 1932 outback crime novelist Arthur Upfield describes a beautiful Aboriginal girl in terms of the overpowering 'lure' of her 'black velvet cheeks' for a young man who did not know he was 'half-caste'.[53] It was also referenced by a genre of postwar painting, on a surface of actual black velvet which took Indigenous and peasant women and children as its subject (see Figure 5.1).

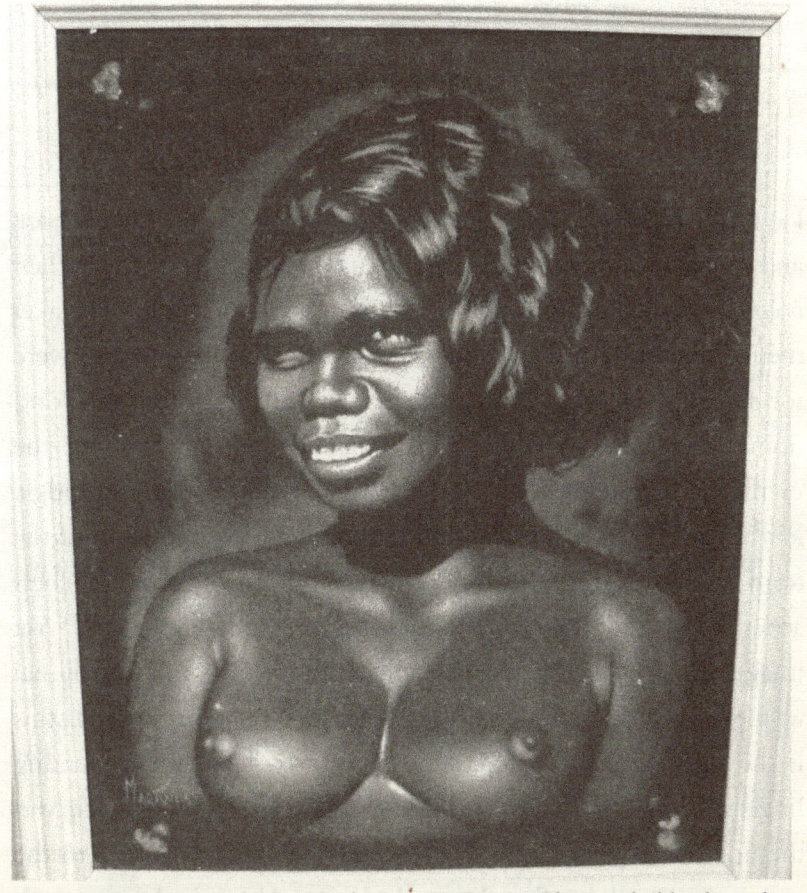

Figure 5.1 'Martinos'. Union Hotel, Gore St, Fitzroy. Photographed by the author

In McGrath's classic and wide-ranging history of the interracial sexual relations referenced by 'black velvet' in the Northern Territory, she notes the term originated as nineteenth-century military slang, and also named an Irish infusion of stout, champagne and cider.[54] From the first, the term belonged to a fraternity of men. It seems a stanza from Henry Lawson's 'Ballad of the rouseabout' first inscribed it in Australian print (since his verse nearly always first appeared in newspapers) as the recourse of the lonely bush itinerant:

I know the track from Spencer's Gulf and north of Cooper's Creek
Where falls the half-caste to the strong, 'black velvet' to the weak
(From gold-top Flossie in the Strand to half-caste and the gin
If they had brains, poor animals! we'd teach them how to sin.)

Lawson's brand of hardknock, and thereby supposedly conversant and impartial, racism grades the sexual access to women by their colour and implies 'full-blood' women were the takings of weaker men, either physically or morally. His boast that such women were too far gone for even bush predators to impart a sense of wrongdoing illuminates the deep ambivalence widely felt about the 'civilising' of natives from those most in contact with them: single lower-class white men. Langton has argued the circulation of the term 'black velvet' gave it 'subliminal power' such that it 'ricochets around most of the sexual images of Aboriginal women.'[55] Yet imagery that nakedly referenced the desirability of Aboriginal women, such as glazed onto this ashtray, was rare; indeed, this is the only image I've found of an Aboriginal woman wearing lingerie (Figure 5.2). Pervading the colonial scene, however, was the unstated frisson (and mostly nostalgia) for visual access to the near-naked bodies of traditionally living Aboriginal women. It

'Black velvet' and 'purple indignation'

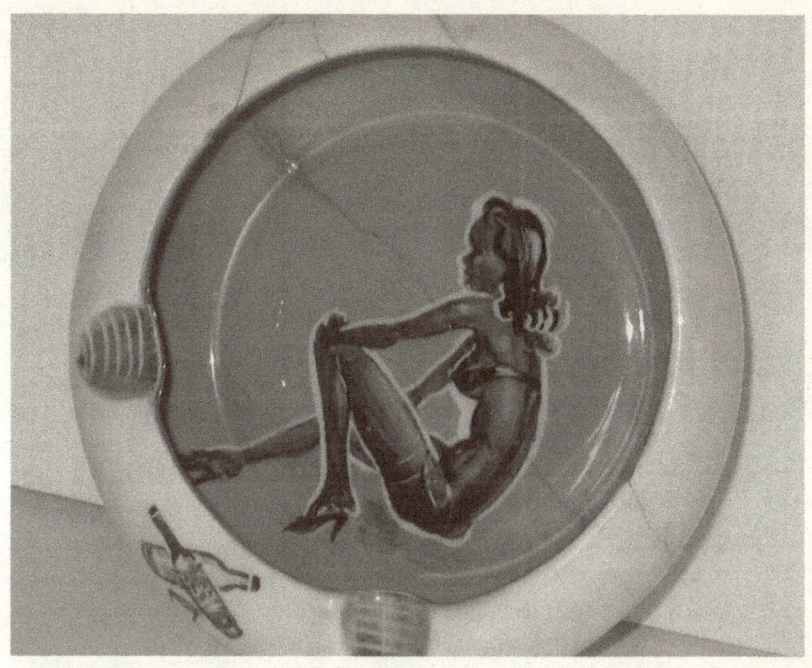

Figure 5.2 Private collection of Colin Chestnut, Sydney. Photographed by the author

was this ethno-porn that Jolliffe in part lampooned by owning up to Aboriginal women's desirability in his popular *Witchetty's Tribe* cartoon series (see Figure 5.3). Recalling Chapter 1, this process by which meaning becomes encased in imagery I have dubbed 'cultural captioning'.

The next overt referencing of 'black velvet' as the trade in Aboriginal women's bodies appeared in print in 1907 in Perth's *Sunday Times*. An anonymous feature by two 'Pressmen' reflected on their travels through the Ashburton region to Onslow, Western Australia. Their pre-emptive audacity in printing the term 'black velvet' was buttressed by their reference to the racialised types 'nigger, buck or gin', whom they claimed were all afflicted with venereal disease and thereby 'dying off at an alarming rate.' They reported that immorality was 'rampant in their camps', and that white men were living with 'black women in camp,

Figure 5.3 *'It's hot. I think I'll change into something cooler'*, Eric Jolliffe, Witchetty's Tribe: Aboriginal Cartoon, no. 4.

[and] sometimes using force to satisfy their brutal passions.' On a number of station homesteads, they'd heard of 'special gins' reserved for 'the managers' benefit'. It was in this context of 'evil association' that these journalists parsed 'black velvet', from 'jokes' shared between managers and station hands to print. Aboriginal women were thus characterised in terms of the 'susceptibility of the "black velvet" about the place while the powers-that-be wink the other eye.'[56] Even without prior impress and reiteration in print to propel 'black velvet' into common parlance, it here appears with a knowing wink. This half-knowing continued to cloak settler expression about interracial sexual activity and white sexual aggression. At Roper River, for instance, the missionary had given the police false information to keep protective husbands from the mission and had been guilty of 'serious offences' against Aboriginal women. But the matter was reported in 1933 as having been 'hushed up'.[57]

Indeed, in print readers were frequently advised that details of sexual engagement by settlers were beyond permissible description and unprintable. In an *Emigrant's Guide* of 1849 the shepherd and stockmen of the bush are described as so degenerate with vice and their activities of such 'barbarism' as to 'dare scarcely be alluded to in print.'[58] Evidence given in court regarding the aggravated assault on an Aboriginal woman in 1881 in Singleton, New South Wales by a group of men was 'unfit for publication', notably because it 'disclosed a state of things highly discreditable to the parties implicated.'[59] Similarly, a few years later the missionary Gribble wrote of abuses by white men that were 'so utterly abominable...as to be altogether unfit for public disclosure.'[60] The same year as the pearling scandal, 1936, missionary Charles Duguid from South Australia spoke of the incidence of cohabitation as 'impossible to exaggerate and for decency's sake in a mixed audience I must moderate my descriptions.'[61] A suppressed language of guarded references to unmentionable acts fed a prurient interest in the native woman, while serving to protect otherwise 'discreditable' white men by drawing a veil over their abuses. Both the rites surrounding her sexuality as well as sexual access by white men construed the Aboriginal woman as a figure of sexual access and excess utterly devoid of agency. It was never considered that Aboriginal women of their own volition might form intimate relations with men of their choosing that were meaningful to them in terms of attraction, pleasure or attachment.

By the time of the pearling fracas, any accusation of indecency by white men had long been easy to dismiss with the argument that native women did not know 'how to set a true value on chastity.' More to the point, Aboriginal men 'shared in the wages of iniquity earned by their women.' Nineteenth-century middle-class constructs of prostitution abnegated procurers of all responsibility. Britain's Contagious Diseases Act of 1866 served as the blueprint for a raft of legislative attempts in colonial Australia to regulate a pool of disease-free women for the sexual outlet of men, particularly men serving in Her Majesty's army or navy, through their registration, compulsory medical examination and confinement in 'lock' hospitals.[62] The prostitute was thought to be at once 'the necessary object of "normal" male sexual needs, but representative of an aberrant form of female sexuality.'[63] Across racial lines, however, 'native' women were always already fallen, and in failing to privatise and constrain sexual access within monogamous marriage it was 'native' men who were deemed most culpable. Thus any quarrels or even murders in Van Diemen's Land were traced as much to the 'depraved excesses of the Aborigines as to the moral turpitude of the whites.' The defence that Aboriginal men were provoked into violence by the rape of their women was dismissed by one query in 1830: 'Did the black women of this Island possess, in the slightest degree, any portion of that delicacy of sentiment which ought to be the distinguishing ornament of her sex?' Significantly no attempt was made to deny the 'atrocities' perpetrated, yet, 'on due reflection it will be observed that the Aboriginal men can have far less to complain of than would appear at first sight.' If not for the yielding of women to the 'lawless desires of white men' and the encouragement by men in this 'nefarious traffic', these men might be 'entitled to our highest compassion.'[64] From a contemporary perspective it is astounding that for these settlers of the nineteenth century the atrocity of rape was a crime principally borne by men due to its infringement of their property rights. The same line of argument appeared in print in 1886 after four 'respected and industrious pioneers' were murdered on the Daly River by 'blood-thirsty savages', who were afterwards suspected by the Aborigines' Friends'

Society of 'outraging' and abducting Aboriginal women. Their defender, Alfred Giles, scoffed at any suggestion of a 'violation of chastity and purity where chasteness is unknown.' The very idea of 'chastity among their women', he said, was 'preposterous. Not less preposterous, therefore, is the idea of the black women being outraged, unless it is by stopping their supply of tobacco.'[65]

In 1905 a Royal Commission on the condition of the natives undertaken by Walter Roth, Assistant Protector of Aborigines in Queensland, altered the language by which the sexual traffic of Aboriginal women and girls became public through print. Measures had been taken to protect Aboriginal women from 'blackbirding' by white pearlers in Western Australia.[66] The tabled report read:

> along the whole coast-line extending from a few miles south of La Grange Bay to the eastern shores of King Sound, drunkenness and prostitution, the former being the prelude to the latter, with consequent loathsome disease, is rife amongst the aborigines. The condition of affairs is mainly due to Asiatic aliens allowed into the State as pearling-boats' crews...The boats call in at certain creeks, ostensibly for wood and water, and the natives flock to these creeks, the men being perfectly willing to barter their women for gin, tobacco, flour, or rice; the coloured crews to whom they are bartered are mostly Malays, Manilamen and Japanese; they frequently take the women off to the luggers...One magistrate considers that the whites are just as much to blame as the coloured crews for the prostitution going on where the boats land for getting wood and water. As a result of their intercourse with aboriginal women, the boats'

crews suffer a good deal from venereal disease, and the loss of their labour is severely felt by the pearlers.[67]

It was in press reports of this inquiry that prostitution between the 'gins and the Malay and other Asiatic pearling crews' was first officially aired to the wider public.[68] Soon after the 1910 Northern Territory Aborigines Act (passed by South Australia) prohibited persons of the 'Asiatic or Negro' races from employing Aboriginal women.[69] The Northern Territory Aboriginals Ordinance of 1911 prohibited white men and Asians from 'habitually consorting' with Aboriginal women and in 1933 such 'carnal knowledge' became an offence.[70]

Already in 1899 concern had been expressed about 'houses' in Mackay said to be servicing Kanakas and Japanese. Raymond Evans found that the Queensland government imported Japanese women to serve as 'suitable outlets' for the 'sexual passion'[71] of 'coloured alien' or migrant workers. Ganter has found Japanese women were classified as prostitutes merely by their presence.[72] Despite a ban placed on the immigration of Japanese women to Queensland in 1898 (and any prostitutes by the Immigration Restriction Act), Japanese prostitutes on Thursday Island were said to enjoy 'a remarkably prosecution-free existence.'[73] Any assurance their presence might have given that sexual activity could be directed through appropriate racial conduits was undone in 1910 by the journalist Frank Fox who reported on 'Malay proas, Chinese junks, and Japanese sampans' as behind the 'vile treatment meted out to the natives.'[74] This preoccupation with Japanese aggression should be situated in the context of Australia's federation movement from the 1890s and Japan's vehement protest against the Immigration Restriction Act of 1901, which grouped their nation with Africa and Polynesia as inferior to Western countries.[75] Anxieties already elevated due to Japan's naval and military victories against Russia and China[76] were heightened by the marked dominance of Japanese contract labourers in the pearling, trepang, mining and sugar industries from the 1880s. The Japanese, anxious to assert national prestige, curtailed the prostitution of Japanese women along Australia's northern shore, signing the 1912 Convention Against Traffic in Women and Children and repatriating many women.[77]

Illicit trafficking, however, did not merely imply the crossing of borders but the contravention of otherwise racially discrete identities, all too often within borders. In 1930, Mary Bennett published her generalised account of Aboriginal women 'wronged' on stations, supplementing their 'meager resources by trading in prostitution' to withstand semi-starvation.[78] Bennett cited raids on stations or 'motor car ruffianism' comprising 'motor car loads of men from bush townships or construction camps bent on "gin-sprees", in other words drink and prostitution orgies.' Yet Bennett also subscribed to the pervasive view that, 'people cannot be robbed of what they do not possess nor native girls of chastity.' It was in this context that she placed the illegal recruiting of natives and other abuses on the northern coastline by pearling luggers. Bennett's complaint did not specify the race of the perpetrators or procurers, however. She gave evidence at the 1934–35 Royal Commission into the 'condition and treatment of Aborigines' in Western Australia headed by H. D. Moseley. The Moseley commission was undoubtedly another turning point in the public disclosure of interracial sex. Bennett argued prostitution of Aboriginal women was 'universal' in the outback and that, while the Aborigines Act purported to protect women, 'some of the police were among the worst offenders.'[79] It was just as mounting evidence of the crimes and misdemeanours of white men was exposed to public view that Australian newspapers seized upon the prostitution of Aboriginal women to Japanese pearlers.

As mentioned, I have covered this print scandal elsewhere, leaving us free to focus on its encrypting in racialised language. The story broke in 1934 when a Presbyterian missionary on Mornington Island in the Gulf of Carpentaria, Reverend Robert H. Wilson, told a reporter that while the 'lower class of white men' were interfering with Aboriginal women, the 'chief source of danger was the visiting Japanese' who were a 'menace to the natives.'[80] Soon after, 'consorting' by white men prompted an ordinance prohibiting the entry of white men into Aboriginal reserves in the Northern Territory.[81] Yet, for Wilson it was the Japanese whose 'very low standards so far as women are concerned' led them to 'ill-treat' Aboriginal women, rousing the ire of their men, who then 'wreak their vengeance on the first white man who comes along.' In the same year *The Argus* reported that the NT Chief Protector of Aborigines Dr Cecil E. Cook had tightened the regulation of Aboriginal women and 'half-castes' ostensibly to afford them greater protection. For Cook unrestricted intermarriage of 'alien coloured races' with Aborigines and 'half-castes' presented a 'grave problem': the result was a 'hybrid coloured population of a very low order.' These 'half-caste coloured aliens' constituted a 'perennial economic and social problem.'[82] Children born of Asian fathers and Aboriginal women did indeed pose a problem to protectors advocating assimilation through biological absorption. For unlike those 'half' and 'quarter-caste' girls whose children's and grandchildren's Aboriginality would ultimately be extinguished by their partnering with white men, these 'half-caste coloured aliens' embodied miscegenation with none of the perceived benefits of assimilation – infamously of 'breeding out the colour.' It is little known that this directive by

Cook in his 1932–33 report was as much a defensive response to Asian–Aboriginal cohabitation as an endorsement of whites and 'half-castes' living together. The full statement reads,

> In the Territory the mating of an aboriginal with any person other than an aboriginal is prohibited. The mating of coloured aliens with any female of part aboriginal blood is also forbidden. Every endeavour is being made to breed out the colour by elevating female half-castes to the white standard with a view to their absorption by mating into the white population.[83]

Within this obscene racial husbandry described by the term 'mating', Asian–Aboriginal children comprised a new and unwelcome racial element in Australia, combining two elements already targeted for eradication, first through the Immigration Restriction Act and then just as the policy of assimilation was being adopted by most states.[84]

Paisley argues the economic, demographic and cultural changes to Darwin during this period exacerbated racial tensions. While white men set about dispensing with any impediments to their freedom of movement, the whereabouts and movements of Aboriginal people were an increasing focus of both administrators and townspeople in Darwin as anxiety about venereal disease, opium use and leprosy within the Aboriginal community 'politicised their social and sexual interactions.'[85] In 1927, *The Argus* reported that Darwin Town Council protested the 'chaining of lubras' at its infamous compound. The report reasoned the 'lubras' had to be chained by the leg because they were diseased and would not 'submit' to treatment; they could 'run rapidly' and 'climb with ease'; they could slip handcuffs with their very small hands; it was 'almost impossible to hold them in captivity.'[86] Under a permit and curfew system instituted by Cook, Aboriginal people were issued with 'dogtags' for identification. An influx of Anglo-Australian men and a steady increase in the presence of white women, accompanied by high unemployment, exacerbated anxiety over Aboriginal people employed in the township.

A protective sentiment, particularly towards 'half-caste' Aboriginal girls – earmarked for marriage with white men to produce paler children – intensified as the presence of Chinese, Malay, Koepanger (single men indentured from Southeast Asia) and Japanese pearlers grew along Australia's northern coast. Lorna Kaino argues relations of reciprocity and exchange established from trade and cohabitation between Macassan traders and Aborigines continued in relations with the now Japanese, Malaysians, Indonesians, Chinese and Singaporeans, Timorese and Filipinos in the pearling and trepanger industries.[87] But as Paisley reports, it was the Koepangers who were more ostracised and blamed for the spread of venereal disease, along with Japanese and Malays, by concerned Australians such as the Woman's Christian Temperance Union.[88] The introduction of opium and gambling among 'detribalised' men was attributed to the Chinese. Referred to as the 'flotsam and jetsam of the Pacific',[89] these multifarious nationals comprised the undifferentiated entity 'alien' and 'Asiatic'.[90] The pearling industry relied on 'coloured' labour and Japanese and another nationals were thereby exempted from the Immigration Restriction Act in 1915.[91] Yet, under the Pearling Act of 1912 it was illegal for Japanese to own an interest in a pearling operation. The divers worked under extremely difficult conditions. Over 600 Japanese men died between 1878 and 1941 working in the Torres Strait.[92] According to Michael Schapers's account of race riots in Broome in 1920, European-Australian pearling masters 'deliberately structured the workforce along ethnic lines in an attempt to divide and rule.'[93] Mary Durack described the social hierarchy of the port: 'white pearlers were the aristocracy, the Japanese and Chinese the brains, the Asiatic crews the serfs and the Aborigines the scavengers.'[94] Ernestine Hill also reflected enthusiastically on employment protocols on the islands between Broome and Wyndham as 'simple', at least between white and black, given that once you had attained a licence, hired a lugger and got a permit to employ natives, 'the native labour does the rest' since for a stick of tobacco, cast off 'gay rags' and rations, the 'tribes are yours to command.' Hill continues with characteristic abandon,

> They will man the ship, feed the family, track up the dingoes, plant the pea-nuts, pick up the pearl shell, smoke the trepang, look after the vegetable garden, build the house, do the housework and mind the baby with a smile that never comes off if you treat them properly… and there is always the chance that one of them, in his naïve simplicity, will hand over a £1000 pearl for an extra stick of tobacco.[95]

Elided of course was the sexual labour of women, so often assumed as another perk of the contract, such as it was. This was met mostly with indifference until the 'Asiatic', ranked below even 'low-caste' European-heritage men, entered into relations with Aboriginal women.

Tensions spilled over in the 1932–33 killings of Japanese that followed a string of deaths of up to seventy-five non-Aborigines in mutinies and escapes over decades.[96] Sympathy arising from the Caledon Bay case was expressed in terms of Aboriginal men protecting their women from violent Japanese.[97] Anthropologist Donald Thompson's report taken from the elder Wonggo (father of the three warriors jailed for life and then released after Thompson's advocacy) was that he was defending his land and people from 'the white and Japanese despoilers of their women',[98] though Fred Gray, an English trepanger fishing at the site and friendly with the Balamumu, stated that Wonggo did not complain of Japanese violence against women or of them reneging on any payment.[99] However, as the pearling scandal unfolded, sympathy turned against Aboriginal men who were scapegoated as 'trafficking' to the Japanese, who simultaneously 'poached'. Thus Aboriginal women remained abused and without recourse to protection except from white men. A series of reports emerged in the press from September 1935, including 'Blacks sell womenfolk to lugger crews' in *The Argus*;[100] 'Reports of sale of lubras' in *The Sydney Morning Herald*;[101] 'Black women exploited' in *The Herald*;[102] 'Lubras on luggers' in *The Canberra Times*;[103] 'Japanese pearl poachers' in *The Daily Telegraph*;[104] 'Lubras sold. Japanese hamper mission work. Barter increases' in *The Sydney Morning Herald*;[105] 'Lubras on pearling vessels' in *The Northern Standard*;[106] and 'Native girls in luggers' in *The Herald*.[107] Run together the semiotics of these headlines show a suturing of poaching to prostitution. An illicit sexual trade attracted a competing masculinity to the nation's unprotected and vulnerable shores. Colloquial language, such as 'lubra', designates the sexuality of Aboriginal women as an exploited yet squandered commodity by 'blacks' who, like the Japanese, comprise a category evacuated of all else but sexual vice. Yet, nowhere did the Australian colloquialism 'black velvet' appear in this print scandal.

Reports appearing of the 'Sordid traffic in Aboriginal girls', in *The Argus* and *The Canberra Times*,[108] spurred the government to action.[109] Monsignor Gsell, Principal of the Bathurst Island Catholic Mission Station, reported that girls as young as ten years were sent to the luggers and at first protested vigorously, but eventually they went to the luggers of their own will, 'attracted by the lucrative gifts they receive from the Japanese.' Gsell intimates that this suggestion of consent is obviated by the vulnerability of children. Adult women's consent was only raised in terms of the violation of men's property: the women were thought to have no property in their own persons, and no modesty by which to protect it. The sexual vulnerability of children did not persist as a driver for government intervention since preventing miscegenation rather than ensuring child protection was in fact the primary moral impetus. There was also a sense at that time that Aboriginal children were sexually precocious.[110]

As we earlier observed, unease created by the children of white and black sexual liaisons right at this time was being salved through the doctrine of biological absorption – casuistry for the doctrine of assimilation. This was about to be formalised as Commonwealth policy at the 1937 meeting of the Aboriginal Protectors' Heads of State (excepting J. W. Bleakley, Chief Protector of Queensland, who was a preservationist and did not sanction biological absorption). As noted earlier, 'Asiatic–Aboriginal' children could not be 'absorbed'. They not only doubled rather than halved the problem of race within eugenic discourse, they indigenised a racial element – broadly the 'Asiatic' – that had, since the Chinese presence in the gold rush, incited fears of 'swamping'. But as Reynolds details, the desire of trade conflicted with demands for racial unity, or homogeneity. The mobility of 'asiatics', but not goods, had begun to be restricted by the 1876 Queensland Goldfields Act.[111] By 1936 calls for coastal patrols of foreign vessels due to the sexual abuse of Aboriginal women was hitched to notions of border protection and as articulated through the White Australia policy. Gsell provided potent imagery of sexual and racial transgression mapped onto a remote, unprotected border. It is little wonder Aboriginal men were initially suspected of colluding with invading Japanese during the war years.[112]

The *Canberra Times* article came immediately before the House of Representatives via Mr McCall (United Australia Party, NSW) who the next day was reported to have been assured by the Minister for the Interior, Thomas Paterson, that enquiries were already being made and that the allegations would be fully investigated.[113] For *The Argus,* Gsell's revelations of 'interference with lubras' spelt 'flagrant invasions of territorial waters by the Japanese.'[114] The paper sent its 'special representative' in Darwin to assess the effectiveness of patrols by the *Larrakia,* the Federal Government's patrol boat, but deemed it ineffective and futile and urged more effective policing of the northern coastline. *The Argus* said the women had told their representative that they were either attracted to the 'lavish supplies of tobacco' or 'beaten into submission by their husbands who had been promised food by the Japanese.'[115] Once again it was the 'aborigines' readiness to trade their women' that monopolised attention and women's possible relations of mutual exchange with Japanese was passed over. It was certainly never considered that the encounter between Japanese men and Aboriginal women might be enacted within diverse behaviours as distinct from each other as consensual cohabitation, to contractual soliciting, to abduction and rape. Aboriginal women and Japanese men each had singular sexual modalities – prostitution and aggression.

In one of the few responses that recognised the pressures on Aboriginal economies, a meeting convened by the Australian Aborigines' League passed a resolution noting that 'insufficient, food supply' was 'one of the chief reasons why the native men sell their women'. The AAL urged the Commonwealth Government to 'provide more adequate rations and to increase the grant to missions for expenditure on food, including meat.' It also called for the provision of a more effective patrol of the coasts.[116] Along with Bennett, this was a rare acknowledgement that prostitution was a response to economic rather than moral shortfall.[117] As early as 1826, newcomer incursions had already disrupted local economies. Konishi cites nineteenth-century explorer Dumont d'Urville who seemed to revel in finding people begging at a Malay trepang camp. He described fishermen amusing themselves by throwing a handful of rice on the ground to watch a rush of Aborigines swallow 'handfuls of sand in which were mixed a few grains of rice to assuage their hunger'.[118] Then, as in the interwar period, the degradation of loss of livelihood was attributed to native incompetence rather than disruption to economy. Gsell called for more funding for mission rations as a means to undercut recourse to prostitution.

The *Canberra Times* quickly became dissatisfied with the government response to the affair, airing the Reverend J. W. Burton's address to the Australian Missionary Conference in which he accused the Commonwealth of 'shirking its responsibilities and creating a "STAIN ON OUR HONOUR" [original emphasis].'[119] Like 'velvet', 'stain' is evocative language suggesting a kind of racial incontinence. *The Argus,* too, reported Burton's address in which he spoke of the treatment of 'our' Aboriginal women by 'salacious brutes' from luggers, claiming that his evidence of their mistreatment, if published, would cause Australians to become 'purple with indignation'.[120] Paterson rebuked Burton, arguing, as of old, 'it was the aborigines themselves who acquiesced because the men freely bartered their women to the crews of the luggers in return for flour tobacco &c.'[121] The honorary secretary of St Joan's Political and Social Alliance in Melbourne, Miss Flynn, endorsed his view, quoting from a letter by Gsell in which he argued that 'too much emphasis had been laid upon the value of Government protection.' Gsell instituted a novel approach in which he targeted children for education, by buying 135 little girls as brides to 'save them from child marriage, polygamy and prostitution.'[122] Gsell was later referred to as 'the Bishop with a hundred wives'.[123] As Ganter found in her study of Moravian missionary Nicolas Hey at Mapoon and the prohibitions he placed on polygamy, Gsell had likewise 'successfully appropriated the role of the male elders in allocating material resources and regulating sexual relations: he had restructured social relations from polygamous gerontocracy to monogamous patriarchy.'[124] Meanwhile, eleven Japanese luggers were fired on with 'several bursts of machine gun' at Guribah Island in early April 1937 and seventeen luggers boarded. They were assembled, the 'restrictions against illegal landings on the Australian coastline' were explained to them, and they were released, to avoid 'international complications'.[125]

Riled, *The Argus* then attacked the government for the 'cool manner' in which it had admitted the traffic in Aboriginal women to foreign craft had been 'common knowledge for years', even of Japanese 'invading' Aboriginal reserves. *The Argus* fulminated,

> yet the Cabinet is only now preparing to consider this hideous scandal, which is a disgrace to Australia's name. There has been evidence in the recent episode a disposition to be lenient with the intruders so as to avoid

possible international complications. Australians generally would not desire the Government's solemn duty of protecting the aborigines to be left undone because of such unworthy timidity.[126]

The Anglican Synod of Ballarat was likewise incensed, demanding, 'Why is it that the great British Empire behaves like a damned coward when it faces any foreign power in the world except Germany?' The Reverend B. H. Dewhurst also criticised the failure of Australian authorities to 'take prompt action to protect aboriginal women in the north against raiders from another country.' Dewhurst insisted, 'Whoever heard of a Government that allowed nationals of a foreign power to interfere with its women and decline to make a protest?'[127] Only five years before war, Australians were up in arms at an infringement of national sovereignty in the persons of its 'native women'. Within a week their calls would be answered. The NT Aboriginal Ordinance was amended to allow for the confiscation of 'foreign pearl shell poachers' found illegally in the vicinity of Aboriginal reserves on the coastline of the Northern Territory or Western Australia. Australian territorial waters were thus closed to foreign vessels as a 'protective measure' afforded to Aboriginal women from the 'attentions of the crews of foreign pearling craft' by their 'invasion of these waters' from Darwin to Arnhem Land.[128] Paterson briefed delegates to the 1937 Initial Conference of Commonwealth and State Aboriginal Authorities, the first meeting of the heads of the state Aboriginal protection and welfare boards, at which the doctrine of biological absorption was formalised as policy.[129] And in early 1941 Vestey's agreed to relinquish its lease over Melville Island, while the Tiwi Islands were gazetted as an Aboriginal reserve with a control base established at Garden Point.[130]

Paterson continued to stress the difficulty of government intervention against Aboriginal men trafficking their women. He wrote to the Ballarat branch of the Labor Party to assure them. 'Members of your branch', wrote the minister, 'can rest assured that nothing is being left undone to protect aboriginal women, despite the practice of selling them engaged in by their own kith and kin.'[131] Meanwhile, accusations that Australian-owned pearling lugger crews, and not crews of oversea luggers, were guilty of the worst excesses were made by the Wesley Church.[132] Paterson asserted to *The Argus* that 'The Patrol Service has come to stay', as long as 'a vestige of the traffic in aboriginal women remained, a traffic which is carried on by male aboriginals who barter their women for flour and tobacco, and must be utterly stamped out.' Paterson was determined, he said, that 'any person, white or coloured, who engages in unlawful poaching or immoral trafficking in aborigines may expect the penalty of the law.'[133] His words collocate poaching and prostitution, reinforcing that settler sexual access to Indigenous women was intrinsic to access to land and resource extraction. Again he ran the two offences together, assuring 'protection would now be afforded aboriginal women from the attentions of the crews of foreign pearling craft', adding that steps would also be taken to 'assure prompt action to deal with vessels found illegally in territorial waters.' Poaching specifically invokes the illegal removal of resources by 'aliens'. Trafficking, as distinct from trading, refers to the illegal exploitation of contraband materials and has come to refer to arms, drugs and human smuggling across borders. The new measures were run together in print reports:

> Action to provide for the effective policing of valuable pearl shell beds in Australian territorial waters and to

'Black velvet' and 'purple indignation'

guard against interference with aboriginal women by the crews of foreign pearling luggers, was taken yesterday by the Commonwealth Government, under amendments of the Aboriginal Ordinance proclaimed in a special Commonwealth gazette.[134]

Placed together here the trespass over Aboriginal women's bodies is seamlessly drawn into the trespass of national sovereignty. But nowhere in this print maelstrom did 'black velvet' appear.

After hostilities commenced, Japanese were accused of having 'fraternised with the aborigines, whose women they wronged. Pretending friendship, they were a most evil influence along the coasts of North Australia.' However, the image of Aboriginal men was rehabilitated. The 'blackfellows' of North Australia 'proved their worth as "allies"' and as 'good companions' to Australian soldiers in guarding the northern coast.[135] Indeed, during the war men from Caledon Bay were pictured in *Wild Life Magazine*.[136] The 'fine character in the faces and bearing of these men' showed they 'prove to be noble and loyal.' Their previous reputation for ferocity had only derived from 'a determination to preserve their land and their kindred from the depredations of intruders, whether white or yellow', though needless to say their 'main grievance was the visits of the Japanese pearlers, who used to carry off their women.'[137] As Aboriginal men became defenders of the northern coast they were reinstated as defenders of their women. Within frontier masculinity, Japanese men were presented as invaders who plundered and raped. It was an image that settler-colonial men could least face about themselves and perhaps for this reason had to be resolutely repelled.

Figure 5.4 'Black Velvet', in People, *14 November 1956, Bauer Media Ltd. Courtesy National Library of Australia; NQ 059.4 PEO*

The scandal of the 'lubra trade' on our northernmost shores did not alter the slanting references to 'black velvet' in print. Xavier Herbert, for example, decided against keeping it as the original title of his 1938 novel *Capricornia*. When fighting with Japan ceased and panic about 'alien coloured' sexual transgression subsided, 'black velvet' was revealed to the public, almost as the

'Black velvet' and 'purple indignation'

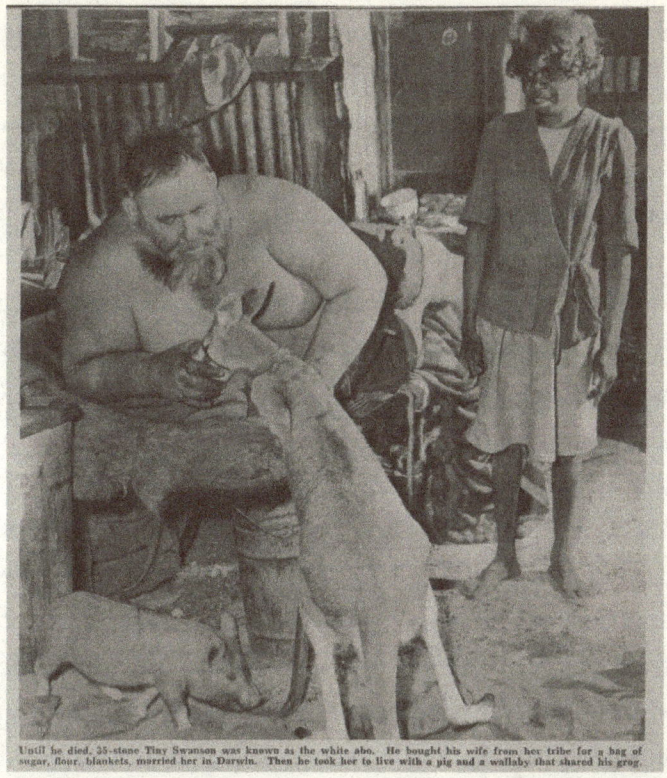

Figure 5.5 'Black Velvet', in People, *14 November 1956, Bauer Media Ltd. Courtesy National Library of Australia; NQ 059.4 PEO*

unveiling of a national secret, by *People* magazine in 1956. *People* was a Fairfax publication and the first Australian weekly to feature a topless model. Its exposure of 'black velvet' was bound to excite salacious interest, yet the author was a Walkley award-winning journalist and relatively sympathetic (see Figure 5.4).[138] Harry Cox sets a vivid scene round a fire on a northern Australian cattle station from which white men took black girls into the stunted shrub. Cox argued this 'hush-hush' practice was known all over northern Australia and went back to the first white settlers. But due to the impacts of 'persecution, ill-treatment and near slavery' and epidemic disease, and most importantly the growing presence of white women, the phenomenon of 'black velvet' had declined.

'The white man is no longer lonely',[139] Cox declared, and he also felt a 'belated sense of shame.' But for the 'aboriginal harlot' it was too late. By giving her money or trinkets she had learnt she could 'make a trade of it.' Cox did not see 'black velvet' as exclusive to the north and he linked it expressly to Aborigines being 'hunted' from their lands, to white 'superior airs' and to a 'general policy of destroying the natives' personal integrity, of humiliating and ill-treating them, and generally taking from them all their human rights.' Interestingly, the Japanese now figure benignly in Cox's exposé as members of an 'oasis of tolerance' for people of 'mixed blood' in Broome. Cox's exemplar was found in the prospector and 35-stone 'Tiny Swanson', conveying the side-show excess of white men who married Aboriginal women (see Figure 5.5). Swanson was well known in the Northern Territory for strong-man feats, but perhaps most famous posthumously for requiring a two-tonne crane to lift his body into his grave (he died of kidney failure, aged fifty-eight). A report on his death included this cartoon (Figure 5.6) and Cox described his living arrangements as anarchic with chooks and a drunken pig roaming through the marital shed. Tiny reputedly carried a pet kangaroo under one arm, and his wife, Ruby, under the other.[140] Clearly, 'black velvet' continued to describe marginal sexual relations within the remotest reaches of the interior. Though it specified white–Aboriginal relations, it took in the full 'spectrum' of sexual activity when it came to Aboriginal women, from rape to prostitution and marriage.

The obscured, yet widely circulated, term 'black velvet' operated linguistically as slang euphemism – an innocuous phrase that replaced an offensive social relation. It specifically masked the widely known, yet publicly repressed, phenomenon of interracial cohabitation, as well as white men's sexual aggression. Compared to

'Black velvet' and 'purple indignation'

the blinding print exposure of Japanese men's sexual relations with Aboriginal women and girls, 'black velvet' euphemised a register of touch that was racially specific from white men to Aboriginal women. As Bhabha argues, such counter-narratives of the nation 'continually evoke and erase its totalizing boundaries – both actual and conceptual – [and] disturb those ideological maneuvers through which "imagined communities" are given essentialist identities.'[141] For settlers, 'black velvet' denoted Aboriginal women as a collective, tactile surface of moral oblivion accessible to white men exclusively – women who were devoided of any interiority of values, family attachment, or responsibilities to land, custodianship

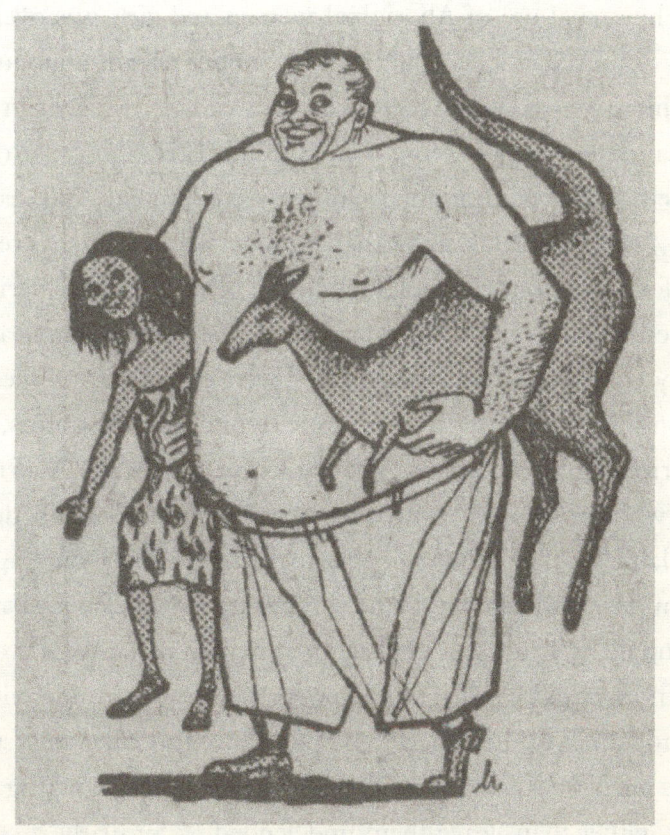

Figure 5.6 'Territorians are mourning for Tiny', The Sun-Herald, 12 December 1954. Courtesy National Library of Australia. JAF Newspaper 079.94 SUN

or law, let alone sexual agency. The specifically white men 'interfering' in, or forming enduring attachments to, black women's bodies, instated an epidermal economy that went largely euphemised. Yet, this sexually transmitted colloquialism consummated colonial entitlement to the resources of the land. Its restricted use conveyed the 'multi-national' localities of northern-shore pearling communities in the Northern Territory, Western Australia and the Torres Strait, and the role of Indigenous women in creating 'a place of conjunction or a site of convergence between different places, cultures, and nations'[142] that had to be suppressed under White Australia.

The sexual use of Aboriginal women and girls was over and again dismissed as a necessary evil in frontier terrain unpopulated by white women, who were themselves cast as negligent in their marital duties to pioneering men and ultimately the cause of the problem.[143] Since Aboriginal women were 'amoral' and, as Hill put it, 'easy for the taking'[144] the argument about who was responsible for access to their bodies fell to the men, who were variously accused of being tyrannical squanderers if they were black, poachers if they were Asian, exploiters if they were lower-class whites and responsible protectors if they were white administrators, missionaries or humanitarians. The argument that it was Aboriginal men who prostituted women to Japanese surfaced again during the claim by the Yolngu people in the Supreme Court against Commonwealth leasing of land at Yirrkala to Nabalco for bauxite mining in 1971. In fact, Yirrkala men refused requests for women from miners and women would not gather near the mine without the protection of their men.[145] Bennett, too, had cited an instance where men on a station refused to muster without taking their wives, rather than 'leave them undefended'.[146] Similarly, a central claim by Aboriginal stockmen in the Wave Hill walk-off – which

'Black velvet' and 'purple indignation'

set in motion campaigns for equal wages and added momentum to land rights – was that they were deliberately rostered to work that removed them from the camp, leaving women vulnerable to white ringers.[147] Black female sexuality has been described by Hortense Spillers as the site of unrecognisable femininity, 'unvoiced, misseen'.[148] The sexual histories of Aboriginal women are suppressed, distorted and misappropriated.

The halting, slanted use of 'black velvet' demonstrates that sexual and political dominance are indeed a 'homology' in Western colonialism, replete with hidden truth claims.[149] Yet, it also reveals the role of language, its expressions and suppressions, in adding to the porousness and incompleteness of colonial state power that Burton has emphasised in her work, 'due as much to the permeability of national/colonial borders as it was to the political instability of political regimes grounded in a normative heterosexual order.'[150] In its racialised denotation it attempted to shore up the borders of 'an unregulated "promiscuity" of categories [that] was occurring in the tropics.'[151] Its very elision in the instance of Japanese and Aboriginal sexual unions mapped sexual and racial coordinates. Through boastful colloquial classification, territorially distinct, nationally discrete sexual domains were linked to permissible trade and protected territory. The possessive impulse thus permeating its meaning, we can see, was flouted by Aboriginal women through the varied intimacies with which they engaged the Japanese pearl fishers to their economies and bodies. By the term 'black velvet', settlers' attempts to control Aboriginal women's desires, their connections and their dealings, along with their victimisation, was rendered as surface effect. In their intimacies with Japanese, Aboriginal women resisted the touch of white men as any claim to possession or as constraining them within national bounds.

6

'ABSOLUTE FRIGHTS': APPEARANCE AND ELDERS

A familiar figure appears to us in J. G. Wood's *Natural History of Man,* published in 1880. He celebrates the grace and symmetry of Aboriginal men, but women, particularly aged women, were derided and scorned. In general Wood found women 'much inferior to the men in appearance' but he singled out women who had reached their later years as 'hideous and hag-like' and attributed their 'deterioration' to their 'exceedingly hard life'. Wood goes on, without restraint, to describe the disturbing lithograph by Angas which we saw in Chapter 3:

> The old Australian woman certainly does not possess the projecting jaws, the enormous mouth, and the sausage-like lips of the African, but she exhibits a type of hideousness peculiarly her own. Her face looks like a piece of black parchment strained tightly over the skull, and the mop-like, unkempt hair adds a grotesque element to the features which only makes them still more repulsive. The breasts reach to the waist, flat, pendent, and swinging about at every movement; her body is so shrunken that each rib stands out boldly, the skin being drawn deeply in between them, and the limbs shrivel up until they look like sticks, the elbows and knees projecting like knots on a gnarled branch...There was one old

'Absolute frights': appearance and elders

woman in particular, who exemplified strongly all the characteristics which have just been described; and so surpassingly hideous, filthy, and repulsive was she, that she looked most like one of the demoniacal forms that Callot was so fond of painting than a veritable human creature. Indeed, so very disgusting was her appearance, that one of the party was made as ill as if he had taken an emetic.[1]

We can surmise from this description that the woman was severely malnourished and barely eking out an existence marred by extreme privation. The given scene is presented as abject, rather than tragic or indeed reprehensible. No doubt this disavowal elicited visceral responses in newcomers and provided the rationale not to assist or seek reparation for people who were clearly in torment and probably gravely ill. Wood declines to reproduce the Angas sketch, 'Not wishing to shock my readers by the portrait of this wretched creature, I have introduced on page 6 two younger females of the same tribe.' He notes that the old woman whose portrait he withheld, 'was clothed in the paingkoont, and wore no other raiment, so that the full hideousness of her form was exposed to view.'[2] But what exactly was exposed to settlers by the condition of this frail, elderly, ailing woman? What exactly did they feel compelled to hide from view under the guise of decorum, yet imprint in majuscule text? For the recursive discursive violence against aged Aboriginal women in colonial print is so graphic and vicious it reads as though stamped by bloodied all caps much like toecaps.

Wood's belief that Aboriginal women aged prematurely due to hardships – usually inflicted by their 'brutish' husbands, but also because their bodies were unclad and unsheltered from harsh elements – was widely shared. His comparison with African women was a nod to the purportedly impartial observation informing comparative physiognomy at the time. His inkling that his readers would receive the 'native belle' as a more digestible representative for Aboriginal womanhood was canny. Having indulged their imaginations in the 'dark belles of the gum forest',[3] readers should, it seemed, be forewarned about the unsightly Aboriginal woman elder. This figure was referenced as a sinister denouement to colonial curiosity. Readers were advised they were shielded from the mortification that such women, particularly diseased, plainly suffering, and possibly starving women, could impart. The very visual access to the feminine body that tribeswomen afforded print consumers was suppressed yet referenced when it came to older women. The term 'unsightly' describes precisely this peek-a-boo dynamic, invoking to the mind's eye what should not be seen while casting a malevolent presence within the fraught colonial encounter and landscape. The obligation on aging, postmaternal women to not offend newcomer men by exposing themselves to view affords us a revealing glimpse into the significance of perceptual relations to the settler-colonial project, the exchange of looks between men and women across the cleave of race and the legitimacy granted to certain native bodies, particularly young, 'comely' or athletic naked bodies, in the colonial scene. Most curiously, elder women were not enjoined to adopt European dress, so beyond the ken of decorum were they; they instead embodied the edict of dying race theory, no less because they appeared more fragile than elder men who were noted as robust and agile. Racial difference was foremost in these European visions of the Australian 'native' woman, as was a look riveted by the twin compulsions of aversion and allure. The concern of this final chapter is newcomers' attention to Aboriginal women's physical characteristics and their compulsion to record (and publish) their

'Absolute frights': appearance and elders

very visceral responses as both impartial scientific observation and as testimony of their own sense of decorum. We return to earlier print fragments and pursue their reiteration into the twentieth century to decipher this encoding of aged Aboriginal women as inimical and anomalous to the colonial scene. We uncover a pattern of meaning through a scatter of recursive descriptions to gauge settler-colonial perceptual relations across the typeset and the significance of age to these colonial, gendered encounters.

The impact of settler incursions into Aboriginal lands was graphically marked over visually accessible Aboriginal bodies, yet injury, disease and privation were held up as proofs of 'savage' custom, race destiny and vagrancy. The inescapable presence of elder women, as we saw with the Angas lithograph, recast the landscape as hostile, malevolent and melancholic. Angas wrote of such 'attenuated' beings appearing unaccountably 'wretched' in the idyllic 'aromatic' and 'flower-spangled' landscape. Elder women also embodied anxiety about a spectral and eerie landscape that was both desolate and entrapping. The less human and more wraith-like they appeared, the more they embodied a settler dread that *terra nullius* would always be haunted by visions of a watching spectre, crouched and brooding, disturbing the peace. A short story printed in a US newspaper described the 'lubra' of an Aboriginal spearing suspect as a 'tall, thin, ill-favoured woman, whose years had passed the twenty-five, or thereabout, which spell middle-age for her sex and race. One eye squinted so much only a segment of the iris showed, with sinister effect.'[4] The project of settlement was disturbed by this antediluvian presence, which contrasted with the endearing and dirigible 'piccaninny' simply by having grown old in situ without the 'guidance' of missionary dormitories or through child removal to training institutes. The elder exposed to view that settlers were not taking up a new world, but rather one ancient, sentient and self-knowing in ways that newcomers could not comprehend.

Descriptions of the physical characteristics, or visual identity, of indigenous peoples are central to colonial discourse. In their exploratory voyages Europeans conflated the quasi-scientific spectacle of ethnology, exoticism and landscape against contemporary ideals of feminine beauty. Encounters with the visual markers of racial difference were primary to the experience of colonial expansion. Aspects of racialised physical appearance, such as headdresses and clothing had been exhibited in international expositions, metropolitan museums and travelling circuses, as well as through refining and industrialising image reproduction, print media and, later, photography. Notions of feminine visibility, too, related to urbanisation, workforce participation, consumption and leisure, would dramatically alter from the 1880s. The emotive language that was woven through anthropometrics also evinced much about the standing of elderly women for Europeans and the importance of their coverings to propriety.

The perception of beauty, or its lack, should have been incompatible with the disinterested gaze of science. It could not be quantified, described or categorised without implicating both subjective evaluation and unexamined societal conventions. And yet appearance is continually referenced in the colonial encounter. 'Prominent superciliary arches' (above the eyes), the 'elongated dolichocephalic (long-headed) skull', the 'well-formed, lithe' 'erect carriage' and 'absence of calves', delicate bones and lank, wavy hair – these evinced the racial category, racial origin and racial destiny of the Australian Aborigine.[5] Despite its dubious scientific status, the appraisal of visual identity was implicated in the ethnological and anthropological gaze. From the 1860s it informed ideas of racial difference and ranking on the ladder of evolutionary hierarchy. Through increasingly probing measurements of native bodily intervals, a clearer picture of the racially ordained worth of Europeans was reflected back to them, particularly in contrast to the purportedly broken-down native woman elder. Ethnological interest in the racial test of beauty informed the logic of scientific spectacle (and its commercialisation), and cast both the monstrous or differently beautiful native woman as specimen and signifier of racial difference. The distinction between European and indigenous women was made not just through their respective physical measures, but also through their very different relation to feminine beauty and its racially distinct modalities of visibility in colonial modernity: indigenous women were exhibited, whereas modern white women increasingly, from the time of Wood's publication, exhibited themselves.

The nakedness of the New Hollander, as is by now well established, was a key descriptor for their ranking as 'primitive' and as living in a 'state of nature', or *'in puris naturalibus'*.[6] This was variously confronting, picturesque, repugnant and impressive to settlers. As clothes became part of the banal and everyday exchange on the colonial frontier, their very visible wear and tear on the bodies of Aborigines, clad in this 'thin veneer of civilisation', seemed an almost intolerable display of unassimilable European values and the attrition of these social rudiments, as well as the deteriorating health of Aboriginal bodies.[7] As Jean Comaroff has argued, colonial subjects were fashioned as much by 'the circulation of stylized objects as from brute force or bureaucratic fiat.'[8] Clothes were 'commodities and accoutrements of a civilized self' but they became something other, and something descriptive of otherness when worn – in both senses of the word – by Aborigines. Injunctions, even ordinances, required Aborigines to don coverings within town boundaries[9] and in the Northern Territory

Aboriginal women were prohibited from wearing male clothing in the company of white men,[10] foreclosing on the 'drover's boy' phenomenon in which women and girls were disguised so drovers could avoid being prosecuted for their abduction or concubinage. Yet, for all the settlers' horror of being exposed to elder women's bodies, these injunctions did not seem particularly directed against them. There was an aspect to their exposure that seemed fitting, namely to harsh elements.

Offence taken at exposure to elder women was compounded by race and gender. In a travelogue of the 1820s by Robert Mudie, 'native Australians' were described as having 'slender claims' to 'personal beauty'. He then calibrates the insignia of the primitive grotesque in disproportionate heads, 'frizzled hair' smeared with grease and ochre, flat noses with distended nostrils, hollow eyes, 'bushy and projecting eyebrows', 'uncommonly large' mouths, thick lips, flat noses and general similarity to orangutangs. Mudie, too, ascribed the loss of young women's looks to 'the hardships they are made to undergo, the inferior nature of their food, and the treatment they receive.' He described the sartorial gaffes of the native, claiming they wore everything given to them as head ornaments. A defence of the 'well meaning ladies of Port Jackson' was raised for they were 'equally astonished and shocked when their sable protégés soon after presented themselves to give thanks, just as nude rearward as before, but with tatters of the *femoralia* [breeches] tastefully gummed around their ears, as a substitute for wigs.'[11]

Spectacularisation of the native woman formed part of what Rosalyn Poignant calls 'the living fermentation that produced modernity.' She argues that colonial representations were 'arenas for the representation of cultural difference, which paralleled the development of ideas about the classification of human types –

ideas that served to define and maintain cultural differences and distance within colonialism's cultures.'[12] Constructs of feminine beauty or its lack operated within colonialism's expanding repertoire of representations of the native woman, supplying European fascination in the physical descriptors of racial difference. If beauty or its lack articulated racial difference and excluded Indigenous women from the category 'modern', as I've argued elsewhere,[13] it did so from within the wider discursive field and visual scene of colonial modernity of which press was a key cultural infrastructure. Let's set the scene for these peculiarly colonial perceptual relations in which the elder Aboriginal woman was allotted with gorgon-like potencies.

In the period that encompasses first-contact scenarios in Australia – from William Dampier's 1688 visit, to the settlement of colonies into the 1850s – Europeans conventionalised 'ways of seeing'[14] along the sightlines of colonial expansion. Along with the surveying and mapping of geographies, the refinement of visual technologies framed first-contact encounters within an increasingly ocularcentric worldview. Ocularcentrism is the privileging of vision in the production of knowledge above all senses: the historical shift to thinking in terms of seeing.[15] Detached, disinterested objectivism was a cultural tendency of the Enlightenment.[16] It created a split between the object observed and the observing subject, which persisted into the modern instrumental gaze, and posited the sexual differentiation of the looking subject as masculine and the looked-at object as feminine.[17] The colonial gaze supplemented this binary opposition by feminising the geographies and indigenous bodies it surveyed.

This 'conquest of the world as perspective',[18] by which objects were perceived as arrayed across an exterior field, has also been described as a defining lineament of modernity.[19] The scientific revolution and its extension of the human gaze through ocular apparati, such as the refracting telescope, unleashed an exploratory, surveying gaze. Martin Jay argues that this 'mapping impulse' facilitated 'a more active search for controlling and dominating the earth.'[20] As we've seen, the expansion of literacy, the invention of the woodblock, the outreach of transportation and communication through imperial trade routes created new prospects for the dissemination of European accounts of the 'native', particularly through the syndication and reiteration of tropes.[21] New interest in the manners and customs of the native were intently focused on their appearance as a means to assess 'the racial hierarchies at modernity's heart.'[22] Concomitantly, image production would become increasingly industrialised and commercialised from the use of commercial half-tone screens in 1890, enabling the reproduction of photographs in the burgeoning illustrated press as well as in picture postcards and picture atlases.[23] The native woman was a 'striking ornament' of romanticised and aestheticised nature, racial difference and colonial conquest, yet older women were seen as monstrous and a rung down the ladder of racial hierarchy.

The face-off of European and indigenous peoples in early colonial encounters impelled new and enduring literary, scientific and artistic conventions, themselves enmeshed in prevailing representational regimes. As we know, cannibalism, infanticide and polygamy were the tripartite underpinnings of savagery, and they were accompanied by sexual promiscuity and imbued with emotional volatility and treachery.[24] But meanings of savagery were also derived from visual impressions, under the influence of the ascendant science of physiognomy, with its measures of difference popularised in print. They were also shaped by mutually incomprehensible languages which forced visual encounters to the fore as the locus of colonial comprehension. In 1841 *The Colonial Magazine* identified Aborigines as of the Alfourou race, and skidded off into a description of their

> repulsive appearance: – flat noses, with thick, wide nostrils; projecting cheek bones, large eyes, wide mouth, thick lips, prominent teeth, long and slender legs, black, lank, dishevelled hair; deep dirty-brown or black skin. They go naked, and cover themselves with dirt and filth; make incisions in their bodies, wear pieces of stick in their noses, and many have the two centre front teeth extracted.[25]

Significantly, it observed, 'their women are still more ugly than the men', and this perception spun off, entrapping Aboriginal women in an ouroboros of vilification.

From the earliest encounters, the Australian 'native' was remarked on as elaborately unclothed. Captain James Cook remarked, 'They were quite naked, and wore no ornaments, unless we consider as such, and as proof of their love of finery, some large punctures or ridges raised on different parts of their bodies, some in straight and others in curved lines.' He rather lyrically referred to these cicatrised markings, made from rubbing ash or clay into incisions, as 'embroidery of their persons'.[26] While he noted the children were 'pretty', a less favourable report was made of 'the persons of the women, especially those in advanced years.'[27] The botanical Banks noted that though the 'Indians' of New Holland seem to be 'fond of ornament', they were 'absolutely without apparel'.[28] Determined to find their true colour under the dirt which he claimed 'stuck to their hides from the day of their birth, without their once having attempted to remove it', Banks spat on a finger and rubbed someone to find they resembled chocolate. He was unsure whether their nakedness was due to 'idleness or want of invention.'[29] When the English offered cloth to the Eora they later found the greater part of it 'lying in a heap together, probably as useless lumber, not worth carrying away.' Cook concluded that 'they seemed to set little value upon any thing that we had.'[30]

These early observations seem to struggle to reconcile apparent Indigenous indifference towards English signs of prosperity with extant ideas of the noble savage. They were published in lavishly illustrated exploratory volumes, in which engravings of portraits and groups ensconced in sublime scenery supported the typology of the noble savage and native belle. As Marianna Torgovnick argues, 'primitivist discourse' fulfils Western longings and yearnings for pre-history and accounts of origin. It draws on notions of the natural order to access the essential and play off degeneracy with nobility.[31] Nakedness figured largely along with the attributions of cannibalism, infanticide and polygamy. The noble savage did not so much retreat from the colonial account; rather, the noble and ignoble savages became more polarised, evincing attraction and repulsion, and none more so than the native belle and unsightly elder woman.

While those from the First Fleet were struggling to establish a settlement at Sydney Cove, Mary Wollstonecraft wrote in London that women are 'taught from their infancy that beauty is woman's spectre, the mind shapes the body, and roaming around its gilt cage, only seeks to adore its prison.'[32] This much-cited comment was made at the height of eighteenth-century colonial expansion, particularly in the southern seas of the Pacific. A penal settlement of just over a thousand convicts – only 191 of whom were women[33] – had been established at Sydney Cove just four years before the publication of *A Vindication of the Rights of Woman*.

'Absolute frights': appearance and elders

The women that sailed from Plymouth were among the first European women to enter into the very masculinist colonial scene created from the exploratory voyages of the Antipodes since Abel Tasman in 1642. The publications emanating from the three South Sea voyages of Captain James Cook in 1769, 1772 and 1776, along with the earlier Pacific voyages of Wallis and Bougainville, and later La Pérouse,[34] had impacted profoundly on the European imagination, which became enthralled by the native belle.[35] The native belle suggests the colonial visual scene was contradictory in its invocations of feminine beauty and how it was referenced against so-called civilised femininity. Just as European and Indigenous women were about to engage in the Australian colonial encounter, feminine beauty or its lack would become a defining discourse of racial difference between 'civilised' and 'primitive' women. Wollstonecraft wrote,

> An immoderate fondness for dress, for pleasure, and for sway, are the passions of savages; the passions that occupy those uncivilised beings who have not yet extended the dominion of the mind, or even learned to think with the energy necessary to concatenate that abstract train of thought which produces principles. And that women from their education and the present state of civilised life, are in the same condition, cannot, I think, be controverted.[36]

Something more than the staking out of reason as the exclusive territory of Europeans – which Wollstonecraft argued should rightfully include British women – is at work here. That civilisation should be manifest in the visual effects of women is a significant inference which would in fact inform the investment of white women in beauty techniques, particularly those that spoke of civilised refinement and, increasingly, modern self-mastery. It would also mean that the adopting of European standards of dress and beauty by Indigenous women would be a central concern of missionaries, colonial administrators, commentators and settlers. Occasionally but enduringly, joking references were made about women's shared love of finery across race. In 1863 a self-identified bushman's memoir of the Lachlan River recalls that the 'gins' anointed themselves all over with red or white pipeclay. He concluded, 'So, ladies of this 20th century are not without precedent when following the fashion of the hour.'[37] The problem with Wollstonecraft's earlier invoking of 'savage passions' was that Indigenous forms of beauty suggested that beauty could in fact be uncontrived, unselfconscious and unregulated. Our escort through these archives, the squatter Edward Curr, recalled overhearing a Bangerang man 'extolling the charms of a young woman, that her skin was smooth and bright as the wood of the box-tree off which the bark had been newly stripped.'[38] This was a rare acknowledgement of the criteria by which Indigenous men appreciated feminine beauty. By most accounts the native belle was beholden to no man's gaze. She embodied a form of beauty that was liberated at the incipient moment of Western feminism.

Smith concludes his *European Vision in the South Pacific* by noting that 'it was the initial impressions of the early navigators in the Pacific which made the most fundamental and lasting impression upon the European imagination.'[39] We've seen the way Dampier was recycled and other impressions from first-contact scenarios continued to appear in print, such as in Bonwick's *The Lost Tasmanian Race*, which cites French explorer Péron in detail. Bonwick writes of Péron's disgust at the 'bizarre and the picturesque effects presented' by the nakedness of the women. He described their forms as 'thin and faded', noting, as European men invariably did, the postmaternal breast as 'long and pendant'. The 'bedaubing' of skin with seal fat and the reddening of hair with ochre dust and charcoal repulsed Péron, who singled out 'aged females' for derision due to their 'gross and ignoble figure' and 'fierce and sombre look' imprinted by the yoke of 'misfortune and slavery.' Scars made in mourning and other life-cycle rites were instead attributed to the 'ill-treatment from their ferocious husbands.' But Péron exempted,

> from this general tableau two or three young girls of from fifteen to sixteen years, in whom we distinguished forms agreeable enough, contours sufficiently graceful, and in whom the breast was firm and well-placed, although the nipple was a little too large and too long. These young girls had also something in the expression of their features the most ingenuous, the most affectionate, the most gentle, as if the better qualities of the soul could exist even in the midst of the savage hordes of the human species, the more particular gift of youth, or grace, and of beauty.[40]

As such the ignoble and noble savage continued to bookend the significatory scene of Australian colonialism. This scene, acutely attuned to appearance and racialised visual identity, invoked the native belle and unsightly elder in a discursive shuttle between the twin tendencies of monstrous and romantic native within Western primitivism.[41] The doubling occurred along the axis of age for, while young women were often noted as 'plump and good-looking', older women were 'literally "old hags" – lean and shrivelled, and excessively ugly.'[42] While the native belle clearly demonstrates the operation of gender in colonial discourse, along with the workings of race within the idea of feminine beauty – the unsightly elder woman was also instrumental to defining the parameters of true womanhood.

Appearance was a means to enact racialised power, capable of withholding cultural presence and legitimacy. Our present culture, 'impaled on the effects of first impressions', is shaped by the physiognomic literature of the seventeenth, eighteenth and nineteenth centuries, particularly Johann Casper Lavater's *Essays on Physiognomy* published from 1781 to 1803, which focused on the 'legibility of character through surface manifestations.'[43] Earlier, in 1775, Johann Blumenbach's *On the Natural Variety of Mankind* proposed that humans could be distinguished by physical traits. He categorised humanity into five races, principally differentiated through chromometrics (eye, hair and skin colour): Caucasian or white, Mongolian or yellow, Ethiopian or black, American or red and Malayan or brown. Blumenbach was influenced by the eighteenth-century anatomists Georges Louis Leclerc and Comte de Buffon[44] but his own contribution to the burgeoning science of human variety was to associate physical differences with mental characteristics. This correlation initiated the science of anthropometry with its basis in bodily measurement, particularly craniometry and osteometry. It also informed the pre-industrial idea of beauty as the surface manifestation of inner virtue, an idea which became racialised in the context of colonialism and its scientific spectacularisation of the 'native'. As Paul Taylor notes,

> the most prominent racialist thought took shape under the same intellectual circumstances that in the eighteenth century produced efforts to define an aesthetic morality

'Absolute frights': appearance and elders

centered on the 'beautiful soul' and in the nineteenth century led to the 'science' of physiognomy.[45]

Thus, Dampier's damning appraisal of the New Hollanders was reprinted in 1787, 'They are long visaged, and of a very unpleasing aspect, having not one graceful feature in their faces.'[46] Thomas Watling, who arrived in the nascent New South Wales colony in 1792, wrote to his aunt in Dumfries that Aborigines' 'virtues are so far from conspicuous.' Watling implicated outward appearance with moral traits when he wrote, 'Irascibility, ferocity, cunning, treachery, filth, and immodesty, are strikingly their dark characteristics.'[47] Still decades later, in 1842, *The Penny Magazine* reported 'their countenances betray their treachery and implacability.'[48]

Early European encounters with Australian Aborigines deployed their physical traits in their positioning in the 'great chain of being', the Linnaean taxonomy explored in Chapter 1, that ranged from 'inanimate matter at the bottom to man and the angels at the apex.'[49] For Robert Montgomery Martin, in 1841, the racial difference of the Aborigines of Australia created a spectacle that science would logically turn its gaze to: 'The very condition of this people is most peculiar and anomalous, and presents a picture of human life which is worthy of attention and study.'[50] From the publication of Darwin's *Origin of Species* in 1859, anthropologists ranked races on the evolutionary ladder. Anthropologists from the 1860s such as Henry Huxley sought to 'standardize the portrayal of indigenous people globally'[51] through anthropometric photography. The emergence of the dry-plate in the mid-1880s allowed Australian photographers such as J. W. Lindt and Nicolas Caire to abandon their studios and travel on photographic expeditions as far afield as New Guinea and the South Pacific.[52] Their work contributed to a representational field that distinguished, ordered and administered native populations and often conflated racial difference with visual abjection. Thus the SA Report of the Select Committee of the Legislative Council on the Aborigines in 1860 quotes ethnologist Professor Richard Owen on his calculation of the facial angle and its relationship to intelligence:

> If a line...be drawn from the occipital condyle along the floor of the nostrils, and be intersected by a second touching the most prominent parts of the forehead and upper jaw, the intercepted angle gives, in a general way, the proportions of the cranial activity and the grade of intelligence; it is called a facial angle. In the dog this angle is 20°, in the great chimpanzee, or gorilla, it is 40°, but the prominent superorbital ridge occasions some exaggeration; in the Australian it is 85°, in the European it is 95°. The ancient Greek artists adopted in their *beau ideal* of the beautiful and intellectual, an angle of 100°.[53]

Evidently Professor Owen had not made acquaintance with a pug. Facial angle was a key indice of civilisation, and the 'prognathous' form of skull was set at a 'low' angle among Aborigines.[54]

Even the considered and sympathetic traveller W. F. Ainsworth was not immune to this ranking of racialised visual identity when he wrote in 1860 that, 'The Australians may be considered as living in the lowest state of civilisation' due to 'their lean and half-starved forms, and the disproportionate size of their limbs and head.'[55] Aboriginal bodies evinced this 'lowest state' on the evolutionary ladder, through a tendency for their skeletons to dematerialise in the colonial visual scene as a materialisation

'Absolute frights': appearance and elders

of their dying race destiny. Thus the report of the 1860 Select Committee found that,

> Physically, the aborigines of Victoria, like the other sad decaying remnants of their race in other parts of Australia, are not only misshapen in outline, owing to the marked disproportion between the cranium and the limbs, but they are also characterised by a very great deficiency of bone throughout the skeleton generally. On the extreme frontiers of degraded humanity, their osseous system is evidently dying out...the chemical proportions of the solid textures of the body in the native Australian seem to be diminishing.

The report also noted that,

> a painful resemblance to the *Cretin* at once arrests the eye, and painfully affects the heart with the conviction, that no-where else on the earth does man so obviously indicate in his skeleton – its amount and quality of bone – in his relaxed casts of muscular development, abject mould of features, and entire style, a fatal tendency to extinction.

The report then sets out a table of measurements which is foot-noted with the following caveat, 'No other woman [than Flora] could be persuaded to be weighed or measured.'[56] This painful reminder that native women comprised a database or were cast as props within colonial measures of racial supremacy is also a sign that women resisted these terms of inclusion in the colonial visual scene, an idea we will conclude with.

For the fastidious observers of imperial modernity, looking with disinterest was primary to their roles as informants in an era of science dominated by measurement and marked by 'an avalanche of numbers' in the physical sciences.[57] The identification of beauty in the 'sooty sirens'[58] of Australia amplified the racial distance assumed by the colonial observer or administrator, while paradoxically drawing Indigenous women into the intimate gaze of the exotic. James Clifford comments on the significance of this distancing in constructions of 'primitivism as a white, Western, and preponderantly male quest for an elusive object whose very condition of desirability resides in some form of distance and difference, whether temporal or geographical.'[59] The native belle type was purportedly a naive beauty unwitting of the impact of her beauty. White men salvaged that beauty as a kind of redemption from the ruin of the tribal,[60] and as a show of colonial chivalry. Robert Dawson, who lived first in the settlement at Port Stephens, recorded in his journal that he saw many native girls who were

> very pretty, and, except that their limbs were somewhat too slender, particularly well formed. Their bosoms were full and handsome, their waists small, and the breadth across the loins corresponding with the development of the form above.[61]

The Aboriginal woman was said to 'possess fine dark eyes' and breasts which 'are at first large, firm and hemisphered.'[62] Her 'mouth is large and much developed, but it frequently displays a set of regular and beautiful teeth',[63] 'so even, perfect and beautifully white, that, were they seen by the Cranbourne-alley dentists, their possession would be coveted.'[64] The features of Indigenous women's beauty were different to that of European women either physically, or when mediated through men's different terms of visual access.

In addition, those beauty features were different because they were unselfconscious 'ornaments of nature' considered unadorned by fashioning and artifice. As Wollstonecraft had intimated decades earlier, the European 'sense of beauty' as a manifestation of inner virtue was, by the mid-nineteenth century, beginning to be challenged by modern forms of feminine visibility, such as street anonymity. These new forms of public visibility were insistently differentiated from the spectacle of the native woman, who was situated in an unspoilt landscape, not an urban public. Beauty and its ideological effects were embedded within this altered play of looks in the modern scene. The primitive was emblematic of the 'cradle of civilisation' and attracted the interest of theologians, artists, scholars and revolutionaries. Elazar Barkan believes this nineteenth-century 'enthusiasm was largely generated by an ambition to restore to a humanity aged by modernism its youth.' While there were regional differences in ideas of the primitive, overall colonialism produced 'powerful images in search of primordial origins.'[65] Aboriginal women's appraisal as beautiful or unsightly depended on their status as either unfashioned primitive or assimilated to European propriety; that is, they either embodied natural beauty, or were beautified. But their prospects for beauty were not only delimited and conditional, they were also precluded through age and its construction as monstrous.

The visual politics that assembled 'primitive', 'sexual deviant' and 'physically impaired' into the nexus of race-grotesque has been well established by postcolonial writers.[66] In his analysis of blackness and non-beauty Noel Caroll refers to the Kantian ideal as approaching 'a perfect example of the category or concept of human being': non-beauty is its corollary and 'an inadequate instantiation of the concept of human being.'[67] Tommy Lott documents the slippage between 'primitive' and 'primate' in the 'Negro–ape metaphor' in which Africans became candidates for the 'missing link' in the Linnaean taxonomy.[68] In Australia Aborigines were said to exhibit the most ape-like characteristics, since they belonged to 'one of the most primitive (in the sense of oldest) races of mankind' and were 'a relic of the oldest human stock.'[69] If black men were apes, however, black women were imagined to have sexual union with apes. Native women's *sexuality* was monstrous and this was manifest in either their immodest attractions and in their association with concupiscence and lasciviousness from the Middle Ages or, conversely, their lack of desirability. J. J. Virey in the early nineteenth century stressed the consonance between the native woman's physiology and her physiognomy (her 'horribly flattened nose' and her 'hideous form').[70] As noted earlier, immigrants needed to be forewarned of the spectre of native women's unsightliness. In 1840 advice was proffered to immigrants to 'Australia Felix',

> The men are far more comely than the females, who, except at a very tender age and in a few examples, are withered and decrepit to a disgusting degree, presenting as close a resemblance to a she baboon or ourang outang as it is possible for a human being to assume, either in the course of nature or by imitation.[71]

This notion that women exaggerated the deficiencies of native men recurred.

Aboriginal women were cast as lesser specimens of their men. Angas claimed their skulls were 'worse than those of the men; they are elongated and very narrow, the development of the intellectual organs being remarkably small.'[72] Robert Brown, in his 1873 *Races of Mankind* described the Australian race as a 'finely-made muscular race' but the *'gins* (or women) are not so good-looking as the men, being early exposed to every hardship and brutally used from their very infancy. None of them are particularly good-looking, and some of the old hags are absolutely hideous.'[73] For one author, women's eclipsing of men in beauty was a marker of civilised races, 'but the rule reads backwards in savage races. The Australian black man is often stately and picturesque – his mate is generally hideous.'[74]

Aboriginal women were thereby the most extreme exemplar removed from the European ideal of beauty. Recalling the 1854 dictionary with its entry 'Races of men in Australia': 'The Australian women, still more ugly than the men, have squalid and disgusting forms; the distance which separates them from the beau ideal appears immense in the eyes of an European.'[75] Woods, too, in his introduction to Reverend Taplin (which Taplin felt discredited his book), stated that women, 'except in rare instances, or amongst young girls, are almost hideous', but this was a function of being the 'slaves of their husbands and of the tribes.'[76] For Ramsay Smith men in fact approximated the Greek ideal of beauty in their 'graceful carriage' and 'perfection of elegance' due to their proportionately longer legs and arms to trunk than Europeans. He quotes a doctor who described Aboriginal men as having the 'finest model of the human proportions I have ever met with in muscular development combining perfect symmetry, activity, and strength; while his head might have compared with the antique bust of a philosopher.' Ramsay Smith adds, however, that though the men have 'deep and broad chests' remaining 'lithe, active and supple to a very great age', the women, 'as a rule, "go off" in condition early, probably on account of the hard work and privation to which they are subjected.'[77] Hard work shapes older men into impressive physiques, while it corrodes women away.

The spectacle of racial difference was enmeshed in sexual difference. As McClintock argues, gender and race are 'articulated categories' that 'come into existence *in and through* their relation to each other' [original emphasis].[78] The 'patterns of conventions within multiple systems of representation'[79] oversaw the placement of the 'native' in the 'fantasmatic construction of a purely feminized geography.'[80] Beauty and its lack gave shape to ideologies of gender which were themselves foundational to the endeavours of colonial modernity. As Peg Zeglin Brand argues, 'Deeply embedded in that inchoate matter from which our judgements of value are formed, beauty is inseparable from all that is best and worst in human experience.'[81]

Unsightliness distinguished savagery, although the arch of gender across class and race allowed white men to debase their own women who bore deviant or criminal insignia with savage likeness. When Jane River was placed in the stocks for three hours in 1833 for being 'as drunk as Paddy McWollop's pig' and 'kicking up a bobbery that yer honor might have heard at the top of Nelson's pillar', she was described in *The Sydney Gazette and New South Wales Advertiser* as, 'fat, forty, and in point of fairness on a par with a black gin.'[82] It was unusual for white women to be referenced against Aboriginal women, so extreme was the insult. But what this snippet intimates is that European men used the trope of the savage or native woman to allow themselves full expression of their misogyny towards European women that might otherwise be bridled with chivalry and decorum.

In 1842 *The Penny Magazine* quoted the surveyor Major Mitchell giving full vent to his revulsion for an elder Aboriginal woman. She was

> shortened and shrivelled with age, without clothing; one eye alone saw through the dim decay of nature – several large fleshy excrescences projected from the sides of her head like so many ears, and the jaw-bone was visible through a gash or scar on one side of her chin. The withered arms and hands, covered with earth by digging and scraping for the snakes and worms on which she fed, resembled the limbs and claws of a quadruped.[83]

As surveyor, Mitchell charts the topography of the Aboriginal woman elder's place in the landscape as benighted and decrepit, literally spoiling the view with the contours of her debasement. Mitchell excises her from the vista, with the inference that she was out of place in her own home, or could only be granted admission if likened to an animal. The remains of elder Aboriginal women were even more out of place. In a lecture in Valparaíso, Chile, Dr Richard Cannon described intruding on the body of a deceased woman undergoing mortuary rites until chased off by a 'missionary's revolver'. He 'crept' to the door of a 'beehive shaped hut' to be confronted by the

> ghastly sight of a wife's body fastened up against the central pole of the hut, a spear beneath the chin. The eyes had been removed and were replaced by pieces of Mother of Pearl with pupils painted thereon. These grim staring eyes often visited me in my dreams.[84]

His companion Frank Jardine wanted to steal 'this queer "curio"' but settled for viewing only by paying the husband in tobacco. Jardine was responsible for many Aboriginal deaths, both during affrays while overlanding cattle from Rockhampton to his father's station at Somerset on Cape York and while acting there as police magistrate.[85] Aside from his disrespect for mortuary rites, the ghastliness Cannon evoked in his description of this deceased woman inscribed Aboriginal elder women within the edict of dying race while casting her people as a malevolent presence in their own homeland.

Another lecture, by Palmer, which we dropped in on in Chapter 3 presented a series of 'rude daguerreotypes' of naked Aborigines, which he was at pains to justify against the strictures of decency. He named individual elder women, 'Old Gooseberry' and 'Raymond Terrace Molly', and invoked the classical nudes of Helen and Aphrodite as admired by Zeuxis and Apelles to explain that his models could not have excited such 'enraptured' admiration.[86] Alongside his use of these new visual aids he gives a fulsome and graphic description of Aboriginal women, drawing from the recently published description of central Australian women by the explorer Eyre, which blazons their short stature, acute facial angle, attenuated limbs, distorted stomachs, pigeon toes, and 'flaccid and pendulous' breasts. He includes Eyre's admiration of women in 'early youth', whom are described as proportioned and symmetrical in figure, with jet black eyes shaded by 'long dark lashes'.[87] But, as was often the case, Palmer felt compelled to diverge Aboriginal women into two camps, pleasing and unsightly, for he continued,

> it would be almost impossible to convey an idea of the repulsive ugliness of many of the females who are advanced in years. Most of you have doubtless met with some specimens, but to those who have not, I would say imagine an Egyptian mummy with a flattened nose, enlarged lips, widened mouth, a coating of lamp black, and a frizzled black and grey horse-hair wig, and you

will have some faint notion of an Australian mammy. It would actually be an insult to a female chimpanzee or orang otang to compare it with an old Australian gin.[88]

If young Aboriginal women had been designated as 'there for the taking', older women were fair game, a soft target through which European men could unleash their misogyny and malign womanhood at will. Certainly J. Brunton Stephens's well-known ode 'To a black gin' pulled no punches:

> *Thy nose appeareth but a traverse section;*
> *Thy mouth has no particular direction*
> *A flabby-rimmed abyss of imperfection.*
> *Thy skull development my eye displeases,*
> *Thou wilt not suffer much from brain diseases,*
> *Thy facial angle forty-five degrees is.*
> *The coarseness of thy tresses is distressing,*
> *With grease and raddle firmly coalescing*[89]

This satirical poem was widely circulated, its purported humour created in the tension between native and European classical perceptions of beauty. Brunton Stephens notes, among other things, women's 'bestial lineaments' to underscore the confusion of species they embodied and while he makes a play to his readers' scornful bemusement, the boundary edges of these categories were of great interest to newcomer observers. Brunton Stephens was cited two decades later by a British parliamentarian who confirmed that 'the women are hideously ugly in the face', yet he notes this did not repel pearl fishers, prospectors, and many more white men from treating them 'as civilized brutes generally of the females of savage races.'[90] Construing Aboriginal elder women as unsightly could mitigate accusations of violence. Baden-Powell recalled Charles Henry Eden (who opened Chapter 2) when he described disturbing a camp and frightening the inhabitants away:

> They left behind them, however, two old 'gins' (women), who were about the most repulsive specimens of humanity it has ever been my lot to gaze upon. They stood there shuddering and making fearful squeaks, as if vainly trying to scream, and were evidently in the most abject terror, but unable from their feebleness to run away. They wore not a vestige of clothing, neither did they appear ashamed of exposing their graceful (?) forms to the gaze of a stranger. But I will turn from the thoughts of them as from a nightmare – they were too positively disgusting.[91]

Much as Eden deflected the terror he caused the women who piled themselves in a heap in an effort to protect their children, Baden-Powell can ward off any sympathy for these terrorised aged women by accusing them of exposing themselves and foregrounding their unsightly visual effects. Similarly, in 1914, a response to a letter by a protector of Aborigines decrying ill treatment of Aborigines was published in the *Northern Territory Times and Gazette*:

> When we contrast the difference between the peerless ball-room loveliness of the loveliest types of female beauty of the white race with the absolute hideousness of some of the oldest aboriginal women – we refer particularly to those old decrepit gins who are generally left behind in the camps with a few mangy mongrel dogs – the comparison almost causes one to shriek out

'Absolute frights': appearance and elders

> aloud as if at the climax of a frightful nightmare. Surely it must have been an inexorable fate that bestowed so much upon the one and denied so much to the other. Despite an early and prolonged Bible teaching the writer does not, cannot, and will not love his alleged black brethren, and he regards the profession of those who say they do as either being fanatical or hollow.[92]

Whatever cruelty might be meted out to Aborigines, the spectre of unsightly aged women was again and again a means to dismiss complaints, allay sympathy and foster indiscriminate hatred for their people.

The postmaternal breast was particularly repellent to European men unused to their public exposure, and perhaps accustomed to décolleté uplifted in the ballroom bosom. Curr leant on scientific terms to legitimate his examination, writing, 'The *mammæ* of the female when marriageable are pyriform rather than round, and after the birth of several children become pendulous and somewhat long, but not by any means to a remarkable extent.'[93] The idea that Aboriginal women aged prematurely was particularly focused on their breasts. The 1912–13 *Cyclopedia of Western Australia* ranges through the racialised features we are by now familiar with (lank rather than 'woolly' hair, 'inferior' muscular development, 'absence of calves', 'large and unshapely' mouth), describing the appearance of women as fair when young (even possessing 'nicely-rounded limbs') but with 'any appearance of beauty' prematurely vanishing due to 'overwork and early childbearing'; the 'majority are distinguished even in early womanhood by pendulous breasts and general want of figure'.[94] In a popular 1933 pictorial book, *We Find Australia*, Charles Holmes describes Aboriginal women as 'the most repulsive women I have ever seen', having 'distended stomachs', 'flat and long' breasts, 'terribly gawky' legs and a 'mass of matted mess' for hair. Holmes also took offence at the festooning of breasts in loops of white paint, giving women 'a skeleton-like appearance.'[95] Notably it was the very capacity of women to continue their race that rendered them hideous to newcomers, tying this trope back to the self-extinguishing maternity of the infanticidal cannibal mother.

By the interwar period new anthropological data introduced alternative measures for the breast. Herbert Basedow reported that the breast underwent three stages of development, according to which women were classed: the flat, the full and the hanging breast. To each of these he reported the Aluridja gave a corresponding name: 'Tidjinigajerra' the girl child, 'tidji' the marriageable young woman, and 'konga' the married woman who has born children.[96] Mountford and Harvey in *Oceania* described the process of selection by spirit children for their earthly mothers: 'The spirit child is always on the look-out for pleasant-faced and kindly mothers, particularly those with large breasts.'[97] The notion that breast desirability could be decided by children, according to maternal skill and experience, rather than visual appeal to men, if credible, was a startling reclamation from the gaze of European men. If 'nakedness defined the Western encounter with colonial – and potentially colonial – spaces',[98] it was undoubtedly the sight of postmaternal aged women out of doors that most affronted newcomers. If women hoped their breasts might be sighted by unborn children, their exposure might also be considered a form of resistance to the colonial gaze.

Aboriginal women were deployed as scientific spectacle linked to a sense of urgency to document their 'physical characteristics' before the 'disappearance' of the Aborigine due to the sweeping advance of colonial modernity. Against reports of declining

'Absolute frights': appearance and elders

numbers of Aborigines, the Geographical Society urged the government to fund Spencer, then curator of the Public Library, to model in brown clay a 'complete set of ethnological specimens, male and female, of the Australian aborigine before this ancient race becomes extinct.'[99] But they would not have their wish until June 1933, when the Field Museum of Chicago opened its 'Hall of Man' featuring one hundred bronzed racial types modelled 'from living subjects' by sculptor Malvina Hoffman. In Hoffman's account of the three-year project, she blithely predicts that by the end of the century the primitive races she sculpted would have 'disappeared into the dim records of history.' This recording imperative salvaged the native woman from invisibility to Western eyes and installed her body as artefact into the hallowed halls of public museums. Hoffman's work, she said, 'sensitized' her mind 'like a photographic plate.' Yet the perceptual realism required for the task could not evade conventions of appraising beauty. She explains that the Field Museum's exclusion of the Tasmanian Aborigine was due to their extinction, and adds, 'It was a great relief to me, for they were ugly enough to make celibacy an easy task, and sculpture an impossible one.'[100] Infecundity is here associated with unsightliness, desirability is a function of beauty and dying race becomes the fate of an unsightly people. The inference that knowledge about a disappearing people was less compelling if they were unsightly had been presaged in 1898, in a paper by missionary James Backhouse read before the Royal Society of Tasmania. Backhouse lamented the lack of information on Tasmanian Aborigines, but believed, 'If they had been as picturesque as the Red Indian or the Maori, we should probably have known a great deal more about them.'[101] The quest for scientific record was confused with commodity aesthetics as the print market diversified and became increasingly competitive.

In 1952 Professor MacKenzie wrote in *Mankind* that Aboriginal skull artefacts were 'by the standards of modern man abominably ugly.'[102] The scientist situates beauty as a discernible surface effect of racial difference which, through the cumulative shapes and alignments of physical features, describes the 'standards' of savage variety and distinctness from 'modern man'.

In 1915, just when white Australian women were experiencing forms of visibility that articulated their pleasing identities anew, Aboriginal women were imaged as 'An ugly blot on Australia' in the frontispiece of *The Inlander*, the quarterly magazine published by the Presbyterian Church of Australia. Printing an image, which doesn't bear reproducing here, of a thin woman covered from waist to knee and with a child on her hip, *The Inlanders'* intention was to mobilise in Australian citizens 'more compassionate thought to the care of aged black women in our land.' However, her failure to appear modern confirmed the status of Aboriginal mothers and their grandchildren as literally out of place in the contemporary Australian scene:

> Quite apart from humanitarian consideration for the natives, we feel that the presence of emaciated and often positively diseased blacks is a national danger to us. What may not happen through flies passing from such creatures to settle on little white children on the Inland? Again, what must be the effect on the hearts and minds of little children if compelled to grow accustomed to the sight of 'Blots' in human form?[103]

Her monstrosity is conflated with her Aboriginality, thus placing her outside the category of human, and she should be extirpated from white children's view if she is to take her ordained place in

'Absolute frights': appearance and elders

an appropriate picture of the nation. McClintock argues that racial abjection is required by industrial imperialism 'as its constitutive, inner repudiation.' Through its intricate deployment in other discourses, beauty and its lack became a means to enact that exclusion, and Aboriginal elder women were among those peoples 'expelled and obliged to inhabit the impossible edges of modernity.'[104]

In this typical cartoon from Hugh Maclean (Figure 6.1), whose work we saw in Chapter 4, the simian features and bulk of the Aboriginal cattle-station domestic are pitted against a failure

"Why don't you let her marry Warrigal? I'm paying him good wages."
"She's too plurry good lookin' for Warrigal!"

Figure 6.1 Hugh Maclean in Aussie, 1928.

of Aboriginal perception in the elder looking on.[105] From the earliest settler accounts, Aborigines were renowned for having an uncanny 'quickness of perception'[106] and an almost supernaturally 'keen eye' embodied by the tracker type.[107] However, this 'merely practical understanding' was pitted against a 'defect in the higher style of thought.'[108] As Angas remarked, clearly influenced by phrenology and its assessment of Indigenous skulls, 'Their heads are not wanting in the perceptive faculties, though in the reflective they are deficient.'[109] The appreciation of feminine beauty was elevated to the level of considered reflection, which characterised the European mind. The humour of the Maclean cartoon lies in the gap between the Aboriginal elder's perception of 'good looking' and the assumed white reader's knowing contemplation, which incorporated aesthetic standards. While the joke is on the Aboriginal domestic, it is her failure to measure up to white standards of feminine beauty that is construed as comic.

Cartoons of 1920s black-and-white artists continued this tradition of picturing Aboriginal women as visual anomalies in the Australian modern scene, as we saw in the threshold imagery of Chapter 4.[110] As modernity provided seemingly endless vistas and vantages for the modern girl who could step into public space and take her place, Aboriginal women continued to be characterised as prematurely aging, as enjoying but a 'short-lived time of youth and beauty' due to coming to 'maturity early' but soon growing 'wrinkled, bent, old, miserable and discontented'. This bore no relation, of course, to the endless rounds of removal to reserves and missions that women endured, the theft of their children, or trying to subsist on rations, or wages in lieu. Rather, their lives were assessed as 'one eternal round of toil' and imposts that came exclusively and unrelentingly from their unfeeling men. Moreover, 'the drudgery fall on the women well up in years.'[111] For Charles Barrett, the prolific nature writer, the unsightliness of Aboriginal elder women was a trope he could recycle in each of his many pamphlets. In his 'Blackfellows of Australia' he, too, shuttles from the early beauty of Aboriginal women, noting their 'stately and graceful' walk. But celebrating Aboriginal feminine beauty seemed to require a retributive denouement and the elder woman – in fact not too elderly, but rapidly aged – was, by this time, ready to hand. 'The old women', Barrett screes, 'with their almost bare heads, denuded of hair to make string for their sons-in-law, their wrinkled faces, bleary, fly-infested eyes and skinny limbs, can only be described as repulsive.'[112] Hill was similarly unrestrained when she described one elderly woman as 'an emaciated hag with pendulous lips.'[113] As women came under increasing pressure to maintain their youth through beauty regimes and products, aging prematurely became another means to mark off racial difference. In 1944, *Wild Life Magazine* wrote of women as 'quite attractive in adolescence, but, like too many native peoples, they soon lose their early charm.'[114] Barrett reiterated, this time in *Rydge's* magazine, that 'many of the girls are handsome; but too soon they lose their young charms, becoming ugly and withered *old* women before middle age.'[115]

The repugnant gin was undoubtedly a dominant visual typecast of native women in accordance with longstanding tropes: the inhabitants of the inverted Antipodes;[116] the simian native; the grotesque and degraded colonised. Her impress of starvation and impoverishment was set 'quite apart from humanitarian consideration', as *The Inlander* said. Indeed, this privation was convenient to settlers from the 1830s for whom Australia was the southern paradise with unbounded grazing opportunities, impeded only by the wanderings of the native-grotesque. It is shocking from our perspective that white Australians could bear witness to the manifest privation and distress of aged Aboriginal women and feel compelled not to relieve, but instead only seek to profit in print from the salient visual effects of disease and poverty. Under White Australia and the policy of assimilation, aging prematurely was a commonsense means to imprecate the eradication of a people who could not die off too soon. For the role they had been cast in, as apocryphal to colonial modernity, as evoking an eerie, malevolent land, as succumbing to the edict of dying race, their costume had been decided and it was the exposed, attenuated, unsightly primitive body from which decent newcomers averted their eyes, recording their abhorrence all the while. It is a hideous, confronting archive, but one that bears witness to the misapprehension and possibly fear of settlers when facing off with women who embodied the gravitas and authority of the elder.

Abigail Solomon-Godeau, writing about Gauguin's years in Polynesia, reflects on the expeditionary literature produced by voyagers to the South Seas, foremost Cook, Wallis and Bougainville. She concludes that 'the colonial encounter is first and foremost the encounter with the body of the Other'. This encounter effects force over bodies in the violent process of colonial dispossession, but it is also 'endlessly elaborated within a shadow world of representation – a question of imaginary power over imaginary bodies' that continually elides 'the non-reciprocity of these power relations.'[117] That non-reciprocity was assured through the 'form of objectification' levelled at Aboriginal women. Beauty is necessarily a discourse of ideals and as a system of value beauty excludes many women. It was an apposite discourse, therefore, to deploy across the field of colonial power relations.

The racialising of beauty established and maintained distinct forms of visual identity that then played their part in colonial expansion and consolidation. The unsightly elder woman masked and suppressed the impact of brutal dispossession and misappropriation of Indigenous women's sexuality and labour. Modernity dramatically altered forms of subjectivity through changes to visual identity, and beauty or its lack was a touchstone for restabilising meanings of true womanhood and racial difference. The invocation of the primitive showed how white Australian femininity was so crucially construed around this visually inscribed racial bookending. Modern settler femininity was intelligible through a complex of racial citations of the primitive that repeatedly deployed a visual of Aboriginal aged femininity within the chiasm of print. As ethnological specimen, as tribal native belle, as fashioned to assimilate, or as unsightly, Indigenous women had limited prospects to articulate their own visual identities.

And yet they did. A survey across the typeset divulges white-authored but possibly credible tales of Aboriginal women resisting the terms of their visualisation and confronting their co-option into white visual registers. As Jane Lydon has found, residents of Coranderrk for some decades resisted and exploited the requirements of photographers, demanding escalating payment for posing and refusing to disrobe.[118] In 1870 Brough Smyth reported it was impracticable to obtain complete measurements of Victorians on stations. He wrote,

> They are now clothed, and having regard to the circumstances under which they are now living, it has been deemed inadvisable, even in the interests of science, to prosecute investigations which might raise in their minds feelings of disgust.[119]

Decades on, in 1931, the naturalist T. P. Bellchambers recounted his travels along the Murray. At one camp a woman, Mary, adamantly refused to be photographed. 'I was told: "Oh, she no like 'em picture left when she die. She think that no good."'[120] Basedow, too, encountered resistance despite photographing people 'in a state of utter, and apparently unconscious nudity' with the sexes mixing 'with absolute frankness' and walking about *en deshabille* without attracting the slightest attention or giving the least offence to anyone among themselves.' Basedow then relates an incident of photographing a Daly River 'lubra' 'in an attitude that under other conditions would have been considered most unbecoming.'[121] The woman reported that Basedow had taken a 'wrong picture longa me' and asked the acting district magistrate (Basedow's brother) to report Basedow to the government resident at Port Darwin. Minds that were aware of the colonially inscribed visual signs of the Aboriginal body, while determined to shape those signs, were clearly at work here.

But perhaps the final note should go to a woman reported in Thomas and Joyce's *Women of All Nations* in a story we can only hope to be true for Thomas can hardly be relied upon for credible records. But this anecdote does at least impute some awareness among newcomers of the arbitrary, even ironic nature of racialised dress codes. He wrote of the reply given to a European girl when she asked why a black woman wore a bone in her nose, asserting that white women did not do that.

> The black gin looked her censor up and down and fixed her eyes on her earrings. 'Why you make holes in your ears? No good that! Black gin no do that, pull 'em down your ears like dogs. Plenty good bone in nose, make you sing good. S'posin' cuggil (bad) smell, you put bone longa nose, no smell 'im. Plenty good make hole longa nose, no good make hole longa ears, make 'em hang

down all same dogs!' And with that the old black went off laughing, pulling down the lobes of her ears and barking like a dog.[122]

The tale invites a history still to be woven in the interstices of the colonial archive where Aboriginal elder women, deemed comically unassimilable to white standards of dress, indifferent to youth-defined ideals of beauty and unsightly in the scene of colonial modernity, may well have had the last laugh on cruelly imposed ideals of feminine embodiment.

Throughout this book of lies we have surveyed some of the more disturbing tropes in print impressions of Aboriginal women, each of them a sustained, habitual assault on their dignity. The trope of women elders as unsightly is distressing not only because of the unique and exemplary authority and respect we have come to understand is accorded to Aboriginal elders. This particular form of dehumanising is also painful to witness because of their valiant struggle to protect their children and grandchildren from the worst interventions by white administrators, and to pass on their way of being while coping with their own trauma, deprivation and grief. Compounding this is the reverence we feel for our mothers and grandmothers, and the profound and fierce sense of protection we experience as their bodies become frail and vulnerable. For that very frailty to be cast as monstrous – the visual marks of their suffering and endurance, or disfigurement by accident, assault or intervention, or the traces of mourning and maternity – is itself monstrous. It makes clear how intensely newcomers disregarded Aboriginal women: they missed, for instance, that traces of maternity left on the feminine body awarded greater access to restricted knowledge and thereby bestowed authority on elder women. The disrespect shown by this slur could be dismissed as another low point in settler imaginings of Aboriginal women, one so arrantly hurtful at first glance it seems best consigned to history. But enduring sentiments and attitudes should be confronted, contextualised and excised from our reticulated repertoire of racialised disregard. The recursive chiasm of racism needs to be stopped in its cycle of endless reinvention. And in as much as this recurring denigration always described more accurately what was going on in the minds of newcomers, it occasions taking stock of imaginings of youth and innovation in colonial modernity, of the relation ascribed to dying race and Indigenous longevity, and to prompt us to consider who felt most exposed by Indigenous nakedness and the affront of a woman's lived-in body, living in place.

Conclusion

THE ANATOMY OF RACISM AND MISOGYNY

This book does not propose a way of knowing Aboriginal women that goes beyond 'skin deep', that pretends to be more accurate or truthful. That is not my place, nor my story to tell. Rather it identifies conventions of knowing or shared preoccupations that, through the recursive operation of print, were entrenched in perceptions and ways of relating across race and gender. The intervention of the book is into these vestigial loops of understanding. It finds that marginalising the voices of people that print consumers want to read about, through fallacy, hearsay and supposition, can quickly congeal into types and tropes, cultural fixtures that entrap us in misapprehension, but also forestall any resistance to entrenched meaning. Racism and misogyny entwined through the figure of the Aboriginal woman to indelibly impress indices of difference, suspended in a loop without culmination, in a relay of differentiation without end.

I doubt much of the material in this book will surprise Aboriginal women. I am uneasily aware that the exposure of such enduringly hurtful slurs and insults threatens to add to the reiteration that embeds racism in shared patterns of meaning. I hope exposing these hidden and forgotten distortions to view challenges the 'tissue of errors' that has shrouded settler imaginings of Aboriginal women, and rents this flimsy 'evidence' apart. In the main, colonial print drew Aboriginal women into an appraisal that was ultimately unable to perceive beyond the imprint of its own social norms. The very repetition of these constructs belies that they were ever stabilised or complete, however. We've seen them being reconfigured at various historical junctures, or operating exclusively in certain cultural domains, or being challenged by Aboriginal resistors, or settler-observers committed to rigour or empathy, or simply more willing to shift around their perceptual horizons. We've seen them exaggerated into parody and collapsing under the unbearable lightness of conjecture. If these contrivances and distortions sought the final word in defining Aboriginal women, in a perennial attempt to situate a native womanhood in the nation, closure was perpetually precluded. Understanding the requirement for that hyperbolic reiteration and the stresses these claims came under might suggest ongoing strategic sites for resistance.

Tracing and charting these procedures for maligning, and accounting for the idiosyncratic ways misogyny and racism hinged in Australia, through the interface of transnational syndication and local circumstance, creates a lineage by which to identify residues of national sentiment. For instance, with some rare exceptions, there has always been widespread indifference to violence against Aboriginal women and children, along with a readiness to misappropriate it into a racialised descriptor to justify intrusive and discriminatory administrations. The imperative to secure safety now should be realised within a heightened awareness of these longstanding imprints of racialised gender relations. They should force a reckoning by non-Indigenous, particularly settler-heritage Australians that offers to these women, their mothers, grandmothers and ancestors some solace, dignity, empowerment and redress.

The 'woman question', alive from the eighteenth-century Enlightenment, was demonstrably connected to representations of native femininity and maternity. Conterminous with the exploratory voyages and thickening throughout colonial expansion was debate on the condition of women in commercial society or civilisation. The savage, primitive, native, aboriginal or indigenous woman represented, at either end of the noble/ignoble spectrum, the plenitude of nature or conversely the spectre of abject exposure, subjection to brutal overlords and subsistence in harsh and unaccommodating surrounds. As women insisted on their place in public – as voters and elected representatives, in education and the workforce, in commerce and leisure – they deployed the figure of the subjugated native woman as a measure of the civilising insignia of their own advancement, in a prototype feminism that was ethnocentric and supersessionist. Conversely, the supposed embodiment of sexual innocence, allure and vulnerability by pre-maternal native girls invoked universalising conceptions of humanity, arising from the abolitionist movement, in white feminist and clerical calls for protection against frontier masculinity into the twentieth century. Contact across race under these conditions was profoundly inflected by gender. The colonial project was buttressed by conceptions of a feminised landscape, through a similitude of body and land holding out the promise of sexual access – conflated as it was with visual access. These were collocated with frontier chivalry, a primordial yet self-extinguishing maternity, the domestication of unremunerated labour and dying race. Gender was a constituent element in the making of settler-colonial identities and through which its material reality and perceptual relations, with all their competing and incomplete differentials of power, were organised and negotiated.

How these were writ through print descriptions of Aboriginal women comprises the content of this book. That they had to be written through again and again is its revelation.

Rather than bring neatly to a close this book of white lies, as though the last has now been uttered, it needs to be said that each of the chapters had to be jettisoned of tens thousands of words of quotations and extracts from print media, including newspapers, magazines and reviews. There are reams of this material, a king tide of malice, which betrays a readiness and willingness to disregard Aboriginal women and describes the particular discomfort and enthralment they evoked in newcomers. It reveals the idiosyncratic forms misogyny takes when conjoined with racism – and it early became apparent this conjunction drew from both paradigms – but together the intensity of effect created a new coordinate that, while influenced by imported models, was local in its manifestations. It was in effect European misogyny cast out to the periphery and unleashed.

The archive also reveals how very pernicious and effective the mere function of repetition is in establishing truths in any mediascape. Put simply, racism requires a lot of upkeep and its cultural traction is maintained by reiteration. Granted there were many who attempted to redirect the typeset from disregard to regard, but as print underwent its own expansions, refinements and market consolidations, the types it cast and the tropes it set over time generalised a readership, a public that peopled an idea of nation in which the figure of the Aboriginal woman came to caption a mesh of sentiment ranging from fondness, lust, dependence, chivalry, paternalism, bemusement, disdain, disgust and dread. Within these print impressions it is text and image that conquer the feminine colonised body. The particular imprint of discursive violence, enmeshing these varieties of affect, allowed for a hands-off offensive, interpelating her in symbolic rather than physical violence and thereby effacing her experience of that vehemence. The observational ethos of exploration and settlement textualised and iconographed the bodies of Indigenous women onto which European desires and fears around gender relations were projecting, rapidly altering under the mediascape of colonial modernity.

I was compelled to write this book by the renewed offensive against Aboriginal Australians that commenced with Howard's refusal to apologise to the Stolen Generations, and it was written through the Northern Territory Emergency Response (or Intervention) in 2007 and its later guises under subsequent governments. This work is an artefact of this fraught period in Australian racial history, one of many responses to this redoubled disregard. It hopes to partake of the new regard emerging from the reconciliation movement, anti-intervention efforts, and Indigenous artists revisiting and reworking the colonial archive. All dissipate the momentum by which regimes of knowledge, complex and contradictory as they are, propagate and reconfigure racialised distinctions within the projects of economic and geopolitical dominance.

Skin Deep draws attention to the disregard of Indigenous women as serving the material destruction of their bodies, economies, custodianship, and ways of being in place. It finds the effacement of Aboriginal women's voices and their own ways of appearing in the settler-colonial public was incomplete since gender and race show themselves to be unstable and porous coordinates in the articulation and assignation of national identities. Construing Aboriginal women as infertile, infanticidal, infirm and thereby as embodying their people's terminus, rather than generation, was an alibi for the violence they endured on the frontier and in its aftermath and through the interventions of state administrations. The recursion of these effacing yet exposed constructs of Aboriginal women was advanced through print and its syndications on a global scale. Once aware of how such racial distortions become entrenched, a renewed impetus to resist them at every iteration ought to become part of a nationwide apology and commitment to recognising the dignity of Aboriginal women. By extension, whenever and wherever we hear a misrepresentation advanced in public about a people that contrives to mark them off with exaggerated disparity and disregard, we need to call it out then and there.

Appendix

JOURNAL PUBLICATIONS DEDICATED TO AUSTRALIAN ABORIGINAL WOMEN UNTIL 1959

Extracted from John Greenway, *Bibliography of the Australian Aborigines and the Native Peoples of Torres Strait to 1959*, Angus and Robertson, Sydney, 1963.

J. G. Garson, 'Pelvimetry', *Journal of Anatomical Physionomy*, no. 16, 1822, pp. 106–13.

John Lhotsky, *A Song of the Women of the Menero Tribe near the Australian Alps*, Sydney, 1835[1]

Rev. James Beattie Love, 'A primitive method of making a wooden dish by native women of the Musgrave Ranges, South Australia', *Transactions of the Royal Historical Society of South Australia*, no. 66, 1843, pp. 215–17.

T. R. H. Thomson, 'Observations on the reported incompetency of the "gins" of Aboriginal females of New Holland, to procreate with a native male, after having born half-caste children to a European or white', *Journal of the Ethnological Society of London*, vol. III, 1854, pp. 243–46.

P. Broica, 'Relative sterility of interbreeds between Europeans and Australians or Tasmanians', in *On the Phenomena of Hybridity in the Genus Homo*, London, 1864.

'Childbearing in Australia', *Journal of the Ethnological Society of London*, no. 1, 1868, p. 68.

J. D. Hooker, 'On child-bearing in Australia and New Zealand', *Journal of the Ethnological Society of London*, no. 1, 1869, pp. 68–75.

Lorimer Fison, 'On Australian marriage laws', *Journal Anthropological Institute*, no. 19, 1880, pp. 354–57.

Baron Nicolaus de Mikloukho-Maklay, 'On the practice of ovariotomy by the native of the Herbert River in Queensland', *Proceedings of the Linnean Society of NSW*, no. 6, 1881, pp. 622–24.

Alfred William Howitt and Lorimer Fison, 'From mother-right to father-right', *Journal Anthropological Institute*, vol. 12, no. 1, 1882, pp. 30–46.

Sir John Lubbock, 'On the customs of marriage and systems of relationship among the Australians', *Journal Anthropological Institute*, no. 14, 1885, pp. 292–300.

Georges Raynaud, 'La femme, la marriage, la familie en Australie', *Bulletin de la Société d'ethnographie Paris*, vol. 2, no. 4, 1890, pp. 143–150.
Ernest Favenc, 'An Aborigine wedding', *Science of Man*, vol. 1, no. 2, 1899, p. 256.
Francis Galton, 'Note on Australian marriage systems', *Journal Anthropological Institute*, no. 28, 1889, pp. 70–72.
W. J. Enright, 'The widow's cap of the Australian Aborigines', *Proceedings of the Linnean Society of NSW*, vol. 24, no. 2, 1899, pp. 333–45.
J. Maguire, 'Childbirth in the Wiradjuri tribe', *Science of Man*, vol. 4, no. 7, 1901, pp. 115–16.
Mrs T. Rankin, 'Aboriginal giantess grave', *Science of Man*, vol. 4, no. 5, 1901, p. 81.
Charles Gabriel Seligman, 'Birth and childhood custom', in Haddon, *Reports of the Cambridge Anthropological Expedition to Torres Strait*, no. 5, 1904, pp. 194–200.
Charles Gabriel Seligman, 'Women's puberty customs', in Haddon, *Reports of the Cambridge Anthropological Expedition to Torres Strait*, no. 5, 1904, pp. 201–07.
Charles Gabriel Seligman, 'Torres Strait and New Guinea', in T. A. Joyce (ed.), *Women of all Nations*, vol. 1, 1908, pp. 151–60.
Sir James George Fraser, 'The Australian marriage laws', *Man*, 1908, p. 8.
Harry Stockdale, 'Aborigines: love, courtship and marriage ... women's work', *Antiquarian's Gazette and Art Collectors Guide*, December 1907, pp. 21–24 and March 1908, pp. 59–61.
Northcote Thomas, 'Native women of Australia', in T. A. Joyce and N. W. Thomas (eds), *Women of all Nations*, London, 1908.
Alfred Radcliffe-Browne, 'Beliefs concerning childbirth in some Australian tribes', *Man*, 1912, p. 96.
C. G. Gallichan, *Position of Women in Primitive Society*, London, 1914.
Daisy M. Bates, 'Aboriginal reserves and women patrols', *Perth Sunday Times*, 2 September 1921.
J. Done, 'A girl's puberty custom in Boigu', *Man*, 1923, p. 94.
Dr William Warner, 'Native morals: black flappers' coy ways', *Sydney Sun*, 23 September 1924; and *Western Mail*, 20 October 1927, p. 40.
Ernest Jones, 'Mother right and the sexual ignorance of savages', *International Journal of Psycho-Analysis,* vol. 6, part 2, 1925, p. 106.
Daisy M. Bates, 'Aboriginal cannibals: mothers who eat their babies', *Adelaide Register,* 8 March 1927; *The Horsham Times,* 1 May 1928, p. 4; and *The Register,* 8 March 1928, p 10.
'Women's work in the Torres Straits', *Australian Women's Mirror,* 26 June 1928, pp. 12, 54.

Appendix

John Burton Cleeland, 'Difficult birth of a pure-blooded Australian Aboriginal woman', *Medical Journal of Australia*, 1928, p. 219.

C. M. T. Cooke, 'Status of Aboriginal women in Australia', *Proceedings of the Pan-Pacific Women's Conference*, no. 2. 1930, pp. 127–45.

Lloyd Warner, 'Birth control in primitive society', *Birth Control Review*, New York, no. 4, 1931, pp. 105–07.

Frederick Wood-Jones, 'A small headed type of female Australian', *Man*, 1932, p. 45.

Ngoondaw Gladys, 'Saint George', Mount Margaret Aboriginal Mission, 1935.

Pater Wilhelm Schmidt, 'The position of women with regard to property in primitive society', *American Anthropology*, no. 37, 1935, pp. 244–56.

Francis Grosvenor, 'The vagaries of black sister. A human story from the North', *Aborigines' Protector*, vol. 1, no. 2, June 1936, pp. 14–15.

Mary Montgomery Bennett, 'The Aboriginal mother in Western Australia', a paper read to the British Commonwealth League Conference, London, June 1933.

Helen Skardon, 'The house gins', *Walkabout*, no. 3, March 1937, pp. 46–49.

D. A. Dowling, 'Unusual endocrine disturbances of Aboriginal sisters', *Medical Journal of Australia*, no. 24, 27 March 1937, pp. 474–75.

Donald Thomson, 'The Australian native woman as food producer', *Illustrated London News*, 22 October 1938, pp. 730–73.

Alfred Radcliffe-Browne, 'Motherhood in Australia', *Man*, 1938, p. 14.

Phyllis M. Kaberry, 'The life and secret ritual of Aboriginal women in the Kimberleys', *Mankind*, vol. 2, no. 7, September 1939, p. 223.

Charles Pearcy Mountford and H. K. Fry, 'Women of the Adnjamatna tribe of the Northern Flinders Ranges, South Australia', *Oceania*, vol. 12, no. 2, December 1941, pp. 155–62.

Roy Hamilton Goddard, 'Kopi: funerary skull caps', *Mankind*, vol. 2, no. 2, August 1946, pp. 25–27.

J. De Vidas, 'Childbirth among the Aranda, Central Australia', *Oceania*, vol. 17, no. 2, December 1947, pp. 117–19.

A. J. Pearce, *Native Women are Slaves*, Melbourne, 1947.

Daniel Sutherland Davidson, 'Mourning caps of the Australian Aborigines', *Proceedings of the American Philosophical Society*, no. 92, 1948, pp. 57–70.

B. Strehlow, 'Glimpses of lubra life in Central Australia', *Aborigines' Friends Association Annual Report*, 1949, pp. 33–35.

Géza Róheim, 'Dreams of women of Central Australia', *Psychiatric Quarterly*, no. 24, 1950, pp. 35–64.

Catherine Berndt, 'Expression of grief among Aboriginal women', *Oceania*, vol. 22, no. 4, June 1950, pp. 286–332.

E. R. Lawrie, 'Educational work among native women and children, *Aborigines' Friends Association Annual Report*, 1951, pp. 23–25.

Jacques Villeminot, 'Central Australia: Pidjindjara women's secret chanting', Sydney University Phonograph Record, no. 71, 1953.

Alex Norton, 'The life of Aboriginal women in Australia', *ABC Weekly*, 8 December 1956, p. 14.

H. V. V. Noone, 'The woman and the sacred bora ring', *Dawn*, no. 7, March 1958, p. 11.

NOTES

Introduction

1. Norman Laird, 'Aborigine girl', *Walkabout*, vol. 12, no. 12, 1 October 1946, pp. 20–21, p. 20.
2. A. M. Duncan-Kemp, *Where Strange Paths Go Down*, W. R. Smith and Paterson, Brisbane, 1964, p. 297.
3. Mrs Aeneas Gunn, *We of the Never Never*, A. Moring, London, 1905; Daisy Bates, *Passing of the Aborigines*, John Murray, London, 1944; Mary Durack, *Kings in Grass Castles*, Constable, London, 1959.
4. Mrs D. Duncan-Kemp, Duncan-Kemp's daughter-in-law, personal correspondence with the author, July 2011.
5. See, for instance, Robin Barrington's study of the photographs used by Bates in 'Unravelling the Yamaji imaginings of Alexander Morton and Daisy Bates', *Aboriginal History*, vol. 39, 2016, pp. 27–62.
6. Marcia Langton, *'Well, I heard it on the radio and I saw it on the television …' An Essay for the Australian Film Commission on the Politics and Aesthetics of Filmmaking by and about Aboriginal People and Things*, Australian Film Commission, Sydney, 1993, p. 45.
7. L. Conor, 'The 'lubra' type in Australian imaginings of Aboriginal women from 1836–1973', *Gender and History*, vol. 25, no. 2, July 2013, pp. 230–51.
8. Ernestine Hill, *The Great Australian Loneliness*, Robertson and Mullens, Melbourne, 1943, p. 230.
9. Homi Bhabha, *The Location of Culture*, Routledge, London, 1994, p. 79.
10. Frantz Fanon, *Black Skin, White Masks*, Grove Press, New York, 1967, p. 112.
11. Anne Maxwell, *Colonial Photography and Exhibitions: Representations of the 'Native' and the Making of European Identities*, Leicester University Press, London, 1991, pp. 13, 189.
12. Anne McClintock, *Imperial Leather: Race, Gender and Sexuality in the Colonial Contest*, Routledge, New York, 1995, p. 353.

13 Hugh Maclean, 'Dry gin', 1929, reproduced in Patricia Rolfe, *The Journalistic Javelin: An Illustrated History of the Bulletin*, Wildcat Press, Sydney, 1979, ill. 197.
14 L. Conor, 'The primitive woman in the colonial scene', in *The Spectacular Modern Woman: Feminine Visibility in the 1920s*, Indiana University Press, Bloomington, 2004, pp. 175–208.
15 Geoffrey Blainey, *John Latham Memorial Lecture*, 1993; and 'Drawing up a balance sheet of our history', *Quadrant*, vol. 37, nos. 7–8, July/August, 1993.
16 'Civilised girls from the vicinity of Townsville', in Carl Lumholtz, *Among Cannibals: An Account of Four Years Travel in Australia*, Charles Scribner's Sons, London, 1889, p. 341.
17 The CP in CPAULLK.A is conjoined which may indicate the engraver's initials. Despite holding an extensive file on Scribner and Sons, the American Archive of Art does not have information on either the photographer or the engraver. H. J. Gibbney, 'Lumholtz, Carl Sophus (1851–1921)', *Australian Dictionary of Biography*, vol. 5, Melbourne University Press, Melbourne, 1975.
18 Gibbney, 'Lumholtz, Carl Sophus', *ADB*.
19 Lumholtz, *Among Cannibals*, p. 346.
20 Henry G. Lamond, 'Dark ladies', *Walkabout*, May 1964, pp. 34–36. My thanks to Clare Wright for bringing this article to my attention.
21 Karen Donnelly, 'The discovery of a 19th century photographer, Thomas Cleary', *Bulletin* (Olive Pink Society), vol. 7, nos 1–2, 1995, pp. 9–21.
22 Andrew Sayers, 'McRae, Tommy (1835–1901)', *Australian Dictionary of Biography*, National Centre of Biography, Australian National University, accessed 8 October 2015, <http://adb.anu.edu.au/biography/mcrae-tommy-13074/text23649>.
23 *North Eastern Ensign*, 22 November 1895, cited in Donnelly, *Bulletin*.
24 Deborah Poole, *Vision, Race and Modernity: A Visual Economy of the Andean World*, Princeton University Press, Princeton, 1997, p. 53.
25 Jack T. Patton, 'Aborigines Progressive Association', *The Abo Call*, no. 1, April 1938, p. 3.
26 Gareth Griffiths, 'The myth of authenticity', in Bill Ashcroft, Gareth Griffiths, Helen Tiffin (eds), *The Postcolonial Studies Reader*, Routledge, London, 1995, pp. 237–241, p. 239.
27 J. T. Patton, 'Calling Aborigines: straight talk', *Abo Call*, no. 3, June 1938, p. 1.
28 J. T. Patton, 'Our huge task', *Abo Call*, no. 2, May 1938, p. 1.

29 See Jane Lydon, *Eye Contact: Photographing Indigenous Australians*, Duke University Press, Durham, 2005, p. 38.
30 Barry Judd, '"It's not cricket": Victorian Aboriginal cricket at Coranderrk', in Lynette Russell and John Arnold (eds), *The La Trobe Journal,* Special issue: Indigenous Victorians: repressed, resourceful and respected, no. 85, May 2010, pp. 37–51, p. 42.
31 Michael Taussig, *Mimesis and Alterity: A Particular History of the Senses*, Routledge, New York, 1993, p. 16.
32 Edward Said, *Orientalism: Western Conceptions of the Orient*, Penguin, London, 1978. p. 20.
33 Taussig, *Mimesis and Alterity*, p. 17.
34 *The Last Tasmanian,* 1978, documentary film, ARTIS Films, directed by Tom Haydon.
35 On ABC's *Monday Conference*, 4 September 1979, the filmmaker Tom Haydon, historian Lyndall Ryan, and Aboriginal activist Mike Mansell debated the controversy, Mansell countering the documentary's byline with, 'we are the only race of people on earth who have to daily justify our existence'.
36 Tom O'Regan, 'Documentary in controversy: The Last Tasmanian', *An Australian Film Reader*, 1985, pp. 127–36 <http://wwwmcc.murdoch.edu.au/ReadingRoom/film/Tasmanian.html>, accessed 5 January 2012.
37 ibid.
38 My paternal great-great grandfather, 'Red Mick' O'Connor, fled the approach of Redcoats in Ballymaquirk (County Cork) in 1865, which suggests he was involved in political insurgency. The O'Connors lived at Woodend and were coal burners. My maternal forebears were convicts, William and Thomas Wadley, transported along with 481 rural labourers for machine breaking in the English Swing Riots of the 1830s. The riots were in part an outcome of the Enclosure Acts between 1770 and 1830 which had progressively removed six million acres of common land from the rural poor, leaving them dependent on the dwindling wages from local landowners. When threshing machines were introduced thousands of unemployed targeted farmers' property demanding a minimum wage. The Wadley brothers married Irish sisters, and Thomas's son, my great-great-great grandfather, Thomas Wadley, who also married an Irish woman, settled in Laceby in northeastern Victoria in the 1870s. There is no record in either family of any interaction with Aborigines, and there is no way of knowing my families' interracial relations. Indeed, these lineages provide stories of family origin, but each person mentioned also had four grandparents (I've accounted only for two), telescoping

the possible scenarios out to gainfully employ me in years of dedicated research – only I'm not sure what that would really explain. My thanks to uncles Denis and Gerald O'Connor and distant cousins Trisha and Brian Wadley.

39 Most famously, W. E. H. Stanner's Boyer Lecture, 'The great Australian silence', was broadcast in 1968; C. D. Rowley's *The Destruction of Aboriginal Society* was published in 1970 (Penguin, Ringwood, Vic); Lyndall Ryan's *The Aboriginal Tasmanians* was published in 1981, (Allen and Unwin, Melbourne); Henry Reynolds's *The Other Side of the Frontier: Aboriginal Resistance of the European Invasion of the Australia* appeared in 1981 (Penguin, Ringwood, Vic); Bernard Smith's Boyer Lecture, 'The spectre of Truganini' was broadcast in 1980; and Richard Broome's *The Victorians: Arriving* appeared in 1986 (Fairfax, Syme and Weldon, Sydney). But all were presaged by James Bonwick's *The Lost Tasmanian Race* published in 1884 (S. Low, Marston, Searle, and Rivington, London).

40 Bain Attwood, *Rights for Aborigines*, Allen and Unwin, Crows Nest, 2003.

41 Sara Ahmed, 'The politics of bad feeling', *Australian Critical Race and Whiteness Studies Association Journal*, vol. 1, 2005, pp. 72–85, p. 72.

42 Such declarations can also respond to, or mobilise, Indigenous and non-Indigenous action. As John Howard sought to amend the Racial Discrimination Act in 1997 to undermine native title enshrined through the High Court Wik decision, in consultation with Mirimbiak Nations, I set up and convened the Stick with Wik campaign, selling armbands and ribbons with a send-on postcard protesting his ten-point plan. (By chance I later met Brian Harradine in a caravan park on Magnetic Island and had the opportunity to argue the point outside the camp kitchen.) When Howard declared the Northern Territory Intervention into remote Aboriginal communities, I called a public meeting at the Koorie Heritage Trust and organized a rally at the general post office on behalf of Women for Wik. See L. Conor, 'Howard's desert storm', *Overland*, no. 189, Summer 2007, pp. 12–15; and 'Political science and affective ties', *Arena*, no. 88, April–May 2007, pp. 10–11. I've since argued the anti-Intervention movement has failed to mobilise public support because it has not found a way to talk about violence against women and children in some communities. L. Conor, 'Some hard truths about the intervention', *The Age*, 2 July 2012; and 'It's time to remove the offenders', *The Drum*, ABC Online, 8 March 2012, accessed 23 October 2015, <http://www.abc.net.au/news/2012-03-08/

conor-it27s-time-to-remove-the-offenders/3875014>.
43 Richard Dyer, *White*, Routledge, London, 1997, p. 11.
44 Edith Ellen Hoy, *Harrietville, 115 Years of Continuous Gold Seeking*, Harrietville Historical Society, Harrietville, Vic, *c.* 1967.
45 Edith Ellen Hoy, *Historiette of the Manfields who began their Mt. Buffalo Saga when the Buckland was at its Heyday in the Early 50s*, Harrietville Historical Society, Harrietville, Vic, 1965.
46 'Attacks on the overland routes to Port Phillip', *Historical Records of Victoria, Volume 2A: The Aborigines of Port Phillip 1835–1839*, Victorian Government Printing Office, Melbourne, 1982, pp. 312–42; Reynolds, *The Other Side of the Frontier*, 1981.
47 Judith Bassett, 'The Faithfull massacre at the Broken River, 1838', *Journal of Australian Studies*, vol. 13, no. 24, 1989, pp. 18–34. In an interview Uncle Freddie Dowling corrected the text that the 150 men were Taungerong and Waveroo, and asserted they were Pangerang. See also Morna Sturrock, 'European and Aboriginal conflict in the western district and the north-east of Victoria, in the first decade of white settlement', unpublished, Glen Waverly, 1983.
48 Richard Broome, *Aboriginal Victorians: A History since 1800*, Allen and Unwin, Sydney, 2005, p. 71.
49 Patrick Wolfe, *Settler Colonialism and the Transformation of Anthropology: The Politics and Poetics of an Ethnographic Event*, Cassell, London, 1999, p. 165.
50 William Thomas in Thomas Francis Bride (ed.) *Letters from Victorian Pioneers, Being a Series of Papers in the Early Occupation of the Colony, The Aborigines, etc.*, William Heinemann, Melbourne, 1969 (1898), p. 411.
51 Bassett, 'Faithfull massacre'.
52 Rowley, *Destruction of Aboriginal Society*, p. 151.
53 Quoted in A. Grenfell Price, *White Settlers and Native Peoples*, Georgian House, Melbourne, 1949, p. 111.
54 Cited in Broome, *Aboriginal Victorians*, p. 61.
55 Bassett, 'Faithfull massacre', p. 27.
56 Letter by E. D. Thompson to P. G. King, Colonial Secretary, printed in *Extracts from the Papers and Proceedings of the Aborigines Protection Society*, no. VI, December 1839, William Ball, Arnold, and Co., London, p. 177.
57 Richard Broome, *The Victorians: Arriving*, Fairfax, Syme, Weldon, Sydney, 1986, p. 30.
58 Broome, *Aboriginal Victorians*, p. 82.
59 Governor Gipp established the Border Police at the major river crossings and they were charged with protecting the expanding pastoral

settlement. Bassett, 'Faithfull massacre', p. 32.
60 Rowley, *Destruction of Aboriginal Society*, p. 151.
61 Broome, *Aboriginal Victorians*, p. 81.
62 James Boyce, *1835: The Founding of Melbourne and the Conquest of Australia*, Black Inc., Melbourne, 2011, p. 191.
63 J. Angas and H. Forster, *A History of the Ovens Valley*, self-published, Wangaratta, 1967.
64 Fred Cahir, '"Are you off to the diggings?": Aboriginal guiding to and on the goldfields', in Lynette Russell and John Arnold (eds), *The La Trobe Journal*, Special issue: Indigenous Victorians: repressed, resourceful and respected, no, 85, May 2010, pp. 22–36.
65 Broome, *The Victorians*, p. 32; Broome, *Aboriginal Victorians*, p. 194.
66 Ludwik Krzywicki, *Primitive Society and its Vital Statistics*, MacMillan and Co., London, 1934, p. 316.
67 Broome, *Aboriginal Victorians*, p. 147.
68 Charles Barrett, *Blackfellows: The Story of Australia's Native Race*, Cassell & Co., London, 1942, p. 50.
69 Mary Jane's given name was Luana. Thanks to Pangarang elder and great-grandnephew Freddie Dowling.
70 W. L. Murdoch, Esq., 'Particulars concerning the blacks whose portraits appeared in last issue', *Science of Man*, vol. 3, no. 3, 23 April 1900, pp. 44–47, p. 44.
71 Pangerang elder Freddie Dowling's storytelling can be seen at *Bindagaree 'You see'*, 2014, Culture Victoria, accessed 5 January 2012, <http://cv.vic.gov.au/stories/pangerang-country/11963/bindagaree-you-see/>. Dowling is the author of *No More the Valley Rings with Koorie Laughter* published with Wendy Mitchell, *The Last Dance of the Pangerang*, Wangaratta Historical Society, Wangaratta, 2009.
72 ibid. In his reminiscences, geologist E. J. Dunn described Mary Jane Milawa as the last survivor of the King River tribe, whom he saw camping near Wangaratta in November 1888. Thanks to Dr Fransisco Almeida of Hume Heritage for passing on this reference. My thanks also to Sally Rose and Alison Brash, The Torch (www.thetorch.org.au) for assisting my attempts to contact women in the North East.
73 Sally Morgan, *My Place*, Fremantle Arts Centre Press, Fremantle, 1987.
74 Homi Bhabha, *The Location of Culture*, Routledge, London, 1994, p. 198.
75 The artwork was first 'discovered' by locals Matthew Eather and Leo O'Neil in 1952. In 1962 Aldo Massola wrote to Haha requesting further information and asking to visit the site. However, he announced their whereabouts as his 'find' in *The Age* before she had assurances they

would be protected, causing a stir among locals. See correspondence from John Mulvaney and Aldo Massola to Edith Ellen Hoy, Edith Ellen Hoy Scrapbooks, 119, 119A, 119B, Harrietville Historical Society. See Aldo Massola, 'The rock-shelter at Mudgegonga', *Field Naturalists Club of Victoria*, vol. 83, no. 4, April 1966. The rock-shelter at Mudgegonga doesn't appear in P. J. F. Coutts and D. C. Witter, *A Guide to Recording Archaeological Sites in Victoria*, Records of the Victorian Archaeological Survey no. 3, Aboriginal Affairs Victoria, Melbourne, 1977, accessed 15 March 2014, <http://search.informit.com.au/documentSummary;dn=882700728563068;res=IELIND>.

76 Letter from the Australian Institute of Aboriginal Studies, 27 March 1975, ref SJ.55.
77 Trish Wadley, conversation with the author, 5 January 2012.
78 Chris Healy, *Forgetting Aborigines*, UNSW Press, Sydney, 2008, p. 5.
79 Ann Laura Stoler, *Along the Archival Grain: Epistemic Anxieties and Colonial Sense*, Princeton University Press, Princeton, 2009, p. 20.
80 Some of the Harrietville Historical Society's memorialising included the Guide Alice Plaque at Mt Buffalo; the marking of the Lonely Grave on the Dargo High Plains; and the Mick Dougherty Memorial Seat, the Pioneer's Memorial, the Eric M. Hoy Memorial Water-wheel and the erection of the 'historical flag pole', all in the Harrietville Historical Park. Edith Ellen Hoy Scrapbooks, Harrietville Historical Society.
81 Healy, *Forgetting Aborigines*, p. 205.
82 Bhabha, *Location of Culture*, p. 163.
83 Healy, *Forgetting Aborigines*, p. 158.
84 ibid., p. 178.
85 Robert Young, *White Mythologies: Writing History and the West*, Routledge, London, 1990, p. 1.
86 See Jane Lydon's analysis of a portrait of Ellen of Coorandeerk station by Charles Walter in 1865, in her *Eye Contact: Photographing Indigenous Australians*, Duke University Press, Durham, 2005, p. 43.
87 See Daisy Bates, 'Ngilgi, of many suitors', in *Passing of the Aborigines*, John Murray, London, 1944, p. 63.
88 Bhabha, *Location of Culture*, p. 51.
89 Gayatri Spivak, 'Can the subaltern speak?', in Cary Nelson and Lawrence Grossberg (eds), *Marxism and the Interpretation of Culture*, MacMillan, Houndmills, 1988, pp. 271–313, p. 285.
90 ibid., p. 288.
91 ibid., p. 296.
92 See, for instance, my discussion with Jane Lydon of Nyungar

photo-media artist Dianne Jones in Liz Conor and Jane Lydon (eds), 'Introduction: Double take: reappraising the colonial archive', *Journal of Australian Studies*, special issue, vol. 35, no. 2, June 2011, pp. 137–43.

93 Most famously Keith Windschuttle, *The Fabrication of Aboriginal History, Volume One: Van Diemen's Land 1803–1847*, Macleay Press, Paddington, 2002; Robert Manne (ed.), *Whitewash: On Keith Windschuttle's Fabrication of Aboriginal History*, Black Inc. Agenda, Melbourne, 2003; Stuart MacIntyre and Anna Clark, *The History Wars*, Melbourne University Publishing, Melbourne, 2003.

94 Robert Kenny, *The Lamb Enters the Dreaming: Nathanael Pepper and the Ruptured World*, Scribe, Melbourne, 2007, p. 48.

95 Bronwen Douglas and Chris Ballard (eds), *Foreign Bodies: Oceania and the Science of Race 1750–1940*, ANU Epress, Canberra, 2008, preface.

96 Poole, *Vision, Race and Modernity*, p. 6.

97 Cited in Jennifer L. Morgan, '"Some could suckle over their shoulder": male travelers, female bodies, and the gendering of racial ideology, 1500–1770', *The William and Mary Quarterly*, vol. 54, no. 1, January 1997, pp. 167–192, p. 169.

98 See Marilyn Lake, *Faith: Faith Bandler, Gentle Activist*, Allen and Unwin, Sydney, 2002.

99 Heather Goodall, 'Pearl Gibbs: some memories', *Aboriginal History*, vol. 7, no. 1, 1983, pp. 20–22.

100 Alison Holland, '"Whatever her race a woman is not a chattel": Mary Montgomery Bennet', in Anna Cole, Victoria Katharine Haskins and Fiona Paisley (eds), *Uncommon Ground: White Women and Aboriginal History*, Aboriginal Studies Press, Canberra, 2005, pp. 129–152.

101 Heather Radi, 'Kelly, Emily Caroline (Carrie) (1899–1989)', *Australian Dictionary of Biography*, National Centre of Biography, Australian National University, accessed 15 February 2013, <http://adb.anu.edu.au/biography/kelly-emily-caroline-carrie-12720/text22937>.

102 Sandy Toussaint, 'Preface', in Phyllis Kabbery, *Aboriginal Woman: Sacred and Profane*, Routledge, London, 2004 (1939), p. xi.

103 Phyllis Kabbery, *Aboriginal Woman: Sacred and Profane*, Routledge, London, 1939; Sandy Toussaint, *Phyllis Kaberry and Me: Anthropology, History and Aboriginal Australia*, Melbourne University Press, Melbourne, 1999.

104 Diane E. Barwick, *Rebellion at Coranderrk*, Aboriginal History Inc., Canberra, 1998; Tim Rowse, 'Barwick, Diane Elizabeth (1938–1986)', *Australian Dictionary of Biography*, National Centre of Biography, Australian National University, accessed 15 February 2013, <http://adb.

anu.edu.au/biography/barwick-diane-elizabeth-76/text21837>.
105 Fay Gale (ed.), *Woman's Role in Aboriginal Society*, Australian Institute of Aboriginal Studies, Canberra, 1974.
106 *Women of the Sun*, SBS, 1981. Directed by James Ricketson, David Stevens, Stephen Wallace and Geoffrey Nottage, co-written by Sonia Borg and Hyllus Maris.
107 Diane Bell, *Daughters of the Dreaming*, McPhee Gribble / George Allen and Unwin, Sydney, 1983, p. 90; *Daughters of a Dreaming: A Photographic Exhibition of Koori Women of Southeast Australia*, Museum of Victoria, Melbourne, 1990.
108 Patrick Wolfe, 'Settler colonialism and the elimination of the native', *Journal of Genocide Research*, vol. 8, no. 4, December 2006, pp. 387–409.
109 Laird, 'Aborigine girl', p. 20.
110 Eric White, 'Aborigine Nellie', *Walkabout*, vol. 18, no. 4, 1 April 1952, pp. 42, 44.
111 I approached an anthropologist at the Northern Land Council in an attempt to trace 'Nellie' or her descendants, but she was unable to be identified.
112 Coinciding with the Mabo and Wik cases on native title, a royal commission found the women's business had been fabricated. Files were publicly released without their permission and the breach of confidentiality created a scandal in which the Liberal shadow environment minister was forced to resign. See Ken Gelder and Jane M. Jacobs, 'Promiscuous sacred sites: reflections on secrecy and scepticism in the Hindmarsh Island affair', *Australian Humanities Review*, June–July 1997, accessed 15 March 2014, <http://www.australianhumanitiesreview.org/archive/Issue-June-1997/gelder.html>; Marcia Langton, 'The Hindmarsh Island Bridge affair: how Aboriginal women's religion became an administerable affair', *Australian Feminist Studies*, vol. 11, no. 24, 1996, pp. 211–217, p. 215; A. Stuart, review of 'Secret women's business: the Hindmarsh Island affair', special issue of *Journal of Australian Studies* edited by Lyndall Ryan, *Australian Feminist Studies*, vol. 12, no. 26, 1997, p. 357.
113 See Sharon Huebner's discussion of the complexities of repatriating images and digital technologies in 'Noongar and Koories: interpreting the silences of a colonial archive at Monash University', PhD thesis, Monash Indigenous Centre, Monash University (forthcoming).
114 Rev. Peter Campbell, *Trucanini! Or Lalla Rookh. The Last of the Tasmanian Aborigines,* Hobart, 1876; J. A. Longford, 'Truganini, last princess of Tasmania', *Gentlemen's Magazine*, no. 17, 1876, p. 456;

'Trucanini, queen of Bruni, last of the Tasmanians', *People*, no. 1, 31 June 1951, pp. 43-46; Daisy Bates, 'Fanny Balbuk-Yooreel, the last Swan River (female) native, *Science of Man*, vol. 13, nos 5–6, 1911, pp. 100–101, 119–21; Daisy Bates, 'Ngilgi: an Aboriginal woman's life story', *Australasian*, 23 March 1935; Daisy M. Bates, 'Was she 107? Death of "Nory Ann"', *Western Mail*, 11 December 1924, p. 23; L. G. Chandler, 'Last of her tribe [Mary Woorlong, Kulkyne Tribe, Murray River]', *Wild Life*, vol. 14, no. 2, August 1951, pp. 163–65; Mrs Florrie Munroe, 'The life of queen Mary Ann…a brave woman', *Dawn*, October 1952; 'A grand old lady passes on [Lizzie, Grand Old Lady of Woodenbong Station]', *Dawn*, October 1952.

115 M. S., 'Rosie the tree climber', *Walkabout*, vol. 15, no. 2, February 1949, p. 46.

116 Henry Ling Roth, 'Is Mrs F. C. Smith a last living Aboriginal of Tasmania?', *Journal of the Anthropological Institute*, no. 27, 1898, pp. 451–54. Fanny Cochrane Smith was the last fluent speaker of a Tasmanian language and was proud of her Aboriginality. She sought recognition as the last Tasmanian after her friends William Lanne and Trugernanner died, but her designation as 'half-caste' denied her that status. J. Clark, 'Smith, Fanny Cochrane (1834–1905)', *Australian Dictionary of Biography*, National Centre of Biography, Australian National University, accessed 1 March 2013 <http://adb.anu.edu.au/biography/smith-fanny-cochrane-8466/text14887>.

117 P. Crosbie Morrison, 'Black Aggie', *Wild Life*, vol. 11, no. 5, May 1949, pp. 226–27.

118 Ngoondaw Gladys, 'Saint George', Mount Margaret Aboriginal Mission, 1935. There were two admissions to the mission in 1935, and Wongatha people struggling with drought conditions had been transferred to Mount Margaret after ration depots at the Linden and Morgan stations closed. Following enquiries, AIATSIS advises Ngoondaw Gladys is not listed in its Aboriginal Biographical Index. As her birthplace is unknown it is not possible to trace her to her community or possible descendants. She may be present in the photograph, 'Children at Mount Margaret, 1939', in 'Years of admission of Mount Margaret inmates in 1956 – AIATSIS', accessed 4 March 2013,<http://www.aiatsis.gov.au/ntru/nativetitleconference/conf2007/papers%20and%20presentations/muller.pdf>; M. M. Bennett, *Teaching the Aborigines: Data from Mount Margaret Mission, 1935*; Annual Report, United Aborigines Mission, Mt. Margaret Branch, The Mission, Mt. Margaret, 1957; Margaret Morgan, *Mt Margaret: A Drop in the Bucket*, Mission Publications, Lawson, 1986.

119 Bain Attwood, '"In the name of all my coloured brethren and sisters": a biography of Bessy Cameron', *Hecate* vol. 12, nos 1–2, 1986, pp. 9–53.
120 Here I am paraphrasing Bhabha, *Location of Culture*, p. 47.
121 Marcia Langton, 'Aboriginal art and film: the politics of representation', *Rouge*, 2005, accessed 16 March 2008, <http://www.rouge.com.au/6/aboriginal.html>.
122 Edward M. Curr, *The Australian Race: Its Origins, Languages, Customs, Place of Landing in Australia and the Routes by Which it Spread itself over the Continent*, vol. 1, John Ferres Government Printer, Melbourne, 1886.
123 Ironically, Curr's writings of being an early squatter on Yorta Yorta land was used as a primary source by Justice Olney to scuttle this people's native title claim in 1998. Curr, *Australian Race*, ibid., p. 70.
124 Krzywicki, *Primitive Society*, p. 142.
125 Marji Hill and Alex Barlow, *Black Australia*, Australian Institute of Aboriginal Studies, Canberra, 1978, p. 93.
126 Aileen Moreton-Robinson, *Talkin' up to the White Woman: Indigenous Women and Feminism*, Queensland University Press, Brisbane, 2000, p. 89.
127 ibid., p. 183.
128 Australian Institute for Aboriginal and Torres Strait Islander Studies, 'Guidelines for ethical research in Australian Indigenous studies', AIATSIS, Canberra, 2012, principle 1, p. 2.
129 Eric Michaels, 'A primer of restrictions on picture taking in traditional areas of Aboriginal Australia', *Visual Anthropology*, vol. 4, nos 3–4, 1991, pp. 259–75, p. 259.
130 ibid., p. 260.
131 Taussig, *Mimesis and Alterity*, p. 135.
132 Shino Konishi, '"Wanton with plenty": questioning ethno-historical constructions of sexual savagery in Aboriginal societies, 1788–1803', *Australian Historical Studies*, vol. 39, no. 3, 2008, pp. 356–72, p. 362.
133 Ann Laura Stoler, *Along the Archival Grain: Epistemic Anxieties and Colonial Common Sense*, Princeton, Princeton University Press, p. 2009, p. 44.
134 Konishi, '"Wanton with plenty"', p. 362.
135 Ann Laura Stoler argues for reading 'along' the grain, to follow the archives 'granular rather than seamless texture' in attempting to understand how 'unintelligibilities are sustained' in her *Along the Archival Grain*, p. 53.
136 Martin Lyons, *A History of Reading and Writing in the Western World*, Palgrave MacMillan, New York, 2010, p. 123.
137 Ann Laura Stoler, *Carnal Knowledge and Imperial Power: Race and the*

Intimate in Colonial Rule, University of California Press, Berkeley, 2002, p. 149.
138 F. G. G. Rose, 'Groote Eylandt', *Walkabout*, 1 March 1944, vol. 10, no. 5, (pp. 9–13, 23), p. 12.
139 Bell, *Daughters of the Dreaming*, p. 90.
140 Susan Sontag, *On Photography*, Penguin, Harmondsworth, 1977, p. 59.
141 Roland Barthes, *Mythologies*, Pallidin, London, 1973, p. 119.
142 ibid.
143 Taussig, *Mimesis and Alterity*, p. 21.
144 ibid., p. 35.
145 Nicholas Thomas, *Possessions: Indigenous Art/Colonial Culture*, Thames and Hudson, London, 1987, p. 92.
146 Jurgen Habermas, *The Structural Transformation of the Public Sphere*, Polity Press, Cambridge, 1989, p. 232.
147 ibid., p. 162.
148 Thomas, *Possessions,* p. 231.
149 Francis Jennings, *The Invasion of America: Indians, Colonialism, and the Cant Of Conquest*, University of North Carolina Press, Chapel Hill, 1975.

Chapter 1

1   Chris Healy, *From the Ruins of Colonialism: History as Social Memory*, Cambridge University Press, Cambridge, 1997, p. 95.
2   John Greenway, *Bibliography of the Australian Aborigines and the Native Peoples of Torres Strait to 1959*, Angus and Robertson, Sydney, 1963.
3   See, for instance, William Kring Gregory, 'Australia, the land of living fossils, as exemplified in the proposed exhibition, American Museum', *Natural History*, no. 24, 1924, pp. 5–15; Marcellin Boule, *Fossil Men*, 2nd edn, trans. J. E. and J. Ritchie, Edinburgh, 1923.
4   I am paraphrasing Robert F. Berkhofer in his discussion of the American Boas School of Anthropology. See his *The White Man's Indian: Images of the American Indian from Columbus to the Present,* Vintage, New York, 1979, p. 67. The original phrase, 'the only good Indian is a dead one', derives from General Phil Sheridan. See Patrick Wolfe, 'Land, labor, and difference: elementary structures of race', *American Historical Review*, vol. 106, no. 3, June 2001, fn. 90, p. 891, pp. 866–905. Daisy Bates amended it again, remarking 'with very few exceptions the only good half caste is a dead one', in 'Aboriginal reserves and women patrols', *The Sunday Times*, 2 October 1921, p. 18.
5   Stuart K. Cross, 'On a numerical determination of the relative positions of certain biological types in the evolutionary scale, and of the relative

values of various cranial measurements and indices as criteria', *Proceedings of the Royal Society of Edinburgh*, vol. XXXI, pt. 1, 1910–1911.

6   J. W. Dawson, *Fossil Men and Their Modern Representatives*, London, 1883.

7   Harold V. Mattingley, 'The teeth of some Australian Aboriginal natives, and comparisons with the teeth of prehistoric man', *Commonwealth Dental Review*, vol. XII, 1915, pp. 388–94.

8   Robert Turner and M. J. Boyce, *Australian Aboriginal Signs and Symbols for the Use of Boy Scouts*, Sydney, 1934.

9   J. G. Wood, *The Natural History of Man; being an Account of the Manners and Customs of the Uncivilized Races of Men*, George Routledge and Sons, London, 1880, p. 1.

10 William Ramsay Smith, 'Aborigines', in the *Australian Encyclopedia*, Angus & Robertson, Sydney, 1927, p. 25.

11 'The "abo" as hunter', *Bank Notes*, Commonwealth Bank, December 1932, p. 21, pp. 20–21.

12 S. D. Porteous, *The Psychology of a Primitive People*, Arnold & Co., London, 1929.

13 Due to an 'earlier cessation of brain growth' and 'inferior auditory rote memory'. S. D. Porteous, 'Mentality of Australian Aborigines', *Oceania*, vol. IV, 1933–39, pp. 30–36, p. 32.

14 The study also included 130 men and 127 children. See A. P. Elkin, 'The social life and intelligence of the Australian Aborigine: a review of S. D. Porteous's *Psychology of a Primitive People*', *Oceania*, vol. III, 1932–33, pp. 101–113, p. 110.

15 C. S. Browne, *Australia: A General Account*, Thomas Nelson & Sons, London, 1929, p. 167.

16 Julie Marcus (ed.), *First in their Field: Women and Australian Anthropology*, Melbourne University Press, Melbourne, 1993.

17 Tony Ballantyne, 'What difference does colonialism make? Reassessing print and social change in an age of global imperialism', in Sabrina Alcorn Baron, Eric N. Lindquist and Eleanor F. Shevlin (eds), *Agents of Change: Print Culture Studies after Elizabeth L. Eisenstein*, University of Massachusetts Press, Amherst, 2007, pp. 342–52, p. 343.

18 John A. Hobson, *The Psychology of Jingoism*, Grant Richards, London, 1901, p. 10.

19 ibid., pp. 109, 111–113, 119.

20 Penelope Brown, 'Repetition', *Journal of Linguistic Anthropology*, vol. 9, nos 1–2, June 1991, pp. 223–26, p. 223.

21 Deb Verhoeven, *Sheep and the Australian Cinema*, Melbourne University Press, Melbourne, 2006, p. 4.

22 ibid., p. 7.
23 William Dampier, *New Voyage Around the World,* James Knapton, London, 1697; Adrian Mitchell, *Dampier's Monkey: the South Sea voyages of William Dampier, including William Dampier's unpublished journal,* Wakefield Press, South Australia, 2010.
24 Anna Neill, 'Buccaneer ethnography: nature, culture and nation in the journals of William Dampier', *Eighteenth-Century Studies,* vol. 33, no. 2, 2000, p. 165–80.
25 D. Preston and M. Preston, *A Pirate of Exquisite Mind: The Life of William Dampier, Explorer, Naturalist and Buccaneer,* London, 2004.
26 William Hasty, 'Piracy and the production of knowledge in the travels of William Dampier c1679–1688', *Journal of Historical Geography,* vol. 37, no. 1, 2011, pp. 40–54; G. Barnes and A. Mitchell, 'Measuring the marvelous: science and the exotic in William Dampier', *Eighteenth Century Life,* no. 26, 2002, pp. 45–57.
27 Neill, 'Buccaneer ethnography', p. 168.
28 Marcia Langton, 'Aboriginal art and film: the politics of representation', *Rouge,* 2005, accessed 16 March 2008, <http://www.rouge.com.au/6/aboriginal.html>.
29 Anne Salmond, *Aphrodite's Island: The European Discovery of Tahiti,* Penguin, New Zealand, 2009; Jonathon Lamb, Vanessa Smith and Nicholas Thomas, *Exploration and Exchange: a South Seas Anthology, 1680–1900,* University of Hawai'i Press, Honolulu, 2004; Nicholas Thomas, *Islanders: The Pacific in the Age of Empire,* Yale University Press, New Haven, 2010.
30 Dampier, *New Voyage.*
31 *The History of New Holland,* John Stockdale, London, 1787, p. 27.
32 J. R. McCulloch (ed.), *Dictionary, Geographical, Statistical, and Historical of the Various Countries, Places and Principal Natural Object in the World,* Longman, Brown, Green, and Longmans, London, 1854, pp. 228–31, p. 230.
33 'The Aborigines', public lecture transcribed in the *Empire,* 14 August 1857, p. 2.
34 Albert F. Calvert, *The Discovery of Australia,* George Philip & Son, London, 1893, pp. 40–42.
35 William Dampier quoted in W. Charnley, 'The antiquity of the Aboriginal', *Walkabout,* 1 February 1947, p. 30.
36 Dampier quoted in Samuel Bennett, *The History of Australian Discovery and Colonisation,* Hanson and Bennett, Sydney, 1865, p. 36.
37 See Shino Konishi, 'Idle men: the eighteenth-century roots of the

Indigenous indolence myth', in Ann Curthoys, Frances Peters-Little and John Docker (eds), *Passionate Histories: Myth, Memory and Indigenous Histories*, Aboriginal History Monographs No. 23, ANU ePress, Canberra, 2010, pp. 99–122.
38 *History of New Holland*, p. 30.
39 Dampier quoted in Bennett, *History of Australian Discovery*, p. 37.
40 Calvert, *Discovery of Australia*, p. 42. Reprinted in William Dampier, *Dampier's Voyages*, John Masefield (ed.), E. Grants Richards, London, 1906, p. 456.
41 Trollope visited Australia twice. James Buzard, 'Portable boundaries: Trollope, race and travel', *Nineteenth-Century Contexts*, vol. 32, no. 1, 2001, pp. 5–18.
42 For the relation between literature and travel writing see Tim Fulford, Debbie Lee and Peter J. Kitson, *Literature, Science and Exploration in the Romantic Era: Bodies of Knowledge*, Cambridge University Press, New York, 2004.
43 Anthony Trollope, *Australia and New Zealand*, vol. 1, Chapman and Hall, London, 1873, p. 60.
44 Cited in Buzard, 'Portable boundaries', p. 14.
45 Jill Felicity Durey, 'Modern issues: Anthony Trollope and Australia', *Antipodes*, vol. 21, no. 2, 2007, pp. 179–76, p. 174.
46 Trollope, *Australia and New Zealand*, p. 61.
47 Dampier, *Dampier's Voyages*, p. 453.
48 Hal Colebatch (ed.), *A Story of a Hundred Years: Western Australia, 1829–1929*, Government Printer, Perth, 1929, p. 111.
49 Albert F. Calvert, *The Aborigines of Western Australia*, W. Milligan & Co., London, 1892, p. 9.
50 Calvert, *Discovery of Australia*, p. 41.
51 Doris Anne Chadwick, 'To the new land', *The New South Wales School Magazine of Literature for Our Boys and Girls*, vol. 37, no. 2, 1 July 1952, pp. 153–57, p. 155.
52 See Greenway, *Bibliography of the Australian Aborigines*, p. 107, entry no. 2564.
53 ibid., p. 320, entry no. 8947.
54 Calvert, *Discovery of Australia*, p. 45.
55 Dampier, *New Voyage*, chapter 16.
56 Neill, 'Buccaneer ethnography', p. 171.
57 See Louis Montrose, 'The work of gender in the discourse of discovery', *Representations*, Special issue: The new world, no. 33, Winter, 1991, pp. 1–41.

58 Wolfe, 'Land, labour and difference', p. 878.
59 Neill, 'Buccaneer ethnography', p. 167.
60 *History of New Holland*, p. 235.
61 John Marra, *Journal of the Resolution's voyage, in 1772, 1773, 1774, and 1775, on discovery to the southern hemisphere, by which the non-existence of an undiscovered continent, between the Equator and the 50th degree of southern latitude is demonstratively proved: also a journal of the Adventure's voyage, in the years 1772, 1773, and 1774*, F. Newbery, London, 1775; James Cook, *A voyage towards the South Pole, and Round the World: performed in His Majesty's ships the Resolution and Adventure, in the years 1772, 1773, 1774, and 1775 / written by James Cook, Commander of the Resolution. In which is included Captain Furneaux's narrative of his proceedings in the Adventure during the separation of the ships. In two volumes. Illustrated with maps and charts, and a variety of portraits of persons and views of places drawn during the Voyage by Mr. Hodges and engraved by the most eminent Masters*, W. Strahan and T. Cadell, London, 1777. (None of the above contain the third voyage of 1776–79 from which the Webber drawing is derived.)
62 Deirdre Coleman, *Romantic Colonization and British Anti-Slavery*, Cambridge University Press, Cambridge, 2005, pp. 173–80.
63 James Cook, *Voyages in the Southern Hemisphere*, vols II–III, p. 579, accessed 2 March 2013, <http://southseas.nla.gov.au/journals/hv23/minor_title.html>; *History of New Holland*, p. 180.
64 *History of New Holland*, p. 190.
65 Johann Kaspter Lavater, *Physiognomische Fragmente zur Beförderung der Menschenkenntnis und Menschenliebe,* Orell Füssli, Zurich, 1775–1778; see also Ellis Shookman (ed.), *The Faces of Physiognomy: Interdisciplinary Approaches to Johann Caspar Lavater*, Camden House, Columbia, 1993.
66 Phillipa Levine, 'States of undress: nakedness and the colonial imagination', *Victorian Studies*, vol. 50, no. 2, 2008, p. 189–219.
67 Adeline Masquelier, *Dirt, Undress, and Difference: Critical Perspectives on the Body's Surface,* Indiana University Press, Bloomington, 2005.
68 *Captain Cook's Journal During his first Voyage round the World made in H.M. Bark 'Endeavour' 1768–1771*, Elliot Stock, London, 1893, entry dated 12 July 1770.
69 'Authentic letter from Botany Bay', *The London Chronicle*, no. 5084, 5 May 1789, p. 435.
70 ibid.
71 Lea Holcombe, *Wives and Property: Reform of the Married Women's Property Law in Nineteenth-century England*, University of Toronto Press, Toronto, 1983.

72 Catherine Hall and Leonore Davidoff, *Family Fortunes: Men and Women of the English Middle Class 1780–1850*, Routledge, London, 1987; Alice Clark, *Working Life of Women in the Seventeenth Century*, Frank Cass, Oxon, 1919; Amanda Flather, *Gender and Space in Early Modern England*, Boydell, Suffolk, 2007.

73 Rudiger Joppein and Bernard Smith, *The Art of Captain Cook's Voyages*, vol. 3, Yale University Press, New Haven, 1985–88, p, 2; Geoff Quilley, *The Captain's Artist: The Career of John Webber R. A., Smoking Coasts and Ice-Bound Seas: Cooks Voyage to the Arctic*, Catalogue to the Exhibition at the Captain Cook Memorial Museum, Whitby, 2008, pp. 13–21.

74 George William Anderson (ed.), *A New, Authentic, and Complete Collection of Voyages Round the World undertaken and performed by Royal authority. Containing a new...account of Captain Cook's...Voyages,* Alex Hogg, London, 1784, p. 424. Engraver probably Johann Fritzsch.

75 Angela Rosenthal, 'Raising hair', *Eighteenth-Century Studies*, vol. 38, no. 1, Fall 2004, pp. 1–16; see also Shino Konishi, '"Tied in rolled knots and powdered with ochre": Aboriginal hair and eighteenth-century cross-cultural encounters', in Shino Konishi, Leah Lui-Chivizhe and Lisa Slater (eds), *Borderlands*, Special issue: Indigenous bodies, vol. 7, no. 2, 2008.

76 Philipe Despoix, 'The exchanged portrait and the lethal picture: visualisation techniques and native knowledge in Samuel Hearne's sketches from his trek to the Arctic Ocean and John Webber's record of the Northern Pacific', *Eighteenth Century Fiction*, vol. 23, no. 4, 2011, pp. 667–89.

77 Ter Ellingson, *The Myth of the Noble Savage,* University of California Press, Berkeley, 2001.

78 Denis Diderot, *Supplément au voyage de Bougainville*, H. Dieckmann, Geneva, 1955 (first published 1796, written 1772); Jean Jacques Rousseau, *A Dissertation on the Origin and Foundation of Inequality among Mankind*, trans. from the French, London, 1773–74.

79 Bernard Smith, *European Vision and the South Pacific*, Harper and Row, Sydney, 1985 (1969), p. 326.

80 Liz Conor, '"This striking ornament of nature": the "native belle" in the Australian colonial scene', Claire Colebrook and Rita Felski (eds), *Feminist Theory*, vol. 7, no. 2, August 2006, pp. 197–218.

81 Sydney Parkinson, *A journal of a voyage to the South Seas, in His Majesty's ship, the Endeavour / faithfully transcribed from the papers of the late Sydney Parkinson...: embellished with views and designs, delineated by the Author, and*

engraved by capital artists, Stanfield Parkinson, London, 1773 (not widely available until 1784).
82 *Journal of the Right Hon. Sir Joseph Banks during Captain Cook's first voyage in H.M.S. Endeavour in 1768–71 to Terra del Fuego, Otahite, New Zealand, Australia, the Dutch East Indies, etc.,* Sir Joseph D. Hooker (ed.), Macmillan, London, 1896.
83 Cook, *A Voyage towards the South Pole.*
84 Anderson, *A New, Authentic, and Complete Collection of Voyages Round the World,* p. 424.
85 John Hawkesworth, *An account of the voyages undertaken by the order of His present Majesty, for making discoveries in the southern hemisphere, and successively performed by Commodore Byron, Captain Wallis, Captain Carteret, and Captain Cook, in the Dolphin, the Swallow, and the Endeavour: drawn up from the journals which were kept by the several commanders and from the papers of Joseph Banks,* W. Strahan and T. Cadell, London, 1773.
86 Margaret Jolly, 'Colonial and postcolonial plots in histories of maternities and modernities', in Kalpana Ram and Margeret Jolly (eds), *Maternities and Modernities: Colonial and Postcolonial Experiences in Asia and the Pacific,* Cambridge University Press, Cambridge, 1998, pp. 1–24, p. 4.
87 See Henrietta Moore, quoted in Felicity A. Nussbaum, '"Savage" mothers: narratives of maternity in the mid-eighteenth century,' *Cultural Critique,* no. 20, Winter, 1991–92), p. 124.
88 Londa Schiebinger, 'Why mammals are called mammals: gender politics in eighteenth-century natural history', *The American Historical Review,* vol. 98, no. 2, 1993, pp. 382–411, p. 385, fn. 12.
89 Linneaus made an important distinction between *Mammalia* and *Primate,* even so his inclusion of mankind in the animal kingdom was scandalous and the argument raged well beyond Darwin proposing in 1859 that the mechanism of evolution was natural selection. Caroli Linneai, *Systema Naturae per Regna Tria Naturae, Secundum Classes, Ordines, Genera, Species, cum Characteribus, Differentiis, Synominis, Locis* [System of nature through the three kingdoms of nature, according to classes, orders, genera, and species, with [generic] characters, [specific] differences, synonyms and places], 10th edn, Holmiae, Laurentii Salvii, Stockholm, 1758.
90 Schiebinger, 'Why mammals are called mammals', p. 404.
91 Carolyn Merchant, *The Death of Nature: Women, Ecology and the Scientific Revolution,* Permagon, San Francisco, 1983.
92 Schiebinger, 'Why mammals are called mammals'.
93 I'm not aware of any instance of Aboriginal women wet-nursing for settler women. Certainly in the exploratory voyages this concept is

unlikely to have been applied to them. Schiebinger, 'Why mammals are called mammals', p. 407.
94 See Smith, *European Vision*, p. 326.
95 Tony Hughes-d'Aeth, *Paper Nation: The Story of the Picturesque Atlas of Australasia, 1886–1888,* Melbourne University Press, Melbourne, 2001, p. 84; see Hendrik Kolenberg and Anne Ryan, 'Australian prints in the gallery's collection', Art Gallery of NSW, Sydney, 1998; W. Sandby, *The History of the Royal Academy of Arts,* Longman, Green, Longman, Roberts, & Green, London, 1862; Michael Bryan, *Bryan's Dictionary of Painters and Engravers,* Macmillan, New York, 1903; William Moore, *The Story of Australian Art,* Angus and Robertson, Sydney, 1934; Algernon Graves, *The Royal Academy Exhibitors,* H. Graves, London, 1905.
96 Nicolas Thomas, *In Oceania: Visions, Artefacts, Histories,* Duke University Press, Durham, 1997, p. 13.
97 ibid.
98 John White, *Journal of a Voyage to New South Wales,* 1757/8–1832, accessed 26 July 2011, <http://gutenberg.net.au/ebooks03/0301531h.html#platelist>.
99 'Mr White decorating a female of New South Wales', artist Charles Ansell, engraver Augustine Birrell. Published in London in 1790 as *The Journal of Voyage to New South Wales,* then for the periodical *Historical Magazine, or, Classical Library of Public Events,* vol. 3, 1791, p. 20.
100 Arthur M. Hind, *A History of Engraving and Etching: From the 15th Century to the year 1914,* Dover Publications, New York, 1963.
101 Elizabeth L. Eisenstein, *The Printing Revolution in Early Modern Europe,* 2nd edn, Cambridge University Press, New York, 2005, p. 6.
102 Martyn Lyons uses this phrase referring to popular culture in terms of the difficulty inherent in distinguishing popular and elite cultures since they infiltrated each other, in his *A History of Reading and Writing in the Western World,* Palgrave Macmillan, New York, 2010, p. 74.
103 Jürgen Habermas, *The Structural Transformation of the Public Sphere,* Polity Press, Cambridge, 1989, p. 181.
104 Tony Ballantyne, 'What difference does colonialism make? Reassessing print and social change in an age of global imperialism', in Alcorn Baron, Lindquist and Shevlin (eds), *Agents of Change,* pp. 342–52, p. 344.
105 Lyons, *History of Reading and Writing in the Western World,* p. 94.
106 Eisenstein, *The Printing Revolution,* p. xviii.
107 Alcorn Baron, Lindquist and Shevlin (eds), *Agents of Change,* p. 160.
108 Gérard Genette, *The Architext: An Introduction,* University of California Press, Berkeley, 1991, pp. 83–84.

109 'Farther particulars to the Botany Bay expedition', *The London Chronicle*, 26–28 March 1789.
110 John White, 'The inhabitants of New South Wales', *The Historical Magazine, or, Classical Library of Public Events*, vol. 3, 1 March 1791, p. 20.
111 ibid.
112 'White's journal of a journey to New South Wales', *The Monthly Review, or, Literary Journal*, vol. 4, January–April 1791, p. 322.
113 Laura Rosenthal, *Infamous Commerce: Prostitution in Eighteenth-Century British Literature and Culture*, Cornell University Press, Ithaca, 2006, p. 180.
114 John White, 'Journal of a journey to New South Wales' (extract), *The London Review and Literary Journal*, vol. 18, August 1790; also *The European Magazine, and London Review*, (Philological Society of London), July–December 1790, p. 105.
115 White, 'Journal of a journey to New South Wales', p. 106.
116 ibid.
117 'Account of Rio de Janiero', *The Edinburgh Magazine, or Literary Miscellany*, July 1790, p. 255.
118 Johann Blumenbach classed humanity into five varieties only five years before Cook's landfall in Botany Bay: Caucasian, Mongolian, Malayan, Ethiopian and American. Johann Blumenbach, *On the Natural Variety of Mankind*, in *The Anthropological Treatises of Johann Friedrich Blumenbach*, trans. Thomas Bendyshe, 3rd edn, Longman, Green, Longman, Roberts and Green, London, 1865 (1795).
119 John White, *Journal of a Voyage to New South Wales*, Royal Australian Historical Society, with Angus and Robertson, 1962, p. 99.
120 Jonathon Crary, *Techniques of the Observer: On Vision and Modernity in the Nineteenth Century*, MIT Press, London, 1994, p. 96.
121 ibid.
122 See Joy Damousi, *Depraved and Disorderly: Female Convicts, Sexuality and Gender in Colonial Australia*, Cambridge University Press, Cambridge, 1997, p. 42.
123 Douglas, a Waterloo veteran, returned as an adult to his mother in Sydney who was by then married to a prominent settler. Rex Rienits, 'White, John (1756–1832)', *Australian Dictionary of Biography*, National Centre of Biography, Australian National University, accessed 26 July 2011, <http://adb.anu.edu.au/biography/white-john-2787/text3971>. Jackie French has written a children's novel based on Douglas and an Aboriginal child White adopted: *Nanberry: Black Brother White*, Harper Collins, 2011.

124 The idea of reading as poaching comes from Michel de Certeau. He places reading within a 'private hunting reserve' in which interpretation is authorised by those in positions of social power. It's interesting to think of print syndication as a kind of poaching. Michel de Certeau, 'Reading as poaching', *The Practice of Everyday Life*, University of California Press, 1988, p. 172.

125 Smith, *European Vision*, p. 197.

126 John West-Sooby, interview, 'The French gaze', *Hindsight*, ABC radio, accessed 15 November 2011 <http://www.abc.net.au/rn/hindsight/stories/2011/3278530.htm>.

127 Quoted by Stephanie Pfenningwerth, interview, 'The French gaze'.

128 Smith, *European Vision*, p. 197.

129 The invention of the rotary newspaper press would follow in 1814 and web-fed cylinder presses meant that from 1820 to 1870 the number of pages that could be printed per hour rose from 4,000 to 168,000. John Arnold, 'Printing technology and book production', in Martyn Lyons and John Arnold, *A History of the Book in Australia 1891–1945: A National Culture in a Colonised Market,* University of Queensland Press, Brisbane, 2001, pp. 104–112, p. 105.

130 Lyons, *History of Reading and Writing*, p. 138.

131 François Péron, *Voyage of Discovery to the Southern Hemisphere Performed by Order of the Emperor Napoleon, During the Years 1801, 1802, 1803, and 1804*, Richard Phillips, London, 1809. Illustrated by Lesueur and Petit, the book was printed in Paris by De l'Imprimerie Imperiale in 1807.

132 In Britain and France, mass literacy had been achieved before the advent of free and compulsory education by 1800, though women still trailed behind men. Lyons, *History of Reading and Writing*, p. 94.

133 ibid., p. 121.

134 Habermas, *Structural Transformation of the Public Sphere*, p. 181.

135 Smith, *European Vision*, p. 201.

136 Francois Duprat, *Histoire de l'Imprimerie imperiale de France; suivie des specimens des types etrangers et francais*, De l'Imprimerie imperiale, Paris, 1861. <http://www.archive.org/stream/histoiredelimpri00dupruoft#page/n3/mode/2up>.

137 Cited in Alcorn Baron, Linquist, Shevlin, *Agents of Change,* p. 164. In 1819 the publishing industry in France, including the periodical press, generated over 21 million francs annually. See Christine Haynes, *Lost Illusions: The Politics of Publishing in Nineteenth-Century France*, Harvard University Press, Cambridge, 2010, p. 2.

138 Kai-wing Chow, 'Reinventing Gutenberg: woodblock and

moveable-type printing in Europe and China', in Alcorn Baron, Lindquist and Shevlin, *Agents of Change,* pp. 167–192, p, 178.

139 Cited in Smith, *European Vision,* p. 198.

140 ibid.

141 See Margaret Sanky, 'Perceptions of the Aborigines recorded during the Baudin expedition: the dynamics of first encounter', in Bruce Bennett (ed.), *Australia in between Cultures, Specialists Session papers from the 1998 Australian Academy of the Humanities Symposium,* Australian Academy of the Humanities, Canberra, 1999, pp. 55–76; Margaret Sanky, Jean Fornasiero and Peter Cowley (eds), 'The Baudin expedition 1800–1804', *Australian Journal of French Studies,* special issue, vol. 41, no. 2, 2004.

142 Colin Dyer, *The French Explorers and the Aboriginal Australians, 1772–1839,* University of Queensland Press, Brisbane, 2005, p. 7.

143 Joseph-Marie Degérando's 'The observation of savage peoples' served as the basis for the *General Instruction to Travellers,* published by the Ethnological Society of Paris in 1840. His manual was to become 'the principle standards of ethnographical fieldwork one century later'. See Antonius Robbin and Jeffrey Sluka (eds), *Ethnographic Fieldwork: An Anthropological Reader,* Blackwell, Oxford, 2007, p. 30.

144 Degérando, 'The observation of savage peoples', in Robbin and Sluka (eds), *Ethnographic Fieldwork,* pp. 33–39, p. 34.

145 Robbin and Sluka (eds), *Ethnographic Fieldwork,* p. 30.

146 Degérando, 'The observation of savage peoples', p. 37.

147 Smith, *European Vision,* p. 199.

148 Shino Konishi, 'Francois Péron and the Tasmanians: an unrequited romance', *Inside Story,* accessed 21 July 2011, <http://inside.org.au/an-unrequited-romance/>.

149 Cited in James Bonwick, *The Lost Tasmanian Race,* Sampson Low, Marston, Searle, and Rivington, London, 1884, p. 11, and in Anna Haebich, *Broken Circles: Fragmenting Indigenous Families 1800–2000,* Freemantle Arts Centre Press, Fremantle, 2000, p. 65.

150 Cited in Bonwick, *Lost Tasmanian Race,* p. 11.

151 Baudin had noted the people at Esperance, as they came to call it, in Western Australia, also 'smear various parts of their faces with charcoal'. Quoted in 'The French gaze', *Hindsight.* On their first meeting with Ouré Ouré, she had also applied charcoal to her own face. Pierre-Bernard Milius, who was promoted to commander after the death of Baudin, also noted in his journal that women smeared a mix of charcoal and saliva on their faces and presumed it was in the pursuit of beauty. Venus could be found, he remarked, in this country's coal mines. J.

Bonnemains and P. Haughel, *Récit du Voyage aux Terres Australes de Pierre-Bernard Milius,* Société havraise d'Etudes diverses, Le Havre, 1987, p. 35.
152 Cited in Geoffrey Dutton, *White on Black: The Australian Aborigine Portrayed in Art*, Macmillan, Melbourne, 1974, p. 23.
153 Jolanta T. Pekacz, 'The salonnieres and the philosophies in old regime France: the authority of aesthetic judgment', *Journal of the History of Ideas*, vol. 60, no. 2, 1999, pp. 277–97.
154 Smith, *European Vision*, p. 199.
155 Eisentein, *Printing Revolution*, p. 65.
156 *Enterrement des Naturels de l'Australie / Naturel de l'Australie / Femme de la Tasmanie*, published in Paris between 1822 and 1843 by Jules Boilly after Louis De Sainson for Rear Admiral Dumont d'Urville, from the *Voyage pittoresque autour du monde: avec des portraits de sauvages d'Amérique, d'Asie, d'Afrique, et des îles du Grand ocean; des paysages, des vues maritimes, et plusieurs objets d'histoire naturelle*, Louis Choris, De l'Imprimerie de Firmin Didot, Paris.
157 Stanley Fish, *Is There a Text in this Class*, Harvard University Press, Cambridge, 1980, pp. 147–74.
158 Ballantyne, 'What difference does colonialism make?', p. 345.
159 P. Bourdieu and Loïc J. D. Wacquant, *An Invitation to Reflexive Sociology*, University of Chicago Press, Chicago, 1992, p. 119.
160 Lyons, *History of Reading and Writing*, p. 29.
161 I detail the relation between typography and typology in my 'Moveable parts: press and loom in colonial typologies', in Liz Conor (ed.), *Interventions,* Special issue: Types and typologies, vol. 17, no. 2, 2015, pp. 229–57.
162 Simmel, 'The nobility' [1908], in Donald Levine (ed.), *On Individuality and Social Forms,* University of Chicago Press, Chicago, 1971, pp. 199–213, p. 213.
163 Edward Duyker, interview, 'The French gaze', *Hindsight*. See also his *François Péron: An Impetuous Life*, Melbourne University Press, Melbourne, 2006.

Chapter 2
1 Regina Ganter, 'Letters from Mapoon: colonising Aboriginal gender', *Australian Historical Studies*, vol. 30, no. 113, 1999, pp. 267–85, p. 282.
2 The *Eva* left Cleveland Bay for Port Hinchinbrook with five crew and a passenger a few hours before a hurricane hit Townsville on 4 March 1867. It was thought all were lost. *The Mercury*, 6 April 1867, p. 2; Ian

J. McNiven, Lynette Russell, and Kay Schaffer (eds), *Constructions of Colonialism: Perspectives on Eliza Fraser's Shipwreck,* Leicester University Press, London, 1998; Barbara Creed and Jeanette Hoorn (eds), *Body Trade: Captivity, Cannibalism and Colonialism in the Pacific,* Routledge, New York, 2001.

3 A whaleboat was reported to have been sent from Bowen, in 'Telegraph despatches', *The Mercury,* 5 November 1867, p. 2. It carried searchers from Cardwell, including the police magistrate, for the *Eva* through the Palm Islands, but found no trace. 'The missing schooner Eva', *The Australian News for Home Readers,* 28 May 1867, p. 12; 'The trip of the steamer Black Prince to Rockingham Bay, and search for the missing schooner Eva', *The Sydney Morning Herald,* 24 April 1867, p. 2; Dorothy Jones, 'Eden, Charles Henry (1839–1900)', *Australian Dictionary of Biography,* National Centre of Biography, Australian National University, accessed 26 January 2012, <http://adb.anu.edu.au/biography/eden-charles-henry-3466/text5301>.

4 Eliza Fraser was the wife of the captain of the *Stirling Castle,* a brig shipwrecked on the coast of Queensland in May 1836. Her stay of three months with the people of Fraser Island was described as capture and enslavement at the time, though Aboriginal descendants argue their ancestors assisted the castaways. See Kay Schaffer, *In the Wake of First Contact: The Eliza Fraser Stories,* Cambridge University Press, Melbourne, 1995; McNiven, Russell and Schaffer, *Constructions of Colonialism.*

5 Charles Henry Eden, 'An Australian search party', in H. W. Bates, *Illustrated Travels: A Record of Discovery, Geography and Adventure,* Cassell, Petter and Galpain, London, 1869, pp. 128, 153, 157–201.

6 'New South Wales. Murder of a native of Glasgow', *The Glasgow Daily Herald,* 5 March 1862, p. 4.

7 A massacre on the Murray in October 1834 by Governor Stirling and a party of 'horse' after the murder of a British soldier and three others was related thus, 'On coming upon them, it appears that the British horse charged this tribe without any parley, and killed fifteen of them, not, as it seems, confining their vengeance to the actual murderers. After the rout, the women who had been taken prisoner were dismissed, having been informed, 'that the punishment has been inflicted because of the misconduct of the tribe; that the women and children had been spared; but if any other person should be killed by them, not one would be allowed to remain on this side of the mountains.' Evidence given to the 1838 Select Committee, *Information respecting the aborigines in the British Colonies: circulated by direction of the Meeting for Sufferings, being principally*

extracts from the report presented to the House of Commons, by the Select Committee appointed on that subject, Darton and Harvey, London, 1838, p. 11. In 1879 in Cooktown, native troopers avenging the wounding of Captain Skyes and Mr Hartley, 'hemmed the blacks within a narrow gorge' at Cape Bedford, shot down twenty-four men, waited for four who had escaped to sea to drown, 'hunted up the remainder of the gins, and having found a meerschaum pipe and tomahawk in their possession belonging to Mr. Hartley, the inspector was satisfied he had not killed innocent people. This was explained to the lubras, and they were then permitted to go away'. *The Brisbane Courier*, 1 March 1879, p. 6.

8   A 'Lubra (a native woman)' was reportedly pursued on camels during an 1872 expedition to WA via Alice Springs. She managed to outrun her assailants but her small boy, an 'urchin', was captured. He later snuck away from camp. 'Across Australia', in *The Friend: A Religious and Literary Journal*, 30 October 1875, vol. 49, no. 11, p. 83. John Batman, the syphilitic founder of Melbourne, used women as envoys in Tasmania in 1830 to induce Aborigines to leave an area near Launceston sought by settlers. Batman received a land grant of 2,000 acres for his services to this 'Black War', and each of his assisting 'Sydney Blacks' was gifted 100 acres. The women went unrewarded, as women were not landholders as far as settlers were concerned. An extract from Batman's journal describes how he had two women mediate his attempt to 'bring in' a friendly tribe near Launceston, 24 May 1830. The women reported men from Piper River had shot and killed an Aboriginal woman and others were 'very illtreated'. 'Life of John Batman' in James Bonwick, *Port Phillip Settlement*, Sampson, Low, Marsto, Searle & Rivington, London, 1883, p. 168.

9   It isn't known whether Eden mounted a search for the *Eva* acting as police magistrate of Cardwell, even though others had proved fruitless. The police magistrate at Cardwell was part of the search party that requisitioned the whaleboat, but Eden did not take up that position until the following year. The *Eva* was never discovered and Eden may have led another search party from Cardwell after taking up the police magistrate appointment.

10 Eden, 'An Australian search party', pp. 128, 153, 157–201.

11 ibid.

12 Robert Hogg, 'Performing manliness: "unmanly" men on British frontiers in the mid-nineteenth century', *Journal of Australian Studies*, vol. 35, no. 3, 2011, pp. 355–72.

13 Robert Hogg, 'The unmanly savage: "Aboriginalism" and subordinate

masculinities on the Queensland frontier', *Crossings,* March 2006, pp. 10.3–11.1.

14 Patrick Wolfe, 'Settler colonialism and the elimination of the native', *Journal of Genocide Research,* vol. 8, no. 4, 2006, pp. 387–409.

15 Inga Clendinnen, *Dancing with Strangers,* Text, Melbourne, 2003, pp. 159–60. See Shino Konishi's critique of Clendinnen in '"Wanton with plenty": questioning ethno-historical constructions of sexual savagery in Aboriginal societies, 1788–1803', *Australian Historical Studies,* vol. 39, no. 3, 2008, pp. 356–72; and S. Konishi, 'Representing Aboriginal masculinity in Howard's Australia', in R. L. Jackson II and M. Balaji (eds), *Global Masculinities and Manhood,* University of Illinois Press, Champaign, 2011, pp. 161–85.

16 N. Ruddick, 'Courtship with a club: wife-capture in prehistoric fiction, 1865–1914', *Yearbook of English Studies,* vol. 37, no. 2, 2007, pp. 45–63, p. 45. Lisa O'Connell, '"Matrimonial ceremonies displayed", popular ethnography and enlightened imperialism', *Eighteenth-Century Life,* vol. 26, no. 3, 2002, pp. 98–116.

17 Shino Konishi, *The Aboriginal Male in the Enlightenment World,* Pickering and Chatto, London, 2012, pp. 71–78.

18 O'Connell, '"Matrimonial ceremonies displayed"', p. 99.

19 ibid.

20 Ann McGrath has argued that the characterising of Aboriginal sexual savagery allowed early explorers to portray themselves as chivalrous saviours of coquettish women, in her '"The white man's looking glass": Aboriginal–colonial gender relations at Port Jackson', *Australian Historical Studies,* vol. 24, no. 99, 1990, pp. 186–206.

21 Martyn Lyons, *A History of Reading and Writing in the Western World,* Palgrave Macmillan, New York, 2010.

22 John Arnold, 'Printing technology and book production', in Martyn Lyons and John Arnold, *A History of the Book in Australia 1891–1945: A National Culture in a Colonised Market,* University of Queensland Press, Brisbane, 2001, pp. 104–112, p. 105.

23 See Bernard Cohn, *Colonialism and its Forms of Knowledge: The British in India,* Princeton University Press, Princeton, 1996; Walter Mignolo, *The Dark Side of the Renaissance: Literacy, Territoriality and Colonization,* University of Michigan Press, Ann Arbor, 1995; Tony Ballantyne, 'What difference does colonialism make? Reassessing print and social change in an age of global imperialism', in Sabrina Alcorn Baron, Eric N. Lindquist and Eleanor F. Shevlin, *Agents of Change: Print Culture Studies after Elizabeth L. Eisenstein,* University of Massachusetts Press,

Amherst, 2007, pp. 342–52.
24 Godfrey Charles Mundy, cited in Patty O'Brien, 'The gaze of the "ghosts": images of Aboriginal women in New South Wales and Port Phillip (1800–1850)', in Jan Kociumbas (ed.), *Maps, Dreams and History: Race and Representation in Australia,* Department of History Study Series, No. 8, Sydney University, Sydney, 1998, p, 365.
25 See Joan Perkin, *Women and Marriage in Nineteenth-Century England,* Routledge, London, 1989.
26 R. H. Barnes, 'Marriage by capture', *Journal of the Royal Anthropological Institute,* vol. 5, no. 1, 1999, p. 57.
27 'When there is a death to be revenged, or an enemy to be punished, or a quarrel to be adjusted, some nude old virago will be seen pacing backwards or forwards with great rapidity, pouring forth in a declamatory tone – a sort of chant – a volley of abuse against the adverse party and calling her own people to take signal vengeance by tearing out his liver, or otherwise tormenting him; and it is surprising what an effect this often has on the men', in R. Brough Smyth, *The Aborigines of Victoria: with notes relating to the Habits of the Natives of Other Parts of Australia and Tasmania,* vol. II, John Ferres, Melbourne, 1878, p. 270.
28 This came from the prolific but 'careless' writer and traveller Alfred Calvert, who claimed in 1892 of the Aborigines of WA that, 'any hesitation' by men to fulfil their obligations to revenge a death and his 'wives will have nothing to say to him, the old women will scold him, and no single girl will even glance at him'. Albert F. Calvert, *The Aborigines of Western Australia,* W. Milligan & Co., London, 1892, p. 23. See also Wendy Birman, 'Calvert, Albert Frederick (1872–1946)', *Australian Dictionary of Biography,* National Centre of Biography, Australian National University, accessed 31 January 2012, <http://adb.anu.edu.au/biography/calvert-albert-frederick-5469/text9293>.
29 Clem Cleveson, missionary at Yirrkala, describes a woman who, 'For an hour or more, stark naked, switching flies off herself with a bunch of twigs, she strode up and down haranguing and insulting her menfolk accusing them of cowardice and laziness.' Of course, Cleveson was able to 'get her out the way' and defuse the conflict. In his 'The skull of peace', *People,* 19 February 1958, pp. 7–11, p. 9.
30 James Bonwick, *The Lost Tasmanian Race,* Sampson Low, Marston, Searle, and Rivington, London, 1884, p. 142.
31 Stoler, *Along the Archival Grain,* p. 2.
32 Henri Perron d'Arc, *Aventures d'un voyageur en Australie: neuf mois de sejour chez les Nagarnooks,* 2nd edn, Hachette, Paris, 1870. Ferguson 14036.

Vieille femme haranguant des natifs was exhibited in 'Early images of the Australian Aborigines: an exhibition of material from the Monash University Rare Book Collection', 14 October – 29 November 1993.

33 Colin Thornton-Smith, 'French perceptions of the colony of Victoria – facts, fiction and euphoria', *Explorations: A Journal of French Australian Connections*, accessed 7 February 2012, <http://www.msp.unimelb.edu.au/index.php/explorations/article/view/11/10>.

34 Perron d'Arc, *Aventures d'un voyageur en Australie*, pp. 251–54, Google Books, accessed 13 April 2012, <http://books.google.com.au/books?id=E9IpAAAAYAAJ&q=woman#v=onepage&q=femme&f=false>. My thanks to John O'Connor for translating.

35 Maurice Agulhon, *Marianne into Battle: Republican Imagery and Symbolism in France, 1789–1880*, trans. Janet Lloyd, Cambridge University Press, New York, 1981.

36 Joan Landes, *Women and the Public Sphere in the Age of the French Revolution*, Cornell University Press, Ithaca, 1988.

37 Perron d'Arc's *Aventures d'un voyageur en Australie neuf mois de sejour chez les Nagarnooks*, p. 251. My thanks to John O'Connor for translating.

38 ibid., p. 254.

39 ibid., p. 251.

40 Thomas. Welsby, *The Discoverers of the Brisbane River*, H. J. Diddams & Co., Brisbane, 1913, p. 32.

41 It was thought to be the first notation of Aboriginal song in 1835 (in fact the first transcription derives from the 1802 Baudin expedition. The notation was probably by Charles Lesueur and appeared in François Péron's atlas, *Voyage de découvertes aux terres australes*, De l'Imprimerie Imperiale, Paris, 1807–1816. See Nicole Saintelan, '"Music – if it may so be called": perception and response in the documentation of Aboriginal music in Aboriginal Australia', unpublished MA thesis, University of New South Wales, 1993, p. 12. See also Saintelan's account of the arrangement by Lhotsky of the women of Mereno's song for parlour sheet music, p. 52.

42 Susan Leonardi and Rebecca Pope, *The Diva's Mouth: Body, Voice, Prima Donna Politics*, Rutgers University, New Brunswick, 2008.

43 Louis de Gaya, *Ceremonies nuptiales de toute les nations*, Paris, 1680.

44 O'Connell, '"Matrimonial ceremonies displayed"', p. 109.

45 Schaffer, *In the Wake of First Contact*, p. 3.

46 ibid., p. 2.

47 ibid., p. 3.

48 Angela Woollacott, 'Frontier violence and settler manhood', *History*

Australia, vol. 6, no. 1, 2009, pp. 11.1–11.15.
49 See A. James Hammerton, *Cruelty and Companionship: Conflict in Nineteenth Century Married Life*, Routledge, London, 1992; Kate Lawson and Lyn Shakinovsky, *The Marked Body: Domestic Violence in Nineteenth Century Literature*, SUNY Press, Albany, p. 2.
50 David Collins, *An Account of the English Colony in New South Wales: with Remarks on the Dispositions, Customs, Manners, Etc. of the Native Inhabitants of that Country. To which are added, some particulars of New Zealand; compiled, by permission, from the Mss. of Lieutenant-Governor King*, vol. I., T. Cadell Jun. and W. Davies, London, 1798.
51 Collins, 'Appendix V: Courtship and marriage', in *An Account of the English Colony in New South Wales*.
52 George Barrington, *The History of New South Wales: including Botany Bay...*, M. Jones, London, 1802.
53 Toby R. Benis, 'Criminal transport: George Barrington and the colonial cure', *Australian Literary Studies*, vol. 20, no. 2, 2002, pp. 167–77, p. 167.
54 'Barrington, George (1755–1804)', *Australian Dictionary of Biography*, National Centre of Biography, Australian National University, accessed 29 January 2012, <http://adb.anu.edu.au/biography/barrington-george-1746/text1935>.
55 Nathan Garvey, *The Celebrated George Barrington: A Spurious Author, the Book Trade and Botany Bay*, Horden House, Potts Point, 2008.
56 Barrington, *The History of New South Wales*, p. 35.
57 ibid., p. 36.
58 Hogg, 'The unmanly savage'.
59 As Lyn Hunt argues, the policing of pornography galvanised Europe in response to explicit material circulated as political criticism during the French Revolution. By the time of 'Barrington', self-conscious pornographers sought purely commercial gain through a fraternity of male readers. L. Hunt, *The Invention of Pornography: Obscenity and the Origins of Modernity, 1500–1800*, Zone Books, New York, 2003, p. 42.
60 See Shino Konishi's discussion of the discursive setting for European comparisons between civilised and uncivilised marriage and sexual behaviour in her 'Depicting sexuality: a case study of the Baudin expedition's Aboriginal ethnography', *Australian Journal of French Studies*, vol. 61, no. 2, 2004, pp. 98–118.
61 M. J. D. Roberts, *Making English Morals: Voluntary Association and Moral Reform*, Cambridge University Press, Cambridge, 2004, p. 35.
62 Explicit imagery and text steadily grew from the middle of the eighteenth century and flourished from the nineteenth. Jeffrey Weeks,

Sex, Politics and Society: The Regulation of Sexuality since 1800, Longman, London, 1989, p. 84.
63 Watkin Tench, *A complete account of the settlement at Port Jackson, in New South Wales, including an accurate description of the colony; of the natives; and of its natural productions*, G. Nicol and J. Sewell, London, 1793; Konishi, 'Depicting sexuality', p. 104.
64 Konishi, 'Depicting sexuality', p. 104.
65 ibid.; Konishi, '"Wanton with plenty"'. The Leroy engraving first appeared in *Voyage de découvertes aux terres australes* (Paris, 1807–1816), the second volume of which the French cartographer-surveyor Freycinet completed after Péron's death. Freycinet was invited to complete the account of the Baudin expedition. He had charge of the ship *Le Naturaliste* of that expedition and was then put in command of the *Casuarina*, which Baudin purchased in Sydney from Governor King. Leslie R. Marchant, 'Freycinet, Louis-Claude Desaulses de (1779–1842)', *Australian Dictionary of Biography*, National Centre of Biography, Australian National University, accessed 29 January 2012, <http://adb.anu.edu.au/biography/freycinet-louis-claude-desaulses-de-2226/text1949>.
66 Konishi, 'Depicting sexuality', p. 101.
67 ibid., p. 103.
68 Domeny de Rienzi, *Océanie; ou, Cinquième Partie du Monde: Revue Geographique at Ethnographique de la Malaise, se la Micronesie, de la Polynesie, et de la Melanasie*, Firmin Didot, Paris, 1836, p. 178.
69 Bronwen Douglas and Chris Ballard, *Foreign Bodies, Oceania and the Science of Race 1750–1940*, ANU ePress, Canberra, 2008.
70 Cited in ibid.
71 Unknown artist, lithograph, *Hochzeits-ceremonie der Neuhollander, Ceremonie d'un Mariage*, c. 1840.
72 Mudie, *The Picture of Australia*, p. 256.
73 O'Connell, '"Matrimonial ceremonies displayed"', p. 100.
74 Mudie, *The Picture of Australia*, p. 256.
75 Patricia Grimshaw and Graham Willet, 'Women's history and family history: an exploration of colonial family structure', in Norma Grieve and Pat Grimshaw (eds), *Australian Women: Feminist Perspectives*, Oxford University Press, Melbourne, 1981, pp. 134–155, p. 136.
76 J. R. McCulloch (ed.), *Dictionary, Geographical, Statistical, and Historical of the Various Countries, Places and Principal Natural Objects in the World*, Longman, Brown, Green, and Longmans, London, 1854, pp. 228–231, p. 229.

77 Robert Brown, *The Races of Mankind*, vol. II, Cassell, Petter & Galpin, London, 1873–76, p. 120.
78 Lieutenant R. N. Breton, *Excursions in New South Wales, Western Australia, & Van Dieman's Land, During the Years 1830, 1831, 1832 & 1833*, Richard Bentley, London, 1834. Reprinted New York, 1970, p. 178.
79 'Reverend William Yate', *Queer History: New Zealand Gay, Lesbian, Bisexual and Transgender New Zealand History*, accessed 10 February 2012, <http://www.gaynz.net.nz/history/Yate.html>.
80 D. Coates, John Beecham and William Ellis, *Christianity the Means of Civilization: Shown in Evidence given before a Committee of the House of Commons on Aborigines*, R. B. Seeley and W. Burnside, London, 1837, p. 265.
81 Jonathan Crary, *Techniques of the Observer: On Vision and Modernity in the Nineteenth Century*, MIT Press, Cambridge, 1990, p. 285.
82 P. H. F. Phelps, *Native Scenes [snakes, birds & marine life]*, unpublished album, c. 1840–49. Dixon State Library of New South Wales, accessed 9 February 2012, <http://acms.sl.nsw.gov.au/item/itemDetailPaged.aspx?itemID=447925>.
83 Richard Altick, *Punch: The Lively Youth of a British Institution, 1841–1851*, Ohio State University Press, Columbus, 1997.
84 Phelps, *Native Scenes*.
85 Contemporary anthropologists and sociologists argue bride capture is a highly ritualised rite of passage, with most incidents 'in reality a "sham" capture, which often takes place with the tacit approval of both the husband's and wife's families, sometimes even after a formal betrothal ceremony'. Anil Aggrawal, 'Bride capture', *Encyclopedia of Law & Society: American and Global Perspectives*, Sage, Thousand Oaks, 2007, pp. 135–36; *SAGE Reference Online*, accessed 29 January 2012, <http://sage-ereference.com.ezp.lib.unimelb.edu.au/view/law/n65.xml?rskey=Udcodf&result=1&q=Bride%20Capture>.
86 R. H. Davies, 'On the Aborigines of Van Diemen's Land, *Tasmanian Journal of Natural Science*, vol. 2, no. 11, p. 413, pp. 409–420.
87 W. W. Thorpe, 'Some mutilatory rites practised by the Australian Aborigines', *Mankind*, vol. 1, no. 6, p. 131, pp. 124–131.
88 Bronislaw Malinowski, *The Family Among the Australian Aborigines: A Sociological Study*, University of London, Press, London, 1913, p. 71.
89 ibid., p. 73.
90 ibid., p. 75.
91 John F. McLennan, *Primitive Marriage: An Inquiry into the Origin of the Form of Capture in Marriage Ceremonies*, Adam and Charles Black, Edinburgh, 1865, p. 76.

92 Sir George Grey, cited in Alan Moorehead, *The Fatal Impact: An Account of the Invasion of the South Pacific 1767–1840*, Penguin, Harmondsworth, 1966, pp. 157–58.
93 'Newsletter of Australia: A Narrative to Send to Friends', no. 58, June 1861.
94 Engraving attributed to George Strafford, *Illustrated Melbourne Post*, May 1862, p. 36.
95 Review of Charles Baker, *Sydney and Melbourne: with Remarks on the Present State and Future Prospects of New South Wales, and Practical Advice to Emigrants of various Classes; to which is added a Summary of the Route Home by India, Egypt &c.*, Smith, Elder, and Co., London, 1845, in *The Maitland Mercury & Hunter River General Advertiser*, 7 January 1846, p. 4.
96 Patrick Collins, 'Finney Eldershaw's suspect memoirs', in corrections to his *Goodbye Bussamarai*, accessed 11 February 2012, <http://www.goodbyebussamarai.com/page8.htm>.
97 F. Eldershaw, *Australia as it really is, in its Life, Scenery & Adventure with the Character, Habits, and Customs of the Aboriginal Inhabitants, and the Prospects and Extent of its Goldfields*, Darton and Co., London, 1854, p. 96.
98 ibid., p. 83.
99 ibid., p. 95. This account also appears in Henry Reynolds, *Dispossession: Black Australians and White Invaders,* Allen and Unwin, Sydney, 1989, pp. 42–44.
100 'Australian blacks', *Chambers's Journal of Popular Literature Science and the Arts*, vol. XLI, no. 43, 22 October 1864, pp. 686–88, p. 687.
101 'Wooing as practised by the Australian Blacks', *The Golden Era*, 8 January 1865, p. 5.
102 McLennan, *Primitive Marriage*, pp. 302–06.
103 Richard Yeo, 'Science and intellectual authority in mid-nineteenth-century Britain: Robert Chambers and "Vestiges of the Natural History of Creation"', *Victorian Studies*, vol. 28, no. 1, 1984, pp. 5–31.
104 Liz Conor, 'Moveable parts: press and loom in colonial typologies', in Liz Conor (ed.), *Interventions,* Special issue: Types and typologies, vol. 17, no. 2, 2015, pp. 229–57.
105 Douglas Lorimer, 'Theoretical racism in late-Victorian anthropology, 1870-1900', *Victorian Studies*, vol. 31, no. 3, 1988, p. 405–30; Walter Houghton, 'Periodical literature and the articulate classes', in J. Shattock and M. Wolff (eds), *The Victorian Periodical Press: Samplings and Soundings*, Leicester University Press, Leicester, 1982.
106 John Lubbock, *The Origin of Civilisation and the Primitive Condition of Man: Mental and Social Conditions of Savages*, Spottiswoode and Co, London, 1870.

107 Lubbock cited in Ruddick, 'Courtship with a club', pp. 45–63.
108 Patrick Wolfe, *Settler Colonialism and the Transformation of Anthropology: The Politics and Poetics of an Ethnographic Event*, Cassell, London, 1999, pp. 74–75.
109 Micaela di Leonardo, *Gender at the Crossroads of Knowledge: Feminist Anthropology in the Postmodern Era*, University of California Press, Berkeley, 1991, p. 8.
110 Wolfe, *Settler Colonialism and the Transformation of Anthropology*, p. 83.
111 ibid., p. 84.
112 John Turnbull, *A Voyage round the World: in the years 1800, 1801, 1802, 1803, and 1804, in which the author visited the principal islands in the Pacific Ocean and the English settlements of Port Jackson and Norfolk Island*, volume 1, Richard Phillips, London, 1805, pp. 81–82.
113 Turnbull, *A Voyage round the World*, p. 82.
114 McLennan, *Primitive Marriage*, pp. 74–75.
115 ibid., p. 74.
116 ibid., p. 75.
117 Lynne Nead, *Myths of Sexuality: Representations of Women in Victorian Britain*, Basil Blackwell, Oxford, 1988.
118 George Stocking, *Victorian Anthropology*, Free Press, New York, 1991, p. 316.
119 Augustus Oldfield, 'On the Aborigines of Australia', *Transactions of the Ethnological Society of Great Britain*, no. 3, 1865, pp. 215–98, p. 251.
120 Brown, *The Races of Mankind*, p. 118.
121 ibid.
122 Robert J. C. Young, 'Egypt in America: *Black Athena*, racism and colonial discourse', in Ali Rattansi and Sallie Westwood (eds), *On the Western Front: Studies in Racism, Modernity and Identity*, Polity Press, Cambridge, 1994, pp. 150–69, p. 26.
123 William Thomas, in C. E. Sayers (ed.), Thomas Francis Bride (ed.), *Letters from Victorian Pioneers, Being a Series of Papers in the Early Occupation of the Colony, The Aborigines, etc.*, William Heinemann, Melbourne, 1969 (1898), p. 400.
124 Thomas was the 'most influential witness at the 1858–59 select committee of the Legislative Council on Aborigines. His recommendation to establish reserves and supply depots throughout Victoria was accepted in a modified form and in 1860 became the policy implemented by the new Central Board for the Protection of Aborigines'. D. J. Mulvaney, 'Thomas, William (1793–1867)', *Australian Dictionary of Biography*, National Centre of Biography, Australian

125 Brough Smyth, *The Aborigines of Victoria*, pp. 76–77.
126 ibid., pp. 76–77.
127 Michael Hoare, 'Smyth, Robert Brough (1830–1889)', *Australian Dictionary of Biography*, National Centre of Biography, Australian National University, accessed 10 February 2012, <http://adb.anu.edu.au/biography/smyth-robert-brough-4621/text7609>.
128 Largely on the work of Lorimer Fison, G. B. Halford, A. Howitt and J. Milligan. See Hoare, 'Smyth, Robert Brough (1830–1889)', *Australian Dictionary of Biography*.
129 John Wesley, 'Thoughts on slavery', R. Hawes, London, 1774.
130 'Ode for the Queen's birthday' in James Boswell, *The Scots Magazine*, vol. 38, 1776, p. 45; Mrs Hughes, 'A description of the tomb of Werter', *The Gentlemen's Magazine*, vol. 57, 1785, p. 385; 'Nature with streaming eyes and heaving breast', in Alexander Lindsay and Margaret MacFadden Smith (eds), *Index of English Literary Manuscripts*, vol. 3, part 4, 1997, p. 475.
131 'Reflections on unreasonable sorrow', *The Lady's Magazine: Entertaining Companion for the Fair Sex Appropriated Solely for their Use and Amusement*, October 1778, p. 520.
132 Fannie A. Beers, *Memories. A Record of Personal Experience and Adventure During Four Years of War*, J. B. Lippencott, Philadephia, 1888, p. 157.
133 Konishi, 'Depicting sexuality', p. 104.
134 Thomas in Bride, *Letters from Victorian Pioneers*, p. 429.
135 Augustus Henry Keane, 'Australian culture', *St James's Magazine*, vol. 4, no. 40, 1881, pp. 220–236, p. 224.
136 ibid., p. 223.
137 ibid.
138 Lorimer, 'Theoretical racism', p. 415.
139 See Elazar Barkan, 'Rethinking orientalism: representations of "primitives" in western culture at the turn of the century', *History of European Ideas*, vol. 15, nos 4–6, 1992, pp. 759–65, p. 761.
140 'Mr John Bulmer, Lake Tyers, Gippsland, MS', cited in Brough Smyth, *The Aborigines of Victoria*, p. 77.
141 Edward M. Curr, *Recollections of Squatting in Victoria then called the Port Phillip District (from 1841–1851)*, G. Robertston, Melbourne, 1883, p. 141.
142 ibid., p. 140.
143 ibid., p. 142.
144 ibid., p. 145.

145 'An Aboriginal marriage', *The Sydney Mail*, 9 June 1883, p. 6.
146 Edward M. Curr, *The Australian Race: Its Origins, Languages, Customs, Place of Landing in Australia and the Routes by which it spread itself over the Continent*, vol. 2, John Ferres Government Printer, Melbourne, 1886, p. 196.
147 James A. Farrer, *Primitive Manners and Customs*, Chatto & Windus, London, 1879, p. 228.
148 Farrer, *Primitive Manners and Customs*, p. 230.
149 Lorimer Fison and Alfred William Howitt, *Kamilaroi and Kurnai: group marriage customs and relationship, and marriage by elopement drawn chiefly from the usage of the Australian Aborigines; also, The Kurnai tribe, their customs in peace and war*, George Robinson, Melbourne, 1879, p. 200.
150 ibid., p. 200 fn.
151 ibid.
152 George T. Bettany, *The Red, Brown, and Black Men of America and Australia and their White Supplanters*, Ward, Lock and Co., London, 1890, p. 213.
153 Reverend George Taplin, *The Narrinyeri: An Account of the Tribes of the South Australian Aborigines*, E. S. Wigg & Son, Adelaide, 1879, pp. 11–12.
154 J. D. Woods, 'Introduction', in Reverend George Taplin, *The Native Tribes of South Australia*, E. S. Wigg & Son, Adelaide, 1879, p. xxxi.
155 W. E. H. Stanner, 'Howitt, Alfred William (1830–1908)', *Australian Dictionary of Biography*, National Centre of Biography, Australian National University, accessed 11 February 2012, <http://adb.anu.edu.au/biography/howitt-alfred-william-510/text6037>.
156 A. W. Howitt and Rev. L. Fison, 'From mother-right to father-right', *Journal of the Anthropological Institute of Great Britain and Ireland*, vol. 12, 1883, pp. 30–46, p. 36.
157 Baldwin Spencer and Frank J. Gillen, *The Native Tribes of Central Australia*, Dover, New York, 1968 (1899), p. 555.
158 *The Illustrated Handbook of Western Australia (Paris International Exhibition 1900)*, Government Printer, Perth, 1900, pp. 46–49, p. 46.
159 'Australian Aborigines – II', *The Nation*, vol. 81, no. 2100, 28 September 1905, pp. 261–63, p. 262.
160 Joyce and Thomas, *Women of All Nations*, p. 139.
161 G. Fox, 'Ethnology: the Australian Aborigines', *Science of Man*, vol. X, no. 4, 20 August 1908, pp. 57–61, p. 60.
162 ibid., p. 61.
163 K. R. Cramp, *A Series of Lessons on Aboriginal Life*, Education Society, William Applegate Gullick, Government Printer, Sydney, 1910, p. 8.

164 Malinowski, *The Family Among the Australian Aborigines*, p. 52.
165 ibid., p. 53.
166 ibid., p. 54.
167 ibid., p. 60.
168 ibid., p. 66.
169 ibid., p. 260.
170 H. E. A. Meyer, quoted in Malinowski, *The Family Among the Australian Aborigines*.
171 L. T. Hobhouse and G. C. Wheeler, *The Material Culture and Social Institutions of the Simpler Peoples*, Chapman & Hall, London, 1915, p. 156.
172 See, for instance, Mary Lyndon Shanley, *Feminism, Marriage, and the Law in Victorian England, 1850–1895*, Princeton University Press, Princeton, 1993.
173 George Bennett, *Wanderings in New South Wales, Batavia, Pedir Coast, Singapore, and China; Being the Journal of a Naturalist in those Countries during 1832, 1833, and 1834*, vol. 1, Richard Bentley, London, 1834, p. 250.
174 A. H. Chisholm, 'Bennett, George (1804–1893)', *Australian Dictionary of Biography*, National Centre of Biography, Australian National University, accessed 27 January 2012, <http://adb.anu.edu.au/biography/bennett-george-1770/text1981>.
175 *Colonial Intelligencer or Aborigines' Friend Comprising the Transactions of the Aborigines Protection Society; Interesting Intelligence Concerning the Aborigines of Various Climes and Articles upon Colonial Affairs*, J. Ollivier and Messrs Ward, London, 1847–48, p. 42.
176 Kinahan Cornwallis, *A Panorama of the New World in Two Volumes*, vol. 1, T. C. Newby, London, 1859, p. 192.
177 *The Argus*, 13 September 1860, p. 4.
178 Keane, 'Australian culture', p. 223, pp. 220–236.
179 Augustus Henry Keane, *Man, Past and Present*, Cambridge University Press, London, 1899, revised edition 1920, p. 427.
180 Wood, *The Natural History of Man*, p. 71.
181 ibid.
182 ibid., p. 72.
183 Rev J. H. Sexton, *Australian Aborigines*, Hunkin, Ellis & King, Adelaide, 1944, p. 125.
184 ibid., p. 88.
185 ibid., p. 126.
186 Diane E. Barwick, 'And the ladies are lubras now', in Fay Gale (ed.), *Woman's Role in Aboriginal Society*, 3rd edn, Australian Institute of Aboriginal Studies, Canberra, 1978, p. 52.

187 ibid., p. 61.
188 Catherine H. Berndt, 'Digging sticks and spears, or the two-sex model', in Fay Gale (ed.), *Woman's Role in Aboriginal Society*, 3rd edn, Australian Institute of Aboriginal Studies, Canberra, 1978, pp. 64–84, p. 80.
189 ibid., p. 70.
190 ibid., p. 80.
191 ibid., p. 78.
192 Annette Hamilton, 'A complex strategical situation: gender and power in Aboriginal Australia', in Norma Grieve and Patricia Grimshaw (eds), *Australian Women: Feminist Perspectives,* Oxford University Press, Melbourne, 1981, pp. 69–85, p. 79.
193 Malinowski cited in Phyllis M. Kaberry, *Aboriginal Woman: Sacred and Profane*, Routledge, London, 1939, p. 15.
194 Kaberry, *Aboriginal Woman: Sacred and Profane*, p. 23.
195 See, for example, *The Canberra Times*, 6 January 1976, p. 3.
196 Brown, *The Races of Mankind*, p. 120. Brown also claimed that females cannot inherit the land, p. 123.
197 Roderick J. Flanagan, *The Aborigines of Australia*, Edward F. Flanagan and George Robertson and Company, Sydney, 1888, p. 75.
198 Bettany, *The Red, Brown, and Black Men of America and Australia and their White Supplanters*, p. 202.
199 David W. Carnegie, *Spinifex and Sand: A Narrative of Five Years Pioneering and Exploration in Western Australia*, C. Arthur Pearson, London, 1898, p. 347.
200 William D. Boyce, *Illustrated Australia and New Zealand*, Rana McNally & Company, Chicago, 1922, p. 9.
201 Charles H. Holmes, *We Find Australia*, Hutchinson & Co., London, 1933, p. 142.
202 A. M. Duncan-Kemp, *Where Strange Paths Go Down*, W. R. Smith and Patterson, Brisbane, 1964, p. 287.
203 Breton, *Excursions in New South Wales, Western Australia, & Van Dieman's Land*, p. 177.
204 'Aborigines of Van Diemen's Land', *The Penny Magazine*, vol. XI, no. 634, 1842, pp. 195–96.
205 Timothy Bottoms, *Conspiracy Of Silence: Queensland's Frontier Killing Times,* Allen and Unwin, Sydney, 2013; Dirk A. Moses, *Genocide and Settler Society: Frontier Violence and Stolen Indigenous Children in Australian History*, Berghahn Books, New York, 2005. Ryan, Reynolds and Evans have also published recently on the frontier. See, for example, Lyndall Ryan, *Tasmanian Aborigines – A History since 1803*, Allen & Unwin, Sydney, 2013.

206 Thirteen women were reported to have themselves murdered mostly Aboriginal men, and five women allegedly committed assaults. Ten women were reported as being used as informants, and their role as go-betweens across cultures and intertribally was noted.
207 This massacre came to light through a letter to *The Bulletin*, written by a resident of Morinish. 'Barbarous outrage by the native police', *The Queenslander,* 29 June 1867, p. 6.
208 See, for instance, 'The murdered orderly', which detailed a revenge raid on a camp of Queensland 'savages' after the spearing of a Hungarian overseer. In *All the Year Round*, 'conducted' (meaning founded and owned) by Charles Dickens, vol. 18, no. 446, November 1867, pp. 469–70.
209 George Nelson, ten years, and Randell Bass, thirteen years, were fined the costs of the case, 4s 9d each. *The West Australian*, 7 April 1887, p. 3.
210 Richardson (a butcher) and Jenkins (a timber getter) were arrested at Kilcoy, Queensland, but the case for the Crown was abandoned since 'it was impossible to make the principal witnesses understand the nature of an oath or a declaration' due to the wording of the Oaths Amendment Act of 1876. *The Brisbane Courier*, 16 April 1880, p. 3; *The Argus*, 14 April 1880, p. 5.
211 *The Brisbane Courier*, 8 November 1895, p. 5.
212 Seven women and children were killed with tomahawks at Cape Otway by Barabool men, overseen by the Surveyor Smythe who, having orchestrated and overseen their carnage, casts himself as hapless bystander and the rescuer of one girl. 'Port Phillip', *The Maitland Mercury & Hunter River General Advertiser*, 9 September 1846, p. 4. For an account of the Port Philip Native Police Corps, disbanded in 1852, Henry Hutchinson Smythe and his relationship with the Mornington Peninsula peoples, see Marie Fels, *Good Men and True: The Aboriginal Police of the Port Phillip District 1837–1853*, Melbourne University Press, Melbourne, 1988, p. 355.
213 A young girl was shot through both legs and crippled. Her mother was wounded with buckshot when she attempted to carry her away as were another boy and girl trying to remove her from the line of fire. A year and a half earlier four women were abducted from this community during a similar raid. Letter from J. H. Wedge, surveyor at 'Bearpurt', to the Colonial Secretary of VDL in 1836, cited in James Bonwick, *Port Phillip Settlement*, Sampson Low, Marston, Searle, & Rivington, London, 1883, p. 506. On Bonwick's history, see Lyndall Ryan, '"Hard evidence": the debate about massacre in the black war of Tasmania', in

Frances Peters-Little, Ann Curthoys and John Docker (eds), *Passionate Histories: Myth, Memory and Indigenous Australia,* ANU ePress, Canberra, pp. 39–50, p. 42.

214 Superintendent Donald M'Laughlan at Mr H. Eckford's station, Burron Burron, attacked a local camp with 'Black Harry' using firearms and cutlass 'indiscriminately'. No magisterial inquiry was made, nor warrant for the assailants' apprehension, nor coroner's inquest made on the bodies. *The Maitland Mercury & Hunter River General Advertiser,* 15 March 1854, p. 2.

215 Dr M'Cartney was charged with striking John Campbell. *The Maitland Mercury & Hunter River General Advertiser,* 4 February 1952, p. 2.

216 *The Courier* (Hobart), 4 September 1850, p. 3.

217 This particular report was compiled from a letter from Port Darwin and published in the *Sydney Morning Herald,* drawn from a special correspondent of the Melbourne *Argus* who visited the Torres Straits. 'Occasional notes', *Pall Mall Gazette,* 25 May 1882, p. 3.

218 Henry Reynolds, *This Whispering in our Hearts,* Allen and Unwin, Sydney, 1998.

219 *Report from the Select Committee on the Native Police Force and the Condition of the Aborigines Generally together with the proceedings of the Committee and minutes of evidence,* Fairfax and Belbridge, Brisbane, 1861.

220 *The Argus,* 28 September 1861, p. 5.

221 *The Brisbane Courier,* 14 December 1867, p. 7.

222 *The Argus,* 29 September 1881, p. 8.

223 *The Argus,* 4 October 1881, p. 5.

224 *The Brisbane Courier,* 19 October 1881, p. 3.

225 *Northern Territory Times and Gazette,* 22 July 1882, p. 3.

226 *Northern Territory Times and Gazette,* 21 March 1885, p. 3.

227 *The Courier,* 11 July 1863, p. 3.

228 *The Mercury,* 8 February 1910, p. 3.

229 See also Fiona Paisley, 'Race hysteria, Darwin 1938', *Australian Feminist Studies,* vol. 16, no. 34, 2001, pp. 43–59.

230 *The Canberra Times,* 14 November 1933, p. 1.

231 *The Canberra Times,* 15 November 1933, p. 3.

232 *The Courier-Mail,* 18 November 1933, p. 13.

233 *The Courier-Mail,* 24 April 1934, p. 13.

234 *The Brisbane Courier,* 2 November 1875, p. 3.

235 'An Aboriginal woman attacked', *The West Australian,* 30 December 1895, p. 6.

236 *The Perth Gazette and Independent Journal of Politics and News,* 10 February 1849, p. 3.

237 *The Brisbane Courier*, 20 August 1881, p. 6.
238 'Outrage on a gin', *The Argus*, 15 November 1884, p. 9.
239 *The Mercury*, 22 November 1884, p. 3.
240 *The Argus,* 26 November 1884, p. 10.
241 *The Advertiser*, 7 August 1901, p. 4.
242 Edward W. Said, *Orientalism: Western Conceptions of the Orient*, 4th edn, Penguin, London, 1995 (1978), p. 187.

Chapter 3

1   Louise Jordan Miln (1864–1933) travelled to Australia in October 1888 with her husband, English Shakespearean actor George Crighton Miln. His company toured Australia for two years and then the Far East. See Stanley Wells and Sarah Stanton (eds), *The Cambridge Companion to Shakespeare on Stage*, Cambridge University Press, Cambridge, 2002, p. 202.
2   Louise Jordan Miln, *Little Folks of Many Lands,* John Murray, London, 1899, pp. 142–43.
3   Edward W. Said, *Orientalism: Western Conceptions of the Orient*, 4th edn, Penguin, London, 1995 (1978), pp. 57, 87.
4   Aboriginal mothers recently have felt under increased scrutiny since the NT Intervention and through the intergenerational legacy of this charge of incompetence. See Kelly Briggs, 'Aboriginal mothers like me still fear that our children could be taken away', *The Guardian*, 21 January 2014, accessed 22 January 2014, <http://www.theguardian.com/commentisfree/2014/jan/21/aboriginal-mothers-like-me-still-fear-that-our-children-could-be-taken-away>.
5   Lieutenant R. N. Breton claimed in 1834 that 'native women', in various parts of the colony, 'sometimes put their children to death, in order that they may be enabled to suckle the whelps of dogs.' He at least found the idea 'too monstrous' to believe but insisted suckling of whelps was 'well known to be the case.' Such a practice contravened new relations in animal husbandry forged by the agrarian revolution. Breton, *Excursions in New South Wales, Western Australia, & Van Dieman's Land, During the Years 1830, 1831, 1832 & 1833*, New York, 1970 (1834), p. 170.
6   Protector William Thomas's count is discussed in Marguerita Stephens, *White Without Soap: Philanthropy, Caste and Exclusion in Colonial Victoria. A Political Economy of Race*, Melbourne University Book Custom Centre, Melbourne, 2010, p. 65. See also M. Stephens, 'Infanticide at Port Phillip: Protector William Thomas and the witnessing of things unseen', *Aboriginal History*, vol. 38, 2014, pp. 109–30.

7   See, for example, a report on this select committee in *The Maitland Mercury & Hunter River General Advertiser*, 27 December 1835, p. 2.
8   Laila Williamson, 'Infanticide: an anthropological analysis', in M. Kohl (ed.), *Infanticide and the Value of Life*, Prometheus, New York, 1978, p. 61.
9   Anne-Marie Kilday, *A History of Infanticide in Britain, c. 1600 to the Present*, Palgrave MacMillan, Houndsmills, 2013.
10 Gillian Cowlishaw, 'Infanticide in colonial Australia', *Oceania*, vol. 48, no. 4, 1978, pp. 262–82, p. 266.
11 Kilday, *History of Infanticide in Britain*, p. 7.
12 Kathryn Mosely, 'The history of infanticide in western society', *Issues in Law & Medicine*, vol. 1, no. 5, 1986, pp. 345–61; Judith Allen, 'Octavius Beale re-considered: infanticide, baby-farming and abortion in NSW 1880-1939', in Sydney Labour History Group, *What Rough Beast, The State and Social Order in Australian History*, Allen & Unwin, Sydney, 1982, pp. 111–29.
13 Stephens, *White Without Soap*, p. 72.
14 Stephens cites the medical report of dispenser H. G. Jones, who treated people, including children, for syphilis in the Melbourne and Western Port districts in May 1832. See Marguerita Stephens, 'A word of evidence: shared tales about infanticide and "others not us" in colonial Victoria', in Jane Carey and Claire McLisky (eds), *Creating White Australia*, Sydney University Press, Sydney, 2009, pp. 175–194, p. 187. Alan Gray provides a close analysis of the Daly River Mission Baptismal Register, from which it may be possible to extrapolate the very high rate of Aboriginal infant mortality. See his 'Aboriginal fertility at the time of European contact: the Daly River Mission Baptismal Register', *Aboriginal History*, vol. 7, 1983, pp. 80–89. Patricia Jalland notes that the deaths of Aborigines were trivialised in her *Australian Ways of Death: A Social and Cultural History, 1840–1918*, Oxford University Press, Melbourne, 2002, p. 242.
15 Mark Jackson (ed.), *Infanticide: Historical Perspectives on Child Murder and Concealment, 1550–2000*, Ashgate, Burlington, 2002; Kilday, *History of Infanticide in Britain*.
16 In 1883 two sisters, Florence and Fanny Parker, were charged at Rockhampton with the murder of Florence's illegitimate child. Fanny struck the child with a stick and then wrapped it in a rag, took it to the back of the sheep-yard, struck it with a tomahawk to the back and buried it in a shallow hole, because 'it has no father'. A witness alleged that an Aboriginal woman had killed a half-caste baby born on a wagon at the Parker's hotel and given it to the pigs. The sisters were sentenced

to two years' imprisonment. *The Argus*, 2 May 1883, p. 9.
17 Annie Cossins, *The Baby Farmers: A Chilling Tale of Missing Babies, Shameful Secrets and Murder in 19th Century Australia*, Allen and Unwin, Sydney, 2013.
18 '"Baby-farming" in England', *Freeman's Journal*, 24 September 1870, p. 13.
19 The Indian or Sepoy mutiny was an uprising against the East India Company, which started in the town of Meerut and spread to other regions of company-controlled India until the East India Company dissolved in June 1858. See Christopher Herbert, *War of No Pity: The Indian Mutiny and Victorian Trauma*, Princeton University Press, Princeton, 2007.
20 Stephens, 'A word of evidence', p. 190.
21 Revised by linguists at the Victorian Aboriginal Corporation for Languages. See Stephens, 'Infanticide at Port Phillip'.
22 Stephens, 'Infanticide at Port Phillip'.
23 Cowlishaw, 'Infanticide in colonial Australia', pp. 263, 267.
24 Lynette Russell, '"Dirty domestics and worse cooks": Aboriginal women's agency and domestic frontiers, southern Australia, 1800–1850', *Frontiers: A Journal of Women's Studies*, vol. 28, nos 1–2, 2007, pp. 18–46.
25 Stephens, 'Infanticide at Port Phillip'; see also Geoffrey Sanborn, *The Sign of the Cannibal*, Duke University Press, Durham and London, 1998; Satadru Sen, 'The savage family: colonialism and female infanticide in nineteenth century India', *Journal of Women's History*, vol. 14, no. 3, 2002.
26 Human Rights and Equal Opportunity Commission, *Bringing Them Home: The Report of the National Inquiry into the Separation of Aboriginal and Torres Strait Islander Children from their Families*, Human Rights and Equal Opportunity Commission, Sydney, 1997.
27 Anna Haebich, *Broken Circles: Fragmenting Indigenous Families 1800–2000*, Freemantle Arts Centre Press, Fremantle, 2000. See also Fiona Paisley, *Loving Protection: Australian Feminism and Aboriginal Women's Rights 1919–1939*, Melbourne University Press, Melbourne, 2000; Victorian Haskins, *One Bright Spot*, Palgrave MacMillan, Basingstoke, 2005; Margaret Jacobs, *White Mother to a Dark Race: Settler Colonialism, Maternalism, and the Removal of Indigenous Children in the American West and Australia 1880–1940*, University of Nebraska Press, Lincoln, 2009.
28 I explore the question of Indigenous child disinheritance in my 'The "piccaninny": racialised childhood, disinheritance, acquisition and child beauty', *Postcolonial Studies*, vol. 15, no. 1, 2012, pp. 45–68.
29 John Hawkesworth, *An Account of the Voyages Undertaken by the Order of*

his Present Majesty, for making Discoveries in the Southern Hemisphere…, W. Strahan and T. Cadell, London, 1773, p. 208.

30 Patrick Brantlinger explores the 'fantasy of auto-genocide' in his *Dark Vanishings: Discourse on the Extinction of Primitive Races 1800–1930*, Cornell University Press, Ithaca, 2003, p. 2.

31 Paul E. de Strzelecki, *Physical Description of New South Wales and Van Diemen's Land. Accompanied by a geological map, sections, and diagrams, and figures of the organic remains*, facsimile edn, Libraries Board of South Australia, 1967 (1845), pp. 343–47. Cited in Russell McGregor, *Imagined Destinies: Aboriginal Australians and the Doomed Race Theory*, Melbourne University Press, Melbourne, 1997, prologue fn. 32; Charles Darwin, *The Descent of Man and Selection in Relation to Sex*, Princeton University Press, Princeton, 1981 (1879), p. 221. Stephens traces the Strzelecki debate in the third chapter of *White Without Soap*, pp. 104–125. In 1852, a naturalist and surgeon of the Royal Navy, T. R. H. Thomson (who took part in the Niger expedition of 1841), published 'Observations of the reported incompetency of the "gins" or Aboriginal females of New Holland, to procreate with a native male after having borne half-caste children to a European or white'. Thomson reasoned their infertility was because, in 'partaking of the white man's comforts, she is too often the recipient of his vices.' These included drinking rum, smoking tobacco and smallpox, but nowhere does he mention venereal disease. The resulting babies were 'swept off' because of the 'disposition on the part of the gins to get rid of the trouble of ending and carrying about their offspring.' In *Journal of the Ethnological Society of London*, vol. 3, 1854, pp. 243–46.

32 In this subsequent reiteration the author signed himself 'Aboriginal', 'Ethnology: the case of the Aborigines', *Science of Man*, vol. 10, no. 4, November 1907, p. 56, pp. 55–57. Strzelecki was cited in 1854 as accounting for the 'disappearance of the savage races', in 'Races of men in Australia', in J. R. McCulloch (ed.), *Dictionary, Geographical, Statistical, and Historical of the Various Countries, Places and Principal Natural Object in the World,* Longman, Brown, Green, and Longmans, London, 1854, p. 230, pp. 228–31. Dr Karl Scherzer in 1858 observed a mother with a child 'whose features and complexion were obviously the result of white parentage on one side'. He declared Strzelecki's theory 'a complete delusion'. See his *Narrative of the Circumnavigation of the Globe by the Austrian Frigate Novara Undertaken by Order of the Imperial Government in the Years 1857, 1858 & 1859*, vol. III, Saunders, Otley, and Co., London, 1863, p. 32. For a detailed analysis of Strzelecki's theory of dying race,

see McGregor, *Imagined Destinies,* p. 15.
33 *Colonial Intelligencer or Aborigines' Friend,* vol. III, no. XLIII, Ollivier and Ward, London, November 1851, p. 312.
34 Rev. J. H. Sexton, *Australian Aborigines,* Hunkin, Ellis & King, Adelaide, 1944, p. 26.
35 Jennifer Lyle Morgan, 'Labouring women, enslaved women: reproduction and slavery in Barbados and South Carolina, 1650–1750', unpublished PhD thesis, Duke University, 1995.
36 See Ruth Perry, 'Colonizing the breast: sexuality and maternity in eighteenth-century England', *Journal of the History of Sexuality,* Special issue, Part 1: The state, society, and the regulation of sexuality in modern Europe, vol. 2, no. 2, 1991, pp. 204–34.
37 Felicity A. Nussbaum, '"Savage" mothers: narratives of maternity in the mid-eighteenth century', *Cultural Critique,* no. 20, Winter, 1991–92, p. 126.
38 See Perry, 'Colonizing the breast', p. 206. Perry argues new exhortations on women to breastfeed appropriated and colonised their bodies for procreation and domesticity.
39 Stephens, *White Without Soap,* p. 64.
40 David Collins, *An Account of the English Colony in New South Wales…,* T. Cadell and W. Davies, London, 1798, p. 607.
41 McCulloch, 'Collins' N S. Wales, app. P. 601', p. 229. Another report of such a burial – said to be 'strongly illustrative of the habits of the aborigines' – appeared in *The Maitland Mercury & Hunter River General Advertiser,* 30 November 1850, p. 2. The 'blacks' were 'interrogated' on the subject and reportedly explained that 'it was always their custom under similar circumstances to inter the child with the mother'.
42 Thomas R. Malthus, 'The checks to population in the lowest stages of human society', in *An Essay on the Principle of Population,* J. M. Dent, London, 1973, pp. xxiv, 284, cited in Stephens, *White Without Soap,* p. 71.
43 'The Aborigines of Australia', *Empire,* 30 November 1853, p. 3.
44 Stephens, 'A word of evidence', p. 183.
45 Stephens, *White Without Soap,* p. 72.
46 Sen, 'The savage family', pp. 53–81.
47 Stephens, 'A word of evidence', p. 182.
48 Cowlishaw, 'Infanticide in colonial Australia', p. 264.
49 'Journal of an excursion to Brisbane Water', *The Australian,* 20 December 1826, p. 3.
50 *The New Monthly Magazine and Literary Journal,* part II, Henry Colburn, London, 1828, pp. 216–23, p. 220.

Notes

51 Lorenzo Veracini, *Settler Colonialism: A Theoretical Overview*, Palgrave Macmillan, Houndsmills, 2010, p. 66.
52 L. F. Fitzhardinge, 'Cunningham, Peter Miller (1789–1864)', *Australian Dictionary of Biography*, National Centre of Biography, Australian National University, accessed 5 July 2013, <http://adb.anu.edu.au/biography/cunningham-peter-miller-1942/text2325>.
53 This work ran into three editions and was translated into German. Peter Cunningham, *Two Years in New South Wales: A Series of Letters, comprising, Sketches of the Actual State of Society in that Colony...* vol. 2, Henry Colburn, London, 1827, p. 42.
54 Breton, *Excursions in New South Wales*, p. 169.
55 Cited in Colin Groves, 'Australia for the Australians', *Australian Humanities Review*, June 2002, accessed 5 July 2013, <http://www.australianhumanitiesreview.org/archive/Issue-June-2002/groves.html>.
56 Robert Mudie, *The Picture of Australia: Exhibiting New Holland, Van Diemen's Land, and all the Settlements, From the First at Sydney to the Last at the Swan River*, Whittaker, Treacher, and Co., London, 1829, p. 257.
57 ibid., p. 266.
58 Annette Hamilton, 'Bond slaves of Satan: Aboriginal women and the mission dilemma', in Margaret Jolly and Martha MacIntyre (eds), *Family and Gender in the Pacific*, Cambridge University Press, Melbourne, 1989, pp. 236–58.
59 *The Hobart Town Courier*, 23 October 1835, p. 2.
60 Anna Johnston, *The Paper War: Morality, Print Culture, and Power in Colonial New South Wales*, UWA Publishing, Perth, 2011, p. 13.
61 Michiel van Groesen, *The Representations of the Overseas World in the De Bry Collection of Voyages (1590–1634)*, Leiden, Boston, 2008.
62 See Gananath Obeyesekere, *The Apotheosis of Captain Cook: European Mythmaking in the Pacific*, Princeton University Press, New Jersey, 1992.
63 In an extract of Cook's journal he states that he found no grounds for 'the least hint' of cannibalism during his coastal stays to New Holland. Description attributed to Cook, in the *London Chronicle*, no. 4655, 19–21 September 1786, p. 284.
64 Cunningham, *Two Years in New South Wales*, p. 15.
65 Johnston discusses an iteration in the *Monitor* in 1927. See her *Paper War*, p. 119.
66 John Helder Wedge, *Journey to Examine the Country West of Indented Head*, cited in Stephens, *White Without Soap*. There are no press references to infanticide in Van Diemen's Land prior to 1835. Henry Ling Roth devotes a section of text which cites G. A. Robinson, who Stephens also

shows to have relied on hearsay, p. 38; Henry Ling Roth, *The Aborigines of Tasmania*, F. King & Sons, Halifax, 1899, pp. 162–63.
67 Wedge, *Journey to Examine the Country...*, cited in Stephens, *White Without Soap*, p. 72.
68 Robert Dawson, *The Present State of Australia; a Description of the Country, its Advantages, and Prospects, with Reference to Emigration; and a Particular Account of the Manners, Customs, and Condition of its Aboriginal Inhabitants*, extracted in *Asiatic Journal and Monthly Register for British and Foreign India, China and Australasia*, vol. 4, January–April 1830, pp. 120–129, p. 123.
69 'Port Phillip', *Sydney Herald*, 17 November 1836, p. 2.
70 'Settlement at Port Phillip', *Launceston Advertiser*, 26 November 1835, p. 3.
71 John Helder Wedge, 'Journey to examine the country west of indented head', cited in Stephens, *White Without Soap*', p. 93.
72 Stephens, 'Infanticide at Port Phillip'.
73 ibid.
74 'Settlement at Port Phillip', *The Perth Gazette and Western Australian Journal*, 2 April 1836, p. 679.
75 Francis Armstrong, 'Manners and habits of the Aborigines of Western Australia', *The Perth Gazette and Western Australian Journal*, 29 October 1836, p. 790.
76 'The natives', *The Perth Gazette and Western Australian Journal*, 16 September 1837, p. 973.
77 William Thomas in Thomas Francis Bride (ed.), *Letters from Victorian Pioneers, Being a Series of Papers in the Early Occupation of the Colony, The Aborigines, etc.*, William Heinemann, Melbourne, 1969 (1898), p. 84.
78 Cited in Patty O'Brien, 'The gaze of the "Ghosts": images of Aboriginal women in New South Wales and Port Phillip (1800–1850)', in Jan Kociumbas (ed.), *Maps, Dreams and History: Race and Representation in Australia*, Department of History Study Series no. 8, Sydney University, Sydney, 1998, p. 391.
79 Stephens, 'Infanticide at Port Phillip'.
80 ibid.
81 Stephens, *White Without Soap*, pp. 69–71, 76–77.
82 Though the belief that girls were targeted derived from Indian reports from the 1830s, this shift in the attention of Australian newspapers to Indian infanticide didn't really take wing until the Indian mutiny of 1857.
83 See, for example, the case of the free servant Sarah Coffee, *Hobart Town Courier*, 8 December 1837, p. 3.

84 'Infanticide, or the bohemian mother', *Australasian Chronicle*, 12 December 1840, p. 3.
85 Reverend Joseph Orton, *Aborigines of Australia*, Thoms, London, 1836, pp. 7–8.
86 Editors of the *Port Phillip Gazette* (unnamed), *Latest Information with Regard to Australia Felix, The Finest Province of the Great Territory of New South Wales; including The History, Geography, Natural Resources, Government, Commerce, and Finances of Port Phillip; Sketches of the Aboriginal Population and Advice to Immigrants*, Arden and Strode, Melbourne, 1840, p. 97.
87 Michael Pickering, 'Food for thought: an alternative to "Cannibalism in the Neolithic"', *Australian Archaeology*, no. 28, June 1989, pp. 35–39.
88 M. Pickering, 'Cannibalism amongst Aborigines? A critical review of the literary evidence', unpublished Litt. B. thesis, Australian National University, Canberra, 1985; 'Consuming doubts: What some people ate? Or what some people swallowed?', in Laurence Goldman (ed.), *The Anthropology of Cannibalism*, Bergin and Garvey, London, 1999, pp. 5174.
89 Anne McClintock, *Imperial Leather: Race, Gender and Sexuality in the Colonial Context*, Routledge, New York, 1995, p. 27.
90 'Notes of a residence in the bush, by a lady', *Chambers's Edinburgh Journal*, no. 542, June 1842, pp. 180, 173–75, 179–180.
91 C. G. Teichelmann, *Aborigines of South Australia: Illustrative and Explanatory Notes of the Manners, Customs, Habits and Superstitions of the Natives of South Australia*, Adelaide, Committee of the South Australian Wesleyan Methodist Auxiliary Society, 1841, p. 8.
92 Johnston, *Paper War*, p. 26.
93 Teichelmann, *Aborigines of South Australia*, p. 13.
94 ibid.
95 In 1928 Nathan Miller wrote that children before initiation were thought to be 'a nonentity' and not to 'belong' to the group. Nathan Miller, *The Child in Primitive Society*, Kegan Paul, Trench, Trubner & Co, London, 1928, p. 11.
96 From 1790 to 1809. See Nussbaum, '"Savage" mothers', p. 147 fn. 8.
97 Eileen Janes Yeo, 'The creation of "motherhood" and women's responses in Britain and France, 1750–1914', in *Women's History Review*, vol. 8, no. 2, 1999, p. 201.
98 Johnston, *Paper War*, p. 13.
99 'Dr Penny's lecture on the Milmenrura natives', *South Australian*, 29 June 1841, p. 3.

100 *Queries Respecting the Human Race, to be Addressed to Travellers and Others*, British Association for the Advancement of Science, Taylor, London, 1841.
101 Stephens, *White Without Soap*, pp. 78–79.
102 The circular, with a question on infanticide, was printed in *The Sydney Morning Herald*, 11 September 1835, p. 2, and in *The South Australian Register*, 8 November 1835, p. 4.
103 Stephens, *White Without Soap*, p. 81.
104 'The Aborigines', *The Australian*, 19 October 1841, p. 4.
105 Stephens, *White Without Soap*, p. 81.
106 R. H. Davies, 'On the Aborigines of Van Diemen's Land', reprinted from the *Tasmanian Journal of Natural Science* by the British Association for the Advancement of Science in the (Hobart) *Courier*, 7 March 1846, p. 4.
107 'Australia, Lieut-Colonel Gawler, Mr Ed. John Eyre and the "Atheneum"', in the *Geelong Advertiser and Squatters' Advocate*, 23 May 1846, p. 4.
108 Review of a pamphlet authored by Mr Westgarth, 'A report of the conditions, capabilities and prospects of the Australian Aborigines', *Geelong Advertiser and Squatters' Advocate*, 26 August 1846, p. 1.
109 See Patrick Brantlinger's chapter on the Irish famine in his *Dark Vanishings: Discourse on the Extinction of Primitive Races 1800–1930*, Cornell University Press, Ithaca, 2003, pp. 94–116.
110 *The South Australian Register*, 4 September 1847, p. 4.
111 ibid.
112 ibid.
113 'The scab in sheep act', *South Australian Register*, 12 November 1841, p. 3.
114 'Occupation licenses', *South Australian Register*, 2 October 1847, p. 3.
115 *Maitland Mercury & Hunter River General Advertiser*, 25 September 1847, p. 25; *Moreton Bay Courier*, 9 October 1847, p. 4; *Sydney Chronicle*, 14 October 1847, p. 2; *The Australian*, 15 October 1847, p. 4; *Perth Gazette and Independent Journal of Politics and News*, 2 December 1848, p. 3.
116 'Cannibalism and infanticide in Australia', *London Journal*, vol. 7, no. 163, April 1848, pp. 74, 74–75.
117 George French Angas, *Savage Life and Scenes in Australia and New Zealand*, vol. 1, 2nd edn, Smith, Elder and Co., London, 1847, p. 228. Robert Brown called Angas's claim 'stories', 'more suspicious', possibly even 'exaggerated by the ignorant and prejudiced colonists', in his *The Races Of Mankind: A Popular Description of the Characteristics, Manners and Customs of the Principal Varieties of the Human Family*, Cassell, London, 1873, p. 119.

118 E. J. R. Morgan, 'Angas, George French (1822–1886)', *Australian Dictionary of Biography*, National Centre of Biography, Australian National University, accessed 7 July 2013, <http://adb.anu.edu.au/biography/angas-george-french-1708/text1857>.
119 Angas, *Savage Life and Scenes in Australia and New Zealand*, p. 73.
120 ibid.
121 ibid., p. 183.
122 'An old woman', in Angas, *Savage Life*, p. 184.
123 John Morgan, *The Life and Times of William Buckley thirty-two years a wanderer amongst the aborigines of then unexplored country round Port Phillip, now the province of Victoria*, A. MacDougall, Hobart, 1852, p. 66.
124 Cowlishaw, 'Infanticide in colonial Australia', p. 266.
125 James Bonwick, *William Buckley, the Wild White Man, and his Port Phillip Black Friends*, Nichols, Melbourne, 1856, p. 68.
126 Stephens, 'Infanticide at Port Phillip'.
127 Bonwick, *William Buckley*, pp. 68–71.
128 Stephens, *White Without Soap*, p. 85.
129 William Westgarth, 'The Aborigines', *The Moreton Bay Courier*, 12 September 1846, p. 2; See also his 'A report on the condition, capabilities and prospects of the Australian Aborigines', Herald, Melbourne, 1846; and *Australia Felix*, Oliver & Boyd, Edinburgh, 1848.
130 Stephens, *White Without Soap*, p. 111.
131 *The Courier*, 4 November 1846, p. 4.
132 Stephens, *White Without Soap*, p. 84.
133 'The Aborigines of Australia', *The Moreton Bay Courier*, 4 December 1847, p. 15.
134 'The Wesleyan Mission at Buntingdale', *Geelong Advertiser*, 29 October 1847, p. 1.
135 Francis Tuckfield, 'Mission to the Aborigines', *Geelong Advertiser*, 5 November 1847, p. 1.
136 'Correspondence. Buntingdale and the Aborigines', *Geelong Advertiser*, 26 November 1847, p. 1.
137 Heather Le Griffon, *Campfires at the Cross: An Account of the Bunting Dale Aboriginal Mission 1839–1951 at Birregurra, Near Colac, Victoria: with a Biography of Francis Tuckfield*, Australian Scholarly Publishing, Melbourne, 2006.
138 'History of Colac', *The Colac Herald*, 11 January 1889, p. 3; 25 January 1889, p. 3.
139 'Wesleyan missionary meeting', *Bathurst Free Press*, 15 March 1851, p. 3.
140 'The native mission at Port Lincoln', *South Australian Register*, 14 March

1853, p. 3; and in the *Geelong Advertiser and Intelligencer*, 20 April 1853, p. 25.
141 *The Salvado Memoirs*, trans. E. J. Stormon, University of Western Australia Press, Perth, 1977, p. 85.
142 Johnston, *Paper War*, pp. 105, 19.
143 William Westgarth, *Victoria: Late Australia Felix*, Oliver & Boyd, Edinburgh, 1853.
144 See Edward Beasley, *Mid-Victorian Imperialists: British Gentlemen and the Empire of the Mind,* Routledge, Oxon, 2005, pp. 48–56.
145 Geoffrey Serle, 'Westgarth, William (1815–1889)', *Australian Dictionary of Biography*, National Centre of Biography, Australian National University, accessed 17 July 2013, <http://adb.anu.edu.au/biography/westgarth-william-4830/text8057>.
146 'Review. Victoria; Late Australia Felix', *Launceston Examiner*, 25 February 1854, p. 15.
147 Beasley, *Mid-Victorian Imperialists,* p. 49.
148 *Bathurst Free Press*, 24 August 1850, p. 4.
149 *Geelong Advertiser and Intelligencer*, 16 February 1856, p. 2; see also 'Infanticide and its reproach', *Bathurst Free Press and Mining Journal*, 14 October 1857, p. 4.
150 See, for instance, 'The Chinese in Victoria', *Empire*, 21 October 1856, p. 2; 'The social, political, moral and religious character and aspects of the Indian insurrection', *Empire,* 8 February 1858, p. 3.
151 See *The Cairns Post,* 18 June 1890, p. 3. A 'half-caste' woman was charged with concealing birth and infanticide at St Clair Aboriginal Mission Station near Singleton, NSW. Also reported in *The Maitland Daily Mercury*, 25 November 1907, p. 3.
152 'The Aborigines', public lecture transcribed in *Empire*, 14 August 1857, p. 2.
153 Stephens, *White Without Soap*, pp. 80, 85.
154 Julie Carr, *The Captive White Woman of Gipps Land: In Pursuit of the Legend*, Melbourne University Press, Melbourne, 2001.
155 'The Aborigines', *Empire*, 14 August 1857, p. 2.
156 'Hill, Edward Smith (1819–1880)', *Obituaries Australia*, National Centre of Biography, Australian National University, accessed 13 December 2013, <http://oa.anu.edu.au/obituary/hill-edward-smith-13704/text24487>.
157 Michael Organ, *SMS Novara in Sydney, 1858, Chronology,* 6 September 2008, accessed 13 December 2013, <http://www.uow.edu.au/~morgan/novara15.htm>.

158 Dr Karl Scherzer, *Narrative of the Circumnavigation of the Globe by the Austrian Frigate Novara Undertaken by Order of the Imperial Government in the Years 1857, 1858 & 1859*, vol. III, Saunders, Otley, and Co., London, 1863, p. 33.
159 'Lower Murrumbidgee', *The Sydney Morning Herald*, 6 December 1859, p. 5.
160 ibid.
161 'The Aborigines', *South Australian Register*, 2 December 1861, p. 3.
162 Nancy Wright, 'The problem of Aboriginal evidence in early colonial New South Wales', in Diane Kirkby and Catherine Coleborne (eds), *Law, History, Colonialism: The Reach of Empire*, Manchester University Press, Manchester, 2001, pp. 140–55.
163 *The South Australian Advertiser*, 31 October 1860, p. 3; also in *South Australian Weekly Chronicle*, 3 November 1860, p. 5.
164 'Report of the Select Committee on the Aborigines', *South Australian Register*, 31 October 1860, p. 3.
165 *South Australian Advertiser*, 31 October 1860, p. 3
166 ibid., p. 2.
167 ibid., p. 3.
168 'The Aborigines', *South Australian Register*, 3 January 1861, p. 3.
169 Rev. Dr McCombie, *Australian Sketches*, W. Johnson, London, 1861, p. 155.
170 Bonwick, *William Buckley*, p. 69.
171 *The Courier*, 19 April 1862, p. 2.
172 'Fourteen years with the Aborigines', *Empire*, 7 August 1861, p. 3; 'Fourteen years with the Aborigines', *The Courier*, 15 August 1861, p. 3; 'Fourteen years with the Aborigines', *Ipswich Herald & General Advertiser*, Friday 16 August 1861, p 3, and 23 August 1861, p 4.
173 John Dunmore Lang, *Queensland, Australia: a highly eligible field for emigration, and the future cotton-field of Great Britain: with a disquisition on the origin, manners, and customs of the Aborigines*, Edward Stanford, London, 1861.
174 *The Courier*, 3 October 1861, p. 3; *Sydney Morning Herald*, 9 October 1861, p. 6.
175 Johnston, *Paper War*, p. 115.
176 ibid., p. 162.
177 D. W. A. Baker, 'Lang, John Dunmore (1799–1878)', *Australian Dictionary of Biography*, National Centre of Biography, Australian National University, accessed 17 October 2013, <http://adb.anu.edu.au/biography/lang-john-dunmore-2326/text2953>.

178 See Graham Jenkin, *Conquest of the Ngarrindjeri*, Rigby, Adelaide, 1979.
179 Graham Jenkin, 'Taplin, George (1831–1879)', *Australian Dictionary of Biography*, National Centre of Biography, Australian National University, accessed 16 August 2013, <http://adb.anu.edu.au/biography/taplin-george-4687/text7757>.
180 ibid.
181 'Baker, John (1813–1872)', *Australian Dictionary of Biography*, National Centre of Biography, Australian National University, accessed 25 August 2013, <http://adb.anu.edu.au/biography/baker-john-2920/text4215>.
182 'Point Macleay', *South Australian Register*, 11 April 1867, p. 2.
183 *South Australian Chronicle and Weekly Mail*, 23 May 1874, p. 13.
184 Jenkin, 'Taplin, George (1831–1879)', *Australian Dictionary of Biography*.
185 'The Narrinyeri or tribes of the lakes or Lower Murray', *South Australian Register*, 28 December 1861, p. 3.
186 See Stephens, 'A word of evidence', p. 180.
187 'The Narrinyeri', *South Australian Register*.
188 South Australia Legislative Council, *Report of the Select Committee of the Legislative Council, upon 'the Aborigines;' together with Minutes of Evidence and Appendix*, W. C. Cox, Government Printer, Adelaide, 1860, p. 60, accessed 30 October 2015, <http://aiatsis.gov.au/archive_digitised_collections/_files/archive/removeprotect/92284.pdf>.
189 Dr Karen Hughes, correspondence with the author, 15 August 2013.
190 Stephens, *White Without Soap*, p. 94; Stephens, 'A word of evidence', p. 190.
191 Jenkin, *Conquest of the Ngarrindjeri*, p. 31.
192 Russell, '"Dirty domestics and worse cooks"', pp. 18–46.
193 Cited in Jenkin, *Conquest of the Ngarrindjeri*, pp. 47, 49.
194 Ludwik Krzywicki, *Primitive Society and its Vital Statistics*, MacMillan and Co., London, 1934, pp. 311, 314–16.
195 H. A. E. Meyer, 'Manners and customs of the Encounter Bay tribe, South Australia', G. Dehane, Adelaide, 1846.
196 Reverend George Taplin, *The Narrinyeri: An Account of the Tribes of the South Australian Aborigines*, J. T. Shawyer, Adelaide, 1874, p. 12.
197 'The Narrinyeri or tribes of the lakes or Lower Murray', *South Australian Register*, 28 December 1861, p. 3.
198 Taplin, *The Narrinyeri*.
199 'Aborigines Friends Association', *South Australian Register*, 25 November 1863, p. 3.
200 'Report of the Select Committee on the Aborigines', *South Australian Register*, 31 October 1860, p. 3.

Notes

201 'A visit to Point Macleay', *South Australian Register*, 16 November 1863, p. 3.
202 Cited in Jenkin, *Conquest of the Ngarrindjeri*, p. 124.
203 Cited in Jenkin, *Conquest of the Ngarrindjeri*, p. 82.
204 Dr Lionel Lubbitz, consultant paediatrician at the Royal Children's Hospital, personal correspondence with the author, 29 June 2013.
205 Cited in Edward M. Curr, *The Australian Race: Its Origins, Languages, Customs, Place of Landing in Australia and the Routes by which it spread itself over the Continent*, vol. 2, John Ferres Government Printer, Melbourne, 1886, p. 264.
206 *Bathurst Free Press and Mining Journal*, 1 July 1890, p. 4.
207 *Shoalhaven Telegraph*, 1 February 1905, p. 6.
208 Charles Chewing, *Back in the Stone Age: The Natives of Central Australia*, Angus & Robertson, Sydney, 1936, pp. 120, 118.
209 *South Australian Register*, 24 April 1889, p. 5; 19 March 1889, p. 4.
210 Ronald Murray Berndt and Catherine Helen Berndt, with John E. Stanton, *A World that was: The Yaraldi of the Murray River and the Lakes, South Australia*, University of British Columbia Press, Vancouver, 1993, pp. 138–39.
211 ibid.
212 These Australian cases were corroborated by incidents in Britain. In the year 1862 alone the number of inquests on children held in its metropolitan areas came to 1,103. *Cornwall Chronicle (Launceston)*, 16 July 1862, p. 3.
213 *South Australian Register*, 14 December 1863, p. 2; 'The prevalence of infanticide in London', *Empire*, 2 November 1864, p. 8. 'Murder of babies. An English "fashion"', *Freeman's Journal*, 21 November 1863, p. 2.
214 'The Aborigines in the north', *South Australian Register*, 23 November 1865, p. 2.
215 *Ovens and Murray Advertiser*, 14 October 1865, p. 4.
216 Accessed 14 December 2013, <http://library.sunshinecoast.qld.gov.au/sitePage.cfm?code=noosa-region>.
217 *South Australian Register*, 15 November 1873, p. 4.
218 ibid., reprinted in the *Goulburn Herald and Chronicle*, 6 December 1873, p. 2, and *The Northern Territory Times and Gazette*, 23 January 1874, p. 3.
219 'Law for Aborigines', *Southern Argus*, 13 August 1874, p. 2.
220 Curr mostly attributed depopulation to disease, yet he had been involved in frays along with Captain Dana. Samuel Furphy, '"Our civilisation has rolled over thee": Edward M. Curr and the Yorta Yorta native title case', *History Australia*, vol. 7, no. 3, 2010, pp. 1–54; 'The Australian race', *The*

Sydney Morning Herald, 8 October 1888, p. 8.
221 Brown, *The Races Of Mankind*, p. 119.
222 Unsourced, undated review of Robert Brough Smyth, *The Aborigines of Victoria*, Museum of Victoria, R. E. Johns' scrapbooks, Box 3, c1869–1882, p. 429.
223 'The Australian Aborigines', December 1880, unattributed, unsourced newspaper clipping, Museum of Victoria, R. E. Johns' scrapbooks, Box 3, c1869–1882, p. 526.
224 Largely on the work of Lorimer Fison, G. B. Halford, A. Howitt and J. Milligan. See Michael Hoare, 'Smyth, Robert Brough (1830–1889)', *Australian Dictionary of Biography*, National Centre of Biography, Australian National University, accessed 10 February 2012, <http://adb.anu.edu.au/biography/smyth-robert-brough-4621/text7609>.
225 'The Australian Aborigines', *The Australasian Sketcher with Pen and Pencil*, 15 January 1881, p. 23.
226 In the preface to the missionary J. B. Gribble's *Black but Comely*, the conversion of 'Warrigal Lizzie' is related. She had drunkenly assaulted Gribble outside a store and allegedly took 'her child by the ankles, and swinging it round and round over her head she was on the point of dashing its brains out on the wheels of Mr Gribble's vehicle'. Gribble 'prevented' her and 'managed to take the poor wild woman' to his mission. ('Warragul' means 'wild animal', a name 'given her by the blacks' and a name popularly ascribed to Aboriginal men by whites.) He goes on, 'she is now a Christian widow and mother at the Warangesda Mission Station, on the Murrumbidgee river', giving 'much help' to Mrs Gribble at prayer meetings. John Brown Gribble, *Black but Comely, or, Glimpses of Aboriginal Life in Australia*, Morgan and Scott, London, 1884, pp. 10–11.
227 'The Australian Aborigines', *Australasian Sketcher*, p. 23.
228 *The Argus*, 12 March 1881, p. 4.
229 Peter Corris, 'Dawson, James (Jimmy) (1806–1900)', *Australian Dictionary of Biography*, National Centre of Biography, Australian National University, accessed 8 July 2013, <http://adb.anu.edu.au/biography/dawson-james-jimmy-3381/text5117>.
230 Curr, *Australian Race,* p. 76.
231 'Kamileroi and Kurnai', *South Australian Register,* 18 November 1880, p. 6.
232 Stephens, 'A word of evidence'.
233 Stephens, 'Infanticide at Port Phillip'.
234 'Kamileroi and Kurnai', *South Australian Register,* 18 November 1880, p. 6.
235 Edward M. Curr, *Recollections of Squatting in Victoria then called the Port*

Phillip District (from 1841–1851), G. Robertston, Melbourne, 1883, p. 246.

236 Marylynn Salmon, 'The cultural significance of breastfeeding and infant care in early modern England and America', *Journal of Social History,* vol. 28, no. 2, 1994, pp. 247–69.

237 Gillian Cowlishaw, 'The determinants of fertility among Australian Aborigines', *Mankind,* vol. 13, no. 1, 1981, pp. 37–55.

238 'Review of "Aborigines of Australia"', *South Australian Register,* 14 May 1889, p. 7.

239 D. J. Mulvaney, 'Willshire, William Henry (1852–1925)', *Australian Dictionary of Biography,* National Centre of Biography, Australian National University, accessed 20 December 2013, <http://adb.anu.edu.au/biography/willshire-william-henry-9128/text16101>.

240 William Henry Willshire, *The Land of the Dawning, being Facts gleaned from Cannibals in the Australian Stone Age,* W. K. Thomas & Co., Adelaide, 1896, p. 18.

241 'Australian Aborigines folklore', *The Brisbane Courier,* 18 May 1889, p. 7.

242 *Albury Banner and Wodonga Express,* 12 May 1899, p. 25.

243 See 'Sir Francis Galton', *Encyclopaedia Britannica,* 2015, accessed 17 November 2015, <www.britannica.com/biography/Francis-Galton>.

244 'Darwinism and the Aborigines', *The Queenslander,* 2 November 1889, p. 825.

245 A. Dorothy Aldersey, *Pastoral Pioneers of South Australia,* Lynton Publications, Blackwood, 1974 (facsimile).

246 *Bathurst Free Press and Mining Journal,* 2 April 1890, p. 4.

247 ibid.

248 *The Bacchus Marsh Express,* 27 September 1890, p. 2.

249 *South Australian Register,* 27 February 1899, p. 6.

250 A 'Baby Tower' near 'Shanghae' in which mothers allegedly threw their unwanted children, and which was regularly emptied by the government, was reported in *The Cornwall Chronicle,* 24 May 1862, p. 2.

251 Barrie Reynolds, 'Roth, Walter Edmund (1861–1933)', *Australian Dictionary of Biography,* National Centre of Biography, Australian National University, accessed 24 December 2013, <http://adb.anu.edu.au/biography/roth-walter-edmund-8280/text14509>.

252 'Ethnology. Notes on savage life in the early days of Western Australian settlement', *The Queenslander,* 29 March 1902, p. 674.

253 See, for example, 'The story of the blacks', *The Register,* 27 August 1904, p. 3. Author Charles White recirculated from a range of written accounts of infanticide, including from Taplin and Fyans. His work was

serialised extensively throughout the regional press during 1905. See, for example, *The Shoalhaven Telegraph*, 1 February 1905, p. 6.
254 Alfred Howitt cites a number of settler observers to detail tribal variation in the practice of infanticide, and includes Buckley as one source, in his *Native Tribes of South-east Australia*, Macmillan, London, 1904, pp. 748–51. Print reviews detailed the method of children being knocked on the head and eaten to gain strength. *Western Mail*, 14 January 1905, p. 35.
255 Similarly, Australian ladies in London enthralled its drawing rooms with 'word-pictures' of Aboriginal infanticide. 'Notes from London', *Kalgoorlie Miner*, 1 August 1903, p. 7.
256 *The Advertiser*, 1 November 1902, p. 9.
257 See Rosemary Pringle, 'Octavius Beale and the ideology of the birthrate', *Refractory Girl*, no. 3, 1975, pp. 19–27.
258 'The Royal Commission on the birthrate', *The Sydney Morning Herald*, 5 March 1904, p. 10.
259 G. Fox, 'Ethnology: the Australian Aborigines', *Science of Man*, vol. X, no. 4, 20 August 1908, p. 56, pp. 57–61.
260 Curr, *Australian Race*, p. 76.
261 Krzywicki, *Primitive Society*, p. 144.
262 Carl Lumholtz, *Among Cannibals: An Account of Four Years' Travels in Australia and of Camp Life with the Aborigines of Queensland*, Charles Scribner's Sons, New York, 1889.
263 Bronislaw Malinowski, *The Family Among the Australian Aborigines: A Sociological Study*, University of London, Press, London, 1913, p. 251.
264 W. J. Sollas, *Ancient Hunters and their Modern Representatives*, Macmillan and Co., London, 1924, p. 292; T. Athol Joyce and N. W. Thomas, *Women of All Nations: A Record of Their Characteristics, Habits, Manners, Customs & Influence*, Cassell and Co., London, 1908, p. 134; A. W. Howitt, *The Native Tribes of South-east Australia*, Macmillan and Co., London, 1904, p. 775.
265 'Aboriginal', 'Ethnology: the case of the Aborigines', *Science of Man*, vol. X, no. 4, 20 August 1908, p. 56, pp. 55–57.
266 William Ramsay Smith, 'Aborigines', in *Australian Encyclopedia*, Angus & Robertson, Sydney, 1927, p. 30. Ironically, Ramsay Smith was himself subject to a series of professional inquiries that were found to be compromised by 'procedural irregularities: witnesses were not cross-examined, some testimonies were based on hearsay'. Ronald Elmslie and Susan Nance, 'Smith, William Ramsay (1859–1937)', *Australian Dictionary of Biography*, National Centre of Biography, Australian

National University, accessed 27 December 2013, <http://adb.anu.edu. au/biography/smith-william-ramsay-8493/text14941>.
267 Baldwin Spencer and Francis Gillen, *The Arunta: A Study of a Stone Age People*, Macmillan, London, 1927, pp. 39, 229; Review, *The West Australian*, 21 January 1928, p. 6.
268 See, for instance, J. Huston Edgar, who replied to Dr Basedow's refutation of his characterisation of 'cruel and disgusting' Aboriginal rites by quoting Spencer and Gillen. 'The Aborigines', *The Register*, 27 August 1928, p. 8.
269 Paul Monaghan, review of Bob Reece, *Daisy Bates, Grand Dame of the Desert*, National Library of Australia, Canberra, 2007, in *Aboriginal History*, vol. 34, 2010, pp. 239–41.
270 Jim Anderson, 'A glorious thing is to live in a tent in the infinite: Daisy Bates', in Anna Cole, Victoria Katharine Haskins and Fiona Paisley (eds), *Uncommon Ground: White Women in Aboriginal History*, Aboriginal Studies Press, Canberra, 2005, p. 222.
271 'Aboriginal cannibals', *The Register*, 8 March 1928, p. 10.
272 Monaghan, review of Reece, *Daisy Bates*.
273 Daisy Bates, 'Our cannibals', *The Sydney Morning Herald*, 25 January 1930, p. 21.
274 Anderson, 'A glorious thing is to live in a tent', p. 222.
275 Bates, 'Our cannibals'.
276 Daisy Bates, '"Thus…my days have passed"', *The Australian Women's Weekly*, 13 January 1934, p. 3.
277 Yet, if Bates was privy to men's secrets, in the self-mythologised figure of Kabbarli, she would have forfeited access to women's knowledge, according to Isobel White. See her 'Daisy Bates: legend and reality' in Julie Marcus (ed.), *First in their Field: Women and Australian Anthropology*, Melbourne University Press, Melbourne, 1993, p. 62, pp. 46–65.
278 *The West Australian*, 14 April 1906, p. 4.
279 *Weekly Times*, 29 August 1914, p. 10; 'Aboriginal savages, lawless cannibals', *The Advertiser*, 2 January 1930, p. 14.
280 Phillip Arthur Micklem, 'Aboriginal communism', *The Sydney Morning Herald*, 6 June 1922, p. 6.
281 'Aboriginal savages, lawless cannibals', *The Advertiser*.
282 Reece, *Daisy Bates*, p. 87.
283 Ann Standish, 'Daisy Bates: dubious leadership', 2012, *Seizing the Initiative: Australian Women Leaders in Politics, Workplaces and Communities*, accessed 3 January 2013, <http://www.womenaustralia.info/leaders/sti/standish.html>.

284 See Ronald Niezen, *The Origins of Indigenism: Human Rights and the Politics of Identity*, University of California Press, Berkeley, 2003.
285 Cited in Standish, 'Daisy Bates', p. 100.
286 Bates did not specify language groups so a definite translation is difficult. Beth Sometimes, Big hART project, Ngapartji Ngapartji: Indigenous language in the arts, correspondence with the author, 21 January, 2014.
287 Ernestine Hill, *The Great Australian Loneliness*, Robertson and Mullens, Melbourne, 1942, p. 254.
288 Hill, *Great Australian Loneliness*.
289 George Aiston, self-taught ethnologist of Central Australia who gained the trust of the Wangkangurru. See his 'The desert Aborigines', *Mankind*, vol. 1, no. 12, 1935, p. 6, pp. 5–8; Eric Thonemann in the ghostwritten biography of Budjala/Buludja/Buledja, a Mungari woman of the NT Elsey Station, ventriloquises her disclosure of smothering her first two babies at birth. If credible, she confirms Aiston's startling finding: 'We do not like our children being taken away from us, sometimes we hide, and sometimes we kill them. You white people do not like to hear us talk like that, but I want to tell you the truth'. See H. E. Thonemann, *Tell the White Man; The Life Story of a Lubra*, Collins, Sydney, 1949, p. 67.
290 Meaghan Morris, 'Panorama: the live, the dead and the living', in Graeme Turner (ed.), *Nation, Culture, Text: Australian Cultural and Media Studies*, Routledge, London, 1993, p. 29, pp. 19–58.
291 Morris, 'Panorama', p. 49.
292 Isobel White, in 'Daisy Bates: legend and reality', argues that Bates pioneered 'participant observation' fieldwork.
293 Krzywicki, *Primitive Society*, p. 139.
294 G. P. Walsh, 'Mowbray, Philip Henry Mitchell (Phil) (1845–1903)', *Australian Dictionary of Biography,* National Centre of Biography, Australian National University, accessed 14 January 2014, <http://adb.anu.edu.au/biography/mowbray-philip-henry-mitchell-phil-13116/text23733>.
295 Krzywicki, *Primitive Society*, pp. 126, 124, 133, Appendix V, 135, 137, 547, 142.
296 Alison Holland, '"Whatever her race, a woman is not a chattel": Mary Montgomery Bennett', in Anna Cole, Victoria Haskins and Fiona Paisley (eds), *Uncommon Ground: White Women in Aboriginal History*, Aboriginal Studies Press, Canberra, 2005, pp. 129–52; Fiona Paisley, '"For a brighter day": Constance Ternent Cooke', in Cole, Haskins and Paisley (eds), *Uncommon Ground: White Women in Aboriginal History*,

Aboriginal Studies Press, Canberra, 2005, pp. 172–96.
297 Henry Doyle Moseley, *Royal Commission Appointed to Investigate, Report and Advise Upon Matters in Relations to the Condition and Treatment of Aborigines*, Western Australia, 1934.
298 Paper untitled. Mary Montgomery Bennett also wrote *The Australian Aborigines as a Human Being,* Alston Rivers, London, 1930.
299 'Does Australia mistreat its Aborigines', *The Daily News*, 24 June 1933, p. 16.
300 'Aboriginal females', *Northern Standard*, 4 July 1939, p. 5.
301 See Jane Carey, 'The racial imperatives of sex: birth control and eugenics in Britain, the United States and Australia in the interwar years', *Women's History Review*, vol. 21, no. 5, 2012, pp. 733–52.
302 George G. Hacket, 'Aboriginal natives', *The Advertiser*, 8 January 1930, p. 18.
303 Nussbaum, '"Savage" mothers', p. 126.
304 Patrick Wolfe, *Settler-Colonialism and the Transformation of Anthropology: The Politics and Poetics of an Ethnographic Event*, Cassell, London, 1999, p. 98.
305 David Page, *Man, Where, Whence, and Whither: Being a Glance at Man in his Natural-History Relations*, Edmonston and Douglas, Edinburgh, 1867, p. 80.
306 Cited in Haebich, *Broken Circles,* p. 118.
307 Unattributed, *Pauline Hanson: The Truth*, Ipswich, self-published, 1997, p. 134.
308 Cited in Katherine Biber, 'Cannibals and colonialism', *Sydney Law Review*, vol. 27, 2005, pp. 623–37, p. 626.

Chapter 4

1 *Wonderful Australia in Pictures*, Herald and Weekly Times, Colorgravure, Melbourne, 1949, p. 115.
2 Ironically, in South Australia that displacement would soon be literal and spatial, not temporal, due to British nuclear tests over Maralinga Tjarutja lands between 1956 and 1963.
3 Einstein's theory of special relativity was introduced in his 1905 paper 'On the electrodynamics of moving bodies' (in *The Principle of Relativity,* trans. George Barker Jeffery and Wilfrid Perrett, Methuen and Company, London, 1923); his space/time theory was published under 'Space–time' in the *Encyclopedia Britannica*, 13th edn, 1926.
4 See Stephern Kern's discussion, *The Culture of Time and Space: 1880–1918*, Harvard University Press, Cambridge, 1983, pp. 18–20.

5   Mary Louise Pratt describes imperial contact zones as 'the space of colonial encounters, the space in which peoples geographically and historically separated come into contact with each other and establish ongoing relations, usually involving conditions of coercion, radical inequality, and intractable conflict'. See her *Imperial Eyes: Travel Writing and Transculturation*, Routledge, New York, 1992, p. 6.
6   Liz Conor, '"Strangely clad": enclosure, exposure, and the cleavage of empire', *Journal of Australian Studies*, Special issue: Colonial visual cultures: 'Double take: reappraising the colonial archive', vol. 35, no. 2, 2011, pp. 185–200.
7   Victoria Haskins, 'From the centre to the city: modernity, mobility and mixed descent Aboriginal domestic workers from central Australia', *Women's History Review*, vol. 18, no. 1, 2009, pp. 155–175, p. 155.
8   Lynette Russell, '"Dirty domestics and worse cooks": Aboriginal women's agency and domestic frontiers, southern Australia, 1800–1850', *Frontiers: A Journal of Women's Studies*, vol. 28, nos 1–2, 2007, pp. 18–46.
9   Charles Chauvel and Elsa Chauvel, *Walkabout*, W. H. Allen, London, 1959, p. 178.
10 ibid., p. 132.
11 Robert Montgomery Martin Esq (ed.), 'Aborigines of Australia', *The Colonial Magazine and Commercial-Maritime Journal*, vol. V, May–August 1841, p. 152.
12 Haskins, 'From the centre to the city', p. 155.
13 See Marilyn Lake and Henry Reynolds, *Drawing the Global Colour Line: White Men's Countries and the Question of Racial Equality*, Melbourne University Press, Melbourne, 2008, pp. 13–45.
14 Angela Woollacott, *To Try Her Fortune in London: Australian Women, Colonialism, and Modernity*, Oxford University Press, Oxford, 2001.
15 Lynette Russell, *Roving Mariners: Australian Aboriginal Whalers and Sealers in the Southern Oceans, 1790–1870*, SUNY Press, Albany, 2012.
16 'The Aborigines of Australia', *Chamber's Journal of Popular Literature, Science and Art*, vol. X, no. 516, p. 736.
17 Martin, 'Aborigines of Australia', p. 430.
18 'Extract from M. Commissioner Massie's Report for the New-England District, Armadale, 10 January 1842', *The Colonial Intelligencer*, vol. IV, nos XIV and XV, June and July 1853, p. 266.
19 Daisy Bates, *Passing of the Aborigines*, John Murray, London, 1944.
20 Climbing becomes a significant mode of comportment because the preceding discussion deploys the metaphor of family trees and the diverse evolutionary branches of mankind 'sprouting' from the 'common

stem'. *Wonderful Australia in Pictures*, p. 127.
21 *Wonderful Australia in Pictures*, p. 208.
22 In 1910 Roth described the extent of someone's country by 'their "walkabout"'. See Walter E. Roth, *Records of the Australian Museum*, vol. 8, no. 1, 1910, p. 87.
23 *Wonderful Australia in Pictures*, p. 127.
24 ibid., p. 128.
25 Tjungarrayi was later 'centralised to the government station at Jay Creek, where he produced artefacts for tourists and become their guide.' See Jillian Barnes, 'Resisting the captured image: how Gwoja Tjungurrayi, 'One Pound Jimmy', escaped the 'stone age', in Ingereth MacFarlane and Mark Hannah (eds), *Transgressions: Critical Australian Indigenous Histories*, Aboriginal History Monograph 16, ANU ePress, Canberra, 2007. I have attempted to contact Tjungurrayi's granddaughters but was unable to reach them.
26 Charles Homes, *We Find Australia,* Hutchinson, London, 1932.
27 Barnes, 'Resisting the captured image'.
28 C. S. Browne, *Australia: A General Account*, Thomas Nelson & Sons, London, 1929, p. 225.
29 In the Australian context, the work of Victoria Haskins, Heather Goodall, Lyn Riddett, Fiona Paisley, Lynette Russell and Anna Haebich has closely examined the operation of settler-colonialism in the domestic realm.
30 Anne McClintock, *Imperial Leather: Race, Gender and Sexuality in the Colonial Contest*, Routledge, New York, 1995, p. 36.
31 British colonies tended to be more progressive on a range of issues that would come to be defined as first-wave feminist, such as property rights. Patricia Grimshaw and Graham Willet, 'Women's history and family history: an exploration of colonial family structure', in Norma Grieve and Pat Grimshaw (eds), *Australian Women: Feminist Perspectives*, Oxford University Press, Melbourne, 1981, pp. 134–55.
32 Ann Laura Stoler, *Carnal Knowledge and Imperial Power: Race and the Intimate in Colonial Rule*, University of the California Press, Berkeley, 2002, p. 153.
33 John Gascoigne, *The Enlightenment and the Origins of European Australia*, Cambridge University Press, Cambridge, 2002, p. 148.
34 Editorial, *The Register*, 25 June 1843, p. 3a.
35 Extract from 'South Australia: The Aborigines,' *The Colonial Intelligencer*, vol. IV, nos XIV and XV, June and July 1853.
36 Matthew Romaniello makes a case that separate spheres were not created

but reified under German industrialism. The transference of ideas from cameralism and the Enlightenment transformed the peasant household to the princely court. See his *Productive Men, Reproductive Women: The Agrarian Household and the Emergence of Separate Spheres During the German Enlightenment*, Berghahn Books, New York, 2000; see also Sara Horrell and Jane Humphries, 'Women's labour force participation and the transition to the male-breadwinner family, 1790–1865', in Pamela Sharpe (ed.), *Women's Work: The English Experience 1650–1914*, Arnold, London, 1998.

37 Felicity A. Nussbaum, '"Savage" mothers: narratives of maternity in the mid-eighteenth century', *Cultural Critique*, no. 20, Winter, 1991–92, p. 126.

38 See Dolores Mitchell, 'Images of exotic women in turn-of-the-century tobacco art', *Feminist Studies*, vol. 18, no. 2, 1992, p. 330.

39 Cited in *The Manning Index of South Australian History*, accessed 1 April 2008, <http://www.slsa.sa.gov.au/manning/>.

40 W. J. Sollas, *Ancient Hunters and their Modern Representatives*, MacMilland and Co., London, 1924, p. 290.

41 J. A. Hammerton, *People of All Nations*, Educational Book Co., London, 1920–1938, p. 247, pp. 247–311.

42 For example, see George French Angas, *Savage Life and Scenes in Australia and New Zealand*, vol. 1, 2nd edn, Smith, Elder and Co, London, 1847, p. 81.

43 Gascoigne, *The Enlightenment and the Origins of European Australia*, p. 71.

44 Henry Reynolds argues that explorers looked not for empty land, but for peopled districts, indicating the presence of water. See his *With the White People: The Crucial Role of Aborigines in the Exploration and Development of Australia*, Penguin, Ringwood, 1990, pp. 13–15.

45 Deborah Bird Rose, cited in Patrick Wolfe, *Settler-Colonialism and the Transformation of Anthropology: The Politics and Poetics of an Ethnographic Event*, Cassell, London, 1999, p. 1.

46 For an overview of debates about when 'self-determination' became adopted into government policy terminology, see Tim Rowse, *White Flour, White Power: From Rations to Citizenship in Central Australia*, Cambridge University Press, Cambridge, 1998, pp. 204–07.

47 Annette Hamilton, 'A complex strategical situation: gender and power in Aboriginal Australia', in Norma Grieve and Patricia Grimshaw (eds), *Australian Women: Feminist Perspectives*, Oxford University Press, Melbourne, 1981, pp. 69–85, p. 79.

48 Quoted in Gascoigne, *The Enlightenment*, p. 168.

49 Diane Barwick and Diane Bell argued this was hardly surprising given the 'responsibilities of housewives in our own society were not studied as a form of work like other occupations until 1974'. In 'Women in Aboriginal society: resources for research', in Diane Barwick, Michael Mace and Tom Stannage (eds), *Handbook for Aboriginal and Islander History*, Aboriginal History, Canberra, 1979, p. 180.

50 See Ann McGrath, '"Modern stone-age slavery: images of Aboriginal labour and sexuality', *Labour History*, no. 69, 1995, p. 33.

51 Rev. John Flynn, *The Inlander: A Quarterly Magazine dealing with National Interests from the Outbacker's Point of View*, Gordon and Gotch, Sydney, 1915, p. 23.

52 Homi Bhabha, *The Location of Culture*, Routledge, London, 1994, p. 9.

53 Feminist anthropologist Micaela di Leonardo has noted the 'the anthropological tradition of dichotomising "male" public kinship and "female" domestic kinship – and, of course, of providing "thin descriptions" of the latter', when in fact women's kinship struggles 'are concerned, after all, with the distribution of whatever domestic power is available to women and often also entail female influences on male political actions'. Micaela di Leonardo, *Gender at the Crossroads of Knowledge: Feminist Anthropology in the Postmodern Era*, University of California Press, Berkeley, 1991, p. 8.

54 Malinowski cited in Phyllis M. Kaberry, *Aboriginal Woman: Sacred and Profane*, Routledge, London, 1939, p. 15.

55 Diane E. Barwick, 'And the ladies are lubras now', in Fay Gale (ed.), *Woman's Role in Aboriginal Society*, 3rd edn, Australian Institute of Aboriginal Studies, Canberra, 1978, pp. 52, 57, 61.

56 Catherine H. Berndt, 'Digging sticks and spears, or, the two-sex model', in Fay Gale (ed.), *Woman's Role in Aboriginal Society*, 3rd edn, Australian Institute of Aboriginal Studies, Canberra, 1978, pp. 64–84, p. 80.

57 ibid.

58 Extract from William Henry Suttor, MLC, New South Wales, *Australian Stories Retold and Sketches of Country Life*, Whalan, Bathurst, 1877.

59 See Stephen Muecke's discussion of how modernity incorporates and represses the ancient as represented by traditional indigeneity. *Ancient and Modern: Time Culture and Indigenous Philosophy*, University of New South Wales Press, Sydney, 2004.

60 P. W. Bassett-Smith, 'The Aborigines of north-west Australia', *The Journal of the Anthropological Institute of Great Britain and Ireland*, vol. XXIII, 1894, p. 326, pp. 324–331.

61 'Our northern shores', *Northern Territory Times and Gazette*, 22 July 1924, p. 2.

62 Liz Conor, *The Spectacular Modern Woman: Feminine Visibility in the 1920s*, Indiana University Press, Bloomington, 2004.
63 Charles Barrett and A. S. Kenyon, 'Blackfellows of Australia', Lawrence Kay for Pictorial Newspapers, Melbourne, c. 1936, p. 7.
64 R. H. Croll, 'The original owners', in L. L. Plitzer (ed.), *Centenary Journal*, Melbourne, 1934, p. 137, pp. 39–41, 132, 137, 146.
65 *The Argus*, 11 August 1934, p. 4.
66 Coralie Rees, *Spinifex Walkabout: Hitch-hiking in Remote North Australia*, Australasian Publishing, Sydney, 1953, p. 262.
67 Appears to derive from Eric Joliffe's 'Witchetty's tribe' series of 1952.
68 Allan Marshall, *Ourselves Writ Strange*, F. W. Cheshire, Melbourne, 1948, p. 83.
69 Charles Barrett, illustrated by Ivor Horman, 'An ancient people', *Rydge's*, 1 December 1947, p. 1093.
70 A. M. Duncan-Kemp, *Where Strange Paths Go Down*, W. R. Smith and Patterson, Brisbane, 1964, pp. 73, 103, 131.
71 ibid., p. 34.
72 See Margaret McGuire, 'The legend of the good fella missus', *Aboriginal History*, vol. 14, 1990, pp. 124–151.
73 Mrs Aeneas Gunn, *We of the Never-Never*, Angus and Robertson, Sydney, 1908, p. 43.
74 Mrs Aeneas Gunn, *The Little Black Princess*, Angus and Robertson, Sydney, 1905, p. 175.
75 Lytha, 'Cattle kingdom', *Walkabout*, 1 March 1942, no. 5, p. 12.
76 Deborah Bird Rose, *Hidden Histories: Black stories from Victoria River Downs, Humbert River and Wave Hill Stations*, Aboriginal Studies Press, Canberra, 1991, pp. 30, 211.
77 J. W. Bleakley, 'The Aborigines and half castes of central and north Australia', in Sharman Stone, *Aborigines in White Australia: A Documentary History of the Attitudes Affecting Official Policy and the Australian Aborigine 1697–1973*, Heinemann, South Yarra, 1974, p. 155.
78 Ann McGrath, '"Spinifex fairies": Aboriginal workers in the Northern Territory, 1911–1939', in Elizabeth Windschuttle (ed.), *Women, Class and History: Feminist Perspectives on Australia 1788–1978*, Fontana, Sydney, 1980, p. 255.
79 'Our Aborigines', Minister for Territories, prepared for the National Aborigines' Day of Observance Committee, 12 July 1957, Commonwealth Government Printer, Canberra.
80 Henrietta Drake-Brockman, 'Coloured characters', *Walkabout*, vol. 11, no. 8, 1 June 1945, p. 15.

81 'Christmas day in the far north – a royal visitor', *Supplement to the Illustrated Australian News*, 19 December 1885, p. 226.
82 Duncan-Kemp, *Where Strange Paths Go Down*, p. 226.
83 ibid., p. 34.
84 Bleakley, 'The Aborigines and half castes of central and north Australia', p. 156.
85 McGrath, '"Spinifex fairies"', pp. 239–40.
86 Angela Woollacott, 'White colonialism and sexual modernity: Australian women in the early twentieth-century metropolis', in Antoinette Burton (ed.), *Gender, Sexuality and Colonial Modernities*, Routledge, London, 1999, p. 56.
87 Ernestine Hill, *The Great Australian Loneliness*, Robertson and Mullens, Melbourne, 1942, pp. 218–19.
88 Chauvel and Chauvel, *Walkabout*, p. 189.
89 McGrath, '"Spinifex fairies"', p. 258.
90 Hill, *The Great Australian Loneliness*, p. 133.
91 'Northern Territory kitchen', *The Australian Countryside in Pictures*, Herald Gravure, Melbourne, 1953, p. 218.
92 McClintock, *Imperial Leather*, p. 170.
93 Chauvel and Chauvel, *Walkabout*, p. 189.
94 Hill, *The Great Australian Loneliness*, p. 54.
95 Rowse details the history of equal pay for pastoral workers staged from 1966 to 1968 in *White Flour, White Power*, pp. 127–28.
96 Bhabha, *Location of Culture*, p. 9.
97 McGrath, '"Spinifex fairies"', p. 255.
98 Stan Cross and Mick Paul both sourced from Vane Lindsay, *The Inked-in Image: A Social and Historical Survey of Australian Comic Art*, Hutchinson of Australia, Richmond, 1979. The society is now known as the Australian Cartoonists' Association.
99 Kate Bagnall, 'Across the threshold: white women and Chinese hawkers in the white colonial imaginary', *Hecate,* vol. 28, no. 2, 2002, pp. 9–29.
100 Mary Douglas, *Purity and Danger*, Routledge and Kegan Paul, London, 1966, p. 2.
101 Diane Bell, *Daughters of the Dreaming*, McPhee Gribble / George Allen and Unwin, Sydney, 1983, p. 45.
102 Larissa Behrendt, 'Consent in a (neo) colonial society: Aboriginal woman as sexual and legal "other"', *Australian Feminist Studies*, vol. 15, no. 33, 2000, p. 355.
103 Frank Clune, *Roaming Around Australia*, Hawthorn Press, Melbourne, 1947, pp. 219, 231, 235.

104 Hill, *Great Australian Loneliness*, pp. 99, 169.
105 George Aiston, 'The desert Aborigines', *Mankind*, vol. 1, no. 12, 1935, p. 8.
106 Marilyn Lake, 'Frontier feminism and the marauding white man', *Journal of Australian Studies: Australian Frontiers,* vol. 49, 1996, pp. 12–20; Alison Holland, 'The campaign for women protectors: gender, race and frontier between the wars', *Australian Feminist Studies*, vol. 16, no. 34, 2001, pp. 27–42; Haskins, 'From the centre to the city'.
107 H. D. Moseley, 'Report following the Royal Commission on Aborigines, 24 January 1935', in Sharman Stone, *Aborigines in White Australia: A Documentary History of the Attitudes Affecting Official Policy and the Australian Aborigine 1697–1973*, Heinemann, South Yarra, 1974, p. 167.
108 Alison Holland, 'Feminism, colonialism and aboriginal workers: an anti-slavery crusade', in Ann McGrath and Kay Saunders with Jackie Huggins (eds), *Aboriginal Workers*, Australian Society for the Study of Labour History, Sydney, 1995, p. 57.
109 Masters and Servants Act 1892. Western Australia (55 Vict, No. 28). Susan Jane Hunt, *Spinifex and Hessian: Women's Lives in North-Western Australia 1860–1900*, University of Western Australia Press, Perth, 1986, p. 99.
110 Bates, *Passing of the Aborigines*, pp. 16, 10, 215.
111 Paul James, *Globalism, Nationalism, Tribalism: Bringing Theory Back In*, Sage Publications, London, 2006, p. 184.
112 Eileen Barry, '"Kabbarli" of desert places', *Walkabout*, October, 1966, pp. 14–17, p. 16.
113 ibid.
114 Bhabha, *Location of Culture*, p. 13.
115 Antoinette Burton, 'Introduction: The unfinished business of colonial modernities', in A. Burton (ed.), *Gender, Sexuality and Colonial Modernities*, Routledge, London, 1999, p. 2.

Chapter 5
1   The strife culminated in the infamous Caledon Bay spearing of five trepangers, along with the killings of two white men and one policeman on Woodah Island.
2   Liz Conor, '"Black velvet" and "purple indignation": print responses to Japanese "poaching" of Aboriginal women', *Aboriginal History*, vol. 37, 2013, p. 51–77.
3   Ann Laura Stoler, *Carnal Knowledge and Imperial Power: Race and the*

Intimate in Colonial Rule, University of California Press, Berkeley, 2002, p. 145.
4   Ruth Balint, 'Aboriginal women and Asian men: a maritime history of color in white Australia', *Signs*, vol. 37, no. 3, 2012, pp. 544–54, p. 544.
5   Franchise (1902) and Naturalisation (1903) acts excluded Aboriginal people as well as people from Asian countries from citizenship. See Henry Reynolds, *North of Capricorn: The Untold Story of Australia's North*, Allen and Unwin, Sydney, 2003, p. xi; Museum of Australian Democracy, *Documenting a democracy,* accessed 15 June 2013, <http://foundingdocs.gov.au>.
6   Homi Bhabha, *The Location of Culture*, Routledge, London, 1994, p. 140.
7   See Ann Curthoys, 'An uneasy conversation: the multicultural and the indigenous', in John Docker and Gerhard Fischer (eds), *Race, Colour and Identity in Australia and New Zealand*, UNSW Press, Sydney, 2000, pp. 21–36; Minoru Hokari, 'Anti-minorities history: perspectives on Aboriginal-Asian relations', in Penny Edwards and Shen Yuanfang (eds), *Lost in the Whitewash: Aboriginal–Asian Encounters in Australia, 1901–2001*, Humanities Research Centre, Australian National University, Canberra, 2003, pp. 85–101.
8   Peta Stephenson, 'New cultural scripts: exploring the dialogue between Indigenous and "Asian" Australians', *Journal of Australian Studies*, Special issue: Sojourners and strangers, vol. 27, no. 77, 2003, pp. 57–68.
9   See Ann Laura Stoler's discussion of the notion of interior frontiers in her 'Sexual affronts and racial frontiers: European identities and the cultural politics of exclusion in colonial Southeast Asia', in Frederick Cooper and Ann Laura Stoler (eds), *Tensions of Empire: Colonial Cultures in a Bourgeois World*, University of California Press, Berkeley, 1997, pp. 198–237, p. 199.
10 Elizabeth A. Povinelli, *The Empire of Love: Toward a Theory of Intimacy, Genealogy and Carnality*, Duke University Press, Durham, 2006, p. 1.
11 South Australia Legislative Council, *Report of the Select Committee of the Legislative Council on the Aborigines' Bill*, Paper no. 77, Item no. 854, Adelaide, 1899, cited in Ronald and Catherine Berndt, *From Black to White in South Australia*, F. W. Cheshire, Melbourne, 1951, pp. 54–55.
12 *Canberra Times*, 25 August 1936, p. 1.
13 In debate on the Aborigines Act of 1905, pastoralists successfully lobbied to reduce the minimum fine for cohabiting from 50 to 5 pounds. Anna Haebich, *Broken Circles: Fragmenting Indigenous Families 1800–2000*, Fremantle Arts Centre Press, Fremantle, 2000, p. 239.
14 *Courier-Mail*, 4 January 1934, p. 13.

15 Gayatri Spivak, 'Can the subaltern speak?', in Cary Nelson and Lawrence Grossberg (eds), *Marxism and the Interpretation of Culture*, MacMillan, Houndmills, 1988, pp. 271–313, p. 296.
16 Regina Ganter, 'Letters from Mapoon: colonising Aboriginal gender', *Australian Historical Studies*, vol. 30, no. 113, 1999, pp. 267–85, p. 267.
17 Ann McGrath, '"Spinifex fairies": Aboriginal workers in the Northern Territory, 1911–1939', in Elizabeth Windschuttle (ed.), *Women, Class and History: Feminist Perspectives on Australia 1788–1978*, Fontana, Sydney, 1980.
18 Kay Merry, 'The cross-cultural relationships between the sealers and the Tasmanian Aboriginal women at Bass Strait and Kangaroo Island in the early nineteenth century', *Counterpoints*, vol. 3, no. 1, 2003, pp. 80–88.
19 Victoria Haskins, 'On the doorstep: Aboriginal domestic service as a "contact zone"', *Australian Feminist Studies*, vol. 16, no. 34, 2001, pp. 13–25.
20 The story of the marriage of Okamura and Mary Masatora of Broome and that of their children and grandchildren is told by Fujio Nakano, 'Japanese pearl divers of Broome', *Geo: Australia's National Geographic*, vol. 2, no. 4, 1980, pp. 112–121. For a more detailed telling of their story and that of many such marriages in Broome, see Regina Ganter, 'The Wakayama triangle: Japanese heritage of North Australia', *Journal of Australian Studies*, vol. 23, no. 61, 1999, pp. 55–63; R. Ganter, *Mixed Relations: Asian-Aboriginal Contact in North Australia*, UWA Publishing, Perth, 2006. See also Christine Choo, 'Asian men on the West Kimberley coast 1900–1940', *Studies in Western Australian History*, vol. 16, 1995, pp. 89–111; Stephenson, 'New cultural scripts'.
21 Balint, 'Aboriginal women and Asian men', p. 544; *The Canberra Times*, 25 August 1936; Lorna Kaino, '"Broome culture" and its historical links to the Japanese pearling industry', *Continuum, Journal of Media and Cultural Studies*, vol. 25, no. 4, 2011, pp. 479–90.
22 See Ann McGrath, '"Black velvet": Aboriginal women and their relations with white men in the Northern Territory 1910–1940', in Kay Daniels (ed.), *So Much Hard Work: Women and Prostitution in Australia*, Fontana, Sydney, 1984, pp. 233–97, p. 252.
23 See Sumi Kwaymullina, 'For marbles: Aboriginal people in the early pearling industry of the North-West', *Studies In Western Australian History*, vol. 22, 2001, pp. 53–61, p. 57.
24 Susan Jane Hunt, *Spinifex and Hessian: Women's Lives in North-Western Australia 1860–1900*, University of Western Australia Press, Perth, 1986, p. 103.

25 It was these interventions that led to the uptake of Asian and Islander labour on luggers to replace Aboriginal divers. 1883 saw the appointment of a Commission of Inquiry. M. K. Hill, 'The regulation of Aboriginal women in the Western Australian pearling industry, 1860–1905', unpublished thesis, University of Western Australia, 1994.
26 See Regina Ganter, *The Pearl-shellers of Torres Strait: Resource Use, Development and Decline 1860s-1960s*, Melbourne University Press, Melbourne, 1994, p. 107.
27 Anne McClintock, *Imperial Leather: Race, Gender and Sexuality in the Colonial Contest*, Routledge, New York, 1995, pp. 44, 113.
28 Marianna Torgovnick, *Gone Primitive: Savage Intellects and Modern Lives*, University of Chicago Press, Chicago, 1990, p. 104.
29 See Bernard Smith, *European Vision and the South Pacific*, Harper and Row, Sydney, 1985 (1969), p. 88.
30 'An account of the inhabitants of Otaheite, a lately discovered island in the south-sea', *The London Magazine*, June 1773, p. 266.
31 Roy Porter and Lesley Hall, *The Facts of Life: The Creation of Sexual Knowledge in Britain, 1650–1950*, Yale University Press, New Haven, 1995.
32 'An authentic account of the natives of Otahitee', *The General Evening Post*, no. 7812, 20 March 1784.
33 Michael Taussig, *Mimesis and Alterity: A Particular History of the Senses*, Routledge, New York, 1993, p. 67.
34 Cook quoted in Samuel Bennett, *The History of Australian Discovery and Colonisation*, Hanson and Bennett, Sydney, 1865, p. 106.
35 Shino Konishi, *The Aboriginal Male in the Enlightenment World*, Pickering and Chatto, London, 2012.
36 Joseph D. Hooker (ed.), *Journal of The Right Hon. Sir Joseph Banks*, MacMillan & Co., London, 1896, p. 308.
37 Konishi, *Aboriginal Male,* p. 87.
38 ibid., p. 74.
39 Quoted in Ann McGrath, 'Consent, marriage and colonialism: Indigenous Australian women and colonizer marriages', *Journal of Colonialism and Colonial History*, vol. 6, no. 3, 2005, pp. 1–23.
40 Konishi includes William Robertson's and the Compte de Buffon's earlier appraisal of American Indian men in her study of eighteenth-century attitudes to Aboriginal men's sexuality. See her *Aboriginal Male*, p. 72.
41 Prefacing W. E. T. Young's letter published in 'The natives of South Australia', *The Colonial Intelligencer or Aborigines' Friend,* vol. II, no. XIV, June 1849, p. 215.

42 George Barrington, *The History of New South Wales: including Botany Bay...*, M. Jones, London, 1802, p. 36.
43 Inga Clendinnen, *Dancing with Strangers*, Text, Melbourne, 2003, p. 153.
44 Konishi, *Aboriginal Male*, p. 73.
45 Clendinnen, *Dancing with Strangers*, p. 152.
46 John Gibson, letter printed in 'South Australia', *The Colonial Intelligencer or, Aborigines' Friend*, vol. III, no. XLIII, 1851, p. 315.
47 As discussed in Chapter 2, Konishi explores this question in her '"Wanton with plenty": questioning ethno-historical constructions of sexual savagery in Aboriginal societies, 1788–1803', *Australian Historical Studies*, vol. 39, no. 3, 2008, pp. 356–72.
48 McGrath, '"Black velvet"', p. 248.
49 *Northern Territory Times and Gazette*, 17 June 1915, p. 7.
50 'Stud' denoted Aboriginal women on pastoral stations kept for white station management and hands, much as 'buck' referred to single young Aboriginal men. The NT register of wards was colloquially known as *The Stud Book*. Sidney J. Barker, *The Australian Language*, Currawong Publishing Co., Sydney, 1966, p. 324.
51 Edward M. Curr, *Recollections of Squatting in Victoria then called the Port Phillip District (from 1841–1851)*, G. Robertston, Melbourne, 1883, p. 283.
52 'The Aborigines of Western Australia', in J. S. Battye (ed.), *Cyclopedia of Western Australia*, vol. 1, Hassey and Gillingham, Adelaide, 1912–13, pp. 45–62, p. 50.
53 Arthur W. Upfield, 'The Barrakee mystery', *The Daily News*, 7 May 1932, p. 9.
54 McGrath, '"Black velvet"'.
55 Marcia Langton, *Well, I heard it on the radio and I saw it on the television ...' An Essay for the Australian Film Commission on the Politics and Aesthetics of Filmmaking by and about Aboriginal People and Things*, Australian Film Commission, Sydney, 1993, p. 50.
56 The Gadfly, 'Through the Ashburton', *The Sunday Times*, 16 June 1907, p. 12.
57 *The Argus*, 2 November 1933, p. 9.
58 *Mann's Emigrant's Guide to Australia; including The Colonies of New South Wales, Port Phillip. South Australia, Western Australia, and Moreton Bay*, William Strange, London, 1849, p. 16.
59 The Bench found both defendants guilty, and sentenced John Trunley and Gerald Thompson to each pay a fine of 5 pounds, in default one month's imprisonment. *The Maitland Mercury & Hunter River General*

Advertiser, 3 November 1881, p. 7.
60 John Brown Gribble, *Black But Comely, or, Glimpses of Aboriginal Life in Australia*, Morgan and Scott, London, 1884, p. 26.
61 *The Argus*, 14 May 1936, p. 7.
62 Kay Daniels, 'Prostitution in Tasmania during the transition from penal settlement to "civilised" society', in K. Daniels (ed.), *So Much Hard Work: Women and Prostitution in Australia*, Fontana, Sydney, 1984, pp. 15–86.
63 Daniels (ed.), *So Much Hard Work*, p. 3.
64 *Colonial Times*, 30 April 1830, p. 4.
65 Alfred Giles, *Northern Territory Times and Gazette*, 6 March 1886, p. 3.
66 Hill, 'The regulation of Aboriginal women'.
67 Cited in Kwaymullina, 'For marbles', p. 56.
68 'The Australian blacks', *The Nation*, vol. 80, no. 2077, 20 April 1905, pp. 308–10, p. 310.
69 McGrath, '"Black velvet"', p. 268.
70 ibid., p. 265.
71 Cited in Raymond Evans, '"Soiled doves": prostitution in colonial Queensland', in Daniels (ed.), *So Much Hard Work*, p. 139.
72 By 1897 over a hundred such women were operating in Childers, Innisfail and Cairns; by 1899 nineteen Japanese women worked in Mackay brothels and in 1902 thirty-one Japanese prostitutes, known as *Karayuki-san*, worked on Thursday Island. However, the Queensland police commissioner in 1897 categorised all Japanese women in the colony, aside from the consul's wife, as gaining 'their living by prostitution'. In addition under the Queensland Vagrancy Act of 1930, any house in which an 'Asiatic' woman lived could be considered a brothel. Ganter, 'The Wakayama triangle'; R. Ganter, 'Living an immoral life: "coloured" women and the paternalistic state', *Hecate*, vol. 24, no. 1, 1998, pp. 13–40.
73 Cited in Yuriko Nagata, 'The Japanese in Torres Strait', in Anna Shnukal, Guy Ramsay and Yuriko Nagata (eds), *Navigating Boundaries: The Asian Diaspora in Torres Strait*, Pandanus Books, Canberra, 2004, pp. 138–59.
74 Frank Fox, *Australia*, Adam and Charles Black, London, 1910, p. 140.
75 Marilyn Lake and Henry Reynolds, *Drawing the Global Colour Line: White Men's Countries and the Question of Racial Equality*, Melbourne University Press, Melbourne, 2008.
76 See Yûichi Murakami, 'Australia's immigration legislation, 1893–1901: the Japanese response', in Paul Jones and Vera Mackie (eds), *Relationships:*

Japan and Australia, 1870s–1930s, University of Melbourne, Melbourne, 2001, pp. 45–70; Lake and Reynolds, *Drawing the Global Colour Line.*
77 Nagata, 'Japanese in Torres Strait'.
78 M. M. Bennett, *The Australian Aboriginal as a Human Being,* Alston Rivers, London, 1930, pp. 113, 115, 118.
79 *Argus,* 23 March 1934, p. 10.
80 *Courier-Mail,* 12 January 1934, p. 6.
81 *Argus,* 14 May 1936, p. 7.
82 *Argus,* 30 June 1934, p. 17.
83 Report on the administration of the Northern Territory, 30 June 1933, p. 7.
84 The Pacific Islands Labourers Act (1901) instigated deportation of Melanesians living in Queensland from 1906. See Reynolds, *North of Capricorn,* p. xi; Museum of Australian Democracy <http://foundingdocs.gov.au/item-did-15.html>.
85 Fiona Paisley, 'Race hysteria, Darwin 1938', *Australian Feminist Studies,* vol. 16, no. 34, 2001, pp. 43–59, p. 45.
86 *Argus,* 3 September 1927, p. 33.
87 Kaino, '"Broome culture".
88 Paisley, 'Race hysteria', p. 46.
89 *West Australian,* 31 July 1937, cited in McGrath, '"Black velvet"', p. 277.
90 In fact 'Malay' referred to men from Java, Singapore, and the outer islands of the Dutch East Indies. 'Koepanger' could include men from Timor, the nearby islands of Alor or Solor, and sometimes anyone recruited through the Dutch colonial administrative offices in Koepang. Michael Schaper, 'The Broome race riots of 1920', *Studies in Western Australian History,* no. 16, 1995, pp. 112–132, p. 117.
91 Ronald Moore, 'The management of the West Australian pearling industry, 1860 to 1930', *Great Circle,* vol. 16, no. 2, 1994, pp. 121–138.
92 The divers sought sea pearl oyster *Pinetada maxima,* which was the principal material in the production of buttons and knife handles before plastic became common fare. By 1920, eighty per cent of the world's supply of mother-of-pearl shell came from the northern port town of Broome. Markets contracted from the onset of World War I and the pearling industry came under pressure, which intensified in the 1930s with the production of plastic substitutes, Japanese cultured pearls and the Great Depression. Yuriko Nagata, 'Japanese-Australians in the post-war Thursday Island community', *Queensland Review,* vol. 6, no. 2, 1999, pp. 30–43; Moore, 'Management of the West Australian pearling industry'.

93 Schaper, 'Broome race riots', p. 112.
94 Mary Durack cited in Schaper, 'Broome race riots', p. 118.
95 Ernestine Hill, *The Great Australian Loneliness*, Robertson and Mullens, Melbourne, 1942, pp. 242–43.
96 See Ganter, *Pearl-Shellers of Torres Strait*, p. 45.
97 See Mickey Dewar, 'Death in the gulf: a look at the motives behind the Caledon Bay and Woodah Island killings', *Journal of Northern Territory History*, no. 4, 1993, pp. 1–14, p. 6.
98 Donald Thomson, 'Wonggo of Caledon Bay: an Arnhem Land episode', *The Age*, 25 July 1959, p. 18.
99 'Tragic story of the Caledon Bay massacre', *Advertiser*, 13 October 1933, p. 23.
100 'Blacks sell womenfolk to lugger crews', *Argus*, 20 September 1935.
101 'Reports of sale of lubras', *The Sydney Morning Herald*, 23 September 1935.
102 'Black women exploited', *The Herald* (Melbourne), 24 September 1936.
103 'Lubras on luggers' (almost a slant rhyme with the 1937 film title, *Lovers and Luggers*), *Canberra Times*, 25 August 1936, p. 1.
104 'Japanese pearl poachers', *Daily Telegraph*, 26 May 1936.
105 'Lubras sold. Japanese hamper mission work. Barter increases', *The Sydney Morning Herald*, 25 September 1936.
106 'Lubras on pearling vessels', *Northern Standard*, 25 August 1936.
107 'Native girls in luggers', *The Herald*, 21 June 1937.
108 *The Canberra Times*, 25 September 1936, p. 5.
109 See John Morris, 'The Japanese and the Aborigines: an overview of the efforts to stop the prostitution of coastal and island women', *Journal of Northern Territory History*, no. 21, 2010, pp. 15–36.
110 F. M. Ashley-Montagu, 'The procreative theories of primitive man', *The Realist*, vol. 2, 1929, p. 92, pp. 87–96.
111 Reynolds, *North of Capricorn*, p. xi.
112 See John Morris, 'Potential allies of the enemy: the Tiwi in World War Two', *Journal of Northern Territory History*, no 15, 2004, pp. 77–90.
113 *Argus*, 26 September 1936, p. 5.
114 *Argus*, 31 December 1936, p. 8.
115 ibid.
116 *Argus*, 21 November 1936, p. 27.
117 J. W. Bleakley, Chief Protector of Aborigines in Queensland, noted in his 1928 inquiry into the condition of Aborigines and half-castes in the Northern Territory, 'Women find the temptation to supplement their meagre resources by trading in prostitution too strong to withstand'. Cited in McGrath, '"Black velvet"', p. 254.

118 Dumont d'Urville cited in Konishi, *Aboriginal Male*, p. 165.
119 *Canberra Times*, 6 April 1937, p. 2.
120 *Argus*, 6 April 1937, p. 10.
121 *Argus*, 8 April 1937, p. 12.
122 *Argus*, 6 April 1937, p. 10. 'Owner of 121 "wives". Monsignor Gsell in Sydney', *The Sydney Morning Herald*, 18 September 1937; 'Father Gsell's 150 wives. Subterfuge by a missionary on Bathurst Island', *Parade*, May 1966; 'NT mission priest bought "wives" by the hundred', *Daily Mirror*, 13 August 1980. John Morris argues these girls were thereby exempted from the promise-system of betrothal and could later marry young men of their choosing. See Morris, 'The Japanese and the Aborigines'.
123 The reference came in 1950 from the NT administrator Abbott, who described Gsell's system of buying baby girls from the elder men to stop the 'tribal practice of handing young girls of six or seven over to the old men of the tribe'. Gsell removed them to the mission station, 'where the nuns looked after them, and as they grew up they married Christianized native boys'. Any mention of prostitution to Japanese seems forgotten by 1950.
124 Ganter, 'Letters from Mapoon', p. 279.
125 Soon after two more boats were captured in Boucaut Bay, Arnhem Land, on 10 June 1937 and escorted to Darwin. The crew were released, reportedly because there was no room at Fanny Bay goal. *Argus*, 6 April 1937, p. 9.
126 *Argus*, 7 April 1937, p. 6.
127 *Argus*, 15 April 1937, p. 12.
128 *Canberra Times*, 21 April 1937, p. 1.
129 *Canberra Times*, 22 April 1937, p. 4.
130 See Morris, 'The Japanese and the Aborigines'.
131 *Argus*, 21 June 1937, p. 1.
132 *Argus*, 7 May 1937, p. 7.
133 *Canberra Times*, 22 June 1937, p. 2.
134 *Canberra Times*, 22 April 1937, p. 4.
135 Charles Barrett, *Blackfellows: The Story of Australia's Native Race*, Cassell & Co., London, 1942, p. 12.
136 'People of the territory', *Wild Life Magazine*, June 1944, p. 175.
137 ibid., pp. 175–77. By 1958 the men of Caledon Bay were said to have 'refused to lend their women' to the Japanese trepangers, who slighted them by thinking 'presents of tobacco gave them the right to take any native woman they wanted.' Clem Cleveson, 'The skull of peace', *People*, 19 February 1958, pp. 7–11, p. 7.

138 Harry Cox, 'Black velvet, *People*, 14 November 1956, pp. 27–31, p. 27.
139 ibid., p. 28.
140 'Territorians and mourning for Tiny', *The Sun-Herald*, 12 December 1954, p. 48.
141 Bhabha, *Location of Culture*, p. 149.
142 Hokari, 'Anti-minorities history', p. 10.
143 See, for example, Hill, *Great Australian Loneliness*, p. 230.
144 ibid., p. 230.
145 Ronald Croxford, 'Sunset of Yirrkala, but not of an age-old culture', *Smoke Signals*, vol. 6, no. 4, 1970, pp. 37–41.
146 Bennett, *Australian Aboriginal as a Human Being*, p. 114, fn. 2.
147 Ann McGrath, '"Modern stone-age slavery: images of Aboriginal labour and sexuality', *Labour History*, no. 69, 1995, p. 33.
148 Cited in Lisa B. Thompson, *Beyond the Black Lady: Sexuality and the New African American Middle Class*, Chicago, University of Illinois Press, 2009, p. 8.
149 Victorian Haskins and John Maynard, 'Sex, race and power: Aboriginal men and white women in Australian history', *Australian Historical Studies*, vol. 37, no. 126, 2005, pp. 191–216, p. 206.
150 A. Burton (ed.), *Gender, Sexuality and Colonial Modernities*, Routledge, London, 1999, p. 2.
151 Ross Gibson, *Seven Versions of an Australian Badland*, University of Queensland Press, Brisbane, 2002, p. 169.

Chapter 6

1 J. G. Wood, *The Natural History of Man; being an Account of the Manners and Customs of the Uncivilized Races of Men*, George Routledge and Sons, London, 1880, pp. 3, 5.
2 ibid., p. 6.
3 'The enemy of the Australian and Tasmanian Aborigines', *Scottish Review*, October 1860, pp. 380–92, p. 383.
4 Ernest Dawson, 'The prisoner', *The Living Age*, 14 May 1904, pp. 412–25, p. 418.
5 J. Deniker, *The Races of Man: An Outline of Anthropology and Ethnography*, Walter Scott, London, 1900, p. 477.
6 F. Eldershaw, *Australia as it really is, in its Life, Scenery & Adventure with the Character, Habits, and Customs of the Aboriginal Inhabitants, and the Prospects and Extent of its Goldfields*, Darton and Co., London, 1854, p. 89. Norton uses the same Latin in his 'Stray notes about our Aborigines', in *Science of Man*, vol. IX, no. 8, 1 August 1907, pp. 116–17, p. 117.

7   This phrase first appears in the press in 1883 and was popularised in J. G. Frazer's *The Golden Bough: A Study in Magic and Religion*, 1890, and then again in E. R. Burrough's *Tarzan of the Apes*, first serialised in *The All-Story*, 1912.
8   Jean Comoroff, 'The empire's old clothes: fashioning the colonial subject', in Louise Lamphere, Helena Ragone and Patricia Zavella (eds), *Situated Lives: Gender and Culture in Everyday Life*, New York, Routledge, 1997, pp. 400–420, p. 400.
9   Lieutenant R. N. Breton noted that Aborigines were not permitted to enter Sydney town unless clothed. Breton, *Excursions in New South Wales, Western Australia, & Van Dieman's Land, During the Years 1830, 1831, 1832 & 1833*, New York, 1970 (1834), p. 169.
10 Northern Territory, *Ordinances / The Northern Territory of Australia*, Commonwealth Government Printer, Canberra, 1911–1977; Aboriginals Ordinance 1911 (NT), accessed 28 February 2014, <http://www.findandconnect.gov.au/ref/nt/objects/YD0000001.htm>.
11 Robert Mudie, *The Picture of Australia: Exhibiting New Holland, Van Diemen's Land, and all the Settlements, From the First at Sydney to the Last at the Swan River*, Whittaker, Treacher, and Co., London, 1829, pp. 231, 232–33, 228–29.
12 Rosalyn Poignant, *Professional Savages: Captive Lives and Western Spectacle*, University of New South Wales Press, Sydney, 2004, pp. 8, 60.
13 Liz Conor, *The Spectacular Modern Woman: Feminine Visibility in the 1920s*, Indiana University Press, Bloomington, 2004, Chapter 6.
14 John Berger, *Ways of Seeing*, Penguin, London, 1972.
15 Martin Jay, *Downcast Eyes: The Denigration of Vision in Twentieth-Century French Thought*, University of California Press, Berkeley, 1994, p. 21.
16 Thomas R. Flynn, 'Foucault and the eclipse of vision', in David Levin (ed.), *Modernity and the Hegemony of Vision*, University of California Press, Los Angeles, 1993, p. 274.
17 See my discussion of gender asymmetry in perceptual relations in 'The status of the woman-object', in *The Spectacular Modern Woman*, Chapter 1.
18 Scott McQuire, *Visions of Modernity: Representation, Memory, Time and Space in the Age of the Camera*, Sage, London, 1997, p. 22.
19 David Levin situates the commencement of modernity with 'the "discovery" of perspective and the rationalization of sight in the Italian Renascimento of the fifteenth-century'. Levin (ed.), *Modernity and the Hegemony of Vision*, p. 2.
20 Jay, *Downcast Eyes*, p. 63.

21 ibid., pp. 63, 66.
22 Angela Wollacott, 'White colonialism and sexual modernity: Australian women in the early twentieth century metropolis', in A. Burton (ed.), *Gender, Sexuality and Colonial Modernities*, Routledge, London, 1999, p. 50.
23 Picture postcards emerged in the late 1890s but not until 1902 were they made available in Britain with divided backs for messages and postal addresses. See Christine Cane and Niel Gunson, 'Postcards: a source for Aboriginal biography', *Aboriginal History*, vol. 10, no. 1, 1986, p. 171.
24 Bernard Smith, *European Vision and the South Pacific*, Harper and Row, Sydney, 1985 (1969), pp. 326, pp. 50, 122.
25 'On the varieties of the human race', in Robert Montgomery Martin Esq (ed.), *The Colonial Magazine and Commercial-Maritime Journal*, vol. V, Fisher Son and Co., May–August 1841, London, p. 367.
26 *The History of New Holland*, John Stockdale, London, 1787, pp. 55, 69.
27 Cook quoted in Samuel Bennett, *The History of Australian Discovery and Colonisation*, Hanson and Bennett, Sydney, 1865, p. 106.
28 *History of New Holland*, p. 190.
29 Joseph D. Hooker (ed.), *Journal of the Right Hon. Sir Joseph Banks*, MacMillan & Co., London, 1896, pp. 308, 309.
30 *History of New Holland*, p. 186.
31 Marianna Torgovnick, *Gone Primitive: Savage Intellects and Modern Lives*, University of Chicago Press, Chicago, 1990, p. 46.
32 Mary Wollstonecraft, *A Vindication of the Rights of Woman*, Penguin Books, Harmondsworth, 1982 (1792), p. 131.
33 Also present were the twenty-seven wives of naval officers and colonial administrators. See A. G. L. Shaw, '1788–1810', in Frank Crowley (ed.), *A New History of Australia*, Heinemann, Melbourne, 1974, p. 6.
34 Wallis sailed in 1767 and is known for 'discovering' Tahiti, Bougainville in 1768, and La Perouse in 1785.
35 Liz Conor, '"This striking ornament of nature": the "native belle" in the Australian colonial scene', *Feminist Theory*, vol. 7, no. 2, 2006, pp. 197–218.
36 Wollstonecraft, *Vindication of the Rights of Woman*, p. 311.
37 Andrew Crombie, *After Sixty Years or Recollections of an Australian Bushman*, Watson, Ferguson & Co, Brisbane, 1927, p. 46.
38 Curr, *Recollections of Squatting*, p. 261–62.
39 Smith, *European Vision*, p. 329.
40 Péron cited in James Bonwick, *The Lost Tasmanian Race*, Sampson Low, Marston, Searle, and Rivington, London, 1884, p. 15.
41 Primitivist discourse is 'fundamental to the Western sense of self and Other'. See Torgovnick, *Gone Primitive*, p. 8.

42 Dominic D. Daly, *Digging, Squatting and Pioneering Life in the Northern Territory and South Australia*, Sampson Low, Marston, Searle and Rivington, London, 1887, p. 67.
43 Virginia Blum, *Flesh Wounds: The Culture of Cosmetic Surgery*, University of California Press, Berkeley, 2005, p. 126.
44 Anne Maxwell, *Colonial Photography and Exhibitions: Representations of the 'Native' and the Making of European Identities*, Leicester University Press, London, 1999, p. 38.
45 Paul T. Taylor, 'Malcom's conk and Danto's colors; or four logical petitions concerning race, beauty, and aesthetics', in Peg Zeglin Brand (ed.), *Beauty Matters*, Indiana University Press, Bloomington, 2000, p. 58.
46 *History of New Holland*, p. 27.
47 Quoted in Geoffrey Dutton, *White on Black: The Australian Aborigine Portrayed in Art*, MacMillan, Melbourne, 1974, p. 17.
48 'Aborigines of Australia', *The Penny Magazine*, vol. XI, no. 634, 19 February 1842, pp. 65–67, p. 65.
49 Maxwell, *Colonial Photography*, p. 39. See also Tommy L. Lott, *The Invention of Race: Black Culture and the Politics of Representation*, Malden, Blackwell, 1999, p. 8.
50 'Aborigines of Australia – Swan River. Their public life', in Robert Montgomery Martin, Esq. (ed.), *The Colonial Magazine and Commercial-Maritime Journal*, vol. V, May–August, 1841, p. 424.
51 Maxwell, *Colonial Photography*, p. 41.
52 Tony Hughes-d'Aeth, *Paper Nation: The Story of the Picturesque Atlas of Australasia, 1886–1888*, Melbourne University Press, Melbourne, 2001, p. 191.
53 *Report of the Select Committee of the Legislative Council, upon 'the Aborigines;' together with Minutes of Evidence and Appendix*, South Australian Legislative Council, W. C. Cox, Government Printer, Adelaide, 1860, p. 378, accessed 30 October 2015, <http://aiatsis.gov.au/archive_digitised_collections/_files/archive/removeprotect/92284.pdf>.
54 Albert F. Calvert, The Aborigines of Western Australia, W. Milligan & Co., London, 1892, p. 6.
55 W. F. Ainsworth (ed.), *All Around the World: An Illustrated Record of Voyages, Travels, and Adventures in all Parts of the Globe*, William Collins and Sons, London, 1860 p. 311.
56 'Report of the Select Committee of the Legislative Council on the Aborigines', *The North British Review*, vol. XXXII, February–March 1860, pp. 366–88, pp. 377, 380.
57 See Ian Hacking, *Representing and Intervening: Introductory Topics in the Philosophy of Natural Science*, Cambridge University Press, Cambridge,

1983, p. 234. Quoted in Jonathan Crary, *Techniques of the Observer: On Vision and Modernity in the Nineteenth Century,* MIT Press, Cambridge, 1990, p. 17.

58 From an officer of the First Fleet, quoted in W. E. H. Stanner, 'The history of indifference thus begins', *Aboriginal History,* vol. 1, no. 1, 1977, p. 18.

59 James Clifford, 'Histories of the tribal and the modern', in Kymberly N. Pender (ed.), *Race-ing Art History: Critical Readings in Race and Art History,* Routledge, New York and London, 2002, p. 140; Abigail Solomon-Godeau, 'Going native', *Art in America,* 1989, pp. 119–29, 161 (discussing Gauguin's years in Brittany and Polynesia).

60 See Stephen Muecke's discussion of how modernity incorporates and represses the ancient as represented by traditional indigeneity. *Ancient and Modern: Time Culture and Indigenous Philosophy,* University of New South Wales Press, Sydney, 2004.

61 Robert Dawson, 'State of New South Wales', quoted in 'The Aborigines of Australia', *The Asiatic Journal and Monthly Register for British and Foreign India, China and Australasia,* vol. IV, January–April, 1831, p. 124.

62 The unnamed author disputes the descriptions of M. Bory de St Vincent in *The Westminster Review,* vol. XII, Oct 1829–Jan 1830.

63 George French Angas, 'On the Aboriginal inhabitants of N. S. Wales', *Waugh's Australian Almanac,* James W. Waugh, Sydney, 1858, p. 53.

64 Dr J. B. Clutterbuck's account of 'Port Phillip in 1849' in *The Illustrated London News,* 26 January 1850, p. 53.

65 Elazar Barkan, 'Rethinking orientalism: representations of "primitives" in western culture at the turn of the century', *History of European Ideas,* vol. 15, nos 4–6, 1992, pp. 759–65, p. 761.

66 Anne McClintock, *Imperial Leather: Race, Gender and Sexuality in the Colonial Contest,* Routledge, New York, 1995, p. 44. See also Poignant's analysis of the exhibition of 'freaks', living 'curiosities', the congenitally impaired and exotic indigenous in travelling circuses, fairgrounds, international exhibits, theatres and museums in the nineteenth century. *Professional Savages,* p. 84. See also Maxwell, *Colonial Photography,* p. 82.

67 Noel Carroll, 'Ethnicity, race, and monstrosity: the rhetorics of horror and humor', in Peg Zeglin Brand (ed.), *Beauty Matters,* Indiana University Press, Bloomington, 2000, p. 37.

68 Lott, *Invention of Race,* pp. 7–13.

69 Sander Gilman, 'The hottentot and the prostitute: toward an iconography of female sexuality', in Kymberly N. Pinder (ed.), *Race-ing*

Art History: Critical Readings in Race and Art History, Routledge, New York, 2002, p. 121.

70 William Ramsay Smith, 'Aborigines', in the *Australian Encyclopedia*, Sydney, Angus & Robertson, 1927, p. 16.

71 Editors of the *Port Phillip Gazette* (unnamed), *Latest Information with Regard to Australia Felix, The Finest Province of the Great Territory of New South Wales; including The History, Geography, Natural Resources, Government, Commerce, and Finances of Port Phillip; Sketches of the Aboriginal Population and Advice to Immigrants*, Arden and Strode, Melbourne, 1840, p. 96.

72 George French Angas, *Savage Life and Scenes in Australia and New Zealand*, vol. 1, 2nd edn, Smith, Elder and Co, London, 1847, p. 80.

73 Robert Brown, *The Races Of Mankind: A Popular Description of the Characteristics, Manners and Customs of the Principal Varieties of the Human Family*, Cassell, London, 1873, p. 114.

74 Howard Willoughby, *Australian Pictures: Drawn with Pen and Pencil*, Religious Tract Society, London, 1886, p. 168.

75 J. R. McCulloch, *Dictionary, Geographical, Statistical, and Historical of the Various Countries, Places and Principal Natural Objects in the World*, Longman, Brown, Green, and Longmans, London, 1854, p. 228, pp. 228–31.

76 J. D. Woods, 'Introduction', in Reverend George Taplin, *The Native Tribes of South Australia*, E. S. Wigg & Son, Adelaide, 1879, p. xxxv.

77 Ramsay Smith, 'Aborigines', pp. 18, 20.

78 McClintock, *Imperial Leather*, p. 5.

79 Gilman, 'The hottentot and the prostitute', p. 121, fn. 7.

80 Solomon-Godeau, 'Going native'; see also Clifford, 'Histories of the tribal and the modern', p. 143.

81 Zeglin Brand, *Beauty Matters*, p. xv.

82 *The Sydney Gazette and New South Wales Advertiser*, 22 January 1833, p. 2.

83 'Aborigines of Australia', *The Penny Magazine*, vol. XI, no. 634, 1842, p. 66.

84 Richard Cannon, *Savage Scenes from Australia*, Imprenta del Universo de G. Helfmann, Valparaíso, 1885, p. 17.

85 Frank Jardine married Sana Sola, niece of the Samoan King. Clem Lack, 'Jardine, Francis Lascelles (Frank) (1841–1919)', *Australian Dictionary of Biography*, National Centre of Biography, Australian National University, 1972, accessed 27 February 2014, <http://adb.anu.edu.au/biography/jardine-francis-lascelles-frank-3924/text6117>; Nonie Sharp, *Footprints along the Cape York Sandbeaches*, Aboriginal Studies Press, Canberra, 1992.

Notes

86 Mr J. H. Palmer, *Empire*, 14 August 1857, p. 2.
87 Eyre extract as quoted in '"This striking ornament of nature"', p. 206.
88 Palmer, *Empire*, p. 2.
89 J. Brunton Stephens, 'To a black gin', *Northern Territory Times and Gazette*, 20 April 1878, p. 2. Stephens's verses are reprinted in a collection of published broadcast lectures, Herbert Basedow (ed.), *Coo-ee Talks: A Collection of Lecturettes upon Early Experiences among the Aborigines of Australia delivered from a Wireless Broadcasting Station*, Angus & Robertson, Sydney, 1928, p. 2.
90 Michael Davitt, *Life and Progress in Australasia*, Methuen, London, 1896, pp. 37, 38.
91 B. F. S. Baden-Powell, *In Savage Isles and Settled Lands*, Richard Bentley & Son, London, 1892, p. 118.
92 *Northern Territory Times and Gazette*, 2 April 1914, p. 14.
93 Edward M. Curr, *The Australian Race: Its Origins, Languages, Customs, Place of Landing in Australia and the Routes by which it spread itself over the Continent*, vol. 2, John Ferres Government Printer, Melbourne, 1886, p. 40.
94 'The Aborigines of Western Australia', in J. S. Battye (ed.), *Cyclopedia of Western Australia*, vol. 1, Hassey and Gillingham, Adelaide, 1912–13, p. 51, pp. 45–62.
95 Charles H. Holmes, *We Find Australia*, Hutchinson & Co., London, 1933, p. 134.
96 Herbert Basedow, *Knights of the Boomerang: Episodes from a Life Spent Among the Native Tribes of Australia*, Hesperian Press, Perth, 2004 (1935), p. 7.
97 C. P. Mountford and Alison Harvey, 'Women of the Adnjamatana tribe of the Northern Flinders Ranges, South Australia', *Oceania*, vol. 12, 1941–42, pp. 155–63, p. 156.
98 Philippa Levine, 'States of undress: nakedness and the colonial imagination', *Victorian Studies*, vol. 50, no. 2, 2008, pp. 189–219, p. 192.
99 R. S. Walpole Esq, 'Suggestions as to the origin and geographical distribution of the aborigines of Australia', *The Royal Geographical Society of Australasia* (Victoria), vol. XVII, 1899, p. 62.
100 Malvina Hoffman, *Heads and Tales*, Charles Scribner's Sons, New York, 1936, pp. 11, 13.
101 James Backhouse, 'The Tasmanian Aborigines', in *Papers and Proceedings, Royal Society of Tasmania*, Davies Brothers, Hobart, 1898–1899, pp. 65–73, p. 65.
102 Professor MacKenzie is commenting on the discovery of the Cohuna

skull in Victoria. MacKenzie argued that the upper jaw projection, 'is that of a man in such a primitive form that he had barely learned to stand upright…the skull is that of a male who probably shambled along on all fours most of the time and the projected jaw indicates that he rooted for his food in the ground when necessary. He was undoubtedly extremely hairy and by the standards of modern man abominably ugly.' Quoted in *Mankind*, vol. 4, no. 8, March 1952, p. 315.

103 'About our Aborigines', *The Inlander*, vol. 2, first quarter, 1915, pp. 22, 27.
104 McClintock, *Imperial Leather*, p. 72.
105 Hugh MacClean, *Aussie*, 14 April 1927, p. 10.
106 'The Aborigines', *The Illustrated Australian Magazine*, vol. III, July 1851, p. 48.
107 'Aborigines of Australia', *The Penny Magazine*, vol. XI, 1842, p. 65.
108 'Report of the Select Committee 1860', *The North British Review*, p. 382.
109 Angas, *Savage Life and Scenes*, p. 80.
110 See my discussion of black-and-white artists Hugh Maclean, Mick Paul and B. E. Minns in *The Spectacular Modern Woman*, pp. 182–208.
111 Charles Chewing, *Back in the Stone Age: The Natives of Central Australia*, Angus & Robertson, Sydney, 1936, p. 118.
112 Charles Barrett and A. S. Kenyon, 'Blackfellows of Australia', Lawrence Kay for Pictorial Newspapers, Melbourne, c. 1936, p. 7.
113 Ernestine Hill, 'Black man's day', *Walkabout*, 1 August 1940, pp. 29–47, p. 30.
114 'People of the territory', *Wild Life Magazine*, June 1944, p. 175, pp. 175–77.
115 Charles Barrett, illustrated by Ivor Horman, 'An ancient people', *Rydge's*, 1 December 1947, p. 1093.
116 The Antipodes – meaning 'opposite footed' – had preoccupied Europeans since Cicero speculated that it was an inverted geography inhabited by people with opposite traits, with mouths in their chests who walked upside down. Yohanes Hartadi, 'An allegorical reading of Australia in European imaginative writings and exploration journals', seminar, 12 October 2005, Australian Centre, University of Melbourne.
117 Solomon-Godeau, 'Going native', p. 146.
118 French photographer Désiré Charnay travelled to Coranderrk in 1878 and 'sent them to the devil' when his subjects rose their fee from 5 shillings to 20 in one day. Photographer Robert Brough Smyth noted in 1870 'they are careful in the matter of clothing' and that they would be offended if asked to pose naked. Quoted in Jane Lydon, *Eye Contact:*

Notes

Photographing Indigenous Australians, Duke University Press, Durham, 2005.
119 Brough Smyth cited in Australian and New Zealand Association for the Advancement of Science, *Handbook for Victoria*, H. J. Green Government Printer, Melbourne, 1935, p. 138.
120 T. P. Bellchambers, *A Nature-Lover's Notebook*, Nature Lover's League, Adelaide, 1931, p. 180.
121 Basedow, *Knights of the Boomerang*, p. 2.
122 T. Athol Joyce and N. W. Thomas, *Women of All Nations: A Record of Their Characteristics, Habits, Manners, Customs & Influence*, Cassell and Co., London, 1908, p. 135.

Appendix
1 First recording of Aboriginal song. Arrangement for sheet music advertised four times in the *Sydney Gazette and New South Wales Advertiser* between November and December 1934.

BIBLIOGRAPHY

Primary sources
Books and articles

'The Aborigines of Western Australia', in J. S. Battye (ed.), *Cyclopedia of Western Australia*, vol. 1, Hassey and Gillingham, Adelaide, 1912–13, pp. 45–62.

Ainsworth, W. F. (ed.), *All Around the World: An Illustrated Record of Voyages, Travels, and Adventures in all Parts of the Globe*, William Collins and Sons, London, 1860.

Anderson, George William (ed.), *A New, Authentic, and Complete Collection of Voyages Round the World Undertaken and Performed by Royal Authority. Containing a New...Account of Captain Cook's...Voyages*, Alex Hogg, London, 1784.

Angas, George French, *Savage Life and Scenes in Australia and New Zealand*, vol. 1, 2nd edn, Smith, Elder and Co., London, 1847.

Armstrong, Francis, 'Manners and Habits of the Aborigines of Western Australia', *The Perth Gazette and Western Australian Journal*, 29 October 1836, p. 790.

'Attacks on the overland routes to Port Phillip', *Historical Records of Victoria, Volume 2A: The Aborigines of Port Phillip 1835–1839*, Victorian Government Printing Office, Melbourne, 1982, pp. 312–42.

Australian and New Zealand Association for the Advancement of Science, *Handbook for Victoria*, H. J. Green Government Printer, Melbourne, 1935.

Baden-Powell, B. F. S., *In Savage Isles and Settled Lands*, Richard Bentley & Son, London, 1892.

Barker, Sidney J., *The Australian Language*, Currawong Publishing Co., Sydney, 1966.

Barrett, Charles, *Blackfellows: The Story of Australia's Native Race*, Cassell & Co., London, 1942.

Barrington, George, *The History of New South Wales: Including Botany Bay...*, M. Jones, London, 1802.

Bibliography

Basedow, Herbert (ed.), *Coo-ee Talks: A Collection of Lecturettes upon Early Experiences among the Aborigines of Australia Delivered from a Wireless Broadcasting Station*, Angus & Robertson, Sydney, 1928.

Basedow, Herbert, *Knights of the Boomerang: Episodes from a Life Spent among the Native Tribes of Australia*, Hesperian Press, Perth, 2004 (1935).

Bates, Daisy, *Passing of the Aborigines*, John Murray, London, 1944.

Beers, Fannie A., *Memories. A Record of Personal Experience and Adventure During Four Years of War*, J. B. Lippencott, Philadephia, 1888.

Bellchambers, T. P., *A Nature-Lover's Notebook*, Nature Lover's League, Adelaide, 1931.

Bennett, George, *Wanderings in New South Wales, Batavia, Pedir Coast, Singapore, and China; Being the Journal of a Naturalist in those Countries during 1832, 1833, and 1834*, vol. 1, Richard Bentley, London, 1834.

Bennett, M. M., *The Australian Aboriginal as a Human Being*, Alston Rivers, London, 1930.

Bennett, M. M., *Teaching the Aborigines: Data from Mount Margaret Mission*, 1935.

Bennett, Samuel, *The History of Australian Discovery and Colonisation*, Hanson and Bennett, Sydney, 1865.

Bettany, George T., *The Red, Brown, and Black Men of America and Australia and their White Supplanters*, Ward, Lock and Co., London, 1890.

Bleakley, J. W., 'The Aborigines and half castes of central and north Australia', in Sharman Stone, *Aborigines in White Australia: A Documentary History of the Attitudes Affecting Official Policy and the Australian Aborigine 1697–1973*, Heinemann, South Yarra, 1974, p. 155.

Blumenbach, Johann, *On the Natural Variety of Mankind*, in *The Anthropological* James A. Farrer, *Primitive Manners and Customs*, Chatto & Windus, London, 1879.

Bonwick, James, *William Buckley, the Wild White Man, and his Port Phillip Black Friends*, Nichols, Melbourne, 1856.

Bonwick, James, *Port Phillip Settlement*, Sampson, Low, Marston, Searle & Rivington, London, 1883.

Bonwick, James, *The Lost Tasmanian Race*, Sampson Low, Marston, Searle, and Rivington, London, 1884.

Boule, Marcellin, *Fossil Men*, 2nd edn, trans. J. E. and J. Ritchie, Edinburgh, 1923.

Boyce, William D., *Illustrated Australia and New Zealand*, Rana McNally & Company, Chicago, 1922.

Breton, Lieutenant R. N., *Excursions in New South Wales, Western Australia, & Van Dieman's Land, During the Years 1830, 1831, 1832 & 1833*, New York, Johnson Reprint Corp., 1970 (1834).

Bride, Thomas Francis (ed.), *Letters from Victorian Pioneers, Being a Series of Papers in the Early Occupation of the Colony, The Aborigines, etc.*, ed. by C. E. Sayers, William Heinemann, Melbourne, 1969 (1898).

Brough Smyth, R., *The Aborigines of Victoria: with Notes Relating to the Habits of the Natives of Other Parts of Australia and Tasmania*, vol. II, John Ferres, Melbourne, 1878.

Brown, Robert, *The Races Of Mankind: A Popular Description of the Characteristics, Manners and Customs of the Principal Varieties of the Human Family*, Cassell, Petter & Galpin, London, 1873.

Browne, C. S., *Australia: A General Account*, Thomas Nelson & Sons, London, 1929.

Bryan, Michael, *Bryan's Dictionary of Painters and Engravers*, Macmillan, New York, 1903.

Burrough, E. R., *Tarzan of the Apes*, first serialised in *The All-Story*, 1912.

Calvert, Albert F., *The Aborigines of Western Australia*, W. Milligan & Co., London, 1892.

Calvert, Albert F., *The Discovery of Australia*, George Philip & Son, London, 1893.

Campbell, Rev. Peter, *Trucanini! Or Lalla Rookh. The Last of the Tasmanian Aborigines*, Hobart, 1876.

Cannon, Richard, *Savage Scenes from Australia*, Imprenta del Universo de G. Helfmann, Valparaíso, 1885.

Carnegie, David W., *Spinifex and Sand: A Narrative of Five Years Pioneering and Exploration in Western Australia*, C. Arthur Pearson, London, 1898.

Chauvel, Charles, and Chauvel, Elsa, *Walkabout*, W. H. Allen, London, 1959.

Chewing, Charles, *Back in the Stone Age: The Natives of Central Australia*, Angus & Robertson, Sydney, 1936.

Choris, Louis, *Voyage pittoresque autour du monde: avec des portraits de sauvages d'Amérique, d'Asie, d'Afrique, et des îles du Grand ocean; des paysages, des vues maritimes, et plusieurs objets d'histoire naturelle*, De l'Imprimerie de Firmin Didot, Paris, 1822.

Clark, Alice, *Working Life of Women in the Seventeenth Century*, Frank Cass, Oxon, 1919.

Clune, Frank, *Roaming around Australia*, Hawthorn Press, Melbourne, 1947.

Coates, D., Beecham, John, and Ellis, William, *Christianity the Means of Civilization: Shown in Evidence given before a Committee of the House of Commons on Aborigines*, R. B. Seeley and W. Burnside, London, 1837.

Colebatch, Hal (ed.), *A Story of a Hundred Years: Western Australia, 1829–1929*, Government Printer, Perth, 1929.

Collins, David, *An Account of the English Colony in New South Wales: with*

Bibliography

Remarks on the Dispositions, Customs, Manners, Etc. of the Native Inhabitants of that Country. To which are added, some particulars of New Zealand; compiled, by permission, from the Mss. of Lieutenant-Governor King, vol. 1, T. Cadell Jun. and W. Davies, London, 1798.

Cook, James, *Voyages in the Southern Hemisphere*, vols II–III, 1773, accessed 2 March 2013, <http://southseas.nla.gov.au/journals/hv23/minor_title.html>.

Cook, James, *A voyage towards the South Pole, and Round the World: performed in His Majesty's ships the Resolution and Adventure, in the years 1772, 1773, 1774, and 1775 / written by James Cook, Commander of the Resolution. In which is included Captain Furneaux's narrative of his proceedings in the Adventure during the separation of the ships. In two volumes. Illustrated with maps and charts, and a variety of portraits of persons and views of places drawn during the Voyage by Mr. Hodges and engraved by the most eminent Masters*, W. Strahan and T. Cadell, London, 1777.

Cook, James, *Captain Cook's Journal During his first Voyage round the World made in H.M. Bark 'Endeavour' 1768–1771*, Elliot Stock, London, 1893.

Cornwallis, Kinahan, *A Panorama of the New World in Two Volumes*, vol. 1, T. C. Newby, London, 1859.

Coutts, P. J. F. and Witter, D. C., *A Guide to Recording Archaeological Sites in Victoria*, Records of the Victorian Archaeological Survey no. 3, Aboriginal Affairs Victoria, Melbourne, 1977, accessed 15 March 2014, <http://search.informit.com.au/documentSummary;dn=882700728563068;res=IELIND>.

Cramp, K. R., *A Series of Lessons on Aboriginal Life*, Education Society, William Applegate Gullick, Government Printer, Sydney, 1910.

Crombie, Andrew, *After Sixty Years or Recollections of an Australian Bushman*, Watson, Ferguson & Co, Brisbane, 1927.

Cross, Stuart K., 'On a numerical determination of the relative positions of certain biological types in the evolutionary scale, and of the relative values of various cranial measurements and indices as criteria', *Proceedings of the Royal Society of Edinburgh*, vol. XXXI, pt. 1, 1910–1911.

Cunningham, Peter, *Two Years in New South Wales: A Series of Letters, comprising, Sketches of the Actual State of Society in that Colony...* vol. 2, Henry Colburn, London, 1827.

Curr, Edward M., *Recollections of Squatting in Victoria then called the Port Phillip District (from 1841–1851)*, G. Robertson, Melbourne, 1883.

Curr, Edward M., *The Australian Race: Its Origins, Languages, Customs, Place of Landing in Australia and the Routes by which it spread itself over the Continent*, vol. 1, John Ferres Government Printer, Melbourne, 1886.

Curr, Edward M., *The Australian Race: Its Origins, Languages, Customs, Place of Landing in Australia and the Routes by which it spread itself over the Continent*, vol. 2, John Ferres Government Printer, Melbourne, 1886.

Daly, Dominic D., *Digging, Squatting and Pioneering Life in the Northern Territory and South Australia*, Sampson Low, Marston, Searle & Rivington, London, 1887.

Dampier, William, *New Voyage Around the World*, James Knapton, London, 1697.

Dampier, William, *Dampier's Voyages*, ed. by John Masefield, E. Grants Richards, London, 1906.

Darwin, Charles, *The Descent of Man and Selection in Relation to Sex*, Princeton University Press, Princeton, 1981 (1879).

Davies, R. H., 'On the Aborigines of Van Diemen's Land', reprinted from the *Tasmanian Journal of Natural Science* by the British Association for the Advancement of Science in the (Hobart) *Courier*, 7 March 1846, p. 4.

Davitt, Michael, *Life and Progress in Australasia*, Methuen, London, 1896.

Dawson, J. W., *Fossil Men and Their Modern Representatives*, London, 1883.

Dawson, Robert. *The Present State of Australia; a Description of the Country, its Advantages, and Prospects, with Reference to Emigration; and a Particular Account of the Manners, Customs, and Condition of its Aboriginal Inhabitants*, extracted in *Asiatic Journal and Monthly Register for British and Foreign India, China and Australasia*, vol. 4, January–April 1830.

Degérando, Joseph-Marie, 'The observation of savage peoples' [1800], in Antonius Robbin and Jeffrey Sluka (eds), *Ethnographic Fieldwork: An Anthropological Reader*, Blackwell, Oxford, 2007, pp. 33–39.

Deniker, J., *The Races of Man: An Outline of Anthropology and Ethnography*, Walter Scott, London, 1900, p. 477.

Diderot, Denis, *Supplément au voyage de Bougainville*, H. Dieckmann, Geneva, 1955 (first published 1796, written 1772).

Duncan-Kemp, A. M., *Where Strange Paths Go Down*, W. R. Smith and Paterson, Brisbane, 1964.

Duprat, F. A., *Histoire de l'Imprimerie impériale de France; suivie des specimens des types etrangers et francais*, De l'Imprimerie imperiale, Paris, 1861. <http://www.archive.org/stream/histoiredelimpri00dupruoft#page/n3/mode/2up>.

Durack, Mary, *Kings in Grass Castles*, Constable, London, 1959.

Eden, Charles Henry, 'An Australian search party', in H. W. Bates (ed.), *Illustrated Travels: A Record of Discovery, Geography and Adventure*, Cassell, Petter and Galpain, London, 1869.

Editors of the *Port Phillip Gazette* (unnamed), *Latest Information with Regard to*

Bibliography

Australia Felix, The Finest Province of the Great Territory of New South Wales; including The History, Geography, Natural Resources, Government, Commerce, and Finances of Port Phillip; Sketches of the Aboriginal Population and Advice to Immigrants, Arden and Strode, Melbourne, 1840.

Eldershaw, F., *Australia as it really is, in its Life, Scenery & Adventure with the Character, Habits, and Customs of the Aboriginal Inhabitants, and the Prospects and Extent of its Goldfields*, Darton and Co., London, 1854.

Elkin, A. P., 'The social life and intelligence of the Australian Aborigine: a review of S. D. Porteous's *Psychology of a Primitive People*', Oceania, vol. III, 1932–33, pp. 101–113.

Fison, Lorimer, and Howitt, Alfred William, *Kamilaroi and Kurnai: group marriage customs and relationships, and marriage by elopement drawn chiefly from the usage of the Australian Aborigines; also, The Kurnai tribe, their customs in peace and war*, George Robinson, Melbourne, 1879

Flanagan, Roderick J., *The Aborigines of Australia*, Edward F. Flanagan and George Robertson and Company, Sydney, 1888.

Fox, Frank, *Australia*, Adam and Charles Black, London, 1910.

Fox, G., 'Ethnology: the Australian Aborigines', *Science of Man*, vol. X, no. 4, 20 August 1908, pp. 56–61.

Frazer, J. G., *The Golden Bough: A Study in Magic and Religion*, Macmillan and Co., New York and London, 1890.

Gaya, Louis de, *Ceremonies Nuptiales de toute les Nations*, Etienne Michallet, Paris, 1680.

Gladys, Ngoondaw, 'Saint George', Mount Margaret Aboriginal Mission, 1935.

Graves, Algernon, *The Royal Academy Exhibitors*, H. Graves, London, 1905.

Gregory, William King, 'Australia, the land of living fossils, as exemplified in the proposed exhibition, American Museum', *Natural History*, no. 24, 1924, pp. 5–15.

Grenfell Price, A., *White Settlers and Native Peoples*, Georgian House, Melbourne, 1949.

Extracts from the Papers and Proceedings of the Aborigines Protection Society, no. VI, December 1839, William Ball, Arnold, and Co., London.

Gribble, John Brown, *Black but Comely, or, Glimpses of Aboriginal Life in Australia*, Morgan and Scott, London, 1884.

Gunn, Mrs Aeneas, *We of the Never Never*, A. Moring, London, 1905.

Gunn, Mrs Aeneas, *The Little Black Princess*, Angus and Robertson, Sydney, 1905.

Hammerton, J. A., *People of All Nations*, Educational Book Co., London, 1920–1938.

Hawkesworth, John, *An account of the voyages undertaken by the order of His present Majesty, for making discoveries in the southern hemisphere, and successively performed by Commodore Byron, Captain Wallis, Captain Carteret, and Captain Cook, in the Dolphin, the Swallow, and the Endeavour: drawn up from the journals which were kept by the several commanders and from the papers of Joseph Banks*, W. Strahan and T. Cadell, London, 1773.

Hill, Ernestine, *The Great Australian Loneliness*, Robertson and Mullens, Melbourne, 1943.

The History of New Holland, John Stockdale, London, 1787.

Hobhouse, L. T., and Wheeler, G. C., *The Material Culture and Social Institutions of the Simpler Peoples*, Chapman & Hall, London, 1915.

Hobson, John A., *The Psychology of Jingoism*, Grant Richards, London, 1901.

Hoffman, Malvina, *Heads and Tales*, Charles Scribner's Sons, New York, 1936.

Holmes, Charles H., *We Find Australia*, Hutchinson & Co., London, 1933.

Hooker, Joseph D. (ed.), *Journal of the Right Hon. Sir Joseph Banks during Captain Cook's first voyage in H.M.S. Endeavour in 1768–71 to Terra del Fuego, Otahite, New Zealand, Australia, the Dutch East Indies, etc.*, Macmillan, London, 1896.

Howitt, A. W., and Fison, Rev. L., 'From mother-right to father-right', *Journal of the Anthropological Institute of Great Britain and Ireland*, vol. 12, 1883, pp. 30–46.

Howitt, A. W., *The Native Tribes of South-east Australia*, Macmillan and Co., London, 1904.

The Illustrated Handbook of Western Australia (Paris International Exhibition 1900), Government Printer, Perth, 1900.

Joyce, T. Athol, and Thomas, N. W., *Women of All Nations: A Record of Their Characteristics, Habits, Manners, Customs & Influence*, Cassell and Co., London, 1908.

Kaberry, Phyllis M., *Aboriginal Woman: Sacred and Profane*, Routledge, London, 1939.

Keane, Augustus Henry, *Man, Past and Present*, Cambridge University Press, London, revised edn, 1920 (1899).

Krzywicki, Ludwik, *Primitive Society and its Vital Statistics*, MacMillan and Co., London, 1934.

Lang, John Dunmore, *Queensland, Australia: a highly eligible field for emigration, and the future cotton-field of Great Britain: with a disquisition on the origin, manners, and customs of the Aborigines*, Edward Stanford, London, 1861.

Lavater, Johann Kaspter, *Physiognomische Fragmente zur Beförderung der Menschenkenntnis und Menschenliebe*, Orell Füssli, Zurich, 1775–1778.

Bibliography

Linneai, Caroli, *Systema Naturae per Regna Tria Naturae, Secundum Classes, Ordines, Genera, Species, cum Characteribus, Differentiis, Synominis, Locis* [System of nature through the three kingdoms of nature, according to classes, orders, genera, and species, with [generic] characters, [specific] differences, synonyms and places], 10th edn, Holmiae, Laurentii Salvii, Stockholm, 1758.

Lubbock, John, *The Origin of Civilisation and the Primitive Condition of Man: Mental and Social Conditions of Savages*, Spottiswoode and Co, London, 1870.

Lumholtz, Carl, *Among Cannibals: An Account of Four Years' Travels in Australia and of Camp Life with the Aborigines of Queensland*, Charles Scribner's Sons, New York, 1889.

McCombie, Rev. Dr, *Australian Sketches*, W. Johnson, London, 1861, p. 155.

McCulloch, J. R. (ed.), *Dictionary, Geographical, Statistical, and Historical of the Various Countries, Places and Principal Natural Object in the World*, Longman, Brown, Green, and Longmans, London, 1854.

McLennan, John F., *Primitive Marriage: An Inquiry into the Origin of the Form of Capture in Marriage Ceremonies*, Adam and Charles Black, Edinburgh, 1865.

Malinowski, Bronislaw, *The Family Among the Australian Aborigines: A Sociological Study*, University of London Press, London, 1913.

Malthus, Thomas R., *An Essay on the Principle of Population*, J. M. Dent, London, 1973 (1798).

Mann's Emigrant's Guide to Australia; including The Colonies of New South Wales, Port Phillip. South Australia, Western Australia, and Moreton Bay, William Strange, London, 1849.

Marra, John, *Journal of the Resolution's voyage, in 1772, 1773, 1774, and 1775, on discovery to the southern hemisphere, by which the non-existence of an undiscovered continent, between the Equator and the 50th degree of southern latitude is demonstratively proved: also a journal of the Adventure's voyage, in the years 1772, 1773, and 1774*, F. Newbery, London, 1775.

Marshall, Allan, *Ourselves Writ Strange*, F. W. Cheshire, Melbourne, 1948, p. 83.

Massola, Aldo, 'The rock-shelter at Mudgegonga', *Field Naturalists Club of Victoria*, vol. 83, no. 4, April 1966.

Mattingley, Harold V., 'The teeth of some Australian Aboriginal natives, and comparisons with the teeth of prehistoric man', *Commonwealth Dental Review*, vol. XII, 1915, pp. 388–94.

Meyer, H. A. E., 'Manners and customs of the Encounter Bay tribe, South Australia', G. Dehane, Adelaide, 1846.

Miln, Louise Jordan, *Little Folks of Many Lands,* John Murray, London, 1899.

Miller, Nathan, *The Child in Primitive Society,* Kegan Paul, Trench, Trubner & Co, London, 1928.

Moore, William, *The Story of Australian Art,* Angus and Robertson, Sydney, 1934.

Morgan, John, *The Life and Times of William Buckley thirty-two years a wanderer amongst the aborigines of then unexplored country round Port Phillip, now the province of Victoria,* A. MacDougall, Hobart, 1852.

Morgan, Margaret, *Mt Margaret: A Drop in the Bucket,* Mission Publications, Lawson, 1986.

Mount Margaret Mission, *Annual Report,* United Aborigines Mission, Mt Margaret Branch, 1957.

Mudie, Robert, *The Picture of Australia: Exhibiting New Holland, Van Diemen's Land, and all the Settlements, From the First at Sydney to the Last at the Swan River,* Whittaker, Treacher, and Co., London, 1829.

Orton, Rev. Joseph, *Aborigines of Australia,* Thoms, London, 1836.

Page, David, *Man, Where, Whence, and Whither: Being a Glance at Man in his Natural-History Relations,* Edmonston and Douglas, Edinburgh, 1867.

Parkinson, Sydney, *A journal of a voyage to the South Seas, in His Majesty's ship, the Endeavour / faithfully transcribed from the papers of the late Sydney Parkinson...: embellished with views and designs, delineated by the Author, and engraved by capital artists,* Stanfield Parkinson, London, 1773.

Péron, François, *Voyage de découvertes aux terres australes...,* De l'Imprimerie Imperiale, Paris, 1807.

Péron, François, *Voyage of Discovery to the Southern Hemisphere Performed by Order of the Emperor Napoleon, During the Years 1801, 1802, 1803, and 1804,* Richard Phillips, London, 1809.

Perron d'Arc, Henri, *Aventures d'un voyageur en Australie: neuf mois de sejour chez les Nagarnooks,* 2nd edn, Hachette, Paris, 1870.

Porteous, S. D., *The Psychology of a Primitive People,* Arnold & Co., London, 1929.

Porteous, S. D., 'Mentality of Australian Aborigines', *Oceania,* vol. 4, no. 1, 1933, pp. 30–36.

Queries Respecting the Human Race, to be Addressed to Travellers and Others, British Association for the Advancement of Science, Taylor, London, 1841.

Rees, Coralie, *Spinifex Walkabout: Hitch-hiking in Remote North Australia,* Australasian Publishing, Sydney, 1953.

'Report of the Select Committee of the Legislative Council on the Aborigines', *The North British Review,* vol. XXXII, February–March 1860, pp. 366–88.

Bibliography

Rienzi, Domeny de, *Océanie; ou, Cinquième Partie du Monde: Revue Geographique at Ethnographique de la Malaise, se la Micronesie, de la Polynesie, et de la Melanasie*, Firmin Didot, Paris, 1836.

Rolfe, Patricia, *The Journalistic Javelin: An Illustrated History of the Bulletin*, Wildcat Press, Sydney, 1979.

Roth, Henry Ling, 'Is Mrs F. C. Smith a last living Aboriginal of Tasmania?', *Journal of the Anthropological Institute*, no. 27, 1898, pp. 451–54.

Roth, Henry Ling, *The Aborigines of Tasmania*, F. King & Sons, Halifax, 1899.

Rousseau, Jean Jacques, *A Dissertation on the Origin and Foundation of Inequality among Mankind*, trans. from the French, London, 1773–74.

Sandby, W., *The History of the Royal Academy of Arts*, Longman, Green, Longman, Roberts, & Green, London, 1862.

Scherzer, Dr Karl, *Narrative of the Circumnavigation of the Globe by the Austrian Frigate Novara Undertaken by Order of the Imperial Government in the Years 1857, 1858 & 1859*, vol. III, Saunders, Otley, and Co., London, 1863.

Sexton, Rev. J. H. *Australian Aborigines*, Hunkin, Ellis & King, Adelaide, 1944.

Smith, William Ramsay, 'Aborigines', in *Australian Encyclopedia*, Angus & Robertson, Sydney, 1927, p. 25.

Sollas, W. J., *Ancient Hunters and their Modern Representatives*, Macmillan and Co., London, 1924.

Spencer, Baldwin, and Gillen, Frank J., *The Native Tribes of Central Australia*, Dover, New York, 1968 (1899).

Spencer, Baldwin, and Gillen, Francis, *The Arunta: A Study of a Stone Age People*, Macmillan, London, 1927.

Strzelecki, Paul E. de, *Physical Description of New South Wales and Van Diemen's Land. Accompanied by a geological map, sections, and diagrams, and figures of the organic remains*, facsimile edn, Libraries Board of South Australia, 1967 (1845).

Strzelecki, P. E. de, 'Races of men in Australia', in J. R. McCulloch (ed.), *Dictionary, Geographical, Statistical, and Historical of the Various Countries, Places and Principal Natural Object in the World*, Longman, Brown, Green, and Longmans, London, 1854, pp. 228–31.

Suttor, William Henry, *Australian Stories Retold and Sketches of Country Life*, Whalan, Bathurst, 1877.

Taplin, Rev. George, *The Narrinyeri: An Account of the Tribes of the South Australian Aborigines*, J. T. Shawyer, Adelaide, 1874.

Taplin, Rev. George, *The Native Tribes of South Australia*, E. S. Wigg & Son, Adelaide, 1879. 'Introduction' by J. D. Woods.

Teichelmann, C. G., *Aborigines of South Australia: Illustrative and Explanatory Notes of the Manners, Customs, Habits and Superstitions of the Natives of*

South Australia, Committee of the South Australian Wesleyan Methodist Auxiliary Society, Adelaide, 1841.

Tench, Watkin, *A Complete Account of the Settlement at Port Jackson, in New South Wales, including an Accurate Description of the Colony; of the Natives; and of its Natural Productions*, G. Nicol and J. Sewell, London, 1793.

Thomson, T. R. H., 'Observations of the reported incompetency of the "gins" or Aboriginal females of New Holland, to procreate with a native male after having borne half-caste children to a European or white', *Journal of the Ethnological Society of London*, vol. 3, 1854, pp. 243–46.

Thonemann, H. Eric, *Tell the White Man; The Life Story of a Lubra*, Collins, Sydney, 1949.

Treatises of Johann Friedrich Blumenbach, trans. Thomas Bendyshe, 3rd edn, Longman, Green, Longman, Roberts and Green, London, 1865 (1795).

Trollope, Anthony, *Australia and New Zealand*, vol. 1, Chapman and Hall, London, 1873.

Turnbull, John, *A Voyage round the World: in the years 1800, 1801, 1802, 1803, and 1804, in which the author visited the principal islands in the Pacific Ocean and the English settlements of Port Jackson and Norfolk Island*, volume 1, Richard Phillips, London, 1805.

Turner, Robert, and Boyce, M. J., *Australian Aboriginal Signs and Symbols for the Use of Boy Scouts*, Sydney, 1934.

Welsby, Thomas, *The Discoverers of the Brisbane River*, H. J. Diddams & Co., Brisbane, 1913.

Wesley, John, 'Thoughts on slavery', R. Hawes, London, 1774.

Westgarth, William, *Australia Felix*, Oliver & Boyd, Edinburgh, 1848.

Westgarth, William, *Victoria: Late Australia Felix*, Oliver & Boyd, Edinburgh, 1853.

White, John, *Journal of a Voyage to New South Wales*, 1757/8–1832, accessed 26 July 2011, <http://gutenberg.net.au/ebooks03/0301531h.html#platelist>.

White, John, *Journal of a Voyage to New South Wales*, Royal Australian Historical Society, with Angus and Robertson, 1962.

Willoughby, Howard, *Australian Pictures: Drawn with Pen and Pencil*, Religious Tract Society, London, 1886.

Willshire, William Henry, *The Land of the Dawning, being Facts gleaned from Cannibals in the Australian Stone Age*, W. K. Thomas & Co., Adelaide, 1896.

Wollstonecraft, Mary, *A Vindication of the Rights of Woman*, Penguin Books, Harmondsworth, 1982 (1792).

Wood, J. G., *The Natural History of Man; being an Account of the Manners and*

Bibliography

Customs of the Uncivilized Races of Men, George Routledge and Sons, London, 1880.
Wonderful Australia in Pictures, Herald and Weekly Times, Colorgravure, Melbourne, 1949.

Magazines and periodicals

'The "abo" as hunter', *Bank Notes*, Commonwealth Bank, December 1932, pp. 20–21.
'Aboriginal', 'Ethnology: the case of the Aborigines', *Science of Man*, vol. 10, no. 4, November 1907, pp. 55–57.
'An Aboriginal marriage', *The Sydney Mail*, 9 June 1883, p. 6.
'The Aborigines', *The Illustrated Australian Magazine*, vol. III, July 1851, p. 48.
'The Aborigines', public lecture transcribed in the *Empire*, 14 August 1857, p. 2.
'Aborigines of Australia', *The Penny Magazine*, vol. XI, no. 634, 19 February 1842, pp. 65–67.
'The Aborigines of Australia', *The Asiatic Journal and Monthly Register for British and Foreign India, China and Australasia*, vol. IV, January–April 1831, p. 124.
'Aborigines of Australia – Swan River. Their public life', in Robert Montgomery Martin, Esq. (ed.), *The Colonial Magazine and Commercial-Maritime Journal*, vol. 5, May–August 1841, p. 424.
'The Aborigines of Australia', *Empire*, 30 November 1853, p. 3.
'The Aborigines of Australia', *Chambers's Journal of Popular Literature, Science and Art*, vol. X, no. 516, p. 736.
'Aborigines of Van Diemen's Land', *The Penny Magazine*, vol. XI, no. 634, 1842, pp. 195–96.
'About our Aborigines', *The Inlander,* vol. 2, first quarter, 1915, pp. 22, 27.
'Account of Rio de Janiero', *The Edinburgh Magazine, or Literary Miscellany*, July 1790, p. 255.
'An account of the inhabitants of Otaheite, a lately discovered island in the south-sea', *The London Magazine*, June 1773, p. 266.
'Across Australia', in *The Friend: A Religious and Literary Journal*, 30 October 1875, vol. 49, no. 11, p. 83.
Aiston, George, 'The desert Aborigines', *Mankind*, vol. 1, no. 12, 1935, pp. 5–8.
Angas, George French, 'On the Aboriginal inhabitants of N. S. Wales', *Waugh's Australian Almanac*, James W. Waugh, Sydney, 1858, p. 53.
Ashley-Montagu, F. M., 'The procreative theories of primitive man', *The Realist*, vol. 2, 1929, pp. 87–96.

'The Australian Aborigines', *The Australasian Sketcher with Pen and Pencil*, 15 January 1881, p. 23.

'Australian Aborigines – II', *The Nation*, vol. 81, no. 2100, 28 September 1905, pp. 261–63.

'An authentic account of the natives of Otahitee', *The General Evening Post*, no. 7812, 20 March 1784.

'Australian blacks', *Chambers's Journal of Popular Literature Science and the Arts*, vol. XLI, no. 43, 22 October 1864, pp. 686–88.

'The Australian blacks', *The Nation*, vol. 80, no. 2077, 20 April 1905, p. 310, pp. 308–10.

'Authentic letter from Botany Bay', *The London Chronicle*, no. 5084, 5 May 1789, p. 435.

'"Baby-farming" in England', *Freeman's Journal*, 24 September 1870, p. 13.

Backhouse, James, 'The Tasmanian Aborigines', in *Papers and Proceedings, Royal Society of Tasmania,* Davies Brothers, Hobart, 1898–1899, pp. 65–73.

Bassett-Smith, P. W., 'The Aborigines of north-west Australia', *The Journal of the Anthropological Institute of Great Britain and Ireland*, vol. XXIII, 1894, pp. 324–331.

Barrett, Charles, and Kenyon, A. S., 'Blackfellows of Australia', Lawrence Kay for Pictorial Newspapers, Melbourne, c. 1936, p. 7.

Barrett, Charles, illustrated by Ivor Horman, 'An ancient people', *Rydge's*, 1 December 1947, p. 1093.

Barry, Eileen, '"Kabbarli" of desert places', *Walkabout*, October, 1966, pp. 14–17.

Bates, Daisy, 'Fanny Balbuk-Yooreel, the last Swan River (female) native, *Science of Man*, vol. 13, nos 5–6, 1911, pp. 100–101, 119–21.

Bates, Daisy, 'Aboriginal reserves and women patrols', *The Sunday Times*, 2 October 1921, p. 18.

Bates, Daisy M., 'Was she 107? Death of "Nory Ann"', *Western Mail*, 11 December 1924, p. 23.

Bates, Daisy, '"Thus...my days have passed"', *The Australian Women's Weekly*, 13 January 1934, p. 3.

Bates, Daisy, 'Ngilgi: an Aboriginal woman's life story', *Australasian*, 23 March 1935.

'Cannibalism and infanticide in Australia', *London Journal*, vol. 7, no. 163, April 1848, pp. 74–75.

Chadwick, Doris Anne, 'To the new land', *The New South Wales School Magazine of Literature for Our Boys and Girls*, vol. 37, no. 2, 1 July 1952, pp. 153–57.

Chandler, L. G., 'Last of her tribe [Mary Woorlong, Kulkyne Tribe, Murray River]', *Wild Life*, vol. 14, no. 2, August 1951, pp. 163–65.

Bibliography

Charnley, W., 'The antiquity of the Aboriginal', *Walkabout*, 1 February 1947, p. 30.

'The Chinese in Victoria', *Empire*, 21 October 1856, p. 2.

'Christmas day in the far north – a royal visitor', *Supplement to the Illustrated Australian News*, 19 December 1885, p. 226.

Cleveson, Clem, 'The skull of peace', *People*, 19 February 1958, pp. 7–11.

Clutterbuck, Dr J. B., 'Port Phillip in 1849', *The Illustrated London News*, 26 January 1850, p. 53.

Colonial Intelligencer or Aborigines' Friend Comprising the Transactions of the Aborigines Protection Society; Interesting Intelligence Concerning the Aborigines of Various Climes and Articles upon Colonial Affairs, J. Ollivier and Messrs Ward, London, 1847–48.

Colonial Intelligencer or Aborigines' Friend, vol. III, no. XLIII, Ollivier and Ward, London, November 1851.

'M. Commissioner Massie's Report for the New-England District, Armadale, 10 January 1842', extract, *The Colonial Intelligencer*, vol. IV, nos XIV and XV, June and July 1853, p. 266.

Cox, Harry, 'Black velvet', *People*, 14 November 1956, pp. 27–31.

Croll, R. H., 'The original owners', in L. L. Politzer (ed.), *Centenary Journal*, Melbourne, 1934.

Croxford, Ronald, 'Sunset of Yirrkala, but not of an age-old culture', *Smoke Signals*, vol. 6, no. 4, 1970, pp. 37–41.

Davies, R. H., 'On the Aborigines of Van Diemen's Land, *Tasmanian Journal of Natural Science*, vol. 2, no. 11, 1846, pp. 409–420.

Dawson, Ernest, 'The prisoner', *The Living Age*, 14 May 1904, pp. 412–25.

Drake-Brockman, Henrietta, 'Coloured characters', *Walkabout*, vol. 11, no. 8, 1 June 1945, p. 15.

'The enemy of the Australian and Tasmanian Aborigines', *Scottish Review*, October 1860, pp. 380–92.

'Farther particulars to the Botany Bay expedition', *The London Chronicle*, 26–28 March 1789.

'Father Gsell's 150 wives. Subterfuge by a missionary on Bathurst Island', *Parade*, May 1966.

Flynn, Rev. John, *The Inlander: A Quarterly Magazine dealing with National Interests from the Outbacker's Point of View*, Gordon and Gotch, Sydney, 1915, p. 23.

'Fourteen years with the Aborigines', *Empire*, 7 August 1861, p. 3.

Fox, G., 'Ethnology: the Australian Aborigines', *Science of Man*, vol. X, no. 4, 20 August 1908, pp. 57–61.

Gibson, John, letter printed in 'South Australia', *The Colonial Intelligencer or,*

Aborigines' Friend, vol. III, no. XLIII, 1851, p. 315.

'A grand old lady passes on [Lizzie, Grand Old Lady of Woodenbong Station]', *Dawn,* October 1952.

Hill, Ernestine, 'Black man's day', *Walkabout,* 1 August 1940, pp. 29–47.

Hughes, Mrs, 'A description of the tomb of Werter', *The Gentlemen's Magazine,* vol. 57, 1785, p. 385.

Illustrated Melbourne Post, May 1862, p. 36.

Keane, Augustus Henry, 'Australian culture', *St James's Magazine,* vol. 4, no. 40, 1881, pp. 220–236.

Laird, Norman, 'Aborigine girl', *Walkabout,* vol. 12, no. 12, 1 October 1946, pp. 20–21.

Lamond, Henry G., 'Dark ladies', *Walkabout,* May 1964, pp. 34–36.

London Chronicle, no. 4655, 19–21 September 1786, p. 284.

Longford, J. A., 'Truganini, last princess of Tasmania', *Gentlemen's Magazine,* no. 17, 1876, p. 456.

Lytha, 'Cattle kingdom', *Walkabout,* 1 March 1942, no. 5, p. 12.

M. S., 'Rosie the tree climber', *Walkabout,* vol. 15, no. 2, February 1949, p. 46.

MacClean, Hugh, *Aussie,* 14 April 1927, p. 10.

Mankind, vol. 4, no. 8, March 1952, p. 315.

Martin, Robert Montgomery, Esq (ed.), 'Aborigines of Australia', *The Colonial Magazine and Commercial-Maritime Journal,* vol. V, May–August 1841, p. 152.

'The missing schooner Eva', *The Australian News for Home Readers,* 28 May 1867, p. 12.

Morrison, P. Crosbie, 'Black Aggie', *Wild Life,* vol. 11, no. 5, May 1949, pp. 226–27.

Munroe, Mrs Florrie, 'The life of queen Mary Ann…a brave woman', *Dawn,* October 1952.

'Murder of babies. an English "fashion"', *Freeman's Journal,* 21 November 1863, p. 2.

'The murdered orderly', *All the Year Round,* vol. 18, no. 446, November 1867, pp. 469–70.

Murdoch, W. L., Esq., 'Particulars concerning the blacks whose portraits appeared in last issue', *Science of Man,* vol. 3, no. 3, 23 April 1900, pp. 44–47.

'Nature with streaming eyes and heaving breast', in Alexander Lindsay and Margaret MacFadden Smith (eds), *Index of English Literary Manuscripts,* vol. 3, part 4, 1997, p. 475.

The New Monthly Magazine and Literary Journal, part II, Henry Colburn, London, 1828, pp. 216–23.

Bibliography

'New South Wales. Murder of a native of Glasgow', *The Glasgow Daily Herald*, 5 March 1862, p. 4.

'Newsletter of Australia: A Narrative to Send to Friends', no. 58, June 1861.

'Northern Territory kitchen', *The Australian Countryside in Pictures*, Herald Gravure, Melbourne, 1953, p. 218.

Norton, A. 'Stray notes about our Aborigines', *Science of Man*, vol. IX, no. 8, 1 August 1907, pp. 116–17.

'Notes of a residence in the bush, by a lady', *Chambers's Edinburgh Journal*, no. 542, June 1842, pp. 173–75, 179–180.

'Ode for the Queen's birthday', in James Boswell, *The Scots Magazine*, vol. 38, 1776, p. 45.

'On the varieties of the human race', in Robert Montgomery Martin Esq (ed.), *The Colonial Magazine and Commercial-Maritime Journal*, vol. V, May–August 1841, Fisher Son and Co., London.

Palmer, J. H., *Empire*, 14 August 1857, p. 2.

Patton, Jack T., 'Aborigines Progressive Association', *The Abo Call*, no. 1, April 1938, p. 3.

Patton, Jack T., 'Calling Aborigines: straight talk', *The Abo Call*, no. 3, June 1938, p. 1.

Patton, Jack T., 'Our huge task', The *Abo Call*, no. 2, May 1938, p. 1.

'Mr Penny's lecture on the Milmenrura natives', *South Australian*, 29 June 1841, p. 3.

'People of the territory', *Wild Life Magazine*, June 1944, pp. 175–77.

'The prevalence of infanticide in London', *Empire*, 2 November 1864, p. 8.

'Reflections on unreasonable sorrow', *The Lady's Magazine: Entertaining Companion for the Fair Sex Appropriated Solely for their Use and Amusement*, October 1778, p. 520.

Rose, F. G. G., 'Groote Eylandt', *Walkabout*, 1 March 1944, vol. 10, no. 5, pp. 9–13, 23.

Roth, Walter E., *Records of the Australian Museum*, vol. 8, no. 1, 1910, p. 87.

Shaw, A. G. L., '1788–1810', in Frank Crowley (ed.), *A New History of Australia*, Heinemann, Melbourne, 1974.

'The social, political, moral and religious character and aspects of the Indian insurrection', *Empire*, 8 February 1858, p. 3.

'South Australia: The Aborigines,' extract, *The Colonial Intelligencer*, vol. IV, nos XIV and XV, June and July 1853.

Thorpe, W. W., 'Some mutilatory rites practised by the Australian Aborigines', *Mankind*, vol. 1, no. 6, 1932, pp. 124–134.

'Trucanini, queen of Bruni, last of the Tasmanians', *People*, no. 1, 31 June 1951, pp. 43–46.

Walpole, R. S., Esq, 'Suggestions as to the origin and geographical distribution of the aborigines of Australia', *The Royal Geographical Society of Australasia* (Victoria), vol. XVII, 1899.

The Westminster Review, vol. XII, Oct 1829–Jan 1830.

White, Eric, 'Aborigine Nellie', *Walkabout*, vol. 18, no. 4, 1 April 1952, pp. 42–44.

White, John, 'Journal of a journey to New South Wales' (extract), *The London Review and Literary Journal*, vol. 18, August 1790.

White, John, 'Journal of a journey to New South Wales' (extract), *The European Magazine, and London Review*, (Philological Society of London), July–December 1790, p. 105.

'Mr White decorating a female of New South Wales', artist Charles Ansell, engraver Augustine Birrell, *The Journal of Voyage to New South Wales*, London, 1790.

White, John, 'The inhabitants of New South Wales', *The Historical Magazine, or, Classical Library of Public Events*, vol. 3, 1 March 1791, p. 20.

'White's journal of a journey to New South Wales', *The Monthly Review, or, Literary Journal*, vol. 4, January–April 1791, p. 322.

'Mr White decorating a female of New South Wales', *Historical Magazine, or, Classical Library of Public Events*, vol. 3, 1791, p. 20.

'Wooing as practised by the Australian Blacks', *The Golden Era*, 8 January 1865, p. 5.

Young, W. E. T., in 'The natives of South Australia', *The Colonial Intelligencer or Aborigines' Friend*, vol. II, no. XIV, June 1849, p. 215.

Newspapers

The Advertiser, 'Aboriginal savages, lawless cannibals', 2 January 1930, p. 14; 7 August 1901, p. 4; 1 November 1902, p. 9; George G. Hacket, 'Aboriginal natives', 8 January 1930, p. 18; 'Tragic story of the Caledon Bay massacre', 13 October 1933, p. 23.

The Age, Donald Thomson, 'Wonggo of Caledon Bay: an Arnhem Land episode', 25 July 1959, p. 18.

Albury Banner and Wodonga Express, 12 May 1899, p. 25.

The Argus, 13 September 1860, p. 4; 28 September 1861, p. 5; 14 April 1880, p. 5; 12 March 1881, p. 4; 29 September 1881, p. 8; 4 October 1881, p. 5; 2 May 1883, p. 9; 'Outrage on a gin', 15 November 1884, p. 9; 26 November 1884, p. 10; 3 September 1927, p. 33; 2 November 1933, p. 9; 23 March 1934, p. 10; 30 June 1934, p. 17; 11 August 1934, p. 4; 'Blacks sell womenfolk to lugger crews', 20 September 1935; 14 May 1936, p. 7; 26 September 1936, p. 5; 21 November 1936, p. 27; 31 December 1936,

p. 8; 'Owner of 121 "wives"', 6 April 1937, p. 9; 6 April 1937, p. 10; 8 April 1937, p. 12; 7 April 1937, p. 6; 15 April 1937, p. 12; 7 May 1937, p. 7; 21 June 1937, p. 1.

The Australian, 'Journal of an excursion to Brisbane Water', 20 December 1826, p. 3; 'The Aborigines', 19 October 1841, p. 4; 15 October 1847, p. 4.

Australasian Chronicle, 'Infanticide, or the bohemian mother', 12 December 1840, p. 3.

The Bacchus Marsh Express, 27 September 1890, p. 2.

Bathurst Free Press, 24 August 1850, p. 4; 'Wesleyan missionary meeting', 15 March 1851, p. 3.

Bathurst Free Press and Mining Journal, 'Infanticide and its reproach', 14 October 1857, p. 4; 2 April 1890, p. 4; 1 July 1890, p. 4.

The Brisbane Courier, 14 December 1867, p. 7; 2 November 1875, p. 3; 1 March 1879, p. 6; 16 April 1880, p. 3; 20 August 1881, p. 6; 19 October 1881, p. 3; 'Australian Aborigines folklore', 18 May 1889, p. 7; 8 November 1895, p. 5.

The Cairns Post, 18 June 1890, p. 3.

The Canberra Times, 14 November 1933, p. 1; 15 November 1933, p. 3; 'Lubras on luggers', 25 August 1936, p. 1; 25 September 1936, p. 5; 6 April 1937, p. 2; 21 April 1937, p. 1; 22 April 1937, p. 4; 22 June 1937, p. 2; 6 January 1976, p. 3.

The Colac Herald, 'History of Colac', 11 January 1889, p. 3; 25 January 1889, p. 3.

Colonial Times, 30 April 1830, p. 4.

Cornwall Chronicle (Launceston), 24 May 1862, p. 2; 16 July 1862, p. 3.

The Courier (Hobart), 4 September 1850, p. 3.

The Courier, 4 November 1846, p. 4; 'Fourteen years with the Aborigines', 15 August 1861, p. 3; 3 October 1861, p. 3; 19 April 1862, p. 2; 11 July 1863, p. 3.

The Courier-Mail, 18 November 1933, p. 13; 4 January 1934, p. 13; 12 January 1934, p. 6; 24 April 1934, p. 13.

Daily Mirror, 'NT mission priest bought "wives" by the hundred', 13 August 1980.

The Daily News, Arthur W. Upfield, 'The Barrakee mystery', 7 May 1932, p. 9; 'Does Australia mistreat its Aborigines', *The Daily News*, 24 June 1933, p. 16.

Daily Telegraph, 'Japanese pearl poachers', 26 May 1936.

Geelong Advertiser and Squatters' Advocate, 'Australia, Lieut-Colonel Gawler, Mr Ed. John Eyre and the "Atheneum"', 23 May 1846, p. 4; Review of a pamphlet authored by Mr Westgarth, 'A report of the conditions, capabilities and prospects of the Australian Aborigines', 26 August 1846, p. 1.

Geelong Advertiser, 'The Wesleyan Mission at Buntingdale', 29 October 1847, p. 1; Francis Tuckfield, 'Mission to the Aborigines', 5 November 1847, p. 1; 'Correspondence. Buntingdale and the Aborigines', 26 November 1847, p. 1.

Geelong Advertiser and Intelligencer, 20 April 1853, p. 25; 16 February 1856, p. 2.

Goulburn Herald and Chronicle, 6 December 1873, p. 2

The Herald (Melbourne), William Westgarth, 'A report on the condition, capabilities and prospects of the Australian Aborigines', Melbourne, 1846; 'Black women exploited', 24 September 1936; 'Native girls in luggers', *The Herald,* 21 June 1937.

The Hobart Town Courier, 23 October 1835, p. 2; 8 December 1837, p. 3.

Ipswich Herald & General Advertiser, 'Fourteen years with the Aborigines', 16 August 1861, p 3; 23 August 1861, p 4.

Kalgoorlie Miner, 'Notes from London', 1 August 1903, p. 7.

Launceston Advertiser, 'Settlement at Port Phillip', 26 November 1835, p. 3.

Launceston Examiner, 'Review. Victoria; Late Australia Felix', 25 February 1854, p. 15.

The Maitland Daily Mercury, 25 November 1907, p. 3.

The Maitland Mercury & Hunter River General Advertiser, 27 December 1835, p. 2; Review of Charles Baker, *Sydney and Melbourne*, 7 January 1846, p. 4; 'Port Phillip', 9 September 1846, p. 4; 25 September 1847, p. 25; 30 November 1850, p. 2; 15 March 1854, p. 2; 3 November 1881, p. 7; 4 February 1952, p. 2.

The Mercury, 6 April 1867, p. 2; 'Telegraph despatches', 5 November 1867, p. 2; 22 November 1884, p. 3; 8 February 1910, p. 3.

The Moreton Bay Courier, William Westgarth, 'The Aborigines', 12 September 1846, p. 2; 9 October 1847, p. 4; 'The Aborigines of Australia', 4 December 1847, p. 15.

Northern Standard, 'Lubras on pearling vessels', 25 August 1936; 'Aboriginal females', *Northern Standard*, 4 July 1939, p. 5.

The Northern Territory Times and Gazette, 23 January 1874, p. 3; J. Brunton Stephens, 'To a black gin', 20 April 1878, p. 2; 22 July 1882, p. 3; 21 March 1885, p. 3; Alfred Giles, 6 March 1886, p. 3; 2 April 1914, p. 14; 17 June 1915, p. 7; 'Our northern shores', 22 July 1924, p. 2.

Ovens and Murray Advertiser, 14 October 1865, p. 4.

Pall Mall Gazette, 'Occasional notes', 25 May 1882, p. 3.

The Perth Gazette and Independent Journal of Politics and News, 'Settlement at Port Phillip', 2 April 1836, p. 679; 'The natives', 16 September 1837,

p. 973; 2 December 1848, p. 3; 10 February 1849, p. 3.

The Queenslander, 'Barbarous outrage by the native police', 29 June 1867, p. 6; 'Darwinism and the Aborigines', 2 November 1889, p. 825; 'Ethnology. Notes on savage life in the early days of Western Australian settlement', 29 March 1902, p. 674.

The Register, Editorial, 25 June 1843, p. 3a; 'Aboriginal cannibals', 8 March 1928, p. 10; Charles White, 'The story of the blacks', 27 August 1904, p. 3; 'The Aborigines', 27 August 1928, p. 8.

Shoalhaven Telegraph, 1 February 1905, p. 6.

South Australian Register, 8 November 1835, p. 4; 'The scab in sheep act', 12 November 1841, p. 3; 4 September 1847, p. 4; 'Occupation licenses', 2 October 1847, p. 3; 'The native mission at Port Lincoln', 14 March 1853, p. 3; 'Report of the Select Committee on the Aborigines', 31 October 1860, p. 3; 'The Aborigines', 2 December 1861, p. 3; 'The Aborigines', 3 January 1861, p. 3; 'The Narrinyeri or tribes of the lakes or Lower Murray', 28 December 1861, p. 3; 'A visit to Point Macleay', 16 November 1863, p3; 'Aborigines Friends Association', 25 November 1863, p. 3; 14 December 1863, p. 2; 'Point Macleay', 11 April 1867, p. 2; 23 November 1865, p. 2; 'The Aborigines in the north', 15 November 1873, p. 4; 'Kamileroi and Kurnai', 18 November 1880, p. 6; 19 March 1889, p. 4; 24 April 1889, p. 5; 'Review of "Aborigines of Australia"', 14 May 1889, p. 7; 27 February 1899, p. 6.

The South Australian Advertiser, 31 October 1860, p. 3.

South Australian Weekly Chronicle, 3 November 1860, p. 5.

South Australian Chronicle and Weekly Mail, 23 May 1874, p. 13.

Southern Argus, 'Law for Aborigines', 13 August 1874, p. 2.

The Sun-Herald, 'Territorians and mourning for Tiny', 12 December 1954, p. 48.

The Sunday Times, The Gadfly, 'Through the Ashburton', 16 June 1907, p. 12.

Sydney Chronicle, 14 October 1847, p. 2.

The Sydney Gazette and New South Wales Advertiser, 22 January 1833, p. 2; November and December 1934.

Sydney Herald, 'Port Phillip', 17 November 1836, p. 2.

The Sydney Morning Herald, 11 September 1835, p. 2; 'Lower Murrumbidgee', 6 December 1859, p. 5; 9 October 1861, p. 6; 'The trip of the steamer Black Prince to Rockingham Bay, and search for the missing schooner Eva', 24 April 1867, p. 2; 'The Australian race', 8 October 1888, p. 8; 'The Royal Commission on the birthrate', 5 March 1904, p. 10; Daisy Bates, 'Our cannibals', 25 January 1930, p. 21; Phillip Arthur Micklem, 'Aboriginal communism', 6 June 1922, p. 6; 'Reports of sale of lubras',

23 September 1935; 'Lubras sold. Japanese hamper mission work. Barter increases', 25 September 1936; 'Monsignor Gsell in Sydney', 18 September 1937.
Weekly Times, 29 August 1914, p. 10.
The West Australian, 7 April 1887, p. 3; 'An Aboriginal woman attacked', 30 December 1895, p. 6; 14 April 1906, p. 4; Review of *The Arunta: A Study of a Stone Age People,* 21 January 1928, p. 6.
Western Mail, 14 January 1905, p. 35.

Parliamentary papers

Australia, Parliament, 'Report on the administration of the Northern Territory for the year ended 30th June, 1933', Commonwealth Government Printer, Canberra, 1934.
Department of Territories, 'Our Aborigines', prepared for the National Aborigines' Day of Observance Committee, Commonwealth Government Printer, Canberra, 1957.
Moseley, H. D., *Royal Commission Appointed to Investigate, Report and Advise Upon Matters in Relations to the Condition and Treatment of Aborigines,* Western Australia, 1934.
Queensland Legislative Assembly, *Report from the Select Committee on the Native Police Force and the Condition of the Aborigines Generally together with the proceedings of the Committee and minutes of evidence,* Fairfax and Belbridge, Brisbane, 1861.
Society of Friends, Aborigines' Committee, *Information respecting the aborigines in the British Colonies: circulated by direction of the Meeting for Sufferings, being principally extracts from the report presented to the House of Commons, by the Select Committee appointed on that subject,* Darton and Harvey, London, 1838.
South Australian Legislative Council, *Report of the Select Committee of the Legislative Council, upon 'the Aborigines'; together with Minutes of Evidence and Appendix,* W C. Cox, Government Printer, Adelaide, 1860, accessed 30 October 2015, <http://aiatsis.gov.au/archive_digitised_collections/_files/archive/removeprotect/92284.pdf>.
South Australia Legislative Council, *Report of the Select Committee of the Legislative Council on the Aborigines' Bill,* Paper no. 77, Item no. 854, Adelaide, 1899.

Manuscripts

Australian Institute of Aboriginal Studies, letter, 27 March 1975, ref SJ.55.
Edith Ellen Hoy Scrapbooks, 119, 119A, 119B, Harrietville Historical Society.

Bibliography

Museum of Victoria, R. E. Johns' scrapbooks, Box 3, c. 1869–1882.

Phelps, P. H. F., *Native Scenes [snakes, birds & marine life]*, unpublished album, c. 1840–49. Dixon State Library of New South Wales, accessed 9 February 2012, <http://acms.sl.nsw.gov.au/item/itemDetailPaged.aspx?itemID=447925>.

Secondary sources
Books and articles

Aggrawal, Anil, 'Bride capture', *Encyclopedia of Law & Society: American and Global Perspectives*, Sage, Thousand Oaks, 2007, pp. 135–36; *SAGE Reference Online*, accessed 29 January 2012, <http://sage-ereference.com.ezp.lib.unimelb.edu.au/view/law/n65.xml?rskey=Udcodf&result=1&q=Bride%20Capture>.

Agulhon, Maurice, *Marianne into Battle: Republican Imagery and Symbolism in France, 1789–1880*, trans. Janet Lloyd, Cambridge University Press, New York, 1981.

Ahmed, Sara, 'The politics of bad feeling', *Australian Critical Race and Whiteness Studies Association Journal*, vol. 1, 2005, pp. 72–85.

Aldersey, A. Dorothy, *Pastoral Pioneers of South Australia*, Lynton Publications, Blackwood, 1974 (facsimile).

Allen, Judith, 'Octavius Beale re-considered: infanticide, baby-farming and abortion in NSW 1880–1939', in Sydney Labour History Group, *What Rough Beast, The State and Social Order in Australian History*, Allen & Unwin, Sydney, 1982, pp. 111–29.

Altick, Richard, *Punch: The Lively Youth of a British Institution, 1841–1851*, Ohio State University Press, Columbus, 1997.

Anderson, Jim, 'A glorious thing is to live in a tent in the infinite: Daisy Bates', in Anna Cole, Victoria Katharine Haskins and Fiona Paisley (eds), *Uncommon Ground: White Women in Aboriginal History*, Aboriginal Studies Press, Canberra, 2005.

Angas, J. and Forster, H., *A History of the Ovens Valley*, self-published, Wangaratta, 1967.

Arnold, John, 'Printing technology and book production', in Martyn Lyons and John Arnold, *A History of the Book in Australia 1891–1945: A National Culture in a Colonised Market*, University of Queensland Press, Brisbane, 2001, pp. 104–112.

Attwood, Bain, '"In the name of all my coloured brethren and sisters": a biography of Bessy Cameron', *Hecate*, vol. 12, nos 1–2, 1986, pp. 9–53.

Attwood, Bain, *Rights for Aborigines*, Allen and Unwin, Sydney, 2003.

Australian Institute for Aboriginal and Torres Strait Islander Studies,

'Guidelines for ethical research in Australian Indigenous studies', AIATSIS, Canberra, 2012.

Bagnall, Kate, 'Across the threshold: white women and Chinese hawkers in the white colonial imaginary', *Hecate,* vol. 28, no. 2, 2002, pp. 9–29.

Baker, D. W. A., 'Lang, John Dunmore (1799–1878)', *Australian Dictionary of Biography*, National Centre of Biography, Australian National University, accessed 17 October 2013, <http://adb.anu.edu.au/biography/lang-john-dunmore-2326/text2953>.

'Baker, John (1813–1872)', *Australian Dictionary of Biography*, National Centre of Biography, Australian National University, accessed 25 August 2013, <http://adb.anu.edu.au/biography/baker-john-2920/text4215>.

Balint, Ruth, 'Aboriginal women and Asian men: a maritime history of color in white Australia', *Signs*, vol. 37, no. 3, 2012, pp. 544–54.

Ballantyne, Tony, 'What difference does colonialism make? Reassessing print and social change in an age of global imperialism', in Sabrina Alcorn Baron, Eric N. Lindquist and Eleanor F. Shevlin (eds), *Agent of Change: Print Culture Studies after Elizabeth L. Eisenstein*, University of Massachusetts Press, Amherst, 2007, pp. 342–52.

Barkan, Elazar, 'Rethinking orientalism: representations of "primitives" in western culture at the turn of the century', *History of European Ideas*, vol. 15, nos 4–6, 1992, pp. 759–65.

Barnes, G. and Mitchell, A. 'Measuring the marvelous: science and the exotic in William Dampier', *Eighteenth Century Life*, no. 26, 2002, pp. 45–57.

Barnes, Jillian, 'Resisting the captured image: how Gwoja Tjungurrayi, "One Pound Jimmy", escaped the "stone age"', in Ingereth MacFarlane and Mark Hannah (eds), *Transgressions: Critical Australian Indigenous Histories*, Aboriginal History Monograph 16, ANU ePress, Canberra, 2007.

Barnes, R. H., 'Marriage by capture', *Journal of the Royal Anthropological Institute*, vol. 5, no. 1, 1999, p. 57–73.

Baron, Sabrina Alcorn, Lindquist, Eric N., and Shevlin, Eleanor F. (eds), *Agent of Change: Print Culture Studies after Elizabeth L. Eisenstein*, University of Massachusetts Press, Amherst, 2007.

'Barrington, George (1755–1804)', *Australian Dictionary of Biography*, National Centre of Biography, Australian National University, accessed 29 January 2012, <http://adb.anu.edu.au/biography/barrington-george-1746/text1935>.

Barrington, Robin, 'Unravelling the Yamaji imaginings of Alexander Morton and Daisy Bates', *Aboriginal History*, vol. 39, 2016, pp. 27–62.

Bibliography

Barthes, Roland, *Mythologies*, Pallidin, London, 1973.
Barwick, Diane E., 'And the ladies are lubras now', in Fay Gale (ed.), *Woman's Role in Aboriginal Society*, 3rd edn, Australian Institute of Aboriginal Studies, Canberra, 1978.
Barwick, Diane E., *Rebellion at Coranderrk*, Aboriginal History Inc., Canberra, 1998.
Barwick, Diane, and Bell, Diane, 'Women in Aboriginal society: resources for research', in Diane Barwick, Michael Mace and Tom Stannage (eds), *Handbook for Aboriginal and Islander History*, Aboriginal History, Canberra, 1979.
Bassett, Judith, 'The Faithfull massacre at the Broken River, 1838', *Journal of Australian Studies*, vol. 13, no. 24, 1989, pp. 18–34.
Beasley, Edward, *Mid-Victorian Imperialists: British Gentlemen and the Empire of the Mind*, Routledge, Oxon, 2005.
Behrendt, Larissa, 'Consent in a (neo) colonial society: Aboriginal woman as sexual and legal "other"', *Australian Feminist Studies*, vol. 15, no. 33, 2000p, p. 353–67.
Bell, Diane, *Daughters of the Dreaming*, McPhee Gribble / George Allen and Unwin, Sydney, 1983.
Benis, Toby R., 'Criminal transport: George Barrington and the colonial cure', *Australian Literary Studies*, vol. 20, no. 2, 2002, pp. 167–77.
Berger, John, *Ways of Seeing*, Penguin, London, 1972.
Berkhofer, Robert F., *The White Man's Indian: Images of the American Indian from Columbus to the Present*, Vintage, New York, 1979.
Berndt, Catherine H., 'Digging sticks and spears, or the two-sex model', in Fay Gale (ed.), *Woman's Role in Aboriginal Society*, 3rd edn, Australian Institute of Aboriginal Studies, Canberra, 1978, pp. 64–84.
Berndt, Ronald, and Berndt, Catherine, *From Black to White in South Australia*, F. W. Cheshire, Melbourne, 1951.
Berndt, Ronald Murray, and Berndt, Catherine Helen, with John E. Stanton, *A World that was: The Yaraldi of the Murray River and the Lakes, South Australia*, University of British Columbia Press, Vancouver, 1993.
Bhabha, Homi, *The Location of Culture*, Routledge, London, 1994.
Biber, Katherine, 'Cannibals and colonialism', *Sydney Law Review*, vol. 27, 2005, pp. 623–37.
Birman, Wendy, 'Calvert, Albert Frederick (1872–1946)', *Australian Dictionary of Biography*, National Centre of Biography, Australian National University, accessed 31 January 2012, <http://adb.anu.edu.au/biography/calvert-albert-frederick-5469/text9293>.
Blainey, Geoffrey, 'Drawing up a balance sheet of our history', *Quadrant*, vol. 37, nos. 7–8, 1993.

Blum, Virginia, *Flesh Wounds: The Culture of Cosmetic Surgery*, University of California Press, Berkeley, 2005.

Bonnemains, J., and Haughel, P., *Récit du Voyage aux Terres Australes de Pierre-Bernard Milius,* Société havraise d'Etudes diverses, Le Havre, 1987.

Bottoms, Timothy, *Conspiracy Of Silence: Queensland's Frontier Killing Times,* Allen and Unwin, Sydney, 2013.

Bourdieu, Pierre, and Wacquant, Loïc J. D., *An Invitation to Reflexive Sociology*, University of Chicago Press, Chicago, 1992.

Boyce, James, *1835: The Founding of Melbourne and the Conquest of Australia*, Black Inc., Melbourne, 2011.

Brantlinger, Patrick, *Dark Vanishings: Discourse on the Extinction of Primitive Races 1800–1930*, Cornell University Press, Ithaca, 2003.

Briggs, Kelly, 'Aboriginal mothers like me still fear that our children could be taken away', *The Guardian*, 21 January 2014, accessed 22 January 2014, <http://www.theguardian.com/commentisfree/2014/jan/21/aboriginal-mothers-like-me-still-fear-that-our-children-could-be-taken-away>.

Broome, Richard, *The Victorians: Arriving,* Fairfax, Syme and Weldon, Sydney, 1986.

Broome, Richard, *Aboriginal Victorians: A History since 1800*, Allen and Unwin, Sydney, 2005.

Brown, Penelope, 'Repetition', *Journal of Linguistic Anthropology,* vol. 9, nos 1–2, June 1991, pp. 223–26.

Burton, Antoinette (ed.), *Gender, Sexuality and Colonial Modernities*, Routledge, London, 1999.

Buzard, James, 'Portable boundaries: Trollope, race and travel', *Nineteenth-Century Contexts*, vol. 32, no. 1, 2001, pp. 5–18.

Cahir, Fred, '"Are you off to the diggings?": Aboriginal guiding to and on the goldfields', in Lynette Russell and John Arnold (eds), *The La Trobe Journal,* Special issue: Indigenous Victorians: repressed, resourceful and respected, no. 85, May 2010, pp. 22–36.

Cane, Christine, and Gunson, Niel, 'Postcards: a source for Aboriginal biography', *Aboriginal History*, vol. 10, no. 1, 1986, pp. 171–74.

Carey, Jane, 'The racial imperatives of sex: birth control and eugenics in Britain, the United States and Australia in the interwar years', *Women's History Review*, vol. 21, no. 5, 2012, pp. 733–52.

Carr, Julie, *The Captive White Woman of Gipps Land: In Pursuit of the Legend*, Melbourne University Press, Melbourne, 2001.

Carroll, Noel, 'Ethnicity, race, and monstrosity: the rhetorics of horror and humor', in Peg Zeglin Brand (ed.), *Beauty Matters*, Indiana University Press, Bloomington, 2000, pp. 37–56.

Bibliography

Chisholm, A. H., 'Bennett, George (1804–1893)', *Australian Dictionary of Biography,* National Centre of Biography, Australian National University, accessed 27 January 2012, <http://adb.anu.edu.au/biography/bennett-george-1770/text1981>.

Choo, Christine, 'Asian men on the West Kimberley coast 1900–1940', *Studies in Western Australian History,* vol. 16, 1995, pp. 89–111.

Chow, Kai-wing, 'Reinventing Gutenberg: woodblock and moveable-type printing in Europe and China', in Alcorn Baron, Lindquist and Shevlin, *Agent of Change,* pp. 167–192.

Clark, J., 'Smith, Fanny Cochrane (1834–1905)', *Australian Dictionary of Biography,* National Centre of Biography, Australian National University, accessed 1 March 2013 <http://adb.anu.edu.au/biography/smith-fanny-cochrane-8466/text14887>.

Clendinnen, Inga, *Dancing with Strangers,* Text, Melbourne, 2003.

Clifford, James, 'Histories of the tribal and the modern', in Kymberly N. Pender (ed.), *Race-ing Art History: Critical Readings in Race and Art History,* Routledge, New York and London, 2002.

Cohn, Bernard, *Colonialism and its Forms of Knowledge: The British in India,* Princeton University Press, Princeton, 1996.

Coleman, Deirdre, *Romantic Colonization and British Anti-Slavery,* Cambridge University Press, Cambridge, 2005.

Collins, Patrick, 'Finney Eldershaw's suspect memoirs', in corrections to his *Goodbye Bussamarai,* accessed 11 February 2012, <http://www.goodbye-bussamarai.com/page8.htm>.

Comoroff, Jean, 'The empire's old clothes: fashioning the colonial subject', in Louise Lamphere, Helena Ragone and Patricia Zavella (eds), *Situated Lives: Gender and Culture in Everyday Life,* New York, Routledge, 1997, pp. 400–420.

Conor, Liz, *The Spectacular Modern Woman: Feminine Visibility in the 1920s,* Indiana University Press, Bloomington, 2004.

Conor, Liz, '"This striking ornament of nature": the "native belle" in the Australian colonial scene', in Claire Colebrook and Rita Felski (eds), *Feminist Theory,* vol. 7, no. 2, August 2006, pp. 197–218.

Conor, Liz, 'Howard's desert storm', *Overland,* no. 189, Summer 2007, pp. 12–15.

Conor, Liz, 'Political science and affective ties', *Arena,* no. 88, April–May 2007, pp. 10–11.

Conor, Liz, '"Strangely clad": enclosure, exposure, and the cleavage of empire', in Liz Conor and Jane Lydon (eds), *Journal of Australian Studies,* Special issue: Colonial visual cultures: 'Double take: reappraising the colonial archive', vol. 35, no. 2, 2011, pp. 185–200.

Conor, Liz, 'The "piccaninny": racialised childhood, disinheritance, acquisition and child beauty', *Postcolonial Studies*, vol. 15, no. 1, 2012, pp. 45–68.

Conor, Liz, 'Some hard truths about the intervention', *The Age*, 2 July 2012.

Conor, Liz, 'It's time to remove the offenders', *The Drum*, ABC Online, 8 March 2012, accessed 23 October 2015, <http://www.abc.net.au/news/2012-03-08/conor-it27s-time-to-remove-the-offenders/3875014>.

Conor, Liz, 'The 'lubra' type in Australian imaginings of Aboriginal women from 1836–1973', *Gender and History*, vol. 25, no. 2, July 2013, pp. 230–51.

Conor, Liz, '"Black velvet" and "purple indignation": print responses to Japanese "poaching" of Aboriginal women', *Aboriginal History*, vol. 37, 2013, p. 51–77.

Conor, Liz, 'Moveable parts: press and loom in colonial typologies', in Liz Conor (ed.), *Interventions,* Special issue: Types and typologies, vol. 17, no. 2, 2015, pp. 229–57.

Conor, Liz, and Lydon, Jane (eds), 'Introduction: Double take: reappraising the colonial archive', *Journal of Australian Studies*, Special issue: Colonial visual cultures, vol. 35, no. 2, June 2011, pp. 137–43.

Corris, Peter, 'Dawson, James (Jimmy) (1806–1900)', *Australian Dictionary of Biography*, National Centre of Biography, Australian National University, accessed 8 July 2013, <http://adb.anu.edu.au/biography/dawson-james-jimmy-3381/text5117>.

Cossins, Annie, *The Baby Farmers: A Chilling Tale of Missing Babies, Shameful Secrets and Murder in 19th Century Australia*, Allen and Unwin, Sydney, 2013.

Cowlishaw, Gillian, 'Infanticide in colonial Australia', *Oceania*, vol. 48, no. 4, 1978, pp. 262–82.

Cowlishaw, Gillian, 'The determinants of fertility among Australian Aborigines', *Mankind*, vol. 13, no. 1, 1981, pp. 37–55.

Crary, Jonathon, *Techniques of the Observer: On Vision and Modernity in the Nineteenth Century*, MIT Press, Cambridge, 1994.

Creed, Barbara, and Hoorn, Jeanette (eds), *Body Trade: Captivity, Cannibalism and Colonialism in the Pacific,* Routledge, New York, 2001.

Curthoys, Ann, 'An uneasy conversation: the multicultural and the indigenous', in John Docker and Gerhard Fischer (eds), *Race, Colour and Identity in Australia and New Zealand*, UNSW Press, Sydney, 2000, pp. 21–36.

Damousi, Joy, *Depraved and Disorderly: Female Convicts, Sexuality and Gender in Colonial Australia*, Cambridge University Press, Cambridge, 1997.

Daniels, Kay, 'Prostitution in Tasmania during the transition from penal settlement to "civilised" society', in K. Daniels (ed.), *So Much Hard Work: Women and Prostitution in Australia*, Fontana, Sydney, 1984, pp. 15–86.

Daughters of a Dreaming: A Photographic Exhibition of Koori Women of Southeast Australia, Museum of Victoria, Melbourne, 1990.

de Certeau, Michel, *The Practice of Everyday Life*, University of California Press, Oakland, 1988.

Despoix, Philipe, 'The exchanged portrait and the lethal picture: visualisation techniques and native knowledge in Samuel Hearne's sketches from his trek to the Arctic Ocean and John Webber's record of the Northern Pacific', *Eighteenth Century Fiction*, vol. 23, no. 4, 2011, pp. 667–89.

Dewar, Mickey, 'Death in the gulf: a look at the motives behind the Caledon Bay and Woodah Island killings', *Journal of Northern Territory History*, no. 4, 1993, pp. 1–14.

Donnelly, Karen, 'The discovery of a 19th century photographer, Thomas Cleary', *Bulletin* (Olive Pink Society), vol. 7, nos 1–2, 1995, pp. 9–21.

Douglas, Bronwen, and Ballard, Chris (eds), *Foreign Bodies: Oceania and the Science of Race 1750–1940,* ANU Epress, Canberra, 2008.

Douglas, Mary, *Purity and Danger*, Routledge and Kegan Paul, London, 1966.

Dowling, Freddie, *No More the Valley Rings with Koorie Laughter*, Wangaratta Historical Society, Wangaratta, 2009.

Dowling, Freddie, *The Last Dance of the Pangerang*, Wangaratta Historical Society, Wangaratta, 2009.

Dowling, Freddie, *Bindagaree 'You see'*, 2014, Culture Victoria, accessed 5 January 2012, <http://cv.vic.gov.au/stories/pangerang-country/11963/bindagaree-you-see/>.

Durey, Jill Felicity, 'Modern issues: Anthony Trollope and Australia', *Antipodes*, vol. 21, no. 2, 2007, pp. 170–76.

Dutton, Geoffrey, *White on Black: The Australian Aborigine Portrayed in Art*, Macmillan, Melbourne, 1974.

Duyker, Edward, *François Péron: An Impetuous Life*, Melbourne University Press, Melbourne, 2006.

Dyer, Colin, *The French Explorers and the Aboriginal Australians, 1772–1839*, University of Queensland Press, Brisbane, 2005.

Dyer, Richard, *White*, Routledge, London, 1997.

Einstein, A., 'On the electrodynamics of moving bodies' [1905], in *The Principle of Relativity,* trans. George Barker Jeffery and Wilfrid Perrett, Methuen and Company, London, 1923.

Einstein, A., 'Space–time', *Encyclopedia Britannica*, 13th edn, 1926.

Eisenstein, Elizabeth L., *The Printing Revolution in Early Modern Europe*, 2nd edn, Cambridge University Press, New York, 2005.

Ellingson, Ter, *The Myth of the Noble Savage,* University of California Press, Berkeley, 2001.

Elmslie, Ronald, and Nance, Susan, 'Smith, William Ramsay (1859–1937)', *Australian Dictionary of Biography*, National Centre of Biography, Australian National University, accessed 27 December 2013, <http://adb.anu.edu.au/biography/smith-william-ramsay-8493/text14941>.

Evans, Raymond, '"Soiled doves": prostitution in colonial Queensland', in Kay Daniels (ed.), *So Much Hard Work: Women and Prostitution in Australia*, Fontana, Sydney, 1984, pp. 127–61.

Fanon, Frantz, *Black Skin, White Masks*, Grove Press, New York, 1967.

Fels, Marie, *Good Men and True: The Aboriginal Police of the Port Phillip District 1837–1853*, Melbourne University Press, Melbourne, 1988.

Fish, Stanley, *Is There a Text in this Class*, Harvard University Press, Cambridge, 1980.

Fitzhardinge, L. F., 'Cunningham, Peter Miller (1789–1864)', *Australian Dictionary of Biography*, National Centre of Biography, Australian National University, accessed 5 July 2013, <http://adb.anu.edu.au/biography/cunningham-peter-miller-1942/text2325>.

Flather, Amanda, *Gender and Space in Early Modern England*, Boydell, Suffolk, 2007.

Flynn, Thomas R., 'Foucault and the eclipse of vision', in David Levin (ed.), *Modernity and the Hegemony of Vision,* University of California Press, Los Angeles, 1993, p. 273–86.

'The French gaze', *Hindsight*, ABC radio, 7 August 2011, accessed 15 November 2011 <http://www.abc.net.au/rn/hindsight/stories/2011/3278530.htm>.

French, Jackie, *Nanberry: Black Brother White*, Harper Collins, 2011.

Fulford, Tim, Lee, Debbie and Kitson, Peter J., *Literature, Science and Exploration in the Romantic Era: Bodies of Knowledge*, Cambridge University Press, New York, 2004.

Furphy, Samuel, '"Our civilisation has rolled over thee": Edward M Curr and the Yorta Yorta native title case', *History Australia*, vol. 7, no. 3, 2010, pp. 1–54.

Gale, Fay (ed.), *Woman's Role in Aboriginal Society*, Australian Institute of Aboriginal Studies, Canberra, 1974.

'Galton, Sir Francis', *Encyclopaedia Britannica,* 2015, accessed 17 November 2015, <www.britannica.com/biography/Francis-Galton>.

Ganter, Regina, *The Pearl-shellers of Torres Strait: Resource Use, Development and Decline 1860s–1960s*, Melbourne University Press, Melbourne, 1994.

Bibliography

Ganter, Regina, 'Living an immoral life: "coloured" women and the paternalistic state', *Hecate*, vol. 24, no. 1, 1998, pp. 13–40.

Ganter, Regina, 'Letters from Mapoon: colonising Aboriginal gender', *Australian Historical Studies*, vol. 30, no. 113, 1999, pp. 267–85.

Ganter, Regina, 'The Wakayama triangle: Japanese heritage of North Australia', *Journal of Australian Studies*, vol. 23, no. 61, 1999, pp. 55–63.

Ganter, Regina, *Mixed Relations: Asian–Aboriginal Contact in North Australia*, UWA Publishing, Perth, 2006.

Garvey, Nathan, *The Celebrated George Barrington: A Spurious Author, the Book Trade and Botany Bay*, Horden House, Potts Point, 2008.

Gascoigne, John, *The Enlightenment and the Origins of European Australia*, Cambridge University Press, Cambridge, 2002.

Gelder, Ken, and Jacobs, Jane M., 'Promiscuous sacred sites: reflections on secrecy and scepticism in the Hindmarsh Island affair', *Australian Humanities Review*, June–July 1997, accessed 15 March 2014, <http://www.australianhumanitiesreview.org/archive/Issue-June-1997/gelder.html>.

Genette, Gérard, *The Architext: An Introduction*, University of California Press, Berkeley, 1991.

Gibbney, H. J., 'Lumholtz, Carl Sophus (1851–1921)', *Australian Dictionary of Biography*, vol. 5, Melbourne University Press, Melbourne, 1975.

Gibson, Ross, *Seven Versions of an Australian Badland*, University of Queensland Press, Brisbane, 2002.

Gilman, Sander, 'The hottentot and the prostitute: toward an iconography of female sexuality', in Kymberly N. Pinder (ed.), *Race-ing Art History: Critical Readings in Race and Art History*, Routledge, New York, 2002, p. 119–138.

Goodall, Heather, 'Pearl Gibbs: some memories', *Aboriginal History*, vol. 7, no. 1, 1983, pp. 20–22.

Gray, Alan, 'Aboriginal fertility at the time of European contact: the Daly River Mission Baptismal Register', *Aboriginal History*, vol. 7, 1983, pp. 80–89.

Greenway, John, *Bibliography of the Australian Aborigines and the Native Peoples of Torres Strait to 1959*, Angus and Robertson, Sydney, 1963.

Griffiths, Gareth, 'The myth of authenticity', in Bill Ashcroft, Gareth Griffiths, Helen Tiffin (eds), *The Postcolonial Studies Reader*, Routledge, London, 1995, pp. 237–241.

Grimshaw, Patricia, and Willet, Graham, 'Women's history and family history: an exploration of colonial family structure', in Norma Grieve and Pat Grimshaw (eds), *Australian Women: Feminist Perspectives*, Oxford University Press, Melbourne, 1981, pp. 134–155.

Groves, Colin, 'Australia for the Australians', *Australian Humanities Review*, June 2002, accessed 5 July 2013, <http://www.australianhumanitiesreview.org/archive/Issue-June-2002/groves.html>.

Habermas, Jürgen, *The Structural Transformation of the Public Sphere*, Polity Press, Cambridge, 1989.

Hacking, Ian, *Representing and Intervening: Introductory Topics in the Philosophy of Natural Science*, Cambridge University Press, Cambridge, 1983.

Haebich, Anna, *Broken Circles: Fragmenting Indigenous Families 1800–2000*, Fremantle Arts Centre Press, Fremantle, 2000.

Hall, Catherine, and Davidoff, Leonore, *Family Fortunes: Men and Women of the English Middle Class 1780–1850*, Routledge, London, 1987.

Hamilton, Annette, 'A complex strategical situation: gender and power in Aboriginal Australia', in Norma Grieve and Patricia Grimshaw (eds), *Australian Women: Feminist Perspectives,* Oxford University Press, Melbourne, 1981, pp. 69–85.

Hamilton, Annette, 'Bond slaves of Satan: Aboriginal women and the mission dilemma', in Margaret Jolly and Martha MacIntyre (eds), *Family and Gender in the Pacific*, Cambridge University Press, Melbourne, 1989, pp. 236–58.

Hammerton, A. James, *Cruelty and Companionship: Conflict in Nineteenth Century Married Life,* Routledge, London, 1992.

Hartadi, Yohanes, 'An allegorical reading of Australia in European imaginative writings and exploration journals', seminar, 12 October 2005, Australian Centre, University of Melbourne.

Haskins, Victoria, 'On the doorstep: Aboriginal domestic service as a "contact zone"', *Australian Feminist Studies,* vol. 16, no. 34, 2001, pp. 13–25.

Haskins, Victoria, *One Bright Spot*, Palgrave MacMillan, Basingstoke, 2005.

Haskins, Victoria, 'From the centre to the city: modernity, mobility and mixed descent Aboriginal domestic workers from central Australia', *Women's History Review*, vol. 18, no. 1, 2009, pp. 155–175.

Haskins, Victoria, and Maynard, John, 'Sex, race and power: Aboriginal men and white women in Australian history', *Australian Historical Studies*, vol. 37, no. 126, 2005, pp. 191–216.

Hasty, William, 'Piracy and the production of knowledge in the travels of William Dampier c1679–1688', *Journal of Historical Geography*, vol. 37, no. 1, 2011, pp. 40–54.

Haynes, Christine, *Lost Illusions: The Politics of Publishing in Nineteenth-Century France*, Harvard University Press, Cambridge, 2010.

Healy, Chris, *From the Ruins of Colonialism: History as Social Memory*, Cambridge University Press, Cambridge, 1997.

Bibliography

Healy, Chris, *Forgetting Aborigines*, UNSW Press, Sydney, 2008.

Herbert, Christopher, *War of No Pity: The Indian Mutiny and Victorian Trauma*, Princeton University Press, Princeton, 2007.

'Hill, Edward Smith (1819–1880)', *Obituaries Australia*, National Centre of Biography, Australian National University, accessed 13 December 2013, <http://oa.anu.edu.au/obituary/hill-edward-smith-13704/text24487>.

Hill, M. K., 'The regulation of Aboriginal women in the Western Australian pearling industry, 1860–1905', unpublished thesis, University of Western Australia, 1994.

Hill, Marji, and Barlow, Alex, *Black Australia*, Australian Institute of Aboriginal Studies, Canberra, 1978.

Hind, Arthur M., *A History of Engraving and Etching: From the 15th Century to the year 1914*, Dover Publications, New York, 1963.

Hoare, Michael, 'Smyth, Robert Brough (1830–1889)', *Australian Dictionary of Biography*, National Centre of Biography, Australian National University, accessed 10 February 2012, <http://adb.anu.edu.au/biography/smyth-robert-brough-4621/text7609>.

Hogg, Robert, 'The unmanly savage: "Aboriginalism" and subordinate masculinities on the Queensland frontier', *Crossings,* March 2006, pp. 10.3–11.1.

Hogg, Robert, 'Performing manliness: "unmanly" men on British frontiers in the mid-nineteenth century', *Journal of Australian Studies*, vol. 35, no. 3, 2011, pp. 355–72.

Hokari, Minoru, 'Anti-minorities history: perspectives on Aboriginal–Asian relations', in Penny Edwards and Shen Yuanfang (eds), *Lost in the Whitewash: Aboriginal–Asian Encounters in Australia, 1901–2001*, Humanities Research Centre, Australian National University, Canberra, 2003, pp. 85–101.

Holcombe, Lea, *Wives and Property: Reform of the Married Women's Property Law in Nineteenth-century England*, University of Toronto Press, Toronto, 1983.

Holland, Alison, 'Feminism, colonialism and aboriginal workers: an anti-slavery crusade', in Ann McGrath and Kay Saunders with Jackie Huggins (eds), *Labour History*, Special issue: Aboriginal workers, no. 69, 1995, p. 52–64.

Holland, Alison, 'The campaign for women protectors: gender, race and frontier between the wars', *Australian Feminist Studies*, vol. 16, no. 34, 2001, pp. 27–42.

Holland, Alison, '"Whatever her race a woman is not a chattel": Mary Montgomery Bennet', in Anna Cole, Victoria Katharine Haskins and

Fiona Paisley (eds), *Uncommon Ground: White Women and Aboriginal History*, Aboriginal Studies Press, Canberra, 2005, pp. 129–152.

Horrell, Sara, and Humphries, Jane, 'Women's labour force participation and the transition to the male-breadwinner family, 1790–1865', in Pamela Sharpe (ed.), *Women's Work: The English Experience 1650–1914*, Arnold, London, 1998.

Houghton, Walter, 'Periodical literature and the articulate classes', in J. Shattock and M. Wolff (eds), *The Victorian Periodical Press: Samplings and Soundings*, Leicester University Press, Leicester, 1982.

Hoy, Edith Ellen, *Historiette of the Manfields who began their Mt. Buffalo Saga when the Buckland was at its Heyday in the Early 50s*, Harrietville Historical Society, Harrietville, Vic, 1965.

Hoy, Edith Ellen, *Harrietville, 115 Years of Continuous Gold Seeking*, Harrietville Historical Society, Harrietville, Vic, c. 1967.

Hughes-d'Aeth, Tony, *Paper Nation: The Story of the Picturesque Atlas of Australasia, 1886–1888*, Melbourne University Press, Melbourne, 2001.

Human Rights and Equal Opportunity Commission, *Bringing Them Home: The Report of the National Inquiry into the Separation of Aboriginal and Torres Strait Islander Children from their Families*, Human Rights and Equal Opportunity Commission, Sydney, 1997.

Hunt, Lyn, *The Invention of Pornography: Obscenity and the Origins of Modernity, 1500–1800*, Zone Books, New York, 2003.

Hunt, Susan Jane, *Spinifex and Hessian: Women's Lives in North-Western Australia 1860–1900*, University of Western Australia Press, Perth, 1986.

Jackson, Mark (ed.), *Infanticide: Historical Perspectives on Child Murder and Concealment, 1550–2000*, Ashgate, Burlington, 2002.

Jacobs, Margaret, *White Mother to a Dark Race: Settler Colonialism, Maternalism, and the Removal of Indigenous Children in the American West and Australia 1880–1940*, University of Nebraska Press, Lincoln, 2009.

Jalland, Patricia, *Australian Ways of Death: A Social and Cultural History, 1840–1918*, Oxford University Press, Melbourne, 2002.

James, Paul, *Globalism, Nationalism, Tribalism: Bringing Theory Back In*, Sage Publications, London, 2006.

Jay, Martin, *Downcast Eyes: The Denigration of Vision in Twentieth-Century French Thought*, University of California Press, Berkeley, 1994.

Jenkin, Graham, *Conquest of the Ngarrindjeri*, Rigby, Adelaide, 1979.

Jenkin, Graham, 'Taplin, George (1831–1879)', *Australian Dictionary of Biography*, National Centre of Biography, Australian National University, accessed 16 August 2013, <http://adb.anu.edu.au/biography/taplin-george-4687/text7757>.

Bibliography

Jennings, Francis, *The Invasion of America: Indians, Colonialism, and the Cant Of Conquest*, University of North Carolina Press, Chapel Hill, 1975.

Johnston, Anna, *The Paper War: Morality, Print Culture, and Power in Colonial New South Wales,* UWA Publishing, Perth, 2011.

Jolly, Margaret, 'Colonial and postcolonial plots in histories of maternities and modernities', in Kalpana Ram and Margeret Jolly (eds), *Maternities and Modernities: Colonial and Postcolonial Experiences in Asia and the Pacific*, Cambridge University Press, Cambridge, 1998, pp. 1–24.

Jones, Dorothy, 'Eden, Charles Henry (1839–1900)', *Australian Dictionary of Biography,* National Centre of Biography, Australian National University, accessed 26 January 2012, <http://adb.anu.edu.au/biography/eden-charles-henry-3466/text5301>.

Joppein, Rudiger, and Smith, Bernard, *The Art of Captain Cook's Voyages*, vol. 3, Yale University Press, New Haven, 1985–88.

Judd, Barry, '"It's not cricket": Victorian Aboriginal cricket at Coranderrk', in Lynette Russell and John Arnold (eds), *The La Trobe Journal,* Special issue: Indigenous Victorians: repressed, resourceful and respected, no. 85, May 2010, pp. 37–51.

Kaino, Lorna, '"Broome culture" and its historical links to the Japanese pearling industry', *Continuum, Journal of Media and Cultural Studies*, vol. 25, no. 4, 2011, pp. 479–90.

Kenny, Robert, *The Lamb Enters the Dreaming: Nathanael Pepper and the Ruptured World*, Scribe, Melbourne, 2007.

Kern, Stephen, *The Culture of Time and Space: 1880–1918*, Harvard University Press, Cambridge, 1983.

Kilday, Anne-Marie, *A History of Infanticide in Britain, c. 1600 to the Present*, Palgrave MacMillan, Houndsmills, 2013.

Kolenberg, Hendrik, and Ryan, Anne, 'Australian prints in the gallery's collection', Art Gallery of NSW, Sydney, 1998.

Konishi, Shino, 'Depicting sexuality: a case study of the Baudin expedition's Aboriginal ethnography', *Australian Journal of French Studies*, vol. 61, no. 2, 2004, pp. 98–118.

Konishi, Shino, '"Tied in rolled knots and powdered with ochre": Aboriginal hair and eighteenth-century cross-cultural encounters', in Shino Konishi, Leah Lui-Chivizhe and Lisa Slater (eds), *Borderlands*, Special issue: Indigenous bodies, vol. 7, no. 2, 2008.

Konishi, Shino, '"Wanton with plenty": questioning ethno-historical constructions of sexual savagery in Aboriginal societies, 1788–1803', *Australian Historical Studies*, vol. 39, no. 3, 2008, pp. 356–72.

Konishi, Shino, 'Idle men: the eighteenth-century roots of the Indigenous indolence myth', in Ann Curthoys, Frances Peters-Little and John Docker (eds), *Passionate Histories: Myth, Memory and Indigenous Histories*, Aboriginal History Monographs No. 23, ANU ePress, Canberra, 2010, pp. 99–122.

Konishi, Shino, 'Francois Peron and the Tasmanians: an unrequited romance', *Inside Story*, accessed 21 July 2011, <http://inside.org.au/an-unrequited-romance/>.

Konishi, Shino, 'Represent-ing Aboriginal masculinity in Howard's Australia', in R. L. Jackson II and M. Balaji (eds), *Global Masculinities and Manhood*, University of Illinois Press, Champaign, 2011, pp. 161–85.

Konishi, Shino, *The Aboriginal Male in the Enlightenment World*, Pickering and Chatto, London, 2012.

Kwaymullina, Sumi, 'For marbles: Aboriginal people in the early pearling industry of the North-West', *Studies In Western Australian History*, vol. 22, 2001, pp. 53–61.

Lack, Clem, 'Jardine, Francis Lascelles (Frank) (1841–1919)', *Australian Dictionary of Biography*, National Centre of Biography, Australian National University, 1972, accessed 27 February 2014, <http://adb.anu.edu.au/biography/jardine-francis-lascelles-frank-3924/text6117>.

Lake, Marilyn, 'Frontier feminism and the marauding white man', *Journal of Australian Studies: Australian Frontiers*, vol. 49, 1996, pp. 12–20.

Lake, Marilyn, *Faith: Faith Bandler, Gentle Activist*, Allen and Unwin, Sydney, 2002.

Lake, Marilyn, and Reynolds, Henry, *Drawing the Global Colour Line: White Men's Countries and the Question of Racial Equality*, Melbourne University Press, Melbourne, 2008.

Lamb, Jonathon, Smith, Vanessa and Thomas, Nicholas, *Exploration and Exchange: a South Seas Anthology, 1680–1900*, University of Hawai'i Press, Honolulu, 2004.

Landes, Joan, *Women and the Public Sphere in the Age of the French Revolution*, Cornell University Press, Ithaca, 1988.

Langton, Marcia, *'Well, I heard it on the radio and I saw it on the television …' An Essay for the Australian Film Commission on the Politics and Aesthetics of Filmmaking by and about Aboriginal People and Things*, Australian Film Commission, Sydney, 1993.

Langton, Marcia, 'The Hindmarsh Island Bridge affair: how Aboriginal women's religion became an administerable affair', *Australian Feminist Studies*, vol. 11, no. 24, 1996, pp. 211–217.

Langton, Marcia, 'Aboriginal art and film: the politics of representation', *Rouge*, 2005, accessed 16 March 2008, <http://www.rouge.com.au/6/aboriginal.html>.

Bibliography

The Last Tasmanian, 1978, documentary film, ARTIS Films, directed by Tom Haydon.
Lawson, Kate, and Shakinovsky, Lyn, *The Marked Body: Domestic Violence in Nineteenth Century Literature*, SUNY Press, Albany.
Le Griffon, Heather, *Campfires at the Cross: An Account of the Bunting Dale Aboriginal Mission 1839-1951 at Birregurra, Near Colac, Victoria: with a Biography of Francis Tuckfield*, Australian Scholarly Publishing, Melbourne, 2006.
Leonardi, Susan, and Pope, Rebecca, *The Diva's Mouth: Body, Voice, Prima Donna Politics*, Rutgers University, New Brunswick, 2008.
Leonardo, Micaela di, *Gender at the Crossroads of Knowledge: Feminist Anthropology in the Postmodern Era*, University of California Press, Berkeley, 1991.
Levin, David (ed.), *Modernity and the Hegemony of Vision*, University of California Press, Los Angeles, 1993.
Levine, Phillipa, 'States of undress: nakedness and the colonial imagination', *Victorian Studies*, vol. 50, no. 2, 2008, p. 189–219.
Lindsay, Vane, *The Inked-in Image: A Social and Historical Survey of Australian Comic Art*, Hutchinson of Australia, Richmond, 1979.
Lorimer, Douglas, 'Theoretical racism in late-victorian anthropology, 1870–1900', *Victorian Studies*, vol. 31, no. 3, 1988, p. 405–30.
Lott, Tommy L., *The Invention of Race: Black Culture and the Politics of Representation*, Malden, Blackwell, 1999.
Lydon, Jane, *Eye Contact: Photographing Indigenous Australians*, Duke University Press, Durham, 2005.
Lyons, Martyn, *A History of Reading and Writing in the Western World*, Palgrave MacMillan, New York, 2010.
Lyons, Martyn, and Arnold, John, *A History of the Book in Australia 1891-1945: A National Culture in a Colonised Market*, University of Queensland Press, Brisbane, 2001.
McClintock, Anne, *Imperial Leather: Race, Gender and Sexuality in the Colonial Contest*, Routledge, New York, 1995.
McGrath, Ann, '"Spinifex fairies": Aboriginal workers in the Northern Territory, 1911–1939', in Elizabeth Windschuttle (ed.), *Women, Class and History: Feminist Perspectives on Australia 1788–1978*, Fontana, Sydney, 1980, p. 237–62.
McGrath, Ann, '"Black velvet": Aboriginal women and their relations with white men in the Northern Territory 1910–1940', in Kay Daniels (ed.), *So Much Hard Work: Women and Prostitution in Australia*, Fontana, Sydney, 1984, pp. 233–97.

McGrath, Ann, '"The white man's looking glass": Aboriginal–colonial gender relations at Port Jackson', *Australian Historical Studies,* vol. 24, no. 99, 1990, pp. 186–206.

McGrath, Ann, '"Modern stone-age slavery: images of Aboriginal labour and sexuality', *Labour History,* Special issue: Aboriginal workers, no. 69, 1995, p. 30–51.

McGrath, Ann, 'Consent, marriage and colonialism: Indigenous Australian women and colonizer marriages', *Journal of Colonialism and Colonial History,* vol. 6, no. 3, 2005, pp. 1–23.

McGregor, Russell, *Imagined Destinies: Aboriginal Australians and the Doomed Race Theory,* Melbourne University Press, Melbourne, 1997.

McGuire, Margaret, 'The legend of the good fella missus', *Aboriginal History,* vol. 14, 1990, pp. 124–151.

McNiven, Ian J., Russell, Lynette, and Schaffer, Kay (eds), *Constructions of Colonialism: Perspectives on Eliza Fraser's Shipwreck,* Leicester University Press, London, 1998.

McQuire, Scott, *Visions of Modernity: Representation, Memory, Time and Space in the Age of the Camera,* Sage, London, 1997.

MacIntyre, Stuart, and Clark, Anna, *The History Wars,* Melbourne University Publishing, Melbourne, 2003.

Manne, Robert (ed.), *Whitewash: On Keith Windschuttle's Fabrication of Aboriginal History,* Black Inc. Agenda, Melbourne, 2003.

The Manning Index of South Australian History, accessed 1 April 2008, <http://www.slsa.sa.gov.au/manning/>.

Marchant, Leslie R., 'Freycinet, Louis-Claude Desaulses de (1779–1842)', *Australian Dictionary of Biography,* National Centre of Biography, Australian National University, accessed 29 January 2012, <http://adb.anu.edu.au/biography/freycinet-louis-claude-desaulses-de-2226/text1949>.

Marcus, Julie (ed.), *First in their Field: Women and Australian Anthropology,* Melbourne University Press, Melbourne, 1993.

Masquelier, Adeline, *Dirt, Undress, and Difference: Critical Perspectives on the Body's Surface,* Indiana University Press, Bloomington, 2005.

Maxwell, Anne, *Colonial Photography and Exhibitions: Representations of the 'Native' and the Making of European Identities,* Leicester University Press, London, 1991.

Merchant, Carolyn, *The Death of Nature: Women, Ecology and the Scientific Revolution,* Permagon, San Francisco, 1983.

Merry, Kay, 'The cross-cultural relationships between the sealers and the Tasmanian Aboriginal women at Bass Strait and Kangaroo Island in the early nineteenth century', *Counterpoints*, vol. 3, no. 1, 2003, pp. 80–88.

Michaels, Eric, 'A primer of restrictions on picture taking in traditional areas of Aboriginal Australia', *Visual Anthropology*, vol. 4, nos 3–4, 1991, pp. 259–75.

Mignolo, Walter, *The Dark Side of the Renaissance: Literacy, Territoriality and Colonization*, University of Michigan Press, Ann Arbor, 1995.

Mitchell, Adrian, *Dampier's Monkey: the South Sea voyages of William Dampier, including William Dampier's unpublished journal*, Wakefield Press, South Australia, 2010.

Mitchell, Dolores, 'Images of exotic women in turn-of-the-century tobacco art', *Feminist Studies*, vol. 18, no. 2, 1992, pp. 327–50.

Monaghan, Paul, review of Bob Reece, *Daisy Bates, Grand Dame of the Desert*, National Library of Australia, Canberra, 2007, in *Aboriginal History*, vol. 34, 2010, pp. 239–41.

Montrose, Louis, 'The work of gender in the discourse of discovery', *Representations,* Special issue: The new world, no. 33, Winter 1991, pp. 1–41.

Moore, Ronald, 'The management of the West Australian pearling industry, 1860 to 1930', *Great Circle*, vol. 16, no. 2, 1994, pp. 121–138.

Moorehead, Alan, *The Fatal Impact: An Account of the Invasion of the South Pacific 1767–1840*, Penguin, Harmondsworth, 1966.

Moreton-Robinson, Aileen, *Talkin' up to the White Woman: Indigenous Women and Feminism,* Queensland University Press, Brisbane, 2000.

Morgan, E. J. R., 'Angas, George French (1822–1886)', *Australian Dictionary of Biography*, National Centre of Biography, Australian National University, accessed 7 July 2013, <http://adb.anu.edu.au/biography/angas-george-french-1708/text1857>.

Morgan, Jennifer L., '"Some could suckle over their shoulder": male travelers, female bodies, and the gendering of racial ideology, 1500–1770', *The William and Mary Quarterly*, vol. 54, no. 1, January 1997, pp. 167–192.

Morgan, Sally, *My Place*, Fremantle Arts Centre Press, Fremantle, 1987.

Morris, John, 'Potential allies of the enemy: the Tiwi in World War Two', *Journal of Northern Territory History,* no. 15, 2004, pp. 77–90.

Morris, John, 'The Japanese and the Aborigines: an overview of the efforts to stop the prostitution of coastal and island women', *Journal of Northern Territory History*, no. 21, 2010, pp. 15–36.

Morris, Meaghan, 'Panorama: the live, the dead and the living', in Graeme Turner (ed.), *Nation, Culture, Text: Australian Cultural and Media Studies*, Routledge, London, 1993, pp. 19–58.

Moseley, H. D., 'Report following the Royal Commission on Aborigines, 24 January 1935', in Sharman Stone (ed.), *Aborigines in White Australia: A Documentary History of the Attitudes Affecting Official Policy and the Australian Aborigine 1697–1973*, Heinemann, Melbourne, 1974, p. 167.

Mosely, Kathryn, 'The history of infanticide in western society', *Issues in Law & Medicine*, vol. 1, no. 5, 1986, pp. 345–61.

Moses, Dirk A., *Genocide and Settler Society: Frontier Violence and Stolen Indigenous Children in Australian History*, Berghahn Books, New York, 2005.

Mountford, C. P., and Harvey, Alison, 'Women of the Adnjamatana tribe of the Northern Flinders Ranges, South Australia', *Oceania*, vol. 12, 1941–42, pp. 155–63.

Muecke, Stephen, *Ancient and Modern: Time Culture and Indigenous Philosophy*, University of New South Wales Press, Sydney, 2004.

Mulvaney, D. J., 'Thomas, William (1793–1867)', *Australian Dictionary of Biography*, National Centre of Biography, Australian National University, accessed 10 February 2012, <http://adb.anu.edu.au/biography/thomas-william-2727/text3845>.

Mulvaney, D. J., 'Willshire, William Henry (1852–1925)', *Australian Dictionary of Biography*, National Centre of Biography, Australian National University, accessed 20 December 2013, <http://adb.anu.edu.au/biography/willshire-william-henry-9128/text16101>.

Murakami, Yuichi, 'Australia's immigration legislation, 1893–1901: the Japanese response', in Paul Jones and Vera Mackie (eds), *Relationships: Japan and Australia, 1870s–1930s*, University of Melbourne, Melbourne, 2001, pp. 45–70.

Museum of Australian Democracy, *Documenting a democracy*, accessed 15 June 2013, <http://foundingdocs.gov.au>.

Nakano, Fujio, 'Japanese pearl divers of Broome', *Geo: Australia's National Geographic*, vol. 2, no. 4, 1980, pp. 112–121.

Nagata, Yuriko, 'Japanese-Australians in the post-war Thursday Island community', *Queensland Review*, vol. 6, no. 2, 1999, pp. 30–43.

Nagata, Yuriko, 'The Japanese in Torres Strait', in Anna Shnukal, Guy Ramsay and Yuriko Nagata (eds), *Navigating Boundaries: The Asian Diaspora in Torres Strait*, Pandanus Books, Canberra, 2004, pp. 138–59.

Nead, Lynne, *Myths of Sexuality: Representations of Women in Victorian Britain*, Basil Blackwell, Oxford, 1988.

Neill, Anna, 'Buccaneer ethnography: nature, culture and nation in the journals of William Dampier', *Eighteenth-Century Studies*, vol. 33, no. 2, 2000, p. 165–80.

Niezen, Ronald, *The Origins of Indigenism: Human Rights and the Politics of Identity*, University of California Press, Berkeley, 2003.

Nussbaum, Felicity A., '"Savage" mothers: narratives of maternity in the mid-eighteenth century', *Cultural Critique*, no. 20, Winter 1991–92, p. 123–51.

Obeyesekere, Gananath, *The Apotheosis of Captain Cook: European Mythmaking in the Pacific*, Princeton University Press, New Jersey, 1992.

O'Brien, Patty, 'The gaze of the "ghosts": images of Aboriginal women in New South Wales and Port Phillip (1800–1850)', in Jan Kociumbas (ed.), *Maps, Dreams and History: Race and Representation in Australia*, Braxus Publishing, Sydney, 1998, p, 313–400.

O'Connell, Lisa, '"Matrimonial ceremonies displayed", popular ethnography and enlightened imperialism', *Eighteenth-Century Life*, vol. 26, no. 3, 2002 pp. 98–116.

Oldfield, Augustus, 'On the Aborigines of Australia', *Transactions of the Ethnological Society of Great Britain*, no. 3, 1865, pp. 215–98.

O'Regan, Tom, 'Documentary in controversy: The Last Tasmanian', *An Australian Film Reader*, 1985, pp. 127–36, accessed 5 January 2012, <http://wwwmcc.murdoch.edu.au/ReadingRoom/film/Tasmanian.html>.

Organ, Michael, *SMS Novara in Sydney, 1858, Chronology*, 6 September 2008, accessed 13 December 2013, <http://www.uow.edu.au/~morgan/novara15.htm>.

Paisley, Fiona, *Loving Protection: Australian Feminism and Aboriginal Women's Rights 1919–1939*, Melbourne University Press, Melbourne, 2000.

Paisley, Fiona, 'Race hysteria, Darwin 1938', *Australian Feminist Studies*, vol. 16, no. 34, 2001, pp. 43–59.

Paisley, Fiona, '"For a brighter day": Constance Ternent Cooke', in Cole, Haskins and Paisley (eds), *Uncommon Ground: White Women in Aboriginal History*, Aboriginal Studies Press, Canberra, 2005, pp. 172–96.

Unattributed, *Pauline Hanson: The Truth*, Ipswich, self-published, 1997.

Quilley, Geoff, *The Captain's Artist: The Career of John Webber R.A., Smoking Coasts and Ice-Bound Seas: Cook's Voyage to the Arctic*, Catalogue to the Exhibition at the Captain Cook Memorial Museum, Whitby, 2008.

Perkin, Joan, *Women and Marriage in Nineteenth-Century England*, Routledge, London, 1989.

Perry, Ruth, 'Colonizing the breast: sexuality and maternity in eighteenth-century England', *Journal of the History of Sexuality*, Special issue, Part 1: The state, society, and the regulation of sexuality in modern Europe, vol. 2, no. 2, 1991, pp. 204–34.

Pekacz, Jolanta T., 'The salonnieres and the philosophies in old regime France: the authority of aesthetic judgment', *Journal of the History of Ideas*, vol. 60, no. 2, 1999, pp. 277–97.

Pickering, Michael, 'Cannibalism amongst Aborigines? A critical review of the literary evidence', unpublished Litt. B. thesis, Australian National University, Canberra, 1985.

Pickering, Michael, 'Food for thought: an alternative to "Cannibalism in the Neolithic"', *Australian Archaeology*, no. 28, June 1989, pp. 35–39.

Pickering, Michael, 'Consuming doubts: What some people ate? Or what some people swallowed?', in Laurence Goldman (ed.), *The Anthropology of Cannibalism*, Bergin and Garvey, London, 1999, pp. 51–74.

Poignant, Rosalyn, *Professional Savages: Captive Lives and Western Spectacle*, University of New South Wales Press, Sydney, 2004.

Poole, Deborah, *Vision, Race and Modernity: A Visual Economy of the Andean World*, Princeton University Press, Princeton, 1997.

Porter, Roy, and Hall, Lesley, *The Facts of Life: The Creation of Sexual Knowledge in Britain, 1650–1950*, Yale University Press, New Haven, 1995.

Povinelli, Elizabeth A., *The Empire of Love: Toward a Theory of Intimacy, Genealogy and Carnality*, Duke University Press, Durham, 2006.

Pratt, Mary Louise, *Imperial Eyes: Travel Writing and Transculturation*, Routledge, New York, 1992.

Preston, D. and Preston, M., *A Pirate of Exquisite Mind: The Life of William Dampier, Explorer, Naturalist and Buccaneer*, London, 2004.

Pringle, Rosemary, 'Octavius Beale and the ideology of the birthrate', *Refractory Girl*, no. 3, 1975, pp. 19–27.

Radi, Heather, 'Kelly, Emily Caroline (Carrie) (1899–1989)', *Australian Dictionary of Biography*, National Centre of Biography, Australian National University, accessed 15 February 2013, <http://adb.anu.edu.au/biography/kelly-emily-caroline-carrie-12720/text22937>.

'Reverend William Yate', *Queer History: New Zealand Gay, Lesbian, Bisexual and Transgender New Zealand History*, accessed 10 February 2012, <http://www.gaynz.net.nz/history/Yate.html>.

Reynolds, Barrie, 'Roth, Walter Edmund (1861–1933)', *Australian Dictionary of Biography*, National Centre of Biography, Australian National University, accessed 24 December 2013, <http://adb.anu.edu.au/biography/roth-walter-edmund-8280/text14509>.

Reynolds, Henry, *The Other Side of the Frontier: Aboriginal Resistance of the European Invasion of the Australia*, Penguin, Ringwood, Vic, 1981.

Reynolds, Henry, *Dispossession: Black Australians and White Invaders*, Allen and Unwin, Sydney, 1989.

Bibliography

Reynolds, Henry, *With the White People: The Crucial Role of Aborigines in the Exploration and Development of Australia*, Penguin, Ringwood, 1990.

Reynolds, Henry, *This Whispering in our Hearts*, Allen and Unwin, Sydney, 1998.

Reynolds, Henry, *North of Capricorn: The Untold Story of Australia's North*, Allen and Unwin, Sydney, 2003.

Rienits, Rex, 'White, John (1756–1832)', *Australian Dictionary of Biography*, National Centre of Biography, Australian National University, accessed 26 July 2011, <http://adb.anu.edu.au/biography/white-john-2787/text3971>.

Roberts, M. J. D., *Making English Morals: Voluntary Association and Moral Reform*, Cambridge University Press, Cambridge, 2004.

Romaniello, Matthew, *Productive Men, Reproductive Women: The Agrarian Household and the Emergence of Separate Spheres During the German Enlightenment*, Berghahn Books, New York, 2000.

Rose, Deborah Bird, *Hidden Histories: Black stories from Victoria River Downs, Humbert River and Wave Hill Stations*, Aboriginal Studies Press, Canberra, 1991.

Rosenthal, Angela, 'Raising hair', *Eighteenth-Century Studies*, vol. 38, no. 1, 2004, pp. 1–16.

Rosenthal, Laura, *Infamous Commerce: Prostitution in Eighteenth-Century British Literature and Culture*, Cornell University Press, Ithaca, 2006.

Rowley, C. D., *The Destruction of Aboriginal Society*, Penguin, Ringwood, Vic, 1970.

Rowse, Tim, 'Barwick, Diane Elizabeth (1938–1986)', *Australian Dictionary of Biography*, National Centre of Biography, Australian National University, accessed 15 February 2013, <http://adb.anu.edu.au/biography/barwick-diane-elizabeth-76/text21837>.

Rowse, Tim, *White Flour, White Power: From Rations to Citizenship in Central Australia*, Cambridge University Press, Cambridge, 1998.

Ruddick, N., 'Courtship with a club: wife-capture in prehistoric fiction, 1865–1914', *Yearbook of English Studies*, vol. 37, no. 2, 2007, pp. 45–63.

Russell, Lynette, '"Dirty domestics and worse cooks": Aboriginal women's agency and domestic frontiers, southern Australia, 1800–1850', *Frontiers: A Journal of Women's Studies*, vol. 28, nos 1–2, 2007, pp. 18–46.

Russell, Lynette, *Roving Mariners: Australian Aboriginal Whalers and Sealers in the Southern Oceans, 1790–1870*, SUNY Press, Albany, 2012.

Ryan, Lyndall, *The Aboriginal Tasmanians*, Allen and Unwin, Melbourne, 1981.

Ryan, Lyndall, '"Hard evidence": the debate about massacre in the black war of Tasmania', in Frances Peters-Little, Ann Curthoys and John Docker (eds), *Passionate Histories: Myth, Memory and Indigenous Australia*, ANU Epress, Canberra, 2010, pp. 39–50.

Ryan, Lyndall, *Tasmanian Aborigines – A History since 1803*, Allen & Unwin, Sydney, 2013.

Said, Edward W., *Orientalism: Western Conceptions of the Orient*, 4th edn, Penguin, London, 1995 (1978).

Saintelan, Nicole, '"Music – if it may so be called": perception and response in the documentation of Aboriginal music in Aboriginal Australia', unpublished MA thesis, University of New South Wales, 1993.

Salmon, Marylynn, 'The cultural significance of breastfeeding and infant care in early modern England and America', *Journal of Social History*, vol. 28, no. 2, 1994, pp. 247–69.

Salmond, Anne, *Aphrodite's Island: The European Discovery of Tahiti*, Penguin, Auckland, 2009.

Salvado, Rosendo, *The Salvado Memoirs*, trans. E. J. Stormon, University of Western Australia Press, Perth, 1977.

Sanborn, Geoffrey, *The Sign of the Cannibal*, Duke University Press, Durham and London, 1998.

Sanky, Margaret, 'Perceptions of the Aborigines recorded during the Baudin expedition: the dynamics of first encounter', in Bruce Bennett (ed.), *Australia in Between Cultures, Specialists Session papers from the 1998 Australian Academy of the Humanities Symposium*, Australian Academy of the Humanities, Canberra, 1999, pp. 55–76.

Sanky, Margaret, Fornasiero, Jean and Cowley, Peter, 'The Baudin expedition in review: old quarrels and new approaches', *Australian Journal of French Studies*, vol. 41, no. 2, 2004, pp. 4–14.

Sayers, Andrew, 'McRae, Tommy (1835–1901)', *Australian Dictionary of Biography*, National Centre of Biography, Australian National University, accessed 8 October 2015, <http://adb.anu.edu.au/biography/mcrae-tommy-13074/text23649>.

Schaffer, Kay, *In the Wake of First Contact: The Eliza Fraser Stories*, Cambridge University Press, Melbourne, 1995.

Schaper, Michael, 'The Broome race riots of 1920', *Studies in Western Australian History*, no. 16, 1995, pp. 112–132.

Schiebinger, Londa, 'Why mammals are called mammals: gender politics in eighteenth-century natural history', *The American Historical Review*, vol. 98, no. 2, 1993, pp. 382–411.

Sen, Satadru, 'The savage family: colonialism and female infanticide in nineteenth century India', *Journal of Women's History*, vol. 14, no. 3, 2002.

Serle, Geoffrey, 'Westgarth, William (1815–1889)', *Australian Dictionary of Biography*, National Centre of Biography, Australian National University, accessed 17 July 2013, <http://adb.anu.edu.au/biography/westgarth-william-4830/text8057>.

Shanley, Mary Lyndon, *Feminism, Marriage, and the Law in Victorian England, 1850–1895*, Princeton University Press, Princeton, 1993.

Sharp, Nonie, *Footprints along the Cape York Sandbeaches*, Aboriginal Studies Press, Canberra, 1992.

Shookman, Ellis (ed.), *The Faces of Physiognomy: Interdisciplinary Approaches to Johann Caspar Lavater*, Camden House, Columbia, 1993.

Simmel, G. 'The nobility' [1908], in Donald Levine (ed.), *Georg Simmel on Individuality and Social Forms,* University of Chicago Press, Chicago, 1971, pp. 199–213.

Smith, Bernard, Boyer Lecture, 'The spectre of Truganini', 1980.

Smith, Bernard, *European Vision and the South Pacific*, Harper and Row, Sydney, 1985 (1969).

Solomon-Godeau, Abigail, 'Going native', *Art in America,* 1989, pp. 119–29, 161.

Sontag, Susan, *On Photography*, Penguin, Harmondsworth, 1977.

Spivak, Gayatri, 'Can the subaltern speak?', in Cary Nelson and Lawrence Grossberg (eds), *Marxism and the Interpretation of Culture*, MacMillan, Houndmills, 1988, pp. 271–313.

Standish, Ann, 'Daisy Bates: dubious leadership', 2012, *Seizing the Initiative: Australian Women Leaders in Politics, Workplaces and Communities*, accessed 3 January 2013, <http://www.womenaustralia.info/leaders/sti/standish.html>.

Stanner, W. E. H., Boyer Lecture, 'The great Australian silence', 1968.

Stanner, W. E. H., 'Howitt, Alfred William (1830–1908)', *Australian Dictionary of Biography,* National Centre of Biography, Australian National University, accessed 11 February 2012, <http://adb.anu.edu.au/biography/howitt-alfred-william-510/text6037>.

Stanner, W. E. H., 'The history of indifference thus begins', *Aboriginal History*, vol. 1, no. 1, 1977, pp. 3–26.

Stephens, Marguerita, 'A word of evidence: shared tales about infanticide and "others not us" in colonial Victoria', in Jane Carey and Claire McLisky (eds), *Creating White Australia*, Sydney University Press, Sydney, 2009, pp. 175–194.

Stephens, Marguerita, *White Without Soap: Philanthropy, Caste and Exclusion in Colonial Victoria. A Political Economy of Race*, Melbourne University Book Custom Centre, Melbourne, 2010.

Stephens, Marguerita, 'Infanticide at Port Phillip: Protector William Thomas

and the witnessing of things unseen', *Aboriginal History*, vol. 38, 2014, pp. 109–30.
Stephenson, Peta, 'New cultural scripts: exploring the dialogue between indigenous and "Asian" Australians', *Journal of Australian Studies*, Special issue: Sojourners and strangers, vol. 27, no. 77, 2003, pp. 57–68.
Stocking, George, *Victorian Anthropology*, Free Press, New York, 1991.
Stoler, Ann Laura, 'Sexual affronts and racial frontiers: European identities and the cultural politics of exclusion in colonial Southeast Asia', in Frederick Cooper and Ann Laura Stoler (eds), *Tensions of Empire: Colonial Cultures in a Bourgeois World*, University of California Press, Berkeley, 1997, pp. 198–237.
Stoler, Ann Laura, *Carnal Knowledge and Imperial Power: Race and the Intimate in Colonial Rule*, University of California Press, Berkeley, 2002.
Stoler, Ann Laura, *Along the Archival Grain: Epistemic Anxieties and Colonial Sense*, Princeton University Press, Princeton, 2009.
Stuart, A., Review of Lyndall Ryan (ed.), 'Secret women's business: the Hindmarsh Island affair', Special issue of *Journal of Australian Studies*, no. 48, 1996, *Australian Feminist Studies*, vol. 12, no. 26, 1997, p. 357.
Taussig, Michael, *Mimesis and Alterity: A Particular History of the Senses*, Routledge, New York, 1993.
Taylor, Paul T., 'Malcom's conk and Danto's colors; or four logical petitions concerning race, beauty, and aesthetics', in Peg Zeglin Brand (ed.), *Beauty Matters*, Indiana University Press, Bloomington, 2000.
Thomas, Nicholas, *Possessions: Indigenous Art/Colonial Culture*, Thames and Hudson, London, 1987.
Thomas, Nicolas, *In Oceania: Visions, Artefacts, Histories*, Duke University Press, Durham, 1997.
Thomas, Nicholas, *Islanders: The Pacific in the Age of Empire*, Yale University Press, New Haven, 2010.
Thompson, Lisa B., *Beyond the Black Lady: Sexuality and the New African American Middle Class*, Chicago, University of Illinois Press, 2009.
Thornton-Smith, Colin, 'French perceptions of the colony of Victoria – facts, fiction and euphoria', *Explorations: A Journal of French Australian Connections*, accessed 7 February 2012, <http://www.msp.unimelb.edu.au/index.php/explorations/article/view/11/10>.
Torgovnick, Marianna, *Gone Primitive: Savage Intellects and Modern Lives*, University of Chicago Press, Chicago, 1990.
Toussaint, Sandy, *Phyllis Kaberry and Me: Anthropology, History and Aboriginal Australia*, Melbourne University Press, Melbourne, 1999.
Toussaint, Sandy, 'Preface', in Phyllis Kabbery, *Aboriginal Woman: Sacred and Profane*, Routledge, London, 2004 (1939).

Bibliography

van Groesen, Michiel, *The Representations of the Overseas World in the De Bry Collection of Voyages (1590–1634)*, Leiden, Boston, 2008.

Veracini, Lorenzo, *Settler Colonialism: A Theoretical Overview*, Palgrave Macmillan, Houndsmills, 2010.

Verhoeven, Deb, *Sheep and the Australian Cinema*, Melbourne University Press, Melbourne, 2006.

Walsh, G. P., 'Mowbray, Philip Henry Mitchell (Phil) (1845–1903)', *Australian Dictionary of Biography,* National Centre of Biography, Australian National University, accessed 14 January 2014, <http://adb.anu.edu.au/biography/mowbray-philip-henry-mitchell-phil-13116/text23733>.

Weeks, Jeffrey, *Sex, Politics and Society: The Regulation of Sexuality since 1800*, Longman, London, 1989.

Wells, Stanley and Stanton, Sarah (eds), *The Cambridge Companion to Shakespeare on Stage*, Cambridge University Press, Cambridge, 2002.

White, Isobel, 'Daisy Bates: legend and reality' in Julie Marcus (ed.), *First in their Field: Women and Australian Anthropology,* Melbourne University Press, Melbourne, 1993, pp. 46–65.

Williamson, Laila, 'Infanticide: an anthropological analysis', in M. Kohl (ed.), *Infanticide and the Value of Life*, Prometheus, New York, 1978.

Windschuttle, Keith, *The Fabrication of Aboriginal History, Volume One: Van Diemen's Land 1803–1847*, Macleay Press, Paddington, 2002.

Wolfe, Patrick, *Settler Colonialism and the Transformation of Anthropology: The Politics and Poetics of an Ethnographic Event*, Cassell, London, 1999.

Wolfe, Patrick, 'Land, labor, and difference: elementary structures of race', *American Historical Review*, vol. 106, no. 3, 2001, pp. 866–905.

Wolfe, Patrick, 'Settler colonialism and the elimination of the native', *Journal of Genocide Research*, vol. 8, no. 4, 2006, pp. 387–409.

Women of the Sun, SBS, 1981. Directed by James Ricketson, David Stevens, Stephen Wallace and Geoffrey Nottage, co-written by Sonia Borg and Hyllus Maris.

Woollacott, Angela, 'White colonialism and sexual modernity: Australian women in the early twentieth-century metropolis', in Antoinette Burton (ed.), *Gender, Sexuality and Colonial Modernities,* Routledge, London, 1999, p. 49–62.

Woollacott, Angela, *To Try Her Fortune in London: Australian Women, Colonialism, and Modernity*, Oxford University Press, Oxford, 2001.

Woollacott, Angela, 'Frontier violence and settler manhood', *History Australia*, vol. 6, no. 1, 2009, pp. 11.1–11.15.

Wright, Nancy, 'The problem of Aboriginal evidence in early colonial New

South Wales', in Diane Kirkby and Catherine Coleborne (eds), *Law, History, Colonialism: The Reach of Empire*, Manchester University Press, Manchester, 2001, pp. 140–55.

Yeo, Eileen Janes, 'The creation of "motherhood" and women's responses in Britain and France, 1750–1914', *Women's History Review*, vol. 8, no. 2, 1999, p. 201.

Yeo, Richard, 'Science and intellectual authority in mid-nineteenth-century Britain: Robert Chambers and "Vestiges of the Natural History of Creation', *Victorian Studies*, vol. 28, no. 1, 1984, pp. 5–31.

Young, Robert, *White Mythologies: Writing History and the West*, Routledge, London, 1990.

Young, Robert J. C., 'Egypt in America: *Black Athena*, racism and colonial discourse', in Ali Rattansi and Sallie Westwood (eds), *Racism, Modernity and Identity: On the Western Front*, Polity Press, Cambridge, 1994, Chapter 4.

Unpublished works

Huebner, Sharon, 'Noongar and Koories: interpreting the silences of a colonial archive at Monash University', PhD thesis, Monash Indigenous Centre, Monash University (forthcoming).

Morgan, Jennifer Lyle, 'Labouring women, enslaved women: reproduction and slavery in Barbados and South Carolina, 1650–1750', PhD thesis, Duke University, 1995.

Sturrock, Morna, 'European and Aboriginal conflict in the western district and the north-east of Victoria, in the first decade of white settlement', Glen Waverly, 1983.

Statutes

Masters and Servants Act 1892, Western Australia
The Pacific Islands Labourers Act 1901
Aborigines Act 1905
Aboriginals Ordinance 1911, Northern Territory

INDEX

activism: Aboriginal 12; women's 27, 141, 279. *See also* humanitarians; resistance
Australian Aborigines' League 315
Aborigines' Friends' Association (AFA) 139, 205
Aborigines' Friends' Society 304–5
Aborigines Progressive Association 10
advertising 250, 260
aging, *see* beauty
Ainsworth, W. F. 342
Aiston, George 279
Anderson, George William 61–62
Angas, George French 184–5, 185fig, 197–8, 326–7, 329, 346, 358
Ansell, Charles 66fig, 68
anthropology 5, 12, 27, 47, 111, 118, 126, 129–32, 135, 158, 205, 229, 231, 341; women anthropologists 47, 119, 254, 256 (*see also* Barwick, Diane; Berndt, Catherine; Kaberry, Phyllis). *See also* ethnology
Armstrong, Francis 173
Arra-Maïda 74–78, 75fig, 80fig, 81–86, 88–89
'Asiatic' men 286, 288–9, 292–3, 298, 305–6, 310–11, 313–14. *See also* pearling industry, scandal

assimilation policy 153–4, 161, 236, 254, 257, 267, 279, 290, 308–9, 313, 360
Austin, Robert 223
Australian Institute for Aboriginal and Torres Strait Islander Studies 20, 34

Bairuk 219
Baker, Charles 115
Baker, John 205–6
Bakunji 210
Balbuk-Yooreel, Fanny 31
Bandjin 7
Bandler, Faith 26
Banks, Joseph 61, 64, 293, 294, 335
Barrett, Charles 17, 261, 262, 358–9
Barrington, George 103, 296
Barwick, Dianne 27, 140, 256
Basedow, Herbert 229, 232, 354, 362
Bass Strait 160, 242
Batman, John 166
Bates, Daisy 2, 22, 31, 156, 158–9, 177, 204, 223, 226–31, 234, 237, 241, 246, 272, 280–2
Baudin, Nicolas 74–80, 86, 107, 295
beauty, conceptions of 333, 336–40, 344–5, 347–8, 351, 353, 355–61, 363
Bellchambers, T. P. 361

Index

Benalla 9, 14
Bennett, George 137, 198
Bennett, Mary Montgomery 26, 229, 233, 307, 315, 324
Bennett, Samuel 52
Berndt, Catherine 140, 212–3, 256–7
Berndt, Ronald 212–3
Bibliography of the Australian Aborigines and the Native Peoples of Torres Strait to 1959 44–46, 101, 371–4. *See also* Greenway, John
Bidawal 16
Billibellary 159, 174
Bingham, Henry 180
biological absorption, *see* eugenics discourse
Blainey, Geoffrey 6
Bleakley, J. W. 266, 269, 313
Blumenbach, Johann 340
Boer War 48
Bonwick, James 97, 186, 202, 338
Booandik 209
Bougainville 61, 293, 337, 360
Bowman, William 16
Breton, Lieutenant R. N. 110, 169
bride capture 92, 94, 101–36, 104fig, 106fig, 111fig, 114fig, 220
Bringing Them Home report 161
Broome, Richard 14
Brough Smyth, Robert 97, 124–25, 127, 216–7, 218, 223, 231, 361
Brown, Robert 110, 122, 216, 347
Browne, C. S. 46
Brunton Stephens, J. 351
Buckley, William 171–3, 186, 189, 202
Bulmer, John 127, 130
Bunjil 219
Burton, Rev. J. W. 315–16

Caledon Bay 312, 319
Calvert, Albert 51, 52, 54
Cameron, Bessy 32
Campbell, Kenneth 181–3
Canberra 147–8
cannibalism 156, 171–3, 176, 181, 192, 195, 196, 213, 216, 220, 226–30, 232, 235
cartoons 6, 112, 241, 242, 260, 272, 273–276, 282, 358; Minns, B. E. 273, 276fig; Maclean, Hugh 5fig, 273, 275fig, 357fig, 358; Cross, Stan 273fig; Paul, Mick 274fig; May, Phil 276; Jolliffe, Eric 10, 301–2
Castelli 86
Central Australia 132, 212, 220, 222, 227, 261
Chauvel, Charles 242–3
Chauvel, Elsa 242–4, 244fig, 269, 272
child bestowal 97
child mortality 154–5, 174, 178–9, 181, 187, 211, 233–5, 237, 266–7
child removal 154, 161, 170, 174–5, 200, 201, 205, 211, 230, 233, 238, 254, 279, 290, 369
children, 'half-caste' 160, 169–70, 180, 187, 188, 202, 219, 221–2, 228, 229, 230, 235, 254, 280, 290, 308, 310, 313
cicatrisation, *see* scarification
clothing: European 51, 60, 68–9, 196, 200, 262–3, 281, 328, 331–2, 336, 363; 'drover's boy' 145, 332; footwear 240, 270, 276, 278. *See also* nakedness
Cox, Harry 320fig, 321–22
Clune, Frank 278
Colac tribe 189–90

Index

Col-bé 165–6
Colebatch, Sir Hal 53
Collins, David 102–03, 109, 165–6, 216, 228, 231
colonial archive 6, 7, 24–27, 37–38, 360. *See also* print: archive
colonial chivalry, *see* masculinity: settler gallantry
colonial gaze 58, 258, 262, 300, 328, 331–2. *See also* visual field
communalism 39, 252–4
Conigrave, C. Price 259
contact zones 155, 157, 235, 240, 242, 251
Cook, Dr Cecil E. 230, 308–10
Cook, Constance Ternent 233
Cook, Captain James 56–64, 81, 171, 294, 335–7, 360
Coranderrk 10, 361
Corbett, Sally 17–19, 18fig
Cross, Stan, *see* cartoons
cultural captioning 3, 25, 26, 41, 60, 65, 89, 301
Cunningham, Peter 169–71
Curr, Edward M. 32, 127–9, 160, 215, 217–9, 225, 231, 232, 299, 338, 353

Dampier, William 50–58, 338, 341
Dandan, *see* Toolooa
d'Arc, Henri Perron 98–99
Darwin, Charles 163, 341; social Darwinism 119, 221–2, 240
Davis, James 203
Dawson, James 217–8
Dawson, Robert 172, 344
de Bry, Theodore 171
de Rienzi, Domeny 107–08, 107fig
Degérando, Joseph-Marie 79, 81
depopulation 17, 46, 115–6, 129, 137, 154, 157–8, 166, 187–8, 190–1, 200–2, 209, 219, 222, 226, 355. *See also* 'dying race' theory
Dewhurst, Rev. B. H. 317
Dhudhuroa 16
Diderot 61, 293
disease 17, 70, 102, 154, 157, 160, 162, 178, 200, 209, 233, 266–7, 281, 321, 329, 360; smallpox 17, 166, 178, 209; tuberculosis 178; venereal (including syphilis) 150, 159, 187, 201, 235, 296, 304–6, 309–10
dispossession, *see* land: theft
Djargurd wurrung 217–8
domestic servitude, Aboriginal women's 8, 240–2, 251, 261, 263–4, 266fig, 267–8, 271fig, 272–3, 277–8
domesticity 38, 140, 168, 241–3, 251–2, 254, 256, 263–5, 265fig, 267–8, 270, 272–3, 276–9, 282. *See also* cartoons
Dowling, Freddie 19, 35
Drake-Brockman, Henrietta 267
Dredge, James 137, 180–1
du Fresne, Marion 61, 81
Duguid, Charles 303
Duncan-Kemp, Alice 2, 11, 26, 223, 241, 263, 268, 272
'dying race' theory: 28, 39–40, 154–5, 193, 201–2, 204, 207, 221–2, 224, 228, 229, 235–6, 296, 328, 342–3, 350, 355, 360; linked to gendered violence 137–8; as rationale for child removal 154, 162. *See also* depopulation

Eden, Charles Henry 90–95, 97, 352
education, Aboriginal children's 211

Index

Eldershaw, Finney 116–17
elopement 130, 134. See also bride capture
Empire 51, 166, 195, 203
Enlightenment 56, 61, 76, 89, 99, 251–2, 333
ethnology 56, 60, 72, 78, 109, 118, 133, 197, 219–20, 223, 231, 296, 330–1, 340, 342–3
eugenics discourse 221–2, 234, 236, 313, 317
Evans, Raymond 143, 306
Eyre, Edward John 222, 232, 350

Faithfull, George 15. See also massacres
Farrer, James Anson 129–30
feet, Aboriginal women's. See clothing, footwear
femininity 3, 38, 55, 83, 151, 260, 264, 266, 325, 337–8, 345, 358, 361, 363, 367
feminisation, of land and nature 55, 63, 252, 286, 333, 345, 348, 367
feminism 257, 338, 367
fertility 46, 154–7, 163, 187, 190, 201, 210, 219, 224–5, 233–6, 355
Fison, Lorimer 130–32, 218, 223
Flinders, Matthew 85
Flynn, Rev. John 255
footwear, *see* clothing, footwear
Fox, G. 133, 224
Fraser, Eliza 90, 101
Friday, Kate 9
Fuller, Rev. Edward 214
Furneaux, Tobias 62
Fyans, Captain 188, 195–6

Galton, Francis 221
Gason, Samuel 160, 214–5
gender relations: Aboriginal 73, 95, 96, 251, 254–7; European 252, 257, 367, 369
Gibbs, Pearl 26
Gillen, Francis James 132, 160, 222, 223, 225, 229, 232
Gipps, Governor George 15
Gippsland, *see* Victoria. See also Kurnai
Gladys, Ngoondaw 32
Greenway, John 31–32, 45
Grey, Governor Sir George 114, 121, 184, 209
Gribble, J. B. 232, 303
Gsell, Monsignor 313–16
Gunn, Mrs Aeneas 223, 263–4, 272
Gwoja Tjungarrayi 248fig, 249

'half-caste', *see* children, 'half-caste'
Hasluck, Paul 267
Hawkesworth 61, 162, 293
Haydon, Tom 11–12
Hill, Edward Smith 197–8, 223
Hill, Ernestine 226, 229–231, 241, 269–70, 272, 279, 311, 324, 359
Hindmarsh Island affair 30
history wars 7
Hobson, J. A. 48
Hoffman, Malvina 355
Holmes, Charles 249, 353–4
Howard, John 6
Howitt, Alfred William 130–32, 160, 218–9, 223, 225, 228, 229
Hoy, Edith 13
humanitarians 47, 142, 144–5, 149, 161, 174, 204, 233, 288, 356, 359
Hutchinson, John 16

image reproduction 67, 76–78, 333–4, 336; consumption of images 78, 87

Index

infant mortality, *see* child mortality
infanticide: trope of 116, 152–4, 156–161, 165, 187–9, 190–1, 194–8, 200, 207, 210–12, 214–6, 221–2, 224–6, 230, 238, 354; Aboriginal 156–7, 171–193, 195, 199, 200, 203, 205–6, 209, 213–9, 223, 232, 236; Western/settler 156–7, 175, 194, 199, 213, 214–7, 222–3, 235; in Britain 166, 214; in India 158, 162, 167, 175, 194, 199, 200, 214, 223; in China 175, 194, 199, 200, 214, 223; in Polynesia 214, 223. *See also* depopulation; 'dying race' theory
interracial sex 93, 107, 277–8, 285–90, 292, 294, 297–8, 306–7, 310, 323, 325; policing of 288, 306, 308, 313; as 'low class' 298, 300, 303, 308. *See also* typecasting of Aboriginal women: 'black velvet'

Jaithmathang 16
Japan 286, 306–7, 314, 320
Japanese pearlers 310, 316, 319, 322–25. *See also* pearling industry, scandal
Jardine, Frank 349
Jolliffe, Eric, *see* cartoons
Jones, Henry 155
Joyce, T. Athol 132, 225, 362

Kaberry, Phyllis 26, 47, 140–1, 256
Karuwali 2
Kaurna 177, 253
Kurnai 16, 210, 218–9
Keane, Augustus 125, 138
Kelly, Caroline 26
Kilbangaroo 127–28
King John 177–8

Krzywicki, Ludwik 17, 32, 209, 225, 231, 232–3
Kundangora 17

La Pérouse, Jean-François de 62, 337
labour: Aboriginal 51–52, 53, 168, 180, 255–6, 268–9, 272, 278, 310–11; colonial economy 55, 251, 265–6, 272, 280, 315; industrialism 252, 272. *See also* domestic servitude, Aboriginal women's; slavery
Laird, Norman 28–29
land: theft 21, 24, 201, 207, 240, 253–4, 297; competition for 189, 213; as property 252. *See also* feminisation, of land
Lang, John Dunmore 203–4
The Last Tasmanian, see Haydon, Tom
Lavater, Johann Caspar 57, 340
Lawson, Henry 300
Leroy, Sebastian 106–08, 107fig
Lesueur, Charles-Alexandre 77, 80fig
Linneaus 63–64, 341, 346
literacy 68, 76–7, 89, 95
Luana 19
Lubbock, John 119
Lumholtz, Carl 7–8, 225, 231

McCombie, Rev. Dr 202, 217
McConnel, Ursula 47
McCulloch, John Ramsey 109, 165
Mackay, George 15, 16
Maclean, Hugh, *see* cartoons
McLennan, John F. 115, 118–22, 177, 236
McRae, Tommy 9
Malcomb, Ann 194
Malinowski, Bronislaw 113, 133, 140, 225, 256

Index

Malthus, Thomas 166, 175, 216, 234
Mansell, Michael 11
Maragan 17
marriage: Aboriginal 4, 129–30, 133, 135; European 94, 101, 119, 136, 295, 304; intermarriage 308, 310; marriage rites genre 102–103. *See also* bride capture
Marrula 2
Marshall, Alan 262
masculinity: Aboriginal 100, 296, 319; settler 92, 101–102, 111, 115–16, 124, 136, 243, 269, 286, 319, 333, 337, 367; settler gallantry 55, 93, 95, 135, 138, 289, 295, 298, 312, 344, 367; working class 105
massacres: 90, 116, 143–44; Cape Otway 144; Coniston 249, 291; Hardie's station 145; Faithfull 14–16
maternity 47, 63–4, 164, 175, 179, 217, 233, 236, 252, 263; Aboriginal 56, 161–2, 171, 186–7, 193, 195, 212–13, 219, 228, 230, 232–6, 354, 363. *See also* fertility; typecasting: primordial mother
May, Phil, *see* cartoons
Meyer, H. A. E. 160, 210
Milawa, Mary Jane 17–19, 18fig
Milmenrura 179, 209
Minns, B. E., *see* cartoons
misogyny 7, 70, 348, 351, 363–8
missions: abuse 302; as 'civilising' influence 139, 158, 177–80, 184, 187, 189–91, 205–7, 217, 254, 296; missionary writing 177, 191. *See also* land: competition for; rationing
Mitaka 2

Mitambuta 16
Mitchell, Major 348–9
mobility: Aboriginal women's 280, 309; European women's 241–2, 245, 256–7, 259–61, 282, 330; settler 245–7, 250–2, 283, 309; nomadism 245–7, 250, 252, 276
modernity 8, 9, 260, 272, 276, 282, 332–4, 344–5, 348, 354, 356–8, 361
Monero-Ngarigo 16
monogamy 94, 127, 136, 295. *See also* marriage: European
Moorhouse, Matthew 222
Moreton Bay 100, 187, 188, 197, 203
Morgan, John 186
mortuary rites 155, 176, 183, 193, 195, 197, 217–8, 232, 349
Moseley, H. D., *see* royal commissions: 1934–5 (WA)
motherhood, *see* maternity
Mount Lowry 178
Mowbray, Phil 232
Mudie, Robert 109, 169, 332
Mulvaney, John 20
Mundy, Fitzherbert 16
Murray region 98, 184, 197, 205, 361
Myrtleford 20–21

Nagarnook 98
nakedness 4, 6, 70, 258, 299, 335–6, 338, 350, 354, 362, 364; linked to morality 57–8, 60–2, 294, 331. *See also* colonial gaze
national identity 12, 49, 236, 260, 287, 317, 319, 323, 325
native police 15, 144–5, 148, 220
naturalism: taxonomy 63, 341
Nawagi 7

510

New South Wales 102–03, 129, 157, 166, 167, 169, 179, 180, 200, 204, 228; Sydney 3, 65–66, 109, 221, 303, 332, 336, 341
New Zealand 61–62
newspapers: circulation and syndication 48–49, 67, 77; publication of scientific reviews and abstracts 132, 136, 215–7, 220; reportage 156, 228, 223, 231, 306, 308, 312; editors 183, 194, 212, 218; *Argus* 191, 218, 313–8; *Australian* 167; *Canberra Times* 313–5; *South Australian Register* 181–3
Ngarigu-Currawong 16
Ngarrindjeri 31, 131, 135, 205–11
Ngilgi 22
nomadism, *see* mobility: nomadism
Northern Territory 36, 113, 146, 215, 230, 261, 263, 264, 265–6, 269, 284, 288, 297–8, 306, 308–9, 317, 322, 324, 331, 352
Northern Territory Emergency Response 36, 154, 369
Novara 197–8
Narrinyeri, *see* Ngarrindjeri

Oldfield, Augustus 122
One Pound Jimmy, *see* Gwoja Tjungarrayi
oral-based cultures 88
O'Regan, Tom 11
Orton, Rev. Joseph 175
Otaheite 162–3, 294
Ouré Ouré, *see* Arra-Maïda

Page, David 236
Palmer, J. H. 51, 195–7, 350
Pangerang 9, 14, 17

Parkinson, Sydney 61
pastoralism: frontier 14, 170, 253–5, 268–9, 280; pastoralists 15–17, 205. *See also* land: competition for
Paterson, Thomas 314, 316–18
Patten, Jack 10
Paul, Mick, *see* cartoons
pearling industry 306–7, 310–11; scandal 284–7, 289, 292, 295, 303, 305–8, 311, 313–4, 317–19
Penny, Dr Richard 179, 209
Peramangk 178
Perkins, J. A. 148, 288
Péron, François 74–85, 338–9. *See also* Arra-Maïda
Petit, Nicolas-Martin 74, 75fig, 81, 83, 106–07
Phelps, P. H. F. 111, 111fig
Phillip, Governor 65, 74
photography 34, 362; portraiture 5, 22–23, 25; anthropometric 341–2, 361
physiognomy 4, 57, 109, 328, 334, 340–1
Pink, Olive 47
Pitjantjatjara 230
Point McLeay, *see* South Australia, Raukkan
police 16, 90, 102, 143, 147–9, 215, 220, 234, 280, 307
polygamy 96, 116, 127, 156, 221, 316
pornography 105–6, 301
Porteous, S. D. 46
Port Phillip, *see* Victoria
Praed, Rosa Campbell 224, 231
press, *see* newspapers
primitivist discourse 9, 244, 247, 336, 346
print: archive 7, 10, 67, 84, 284–5, 291, 293, 298, 363, 368–9;

Index

culture 6, 34, 44, 65, 67, 77, 87, 111, 283, 287, 298, 355, 366, 370; industrialisation 6, 9, 11, 47, 68, 77, 95, 235, 330, 334; as instrument of colonialism 47, 62, 68, 88; repetition 48, 49, 88–89, 93, 134, 215, 225, 238, 334, 366, 368; role in knowledge production 62, 69, 76, 118, 198. *See also* colonial archive; newspapers; publishing

property: women as 58–59, 138, 286, 295–6, 304, 313–14, 316–7, 325; women's rights to 58; patriarchal 120–22, 236. *See also* land

prostitution: of Aboriginal women 122, 200, 234, 284, 286–7, 289–90, 292, 296–7, 303–8, 311–13, 315, 318, 324; of Japanese women 306–7

protection policy 254, 288

publishing: London 78, 104–105; French 77, 107; German 108

Queensland 2, 7, 90, 101, 116, 145, 146, 148, 149, 203, 209, 214, 220, 223, 266, 305, 306, 313–14, 350

racial difference: conceptions of 4, 12, 24–26, 28, 48, 60, 89, 102, 240, 264, 272, 282, 286, 328, 330–1, 333, 337, 340, 342, 348, 356, 359–62; measuring of 57, 62, 135, 331, 334, 340, 344, 354. *See also* ethnology

racism 4, 7, 22, 36, 70, 126, 286, 294, 309, 364–6, 368; anti-racism 12, 370. *See also* racial difference

Ramsay Smith, William 45–46, 225, 347

rationing 206, 234, 280, 315, 358

Raukkan, *see* South Australia

Rees, Coralie 261

referendum (1967) 27

reconciliation 12, 369

resistance, Aboriginal 81, 160, 294, 354, 361–2, 366, 370

Reynolds, Henry 14, 143, 145, 245

Robinson, George Augustus 3, 15, 97, 124

Roper River 302

Roth, Walter Edmund 160, 223, 305

Rousseau 61

royal commissions: 1904–05 (NSW) 224; 1905 (Qld) 305; 1934–5 (WA) 233, 280, 307

Ryan, Lyndall 143

Salvado, Rosendo 190

scarification 60, 113–14, 263, 335–6

Scherzer, Karl 197–8

Science of Man 18–19, 133, 224, 225

select committees: 1837 (UK) 110, 166; 1845 (NSW) 155, 180, 187, 255; 1858–9 (Vic) 180, 217; 1860 (SA) 200–1, 205, 208, 211, 342–3; 1861 (Qld) 145; 1899 (SA) 288

self-determination policy 254

settler-colonialism 3, 4, 6, 13–14, 20, 29, 41, 44, 136, 235–6, 240, 250–1, 254, 286, 295, 318, 324–5, 329–30, 330, 336, 339–40, 344, 360; settler-heritage Australians 1, 3, 7, 12, 359, 366

Sexton, Rev. J. H. 139

sexual difference 60, 63, 347–8

sexualisation: of indigenous women 3, 61, 73, 106, 284, 286, 288–90, 293, 300, 303, 312, 319, 346; of women convicts 72–73

Index

sexuality: frontier 14, 269, 288, 297, 304, 324; Aboriginal women's 325. *See also* interracial sex; pearling industry, scandal
sheep: Sheep Act 183; shearing 183; wool export market 15. *See also* pastoralism
slavery 163, 193, 217, 265, 273, 280, 282
smallpox, *see* disease
Sollas, W. J. 225, 253
song, Aboriginal 85, 99, 100–01
South Australia 31, 179, 209, 181–4, 190, 200, 209, 213, 223, 226, 228, 239, 243, 244fig, 253, 303, 342–3; Raukkan 131, 201, 205–6, 211
Spencer, Baldwin 132, 160, 222, 223, 225, 229, 231, 232, 355
squatters, *see* pastoralism: pastoralists
Stanner, W. E. 131
starvation 157, 169, 234, 279, 315, 327, 329, 342, 359. *See also* rationing
Strehlow, T. H. 229
Strzelecki, Paul de 163, 187, 225, 233
Suttor, William Henry 258
Swift, Jonathan 54
Sydney, *see* New South Wales
syphilis, *see* disease

Tahiti 61
Taplin, Rev. George 131, 160, 199–201, 204–13, 225, 228, 232, 347
Tasmania 3, 11, 81–83, 86, 355. *See also* Van Diemen's Land
Taungurung 16
Teichelmann, C. G. 177–9
Thomas, N. W. 132, 225, 362
Thomas, William 14, 123, 155, 159, 174, 186, 216–7, 231
Tiny Swanson 321fig, 322, 323fig

Tiwi Islands 284, 317
Toolooa 209–10
tooth avulsion 55, 113
Torres Strait 262, 310
trafficking, *see* prostitution
travel writing: genre 26, 61, 70–1, 78, 90, 101, 126, 129, 153, 165, 231; British 52, 61, 70–1, 121, 137, 162; French 61, 78, 98, 107–8; settler Australian 109, 137, 167, 169, 171, 241, 261–2, 278. *See also* *Walkabout*
Trollope, Anthony 52
Trugernanner 31
Tuckfield, Francis 189–90
Turnbull, John 121, 130, 135
typecasting 1, 32, 50, 89, 301, 365, 368; of elder Aboriginal women 98, 100, 326–7, 335–6, 339, 346–64; comportment of Aboriginal women 241, 249, 250, 257–9, 261–3, 265; comportment of Aboriginal men 249, 250, 258, 26. *See also* types
types: the native 44, 334; of Aboriginal women: black velvet 3, 278, 284–7, 289, 292–3, 298–9, 299fig, 300–1, 319–25, 320fig; gin 3, 5fig, 280, 282, 283; lubra 3, 261, 264, 269, 272, 282, 283, 288–9, 309, 312, 320; native belle 61, 68, 73, 81–83, 258–9, 261, 296, 328, 336–9, 344, 361; primordial mother 63–64, 82–83, 153–4, 163–5, 176; spinifex fairy 278; stud 3, 222, 298; of Aboriginal men: jacky-jacky 10; myall 47, 248, 249, 282, 283; noble savage 50, 61, 74, 81, 83, 249, 296, 319, 339; buck 222, 282

Index

Van Diemen's Land 56–57, 59fig, 62, 74, 80, 113, 209, 295, 304. *See also* Tasmania
Victoria 9, 13–17, 19–21, 123–24, 143, 150, 181, 184–5, 191–4, 216; Gippsland 14, 123, 196, 210; Port Phillip 14–16, 98, 123, 166, 170, 171–5, 202, 208; Yarra region 125, 159
violence: gendered 92, 95, 102, 137; racialised 93; against Aboriginal women 95–96, 102, 143–50, 242, 366, 369; against elder Aboriginal women 327, 352–3, 363; of white men 102, 142–151, 265, 296; sexual abuse and rape 93, 102, 105, 143, 145, 150, 180, 242, 279, 288, 290–1, 295–7, 302, 303–4, 314, 322
visual field 73, 111, 258, 333, 344–5, 354. *See also* colonial gaze

Wahgunyah 9
Walbri 291
Walkabout 8fig, 29fig, 51, 231, 249, 264, 265fig, 266fig
Walloa 97
Walpiri 41–42
Warakamai 7
Warburg 99
Wautha wurrung 172
Wave Hill 324–5
Wawgroot 128
Waywurru 16
Webber, John 59–62, 59fig, 64–65
Wedge, John Helder 171–3, 186
Welsby, Thomas 100
Westermarck, Edward 127
Western Australia 32, 53–5, 122, 142, 147, 149, 173, 190, 226, 234, 259, 262fig, 280, 292, 301, 310–11, 317, 322, 324, 353
Westgarth, William 187, 191–4
White Australia policy 161, 224, 236, 278, 287, 314, 324, 360
White, Eric 29–30
White, John 65–66, 66fig, 68–74
Willshire, W. H. 220, 231, 265
Wiradjuri 19
Witchetty's Tribe, see Jolliffe, Eric
Woiwurrung 174
Wollstonecraft, Mary 336–8
Wombeetch Puyuun 217
women, Aboriginal 365–8; as agitators of intertribal conflict 97–100, 98fig; autonomy of 160, 178, 209, 235, 291, 294–6, 303, 314, 324–5, 278, 287, 234–6; abduction of 102, 143, 242, 290–2, 305, 332; custodians 33, 56, 191, 208, 209, 213, 363; exchange of 14, 120–21, 131; as forced informants 90; subjugation of 96, 104, 133, 136–9
women, white: writers 223–4; settlers 269–70. *See also* domesticity
Wongatpan 219
Wood, J. G. 138, 326–8, 347
Wurundjeri 16, 35, 173

Ya-itma-thang 17
Yalata 226
Yaldwin, Henry 16
Yate, Rev. William 110–11
Yolngu 324
Yupton (Yeap-tune) 15

514